CHILTON BOOK COMPANY

REPAIR MANUAL

TAURUS·SABLE CONTINENTAL 1986-89

All U.S. and Canadian models of Ford Taurus • Mercury Sable • front wheel drive Continental

Vice President and General Manager JOHN P. KUSHNERICK
Editor-in-Chief KERRY A. FREEMAN, S.A.E.
Managing Editor DEAN F. MORGANTINI, S.A.E.
Senior Editor RICHARD J. RIVELE, S.A.E.
Senior Editor W. CALVIN SETTLE, JR., S.A.E.
Editor JAMES B. STEELE

CHILTON BOOK COMPANY
Radnor, Pennsylvania
19089

CONTENTS

GENERAL INFORMATION and MAINTENANCE

1 How to use this book
2 Tools and Equipment
6 Routine Maintenance

ENGINE PERFORMANCE and TUNE-UP

43 Tune-Up Procedures
43 Tune-Up Specifications

ENGINE and ENGINE OVERHAUL

58 Engine Electrical System
72 Engine Service
73 Engine Specifications

EMISSION CONTROLS

156 Emission Controls System and Service

FUEL SYSTEM

169 Fuel System Service

CHASSIS ELECTRICAL

204 Heating and Air Conditioning
220 Accessory Service
227 Instruments and Switches
234 Lights, Fuses and Flashers
237 Trailer Wiring

7 DRIVE TRAIN

261 Manual Transaxle
275 Clutch
280 Automatic Transaxle

8 SUSPENSION and STEERING

290 Front Suspension
304 Rear Suspension
318 Steering

9 BRAKES

350 Front Disc Brakes
354 Rear Drum Brakes
359 Rear Disc Brakes
365 Specifications

10 BODY

369 Exterior
384 Interior

11 MECHANIC'S DATA

404 Mechanic's Data
406 Glossary
412 Abbreviations
414 Index

188 Chilton's Fuel Economy
and Tune-Up Tips

388 Chilton's Body Repair
Tips

SAFETY NOTICE

Proper service and repair procedures are vital to the safe, reliable operation of all motor vehicles, as well as the personal safety of those performing repairs. This book outlines procedures for servicing and repairing vehicles using safe, effective methods. The procedures contain many NOTES, CAUTIONS and WARNINGS which should be followed along with standard safety procedures to eliminate the possibility of personal injury or improper service which could damage the vehicle or compromise its safety.

It is important to note that repair procedures and techniques, tools and parts for servicing motor vehicles, as well as the skill and experience of the individual performing the work vary widely. It is not possible to anticipate all of the conceivable ways or conditions under which vehicles may be serviced, or to provide cautions as to all of the possible hazards that may result. Standard and accepted safety precautions and equipment should be used during cutting, grinding, chiseling, prying, or any other process that can cause material removal or projectiles.

Some procedures require the use of tools specially designed for a specific purpose. Before substituting another tool or procedure, you must be completely satisfied that neither your personal safety, nor the performance of the vehicle will be endangered.

Although the information in this guide is based on industry sources and is as complete as possible at the time of publication, the possibility exists that the manufacturer made later changes which could not be included here. While striving for total accuracy, Chilton Book Company cannot assume responsibility for any errors, changes, or omissions that may occur in the compilation of this data.

PART NUMBERS

Part numbers listed in this reference are not recommendations by Chilton for any product by brand name. They are references that can be used with interchange manuals and aftermarket supplier catalogs to locate each brand supplier's discrete part number.

SPECIAL TOOLS

Special tools are recommended by the vehicle manufacturer to perform their specific job. Use has been kept to a minimum, but where absolutely necessary, they are referred to in the text by the part number of the tool manufacturer. These tools can be purchased under the appropriate part number, from major tool manufacturers, tool suppliers, or parts outlets. Others for your car can be purchased from your Ford/Mercury dealer or from Owatonna Tool Company, Owatonna, Minnesota 55060. Before substituting any tool for the one recommended, read the SAFETY NOTICE at the top of this page.

ACKNOWLEDGMENTS

The Chilton Book Company expresses appreciation to the Ford Motor Company for the technical information and illustrations contained within this manual.

Copyright © 1989 by Chilton Book Company
All Rights Reserved
Published in Radnor, Pennsylvania 19089, by Chilton Book Company

Manufactured in the United States of America
1234567890   8765432109

Chilton's Repair Manual: Taurus/Sable/Continental 1986–89
ISBN 0-8019-7942-0 pbk.
Library of Congress Catalog Card No. 88-43186

General Information and and Maintenance

HOW TO USE THIS BOOK

Chilton's Repair Manual for Ford Taurus, Mercury Sable, and Lincoln Continental models is intended to teach you more about the inner workings of your car and save you money on its upkeep. The first two chapters will be used the most, since they contain maintenance and tune-up information and procedures. The following chapters concern themselves with the more complex systems. Operating systems from engine through brakes are covered to the extent that we feel the average do-it-yourselfer should get involved as well as more complex procedures that will benefit both the advanced do-it-yourselfer mechanic as well as the professional. This book will explain such things as rebuilding the transaxle and it should be advised that the expertise required, and the investment in special tools makes this task uneconomical and unpractical for the novice mechanic. We will also tell you how to change your own brake pads and shoes, replace spark plugs, perform routine maintenance, and many more jobs that will save you money, give you personal satisfactions, and help you avoid problems.

A secondary purpose of this book is as a reference for owners who want to understand their car and/or their mechanics better. In this case, no tools at all are required.

Before attempting any repairs or service on your car, read through the entire procedure outlined in the appropriate chapter. This will give you the overall view of what tools and supplies will be required. There is nothing more frustrating than having to walk to the bus stop on Monday morning because you were short one gasket on Sunday afternoon. So read ahead and plan ahead. Each operation should be approached logically and all procedures thoroughly understood before attempting any work. Some special tools that may be required can often be rented from local automotive jobbers or

places specializing in renting tools and equipment. Check the yellow pages of your phone book.

All chapters contain adjustments, maintenance, removal and installation procedures, and overhaul procedures. When overhaul is not considered practical, we tell you how to remove the failed part and then how to install the new or rebuilt replacement. In this way, you at least save the labor costs. Backyard overhaul of some components (such as the alternator or water pump) is just not practical, but the removal and installation procedure is often simple and well within the capabilities of the average car owner.

Two basic mechanic's rules should be mentioned here. First, whenever the LEFT side of the car or engine is referred to, it is meant to specify the DRIVER'S side of the car. Conversely, the RIGHT side of the car means the PASSENGER'S side. Second, all screws and bolts are removed by turning counterclockwise, and tightened by turning clockwise, unless otherwise noted.

Safety is always the most important rule. Constantly be aware of the dangers involved in working on or around an automobile and take proper precautions to avoid the risk of personal injury or damage to the vehicle. See the section in this chapter, Servicing Your Vehicle Safely, and the SAFETY NOTICE on the acknowledgment page before attempting any service procedures and pay attention to the instructions provided. There are 3 common mistakes in mechanical work:

1. Incorrect order of assembly, disassembly or adjustment. When taking something apart or putting it together, doing things in the wrong order usually just costs you extra time; however it CAN break something. Read the entire procedure before beginning disassembly. Do everything in the order in which the instructions say you should do it, even if you can't immediately see a reason for it. When you're taking apart

something that is very intricate (for example, a carburetor), you might want to draw a picture of how it looks when assembled at one point in order to make sure you get everything back in its proper position. We will supply exploded views whenever possible, but sometimes the job requires more attention to detail than an illustration provides. When making adjustments (especially tune-up adjustments), do them in order. One adjustment often affects another and you cannot expect satisfactory results unless each adjustment is made only when it cannot be changed by any other.

2. Overtorquing (or undertorquing) nuts and bolts. While it is more common for overtorquing to cause damage, undertorquing can cause a fastener to vibrate loose and cause serious damage, especially when dealing with aluminum parts. Pay attention to torque specifications and utilize a torque wrench in assembly. If a torque figure is not available remember that, if you are using the right tool to do the job, you will probably not have to strain yourself to get a fastener tight enough. The pitch of most threads is so slight that the tension you put on the wrench will be multiplied many times in actual force on what you are tightening. A good example of how critical torque is can be seen in the case of spark plug installation, especially where you are putting the plug into an aluminum cylinder head. Too little torque can fail to crush the gasket, causing leakage of combustion gases and consequent overheating of the plug and engine parts. Too much torque can damage the threads or distort the plug, which changes the spark gap at the electrode. Since more and more manufacturers are using aluminum in their engine and chassis parts to save weight, a torque wrench should be in any serious do-it-yourselfer's tool box.

There are many commercial chemical products available for ensuring that fasteners won't come loose, even if they are not torqued just right (a very common brand is Loctite®). If you're worried about getting something together tight enough to hold, but loose enough to avoid mechanical damage during assembly, one of these products might offer substantial insurance. Read the label on the package and make sure the product is compatible with the materials, fluids, etc. involved before choosing one.

3. Crossthreading. This occurs when a part such as a bolt is screwed into a nut or casting at the wrong angle and forced, causing the threads to become damaged. Crossthreading is more likely to occur if access is difficult. It helps to clean and lubricate fasteners, and to start threading with the part to be installed going straight in, using your fingers. If you encounter ance, unscrew the part and start over

again at a different angle until it can be inserted and turned several times without much effort. Keep in mind that many parts, especially spark plugs, use tapered threads so that gentle turning will automatically bring the part you're threading to the proper angle if you don't force it or resist a change in angle. Don't put a wrench on the part until it's been turned in a couple of times by hand. If you suddenly encounter resistance and the part has not seated fully, don't force it. Pull it back out and make sure it's clean and threading properly.

Always take your time and be patient; once you have some experience, working on your car will become an enjoyable hobby.

TOOLS AND EQUIPMENT

Naturally, without the proper tools and equipment it is impossible to properly service your vehicle. It would be impossible to catalog each tool that you would need to perform each or every operation in this book. It would also be unwise for the amateur to rush out and buy an expensive set of tools an the theory that he may need one or more of them at sometime.

The best approach is to proceed slowly, gathering together a good quality set of those tools that are used most frequently. Don't be misled by the low cost of bargain tools. It is far better to spend a little more for better quality. Forged wrenches, 6 or 12 point sockets and fine tooth ratchets are by far preferable to their less expensive counterparts. As any good mechanic can tell you, there are few worse experiences than trying to work on a car with bad tools. Your monetary savings will be far outweighed by frustration and mangled knuckles.

Certain tools, plus a basic ability to handle tools, are required to get started. A basic mechanics tool set, a torque wrench, and, for 1976 and later models, a Torx bits set. Torx bits are hexlobular drivers which fit both inside and outside on special Torx head fasteners used in various places on your vehicle.

Begin accumulating those tools that are used most frequently; those associated with routine maintenance and tune-up.

In addition to the normal assortment of screwdrivers and pliers you should have the following tools for routine maintenance jobs (your Jeep, depending on the model year, uses both SAE and metric fasteners):

1. SAE/Metric wrenches, sockets and combination open end/box end wrenches in sizes from ⅛" (3mm) to ¾" (19mm); and a spark plug socket ($^{13}/_{16}$") If possible, buy various length socket drive extensions. One break in this department

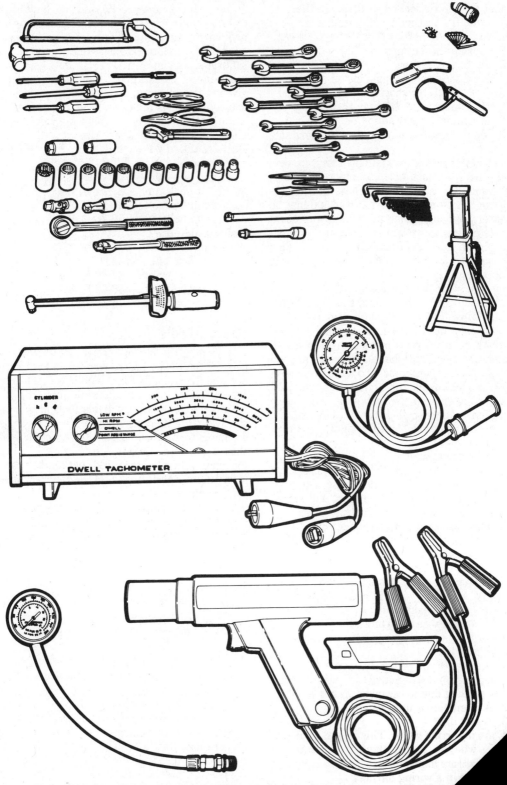

You need only a basic assortment of hand tools for most maintenance and repair

is that the metric sockets available in the U.S. will all fit the ratchet handles and extensions you may already have (¼″, ⅜″, and ½″ drive).

2. Jackstands for support
3. Oil filter wrench
4. Oil filter spout for pouring oil
5. Grease gun for chassis lubrication
6. Hydrometer for checking the battery
7. A container for draining oil
8. Many rags for wiping up the inevitable mess.

In addition to the above items there are several others that are not absolutely necessary, but handy to have around. These include oil-dry (cat box litter works just as well and may be cheaper), a transmission funnel and the usual supply of lubricants, antifreeze and fluids, although these can be purchased as needed. This is a basic list for routine maintenance, but only your personal needs and desires can accurately determine your list of necessary tools.

The second list of tools is for tune-ups. While the tools involved here are slightly more sophisticated, they need not be outrageously expensive. There are several inexpensive tach/dwell meters on the market that are every bit as good for the average mechanic as a $100.00 professional model. Just be sure that it goes to at least 1,200-1,500 rpm on the tach scale and that it works on 4, 6 and 8 cylinder engines. A basic list of tune-up equipment could include:

1. Tach-dwell meter
2. Spark plug wrench
3. Timing light (a DC light that works from the truck's battery is best, although an AC light that plugs into 110V house current will suffice at some sacrifice in brightness)
4. Wire spark plug gauge/adjusting tools
5. Set of feeler blades.

Here again, be guided by your own needs. A feeler blade will set the point gap as easily as dwell meter will read dwell, but slightly less accurately. And since you will need a tachometer anyway ... well, make your own decision.

In addition to these basic tools, there are several other tools and gauges you may find useful. These include:

1. A compression gauge. The screw-in type is slower to use, but eliminates the possibility of a
faulty ~~~~~~~~~~ ng pressure
~~~~~~~~~~ ge

~~~~~~~~~~ s is used for deter-
~~~~~~~~~~ e is current in a
~~~~~~~~~~ if a wire is broken
~~~~~~~~~~ ss.
~~~~~~~~~~ probably find a
~~~~~~~~~~ all but the most
~~~~~~~~~~ dels are perfectly
~~~~~~~~~~ er click (break-

away) type are more precise, and you don't have to crane your neck to see a torque reading in awkward situations. The breakaway torque wrenches are more expensive and should be recalibrated periodically.

Torque specification for each fastener will be given in the procedure in any case that a specific torque value is required. If no torque specifications are given, use the following values as a guide, based upon fastener size:

Bolts marked 6T

6mm bolt/nut − 5-7 ft. lbs.
8mm bolt/nut − 12-17 ft. lbs.
10mm bolt/nut − 23-34 ft. lbs.
12mm bolt/nut − 41-59 ft. lbs.
14mm bolt/nut − 56-76 ft. lbs.

Bolts marked 8T

6mm bolt/nut − 6-9 ft. lbs.
8mm bolt/nut − 13-20 ft. lbs.
10mm bolt/nut − 27-40 ft. lbs.
12mm bolt/nut − 46-69 ft. lbs.
14mm bolt/nut − 75-101 ft. lbs.

Special Tools

Normally, the use of special factory tools is avoided for repair procedures, since these are not readily available for the do-it-yourself mechanic. When it is possible to perform the job with more commonly available tools, it will be pointed out, but occasionally, a special tool was designed to perform a specific function and should be used. Before substituting another tool, you should be convinced that neither your safety nor the performance of the vehicle will be compromised.

When a special tool is indicated, it will be referred to by the manufacturer's part number. Some special tools are available commercially from major tool manufacturers. Others for your car can be purchased from your Ford/Mercury dealer or from the Owatonna Tool Co., Owatonna, Minnesota 55060.

SERVICING YOUR CAR SAFELY

It is virtually impossible to anticipate all of the hazards involved with automotive maintenance and service but care and common sense will prevent most accidents.

The rules of safety for mechanics range from "don't smoke around gasoline," to "use the proper tool for the job." The trick to avoid injuries is to develop safe work habits and take every possible precaution.

Do's

● Do keep a fire extinguisher and first aid kit within easy reach.

• Do wear safety glasses or goggles when cutting, drilling, grinding or prying. If you wear glasses for the sake of vision, then they should be made of hardened glass that can serve also as safety glasses, or wear safety goggles over your regular glasses.

• Do wear safety glasses whenever you work around the battery. Batteries contain sulphuric acid. In case of contact with the eyes or skin, flush the area with water or a mixture of water and baking soda and get medical attention immediately.

• Do use safety stands for any under-car service. Jacks are for raising vehicles; safety stands are for making sure the vehicle stays raised until you want it to come down. Whenever the vehicle is raised, block the wheels remaining on the ground and set the parking brake.

• Do use adequate ventilation when working with any chemicals. Asbestos dust resulting from brake lining wear can cause cancer.

• Do disconnect the negative battery cable when working on the electrical system. The primary ignition system can contain up to 40,000 volts.

• Do follow manufacturer's directions whenever working with potentially hazardous materials. Both brake fluid and antifreeze are poisonous if taken internally.

• Do properly maintain your tools. Loose hammerheads, mushroomed punches and chisels, frayed or poorly grounded electrical cords, excessively worn screwdriver, spread wrenches (open end), cracked sockets can cause accidents.

• Do use the proper size and type of tool for the job being done.

• Do when possible, pull on a wrench handle rather than push on it, and adjust your stance to prevent a fall.

• Do be sure that adjustable wrenches are tightly adjusted on the nut or bolt and pulled so that the face is on the side of the fixed jaw.

• Do select a wrench or socket that fits the nut or bolt. The wrench or socket should sit straight, not cocked.

• Do strike squarely with a hammer to avoid glancing blows.

• Do set the parking brake and block the drive wheels if the work requires that the engine is running.

Don'ts

• Don't run an engine in a garage or anywhere else without proper ventilation – EVER! Carbon monoxide is poisonous. It is absorbed by the body 400 times faster than oxygen. It takes a long time to leave the human body and you can build up a deadly supply of it in you system by simply breathing in a little every day. You may not realize you are slowly poisoning yourself. Always use power vents, windows, fans or open the garage doors.

• Don't work around moving parts while wearing a necktie or other loose clothing. Short sleeves are much safer than long, loose sleeves. Hard-toed shoes with neoprene soles protect your toes and give a better grip on slippery surfaces. Jewelry such as watches, fancy belt buckles, beads or body adornment of any kind is not safe working around a car. Long hair should be hidden under a hat or cap.

• Don't use pockets for tool boxes. A fall or bump can drive a screwdriver deep into you body. Even a wiping cloth hanging from the back pocket can wrap around a spinning shaft or fan.

• Don't smoke when working around gasoline, cleaning solvent or other flammable material.

• Don't smoke when working around the battery. When the battery is being charged, it gives off explosive hydrogen gas.

• Don't use gasoline to wash your hands. There are excellent soaps available. Gasoline may contain lead, and lead can enter the body through a cut, accumulating in the body until you are very ill. Gasoline also removes all the natural oils from the skin so that bone dry hands will suck up oil and grease.

• Don't service the air conditioning system unless you are equipped with the necessary tools and training. Do wear safety glasses, the refrigerant, R-12, is extremely cold and when exposed to the air, will instantly freeze any surface it comes in contact with, including your eyes. Although the refrigerant is normally non-toxic, R-12 becomes a deadly poisonous gas in the presence of an open flame. One good whiff of the vapors from burning refrigerant can be fatal.

IDENTIFICATION

Vehicle Identification Number (VIN)

The official vehicle identification (serial) number (used for title and registration purposes) is stamped on a metal tab fastened to the instrument panel and visible through the driver's side of the windshield from the outside. The vehicle identification (serial) number contains a 17 digit number. The number is used for warranty identification of the vehicle and indicates: manufacturer, type of restraint system, line, series, body type, engine, model year, and consecutive unit number.

Vehicle Certification Label

The Vehicle Certification Label is found on the left door lock face panel or door pillar. The upper half of the label contains the name of the manufacturer, month and year of manufacture, gross weight rating, gross axle weight, and the certification statements pertinent. The certification also repeats the VIN number and gives the color code and the accessories found on the car.

Model Year Identification

The vehicle model year identification can be confirmed by locating the 10th position of the VIN code and using the following chart.

1FABP43M2 J X100001

VIN Code	Year
F	1985
G	1986
H	1987
J	1988
K	1989
L	1990

Vehicle model year for all vehicles—10th position of the VIN

Engine Identification

The vehicle engine identification can be located on the 8th position of the VIN code.

Transaxle Codes

The transmission code is located on the bottom edge of the Vehicle Certification Label.

ROUTINE MAINTENANCE

Major efforts have been undertaken by Ford to improve serviceability and provide reduced scheduled maintenance for our car. This is a built-in savings to you, the owner, in time and dollars.

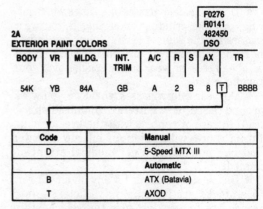

Code	Manual
D	5-Speed MTX III
	Automatic
B	ATX (Batavia)
T	AXOD

Transmission/transaxle identification

Air Cleaner Element and Crankcase Emission Filter

The air cleaner element should be replaced every 30 months or 30,000 miles. More frequent changes are necessary if the car is operated in dusty conditions.

REMOVAL AND INSTALLATION

1. Loosen the air cleaner outlet tube clamp and disconnect the tube.
2. Disconnect the hot air tube (2.5L engine only), PCV inlet tube and the zip tube.
3. Disconnect the cold weather modulator vacuum hose at the temperature sensor (2.5L engine only).
4. Remove the air cleaner and cover retaining screws and the air cleaner assembly.
5. Inspect the inside surfaces of the cover for traces of dirt leakage past the cleaner element as a result of damaged seals, incorrect element or inadequate tightness of the cover retaining clips.
6. Remove the air cleaner element and clean the inside surfaces of the cleaner tray and cover.
7. Install a new air cleaner element, install the cover and assembly. Tighten the retaining clamp to 12-20 ft. lbs.
8. Reconnect all vacuum and air duct hoses and lines.
9. Start the engine and check for vacuum

1FABP18 4 2KZ100001

VIN Code	Displacement		Cylinders	Fuel	Manufacturer
	Liter	CID			
D	2.5 HSC CFI	153	4	Gasoline	Ford
U	3.0 EFI	182	6	Gasoline	Ford
4	3.8 EFI	232	6	Gasoline	Ford
Y	3.0L EFI DOHC	182	6	Gasoline	Yamaha

Engine type, displacement, # of cylinders, fuel type and manufacturer—8th position of the VIN

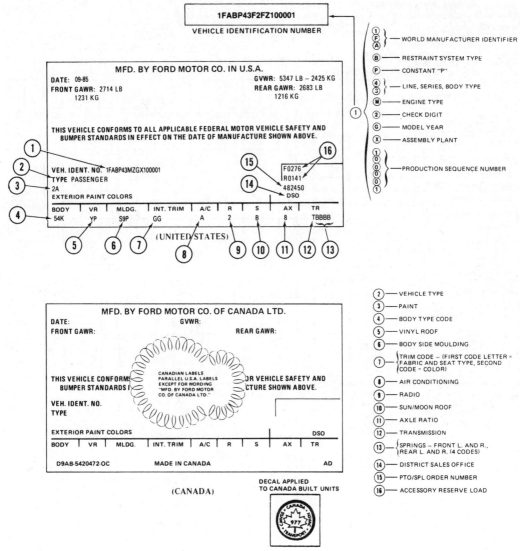

1FABP43F2FZ100001

VEHICLE IDENTIFICATION NUMBER

MFD. BY FORD MOTOR CO. IN U.S.A.

DATE: 09-85

FRONT GAWR: 2714 LB
1231 KG

GVWR: 5347 LB – 2425 KG

REAR GAWR: 2683 LB
1216 KG

THIS VEHICLE CONFORMS TO ALL APPLICABLE FEDERAL MOTOR VEHICLE SAFETY AND BUMPER STANDARDS IN EFFECT ON THE DATE OF MANUFACTURE SHOWN ABOVE.

VEH. IDENT. NO. 1FABP43MZGX100001
TYPE PASSENGER
2A
EXTERIOR PAINT COLORS

BODY	VR	MLDG.	INT. TRIM	A/C	R	S	AX	TR
54K	YP	S9P	GG	A	2	B	8	TBBBB

(UNITED STATES)

F0276
R0141
482450
DSO

- ① ⒡ ⒜ — WORLD MANUFACTURER IDENTIFIER
- ⒝ — RESTRAINT SYSTEM TYPE
- ⒫ — CONSTANT "P"
- ④ ③ — LINE, SERIES, BODY TYPE
- ⒨ — ENGINE TYPE
- ② — CHECK DIGIT
- ⒢ — MODEL YEAR
- ⒳ — ASSEMBLY PLANT
- ① ⓪ ⓪ ⓪ ⓪ ① — PRODUCTION SEQUENCE NUMBER

MFD. BY FORD MOTOR CO. OF CANADA LTD.

DATE: GVWR:

FRONT GAWR: REAR GAWR:

CANADIAN LABELS PARALLEL U.S.A. LABELS EXCEPT FOR WORDING "MFD. BY FORD MOTOR CO. OF CANADA LTD."

THIS VEHICLE CONFORMS ... OR VEHICLE SAFETY AND BUMPER STANDARDS I ... CTURE SHOWN ABOVE.

VEH. IDENT. NO.
TYPE

EXTERIOR PAINT COLORS   DSO

BODY	VR	MLDG.	INT. TRIM	A/C	R	S	AX	TR

D9AB-5420472-OC   MADE IN CANADA   AD

(CANADA)

DECAL APPLIED TO CANADA BUILT UNITS

977

- ② — VEHICLE TYPE
- ③ — PAINT
- ④ — BODY TYPE CODE
- ⑤ — VINYL ROOF
- ⑥ — BODY SIDE MOULDING
- ⑦ — TRIM CODE – (FIRST CODE LETTER = FABRIC AND SEAT TYPE, SECOND CODE = COLOR)
- ⑧ — AIR CONDITIONING
- ⑨ — RADIO
- ⑩ — SUN/MOON ROOF
- ⑪ — AXLE RATIO
- ⑫ — TRANSMISSION
- ⑬ — SPRINGS – FRONT L. AND R., REAR L. AND R. (4 CODES)
- ⑭ — DISTRICT SALES OFFICE
- ⑮ — PTO/SPL ORDER NUMBER
- ⑯ — ACCESSORY RESERVE LOAD

Vehicle Identification and Certification Plates

leaks around both ends of the tube from the air cleaner to the throttle body.

Fuel Filter

The fuel filter provides extremely fine filtration to protect the small metering orifices of the injector nozzles. The filter is a one-piece construction which cannot be cleaned. If the filter becomes clogged or restricted, it should be replaced with a new filter. The filter is located on the underbody next to the right hand front corner of the fuel tank.

REMOVAL AND INSTALLATION

CAUTION: *Always use extreme care when removing and installing any fuel system com-*

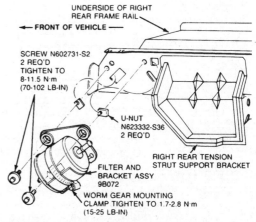

UNDERSIDE OF RIGHT REAR FRAME RAIL
◄— FRONT OF VEHICLE —

SCREW N602731-S2
2 REQ'D
TIGHTEN TO
8-11.5 N·m
(70-102 LB-IN)

U-NUT
N623332-S36
2 REQ'D

RIGHT REAR TENSION STRUT SUPPORT BRACKET

FILTER AND BRACKET ASSY
9B072

WORM GEAR MOUNTING CLAMP TIGHTEN TO 1.7-2.8 N·m (15-25 LB-IN)

Fuel filter mounting—all Taurus/Sable models

CUSTOMER MAINTENANCE SCHEDULE A

Follow Maintenance Schedule A, if your driving habits MAINLY include one or more of the following conditions:
- Short trips of less than 10 miles (16 km) when outside temperatures remain below freezing.
- Operating during HOT WEATHER:
  — Driving in stop-and-go "rush hour" traffic.
- Towing a trailer, using a camper or car-top carrier.
- Operating in severe dust conditions.
- Extensive idling, such as police, taxi or door-to-door delivery service.

SERVICE INTERVAL Perform at the months or distances shown, whichever comes first.	Miles x 1000 / Kilometers x 1000	3 / 4.8	6 / 9.6	9 / 14.4	12 / 19.2	15 / 24	18 / 28.8	21 / 33.6	24 / 38.4	27 / 43.2	30 / 48	33 / 52.8	36 / 57.6	39 / 62.4	42 / 67.2	45 / 72	48 / 76.8	51 / 81.6	54 / 86.4	57 / 91.2	60 / 96
EMISSION CONTROL SERVICE																					
Change Engine Oil (every 3 months) or		X	X	X	X	X	X	X	X	X	X	X	X	X	X	X	X	X	X	X	X
Change Engine Oil Filter (every 3 months) or		X	X	X	X	X	X	X	X	X	X	X	X	X	X	X	X	X	X	X	X
Spark Plugs											X										X
Inspect Accessory Drive Belt(s)											X										X
Replace Air Cleaner Filter ①											X①										X①
Replace Crankcase Filter ①											X①										X①
Replace Engine Coolant (every 36 months) or											X										X
Check Engine Coolant Protection, Hoses and Clamps		ANNUALLY																			
GENERAL MAINTENANCE																					
Inspect Exhaust Heat Shields											X										X
Change Automatic Transaxle Fluid ②											②										②
Inspect Disc Brake Pads and Rotors (Front)											X③										X③
Inspect Brake Linings and Drums ③											③										③
Inspect and Repack Rear Wheel Bearings											X										X

① If operating in severe dust, more frequent intervals may be required — consult your dealer.

② Change automatic transaxle fluid if your driving habits frequently include one or more of the following conditions:
- Operation during HOT WEATHER (above 32°C (90°F)).
- Towing a trailer or using a car top carrier.
- Police, taxi or door-to-door delivery service.

③ If your driving includes continuous stop and go driving or driving in mountainous areas, more frequent intervals may be required.

Vehicle maintenance schedule—unique driving conditions

CUSTOMER MAINTENANCE SCHEDULE B

Follow this Schedule if, generally, you drive your vehicle on a daily basis for several miles and NONE OF THE UNIQUE DRIVING CONDITIONS SHOWN IN SCHEDULE A APPLY TO YOUR DRIVING HABITS.

SERVICE INTERVALS Perform at the months or distances shown, whichever comes first.	Miles x 1000 / Kilometers x 1000	7.5 / 12	15 / 24	22.5 / 36	30 / 48	37.5 / 60	45 / 72	52.5 / 84	60 / 96
EMISSIONS CONTROL SERVICE									
Change Engine Oil and Oil Filter (every 6 months) or		X	X	X	X	X	X	X	X
Replace Spark Plugs					X				X
Change Crankcase Filter					X				X
Inspect Accessory Drive Belt(s)					X				X
Replace Air Cleaner Filter①					X①				X①
Change Engine Coolant (every 36 months) or					X				X
Check Engine Coolant Protection, Hoses and Clamps		ANNUALLY							
GENERAL MAINTENANCE									
Check Exhaust Heat Shields					X				X
Inspect Disc Brake Pads and Rotors (Front)②					X②				X②
Inspect Brake Linings and Drums (Rear)②					X②				X②
Inspect and Repack Rear Wheel Bearing					X				X

①If operating in severe dust, more frequent intervals may be required. Consult your dealer.

②If your driving includes continuous stop-and-go driving or driving in mountainous areas, more frequent intervals may be required.

Vehicle maintenance schedule—normal driving conditions

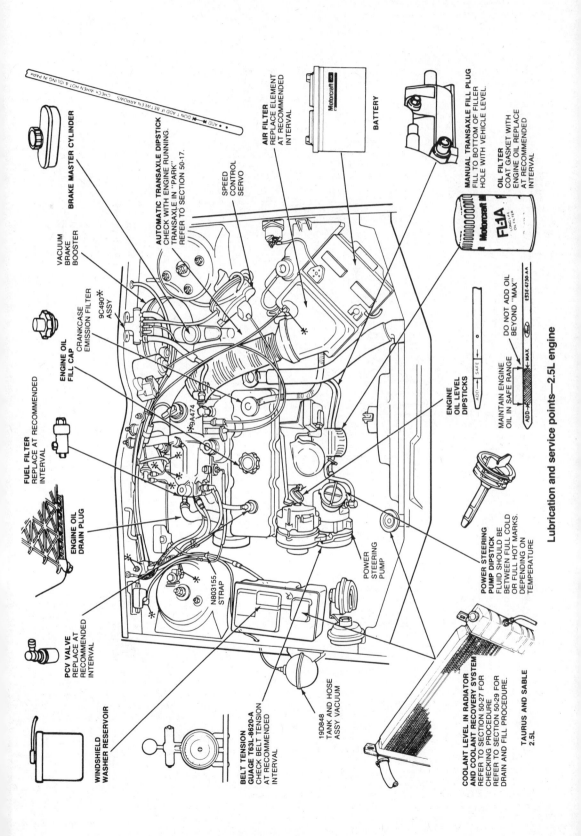

Lubrication and service points—2.5L engine

BRAKE MASTER CYLINDER

CHECK WHEN T HOT & T OIL ING IN PARK
DON T ADD IF BETWEEN ARROWS

AUTOMATIC TRANSAXLE DIPSTICK
CHECK WITH ENGINE RUNNING.
TRANSAXLE IN "PARK"
REFER TO SECTION 50-17.

SPEED CONTROL SERVO

AIR FILTER
REPLACE ELEMENT AT RECOMMENDED INTERVAL

BATTERY

MANUAL TRANSAXLE FILL PLUG
FILL TO BOTTOM OF FILLER HOLE WITH VEHICLE LEVEL.

OIL FILTER
COAT GASKET WITH ENGINE OIL REPLACE AT RECOMMENDED INTERVAL

Motorcraft
F1-A

VACUUM BRAKE BOOSTER

ENGINE OIL FILL CAP

CRANKCASE EMISSION FILTER
9C490*ASSY

FUEL FILTER
REPLACE AT RECOMMENDED INTERVAL

ENGINE OIL DRAIN PLUG

PCV VALVE
REPLACE AT RECOMMENDED INTERVAL

WINDSHIELD WASHER RESERVOIR

BELT TENSION GUAGE T63L-8620-A
CHECK BELT TENSION AT RECOMMENDED INTERVAL

19D848
TANK AND HOSE ASSY VACUUM

N803155 STRAP

ENGINE OIL LEVEL DIPSTICKS

MAINTAIN ENGINE OIL IN SAFE RANGE

DO NOT ADD OIL BEYOND "MAX"

MAX
ADD
SAFE
ADD

POWER STEERING PUMP DIPSTICK
FLUID SHOULD BE BETWEEN FULL COLD OR FULL HOT MARKS. DEPENDING ON TEMPERATURE

POWER STEERING PUMP

COOLANT LEVEL IN RADIATOR AND COOLANT RECOVERY SYSTEM
REFER TO SECTION 50-27 FOR CHECKING PROCEDURE
REFER TO SECTION 50-29 FOR DRAIN AND FILL PROCEDURE.

TAURUS AND SABLE 2.5L

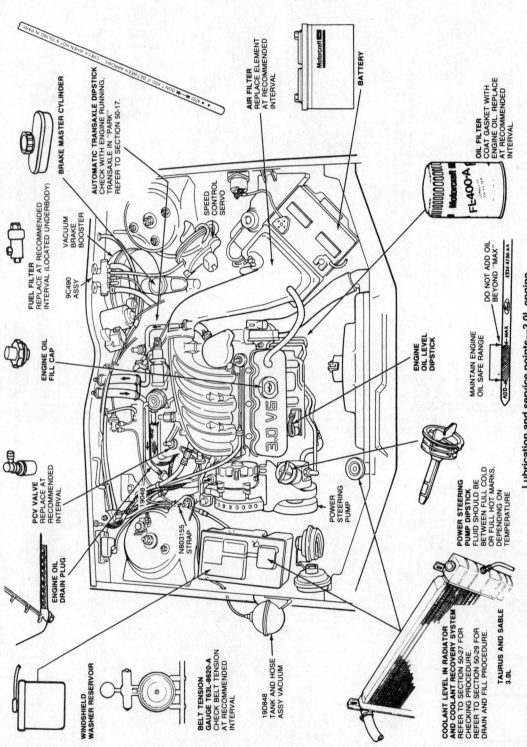

DON'T ADD IF BETWEEN ARROWS. CHECK WHEN HOT & IDLING IN PARK. ◄ ADD ►

BRAKE MASTER CYLINDER

AUTOMATIC TRANSAXLE DIPSTICK
CHECK WITH ENGINE RUNNING, TRANSAXLE IN "PARK". REFER TO SECTION 50-17.

SPEED CONTROL SERVO

AIR FILTER
REPLACE ELEMENT AT RECOMMENDED INTERVAL

BATTERY

OIL FILTER
COAT GASKET WITH ENGINE OIL. REPLACE AT RECOMMENDED INTERVAL.

FUEL FILTER
REPLACE AT RECOMMENDED INTERVAL (LOCATED UNDERBODY)

9C490 ASSY

VACUUM BRAKE BOOSTER

ENGINE OIL FILL CAP

3.0 V6

ENGINE OIL LEVEL DIPSTICK

MAINTAIN ENGINE OIL SAFE RANGE
DO NOT ADD OIL BEYOND "MAX"
MAX
ADD

PCV VALVE
REPLACE AT RECOMMENDED INTERVAL

9048

N803155 STRAP

POWER STEERING PUMP

ENGINE OIL DRAIN PLUG

POWER STEERING PUMP DIPSTICK
FLUID SHOULD BE BETWEEN FULL COLD OR FULL HOT MARKS, DEPENDING ON TEMPERATURE

WINDSHIELD WASHER RESERVOIR

BELT TENSION GAUGE T63L-8620-A
CHECK BELT TENSION AT RECOMMENDED INTERVAL

19D848 TANK AND HOSE ASSY VACUUM

COOLANT LEVEL IN RADIATOR AND COOLANT RECOVERY SYSTEM
REFER TO SECTION 50-27 FOR CHECKING PROCEDURE. REFER TO SECTION 50-29 FOR DRAIN AND FILL PROCEDURE.

TAURUS AND SABLE 3.0L

Lubrication and service points—3.0L engine

3.8L\Engine

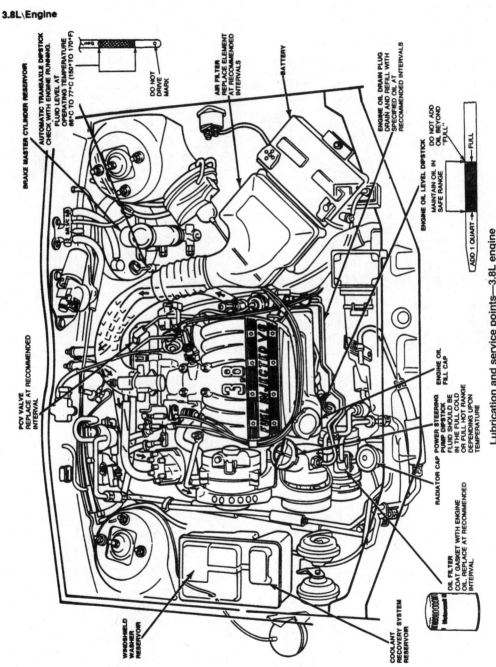

BRAKE MASTER CYLINDER RESERVOIR

AUTOMATIC TRANSAXLE DIPSTICK
CHECK WITH ENGINE RUNNING.
FLUID LEVEL AT
OPERATING TEMPERATURE
66°C TO 77°C (150°TO 170°F)

DO NOT
DRIVE
MARK

AIR FILTER
REPLACE ELEMENT
AT RECOMMENDED
INTERVALS

BATTERY

ENGINE OIL DRAIN PLUG
DRAIN AND REFILL WITH
SPECIFIED OIL AT
RECOMMENDED INTERVALS

ENGINE OIL LEVEL DIPSTICK

MAINTAIN OIL IN
SAFE RANGE

DO NOT ADD
OIL BEYOND
"FULL"

FULL

ADD 1 QUART

PCV VALVE
REPLACE AT RECOMMENDED
INTERVAL

ENGINE OIL
FILL CAP

RADIATOR CAP

POWER STEERING
PUMP DIPSTICK
FLUID SHOULD BE
IN THE FULL COLD
OR FULL HOT RANGE
DEPENDING UPON
TEMPERATURE

OIL FILTER
COAT GASKET WITH ENGINE
OIL. REPLACE AT RECOMMENDED
INTERVAL.

WINDSHIELD
WASHER
RESERVOIR

COOLANT
RECOVERY SYSTEM
RESERVOIR

Lubrication and service points—3.8L engine

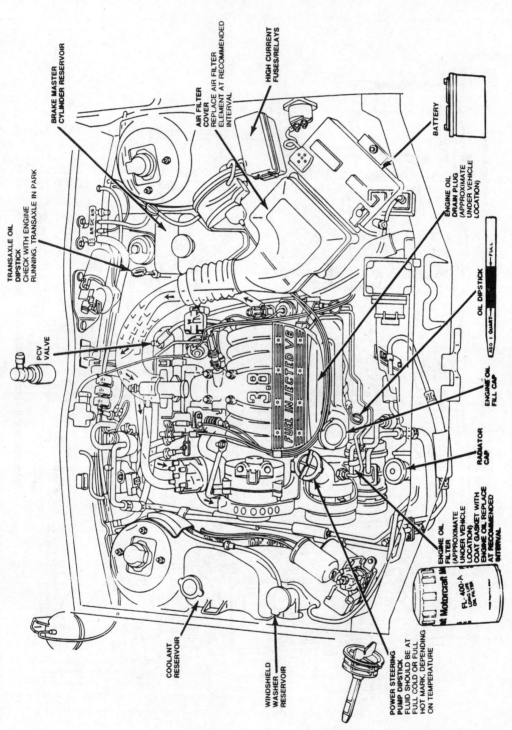

TRANSAXLE OIL
DIPSTICK
CHECK WITH ENGINE
RUNNING, TRANSAXLE IN PARK

BRAKE MASTER
CYLINDER RESERVOIR

AIR FILTER
COVER
REPLACE AIR FILTER
ELEMENT AT RECOMMENDED
INTERVAL

HIGH CURRENT
FUSES/RELAYS

BATTERY

PCV
VALVE

ENGINE OIL
DRAIN PLUG
(APPROXIMATE
UNDER VEHICLE
LOCATION)

OIL DIPSTICK

ADD 1 QUART — FULL

ENGINE OIL
FILL CAP

RADIATOR
CAP

ENGINE OIL
FILTER
(APPROXIMATE
UNDER VEHICLE
LOCATION)
COAT GASKET WITH
ENGINE OIL, REPLACE
AT RECOMMENDED
INTERVAL

Motorcraft
FL-400-A
LONG LIFE
OIL FILTER

POWER STEERING
PUMP DIPSTICK
FLUID SHOULD BE AT
FULL COLD OR FULL
HOT MARK, DEPENDING
ON TEMPERATURE

WINDSHIELD
WASHER
RESERVOIR

COOLANT
RESERVOIR

Lubrication and service points—3.8L engine

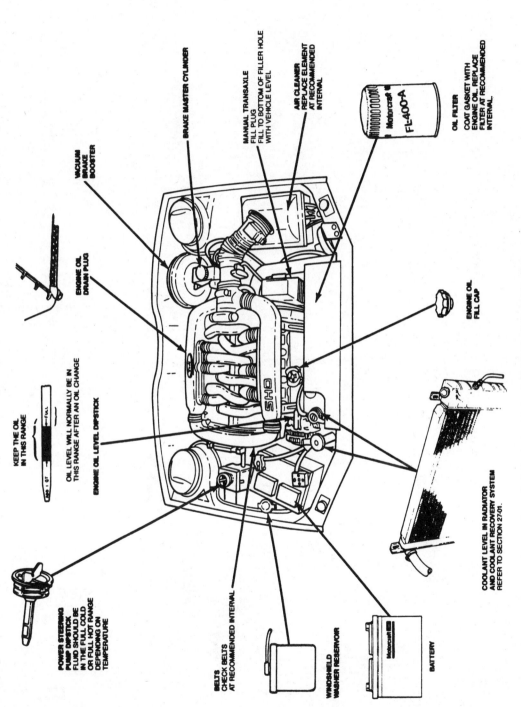

BRAKE MASTER CYLINDER

MANUAL TRANSAXLE
FILL PLUG
FILL TO BOTTOM OF FILLER HOLE
WITH VEHICLE LEVEL

AIR CLEANER
REPLACE ELEMENT
AT RECOMMENDED
INTERVAL

OIL FILTER
COAT GASKET WITH
ENGINE OIL. REPLACE
FILTER AT RECOMMENDED
INTERVAL

VACUUM BRAKE BOOSTER

ENGINE OIL DRAIN PLUG

ENGINE OIL FILL CAP

KEEP THE OIL
IN THIS RANGE

OIL LEVEL WILL NORMALLY BE IN
THIS RANGE AFTER AN OIL CHANGE

ENGINE OIL LEVEL DIPSTICK

POWER STEERING PUMP DIPSTICK
FLUID SHOULD BE
IN THE FULL COLD
OR FULL HOT RANGE
DEPENDING ON
TEMPERATURE

BELTS
CHECK BELTS
AT RECOMMENDED INTERVAL

WINDSHIELD WASHER RESERVOIR

BATTERY

COOLANT LEVEL IN RADIATOR
AND COOLANT RECOVERY SYSTEM
REFER TO SECTION 27-01.

Lubrication and service points—3.0L SHO engine

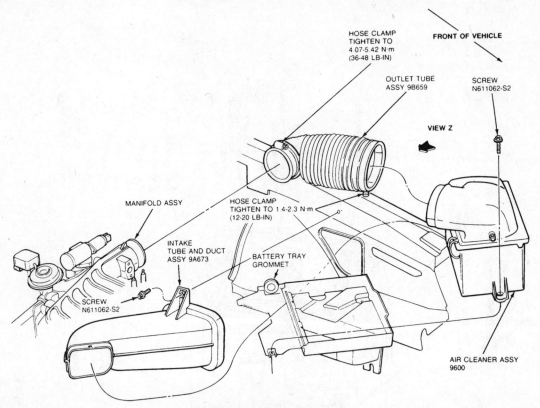

Air intake system—3.0L engine

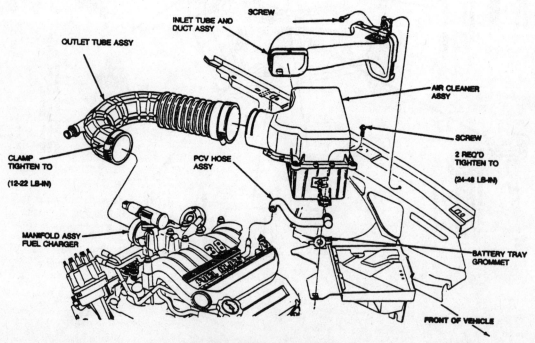

Air intake system—3.8L engine

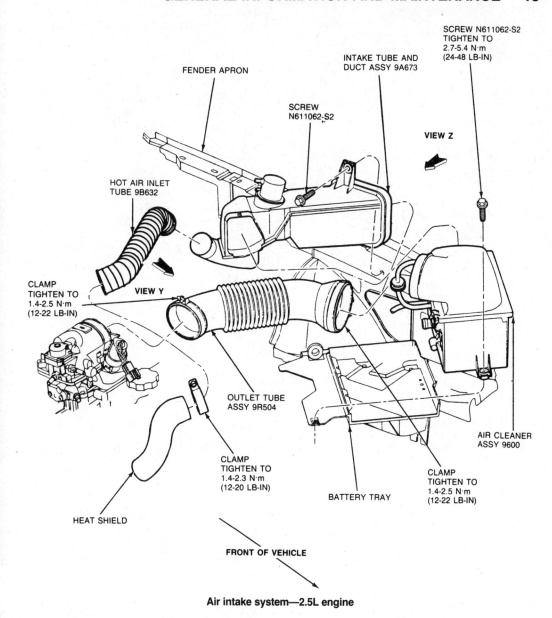

SCREW N611062-S2
TIGHTEN TO
2.7-5.4 N·m
(24-48 LB-IN)

INTAKE TUBE AND
DUCT ASSY 9A673

FENDER APRON

SCREW
N611062-S2

VIEW Z

HOT AIR INLET
TUBE 9B632

CLAMP
TIGHTEN TO
1.4-2.5 N·m
(12-22 LB-IN)

VIEW Y

OUTLET TUBE
ASSY 9R504

AIR CLEANER
ASSY 9600

CLAMP
TIGHTEN TO
1.4-2.3 N·m
(12-20 LB-IN)

BATTERY TRAY

CLAMP
TIGHTEN TO
1.4-2.5 N·m
(12-22 LB-IN)

HEAT SHIELD

FRONT OF VEHICLE

Air intake system—2.5L engine

ponents. *This system is under pressure even while the engine is turned off! Use safety glasses to prevent fuel from getting into your eyes.*

1. With the engine turned OFF, depressurize the fuel system on the EFI engines using special tool T80L-9974-B Fuel Pressure Gauge, or equivalent.

2. Remove the push connect fittings from both side of the fuel filter.

NOTE: *The filter is located on the underbody next to the right hand front corner of the fuel tank. Push connect fitting disconnection procedures are covered in Chapter 5 after Fuel Pumps. The filter's* **flow** *arrow should be noted for installation of the new filter.*

3. Remove the filter from the mounting bracket by loosening the retaining clamp enough to allow the filter to pass through.

4. Install the fuel filter in the bracket, ensuring proper direction of the flow as noted earlier. Tighten the clamp to 15-25 in. lbs.

5. Install the push connect fittings at both ends of the filter.

6. Start the engine and check for fuel leaks.

PCV Valve

No PCV (positive crankcase ventilation) valve is used. Instead, an internal baffle and an orifice control the flow of crankcase gases. (See

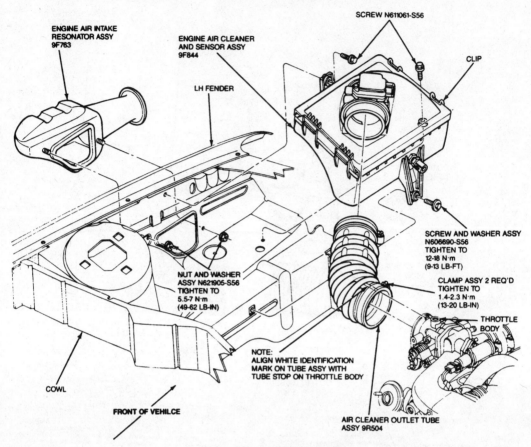

ENGINE AIR INTAKE
RESONATOR ASSY
9F763

ENGINE AIR CLEANER
AND SENSOR ASSY
9F844

SCREW N611061-S56

CLIP

LH FENDER

SCREW AND WASHER ASSY
N606690-S56
TIGHTEN TO
12-18 N·m
(9-13 LB-FT)

NUT AND WASHER
ASSY N621905-S56
TIGHTEN TO
5.5-7 N·m
(49-62 LB-IN)

CLAMP ASSY 2 REQ'D
TIGHTEN TO
1.4-2.3 N·m
(13-20 LB-IN)

THROTTLE
BODY

NOTE:
ALIGN WHITE IDENTIFICATION
MARK ON TUBE ASSY WITH
TUBE STOP ON THROTTLE BODY

COWL

FRONT OF VEHILCE

AIR CLEANER OUTLET TUBE
ASSY 9R504

Air intake system—3.0L SHO engine

Chapter 4 for more details on emission controls).

Evaporative Emission Canister

To prevent gasoline vapors from being vented into the atmosphere, an evaporative emission system captures the vapors and stores them in a charcoal filled canister.

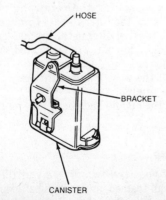

HOSE

BRACKET

CANISTER

Evaporative canister

SERVICING THE EMISSION CANISTER

Since the canister is purged of fumes when the engine is operating, no real maintenance is required. However, the canister should be visually inspected for cracks, loose connections, etc. The emission canister is located on the driver's side fender near the battery. The canister should have no liquid fuel in it and if it does replace it. Replacement is simply a matter of disconnecting the hoses, loosening the mount and replacing the canister.

Battery

Loose, dirty, or corroded battery terminals are a major cause of "no-start." Every 3 months or so, remove the battery terminals and clean them, giving them a light coating of petroleum jelly when you are finished. This will help to retard corrosion.

Check the battery cables for signs of wear or chafing and replace any cable or terminal that looks marginal. Battery terminals can be easily cleaned and inexpensive terminal cleaning tools are an excellent investment that will pay for

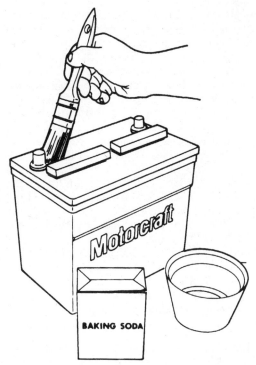

Cleaning the battery with baking soda and water

themselves many times over. They can usually be purchased from any well-equipped auto store or parts department. Side terminal batteries require a different tool to clean the threads in the battery case. The accumulated white powder and corrosion can be cleaned from the top of the battery with an old toothbrush and a solution of baking soda and water.

Unless you have a maintenance-free battery, check the electrolyte level (see Battery under Fluid Level Checks in this chapter) and check the specific gravity of each cell. Be sure that the vent holes in each cell cap are not blocked by grease or dirt. The vent holes allow hydrogen gas, formed by the chemical reaction in the battery, to escape safely.

REPLACEMENT BATTERIES

The cold power rating of a battery measures battery starting performance and provides an approximate relationship between battery size and engine size. The cold power rating of a replacement battery should match or exceed your engine size in cubic inches.

FLUID LEVEL (EXCEPT MAINTENANCE FREE BATTERIES)

Check the battery electrolyte level at least once a month, or more often in hot weather or during periods of extended car operation. The level can be checked through the case on translucent polypropylene batteries; the cell caps must be removed on other models. The electrolyte level in each cell should be kept filled to the split ring inside, or the line marked on the outside of the case.

If the level is low, add only distilled water, or colorless, odorless drinking water, through the opening until the level is correct. Each cell is completely separate from the others, so each must be checked and filled individually.

If water is added in freezing weather, the car should be driven several miles to allow the water to mix with the electrolyte. Otherwise, the battery could freeze.

SPECIFIC GRAVITY (EXCEPT MAINTENANCE FREE BATTERIES)

At least once a year, check the specific gravity of the battery. It should be between 1.20 in.Hg and 1.26 in.Hg at room temperature.

The specific gravity can be check with the use of an hydrometer, an inexpensive instrument available from many sources, including auto parts stores. The hydrometer has a squeeze bulb at one end and a nozzle at the other. Battery electrolyte is sucked into the hydrometer until the float is lifted from its seat. The specific gravity is then read by noting the position of the float. Generally, if after charging, the specific gravity between any two cells varies more than 50 points (0.50), the battery is bad and should be replaced.

It is not possible to check the specific gravity in this manner on sealed (maintenance free) batteries. Instead, the indicator built into the top of the case must be relied on to display any signs of battery deterioration. If the indicator is dark, the battery can be assumed to be OK. If the indicator is light, the specific gravity is low, and the battery should be charged or replaced.

CABLES AND CLAMPS

Once every 6 months, the battery terminals and the cable clamps should be cleaned. Loosen the clamps and remove the cables, negative cable first. On batteries with posts on top, the use of a puller specially made for the purpose is recommended. Damage may occur to battery if proper terminal pullers are not used. These are inexpensive, and available in auto parts stores. Side terminal battery cables are secured with a bolt.

Clean the cable clamps and the battery terminal with a wire brush, until all corrosion, grease, etc. is removed and metal is shiny. It is especially important to clean the inside of the clamp thoroughly, since a small deposit of foreign material or oxidation there will prevent a sound electrical connection and inhibit either starting or charging. Special tools are available

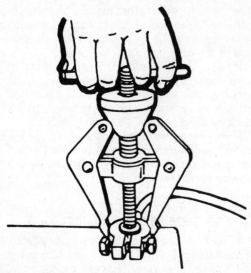

Use a puller to remove the battery cable

for cleaning these parts, one type of conventional batteries and another type for side terminal batteries.

Before installing the cable, loosen the battery holddown clamp or strap, remove the battery and check the battery tray. Clear it of any debris, and check it for soundness. Rust should be wire brushed away, and the metal given a coat of anti-rust paint. Before replacing the battery

wash it with soap and water to remove any dirt. Replace the battery and tighten the holddown clamp or strap securely, but be careful not to overtighten, which will crack the battery case.

After the clamps and terminals are clean, reinstall the cables, negative cable last; do not hammer on the clamps to install. Tighten the clamps securely, but do not distort them. Give the clamps and terminals a thin external coat of grease after installation, to retard corrosion.

Check the cables at the same time that the terminals are cleaned. If the cable insulation is cracked or broken, or if the ends are frayed, the cable should be replace with a new cable of the same length and gauge.

NOTE: *Keep flame or sparks away from the battery; it gives off explosive hydrogen gas. Battery electrolyte contains sulphuric acid. If you should splash any on your skin or in your eyes, flush the affected areas with plenty of clear water; if it lands in your eyes, get medical help immediately.*

Belts

Taurus/Sable and Continental models are equipped with V-ribbed belts. Replacement belts should be of the same type as originally installed. Loose belts will result in slippage and cause improper operation of the driven accessory, power steering, air conditioning, etc. Overtightened belts will put a severe load on accessory bearings and will almost certainly cause them to self destruct.

INSPECTION

Inspect all drive belts for excessive wear, cracks, glazed condition and frayed or broken cords. Replace any drive belt showing the above condition(s).

NOTE: *If a drive belt continually gets cut, the crankshaft pulley might have a sharp projection on it. Have the pulley replaced if this condition continues.*

ADJUSTMENT

NOTE: *Proper adjustment requires the use of the 021-00028 Belt Tension Gauge tool or equivalent.*

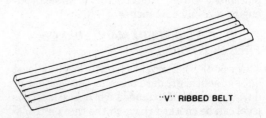

"V" RIBBED BELT

Clean battery cable clamps with a wire brush

6-rib "V" belt

2.5L and 3.8L Engine

The 2.5L and 3.8L engine uses an automatic tensioner and does not require adjustment.

3.0L Engine

The 3.0L engines may have an automatic belt tensioner or an adjustable idler pulley, depending on model.

ALTERNATOR BELT
W/ADJUSTABLE IDLER PULLEY

1. Loosen the alternator adjusting arm bolt and the alternator pivot bolt. Turn the adjusting screw until the belt is adjusted to 120-160 lbs. (new), 80-100 lbs. (used), and 60 lbs. (minimum).

2. Tighten the alternator pivot bolt to 45-57 ft. lbs. (61-76 Nm) and the adjusting bolt to 22-32 ft. lbs. (30-43 Nm), then recheck the belt tension.

POWER STEERING AND AIR CONDITIONING BELTS

1. Loosen the idler pulley and turn the adjusting screw until the belt is adjusted to 150-190 lbs.(new), 140-160 lbs.(used), and 90 lbs. (minimum).

2. Tighten the idler pulley bolt to 52-70 ft. lbs. (70-95 Nm), then recheck the belt tension.
NOTE: *The alternator, power steering, air conditioning drive belt should be checked for tension after both belts are adjusted and the component attaching belts are properly tightened.*

BELT REPLACEMENT

NOTE: *When installing belts on the pulley, ensure that all of the V-grooves are making contact with the pulleys.*

2.5L Engine

1. Insert a ½" breaker bar in the square hole in the tensioner, rotate the tensioner counterclockwise and remove the belt from the pulleys.
CAUTION: *Be careful when removing or installing belts that the tool doesn't slip!*

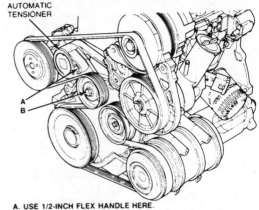

A. USE 1/2-INCH FLEX HANDLE HERE.
B. USE 18mm SOCKET HERE.

V-belt installation—2.5L engine

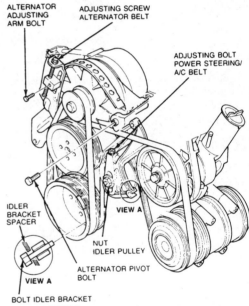

V-belt installation—3.0L engine

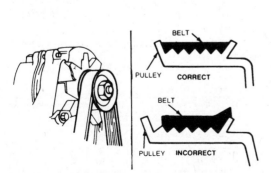

Proper V-belt alignment

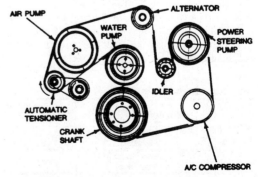

Serpentine belt installation—3.8L engine

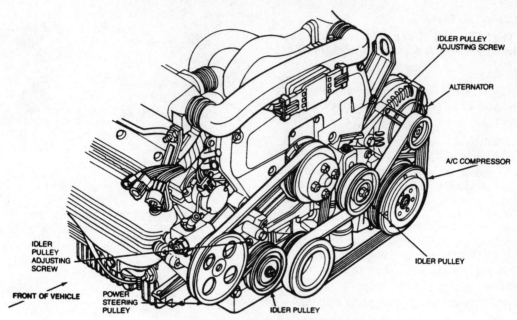

Serpentine belt installation—3.0L SHO engine

2. Install the belt over all pulleys except the alternator pulley.

3. Rotate the tensioner as described in Step 1 and install the belt over the alternator pulley. Check that all the V-grooves make proper contact with the pulleys.

3.0L Engine

ALTERNATOR BELT

1. Loosen the adjusting arm and the pivot bolts.

2. Turn the alternator belt adjusting screw counterclockwise until the old belt can be removed. Remove the belt.

3. Install the new belt over the pulleys. Check that all the V-grooves make proper contact with the pulleys.

4. Adjust the belt tension as outlined in the adjustment procedure.

POWER STEERING AND AIR CONDITIONING BELTS

1. Remove the alternator belt.

2. Loosen the nut on the tensioner pulley.

3. Turn the belt adjusting screw on the tensioner counterclockwise until the belt can be removed. Remove the belt.

4. Install the new belt over the pulleys. Check that all the V-grooves make proper contact with the pulleys.

5. Install the alternator belt as outlined in the adjustment procedure.

6. Adjust the belt tension for both belts as outlined above.

3.8L Engine

1. Remove alternator belt as outlined.

2. Loosen the nut on the tensioner pulley.

3. Insert a ½″ flex handle in square hole in tensioner and rotate tensioner counterclockwise and remove belt from pulleys.

CAUTION: *Use caution when removing or installing belts to ensure that tool does not slip.*

4. Install new belt over all pulleys except alternator pulley making sure all the V-grooves make proper contact with the pulleys.

5. Rotate the tensioner counterclockwise and install belt over alternator pulley. Make sure V-grooves make proper contact with pulleys.

6. Tension will be automatically adjusted by the tensioner.

BELT TENSION SPECIFICATIONS

Belt Type		New Installation		Used Belt Reset		Allowable Minimum	
		N	Lbs	N	Lbs	N	Lbs
6-Rib	Air Conditioning Alternator	980-1180	220-265	660-850	148-192	535	120
4-Rib	Power Steering Water Pump	690-880	154-198	500-700	112-157	357	80

Serpentine belt specifications—3.0L SHO engine

3.0L SHO Engine

ALTERNATOR BELT

1. Loosen the nut in the center of the idler pulley.

2. Loosen the idler adjusting screw until the old belt can be removed and remove the belt.

3. Install the new belt over the pulleys in the proper contact with the pulleys.

4. Adjust the new belt to specifications as follows: Turn the idler pulley nut to the right to tighten the belt to a specification of 220-265 lbs. with a belt tension guage. Torque the idler pulley nut to 25-37 ft. lbs. (34-50 Nm).

POWER STEERING AND AIR CONDITIONING BELT

1. Remove the alternator belt as previously outlined.

2. Loosen the nut on the tensioner pulley.

3. Turn the belt adjusting screw on the tensioner counterclockwise until the belt can be removed.

4. **To install**, position the new belt over the proper pulleys making sure the V-grooves are properly seated. Install the alternator belt as previously outlined. Adjust the power steering and air conditioning belt to a specification of 154-198 lbs. with a belt tension gauge. Adjust the alternator belt as previously outlined.

Hoses

CAUTION: *The cooling fan motor is controlled by a temperature switch. The fan may come on when the engine is off. It will continue to run until the correct temperature is reached. Before working on or around the fan, disconnect the negative battery cable or the fan wiring connector.*

HOSE REPLACEMENT

1. Open the hood and cover the fenders to protect them from scratches.

2. Disconnect the negative (–) battery cable at the battery.

3. Place a suitable drain pan under the radiator and drain the cooling system.

NOTE: *Place a small hose on the end of the radiator petcock, this will direct the coolant into the drain pan.*

CAUTION: *The engine must be cooled down before any hoses may be replaced. If engine is hot, let it cool down for at least an hour. When draining the coolant, keep in mind that cats and dogs are attracted by the ethylene glycol antifreeze, and are quite likely to drink any that is left in an uncovered container or in puddles on the ground. This will prove fatal in sufficient quantity. Always drain the coolant into a sealable container. Coolant should be reused unless it is contaminated or several years old.*

4. After the radiator has drained, position the drain pan under the lower hose. Loosen the lower hose clamps, disconnect the hose from the water pump inlet pipe and allow to drain.

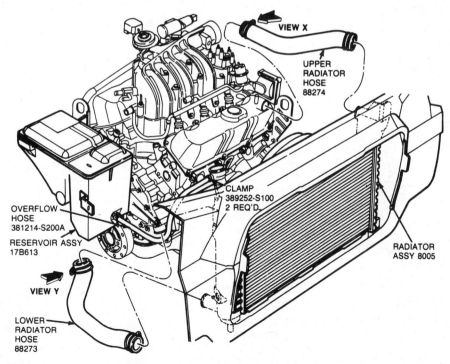

Radiator hose locations—3.0L engine

Disconnect the other end of the hose from the radiator and remove the hose.

5. Loosen the clamps retaining the upper hose, disconnect and remove the hose.

NOTE: *If only the upper hose is to be replaced, drain off enough coolant so the level is below the hose.*

6. If heater hoses need replacement, drain the coolant, loosen the clamps and remove the hose(s).

7. Installation of new hose(s) is in the reverse order of removal.

8. Tighten hoses clamps.

9. Be sure the petcock is closed. Fill the cooling system with the required protection mixture of water and permanent antifreeze. Connect the negative battery cable.

10. Run the engine until normal operating temperature is reached. Shut off the engine and check for coolant leaks. When the engine cools, recheck the coolant level in the radiator, or reservoir container.

Air Conditioning System

GENERAL SERVICING PROCEDURES

The most important aspect of air conditioning service is the maintenance of pure and adequate charge of refrigerant in the system. A refrigeration system cannot function properly if a significant percentage of the charge is lost. Leaks are common because the severe vibration encountered in an automobile can easily cause a cracking or loosening of the air conditioning fittings. As a result, the extreme operating pressures of the system force refrigerant out.

The problem can be understood by considering what happens to the system as it is operated with a continuous leak. Because the expansion valve regulates the flow of refrigerant to the evaporator, the level of refrigerant there is fairly constant. The receiver/drier stores any excess of refrigerant, and so a loss will first appear there as a reduction in the level of liquid. As this level nears the bottom of the vessel, some refrigerant vapor bubbles will begin to appear in the stream of liquid supplied to the expansion valve. This vapor decreases the capacity of the expansion valve very little as the valve opens to compensate for its presence. As the quantity of liquid in the condenser decreases, the operating pressure will drop there and throughout the high side of the system. As the R-12 continues to be expelled, the pressure available to force the liquid through the expansion valve will continue to decrease, and, eventually, the valve's orifice will prove to be too much of a restriction for adequate flow even with the needle fully withdrawn.

At this point, low side pressure will start to drop, and severe reduction in cooling capacity, marked by freeze-up of the evaporator coil, will result. Eventually, the operating pressure of the evaporator will be lower than the pressure of the atmosphere surrounding it, and air will be drawn into the system wherever there are leaks in the low side.

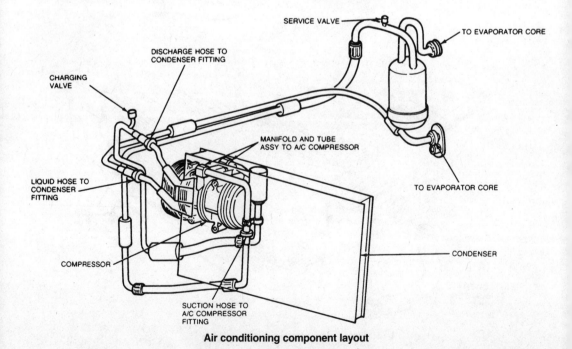

Air conditioning component layout

Because all atmospheric air contains at least some moisture, water will enter the system and mix with the R-12 and the oil. Trace amounts of moisture will cause sludging of the oil, and corrosion of the system. Saturation and clogging of the filter/drier, and freezing of the expansion valve orifice will eventually result. As air fills the system to a greater and greater extent, it will interfere more and more with the normal flows of refrigerant and heat.

A list of general precautions that should be observed while doing this follows:

1. Keep all tools as clean and dry as possible.

2. Thoroughly purge the service gauges and hoses of air and moisture before connecting them to the system. Keep them capped when not in use.

3. Thoroughly clean any refrigerant fitting before disconnecting, in order to minimize the entrance of dirt into the system.

4. Plan any operation that requires opening the system beforehand in order to minimize the length of time it will be exposed to open air. Cap or seal the open ends to minimize the entrance of foreign material.

5. When adding oil, pour it through an extremely clean and dry tube or funnel. Keep the oil capped whenever possible. Do not use oil that has not been kept tightly sealed.

6. Use only refrigerant 12. Purchase refrigerant intended for use in only automotive air conditioning system. Avoid the use of refrigerant 12 that may be packaged for another use, such as cleaning, or powering a horn, as it is impure.

7. Completely evacuate any system that has been opened to replace a component, other than when isolating the compressor, or that has leaked sufficiently to draw in moisture and air. This requires evacuating air and moisture with a good vacuum pump for at least one hour.

If a system has been open for a considerable length of time it may be advisable to evacuate the system for up to 12 hours (overnight).

8. Use a wrench on both halves of a fitting that is to be disconnected, to avoid placing torque on any of the refrigerant lines.

ADDITIONAL PREVENTIVE MAINTENANCE CHECKS

Antifreeze

In order to prevent heater core freeze-up during A/C operation, it is necessary to maintain permanent type antifreeze protection of $+15°F$ ($-9°C$) or lower. A reading of $-15°F$ ($-26°C$) is ideal since this protection also supplies sufficient corrosion inhibitors for the protection of the engine cooling system.

WARNING: *Do not use antifreeze longer than specified by the manufacturer.*

Radiator Cap

For efficient operation of an air conditioned car's cooling system, the radiator cap should have a holding pressure which meets manufacturer's specifications. A cap which fails to hold this pressure should be replaced.

Condenser

Any obstruction or damage to the condenser configuration will restrict the air flow which is essential to its efficient operation. It is therefore, a good rule to keep the unit clean and in proper physical shape.

NOTE: *Bug screens are regarded as obstructions.*

Condensation Drain Tube

This single molded drain tube expels the condensation, which accumulates on the bottom of the evaporator housing, into the engine compartment.

If this tube is obstructed, the air conditioning performance can be restricted and condensation buildup can spill over onto the vehicle's floor.

SAFETY PRECAUTIONS

Because of the importance of the necessary safety precautions that must be exercised when working with air conditioning systems and R-12 refrigerant, a recap of the safety precautions are outlined.

1. Avoid contact with a charged refrigeration system, even when working on another part of the air conditioning system or vehicle. If a heavy tool comes into contact with a section of copper tubing or a heat exchanger, it can easily cause the relatively soft material to rupture.

2. When it is necessary to apply force to a fitting which contains refrigerant, as when checking that all system couplings are securely tightened, use a wrench on both parts of the fitting involved, if possible. This will avoid putting torque on the refrigerant tubing. (It is advisable, when possible, to use tube or line wrenches when tightening these flare nut fittings.)

3. Do not attempt to discharge the system by merely loosening a fitting, or removing the service valve caps and cracking these valves. Precise control is possibly only when using the service gauges. Place a rag under the open end of the center charging hose while discharging the system to catch any drops of liquid that might escape. Wear protective gloves when connecting or disconnecting service gauge hoses.

4. Discharge the system only in a well venti-

lated area, as high concentrations of the gas can exclude oxygen and act as an anesthetic. When leak testing or soldering this is particularly important, as toxic gas is formed when R-12 contacts any flame.

5. Never start a system without first verifying that both service valves are backseated, if equipped, and that all fittings are throughout the system are snugly connected.

6. Avoid applying heat to any refrigerant line or storage vessel. Charging may be aided by using water heated to less than 125°F (52°C) to warm the refrigerant container. Never allow a refrigerant storage container to sit out in the sun, or near any other source of heat, such as a radiator.

7. Always wear goggles when working on a system to protect the eyes. If refrigerant contacts the eye, it is advisable in all cases to see a physician as soon as possible.

8. Frostbite from liquid refrigerant should be treated by first gradually warming the area with cool water, and then gently applying petroleum jelly. A physician should be consulted.

9. Always keep refrigerant can fittings capped when not in use. Avoid sudden shock to the can which might occur from dropping it, or from banging a heavy tool against it. Never carry a refrigerant can in the passenger compartment of a truck.

10. Always completely discharge the system before painting the vehicle (if the paint is to be baked on), or before welding anywhere near the refrigerant lines.

CHECKING FOR OIL LEAKS

Refrigerant leaks show up as oily areas on the various components because the compressor oil is transported around the entire system along with the refrigerant. Look for only spots on all the hoses and lines, and especially on the hose and tubing connections. If there are oily deposits, the system may have a leak, and you should have it checked by a qualified repairman.

NOTE: *A small area of oil on the front of the compressor is normal and no cause for alarm.*

KEEP THE CONDENSER CLEAR

Periodically inspect the front of the condenser for bent fins or foreign material (dirt, bugs, leaves, etc.). If any cooling fins are bent, straighten them carefully with needlenosed pliers. You can remove any debris with a stiff bristle brush or hose.

CAUTION: *Be careful when cleaning condenser fins not to damage core runners. They are made of soft aluminum and can be damaged very easily.*

OPERATE THE AIR CONDITIONING SYSTEM PERIODICALLY

A lot of air conditioning problems can be avoided by simply running the air conditioner at least once a week, regardless of the season. Let the system run for at least 5 minutes a week (even in the winter), and you'll keep the internal parts lubricated as well as preventing the hoses from hardening.

REFRIGERANT LEVEL CHECK

The only way to accurately check the refrigerant level to measure the system evaporator pressures with a manifold gauge set, although rapid on/off cycling of the compressor clutch indicates that the air conditioning system is low on refrigerant. The normal refrigerant capacity is 41 oz. ± 1 oz. for the Taurus/Sable and 40 oz. ± 2 oz. for the Continental.

MANIFOLD TEST GAUGES

Most of the service work performed in air conditioning requires the use of a set of two gauges, one for the high (head) pressure side of the system, sometimes called (discharge) side, the other for the low (suction) side.

The low side gauge records both pressure and vacuum. Vacuum readings are calibrated from 0 to 30 in.Hg and the pressure graduations read from 0 to no less than 60 psi. The high side gauge measures pressure from 0 to at last 600 psi.

Both gauges are threaded into a manifold that contains two hand shut-off valves. Proper manipulation of these valves and the use of the attached test hoses allow the user to perform the following services:

1. Test high and low side pressures.
2. Remove air, moisture, and contaminated refrigerant.
3. Purge the system (of refrigerant).
4. Charge the system (with refrigerant).

The manifold valves are designed so that they have no direct effect on gauge readings, but serve only to provide for, or cut off, flow of refrigerant through the manifold. During all testing and hook-up operations, the valves are kept in a close position to avoid disturbing the refrigeration system. The valves are opened only to purge the system or refrigerant or to charge it.

MANIFOLD GAUGE SET ATTACHMENT

The following procedure is for the attachment of a manifold gauge set to the service gauge port valves. If charge station type of equipment is used, follow the equipment manufacturers instructions.

CAUTION: *The air conditioning system is under high pressure when the engine is run-*

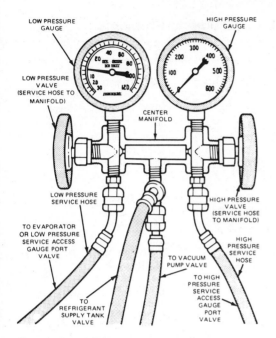

Air conditioning manifold gauge set

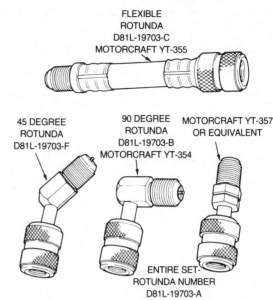

High pressure gauge port valve adapters

ning, When connecting and disconnecting the manifold gauge set make sure the engine is not running.

1. Turn both manifold gauge set valves fully clockwise to close the high and low pressure hoses at the gauge set refrigerant center outlet.

NOTE: *Rotunda high side adapter set D81L-19703-A or Motorcraft Tool YT-354 or 355 or equivalent is required to connect the manifold gauge set or a charging station to the high pressure service access gauge port valve. Check air conditioning component layout diagram in the air conditioning section in this chapter for service access gauge port valve location.*

2. Remove the caps from the high and low pressure service gauge port valves.

3. If the manifold gauge set hoses do not have the valve depressing pins in them, install fitting adapters T71P-19703-S and -R containing the pins on the manifold gauge hoses.

4. Connect the high and low pressure refrigerant hoses to their respective service ports, making sure they are hooked up correctly and fully seated. Tighten the fittings by hand and make sure they are not cross-threaded. Remember that an adapter is necessary to connect the manifold gauge hose to the high pressure fitting.

CHARGING THE SYSTEM

If the system has been completely purged of refrigerant, it must be evacuated before charg-

ing. A vacuum pump should be connected to the center hose of the manifold gauge set, both valves should be opened, and the vacuum pump operated for an hour until the low pressure gauge reads as close to 30 in.Hg as possible. If a part in the system has been replaced or excessive moisture is suspected, continue the vacuum pump operation for about an hour or more.

Close the manifold gauge valves to the center hose, then disconnect the vacuum pump and connect the center hose to a charging cylinder, refrigerant drum or a small can refrigerant dispensing valve. Disconnect the wire harness from the clutch cycling pressure switch and install a jumper wire across the two terminals of the connector. Open the manifold gauge LOW side valve to allow refrigerant to enter the system, keeping the can(s) in an upright position to prevent liquid from entering the system. Only use refrigerant R-12 when charging system which can be purchased at most auto parts stores.

When no more refrigerant is being drawn into the system, start the engine and move the function selector lever to the VENT/HEAT/AC position, the blower switch to HI and depress the air conditioning ON-OFF push button to draw the remaining refrigerant in. Continue to add refrigerant until the specified 40 oz. is reached. Close the manifold gauge low pressure valve and the refrigerant supply valve. Remove the jumper wire from the clutch cycling pressure switch connector and reconnect the pressure switch. Turn the engine off and disconnect the manifold gauge set and install the service port caps.

Troubleshooting Basic Air Conditioning Problems

Problem	Cause	Solution
There's little or no air coming from the vents (and you're sure it's on)	• The A/C fuse is blown • Broken or loose wires or connections • The on/off switch is defective	• Check and/or replace fuse • Check and/or repair connections • Replace switch
The air coming from the vents is not cool enough	• Windows and air vent wings open • The compressor belt is slipping • Heater is on • Condenser is clogged with debris • Refrigerant has escaped through a leak in the system • Receiver/drier is plugged	• Close windows and vent wings • Tighten or replace compressor belt • Shut heater off • Clean the condenser • Check system • Service system
The air has an odor	• Vacuum system is disrupted • Odor producing substances on the evaporator case • Condensation has collected in the bottom of the evaporator housing	• Have the system checked/repaired • Clean the evaporator case • Clean the evaporator housing drains
System is noisy or vibrating	• Compressor belt or mountings loose • Air in the system	• Tighten or replace belt; tighten mounting bolts • Have the system serviced

Sight glass condition
  Constant bubbles, foam or oil streaks
  Clear sight glass, but no cold air
  Clear sight glass, but air is cold
  Clouded with milky fluid
	
	• Undercharged system
	
	• No refrigerant at all
	• System is OK
	• Receiver drier is leaking dessicant
		
		• Charge the system
		
		• Check and charge the system
		
		• Have system checked

Large difference in temperature of lines	• System undercharged	• Charge and leak test the system
Compressor noise	• Broken valves • Overcharged • Incorrect oil level • Piston slap • Broken rings • Drive belt pulley bolts are loose	• Replace the valve plate • Discharge, evacuate and install the correct charge • Isolate the compressor and check the oil level. Correct as necessary. • Replace the compressor • Replace the compressor • Tighten with the correct torque specification
Excessive vibration	• Incorrect belt tension • Clutch loose • Overcharged • Pulley is misaligned	• Adjust the belt tension • Tighten the clutch • Discharge, evacuate and install the correct charge • Align the pulley
Condensation dripping in the passenger compartment	• Drain hose plugged or improperly positioned • Insulation removed or improperly installed	• Clean the drain hose and check for proper installation • Replace the insulation on the expansion valve and hoses
Frozen evaporator coil	• Faulty thermostat • Thermostat capillary tube improperly installed • Thermostat not adjusted properly	• Replace the thermostat • Install the capillary tube correctly • Adjust the thermostat
Low side low—high side low	• System refrigerant is low • Expansion valve is restricted	• Evacuate, leak test and charge the system • Replace the expansion valve
Low side high—high side low	• Internal leak in the compressor—worn	• Remove the compressor cylinder head and inspect the compressor. Replace the valve plate assembly if necessary. If the compressor pistons, rings or

Troubleshooting Basic Air Conditioning Problems (cont.)

Problem	Cause	Solution
Low side high—high side low (cont.)		cylinders are excessively worn or scored replace the compressor
	• Cylinder head gasket is leaking	• Install a replacement cylinder head gasket
	• Expansion valve is defective	• Replace the expansion valve
	• Drive belt slipping	• Adjust the belt tension
Low side high—high side high	• Condenser fins obstructed	• Clean the condenser fins
	• Air in the system	• Evacuate, leak test and charge the system
	• Expansion valve is defective	• Replace the expansion valve
	• Loose or worn fan belts	• Adjust or replace the belts as necessary
Low side low—high side high	• Expansion valve is defective	• Replace the expansion valve
	• Restriction in the refrigerant hose	• Check the hose for kinks—replace if necessary
	• Restriction in the receiver/drier	• Replace the receiver/drier
	• Restriction in the condenser	• Replace the condenser
Low side and high side normal (inadequate cooling)	• Air in the system	• Evacuate, leak test and charge the system
	• Moisture in the system	• Evacuate, leak test and charge the system

Charging From Small Containers

When using a single can air conditioning charging kit, such as is available at local retailers, with engine off, make the connection at the low pressure service port, located on the accumulator/drier. This is very important as connecting the small can to the high pressure port will cause the can to explode. Once the can is connected, charge the system as described above. If a manifold gauge set is being used, the low pressure valve must be closed whenever another can is being connected to the center hose. Hold the cans upright to prevent liquid refrigerant from entering the system and possibly damaging the compressor.

Windshield Wipers

Intense heat from the sun, snow, and ice, road oils and the chemicals used in windshield washer solvent combine to deteriorate the rubber wiper refills. The refills should be replaced about twice a year or whenever the blades begin to streak or chatter.

WIPER REFILL REPLACEMENT

Normally, if the wipers are not cleaning the windshield properly, only the refill has to be replaced. The blade and arm usually require replacement only in the event of damage. It is not necessary (except on new Tridon® refills) to remove the arm or the blade to replace the refill (rubber part), though you may have to position the arm higher on the glass. You can do this turning the ignition switch on and operating the wipers. When they are positioned where they are accessible, turn the ignition switch off.

There are several types of refills and your vehicle could have any kind, since aftermarket blades and arms may not use exactly the same type refill as the original equipment.

Most Anco® styles use a release button that is pushed down to allow the refill to slide out of the yoke jaws. The new refill slides in and locks in place.

Some Trico® refills are removed by locating where the metal backing strip or the refill is wider. Insert a small screwdriver blade between the frame and metal backing strip. Press down to release the refill from the retaining tab.

Other Trico® blades are unlocked at one end by squeezing 2 metal tabs, and the refill is slid out of the frame jaws. When the new refill is installed, the tabs will click into place, locking the refill.

The polycarbonate type is held in place by a locking lever that is pushed downward out of the groove in the arm to free the refill. When the new refill is installed, it will lock in place automatically.

The Tridon® refill has a plastic backing strip with a notch about 1″ (25mm) from the end. Hold the blade (frame) on a hard surface so that the frame is tightly bowed. Grip the tip of the backing strip and pull up while twisting counterclockwise. The backing strip will snap out of the retaining tab. Do this for the remaining

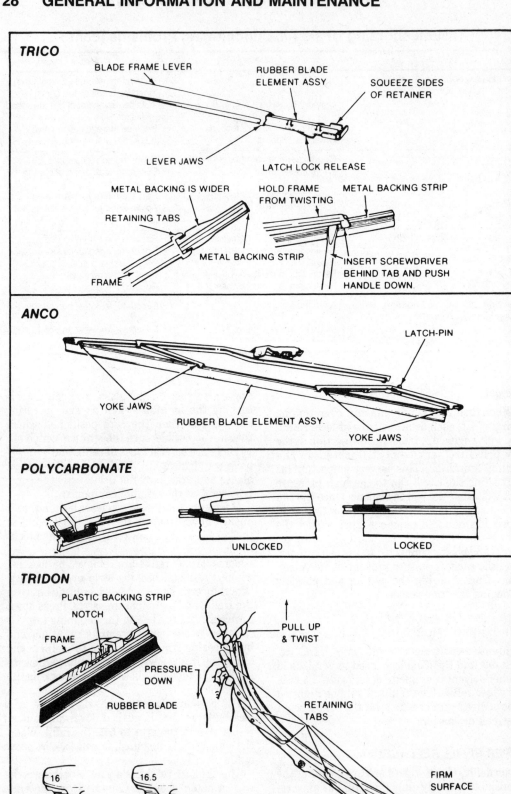

Wiper insert replacement

tabs until the refill is free of the arm. The length of these refills is molded into the end and they should be replaced with identical types.

No matter which type of refill you use, be sure that all of the frame claws engage the refill. Before operating the wipers, be sure that no part of the metal frame is contacting the windshield.

Tires

INFLATION PRESSURE

Tire inflation is the most ignored item of auto maintenance. Gasoline mileage can drop as much as 0.8% for every 1 pound per square inch (psi) of under inflation.

Two items should be a permanent fixture in every glove compartment: a tire pressure gauge and a tread depth gauge. Check the tire air pressure (including the spare) regularly with a pocket type gauge. Kicking the tires won't tell you a thing, and the gauge on the service station air hose is notoriously inaccurate. Also, just looking at the tire does not indicate if it underinflated.

The tire pressures recommended for you car are usually found on a label attached to the door pillar or on the glove box inner cover or in the owner's manual. Ideally, inflation pressure should be checked when the tires are cool. When the air becomes heated it expands and the pressure increases. Every 10° rise (or drop) in temperature means a difference of 1 psi, which also explains why the tire appears to lose air on a very cold night. When it is impossible to check the tires cold, allow for pressure build-up due to heat. If the hot pressure exceeds the cold pressure by more than 15 psi, reduce your speed. Otherwise internal heat is created in the tire. When the heat approaches the temperature at which the tire was cured, during manufacture, the tread can separate from the body.

CAUTION: *Never counteract excessive pressure build-up by bleeding off air pressure (letting some air out). This will only further raise the tire operating temperature.*

Before starting a long trip with lots of luggage, you can add about 2-4 psi to the tires to make them run cooler, but never exceed the maximum inflation pressure on the side of the tire.

TREAD DEPTH

All tires made since 1968 have 8 built-in tread wear indicator bars that show up as ½" wide smooth bands across the tire when ⅟₁₆" of tread remains. The appearance of tread wear indicators means that the tires should be replaced. In fact, many states have laws prohibiting the use of tires with less than ⅟₁₆" of tread

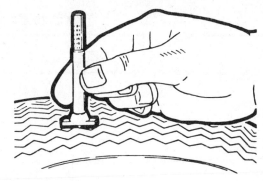

Tire tread depth gauge

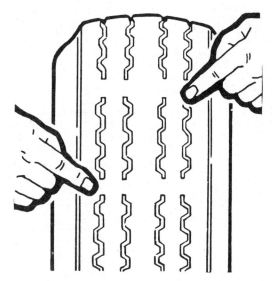

Replace a tire that shows the built-in "bump strip"

remains. The appearance of tread wear indicators means that the tires should be replace. In fact, many states have laws prohibiting the use of tires with less than ⅟₁₆" tread. Tread thickness under ⅟₁₆" is very dangerous on wet road conditions due to hydroplanning.

You can check you own tread depth with an inexpensive gauge or by using a Lincoln head penny. Slip the Lincoln penny into several tread grooves. If you can see the top of Lincoln's head in 2 adjacent grooves, the tires have less than ⅟₁₆" tread left and should be replaced. You can measure snow tires in the same manner by using the tails side of the Lincoln penny. If you see the top of the Lincoln memorial, it's time to replace the snow tires.

CAUTION: *When you replace tires, never mix radial, bias-belted or bias type tires. Use only the tire sizes listed on the tire decal attached to your vehicle on the driver's side door post. Make sure that all tires are the same size, speed rating and load carrying capacity. Use only tire and wheel combinations*

Tire Size Comparison Chart

"Letter" sizes			Inch Sizes	Metric-inch Sizes		
"60 Series"	"70 Series"	"78 Series"	1965–77	"60 Series"	"70 Series"	"80 Series"
			5.50-12, 5.60-12	165/60-12	165/70-12	155-12
		Y78-12	6.00-12			
		W78-13	5.20-13	165/60-13	145/70-13	135-13
		Y78-13	5.60-13	175/60-13	155/70-13	145-13
			6.15-13	185/60-13	165/70-13	155-13, P155/80-13
A60-13	A70-13	A78-13	6.40-13	195/60-13	175/70-13	165-13
B60-13	B70-13	B78-13	6.70-13	205/60-13	185/70-13	175-13
			6.90-13			
C60-13	C70-13	C78-13	7.00-13	215/60-13	195/70-13	185-13
D60-13	D70-13	D78-13	7.25-13			
E60-13	E70-13	E78-13	7.75-13			195-13
			5.20-14	165/60-14	145/70-14	135-14
			5.60-14	175/60-14	155/70-14	145-14
			5.90-14			
A60-14	A70-14	A78-14	6.15-14	185/60-14	165/70-14	155-14
	B70-14	B78-14	6.45-14	195/60-14	175/70-14	165-14
	C70-14	C78-14	6.95-14	205/60-14	185/70-14	175-14
D60-14	D70-14	D78-14				
E60-14	E70-14	E78-14	7.35-14	215/60-14	195/70-14	185-14
F60-14	F70-14	F78-14, F83-14	7.75-14	225/60-14	200/70-14	195-14
G60-14	G70-14	G77-14, G78-14	8.25-14	235/60-14	205/70-14	205-14
H60-14	H70-14	H78-14	8.55-14	245/60-14	215/70-14	215-14
J60-14	J70-14	J78-14	8.85-14	255/60-14	225/70-14	225-14
L60-14	L70-14		9.15-14	265/60-14	235/70-14	
	A70-15	A78-15	5.60-15	185/60-15	165/70-15	155-15
B60-15	B70-15	B78-15	6.35-15	195/60-15	175/70-15	165-15
C60-15	C70-15	C78-15	6.85-15	205/60-15	185/70-15	175-15
	D70-15	D78-15				
E60-15	E70-15	E78-15	7.35-15	215/60-15	195/70-15	185-15
F60-15	F70-15	F78-15	7.75-15	225/60-15	205/70-15	195-15
G60-15	G70-15	G78-15	8.15-15/8.25-15	235/60-15	215/70-15	205-15
H60-15	H70-15	H78-15	8.45-15/8.55-15	245/60-15	225/70-15	215-15
J60-15	J70-15	J78-15	8.85-15/8.90-15	255/60-15	235/70-15	225-15
	K70-15		9.00-15	265/60-15	245/70-15	230-15
L60-15	L70-15	L78-15, L84-15	9.15-15			235-15
	M70-15	M78-15				255-15
		N78-15				

Note: Every size tire is not listed and many size comparisons are approximate, based on load ratings. Wider tires than those supplied new with the vehicle, should always be checked for clearance.

as recommended on the tire decal or by your dealer. Failure to follow these precautions can adversely affect the safety and handling of your vehicle.

TIRE ROTATION

Tire wear can be equalized by switching the position of the tires about every 7,500 miles. Including a conventional spare in the rotation pattern can give up to 20% more tire life.

CAUTION: *Do not include the new SpaceSaver® temporary spare tires in the rotation pattern.*

TIRE STORAGE

Store the tires at proper inflation pressures if they are mounted on wheels. All tires should be

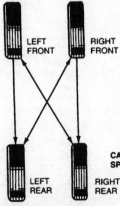

FOUR TIRE ROTATION

LEFT FRONT   RIGHT FRONT

FOUR TIRE ROTATION
ROTATE THE LEFT REAR TIRE TO THE RIGHT FRONT POSITION AND THE RIGHT REAR TO THE LEFT FRONT POSITION. ROTATE THE LEFT FRONT TO THE LEFT REAR AND THE RIGHT FRONT TO THE RIGHT REAR POSITION.

LEFT REAR   RIGHT REAR

CAUTION: DO NOT USE TEMPORAL SPARE TIRES IN THE TIRE ROTATION.

Tire rotation pattern

Troubleshooting Basic Wheel Problems

Problem	Cause	Solution
The car's front end vibrates at high speed	• The wheels are out of balance • Wheels are out of alignment	• Have wheels balanced • Have wheel alignment checked/adjusted
Car pulls to either side	• Wheels are out of alignment • Unequal tire pressure • Different size tires or wheels	• Have wheel alignment checked/adjusted • Check/adjust tire pressure • Change tires or wheels to same size
The car's wheel(s) wobbles	• Loose wheel lug nuts • Wheels out of balance • Damaged wheel • Wheels are out of alignment • Worn or damaged ball joint • Excessive play in the steering linkage (usually due to worn parts) • Defective shock absorber	• Tighten wheel lug nuts • Have tires balanced • Raise car and spin the wheel. If the wheel is bent, it should be replaced • Have wheel alignment checked/adjusted • Check ball joints • Check steering linkage • Check shock absorbers
Tires wear unevenly or prematurely	• Incorrect wheel size • Wheels are out of balance • Wheels are out of alignment	• Check if wheel and tire size are compatible • Have wheels balanced • Have wheel alignment checked/adjusted

kept in a cool, dry place. If they are stored in the garage or basement, do not let them stand on a concrete floor; set them on strips of wood.

FLUIDS AND LUBRICANTS
Engine
FUEL RECOMMENDATIONS

Unleaded gasoline having a Research Octane Number (RON) of 91, or an Antiknock Index of 87 is recommended for your car.

CAUTION: *Leaded gasoline will quickly interfere the operation of the catalytic converter and just a few tankfuls of leaded gasoline will render the converter useless. This will cause the emission of much greater amounts of hydrocarbons and carbon monoxide from the exhaust system, void your warranty and cost a considerable amount of money for converter replacement.*

OIL RECOMMENDATIONS

Oil meeting API classification SF or SF/CC or SF/CD is recommended for use in your vehicle.

Troubleshooting Basic Tire Problems

Problem	Cause	Solution
The car's front end vibrates at high speeds and the steering wheel shakes	• Wheels out of balance • Front end needs aligning	• Have wheels balanced • Have front end alignment checked
The car pulls to one side while cruising	• Unequal tire pressure (car will usually pull to the low side) • Mismatched tires • Front end needs aligning	• Check/adjust tire pressure • Be sure tires are of the same type and size • Have front end alignment checked
Abnormal, excessive or uneven tire wear See "How to Read Tire Wear"	• Infrequent tire rotation • Improper tire pressure • Sudden stops/starts or high speed on curves	• Rotate tires more frequently to equalize wear • Check/adjust pressure • Correct driving habits
Tire squeals	• Improper tire pressure • Front end needs aligning	• Check/adjust tire pressure • Have front end alignment checked

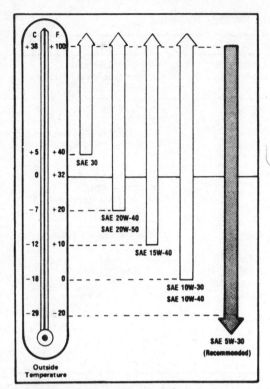

Engine oil viscosity recommendations

Ford has filled your crankcase with SAE 5W-30 and recommends that you continue to use this as long as the outside temperatures do not exceed 100°F (38°C). There are other options however, see the viscosity to temperature chart in this section.

OIL LEVEL CHECK

It is a good idea to check the engine oil each time or at least every other time you fill your gas tank.

1. Be sure your car is on level ground. Shut off the engine and wait for a few minutes to allow the oil to drain back into the oil pan.

2. Remove the engine oil dipstick and wipe clean with a rag.

3. Reinsert the dipstick and push it down until it is fully seated in the tube.

4. Remove the stick and check the oil level. If the oil level is below the lower mark, add one quart.

5. If you wish, you may carefully fill the oil pan to the upper mark on the dipstick with less

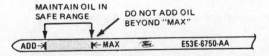

Engine oil level check recommendations

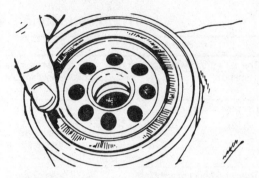

Lubricate the gasket on the new filter with clean engine oil. A dry gasket may not make a good seal and will allow the filter to leak

than a full quart. Do not, however, add a full quart when it would overfill the crankcase (level above the upper mark on the dipstick). The excess oil will generally be consumed at an excessive rate even if no damage to the engine seals occurs.

CHANGING OIL AND FILTER

Change the engine oil and oil filter every 7 months or 7,500 miles. If the car is used in severe service or dusty conditions, change the engine oil and oil filter every 3 months or 3,000 miles. Following these recommended intervals will help keep you car engine in good condition. Dirty oil loses its lubricating qualities and can cause premature wear in your engine.

1. Make sure the engine is at normal operating temperature (this promotes complete draining of the old oil).

2. Apply the parking brake and block the wheels or raise and support the car evenly on jackstands.

3. Place a drain pan of about a gallon and a half capacity under the engine oil pan drain plug. Use the proper size box or socket wrench, loosen and remove the plug. Allow all the old oil to drain. Wipe the pan and the drain plug with a clean rag. Inspect the drain plug gasket, replace if necessary.

4. Reinstall and tighten the drain plug. DO NOT OVERTIGHTEN.

5. Move the drain pan under the engine oil filter. Use a strap wrench and loosen the oil filter (do not remove), allow the oil to drain. Unscrew the filter the rest of the way by hand. Use a rag, if necessary, to keep from burning your fingers. When the filter comes loose from the engine, turn the mounting base upward to avoid spilling the remaining oil.

6. Wipe the engine filter mount clean with a rag. Coat the rubber gasket on the new oil filter with clean engine oil, applying it with a finger. Carefully start the filter onto the threaded engine mount. Turn the filter until it touches the

engine mounting surface. Tighten the filter, by hand, ½ turn more or as recommended by the filter manufacturer.

7. Lower the vehicle to the ground. Refill the crankcase with four quarts of engine oil (five quarts for the 3.0L SHO engine). Replace the filler cap and start the engine. Allow the engine to idle and check for oil leaks. Shut off the engine, wait for several minutes, then check the oil level with the dipstick. Oil level while drop as the filter fills up with oil, Add oil to the proper dipstick level.

Transaxle

SERVICE

Changing the fluid in either the automatic or manual transaxle is not necessary under normal operating conditions. However, the fluid levels should by checked at normal intervals as described previously in this chapter.

If your car is equipped with an automatic transaxle and the region in which you live has severe cold weather, a multi-viscosity automatic transaxle fluid should be used. Ask your dealer about the use of the MV Automatic Transaxle Fluid.

If you operate you car in very dusty conditions, tow a trailer, have extended idling or low speed operation, it may be necessary to change the ATX fluid at regular intervals (20 months, 20,000 miles or more often). Ask your dealer for his recommendations. A description of the fluid change procedure may be found in Chapter 7.

FLUID LEVELS

Manual Transaxle

Each time the engine oil is changed, the fluid level of the transaxle should be checked. The car must be resting on level ground or supported on jackstands (front and back) evenly. To check the fluid, remove the filler plug, located on the upper front (driver's side) of the transaxle with a ⁹⁄₁₆″ wrench.

CAUTION: *The filler plug has a hex-head, do not mistake any other bolts for the filler. Damage to the transaxle could occur if the wrong plug is removed.*

The oil level should be even with the edge of the filler hole or within ¼″ (6mm) of the hole. If the oil is low, add Type F or Dexron®II automatic fluid. Manual transmission type GL is NOT to be used.

NOTE: *A rubber bulb syringe will be helpful in adding the Type F or Dexron®II fluid to the manual transaxle.*

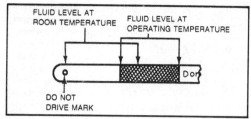

Dipstick markings for the ATX 3-speed automatic transaxle

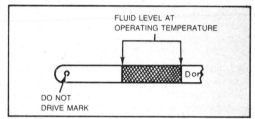

Dipstick markings for the AXOD overdrive automatic transaxle

Automatic Transaxle

A dipstick is provided in the engine compartment to check the level of the automatic transaxle. Check the lubrication and service charts in the beginning of this chapter for dipstick location. Be sure the car is on level ground and that the car's engine and transaxle have reached normal operating temperatures. Start the engine, put the parking brake on the transaxle selector lever in the PARK position. Move the selector lever through all the positions and return to the PARK position. DO NOT TURN OFF THE ENGINE DURING THE FLUID LEVEL CHECK. Clean all dirt from the dipstick cap before removing the dipstick. Remove the dipstick and wipe clean. Reinsert the dipstick making sure it is fully seated. Pull the dipstick out of the tube and check the fluid level. The fluid level should be between the FULL and ADD marks.

If necessary, add enough fluid through the dipstick tube/filler to bring the level to the FULL mark on the dipstick. Use Dexron®II fluid in the ATX 3-speed transaxle, or Ford type H fluid in the AXOD overdrive transaxle.

CAUTION: *Do not overfill. Can cause damage to transaxle. Make sure the dipstick is fully seated.*

If by chance you overfill the transaxle, Thread a small piece of rubber vacuum hose into the dipstick tube until it hits bottom. Using a large turkey baster or equivalent to pull the excess fluid out.

Differential

The differential is incorporated with the transmission, hence transaxle. The transaxle fluid lubricates the differential so any checks or fluid changes can be done by following the procedures above, or in Chapter 7.

Cooling System

LEVEL CHECK

The cooling system of your car contains, among other items, a radiator and an expansion tank. When the engine is running heat is generated. The rise in temperature causes the coolant, in the radiator, to expand and builds up internal pressure. When a certain pressure is reached, a pressure relief valve in the radiator filler cap (pressure cap) is lifted from its seat and allows coolant to flow through the radiator filler neck, down a hose, and into the expansion reservoir.

When the system temperature and pressure are reduced in the radiator, the water in the expansion reservoir is syphoned back into the radiator.

COOLANT CHECK AND CHANGE

On systems without a coolant recovery tank, the engine coolant level should be maintained 1-2″ below the bottom of the radiator filler neck when the engine is at air temperature and 1″ below the bottom of the filler neck when the engine is hot.

On systems with a coolant recovery tank, maintain the coolant level at the level marks on the recovery bottle.

For best protection against freezing and overheating, maintain an approximate 50% water and 50% ethylene glycol antifreeze mixture in the cooling system. Do not mix different brands of antifreeze to avoid possible chemical damage to the cooling system.

Avoid using water that is known to have a high alkaline content or is very hard, except in emergency situations. Drain and flush the cooling system as soon as possible after using such water.

CAUTION: *Cover the radiator cap with a thick cloth before removing it from a radiator in a vehicle that is hot. Turn the cap counterclockwise slowly until pressure can be heard escaping. Allow all pressure to escape from the radiator before completely removing the radiator cap. It is best to allow the engine to cool if possible, before removing the radiator cap.*

NOTE: *Never add cold water to an overheated engine while the engine is not running.*

After filling the radiator, run the engine until it reaches normal operating temperature, to make sure that the thermostat has opened and all the air is bled from the system.

CAUTION: *The cooling fan motor is controlled by a temperature switch. The fan may come on and run when the engine is off. It will continue to run until the correct temperature is reached. Take care not to get your fingers, etc. caught in the fan blades.*

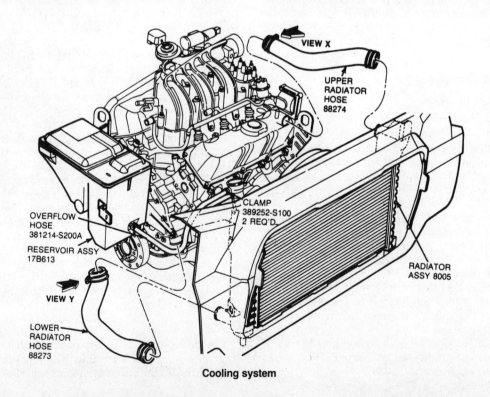

Cooling system

COOLANT SPECIFICATION

This engine has an aluminum cylinder head and requires a special unique corrosion inhibited coolant formulation to avoid radiator damage. Use only a permanent type coolant that meets Ford Specifications such as Ford Cooling System Fluid, Prestone® II or other approved coolants.

DRAINING COOLANT

CAUTION: *When draining the coolant, keep in mind that cats and dogs are attracted by the ethylene glycol antifreeze, and are quite likely to drink any that is left in an uncovered container or in puddles on the ground. This will prove fatal in sufficient quantity. Always drain the coolant into a sealable container. Coolant should be reused unless it is contaminated or several years old.*

To drain the coolant, connect a hose, 457mm long, with an inside diameter of 9.5mm, to the nipple on the drain valve located on the bottom left (driver side) of the radiator. With the en-

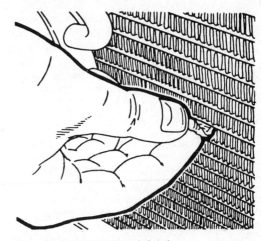

Clean the radiator fins of debris

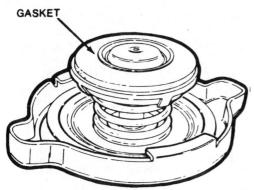

Check the radiator cap gasket for cuts or cracks

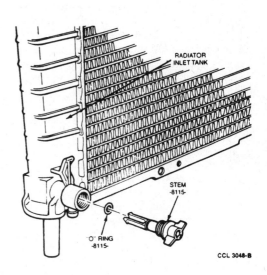

3.0L and 2.5L Engines

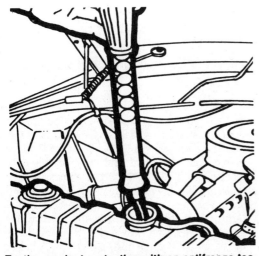

Testing coolant protection with an antifreeze tester

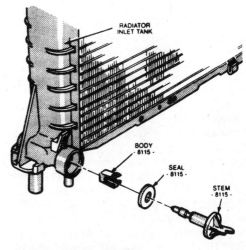

Radiator drain valve location

gine cool, set the heater control to the maximum heat position, remove the radiator cap and open the drain valve or remove the allen head plug (³⁄₁₆″) allowing the coolant to drain into a container. When all of the coolant is drained, remove the 9.5mm hose and close the drain valve.

REPLACING COOLANT

If there is any evidence of rust or scaling in the cooling system, the system should be flushed thoroughly before refilling. With the engine OFF and COOL:

1. Using a funnel, add a 50 percent coolant and 50 percent water solution to the radiator.
2. Reinstall the radiator cap to the pressure relief position by installing the cap to the fully installed position and then backing off to the first stop.
3. Start and idle the engine until the upper radiator hose is warm.
4. Immediately shut off engine. Cautiously remove radiator cap and add water until the radiator is full. Reinstall radiator cap securely.
5. Add coolant to the ADD mark on the reservoir, then fill to the FULL HOT mark with water.
6. Check system for leaks and return the heater temperature control to normal position.

RADIATOR CAP INSPECTION

Allow the engine to cool sufficiently before attempting to remove the radiator cap. Use a rag to cover the cap, then remove by pressing down and turning counterclockwise to the first stop. If any hissing is noted (indicating the release of pressure), wait until the hissing stops completely, then press down again and turn counterclockwise until the cap can be removed.

CAUTION: *DO NOT attempt to remove the radiator cap while the engine is hot. Severe personal injury from steam burns can result.*

Check the condition of the radiator cap gasket and seal inside of the cap. The radiator cap is designed to seal the cooling system under normal operating conditions which allows the build up of a certain amount of pressure (this pressure rating is stamped or printed on the cap). The pressure in the system raises the boiling point of the coolant to help prevent overheating. If the radiator cap does not seal, the boiling point of the coolant is lowered and overheating may occur. If the cap must be replaced, purchase the new cap according to the pressure rating which is specififed for your vehicle.

Prior to installing the radiator cap, inspect and clean the filler neck. If you are reusing the old cap, clean it thoroughly with clear water. After turning the cap on, make sure the arrows align with the overflow hose.

Brake Master Cylinder
LEVEL CHECK

The brake master cylinder is located under the hood, on the left side (drivers side) of firewall. Check the lubrication and service charts for location. Before removing the master cylinder reservoir cap, make sure the vehicle is resting on level ground and clean all the dirt away from the top of the master cylinder. Remove the master cylinder cap.

The Continental is equipped with Anti-lock brakes. To check the fluid level in the anti-lock master cylinder reservoir. Check lubrication and service chart for location of master cylinder.

1. Turn ignition OFF.
2. Pump the brake pedal at least 20 times or until the pedal feel becomes hard, then turn ignition key to ON position.
3. Wait at least 60 seconds to be sure the fluid level is stabilized.
4. The fluid level should be at the MAX line as indicated on the side of the reservoir. If the level is low, remove the cap and add Heavy Duty Brake Fluid (Dot 3) until the MAX line is reached.

The level of the brake fluid should be at the **MAX** mark embossed on the translucent plastic reservoir of the master cylinder. If the level is less than half the volume of the reservoir, check the brake system for leaks. Leaks in the brake system most commonly occur at the rear wheel cylinders or at the front calipers. Leaks at brake lines or at the master cylinder can also be the cause of the loss of brake fluid.

The fluid level lowers due to normal brake shoe wear. After filling the master cylinder to the proper level with brake fluid (Type DOT 3), but before replacing the cap, fold the rubber diaphragm up into the cap, then replace the cap on the reservoir and snap the retaining clip back in place.

Power Steering Pump Reservoir
LEVEL CHECK

Run the engine until it reaches normal operating temperature. While the engine is idling, turn the steering wheel all the way to the right and then left several times. Shut OFF the engine. Open the hood and remove the power steering pump dipstick located on the right side (passenger side) near the front of the engine. Wipe the dipstick clean and reinstall into the pump reservoir. Withdraw the dipstick and note the fluid level shown. The level must show in the hot full range on the dipstick. Add Ford type F automatic transmission fluid or power steering fluid, if necessary, but do not overfill.

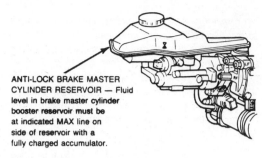

ANTI-LOCK BRAKE MASTER
CYLINDER RESERVOIR — Fluid
level in brake master cylinder
booster reservoir must be
at indicated MAX line on
side of reservoir with a
fully charged accumulator.

Master cylinder location—Continental

Remove any excess fluid with a suction bulb or equivalent.

Windshield Washer Reservoir

LEVEL CHECK

You can fill the washer tank with plain water in the summer time, but the pre-mixed solvents available help dissolve grime and dirt better and provide protection against freezing in the winter. Add fluid through the filler cover when the level drops below the line on the side of the reservoir case.

Rear Wheel Bearings

CAUTION: *When servicing the rear wheel bearings, brake shoes contain asbestos which has been determined to be a cancer causing agent. Never clean the brake surfaces with compressed air! Avoid inhaling any dust from any brake surface! When cleaning brake surfaces, use a commercially available brake cleaning fluid.*

PACKING AND ADJUSTMENT

NOTE: *Sodium-based grease is not compatible with lithium-based grease. Read the package labels and be careful not to mix the two types. If there is any doubt as to the type of grease used, completely clean the old grease from the bearing and hub before replacing.*

Before handling the bearings, there are a few things that you should remember to do and not to do.

Remember to DO the following:
- Remove all outside dirt from the housing before exposing the bearing.
- Treat a used bearing as gently as you would a new one.
- Work with clean tools in clean surroundings.
- Use clean, dry canvas gloves, or at least clean, dry hands.
- Clean solvents and flushing fluids are a must.
- Use clean paper when laying out the bearings to dry.

- Protect disassembled bearings from rust and dirt. Cover them up.
- Use clean rags to wipe bearings.
- Keep the bearings in oil-proof paper when they are to be stored or are not in use.
- Clean the inside of the housing before replacing the bearing.

Do NOT do the following:
- Don't work in dirty surroundings.
- Don't use dirty, chipped or damaged tools.
- Try not to work on wooden work benches or use wooden mallets.
- Don't handle bearings with dirty or moist hands.
- Do not use gasoline for cleaning; use a safe solvent.
- Do not spin-dry bearings with compressed air. They will be damaged.
- Do not spin dirty bearings.
- Avoid using cotton waste or dirty cloths to wipe bearings.
- Try not to scratch or nick bearing surfaces.
- Do not allow the bearing to come in contact with dirt or rust at any time.

The following procedure should be performed whenever the wheel is excessively loose on the spindle or it does not rotate freely.

NOTE: *The rear wheel uses a tapered roller bearing which may feel loose when properly adjusted; this feel should be considered normal.*

1. Raise and support the rear of the vehicle on jackstands.
2. Remove the wheelcover or the ornament and nut covers. Remove the hub grease cap.

NOTE: *If the vehicle is equipped with styled steel or aluminum wheels, the wheels must be removed to remove the dust cover.*

3. Remove the cotter pin and the nut retainer.
4. Back off the hub nut one full turn.
5. While rotating the hub/drum assembly, torque the adjusting nut to 17-25 ft.lb. (23-34 Nm). Back off the adjusting nut ½ turn, then retighten it to 10-15 inch.lb. (0.9-1.5 Nm).
6. Position the nut retainer over the adjusting nut so that the slots are in line with cotter pin hole (without rotating the adjusting nut).
7. Install the cotter pin and bend the ends around the retainer flange.
8. Check the hub rotation. If the hub rotates freely, install the grease cap. If not, check the bearings for damage and replace as necessary.
9. Install the wheel and tire assembly, then lower the vehicle and torque the lug nuts to 80-105 ft.lb. (108-143 Nm).

REMOVAL

CAUTION: *When servicing the rear wheel bearings, brake shoes contain asbestos which has been determined to be a cancer causing agent. Never clean the brake surfaces with compressed air! Avoid inhaling any dust from any brake surface! When cleaning brake surfaces, use a commercially available brake cleaning fluid.*

1. Raise the vehicle and support it safely. Remove the wheel from the hub and drum.

2. Remove the grease cap from the hub, making sure not to damage the cap. Remove the cotter pin, nut retainer, adjusting nut and keyed flat washer from the spindle. Discard the cotter pin.

3. Pull the hub and drum assembly off the spindle being careful not to drop the outer bearing assembly. Remove the outer bearing assembly.

4. Using seal remover 1175-AC or equivalent, remove and discard the grease seal. Remove the inner bearing assembly from the hub.

5. Wipe all grease from the spindle and inside the hub. Cover the spindle with a clean cloth and vacuum all the loose dirt from the brake assembly. Carefully remove the cloth to prevent the dust from falling on the spindle.

6. Clean both bearing assemblies and cups using a suitable solvent. Inspect the bearing assemblies and cups for excessive wear, scratches, pits or other damage. Replace all worn or damaged parts as required.

NOTE: *Allow the solvent to dry before repacking bearings. DO NOT spin dry the bearing with compressed air! Replace bearing cups and races as an assembly, don't mixmatch parts.*

7. If the cups (outer race) are to be replaced, remove them with a slide hammer T50T-100-A and Bearing Cup Puller T77F-1102-A or equivalent.

INSTALLATION

1. If the inner or outer bearing cups (outer race) were removed, install replacement cups using Drive Handle T80T-4000-W and Bearing Cup Replacers T73F-1217-A and T77F-1217-B or equivalent.

WARNING: *DO NOT use the cone and roller assembly to install the cup as this will cause damage to the bearing cup, cone and roller assembly.*

Support the drum hub on a wood block to prevent damage. Be certain the cups (outer race) are properly seated in the hub.

2. Make sure all bearing and spindle surfaces are clean.

3. Using a bearing packer, pack the bearing assemblies with Multi-Purpose Long-Life Lubricant C1AZ-19590-B or equivalent. If a bearing packer is not available, work in as much

grease as possible between the rollers and cages. Grease the cup surfaces.

4. Place the inner bearing cone and roller assembly in the inner cup. Apply a light film of grease to the lips of a new grease seal and install the seal with Rear Hub Seal Replacer T56T-4676-B or equivalent. Be sure the retainer flange is seated all the way around.

5. Apply a light film of grease on the spindle shaft bearing surfaces.

6. Install the hub and drum assembly on the spindle. Keep the hub centered on the spindle to prevent damage to the grease seal and the spindle threads.

7. Install the outer bearing assembly and keyed flat washer on the spindle. Install the adjusting nut finger tight.

8. Follow the procedures shown under "Wheel Bearing Adjustment" above.

OUTSIDE VEHICLE MAINTENANCE

Lock Cylinders

Apply graphite lubricant sparingly thought the key slot. Insert the key and operate the lock several times to be sure that the lubricant is worked into the lock cylinder.

Door Hinges and Hinge Checks

Spray a silicone lubricant on the hinge pivot points to eliminate any binding conditions. Open and close the door several times to be sure that the lubricant is evenly and thoroughly distributed.

Tailgate

Spray a silicone lubricant on all of the pivot and friction surfaces to eliminate any squeaks or binds. Work the tailgate to distribute the lubricant

Body Drain Holes

Be sure that the drain holes in the doors and rocker panels are cleared of obstruction. A small screwdriver can be used to clear them of any debris.

JACKING

Contact points for jacking with either the jack supplied with the car, or with a floor jack are located on the side rocker flanges as shown in the illustration. Always block the axle that is not being raised and never climb under car unless it is being held up with support stands.

Lubrication Recommendations

Item	Part Name
Hinges, Hinge Checks and Pivots*	Polyethylene Grease
Hood Latch and Auxiliary Catch	Polyethylene Grease
Lock Cylinders	Lock Lubricant
Steering Gear (Rack and Pinion)	Hypoid Gear Lube
Steering-Power (Pump Reservoir)	Auto. Trans. Fluid—Type F
Transmission (Automatic)	Auto. Trans. Fluid—Type H
Transmission (Manual)	Auto. Trans. Fluid—Dexron® II or Type F
Engine Oil	5W30
	10W40
	10W30
	20W40
	SAE 30
	15W40
Speedometer Cable	Speedometer Cable Lube
Engine Coolant	Cooling System Fluid
CV Joints	CV Joint Bearing Grease
Brake Master Cylinder	H.D. Brake Fluid—DOT 3
Brake Master Cylinder Push Rod and Bushing	SAE 10W-30 Engine Oil
Drum Brake Shoe Ledges	High Temp. Grease
Parking Brake Cable	Polyethylene Grease
Brake Pedal Pivot Bushing	SAE 10W-30 Engine Oil
Clutch Pedal Pivot Bushing	SAE 10W-30 Engine Oil

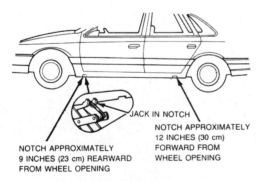

JACK IN NOTCH

NOTCH APPROXIMATELY 12 INCHES (30 cm) FORWARD FROM WHEEL OPENING

NOTCH APPROXIMATELY 9 INCHES (23 cm) REARWARD FROM WHEEL OPENING

NOTCH LOCATING DIMENSIONS ARE THE SAME FOR STATION WAGON MODELS

USE APPROPRIATE NOTCH (FRONT OR REAR)

Correct jack placement locations

TRAILER TOWING

Towing a trailer puts additional load on your Taurus/Sable, and Continental's engine, drive-train, brakes, tires and suspension. For your safety and the care of your car, make sure the trailer towing equipment is properly matched to the trailer. All towing equipment should be safely attached to the vehicle and of the proper weight class.

NOTE: *Trailer towing should only be attempted with the 3.0L or 3.8L V6 engine!*

The maximum trailer weight that your Taurus/Sable, and Continental can tow is 1,000 lbs. gross trailer axle weight with a maximum tongue load of 100 lbs. and must abide to the following qualifications:

• Any model equipped with a AXOD overdrive transaxle should be shifted to the "D" DRIVE position to avoid excessive shifting between the overdrive and third gears.

• Auxiliary oil coolers are recommended for the power steering system and the automatic transaxle during long distance towing (greater than 50 miles, towing in hilly terrain or frequent towing).

• Vehicle speed no higher than 55 mph is

recommended while towing a 1,000 lb. GVW (Gross Vehicle Weight) trailer.

Trailer Hitches

Choose a proper hitch and ball and make sure its location is compatible with that of the trailer. Use a good weight carrying hitch that uniformly distributes the trailer tongue loads through the underbody structure for towing trailers up to 1,000 lbs.

Under no circumstances should a single or multiclamp type hitch be installed on your car, damage to the bumper would result. Nor should any hitch which attaches to the axle be used. Underbody mounted hitches are acceptable if installed properly. Never attach safety chains to the bumper.

TOWING TIPS

Before starting on a trip, practice turning, stopping and backing up in an area away from other traffic (such as a deserted shopping center parking lot) to gain experience in handling the extra weight and length of the trailer. Take enough time to get the feel of the vehicle/trailer combination under a variety of situations.

Skillful backing requires practice. Back up slowly with an assistant acting as a guide and watching for obstructions. Use both rear view mirrors. Place your hand at the bottom of the steering wheel and move it in the direction you want the rear of the trailer to swing. Make small corrections, instead of exaggerated ones, as a slight movement of the steering wheel will result in a much larger movement of the rear of the trailer.

Allow considerable more room for stopping when a trailer is attached to the vehicle. Keep in mind, the car/trailer combination is a considerable increase in the weight that your car's brakes have to bring to a stop. If you have a manual brake controller, lead with the trailer brakes when approaching a stop. Trailer brakes are also handy for correcting side sway. So just touch them for a moment without using your vehicle brakes and the trailer should settle down and track straight again.

To assist in obtaining good handling with the car/trailer combination, it is important that the trailer tongue load be maintained at approximately 10-15% of the loaded trailer weight.

Check everything before starting out on the road, then stop after you've traveled about 50 miles and double-check the trailer hitch and electrical connections to make sure everything is still OK. Listen for sounds like chains dragging on the ground (indicating that a safety chain has come loose) and check your rear view mirrors frequently to make sure the trailer is still there and tracking properly. Check the trailer wheel lug nuts to make sure they're tight and never attempt to tow the trailer with a space saver spare installed on the car.

Remember that a car/trailer combination is more sensitive to cross winds and slow down when crossing bridges or wide open expanses in gusty wind conditions. Exceeding the speed limit while towing a trailer is not only illegal, it is foolhardy and invites disaster. A strong gust of wind can send a speeding car/trailer combination out of control.

Because the trailer wheels are closer than the towing vehicle wheels to the inside of a turn, drive slightly beyond the normal turning point when negotiating a sharp turn at a corner. Allow extra distance for passing other vehicles and downshift if necessary for better acceleration. Allow at least the equivalent of one vehicle and trailer length combined for each 10 mph of road speed.

Finally, remember to check the height of the loaded car/trailer, allowing for luggage racks, antenna, etc. mounted on the roof and take note of low bridges or parking garage clearances.

VEHICLE TOWING

Whenever you are towing another vehicle, or being towed, make sure the strap or chain is sufficiently long and strong. Straps are recommended because they have more stretch then a chain. Attach the strap or chain securely at a point on the frame, shipping tie-down slots are provided on the front and rear of you car and should be used. Never attach a strap or chain to any steering or suspension part. Never try to start the vehicle when being towed, it might run into the back of the tow car. Do not allow too much slack in the tow line, the towed car could run over the line and damage to both cars could occur. If your car is being towed by a tow truck, the towing speed should be limited to 50 mph with the driving wheels off the ground. If it is necessary to tow the car with the drive wheels on the ground, speed should be limited to no more then 35 mph and the towing distance should not be greater than 50 miles. If towing distance is more than 50 miles the front of the car should be put on dollies.

NOTE: *If the car is being towed with the front (drive) wheels on the ground, never allow the steering lock to keep the wheels straight, damage to the steering could occur. In general, don't do this! A new transaxle will cost you a lot more than a reasonable towing service. Remember the old saying, "you can pay me now, or you can pay me later".*

JUMP STARTING A DEAD BATTERY

The chemical reaction in a battery produces explosive hydrogen gas. This is the safe way to jump start a dead battery, reducing the chances of an accidental spark that could cause an explosion.

Jump Starting Precautions

1. Be sure both batteries are of the same voltage.
2. Be sure both batteries are of the same polarity (have the same grounded terminal).
3. Be sure the vehicles are not touching.
4. Be sure the vent cap holes are not obstructed.
5. Do not smoke or allow sparks around the battery.
6. In cold weather, check for frozen electrolyte in the battery. Do not jump start a frozen battery.
7. Do not allow electrolyte on your skin or clothing.
8. Be sure the electrolyte is not frozen.
CAUTION: *Make certain that the ignition key, in the vehicle with the dead battery, is in the OFF position. Connecting cables to vehicles with on-board computers will result in computer destruction if the key is not in the OFF position.*

Jump Starting Procedure

1. Determine voltages of the two batteries; they must be the same.
2. Bring the starting vehicle close (they must not touch) so that the batteries can be reached easily.
3. Turn off all accessories and both engines. Put both cars in Neutral or Park and set the handbrake.
4. Cover the cell caps with a rag—do not cover terminals.
5. If the terminals on the run-down battery are heavily corroded, clean them.
6. Identify the positive and negative posts on both batteries and connect the cables in the order shown.
7. Start the engine of the starting vehicle and run it at fast idle. Try to start the car with the dead battery. Crank it for no more than 10 seconds at a time and let it cool off for 20 seconds in between tries.
8. If it doesn't start in 3 tries, there is something else wrong.
9. Disconnect the cables in the reverse order.
10. Replace the cell covers and dispose of the rags.

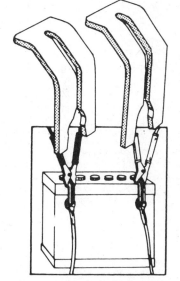

Side terminal batteries occasionally pose a problem when connecting jumper cables. There frequently isn't enough room to clamp the cables without touching sheet metal. Side terminal adaptors are available to alleviate this problem and should be removed after use.

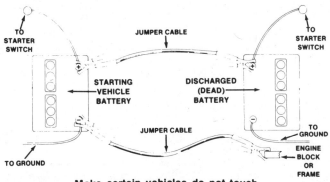

TO STARTER SWITCH

JUMPER CABLE

TO STARTER SWITCH

STARTING VEHICLE BATTERY

DISCHARGED (DEAD) BATTERY

JUMPER CABLE

TO GROUND

TO GROUND

ENGINE BLOCK OR FRAME

Make certain vehicles do not touch

This hook-up for negative ground cars only

PUSHING

Push starting is not recommended on cars with a catalytic converter. Gas accumulation in the converter will cause damage to the system. Also you can't push start a Taurus/Sable with an automatic transaxle anyway.

Capacities

Year	No. Cylinder Displacement liter (cu. in.)	Engine Crankcase		Transmission (pts.)		Drive Axle (pts.)	Fuel Tank (gals.)	Cooling System (qts.)
		With Filter	Without Filter	MT	AT			
1986	2.5L (154)	5.0	4.5	6.2	①	②	③	8.3
	3.0L (182)	4.5	4.0	—	①	②	③	11.0
1987–88	2.5L (154)	5.0	4.5	6.2	④	②	③	8.3
	3.0L (182)	4.5	4.0	—	④	②	③	11.0
1989	2.5L (154)	5.0	4.5	6.2	④	②	③	8.3
	3.0L (182)	4.5	4.0	—	④	②	③	11.0
	3.8L (232)	5.0	4.5	—	④	②	③	12.1
	3.8L SHO (182)	5.0	4.5	6.1	—	②	③	8.5

① Automatic transaxles with overdrive—10.9 qts.
Standard automatic transaxle—8.3 qts.
② Included in the transmission capacity
③ Standard fuel tank is 16.0 gallons. Optional extended range fuel tank is 18.6 gallons.
④ Automatic transaxles with overdrive—13.1 qts.
Standard automatic transaxle—8.4 qts.

Follow this Schedule if, generally, the vehicle is operated on a daily basis for more than 10 miles and NONE OF THE DRIVING CONDITIONS SHOWN IN SCHEDULE A APPLY TO OWNER'S DRIVING HABITS.

SERVICE INTERVALS Perform at the months or distances shown, whichever comes first. Miles x 1000	7.5	15	22.5	30	37.5	45	52.5	60
Kilometers x 1000	12	24	36	48	60	72	84	96
EMISSIONS CONTROL SERVICE								
Change Engine Oil and Oil Filter (every 6 months) or	X	X	X	X	X	X	X	X
Replace Spark Plugs — 3.0L SHO V6 (Platinum)								X
Replace Cam Belt and Adjust Valve Lash. 3.0L SHO V6								X
Inspect Accessory Drive Belt(s)				X				X
Replace Air Cleaner Filter①				X①				X①
Change Engine Coolant (every 36 months) or				X				X
Check Engine Coolant Protection, Hoses and Clamps				ANNUALLY				
GENERAL MAINTENANCE								
Check Exhaust Heat Shields				X				X
Inspect Disc Brake Pads and Rotors (Front and Rear)②				X②				X②
Inspect and Repack Rear Wheel Bearing				X				X

① If operating in severe dust, more frequent intervals may be required. Consult your dealer.

② If vehicle operation includes continuous stop-and-go driving or driving in mountainous areas, more frequent intervals may be required.

Vehicle maintenance schedule—3.0L SHO engine

Engine Performance and Tune-Up

2

TUNE-UP PROCEDURES

In order to extract the full measure of performance and economy from your engine it is essential that it be properly tuned at regular intervals. A regular tune-up will keep your vehicle's engine running smoothly and will prevent the annoying minor breakdowns and poor performance associated with an untuned engine.

A complete tune-up should be performed every 12,000 miles or twelve months, whichever comes first. This interval should be halved if the vehicle is operated under severe conditions, such as trailer towing, prolonged idling, continual stop and start driving, or if starting or running problems are noticed. It is assumed that

the routine maintenance described in Chapter 1 has been kept up, as this will have a decided effect on the results of a tune-up. All of the applicable steps of a tune-up should be followed in order, as the result is a cumulative one.

If the specifications on the tune-up sticker in the engine compartment disagree with the Tune-Up Specifications chart in this chapter, the figures on the sticker must be used. The sticker often reflects changes made during the production run.

Spark Plugs

A typical spark plug consists of a metal shell surrounding a ceramic insulator. A metal elec-

Tune-Up Specifications

| Year | No. Cylinder Displacement liter (cu. in.) | Spark Plugs | | Ignition Timing (deg.) | | Fuel Pump (psi) | Idle Speed (rpm) ① | | Valve Clearance | |
		Type	Gap (in.)	MT	AT		MT	AT	In.	Ex.
1986	2.5L (154)	AWSF-32C	.044	10B	10B	35–45	725	650	Hyd.	Hyd.
	3.0L (182)	AWSF-32C	.044	—	10B	35–45	—	625	Hyd.	Hyd.
1987–88	2.5L (154)	AWSF-32C	.044	10B	10B	35–45	725	650	Hyd.	Hyd.
	3.0L (182)	AWSF-32C	.044	—	10B	35–45	—	625	Hyd.	Hyd.
1989	2.5 (154)	AWSF-32C	.044	10B	10B	35–45	725	650	Hyd.	Hyd.
	3.0L (182)	AWSF-32C	.044	10B	10B	35–45	—	625	Hyd.	Hyd.
	3.8L (232)	AWSF-44C	0.56	①	①	35–45	①	①	Hyd.	Hyd.
	3.0L SHO (182)	AGSP-32P	0.44	②	—	35–45	800		③	③

NA—Not Available
B—Before Top Dead Center
① The Calibration levels vary from model to model. Always refer to the underhood sticker for your car requirements.
Hyd.—Hydraulic valve lash lifters.
② The initial timing is preset at $10° \pm 2°$B and is not adjustable.
③ Engine cold
   Intake 0.006–0.010 inch (0.15–0.25 mm)
   Exhaust 0.010–0.014 inch (0.25–0.35 mm)

trode extends downward through the center of the insulator and protrudes a small distance. Located at the end of the plug and attached to the side of the outer metal shell is the side electrode. The side electrode bends in at a 90° angle so that its tip is even with, and parallel to, the tip of the center electrode. The distance between these two electrodes (measured in thousandths of an inch) is called the spark plug gap. The spark plug in no way produces a spark but merely provides a gap across which the current can arc. The coil produces anywhere from 20,000 to 40,000 volts which travels to the distributor where it is distributed through the spark plug wires to the spark plugs. The current passes along the center electrode and jumps the gap to the side electrode, and, in do doing, ignites the air/fuel mixture in the combustion chamber.

Spark plugs ignite the air and fuel mixture in the cylinder as the piston reaches the top of the compression stroke. The controlled explosion that results forces the piston down, turning the crankshaft and the rest of the drive train.

The average life of a spark plug is dependent on a number of factors: the mechanical condition of the engine; the type of engine; the type of fuel; driving conditions; and the driver.

When you remove the spark plugs, check their condition. They are a good indicator of the condition of the engine. It it a good idea to remove the spark plugs at regular intervals, such as every 2,000 or 3,000 miles, just so you can keep an eye on the mechanical state of your engine.

A small deposit of light tan or gray material on a spark plug that has been used for any period of time is to be considered normal.

The gap between the center electrode and the side or ground electrode can be expected to increase not more than 0.001″ every 1,000 miles under normal conditions.

When a spark plug is functioning normally or, more accurately, when the plug is installed in an engine that is functioning properly, the plugs can be taken out, cleaned, regapped, and reinstalled in the engine without doing the engine any harm.

When, and if, a plug fouls and beings to misfire, you will have to investigate, correct the cause of the fouling, and either clean or replace the plug.

There are several reasons why a spark plug will foul and you can learn which is at fault by just looking at the plug. A few of the most common reasons for plug fouling, and a description of the fouled plug's appearance, are listed in the Color Section, which also offers solutions to the problems.

SPARK PLUG HEAT RANGE

Spark plug heat range is the ability of the plug to dissipate heat. The longer the insulator (or the farther it extends into the engine), the hotter the plug will operate; the shorter the insulator the cooler it will operate. A plug that absorbs little heat and remains too cool will quickly accumulate deposits of oil and carbon since it is not hot enough to burn them off. This leads to plug fouling and consequently to misfiring. A plug that absorbs too much heat will have no deposits, but, due to the excessive heat, the electrodes will burn away quickly and in some instances, preignition may result. Preignition takes place when plug tips get so hot that they glow sufficiently to ignite the fuel/air mixture before the actual spark occurs. This early ignition will usually cause a pinging during low speeds and heavy loads.

The general rule of thumb for choosing the correct heat range when picking a spark plug is: if most of your driving is long distance, high speed travel, use a colder plug; if most of your driving is stop and go, use a hotter plug. Original equipment plugs are compromise plugs, but most people never have occasion to change their plugs from the factory-recommended heat range.

Ford recommends that spark plugs be changed every 30,000 miles for the 2.5L, 3.0L, and 3.8L engines. The 3.0L SHO engine is equipped with Platinum spark plugs that have a recommended life of 60,000 miles. Under severe driving conditions, those intervals should be halved (except 3.0L SHO). Severe driving conditions are:

1. Extended periods of idling or low speed operation, such as off-road or door-to-door delivery.

2. Driving short distances (less than 10 miles) when the average temperature is below 10°F (−12°C) for 60 days or more.

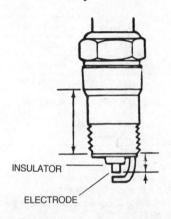

INSULATOR

ELECTRODE

Spark plug heat range

3. Excessive dust or blowing dirt conditions.

When you remove the spark plugs, check their condition. They are in good indicator of the condition of the engine. It is a good idea to remove the spark plugs at regular intervals, such as every 6,000 or so miles, just so you can keep an eye on the mechanical state of the engine.

A small deposit of light tan or gray material on a spark plug that has been used for any period of time is considered normal. Any other color, or abnormal amounts of deposit, indicate that there is something amiss in the engine.

The gap between the center electrode and the side or ground electrode can be expected to increase not more than 0.001″ (0.025mm) every 1,000 miles under normal conditions. When, and if, a plug fouls and begins to misfire, you will have to investigate, correct the cause of the fouling and either clean or replace the plug.

There are several reasons why a spark plug will foul and you can learn which reason is at fault by just looking at the plug. A few of the most common reasons for plug fouling and a description of fouled plug appearance are shown in the Color section.

REPLACING SPARK PLUGS

A Set of spark plugs usually requires replacement every 30,000 miles, (60,000 miles for the 3.0L SHO engine), depending on your style of driving. In normal operation, plug gap increases about 0.025mm for every 1,000-2,500 miles. As the gap increases, the plug's voltage requirement also increases. It requires greater voltage to jump the wider gap and about two to three times as much voltage to fire a plug at higher speeds than at idle.

The spark plugs used in your car require a deep spark plug socket for removal and installation. A special designed pair of plug wire removal pliers is also a good tool to have. The special pliers have cupped jaws that grip the plug wire boot and make the job of twisting and pulling the wire from the plug easier. Damage may occur to the spark plug wire if wire removal pliers are not used.

Check the spark plug gap with a wire feeler gauge

REMOVAL AND INSTALLATION

NOTE: *The original spark plug wires are marked for cylinder location. If replacement wires have been installed, be sure to tag them for proper location. It is a good idea to remove the wires one at a time, service the spark plug, reinstall the wire and move onto the next cylinder.*

For easy access for servicing the spark plugs, remove the air cleaner assembly and air intake tube.

1. Twist the spark plug boot and gently pull it and the wire from the spark plug. This is where the special plug wire pliers come in handy.

CAUTION: *Never pull on the wire itself, damage to the inside conductor could occur.*

2. The plug wire boot has a cover which shields the plug cavity (in the head) against dirt. After removing the wire, blow out the cavity with air or clean it out with a small brush so dirt will not fall into the engine when the spark plug is removed.

3. Remove the spark plug with a spark plug socket. Turn the socket counterclockwise to remove the plug. Be sure to hold the socket straight on the plug to avoid breaking the insulator (a deep socket designed for spark plugs has a rubber cushion built-in to help prevent plug breakage).

4. Once the plug is out, compare it with the spark plug illustrations to determine the engine condition. This is crucial since spark plug readings are vital signs of engine condition and pending problems.

5. If the old plugs are to be reused, clean and regap them. If new spark plugs are to be installed, always check the gap. Use a round wire feeler gauge to check plug gap. The correct size gauge should pass through the electrode gap with a slight drag. If you're in doubt, try the next smaller and one size larger. The smaller gauge should go through easily and the larger should not go through at all. If adjustment is necessary, use the bending tool on the end of the gauge. When adjusting the gap, always bend the side electrode. The center electrode is non-adjustable.

6. Squirt a drop of penetrating oil or anti-seize compound on the threads of the spark plug and install it. Don't oil the threads heavily. Turn the plug in clockwise by hand until it is snug. Be careful not to cross thread the plug

7. When the plug is finger tight, tighten it to the proper torque 17-22 ft. lbs., DO NOT OVERTIGHTEN.

8. Install the plug wire and boot firmly over the spark plug after coating the inside of the

boot and terminal with a thin coat of dielectric compound (Motorcraft D7AZ19A331A or white lithium grease).

9. Proceed to the next spark plug.

CHECK AND REPLACING SPARK PLUG CABLES

Your car is equipped with a electronic ignition system which utilizes 8mm wires to conduct the hotter spark produced. The boots on these wires are designed to cover the spark plug cavities in the cylinder head.

Inspect the wires without removing them from the spark plugs, distributor cap or coil. Look for visible damage such as cuts, pinches, cracks or torn boots. Replace any wires that show damage. If the boot is damaged, it may be replaced by itself. It is not necessary to replace the complete wire just for the boot.

To replace the wire, grasp and twist the boot back and forth while pulling away from the spark plug. Use a special pliers if available.

NOTE: *Always coat the terminals of any wire removed or replaced with a thin layer of dielectric compound.*

When installing a wire be sure it is firmly mounted over or on the plug, distributor cap connector or coil terminal.

FIRING ORDERS

NOTE: *To avoid confusion, tag using a piece of tap, and remove the spark plug wire one at a time, for replacement.*

If new wires have been installed (original wires are marked for cylinder location) and are not identified, or the wires have been removed from the distributor cap, the firing order is: 1-3-4-2 clockwise on the 2.5L 4 cyl. engine and 1-4-2-5-3-6 counterclockwise on the 3.0L and 3.8L 6 cyl. engines.

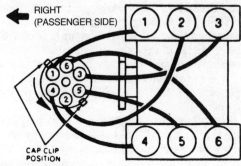

Ford 3800 cc (3.8L)
Firing order: 1–4–2–5–3–6
Distributor rotation: counterclockwise

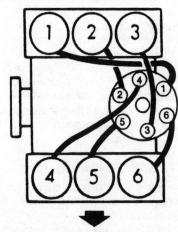

Ford 3000cc 6 cylinder (3.0L)
Firing order: 1–4–5–3–6
Distributor rotation: counterclockwise

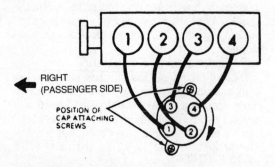

Ford 2500 cc 4 cyl (2.5L)
Firing order: 1–3–4–2
Distributor rotation: clockwise

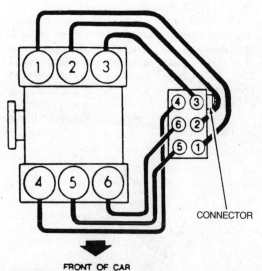

Ford 3.0L SHO 6 cylinder DOHC
Firing order: 1–4–5–3–6
Distributorless Ignition System (DIS)

ELECTRONIC IGNITION SYSTEM

Your car uses an electronic ignition system. The purpose of using an electronic ignition system is: To eliminate the deterioration of spark quality which occur in the breaker point ignition system as the breaker points wore. To extend maintenance intervals. To provide a more intense and reliable spark at every firing impulse in order to ignite the leaner gas mixtures necessary to control emissions.

The breaker points, point actuating cam and the condenser have been eliminated in the solid state distributor. They are replaced by an ignition module and a magnetic pulse-signal generator (pick-up).

A Universal Distributor equipped with a TFI-IV system is used on all Taurus/Sable and Continental models, except for the 3.0L SHO Taurus. TFI stands for Thick Film Integrated which incorporates a molded thermoplastic module mounted on the distributor base. TFI

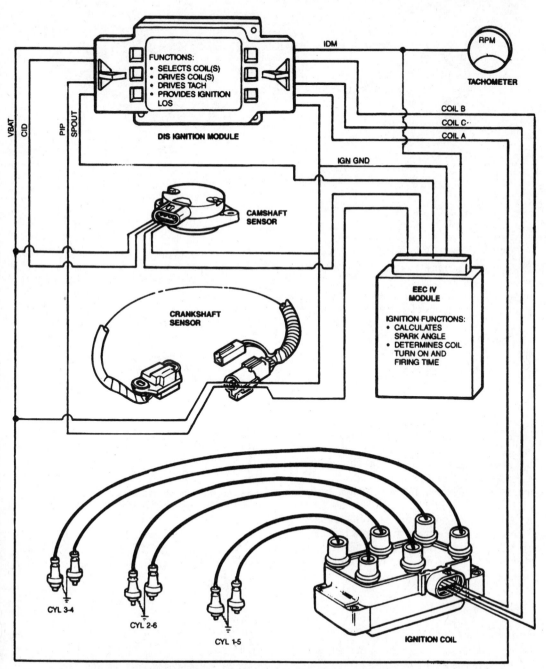

Distributorless ignition system (DIS)—3.0L SHO Taurus

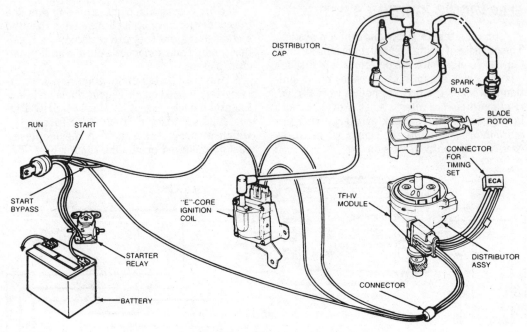

The Taurus/Sable TFI-IV ignition system

also uses an "E" coil which replaces the oil filled design used with earlier systems.

The Universal Distributor equipped with TFI-IV uses a vane switch stator assembly which replace the coil stator. The IV system incorporates provision for fixed octane adjustment and has no centrifugal or vacuum advance mechanisms. All necessary timing requirements are handled by the EEC-IV electronic engine control system.

The 30L SHO Taurus is equipped with a Distributorless Ignition System (DIS). As the name implies, there is no conventional distributor assembly in the engine. The DIS systerm is new for 1989 models only. DIS system consists of: a crankshaft timing sensor that is a single hall effect magnetic switch which is activated by three vanes on the crankshaft timing pulley, a camshaft sensor that is a single hall effect magnetic switch also, but is activated by a single vane driven by the camshaft. An ignition module receives the signal from the crankshaft sensor, camshaft sensor, and spout information for the EEC-IV module, and an ignition coil pack that houses the spark plug wires like the conventional distributor cap.

IGNITION TIMING

ADJUSTMENT

The locations of the timing marks on the 2.5L engine are as follows:
a. Manual transaxles – the timing marks

are located on the flywheel and visible through a hole in the top of the transaxle case. To view the timing marks, a cover plate on top of the transaxle must be removed.

b. Automatic transaxles – the timing marks are visible through a hole in the transaxle case. There is no cover plate.

The 3.0L, 3.0L SHO, and 3.8L engines em-

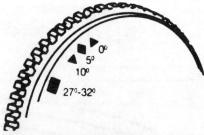

View of the timing marks on the flywheel—2.5L engine with A/T

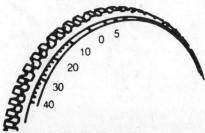

View of the timing marks on the flywheel—2.5L engine with M/T

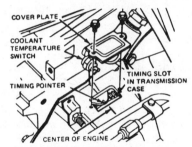

Location of the timing marks—2.5L engine with M/T

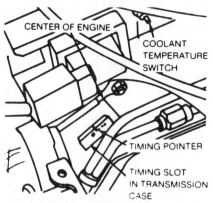

Location of the timing marks—2.5L engine with A/T

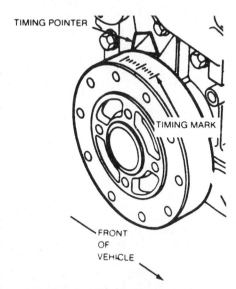

View of the timing marks on the 3.0L engine

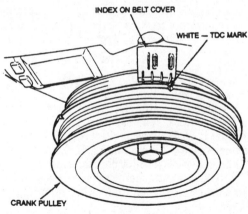

Timing marks on the 3.0L SHO engine

axle cover plate which allows access to the timing marks.

3. Using a white chalk or paint mark, mark the specified timing mark and pointer.

4. Near the distributor, disconnect the inline spout connector. The spout connector is the center wire between the Electronic Control Assembly (ECA) connector and the Thick Film Ignition (TFI) module. Check ignition system diagram in this section for connector location.

5. Connect an inductive type timing light (Rotunda tool No. 059-00006) to the No. 1 spark plug wire. Check firing order for No. 1 plug wire. DO NOT puncture the ignition wire with any type of probing device.

NOTE: *The high ignition coil currents generated in the EEC-IV ignition system may falsely trigger the timing lights with capacitive or direct connect pick-ups. It is necessary that an inductive type timing light be used in this procedure.*

6. Connect a tachometer (Rotunda tool No. 099-00003) to the ignition coil.

NOTE: *The ignition coil electrical connector allows a test lead with an alligator clip to be*

ploy timing marks on the crankshaft pulley and a timing pointer near the pulley.

1. Place the transaxle in the Park (ATX) or Neutral (MTX) position.

2. Open the hood and clean the timing marks with a stiff brush or solvent. On the 2.5L, MTX models, it will be necessary to remove the trans-

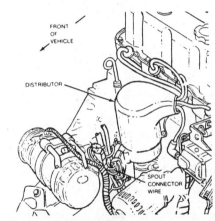

View of the in-line spout connector

connected to it's dark green/yellow dotted wire terminal without removing the connector. Be careful not to ground the alligator clip, for permanent damage will result to the coil.

7. Start the engine and allow it run until the normal operating temperature is reached.

8. Check the engine idle rpm, if it is not within specifications, adjust as necessary. After the rpm has been adjusted or checked, aim the timing light at the timing marks. If they are not aligned, loosen the distributor clamp bolts slightly and rotate the distributor body until the marks are aligned under the timing light illumination.

CAUTION: *Do not rotate the distributor using the distributor cap because you may get a severe shock. Hold the distributor body when adjusting timing.*

9. Tighten the distributor clamp bolts and recheck the ignition timing. Re-adjust the idle speed (if necessary).

10. Turn the engine OFF, remove the test equipment, reconnect the inline spout connector to the distributor and reinstall the cover plate on the MTX models.

3.0L SHO engine

The SHO engine is equipped with the Distributorless Ignition System (DIS). The ignition timing is preset at 10 ± 2 degrees BTDC and is not adjustable.

TACHOMETER HOOKUP

On models (TFI) equipped with an "E" type coil, the tach connection is made at the back of the wire harness connector at the coil. A cut-out is provided and the tachometer lead wire alligator clip can be connected to the dark green/yellow dotted wire of the electrical harness plug.

Universal Distributors
ADJUSTMENTS

Provisions have been incorporated in the universal distributor to allow fixed adjustment capability for octane needs. The adjustment is the accomplished by replacing the standard 0° rod located in the distributor bowl with a 3° or 6° retard rod which are released for service only.

CAUTION: *Do not change the timing by using different octane rods, as Federal Emission Requirements will be affected.*

Octane Rod
REMOVAL

1. Remove cap and rotor for visual access.
2. Locate the octane adjustments boss and remove retaining screw.
3. Slide rod/grommet out to a point where rod can be disengaged from stator retaining post.

NOTE: *Retain grommet for use with new rod.*

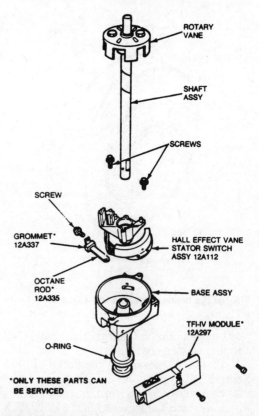

Octane rod location

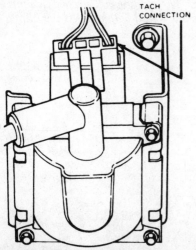

View of the tachometer connecting point of the "E" coil

INSTALLATION

1. Install grommet on new service rod and reinstall in the distributor, making sure to capture the stator post.

2. Install retaining screw and tighten to 15-35 in. lbs.

3. Replace cap and rotor. Tighten caps screws to 33-43 in. lbs. and rotor to 25-35 in. lbs.

NOTE: *Except for the cap, rotor, TFI-IV module, O-ring and octane rod, no other distributor assembly parts are replaceable. There is no calibration required with the universal distributor.*

VALVE LASH

ADJUSTMENT

3.0L SHO Engine

The 3.0L SHO Engine is equipped with mechanical valve tappets. A valve lash adjustment is required after 60,000 miles when operated at normal operating conditions. When performing this procedure, the timing belt should be replaced at this time.

1. Disconnect the negative (–) battery cable.

2. Remove the intake manifold assembly and the cylinder head (valve) covers as outlined.

   a. Partially drain the engine cooling system.

   b. Disconnect the negative (–) battery cable.

   c. Disconnect the electrical and vacuum connectors from the intake manifold.

   d. Remove the air cleaner tube.

   e. Disconnect the coolant lines and throttle cables.

   f. Remove the four upper intake retaining bolts.

   g. Loosen lower bolts and remove the brackets.

   h. Remove the 12 intake-to-cylinder head retaining bolts.

   i. Remove the intake assembly from the vehicle.

3. Insert a feeler gauge under the cam lobe at the 90 degree angle to the camshaft as shown in the illustration.

   a. Valve Lash Intake: 0.15-0.25mm Cold.

   b. Valve Lash Exhaust: 0.25-0.35mm Cold.

4. Adjust the valve clearance by inserting a Tappet Compressor tool part No. T89P-6500-A or equivalent, under the camshaft next to the lobe and rotate downward to depress the bucket tappet.

5. Insert a Tappet Holding tool part No. T89P-6500-B or equivalent and remove the compressor tool.

6. Using a Pick tool part No. T71P-19703-C or equivalent. Lift the adjusting shim and remove the shim with a magnet.

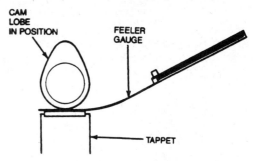

CAM LOBE IN POSITION   FEELER GAUGE   TAPPET

Valve lash check—3.0L SHO engine

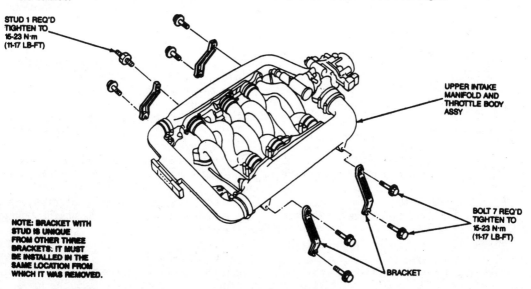

STUD 1 REQ'D TIGHTEN TO 15-23 N·m (11-17 LB-FT)

UPPER INTAKE MANIFOLD AND THROTTLE BODY ASSY

BOLT 7 REQ'D TIGHTEN TO 15-23 N·m (11-17 LB-FT)

NOTE: BRACKET WITH STUD IS UNIQUE FROM OTHER THREE BRACKETS; IT MUST BE INSTALLED IN THE SAME LOCATION FROM WHICH IT WAS REMOVED.

BRACKET

Intake manifold removal

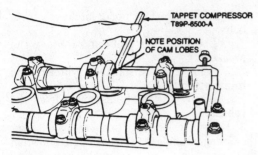

Valve tappet compressor

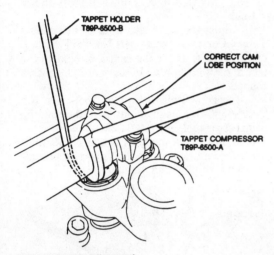

Valve tappet holding tool

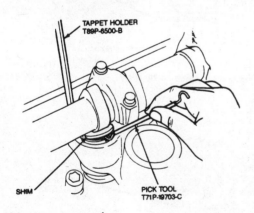

Valve tappet removal

7. Determine the size of the shim by the numbers on the bottom face of the shim or by measuring it with a micrometer. Install replacement shim with the numbers facing down and properly seated.

8. Release the tappet holder by installing the tappet compressor tool.

9. Repeat this procedure for each valve by rotating the engine crankshaft.

10. After the valve lash clearances are checked and adjusted, inspect all valve shims to ensure that they are fully seated in their bucket tappets.

11. Install new cylinder head (valve) cover gaskets and covers.

12. Install the intake manifold assembly. Refer to the "Intake Manifold" removal and installation procedures in chapter 3.

13. Connect the negative (−) battery cable.

14. Start the engine and check for leaks.

2.5L, 3.0L, and 3.8L Engines:

The intake and exhaust valves are driven by the camshaft, working through hydraulic lash adjusters. The lash adjusters eliminate the need for periodic valve lash adjustments.

FUEL SYSTEM ADJUSTMENTS

Idle Speed and Mixture
ADJUSTMENT
2.5L CFI Engine

NOTE: *The curb idle and fast idle speeds are controlled by the EEC-IV computer and the idle speed control (ISC) device. If the control system is operating correctly, the speeds are fixed and should not be changed.*

1. Apply the parking brake and block the wheels.

NOTE: *If equipped with an ATX and an automatic parking brake, ALWAYS place the transaxle in Reverse (not Drive) when checking the idle speed in gear.*

2. Start the engine and allow it run until normal operating temperatures are reached; make sure that all of the accessories are turned Off. Connect a tachometer to the ignition coil connector, described in the tachometer hookup procedure in this section.

3. Check the vacuum lines for leaks.

4. Place the transaxle in Drive (or Reverse) for ATX or Neutral for MTX and allow the engine to operate for two minutes. The idle speed should be within specifications listed on the underhood decal.

NOTE: *If the electric cooling fan turns ON during this procedure, wait for it to turn OFF before proceeding.*

5. If equipped with an ATX, place it in Neutral, the idle speed should increase about 100 rpm.

6. Lightly step on and off the accelerator, the engine speed should return to the specifications on the decal.

7. If the engine speed remains high, repeat the checking sequence.

8. If the curb idle speed remains above the underhood specifications, perform the following procedures:

a. Verify that the throttle linkage is free and unobstructed. If equipped with cruise control, make sure that it is not holding the throttle open.

NOTE: *If the throttle lever is not in contact with the idle speed control (ISC) motor, while the engine is running, but is being held open by the throttle stop adjusting screw (TSAS), this screw must be adjusted.*

b. Turn the engine OFF and remove the air cleaner. Find the self-test and the self-test input (STI) connectors in the engine compartment.

c. Using a jumper wire, connect it between the self-test input (STI) connector and the signal return pin on the self-test connector.

d. Turn the ignition switch ON but do not start the engine.

e. Wait for 10-15 seconds, the idle speed control (ISC) plunger will fully contract; if not, inspect the ISC.

f. Turn the ignition switch OFF and wait for 10-15 seconds, then remove the jumper wire and disconnect the ISC electrical connector from the electrical harness.

g. Remove the throttle body from the engine. Using an ice pick, puncture and remove the throttle stop adjusting screw cover plug, then replace the screw.

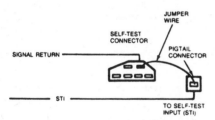

Connecting a jumper wire between the self-test and the self-test input connectors

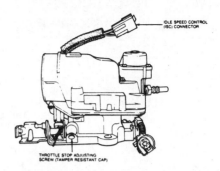

View of the throttle body—2.5L CFI engine

h. Reinstall the throttle body to the engine. Start and stabilize the engine, then set idle speed according to the underhood decal by adjusting the throttle stop screw.

i. Reconnect the ISC electrical harness.

9. Turn the engine OFF and disconnect the tachometer.

3.0L EFI Engine

NOTE: *The curb idle speed rpm is controlled by the EEC-IV computer (ECM) and the idle speed control (ISC) air bypass valve assembly. The throttle stop screw is factory set and does not directly control the idle speed. Adjustment to this setting should be performed only as part of a full EEC-IV diagnosis of irregular idle conditions or idle speeds. Failure to accurately set the throttle plate stop position as described in the following procedure could result in false idle speed control.*

1. Apply the parking brake, turn the A/C control selector OFF and block the wheels.

2. Connect a tachometer and an inductive timing light to the engine. Start the engine and allow it to reach normal operating temperatures.

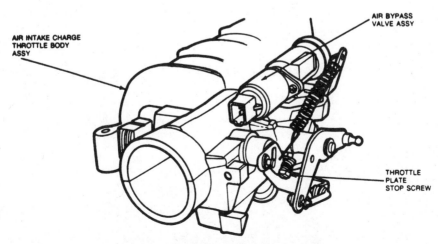

View of the throttle body—3.0L EFI engine

Troubleshooting Engine Performance

Problem	Cause	Solution
Hard starting (engine cranks normally)	• Binding linkage, choke valve or choke piston	• Repair as necessary
	• Restricted choke vacuum diaphragm	• Clean passages
	• Improper fuel level	• Adjust float level
	• Dirty, worn or faulty needle valve and seat	• Repair as necessary
	• Float sticking	• Repair as necessary
	• Faulty fuel pump	• Replace fuel pump
	• Incorrect choke cover adjustment	• Adjust choke cover
	• Inadequate choke unloader adjustment	• Adjust choke unloader
	• Faulty ignition coil	• Test and replace as necessary
	• Improper spark plug gap	• Adjust gap
	• Incorrect ignition timing	• Adjust timing
	• Incorrect valve timing	• Check valve timing; repair as necessary
Rough idle or stalling	• Incorrect curb or fast idle speed	• Adjust curb or fast idle speed
	• Incorrect ignition timing	• Adjust timing to specification
	• Improper feedback system operation	• Refer to Chapter 4
	• Improper fast idle cam adjustment	• Adjust fast idle cam
	• Faulty EGR valve operation	• Test EGR system and replace as necessary
	• Faulty PCV valve air flow	• Test PCV valve and replace as necessary
	• Choke binding	• Locate and eliminate binding condition
	• Faulty TAC vacuum motor or valve	• Repair as necessary
	• Air leak into manifold vacuum	• Inspect manifold vacuum connections and repair as necessary
	• Improper fuel level	• Adjust fuel level
	• Faulty distributor rotor or cap	• Replace rotor or cap
	• Improperly seated valves	• Test cylinder compression, repair as necessary
	• Incorrect ignition wiring	• Inspect wiring and correct as necessary
	• Faulty ignition coil	• Test coil and replace as necessary
	• Restricted air vent or idle passages	• Clean passages
	• Restricted air cleaner	• Clean or replace air cleaner filler element
	• Faulty choke vacuum diaphragm	• Repair as necessary
Faulty low-speed operation	• Restricted idle transfer slots	• Clean transfer slots
	• Restricted idle air vents and passages	• Clean air vents and passages
	• Restricted air cleaner	• Clean or replace air cleaner filter element
	• Improper fuel level	• Adjust fuel level
	• Faulty spark plugs	• Clean or replace spark plugs
	• Dirty, corroded, or loose ignition secondary circuit wire connections	• Clean or tighten secondary circuit wire connections
	• Improper feedback system operation	• Refer to Chapter 4
	• Faulty ignition coil high voltage wire	• Replace ignition coil high voltage wire
	• Faulty distributor cap	• Replace cap
Faulty acceleration	• Improper accelerator pump stroke	• Adjust accelerator pump stroke
	• Incorrect ignition timing	• Adjust timing
	• Inoperative pump discharge check ball or needle	• Clean or replace as necessary
	• Worn or damaged pump diaphragm or piston	• Replace diaphragm or piston

Troubleshooting Engine Performance (cont.)

Problem	Cause	Solution
Faulty acceleration (cont.)	• Leaking carburetor main body cover gasket	• Replace gasket
	• Engine cold and choke set too lean	• Adjust choke cover
	• Improper metering rod adjustment (BBD Model carburetor)	• Adjust metering rod
	• Faulty spark plug(s)	• Clean or replace spark plug(s)
	• Improperly seated valves	• Test cylinder compression, repair as necessary
	• Faulty ignition coil	• Test coil and replace as necessary
	• Improper feedback system operation	• Refer to Chapter 4
Faulty high speed operation	• Incorrect ignition timing	• Adjust timing
	• Faulty distributor centrifugal advance mechanism	• Check centrifugal advance mechanism and repair as necessary
	• Faulty distributor vacuum advance mechanism	• Check vacuum advance mechanism and repair as necessary
	• Low fuel pump volume	• Replace fuel pump
	• Wrong spark plug air gap or wrong plug	• Adjust air gap or install correct plug
	• Faulty choke operation	• Adjust choke cover
	• Partially restricted exhaust manifold, exhaust pipe, catalytic converter, muffler, or tailpipe	• Eliminate restriction
	• Restricted vacuum passages	• Clean passages
	• Improper size or restricted main jet	• Clean or replace as necessary
	• Restricted air cleaner	• Clean or replace filter element as necessary
	• Faulty distributor rotor or cap	• Replace rotor or cap
	• Faulty ignition coil	• Test coil and replace as necessary
	• Improperly seated valve(s)	• Test cylinder compression, repair as necessary
	• Faulty valve spring(s)	• Inspect and test valve spring tension, replace as necessary
	• Incorrect valve timing	• Check valve timing and repair as necessary
	• Intake manifold restricted	• Remove restriction or replace manifold
	• Worn distributor shaft	• Replace shaft
	• Improper feedback system operation	• Refer to Chapter 4
Misfire at all speeds	• Faulty spark plug(s)	• Clean or replace spark plug(s)
	• Faulty spark plug wire(s)	• Replace as necessary
	• Faulty distributor cap or rotor	• Replace cap or rotor
	• Faulty ignition coil	• Test coil and replace as necessary
	• Primary ignition circuit shorted or open intermittently	• Troubleshoot primary circuit and repair as necessary
	• Improperly seated valve(s)	• Test cylinder compression, repair as necessary
	• Faulty hydraulic tappet(s)	• Clean or replace tappet(s)
	• Improper feedback system operation	• Refer to Chapter 4
	• Faulty valve spring(s)	• Inspect and test valve spring tension, repair as necessary
	• Worn camshaft lobes	• Replace camshaft
	• Air leak into manifold	• Check manifold vacuum and repair as necessary
	• Improper carburetor adjustment	• Adjust carburetor
	• Fuel pump volume or pressure low	• Replace fuel pump
	• Blown cylinder head gasket	• Replace gasket
	• Intake or exhaust manifold passage(s) restricted	• Pass chain through passage(s) and repair as necessary
	• Incorrect trigger wheel installed in distributor	• Install correct trigger wheel

Troubleshooting Engine Performance (cont.)

Problem	Cause	Solution
Power not up to normal	• Incorrect ignition timing	• Adjust timing
	• Faulty distributor rotor	• Replace rotor
	• Trigger wheel loose on shaft	• Reposition or replace trigger wheel
	• Incorrect spark plug gap	• Adjust gap
	• Faulty fuel pump	• Replace fuel pump
	• Incorrect valve timing	• Check valve timing and repair as necessary
	• Faulty ignition coil	• Test coil and replace as necessary
	• Faulty ignition wires	• Test wires and replace as necessary
	• Improperly seated valves	• Test cylinder compression and repair as necessary
	• Blown cylinder head gasket	• Replace gasket
	• Leaking piston rings	• Test compression and repair as necessary
	• Worn distributor shaft	• Replace shaft
	• Improper feedback system operation	• Refer to Chapter 4
Intake backfire	• Improper ignition timing	• Adjust timing
	• Faulty accelerator pump discharge	• Repair as necessary
	• Defective EGR CTO valve	• Replace EGR CTO valve
	• Defective TAC vacuum motor or valve	• Repair as necessary
	• Lean air/fuel mixture	• Check float level or manifold vacuum for air leak. Remove sediment from bowl
Exhaust backfire	• Air leak into manifold vacuum	• Check manifold vacuum and repair as necessary
	• Faulty air injection diverter valve	• Test diverter valve and replace as necessary
	• Exhaust leak	• Locate and eliminate leak
Ping or spark knock	• Incorrect ignition timing	• Adjust timing
	• Distributor centrifugal or vacuum advance malfunction	• Inspect advance mechanism and repair as necessary
	• Excessive combustion chamber deposits	• Remove with combustion chamber cleaner
	• Air leak into manifold vacuum	• Check manifold vacuum and repair as necessary
	• Excessively high compression	• Test compression and repair as necessary
	• Fuel octane rating excessively low	• Try alternate fuel source
	• Sharp edges in combustion chamber	• Grind smooth
	• EGR valve not functioning properly	• Test EGR system and replace as necessary
Surging (at cruising to top speeds)	• Low carburetor fuel level	• Adjust fuel level
	• Low fuel pump pressure or volume	• Replace fuel pump
	• Metering rod(s) not adjusted properly (BBD Model Carburetor)	• Adjust metering rod
	• Improper PCV valve air flow	• Test PCV valve and replace as necessary
	• Air leak into manifold vacuum	• Check manifold vacuum and repair as necessary
	• Incorrect spark advance	• Test and replace as necessary
	• Restricted main jet(s)	• Clean main jet(s)
	• Undersize main jet(s)	• Replace main jet(s)
	• Restricted air vents	• Clean air vents
	• Restricted fuel filter	• Replace fuel filter
	• Restricted air cleaner	• Clean or replace air cleaner filter element
	• EGR valve not functioning properly	• Test EGR system and replace as necessary
	• Improper feedback system operation	• Refer to Chapter 4

3. Unplug the spout line (at the distributor). Check ignition system diagram for location. Check and/or adjust the ignition timing to 8-12° BTDC.

4. Shut the engine OFF and disconnect the electrical connector from the air bypass valve assembly. Remove the PCV entry line from the PCV valve.

5. Using the orifice (5mm dia.) tool No. T86P-9600-A, install it the PCV entry line.

6. Start the engine. Place the transaxle in Drive (ATX) or Neutral (MTX). Disconnect the electrical connector from the electric cooling fan.

7. Check and/or adjust (if necessary) the idle speed to 595-655 rpm by turning the throttle plate stop screw.

8. After adjusting the idle speed, turn Off the engine and wait for 3-5 minutes.

9. Start the engine and confirm that the idle speed is now adjusted to specifications, if not, readjust as necessary.

10. Turn the engine OFF and remove the orifice. Reconnect the PCV entry line, the spout line, the ISC motor and the electric cooling fan.

11. Make sure that the throttle plate is not stuck in the bore and that the throttle plate stop screw is setting on the rest pad with the throttle closed. Correct any condition that will not allow the throttle to close to the stop set position.

12. Restart the engine. After 3-5 minutes of operation, the engine idle speed should be at specifications.

3.8L EFI Engine

NOTE: *Like the 3.0L EFI engine, the curb idle speed rpm is controlled by the EEC-IV computer (ECM) and the idle speed control (ISC) air bypass valve assembly. The throttle stop screw is factory set and does not directly control the idle speed. Adjustment to this setting should be performed only as part of a full EEC-IV diagnosis of irregular idle conditions or idle speeds. Failure to accurately set the throttle plate stop position as described in the following procedure could result in false idle speed control.*

1. Apply the parking brake, turn the A/C control selector OFF and block the wheels.

2. Connect a tachometer and an inductive timing light to the engine. Start the engine and allow it to reach normal operating temperatures.

3. Start the engine and run it at 2500 rpm for at least 30 seconds

4. With rear wheels blocked, place transmission selector in DRIVE.

5. Disconnect the Idle Speed Control-Air By-

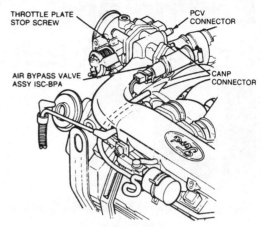

Idle stop screw—3.0L SHO engine

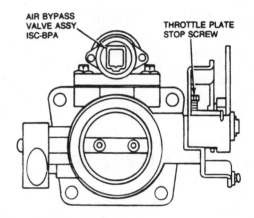

View of the throttle body

pass Solenoid, located above the throttle body assembly.

6. Back out the throttle stop screw to 550 ± 20 rpm then back out an additional ½ turn.

3.0L SHO Engine

1. Block the front wheels, apply the emergency brake, start the engine, and place the transmission selector in NEUTRAL.

2. Unplug the spout line and verify that the ignition timing is base 10 ± 2 degrees BTDC using an inductive timing light.

3. Remove the PCV hose form the throttle body and plug it.

4. Disconnect the Idle Speed Control Air Bypass Solenoid.

5. Check the tachometer to see if it is reading 800 ± 30 rpm. Turn the throttle plate adjusting screw to specifications.

6. Reconnect the Idle Speed Control Air Bypass Solenoid, PCV hose, and check the rpm again.

Engine and Engine Overhaul

3

ENGINE ELECTRICAL

Understanding the Engine Electrical System

The engine electrical system can be broken down into three separate and distinct systems:

1. The starting system
2. The charging system
3. The ignition system.

BATTERY AND STARTING SYSTEM

Basic Operating Principles

The battery is the first link in the chain of mechanisms which work together to provide cranking of the automobile engine. In most modern cars, the battery is a lead/acid electrochemical device consisting of six two-volt (2 V) subsections connected in series so the unit is capable of producing approximately 12 V of electrical pressure. Each subsection, or cell, consists of a series of positive and negative plates held a short distance apart in a solution of sulfuric acid and water. The two types of plates are of dissimilar metals. This causes a chemical reaction to be set up. It is this reaction which produces current flow from the battery when its positive and negative terminals are connected to an electrical appliance such as a lamp or motor. The continued transfer of electrons would eventually convert the sulfuric acid in the electrolyte to water, and make the two plates identical in chemical composition. As electrical energy is removed from the battery, its voltage output tends to drop. Thus, measuring battery voltage and battery electrolyte composition are two ways of checking the ability of the unit to supply power. During the starting of the engine, electrical energy is removed from the battery. However, if the charging circuit is in good condition and the operating conditions are normal, the power removed from the battery will be replaced by the generator (or alternator) which will force electrons back through the battery, reversing the normal flow, and restoring the battery to its original chemical state.

The battery and starting motor are linked by very heavy electrical cables designed to minimize resistance to the flow of current. Generally, the major power supply cable that leaves the battery goes directly to the starter, while other electrical system needs are supplied by a smaller cable. During starter operation, power flows from the battery to the starter and is grounded through the car's frame and the battery's negative ground strap.

The starting motor is a specially designed, direct current electric motor capable of producing a very great amount of power for its size. One thing that allows the motor to produce a great deal of power is its tremendous rotating speed. It drives the engine through a tiny pinion gear (attached to the starter's armature), which drives the very large flywheel ring gear at a greatly reduced speed. Another factor allowing it to produce so much power is that only intermittent operation is required of it. This, little allowance for air circulation is required, and the windings can be built into a very small space.

NOTE: *Because of the small allowance for air circulation in the starter motor, cranking the engine for more than 30 seconds at a time can overheat and cause damage to the starter.*

The starter solenoid is a magnetic device which employs the small current supplied by the starting switch circuit of the ignition switch. This magnetic action moves a plunger which mechanically engages the starter and electrically closes the heavy switch which connects it to the battery. The starting switch circuit consists of the starting switch contained within the ignition switch, a transmission neutral safety switch or clutch pedal switch, and the wiring necessary to connect these in series with the starter solenoid or relay.

A pinion, which is a small gear, is mounted to a one-way drive clutch. This clutch is splined to the starter armature shaft. When the ignition switch is moved to the **start** position, the solenoid plunger slides the pinion toward the flywheel ring gear via a collar and spring. If the teeth on the pinion and flywheel match properly, the pinion will engage the flywheel immediately. If the gear teeth butt one another, the spring will be compressed and will force the gears to mesh as soon as the starter turns far enough to allow them to do so. As the solenoid plunger reaches the end of its travel, it closes the contacts that connect the battery and starter and then the engine is cranked.

As soon as the engine starts, the flywheel ring gear begins turning fast enough to drive the pinion at an extremely high rate of speed. At this point, the one-way clutch begins allowing the pinion to spin faster than the starter shaft so that the starter will not operate at excessive speed. When the ignition switch is released from the starter position, the solenoid is de-energized, and a spring contained within the solenoid assembly pulls the gear out of mesh and interrupts the current flow to the starter.

Some starters employ a separate relay, mounted away from the starter, to switch the motor and solenoid current on and off. The relay thus replaces the solenoid electrical switch, but does not eliminate the need for a solenoid mounted on the starter used to mechanically engage the starter drive gears. The relay is used to reduce the amount of current the starting switch must carry.

THE CHARGING SYSTEM

Basic Operating Principles

The automobile charging system provides electrical power for operation of the vehicle's ignition and starting systems and all the electrical accessories. The battery services as an electrical surge or storage tank, storing (in chemical form) the energy originally produced by the engine driven generator (alternator). The system also provides a means of regulating generator (alternator) output to protect the battery from being overcharged and to avoid excessive voltage to the accessories.

The storage battery is a chemical device incorporating parallel lead plates in a tank containing a sulfuric acid/water solution. Adjacent plates are slightly dissimilar, and the chemical reaction of the two dissimilar plates produces electrical energy when the battery is connected to a load such as the starter motor. The chemical reaction is reversible, so that when the generator is producing a voltage (electrical pressure) greater than that produced by the battery, electricity is forced into the battery, and the battery is returned to its fully charged state.

The vehicle's generator is driven mechanically, through V-belts, by the engine crankshaft. It consists of two coils of fine wire, one stationary (the stator), and one movable (the rotor). The rotor may also be known as the armature, and consists of fine wire wrapped around an iron core which is mounted on a shaft. The electricity which flows through the two coils of wire (provided initially by the battery in some cases) creates an intense magnetic field around both rotor and stator, and the interaction between the two fields creates voltage, allowing the generator to power the accessories and charge the battery.

There are two types of generators: the earlier is the direct current (DC) type. The current produced by the DC generator is generated in the armature and carried off the spinning armature by stationary brushes contacting the commutator. The commutator is a series of smooth metal contact plates on the end of the armature. The commutator is a series of smooth metal contact plates on the end of the armature. The commutator plates, which are separated from one another by a very short gap, are connected to the armature circuits so that current will flow in one directions only in the wires carrying the generator output. The generator stator consists of two stationary coils of wire which draw some of the output current of the generator to form a powerful magnetic field and create the interaction of fields which generates the voltage. The generator field is wired in series with the regulator.

Newer automobiles use alternating current generators or alternators, because they are more efficient, can be rotated at higher speeds, and have fewer brush problems. In an alternator, the field rotates while all the current produced passes only through the stator winding. The brushes bear against continuous slip rings rather than a commutator. This causes the current produced to periodically reverse the direction of its flow. Diodes (electrical one-way switches) block the flow of current from traveling in the wrong direction. A series of diodes are wired together to permit the alternating flow of the stator to be converted to a pulsating, but unidirectional flow at the alternator output. The alternator's field is wired in series with the voltage regulator.

The regulator consists of several circuits. Each circuit has a core, or magnetic coil of wire, which operates a switch. Each switch is connected to ground through one or more resistors. The coil of wire responds directly to system voltage. When the voltage reaches the required level, the magnetic field created by the winding of wire closes the switch and inserts a resistance into the generator field circuit, thus reducing the output. The contacts of the switch cycle open and close many times each second to precisely control voltage.

While alternators are self-limiting as far as maximum current is concerned, DC generators employ a current regulating circuit which responds directly to the total amount of current flowing through the generator circuit rather than to the output voltage. The current regulator is similar to the voltage regulator except that all system current must flow through the energizing coil on its way to the various accessories.

Distributor

The distributor is a new universal gear driven design with a die cast base that incorporates an integrally mounted TFI-IV (Thick Film Ignition) ignition module, a "Hall Effect" vane switch stator assembly and provision for a fixed octane adjustment. The new design eliminates the conventional centrifugal and vacuum advance mechanisms.

REMOVAL AND INSTALLATION

The location of the distributor on the 2.5L engine is in front of the valve cover above the oil filter. On the 3.0L engine, it is located on the left side next to upper intake manifold. On the 3.8L engine, the distributor is located on the right side next to the alternator.

1. Disconnect the primary wiring connector from distributor. Check distributor diagrams for proper location of connector.

NOTE: *Before removing the distributor cap, mark the relationship of the No. 1 wire tower on the distributor base.*

2. Using a screwdriver, remove distributor cap (with the wires attached) and position it aside.

3. Turn the crankshaft to align the rotor with the No. 1 tower position, then remove the rotor.

4. Remove the TFI-IV harness connector.

NOTE: *Some engines may be equipped with a security type distributor hold down bolt. Using the tool No. T82L-12270-A, remove the distributor hold down bolt.*

5. Remove the distributor holddown bolt/clamp and the distributor; be careful not to disturb the intermediate driveshaft.

6. If the engine has been disturbed (crankshaft rotated), perform the following procedures:

a. Remove the No. 1 spark plug.

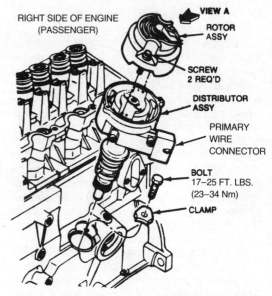

Distributor connection—2.5L, 3.0L and 3.8L Taurus/Sable engines

b. Rotate the crankshaft until the No. 1 piston is on top of the compression stroke. Your should be able to feel the compression pressure being forced out of the No. 1 spark plug hole. Align timing marks for correct initial timing.

c. Position the distributor shaft so that the center of the rotor is pointing toward the mark previously made on distributor base.

d. Continue rotating slightly so that the leading edge of the rotor is centered in the vane switch stator assembly.

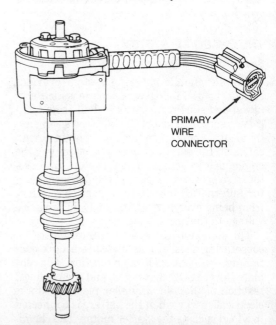

Distributor connection—3.8L Continental

e. Rotate distributor in the block to align the leading edge and the vane switch stator assembly, then verify that the rotor is pointing to the No. 1 cap terminal.

f. Install the distributor hold down bolt and clamp; DO NOT tighten it at this time. NOTE: *If the rotor and vane switch stator cannot be aligned by rotating the distributor in the block, pull the distributor out of block (enough) to disengage the distributor gear and rotate the distributor shaft to engage a different distributor gear tooth. Repeat Step 1 as necessary.*

7. Reinstall the electrical harness connector to the distributor.

8. Install the distributor cap/ignition wire assembly. Check that the ignition wires are securely connected to the distributor cap and spark plugs. Torque the distributor cap screws to 18-23 in. lbs.

9. Using an inductive timing light, set the initial timing by referring to the Vehicle Emission Control Information Decal.

10. Torque the distributor hold down bolt to 17-25 ft. lbs.

11. Check and/or adjust the initial timing (if necessary).

Ignition Coil

TESTING

EEC-IV

At the center terminal on the distributor cap, follow the coil wire to the end. This is the ignition coil "E" type.

1. Make sure transmission is in PARK and ignition is turned OFF.

2. Separate the wiring harness connector from the ignition module at the distributor. Inspect for dirt, corrosion and damage. Reconnect harness if no problem found.

NOTE: *Push connector tabs to separate.*

3. Attach a 12 volt DC test light between coil Tach terminal and engine ground. Crank engine, if the light flashes or lights continuous.

a. Turn ignition switch OFF

b. Disconnect ignition coil connector on top of the coil and inspect for dirt, corrosion and damage.

c. Measure the ignition coil primary resistance, using an ohm Ω meter, from positive ($+$) to negative ($-$) terminal of ignition coil. Check coil diagram A for terminal location.

d. The ohmmeter reading should be 0.3-1.0Ω. If the reading is less than 0.3Ω or greater than 1.0Ω, the ignition coil should be replaced.

e. Measure the coil secondary resistance, using an ohmmeter, connect it to the negative ($-$) terminal and high voltage terminal.

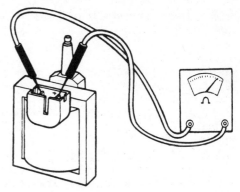

Testing ignition coil primary resistance (ohms)

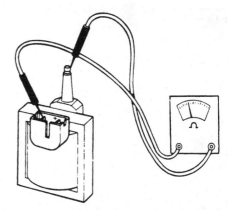

Testing ignition coil secondary resistance (ohms)

f. The resistance should be 6,500-11,500Ω with the ohm meter set on $\Omega \times 1000$. If the reading is less than 6,500Ω or greater than 11,500Ω, replace the coil.

DIS (Distributorless Ignition System)

The DIS ignition coil pack contains three separate ignition coils which are controlled by the DIS module through three coil leads. Each coil fires two spark plugs simultaneously, one plug on the compression stroke and the other on the exhaust stroke. Testing the coil on the DIS system requires special diagnostic equipment. This equipment can be purchased through the dealer or aftermarket suppliers, but is not recommended because the price is not practical for a few times used.

REMOVAL AND INSTALLATION

Except 3.0 SHO Engine

1. Make sure ignition is turned OFF.

2. Remove the high voltage and ignition terminal from the ignition coil.

3. Remove the four bolts that hold the coil on the car body.

4. Install the new coil.

5. Coat the high voltage terminal with dielec-

tric compound and reinstall the coil wire and ignition terminal.

3.0L SHO Engine

1. Disconnect the negative (−) battery cable.
2. Remove the cover from the coil pack and disconnect the electrical connector.
3. Remove the spark plug wires by squeezing the locking tabs to release the coil boot retainers.
4. Remove the four coil pack mounting screws and the coil.
5. **To install:** place new coil on the mounting bracket and torque the screws to 40-62 in. lbs. Connect the spark plug wires and electrical connectors. Install the coil pack cover. Connect the negative (−) battery cable.

Thick Film Ignition Module

TESTING

1. Make sure ignition is turned OFF.
2. Remove coil wire and ground it to car body.
3. Attach the negative (−) volt meter lead to the distributor base.
4. Disconnect the pin in-line connector near the distributor and attach positive (+) volt meter lead to the TFI module side of connector. Check the module testing diagram in this section for terminal location and voltage specifications.
5. Turn the ignition to the ON position.
6. Bump the starter so that the engine rotates a small amount and stops. Record the voltage reading. (Allow sufficient time for the

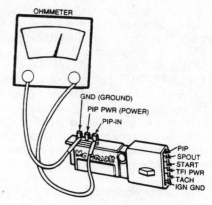

Measure Between These Terminals	Resistor Should Be
● GND - PIP In	Greater than 500 Ohms
● PIP PWR - PIP In	Less than 2K Ohms
● PIP PWR - TFI PWR	Less than 200 Ohms
● GND - IGN GND	Less than 2 Ohms
● PIP In - PIP	Less than 200 Ohms

Module testing locations (ohms)

digital voltage reading to stabilize before taking measurement).

7. The voltage reading should be 70 percent of battery voltage.
8. If the voltage is less than 70 percent, remove the distributor from the engine to test the module and stator.
9. Remove the TFI module from the distributor by removing the two mounting screws. Be careful not to damage stator terminals when pulling module out of distributor.

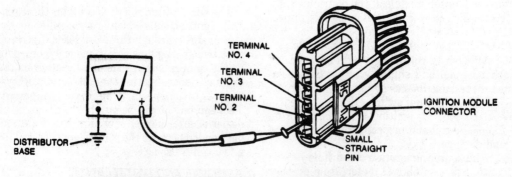

Connector Terminal	Wire/Circuit	Ignition Switch Test Position
#2	To Ignition Coil (−) Terminal	Run
#3	Run Circuit	Run and Start
#4	Start Circuit	Start

Wiring harness testing locations (volts)

10. Measure resistance between the TFI module by using an ohmmeter. Place one meter terminal on the ground terminal and place the second meter terminal on the PIP-IN terminal on the module. Check module testing diagram in this section for terminal location and ohm specifications.

11. After recording ohm resistances, if the readings are within specifications replace the stator assembly in the distributor. If the readings are NOT within specifications replace the module assembly.

REMOVAL AND INSTALLATION

1. Disconnect the negative (−) battery cable.

2. The coil pack is located on the right (passenger) side of the upper intake manifold.

3. Disconnect the input and output wire connectors at the module.

4. **To install:** apply a uniform coating of Heat Sink Grease part No. ESF-M99G123-A or equivalent to the mounting surface of the DIS module. Install the four mounting screws and connect the two wire connectors.

Alternator

The alternator charging system is a negative (−) ground system which consists of an alternator, a regulator, a charge indicator, a storage battery and wiring connecting the components, and fuse link wire.

The alternator is belt-driven from the engine. Energy is supplied from the alternator/regulator system to the rotating field through two brushes to two slip-rings. The slip-rings are mounted on the rotor shaft and are connected to the field coil. This energy supplied to the rotating field from the battery is called excitation current and is used to initially energize the field to begin the generation of electricity. Once the alternator starts to generate electricity, the excitation current comes from its own output rather than the battery.

The alternator produces power in the form of alternating current. The alternating current is rectified by 6 diodes into direct current. The direct current is used to charge the battery and power the rest of the electrical system.

When the ignition key is turned on, current flows from the battery, through the charging system indicator light on the instrument panel, to the voltage regulator, and to the alternator. Since the alternator is not producing any current, the alternator warning light comes on. When the engine is started, the alternator begins to produce current and turns the alternator light off. As the alternator turns and produces current, the current is divided in two ways: part to the battery to charge the battery

and power the electrical components of the vehicle, and part is returned to the alternator to enable it to increase its output. In this situation, the alternator is receiving current from the battery and from itself. A voltage regulator is wired into the current supply to the alternator to prevent it from receiving too much current which would cause it to put out too much current. Conversely, if the voltage regulator does not allow the alternator to receive enough current, the battery will not be fully charged and will eventually go dead.

The battery is connected to the alternator at all times, whether the ignition key is turned on or not. If the battery were shorted to ground, the alternator would also be shorted. This would damage the alternator. To prevent this, a fuse link is installed in the wiring between the battery and the alternator. If the battery is shorted, the fuse link is melted, protecting the alternator.

PRECAUTIONS

To prevent serious damage to the alternator and the rest of the charging system, the following precautions must be observed:

• When installing a battery, make sure that the positive cable is connected to the positive terminal and the negative to the negative terminal.

• When jump-starting the vehicle with another battery, make sure that like terminals are connected. This also applies when using a battery charger.

• Never operate the alternator with the battery disconnected or otherwise on an uncontrolled open circuit. Double-check to see that all connections are tight.

• Do not short across or ground any alternator or regulator terminals.

• Do not try to polarize the alternator.

• Do not apply full battery voltage to the field connector.

• Always disconnect the battery ground cable before disconnecting the alternator lead.

CHARGING SYSTEM TROUBLESHOOTING

There are many possible ways in which the charging system can malfunction. Often the source of a problem is difficult to diagnose, requiring special equipment and a good deal of experience. This is usually not the case, however, where the charging system fails completely and causes the dash board warning light to come on or the battery to become dead. To troubleshoot a complete system failure only two pieces of equipment are needed: a test light, to determine that current is reaching a certain point; and a current indicator (ammeter), to determine the direction of the current flow and its measurement in amps.

This test works under three assumptions:

1. The battery is known to be good and fully charged.

2. The alternator belt is in good condition and adjusted to the proper tension.

3. All connections in the system are clean and tight.

NOTE: *In order for the current indicator to give a valid reading, the car must be equipped with battery cables which are of the same gauge size and quality as original equipment battery cables.*

1. Turn off all electrical components on the car. Make sure the doors of the car are closed. If the car is equipped with a clock, disconnect the clock by removing the lead wire from the rear of the clock. Disconnect the positive battery cable from the battery and connect the ground wire on a test light to the disconnected positive battery cable. Touch the probe end of the test light to the positive battery post. The test light should not light. If the test light does light, there is a short or open circuit on the car.

2. Disconnect the voltage regulator wiring harness connector at the voltage regulator. Turn on the ignition key. Connect the wire on a test light to a good ground (engine bolt). Touch the probe end of a test light to the ignition wire connector into the voltage regulator wiring connector. This wire corresponds to the **I** terminal on the regulator. If the test light goes on, the charging system warning light circuit is complete. If the test light does not come on and the warning light on the instrument panel is on, either the resistor wire, which is parallel with the warning light, or the wiring to the voltage regulator, is defective. If the test light does not come on and the warning light is not on, either the bulb is defective or the power supply wire form the battery through the ignition switch to the bulb has an open circuit. Connect the wiring harness to the regulator.

3. Examine the fuse link wire in the wiring harness from the starter relay to the alternator. If the insulation on the wire is cracked or split, the fuse link may be melted. Connect a test light to the fuse link by attaching the ground wire on the test light to an engine bolt and touching the probe end of the light to the bottom of the fuse link wire where it splices into the alternator output wire. If the bulb in the test light does not light, the fuse link is melted.

4. Start the engine and place a current indicator on the positive battery cable. Turn off all electrical accessories and make sure the doors are closed. If the charging system is working properly, the gauge will show a draw of less than 5 amps. If the system is not working prop-

erly, the gauge will show a draw of more than 5 amps. A charge moves the needle toward the battery, a draw moves the needle away from the battery. Turn the engine off.

5. Disconnect the wiring harness from the voltage regulator at the regulator at the regulator connector. Connect a male spade terminal (solderless connector) to each end of a jumper wire. Insert one end of the wire into the wiring harness connector which corresponds to the **A** terminal on the regulator. Insert the other end of the wire into the wiring harness connector which corresponds to the **F** terminal on the regulator. Position the connector with the jumper wire installed so that it cannot contact any metal surface under the hood. Position a current indicator gauge on the positive battery cable. Have an assistant start the engine. Observe the reading on the current indicator. Have your assistant slowly raise the speed of the engine to about 2,000 rpm or until the current indicator needle stops moving, whichever comes first. Do not run the engine for more than a short period of time in this condition. If the wiring harness connector or jumper wire becomes excessively hot during this test, turn off the engine and check for a grounded wire in the regulator wiring harness. If the current indicator shows a charge of about three amps less than the output of the alternator, the alternator is working properly. If the previous tests showed a draw, the voltage regulator is defective. If the gauge does not show the proper charging rate, the alternator is defective.

REMOVAL AND INSTALLATION

The engines are equipped with V-ribbed belts. To increase the belt life, make sure that the V-grooves make proper contact on the pulleys.

2.5L Engine

1. Disconnect the negative (−) battery cable.

2. Place a ½″ flex handle in the square hole of the belt tensioner or an 18mm socket on the tensioner pulley nut.

3. Turn the tensioner counterclockwise and remove the drive belt.

4. At the back of the alternator, label and disconnect the electrical connectors.

NOTE: *The alternator uses a push-on wiring connector on the field and stator connections. Depress the locking tab when removing the electrical connector from the alternator.*

5. Remove the mounting bolts and the alternator from the vehicle.

6. **To install:** reverse the removal procedures. Torque the alternator-to-engine bolts to 45-57 ft. lbs.

7. To install the drive belt, place it on the

pulleys (except the alternator), turn the tensioner counterclockwise and position the belt on the alternator pulley so that the V-grooves are aligned correctly. Check the V-belt routing diagram in chapter 1 for proper belt location.

3.0L and 3.8L Engines
Including Continental

1. Disconnect the negative (–) battery cable.
2. Remove the alternator adjusting arm bolt and the drive belt.
3. At the back of the alternator, label and disconnect the electrical connectors.

NOTE: *The alternator uses a push-on wiring connector on the field and stator connections. Depress the locking tab when removing the electrical connector from the alternator.*

4. Remove the pivot bolt and the alternator from the vehicle.
5. **To install:** reverse the removal procedures. Adjust the drive belt tension. Check the V-belt routing diagram in chapter 1 for proper belt location. Torque the pivot bolt to 45-57 ft. lbs., and the adjusting arm bolt to 22-32 ft. lbs.

3.0L SHO Engine

1. Disconnect the negative (–) battery cable.
2. Remove the battery and tray assembly.
3. Disconnect the electrical harness connectors at the alternator.
4. Loosen the belt tensioner and remove the belt from the pulley. Refer to the "Alternator Belt" removal and installation procedures in chapter 2.

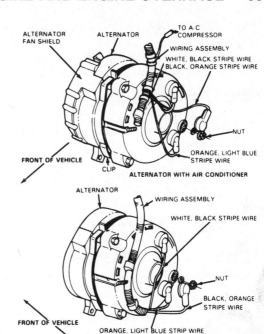

Harness connections for alternators

5. Remove the one mounting bolt at the front of the alternator and the two bolts at the rear.
6. Remove the alternator from the vehicle.
7. **To install:** position the alternator in the mounting brackets and install the three bolts. Torque the front bolts to 36-53 ft. lbs. and the rear bolts to 25-37 ft. lbs.

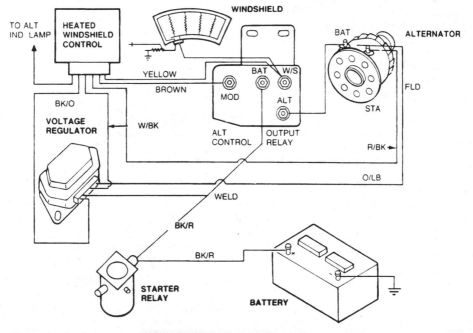

Charging system layout—Continental

8. Connect the electrical connectors. Install the battery tray and the battery.

9. Adjust the belt tension to 148-192 lbs. for a used belt and 220-265 lbs. for a new belt.

Voltage Regulator

NOTE: *Two types of regulators are used, depending on the engine, the alternator output, and the type of dash mounted charging indicator used (light or ammeter). The regulators are 100% solid state, calibrated and preset by the manufacturer. No readjustments are required or possible.*

REMOVAL AND INSTALLATION

External

1. Disconnect the negative (−) battery cable.

2. Disconnect the electrical connectors from the regulator. Make sure the connectors are free of any dirt and corrosion.

3. Remove the regulator mounting screws and the regulator.

4. **To install:** reverse the removal procedures.

5. Test the system for proper voltage regulation.

Internal

1. Disconnect the negative (−) battery cable.

2. At the rear of the alternator, disconnect the electrical connector from the regulator.

3. Remove the regulator-to-alternator screws and the regulator. If necessary, remove the brush holder-to-regulator screws and the brush holder from the regulator.

4. If the brush holder was removed from the regulator, install it using the following procedure:

a. Push the brushes into the brush holder and install a stiff wire (in the brush holder pin hole) to hold the brushes in place.

b. Align the brush holder with the regula-

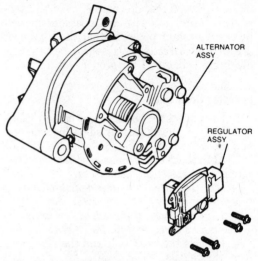

ALTERNATOR ASSY

REGULATOR ASSY

Internal regulator mounting

tor and torque the screws to 20-30 in. lbs.

c. When the regulator/brush holder assembly is installed on the alternator, remove the wire retainer from the brush holder.

NOTE: *If the wire is not removed from the brush holder, a short circuit will result and destroy the regulator.*

5. To install, reverse the removal procedures. Torque the regulator-to-alternator screws to 25-35 in. lbs.

Battery

REMOVAL AND INSTALLATION

1. Loosen the battery cable bolts and spread the ends of the battery cable terminals.

2. Disconnect the negative (−) battery cable first.

3. Disconnect the positive (+) battery cable.

4. Remove the battery holddown.

5. Wearing heavy gloves, remove the battery from under the hood. Be careful not to tip the

Alternator Specifications

Supplier	Stamp Color	Rating		Field Current Amps @ 12V ①	Slip-Ring. Turning mm (inches)		Brush Length mm (inches)		Pulley Nut	
		Amperes @ 15V	Watts @ 15V		Min. Dia.	Max Runabout	New	Wear-Limit	ft. lbs.	(N-m)
Ford	Orange	40	600	4.0	31 (1.22)	0.013 (0.0005)	12.19 (0.480)	6.35 (1/4)	60–100	(82–135)
Ford	Black	65	975	4.0	31 (1.22)	0.013 (0.0005)	12.19 (0.480)	6.35 (1/4)	60–100	(82–135)
Ford	Green	60	900	4.0	31 (1.22)	0.013 (0.0005)	12.19 (0.480)	6.35 (1/4)	60–100	(82–135)
Ford	Red	40 HE	600	4.0	31 (1.22)	0.013 (0.0005)	12.19 (0.480)	6.35 (1/4)	60–100	(82–135)

① A Field Current of 4 amps is used with solid state regulation.

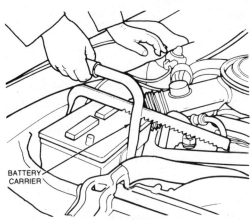

Removing the battery from the car

battery and spill acid on yourself or the car during removal.

6. **To install:** wearing heavy gloves, place the battery in its holder under the hood. Use care not to spill the acid.

7. Install the battery holddown.

8. Install the positive (+) battery cable first.

9. Install the negative (−) battery cable.

10. Apply a light coating of white lithium grease or equivalent to the cable ends to prevent corrosion.

Starter

DIAGNOSIS

Starter Won't Crank The Engine

1. Dead battery.

2. Open starter circuit, such as:
   a. Broken or loose battery cables.
   b. Inoperative starter motor solenoid.
   c. Broken or loose wire from ignition switch to solenoid.
   d. Poor solenoid or starter ground.
   e. Bad ignition switch.

3. Defective starter internal circuit, such as:
   a. Dirty or burnt commutator.
   b. Stuck, worn or broken brushes.
   c. Open or shorted armature.
   d. Open or grounded fields.

4. Starter motor mechanical faults, such as:
   a. Jammed armature end bearings.
   b. Bad bearings, allowing armature to rub fields.
   c. Bent shaft.
   d. Broken starter housing.
   e. Bad starter drive mechanism.
   f. Bad starter drive or flywheel-driven gear.

5. Engine hard or impossible to crank, such as:
   a. Hydrostatic lock, water in combustion chamber.

b. Crankshaft bearings seized.
c. Piston or ring seizing.
d. Bent or broken connecting rod.
e. Seizing of connecting rod bearings.
f. Flywheel jammed or broken.

Starter Spins Freely, Won't Engage

1. Sticking or broken drive mechanism.
2. Damaged ring gear.

REMOVAL AND INSTALLATION

1. Disconnect the negative (−) battery cable and the cable from the starter.

2. Raise and support the front of the vehicle safely and block the rear wheels.

3. From the upper starter stud bolt, remove the cable support and ground cable connection.

4. Remove the starter brace and the starter.

5. Remove the three starter-to-bell housing bolts (2.5L and 3.8L engines) or the two starter-to-bell housing bolts (3.0L engine).

6. If equipped with an ATX, remove the starter between the sub-frame and radiator. If equipped with a MTX, remove the starter between the sub-frame and the engine.

7. To install, place starter between the sub-frame and radiator or engine (depending on transmission). Position the starter in the bell housing and align the bolt holes. Install the starter bolts and torque them to 30-40 ft. lbs.

OVERHAUL

Brush Replacement

1. Remove the top cover by taking out the retaining screw. Loosen and remove the two through bolts (long bolts that run the length of the starter). Remove the starter drive end housing and the starter drive plunger lever return spring.

2. Remove the starter drive plunger lever pivot pin and lever, and remove the armature.

3. Remove the brush end plate.

4. Remove the ground brush retaining screws from the frame and remove the brushes.

5. Cut the insulated brush leads from the field coils, as close to the field connection point as possible.

6. Clean and inspect the starter motor. Check the exploded view of the starter motor in this section.

7. Replace the brush end plate if the insulator between the field brush holder and the end plate is cracked or broken.

8. Position the new insulated field brushes lead on the field coil connections. Position and crimp the clip provided with the brushes to hold the brush lead to the connection. Solder the lead, clip, and connection together using a resin core solder. Use a 300W soldering iron.

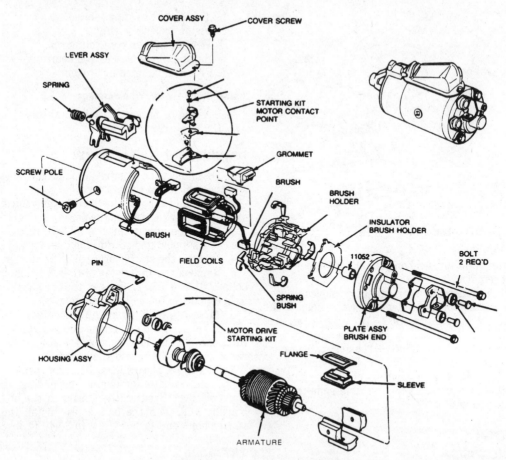

Exploded view of starter motor

9. Install the ground brush leads to the frame with the retaining screws.

10. Clean the armator with special armator paper or very fine emory paper.

11. Position the brush end plate to the starter frame, with the end plate boss in the frame slot.

12. Install the armature in the starter frame.

13. Install the starter drive gear plunger lever to the frame and starter drive assembly, and install the pivot pin.

14. Partially fill the drive end housing bearing bore with grease (approximately ¼ full). Position the return spring on the plunger lever, and the drive end housing to the starter frame. Install the through-bolts and tighten to specified torque (55-75 in. lbs.). Be sure that the stop

ring retainer is seated properly in the drive end housing.

15. Install the armator brushes in the brush holders. Center the brush springs on the brushes.

16. Position the plunger lever cover and brush cover band, with its gasket, on the starter. Tighten the band retaining screw.

17. Connect the starter to a battery to check its operation.

STARTER DRIVE REPLACEMENT

1. Remove the starter from the engine.

2. Remove the starter drive plunger lever cover.

3. Loosen the through-bolts just enough to

Starter Specifications

Years	Engine Ltr. (CID)	Current Draw Normal Load (Amps)	Lock Test		No-Load Current Draw (Amps)	Engine Cranking Speed (rpm)	Brush Length (in.)	Brush Spring Tension (oz.)
			Volts	Torque (ft. lb.)				
'86–'87	2.5L (154)	150–250	5	9.5	80	190–260	0.45	80
	3.0L (182)	150–250	5	9.5	80	190–260	0.45	80

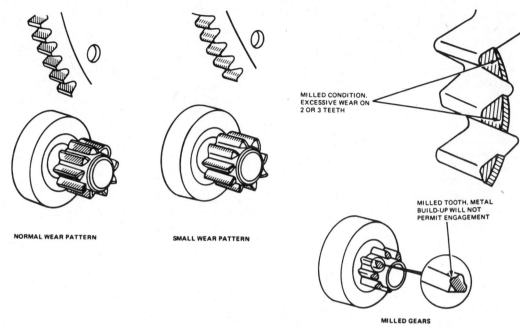

MILLED CONDITION.
EXCESSIVE WEAR ON
2 OR 3 TEETH

MILLED TOOTH. METAL
BUILD-UP WILL NOT
PERMIT ENGAGEMENT

NORMAL WEAR PATTERN

SMALL WEAR PATTERN

MILLED GEARS

Starter drive gear wear patterns

allow removal of the drive end housing and the starter drive plunger lever return spring.

4. Remove the pivot pin which attaches the starter drive plunger lever to the starter frame and remove the lever.

5. Remove the stop ring retainer and stop ring from the armature shaft.

6. Remove the starter drive from the armature shaft.

7. Inspect the teeth on the starter drive. If they are excessively worn, inspect the teeth on the ring gear of the flywheel. If the teeth on the flywheel are excessively worn, the flywheel ring gear should be replaced.

8. Apply a thin coat of white grease to the armature shaft, in the area in which the starter drive operates.

9. Install the starter drive on the armature shaft and install a new stopring.

10. Position the starter drive plunger lever on the starter frame and install the pivot pin. Make sure the plunger lever is properly engaged with the starter drive.

11. Install a new stop ring retainer on the armature shaft.

12. Fill the drive end housing bearing ¼ full with grease.

13. Position the starter drive plunger lever return spring and the drive end housing to the starter frame.

14. Tighten the starter through-bolts to 55-75 in. lbs.

15. Install the starter drive plunger lever cover and the brush cover band on the starter.

16. Install the starter.

ENGINE MECHANICAL

Engine Overhaul

Most engine overhaul procedures are fairly standard. In addition to specific parts replacement procedures and complete specifications for each individual engine. This chapter is also a guide to acceptable rebuilding procedures. Examples of standard rebuilding practice are shown and should be used along with specific details concerning your particular engine.

Competent and accurate machine shop services will insure maximum performance, reliability and engine life. In most instances, it is more profitable for the do-it-yourself mechanic to remove, clean and inspect the component, buy the necessary parts and deliver these to a shop for actual machine work.

On the other hand, much of the rebuilding work (crankshaft, block, bearings, piston rods, and other components) is well within the scope of the do-it-yourself mechanic.

TOOLS

The tools required for an engine overhaul or parts replacement will depend on the depth of your involvement. With few exceptions, they will be the tools found in any mechanic's tool kit (see Chapter 1). More in-depth work will require some or all of the following:

• Dial indicator (reading in thousandths) mounted on a universal base

• Micrometers and telescope gauges

• Jaw and screw-type pullers

- Scraper
- Valve spring compressor
- Ring groove cleaner
- Piston ring expander and compressor
- Ridge reamer
- Cylinder hone or glaze breaker
- Plastigage®
- Engine hoist and stand

The use of most of these tools is illustrated in this chapter. Many can be rented for a one-time use from a local parts jobber or tool supply house specializing in automotive work. Occasionally, the use of special tools is called for. See the information on Special Tools and Safety Notice in the front of this book before substituting another tool.

INSPECTION TECHNIQUES

Procedures and specifications are given in this chapter for inspecting, cleaning and assessing the wear limits of most major components. Other procedures such as Magnaflux® and Zyglo® can be used to locate material flaws and stress cracks. Magnaflux® is a magnetic process applicable only to ferrous materials. The Zyglo® process coats the material with a fluorescent dye penetrant and can be used on any material. Checking for suspected surface cracks can be more readily made using spot check dye. The dye is sprayed onto the suspected area, wiped off and the area sprayed with a developer. Cracks will show up brightly.

OVERHAUL NOTES

Aluminum has become extremely popular for use in engines, due to its low weight. Observe the following precautions when handling aluminum parts:

- Never hot tank aluminum parts; the caustic hot-tank solution will dissolve the aluminum.
- Remove all aluminum parts (identification tag, etc.) from engine parts prior to the hot tanking.
- Always coat threads lightly with engine oil or anti-seize compounds before installation, to prevent seizure.
- Never over torque bolts or spark plugs, especially in aluminum threads.

When assembling the engine, any parts that will be in frictional contact must be prelubed to provide lubrication at initial start-up. Any product specifically formulated for this purpose can be used, but engine oil is not recommended as a prelube.

When semi-permanent (locked, but removable) installation of bolts or nuts is desired, threads should be cleaned and coated with Loctite® or other similar, commercial non-hardening sealant.

REPAIRING DAMAGED THREADS

Several methods of repairing damaged threads are available. Heli-Coil® (shown here), Keenserts® and Microdot® are among the most widely used. All involve basically the same principle (drilling out stripped threads, tapping the hole and installing a prewound insert), making welding, plugging and oversize fasteners unnecessary.

Two types of thread repair inserts are usually supplied: a standard type for most Inch Coarse, Inch Fine, Metric Course and Metric Fine thread sizes and a spark lug type to fit most spark plug port sizes. Consult the individual manufacturer's catalog to determine exact applications. Typical thread repair kits will con-

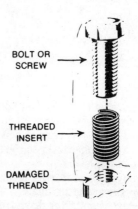

Damaged bolt holes can be repaired with thread repair inserts

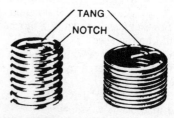

Standard thread repair insert (left) and spark plug thread insert (right)

Drill out the damaged threads with specified drill. Drill completely through the hole or to the bottom of a blind hole

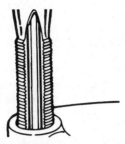

With the tap supplied, tap the hole to receive the thread insert. Keep the tap well oiled and back it out frequently to avoid clogging the threads

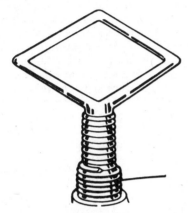

Screw the threaded insert onto the installation tool until the tang engages the slot. Screw the insert into the tapped hole until it is ¼–½ turn below the top surface. After installation break off the tang with a hammer and punch

tain a selection of prewound threaded inserts, a tap (corresponding to the outside diameter threads of the insert) and an installation tool. Spark plug inserts usually differ because they require a tap equipped with pilot threads and a combined reamer/tap section. Most manufacturers also supply blister packed thread repair inserts separately in addition to a master kit containing a variety of taps and inserts plus installation tools.

Before attempting a repair to a threaded hole, remove any snapped, broken or damaged bolts or studs. Penetrating oil can be used to free frozen threads. The offending item can be removed with locking pliers or with a screw or stud extractor. After the hole is clear, the thread can be repaired.

CHECKING ENGINE COMPRESSION

A noticeable lack of engine power, excessive oil consumption and/or poor fuel mileage measured over an extended period are all indicators of internal engine wear. Worn piston rings, scored or worn cylinder bores, blown head gas-

The screw-in type compression gauge is more accurate

kets, sticking or burnt valves and worn valve seats are all possible culprits here. A check of each cylinder's compression will help you locate the problems.

As mentioned in the Tools and Equipment section of Chapter 1, a screw-in type compression gauge is more accurate that the type you simply hold against the spark plug hole, although it takes slightly longer to use. It's worth it to obtain a more accurate reading. Follow the procedures below.

1. Warm up the engine to normal operating temperature.

2. Remove all spark plugs.

3. Disconnect the high tension lead from the ignition coil and ground it to the engine block.

4. Disconnect all fuel injector electrical connections.

5. Coat gauge threads with grease and screw the compression gauge into the No. 1 spark plug hole until the fitting is snug.

NOTE: *Be careful not to crossthread the plug hole. On aluminum cylinder heads use extra care, as the threads in these heads are easily ruined.*

6. Have an assistant depress the accelerator pedal fully. Then, while you read the compression gauge, ask the assistant to crank the engine two or three times in short bursts using the ignition switch.

7. Read the compression gauge at the end of each series of cranks, and record the highest of these readings. Repeat this procedure for each of the engine's cylinders. Maximum compression should be 175-185 psi. A cylinder's compression pressure is usually acceptable if it is not less than 80% of maximum. The difference between each cylinder should be no more than 12-14 psi.

8. If a cylinder is unusually low, pour a tablespoon of clean engine oil into the cylinder through the spark plug hole and repeat the compression test. If the compression comes up after adding the oil, it appears that the cylinder's piston rings or bore are damaged or worn

because the oil temporarily seals the piston rings. If the pressure remains low, the valves may not be seating properly (a valve job is needed), or the head gasket may be blown near that cylinder. If compression in any two adjacent cylinders is low, and if the addition of oil doesn't help the compression, there is leakage past the head gasket. Oil or coolant in the combustion chamber can result from this problem. There may be evidence of water droplets on the engine dipstick when a head gasket has blown. White smoke coming out of the exhaust, usually means that the headgasket is blown.

Engine

REMOVAL AND INSTALLATION

2.5L Engine

1. Relieve the fuel system pressure as follows; First, disconnect the electrical connector at the inertia switch, located on the rear door hinge support above the left inner wheel house on the Taurus/Sable and Continental sedan and on the rear lower corner pillar reinforcement on the station wagon. Then crank the engine for 15 seconds.

2. **ATX only:** Rotate the engine until the flywheel timing marker is aligned with the timing pointer.

3. **ATX only:** Mark the crankshaft pulley at the 12 o'clock position (TDC). Rotate the crankshaft pulley mark to the 6 o'clock (BTDC) position.

4. Disconnect the battery negative (−) cable.

5. Mark the position of the hood hinges and remove the hood.

6. Remove the air cleaner assembly.

7. Position a drain pan under the radiator and drain the radiator coolant. Close the drain valve after all coolant is drained.

CAUTION: *When draining the coolant, keep in mind that cats and dogs are attracted by the ethylene glycol antifreeze, and are quite likely to drink any that is left in an uncovered container or in puddles on the ground. This will prove fatal in sufficient quantity. Always drain the coolant into a sealable container. Coolant should be reused unless it is contaminated or several years old.*

8. Disconnect the upper radiator hose at the engine.

9. Disconnect and mark, for ease of installation, the wiring assembly and vacuum lines as necessary.

10. Disconnect the crankcase ventilation hose at the valve cover and the intake manifold.

11. Disconnect the fuel lines at the throttle body.

12. Disconnect the heater hoses at the throttle body.

13. Disconnect the ground wire at the engine.

14. Disconnect the accelerator cable and the throttle valve control cable at the throttle body.

15. Discharge the air conditioning system, if so equipped. Remove the pressure and suction lines from air conditioning compressor. Be sure to plug all open air conditioning lines to prevent moisture from entering system.

16. **MTX only:** Remove the engine damper brace.

17. Remove the drive belt.

18. Remove the water pump pulley.

19. Remove the air cleaner-to-canister hose.

20. Raise the vehicle on a hoist.

21. Drain the engine oil.

CAUTION: *The EPA warns that prolonged contact with used engine oil may cause a number of skin disorders, including cancer! You should make every effort to minimize your exposure to used engine oil. Protective gloves should be worn when changing the oil. Wash your hands and any other exposed skin areas as soon as possible after exposure to used engine oil. Soap and water, or waterless hand cleaner should be used.*

22. Remove the engine oil filter.

23. Disconnect the starter cable and remove the starter motor.

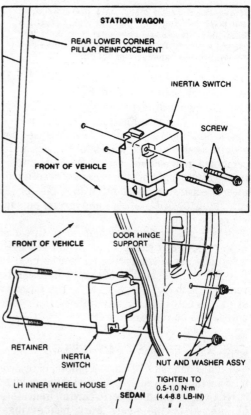

STATION WAGON
REAR LOWER CORNER PILLAR REINFORCEMENT
INERTIA SWITCH
SCREW
FRONT OF VEHICLE
FRONT OF VEHICLE
DOOR HINGE SUPPORT
RETAINER
INERTIA SWITCH
NUT AND WASHER ASSY
LH INNER WHEEL HOUSE
SEDAN
TIGHTEN TO 0.5-1.0 N·m (4.4-8.8 LB-IN)

Inertia switch location

General Engine Specifications

Year	No. Cylinder Displacement liter (cu. in.)	Fuel System Type	Net Horsepower @ rpm	Net Torque @ rpm (ft. lbs.)	Bore x Stroke (in.)	Compression Ratio	Oil Pressure @ rpm
1986	2.5L (154)	CFI	88 @ 4600	130 @ 2800	3.68 x 3.62	9.7:1	55–70 @ 2000
	3.0L (182)	EFI	140 @ 4800	160 @ 3000	3.50 x 3.15	9.3:1	40–60 @ 2000
1987	2.5L (154)	CFI	88 @ 4600	130 @ 2800	3.68 x 3.62	9.7:1	55–70 @ 2000
	3.0L (182)	EFI	140 @ 4800	160 @ 3000	3.50 x 3.15	9.3:1	40–60 @ 2000
1988	2.5L (154)	CFI	88 @ 4600	130 @ 2800	3.70 x 3.60	9.0:1	55–70 @ 2000
	3.0L (182)	EFI	140 @ 4800	160 @ 3000	3.50 x 3.10	9.3:1	55–70 @ 2000
	3.8L (232)	SEFI	140 @ 3800	215 @ 2200	3.81 x 3.39	9.0:1	40–60 @ 2000
1989	3.0L (182)	EFI	140 @ 4800	160 @ 3000	3.50 x 3.10	9.3:1	55–70 @ 2000
	3.8L (232)	SEFI	140 @ 3800	215 @ 2200	3.81 x 3.39	9.0:1	40–60 @ 2000
	3.0L SHO (182)	SEFI	220 @ 6200	200 @ 4800	3.50 x 3.15	9.8:1	40–60 @ 2500

CFI—Central Fuel Injection
EFI—Electronic Fuel Injection
SEFI—Sequential Electronic Fuel Injection

Valve Specifications

Year	No. Cylinder Displacement liter (cu. in.)	Seat Angle (deg.)	Face Angle (deg.)	Spring Test Pressure (lbs. @ in.)	Spring Installed Height (in.)	Stem-to-Guide Clearance (in.)		Stem Diameter (in.)	
						Intake	Exhaust	Intake	Exhaust
1986	2.5L (154)	45	45	182 @ 1.03	1.49	0.0018	0.0023	0.3422	0.3418
	3.0L (182)	45	44	185 @ 1.11	1.85	0.0001–0.0027	0.0015–0.0032	0.3126	0.3121
1987	2.5L (154)	45	45	182 @ 1.03	1.49	0.0018	0.0023	0.3422	0.3418
	3.0L (182)	45	44	185 @ 1.11	1.85	0.0001–0.0027	0.0015–0.0032	0.3126	0.3121
1988	2.5L (154)	45	45	182 @ 1.03	1.49	0.0018	0.0023	0.3422	0.3418
	3.0L (182)	45	44	185 @ 1.11	1.85	0.0001–0.0027	0.0015–0.0032	0.3126	0.3121
	3.8L (232)	45	44	190 @ 1.28	2.02	0.0010–0.0028	0.0015–0.0033	0.3423–0.3415	0.3418–0.3410
1989	2.5L (154)	45	45	182 @ 1.03	1.49	0.0018	0.0023	0.3422	0.3418
	3.0L (182)	45	44	185 @ 1.11	1.85	0.0001–0.0027	0.0015–0.0032	0.3126	0.3121
	3.8L (232)	45	44	190 @ 1.28	2.02	0.0010–0.0028	0.0015–0.0033	0.3423–0.3415	0.3418–0.3410
	3.0L SHO (182)	45	45.5	188 @ 1.52	1.76	0.0010–0.0023	0.0012–0.0025	0.2346–0.2352	0.2344–0.2350

24. **ATX only:** Remove the converter nuts and position the mark, made previously, on the crankshaft pulley as close to the 6 o'clock position (BTDC) as possible with the converter stud visible.

NOTE: *The flywheel timing marker must be in the 6 o'clock (BTDC) position for the proper engine removal and installation.*

25. Remove the engine insulator (motor mount) nuts.
26. Disconnect the exhaust pipe from the manifold.
27. Disconnect the canister bracket from the engine.
28. Disconnect the halfshaft bracket from the engine.

Camshaft Specifications
(All measurements given in inches)

| Year | No. Cylinder Displacement | Journal Diameter | | | | | Lobe Lift | | Bearing Clearance | Camshaft Endplay |
		1	2	3	4	5	In.	Ex.		
1986–89	4-154 (2.5L)	2.006–2.008	2.006–2.008	2.006–2.008	2.006–2.008	2.006–2.008	0.249	0.239	0.001–0.003	0.009
	6-182 (3.0L)	2.0074–2.0084	2.0074–2.0084	2.0074–2.0084	2.0074–2.0084	2.0074–2.0084	0.260	0.260	0.001–0.003	0.005
	6-232 (3.8L)	2.0505–2.0515	2.0505–2.0515	2.0505–2.0515	2.0505–2.0515	2.0505–2.0515	0.240	0.241	0.001–0.003	①
	6-182 (3.0L SHO)	1.2189–1.2195	1.2189–1.2195	1.2189–1.2195	1.2189–1.2195	1.2189–1.2195	0.335	0.315	0.001–0.0026	0.012

① The camshaft is retained by a spring; there is no end play.

Crankshaft and Connecting Rod Specifications
All measurements are given in inches.

| Year | No. Cylinder liter (cu. in.) | Crankshaft | | | | Connecting Rod | | |
		Main Brg. Journal Dia.	Main Brg. Oil Clearance	Shaft End-play	Thrust on No.	Journal Diameter	Oil Clearance	Side Clearance
1986	2.5L (154)	2.2489–2.2490	0.0008–0.0015	0.004–0.008	3	2.1232–2.1261	0.0008–0.0015	0.0035–0.0105
	3.0L (182)	2.5190–	0.0010–0.0014	0.004–0.008	3	2.1253–2.1240	0.0010–0.0014	0.0060–0.0140
1987	2.5L (154)	2.2489–2.2490	0.0008–0.0015	0.004–0.008	3	2.1232–2.1240	0.0008–0.0015	0.0035–0.0105
	3.0L (182)	2.5190–	0.0010–0.0014	0.004–0.008	3	2.1253–2.1261	0.0010–0.0014	0.0060–0.0140
1988	2.5L (154)	2.2489–2.2490	0.0008–0.0015	0.004–0.008	3	2.1232–2.1261	0.0008–0.0015	0.0035–0.0105
	3.0L (182)	2.5190–2.5198	0.0010–0.0014	0.004–0.008	3	2.1253–2.1261	0.0010–0.0014	0.0060–0.0140
	3.8L (232)	2.5190–2.5198	0.0010–0.0014	0.004–0.008	3	2.3103–2.3111	0.0010–0.0014	0.0047–0.0114
1989	2.5L (154)	2.2489–2.2490	0.0008–0.0015	0.004–0.008	3	2.1232–2.1261	0.0008–0.0015	0.0035–0.0105
	3.0L (182)	2.5190–2.5198	0.0010–0.0014	0.004–0.008	3	2.1253–2.1261	0.0010–0.0014	0.0060–0.0140
	3.8L (232)	2.5190–2.5198	0.0010–0.0014	0.004–0.008	3	2.3103–2.3111	0.0010–0.0014	0.0047–0.0114
	3.0L SHO (182)	2.5187–2.5197	0.0011–0.0022	0.0008–0.0087	3	2.0463–2.0472	0.0009–0.0022	0.0063–0.0123

29. Remove the lower engine-to-transmission attaching (bell housing) bolts.
30. Disconnect the lower radiator hose at the tube.
31. Lower the hoist and vehicle.
32. Position a floor jack under the transmission.
33. Disconnect and plug the power steering lines at the pump.
34. Install lifting eyes part No.D81L-6000-D and a engine support tool part No. D79P-6000-A.
35. Attach lifting equipment to support the engine and remove the upper engine-to-transmission attaching bolts.
36. Remove the engine from vehicle.

To install:

37. Install lifting eyes, an engine support tool part No. D79P-6000-A, and the lifting equipment.
NOTE: *The flywheel timing marker must be in a 6 o'clock (BTDC) position for proper engine removal and installation. (ATX only).*
38. Remove the engine from the stand and position in vehicle.
39. Remove the lifting equipment and lifting eyes.

40. Install the upper engine-to-transmission (bell housing) bolts and tighten. Use a floor jack under the transmission to aid alignment.
41. Connect the power steering lines to pump.
42. Raise the vehicle.
43. Connect the lower radiator hose to the tube.
44. Install the lower engine-to-transmission attaching bolts and tighten.
45. Connect the halfshaft bracket to engine.
46. Connect the canister bracket to engine.
47. Connect the exhaust pipe to the manifold.
48. Install the engine insulator (motor mount) nuts and tighten.
49. **ATX only:** Position the mark on the crankshaft pulley as close to the 6 o'clock position (BTDC) as possible, and install the converter nuts and tighten.
50. Position the starter motor and install the attaching bolts and tighten.
51. Connect the starter cable.
52. Install the oil filter. Check to ensure the oil drain plug is installed.
53. Lower the vehicle.
54. Install the air cleaner-to-canister hose.
55. Install the water pump pulley.
56. Install the drive belt and adjust tension.

Piston and Ring Specifications

All measurements are given in inches.

Year	No. Cylinder Displacement liter (cu. in.)	Piston Clearance	Ring Gap			Ring Side Clearance		
			Top Compression	Bottom Compression	Oil Control	Top Compression	Bottom Compression	Oil Control
1986	2.5L (154)	0.0012–0.0022	0.008–0.016	0.008–0.016	0.015–0.055	0.0020–0.0040	0.0020–0.0040	Snug
	3.0L (182)	0.0014–0.0022	0.010–0.020	0.010–0.020	0.010–0.049	0.0012–0.0031	0.0012–0.0031	Snug
1987	2.5L (154)	0.0012–0.0022	0.008–0.016	0.008–0.016	0.015–0.055	0.0020–0.0040	0.0020–0.0040	Snug
	3.0L (182)	0.0014–0.0022	0.010–0.020	0.010–0.020	0.010–0.049	0.0012–0.0031	0.0012–0.0031	Snug
1988	2.5L (154)	0.0012–0.0022	0.008–0.016	0.008–0.016	0.015–0.055	0.002–0.004	0.002–0.004	Snug
	3.0L (182)	0.0014–0.0022	0.010–0.020	0.010–0.020	0.010–0.049	0.0012–0.0031	0.0012–0.0031	Snug
	3.8L (232)	0.0014–0.0032	0.010–0.020	0.010–0.020	0.0150–0.0583	0.0016–0.0037	0.0016–0.0037	Snug
1989	2.5L (154)	0.0012–0.0022	0.008–0.016	0.008–0.016	0.015–0.055	0.002–0.004	0.002–0.004	Snug
	3.0L (182)	0.0014–0.0022	0.010–0.020	0.010–0.020	0.010–0.049	0.0012–0.0031	0.0012–0.0031	Snug
	3.8L (232)	0.0014–0.0032	0.010–0.020	0.010–0.020	0.0150–0.0583	0.0016–0.0037	0.0016–0.0037	Snug
	3.0L SHO (182)	0.0012–0.0020	0.012–0.018	0.012–0.018	0.008–0.020	0.0008–0.0024	0.0006–0.0022	0.0024–0.0059

57. **MTX only:** Install the engine damper brace.

58. Connect the pressure and suction lines to the air conditioning compressor, if equipped and evacuate the system.

59. Connect the accelerator cable and throttle valve control cable at the throttle body.

60. Connect the ground wire at the engine.

61. Connect the heater hoses at the throttle body.

62. Connect the fuel lines at the throttle body.

63. Connect the crankcase ventilation hose at the valve cover and intake manifold.

64. Connect the engine control sensor wiring assembly and vacuum lines.

65. Connect the upper radiator hose at engine.

66. Install the air cleaner assembly.

67. Connect the battery negative (–) cable.

68. **ATX only:** Rotate the engine until the flywheel timing marker is aligned with the timing pointer.

69. Install the timing window cover at transmission.

70. Connect the electrical connector at the inertia switch.

71. Fill the cooling system.

72. Fill with the proper motor oil to the required level.

73. Install the hood.

74. Charge the air conditioning system, if so equipped.

75. Check all fluid levels (power steering, ATX, MTX).

76. Start the vehicle and check for leaks.

3.0L Engine

• The engine assembly is removed out the top without the transaxle.

• Support the front (bell housing) end of the transaxle with a floor jack before disconnecting the transaxle from the axle.

• Lift the engine as outlined in the lifting points procedure below.

Attach engine supports as follows:

a. Attach an Engine Lifting Bracket part No. D81L-6001-D to the LH rear cylinder with a bolt, M10 × 1.5 × 20.

Torque Specifications
All readings in ft. lbs.

Year	No. Cylinder Displacement liter (cu. in.)	Cylinder Head Bolts	Main Bearing Bolts	Rod Bearing Bolts	Crankshaft Pulley Bolts	Flywheel Bolts	Manifold Intake	Manifold Exhaust	Spark Plugs
1986	2.5L (154)	①	51–66	21–26	140–170	54–64	15–23	20–30 ②	5–10
	3.0L (182)	③	65–81	④	141–169	54–64	⑤	20–30 ②	5–10
1987	2.5L (154)	①	51–66	21–26	140–170	54–64	15–23	20–30 ③	5–10
	3.0L (182)	③	65–81	④	141–169	54–64	⑤	20–30 ②	5–10
1988	2.5L (154)	①	51–66	21–26	140–170	54–64	15–23	20–30 ②	5–10
	3.0L (182)	③	65–81	④	141–169	54–64	⑤	20–30 ②	5–10
	3.8L (232)	⑥	65–81	31–36	93–121	54–64	⑦	20–30 ②	5–11
1989	2.5L (154)	①	51–66	21–26	140–170	54–64	15–23	20–30 ②	5–10
	3.0L (182)	③	65–81	④	141–169	54–64	⑤	20–30 ②	5–10
	3.8L (182)	⑥	65–81	31–36	93–121	54–64	⑦	20–30 ②	5–11
	3.0L SHO (182)	⑧	58–65	33–36	112–127	51–58	12–17	26–38	7–15

① Tighten in two steps: 52–59 ft. lbs. and then the final torque at 70–76 ft. lbs.
② Tighten in two stages.
③ Tighten in two steps: 48–54 ft. lbs. and then the final torque of 63–80 ft. lbs.
④ Tighten to 20–28 ft. lbs. and then back off the nuts a minimum of two revolutions; then apply the final torque of 20–25 ft. lbs.
⑤ Tighten in three steps: 11, 18 and the final torque of 24 ft. lbs.
⑥ A. Tighten in four steps: 37, 45, 52, and the final torque of 59 ft. lbs.
   B. Back off all bolts 2–3 revolutions
   C. Repeat step A.
⑦ Tighten in three steps: 7, 15, and the final torque of 24 ft. lbs.
⑧ Tighten in two steps: 37–50 ft. lbs. and the final torque of 62–68 ft. lbs.

b. The engine plant lifting eye should still be on RH front cylinder head. If not, install a second lifting bracket as in Step A. If the engine is being removed, attach lifting chains from the lifting brackets and the lifting equipment. If the engine is to be supported during a service procedure, proceed with Step C.

c. Place the Engine Support Bars part No. D79P-6000-A or equivalent across the engine over each rocker arm cover and attach the chains to the bars and lifting brackets.

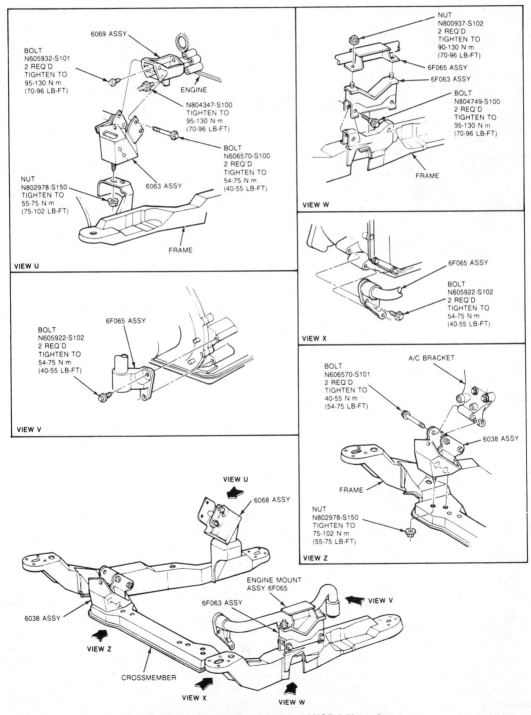

Engine and transaxle mounting—AXOD 2.5L engine

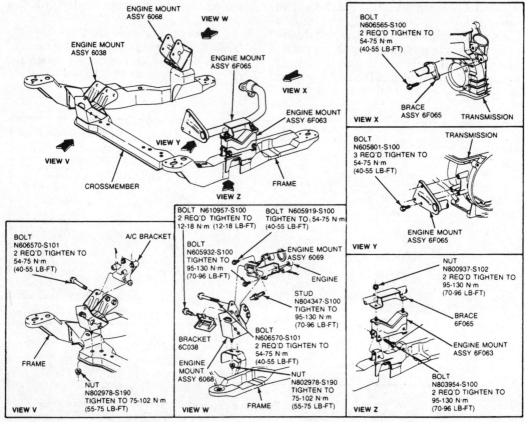

Engine and transaxle mounting—ATX (CLC) 2.5L engine

When only the two support points above are used, the engine assembly will hang slightly down at the rear (approximately 5°) with the transaxle attached. With the transaxle removed, the engine assembly will hang slightly down at the front (approximately 15°) because of the weight of the accessories.

To eliminate either or both of these tilts, attach supports as follows:

a. For the forward tilt, attach a chain from the LH front support bar to the stud on the No. 4 exhaust runner.

b. For the rearward tilt, attach a chain from the RH rear support bar to the exhaust manifold between the No. 2 and No. 3 exhaust runner.

NOTE: *The support hook or chain must angle forward to the front attaching point. Damage WILL result if it runs across the throttle cable or throttle valve mechanism.*

1. Disconnect the battery cables from the battery. Place a drain pan under the radiator and drain the cooling system. Using a scribing tool, mark the hood hinge location and remove the hood.

CAUTION: *When draining the coolant, keep in mind that cats and dogs are attracted by the ethylene glycol antifreeze, and are quite likely to drink any that is left in an uncovered container or in puddles on the ground. This will prove fatal in sufficient quantity. Always drain the coolant into a sealable container. Coolant should be reused unless it is contaminated or several years old.*

2. If equipped with air conditioning, remove the compressor and move it aside; DO NOT discharge the air conditioning system.

3. Remove the air cleaner assembly, the battery and the battery tray.

4. Remove the integrated relay controller, the cooling fan and the radiator with fan shroud. Remove the engine bounce damper bracket from the shock tower.

5. Remove the evaporative emission line, the upper/lower radiator hose and the starter brace.

6. Remove the exhaust pipes from both exhaust manifolds. Remove and plug the power steering pump lines.

7. Bleed the pressure from the fuel system by removing the wire connection from the inertia switch and crank the engine for 15 seconds.

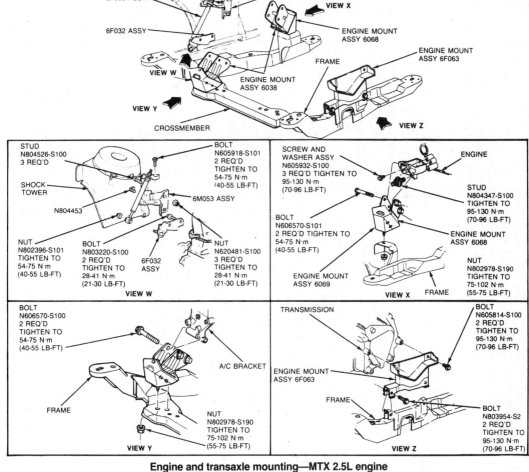

Engine and transaxle mounting—MTX 2.5L engine

Check inertia switch location diagram in this section. Remove the fuel lines. Remove and tag all of the necessary vacuum lines.

8. Disconnect the ground strap, the heater hoses, the accelerator cable linkage, the throttle valve linkage and the speed control cable (if equipped).

9. Disconnect the electrical cable connectors from the following items: the alternator, the air conditioning clutch, the oxygen sensor, the ignition coil, the radio frequency suppressor, the cooling fan voltage resistor, the engine coolant temperature sensor, the thick film ignition module, the fuel injectors, the ISC motor wire, the throttle position sensor, the oil pressure sending switch, the ground wire, the block heater (if equipped), the knock sensor, the EGR sensor and the oil level sensor.

10. Remove the engine mounting bolts and engine mounts. Remove the transaxle-to-engine (bell housing) mounting bolts and the transaxle brace assembly.

11. Connect an engine lifting plate and a ver-

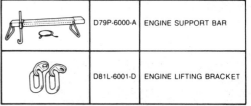

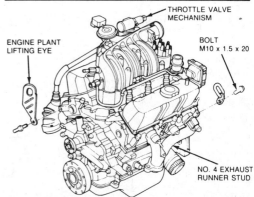

Engine support tools and location—3.0L engine

△ Service:
1. Disconnect battery cables
2. Drain radiator
3. Discharge A/C

☐ Remove/install
10. Air cleaner assembly
11. Battery and tray
12. Integrated relay controller, cooling fan radiator and shroud
13. Bounce damper bracket on shock tower

○ Disconnect/connect:
20. Evaporative emission line
21. Upper radiator hose
22. Starter brace
23. Lower radiator hose
24. Exhaust manifold at pipe
25. Power steering pump lines
26. Fuel lines
27. Vacuum lines
28. Exhaust manifold at pipe
29. Ground strap
30. Heater lines
31. Accelerator cable linkage
    Throttle valve linkage
    Speed control cable

○ Disconnect/connect-wiring:
40. Alternator
41. A/C clutch
42. EGO sensor

Engine remove/disconnect points—3.0L engine

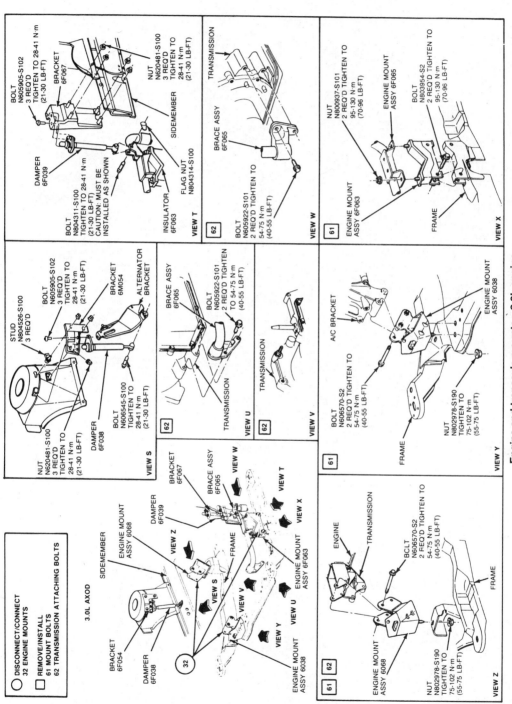

Engine and transaxle mounts—3.0L engine

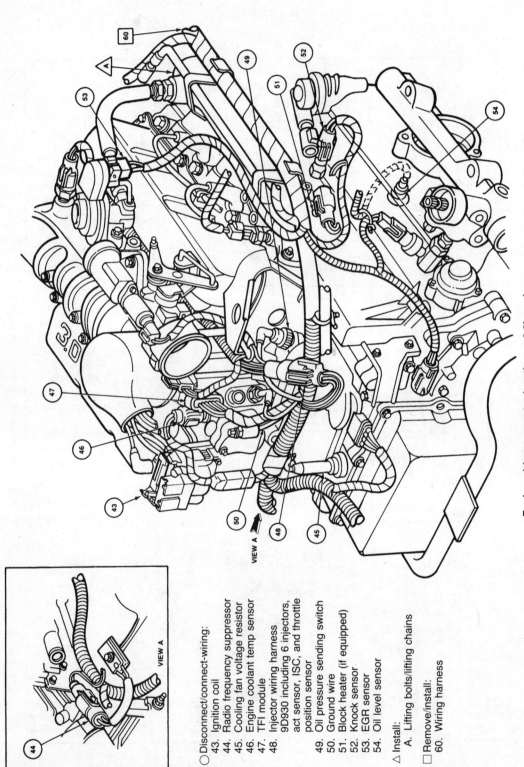

Engine wiring connector locations—3.0L engine

○ Disconnect/connect-wiring:
43. Ignition coil
44. Radio frequency suppressor
45. Cooling fan voltage resistor
46. Engine coolant temp sensor
47. TFI module
48. Injector wiring harness 9D930 including 6 injectors, act sensor, ISC, and throttle position sensor
49. Oil pressure sending switch
50. Ground wire
51. Block heater (if equipped)
52. Knock sensor
53. EGR sensor
54. Oil level sensor

△ Install:
A. Lifting bolts/lifting chains

☐ Remove/install:
60. Wiring harness

tical hoist to the engine, then remove the engine from the vehicle. Make sure everything is disconnected when pulling engine out. Remove the main wire harness from the engine.

To install:

12. Install lifting eyes, an engine support tool part No. D79P-6000-A, and the lifting equipment.

NOTE: *The flywheel timing marker must be in a 6 o'clock (BTDC) position for proper engine removal and installation. (ATX only).*

13. Remove the engine from the stand and position in vehicle.

14. Remove the lifting equipment and lifting eyes.

15. Install the upper engine-to-transmission (bell housing) bolts and tighten. Use a floor jack under the transmission to aid alignment.

16. Connect the power steering lines to pump.

17. Raise the vehicle.

18. Connect the lower radiator hose to the tube.

19. Install the lower engine-to-transmission (bell housing) attaching bolts and tighten.

20. Connect the halfshaft bracket to engine.

21. Connect the canister bracket to engine.

22. Connect the exhaust pipes to the manifolds.

23. Install the engine insulator (motor mount) nuts and tighten.

24. **ATX only:** Position the mark on the crankshaft pulley as close to the 6 o'clock position (BTDC) as possible, and install the converter nuts and tighten.

25. Position the starter motor and install the attaching bolts and tighten.

26. Connect the starter cable.

27. Install the oil filter. Check to ensure the oil drain plug is installed.

28. Lower the vehicle.

29. Install the air cleaner-to-canister hose.

30. Install the water pump pulley.

31. Install the drive belt and adjust tension.

32. **MTX only:** Install the engine damper brace.

33. Connect the pressure and suction lines to the air conditioning compressor, if equipped and evacuate system.

34. Connect the accelerator cable and throttle valve control cable at the throttle body.

35. Connect the ground wire at the engine.

36. Connect the heater hoses at the throttle body.

37. Connect the fuel lines at the throttle body.

38. Connect the crankcase ventilation hose at the valve cover and intake manifold.

39. Connect the engine control sensor wiring assembly and vacuum lines.

40. Connect the upper radiator hose at engine.

41. Install the air cleaner assembly.

42. Connect the battery negative (−) cable.

43. **ATX only:** Rotate the engine until the flywheel timing marker is aligned with the timing pointer.

44. Install the timing window cover at transmission. (2.5L only)

45. Connect the electrical connector at the inertia switch.

46. Fill the cooling system.

47. Fill with the proper motor oil to the required level.

48. Install the hood.

49. Charge the air conditioning system, after evacuation, if so equipped.

50. Check all fluid levels (power steering, ATX, MTX).

51. Start the vehicle.

Check for leaks.

3.8L Engine

• The engine assembly is removed out the top without the transaxle.

• Support the front (bell housing) end of the transaxle with a floor jack before disconnecting the transaxle from the axle.

• Lift the engine as outlined in the lifting points procedure below.

Attach engine supports as follows:

a. Attach an Engine Lifting Bracket part No. D81L-6001-D to the LH rear cylinder with a bolt, M10x1.5x20.

b. The engine plant lifting eyes should still be on the RH front cylinder head. If not, install a second lifting bracket as in Step A. If the engine is being removed, attach lifting chains from the lifting brackets and the lifting equipment. If the engine is to be supported during a service procedure, proceed with Step C.

c. Place the Engine Support Bars part No. D79P-6000-A or equivalent across the engine over each rocker arm cover and attach the chains to the bars and lifting brackets.

1. Position a drain pan under the radiator and drain the radiator coolant. Close the drain valve after all coolant is drained.

CAUTION: *When draining the coolant, keep in mind that cats and dogs are attracted by the ethylene glycol antifreeze, and are quite likely to drink any that is left in an uncovered container or in puddles on the ground. This will prove fatal in sufficient quantity. Always drain the coolant into a sealable container. Coolant should be reused unless it is contaminated or several years old.*

2. Disconnect the battery negative (−) ground cable.

3. Disconnect wiring connector retaining the underhood lamp.

4. Mark the position of hood hinges and remove hood. Be careful not to scratch paint finish.

5. Remove the oil level indicator tube.

6. Disconnect the alternator to voltage regulator wiring assembly.

7. Remove the radiator upper sight shield.

8. Remove the engine cooling fan motor relay retaining bolts.

9. Position the cooling fan motor relay out of the way.

10. Remove the air cleaner assembly.

11. Disconnect the transaxle oil cooler inlet and outlet tubes.

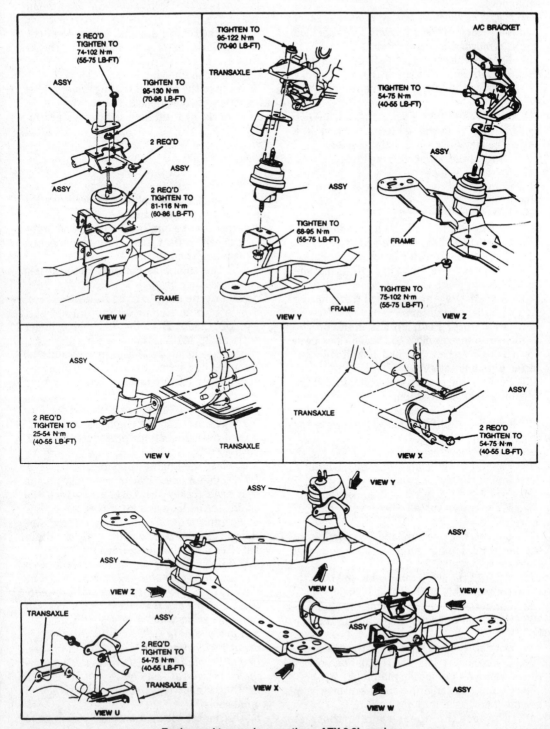

Engine and transaxle mounting—ATX 3.8L engine

12. Remove the fan shroud.
13. Remove the upper radiator hose.
14. Disconnect the transaxle oil cooler inlet and outlet tubes.
15. Disconnect the heater hoses.
16. Disconnect the power steering pressure hose assembly.
17. Discharge and plug the air conditioning system.
18. Disconnect the compressor to condenser line.
19. Remove the radiator coolant recovery reservoir, wiring shield, and accelerator cable mounting bracket.
20. Disconnect the fuel inlet and return hose.
21. Disconnect the power steering pump pressure and return tube bracket.
22. Disconnect the engine control sensor wiring, vacuum hoses, and ground wire assembly.
23. Remove the air duct assembly.
24. Disconnect the throttle control valve cable, bulkhead electrical connector and transaxle pressure switches.
25. Remove the bolts retaining transaxle support, and transaxle support from vehicle.
26. Raise the vehicle on hoist and support using jack stands.
27. Position the oil drain pan beneath the car and drain the oil.

CAUTION: *The EPA warns that prolonged contact with used engine oil may cause a number of skin disorders, including cancer! You should make every effort to minimize your exposure to used engine oil. Protective gloves should be worn when changing the oil. Wash your hands and any other exposed skin areas as soon as possible after exposure to used engine oil. Soap and water, or waterless hand cleaner should be used.*

28. Remove the oil filter assembly.
29. Disconnect the heated exhaust gas oxygen sensor assembly.
30. Remove the drive belt, crankshaft pulley, and drive belt tensioner assemblies.
31. Remove the starter motor and catalytic converter housing and inlet pipe (header pipe)
32. Remove the engine LH and RH front support insulator (motor mount) retaining nuts.
33. Disconnect the oil level indicator sensor.
34. Disconnect the lower radiator hose.
35. Remove the engine-to-transaxle (bell housing) bolts and partially lower engine.
36. Remove the engine assembly from car keeping an eye on pieces that are still partially connected. Place engine on a workstand.

To install:

NOTE: *Lightly oil all bolt and stud threads before installation except those specifying special sealant.*

1. Position the engine assembly in vehicle. With the help of a floor jack, move the transaxle up or down to align with engine.
2. Install the engine-to-transaxle (bell housing) bolts.
3. Remove the engine lifting eyes.
4. Tighten the engine-to-transaxle bolts to 30-40 ft. lbs.
5. Connect the oil pressure gauge unit, air conditioning compressor to condenser discharge line, and air conditioning clutch wire.
6. Start evacuating air conditioning system at this time.
7. Connect the heater water hoses, fuel hoses, and vacuum hoses.
8. Connect the engine control module wiring, and transaxle oil cooler inlet and outlet tubes.
9. Install the radiator.
10. Partially raise the vehicle.
11. Install the LH and RH engine front support insulator (motor mount) retaining nuts.
12. Install the starter motor.
13. Connect the lower radiator hose.
14. Install the drive belt tensioner, crankshaft pulley, and converter assemblies.
15. Connect the heated exhaust gas oxygen sensor.
16. Install the oil filter and connect oil level indicator sensor.
17. Lower the vehicle.
18. Install the radiator coolant recovery reservoir, upper radiator hose, and water pump pulley.
19. Connect the alternator-to-voltage wiring and ground wire.
20. Install the accelerator cable mounting bracket.
21. Connect the power steering lines, fan shroud, and radiator electric motor.
22. Install the drive belts.
23. Install the radiator sight shroud, hood, and connect battery negative (–) cable.
24. Refill with engine oil.
25. Refill with engine coolant.
26. Finish evacuating the air conditioning system, pressure test, and recharge system.
27. Start the engine and check for leaks.

3.0L SHO Engine

• The engine assembly is removed out the top without the transaxle.
• Support the front (bell housing) end of the transaxle with a floor jack before disconnecting the transaxle from the axle.
• Lift the engine as outlined in the lifting points procedure below.
• Attach an Engine Lifting Bracket part No. D81L-6001-D to the LH rear cylinder with a bolt, M10x1.5x20.

CAUTION: *When draining the coolant, keep in mind that cats and dogs are attracted by the ethylene glycol antifreeze, and are quite likely to drink any that is left in an uncovered container or in puddles on the ground. This will prove fatal in sufficient quantity. Always drain the coolant into a sealable container. Coolant should be reused unless it is contaminated or several years old.*

1. Disconnect the negative (–) battery cable.

2. Drain the engine cooling system into a suitable container by loosening the drain plug on the left (driver's) side of the radiator.

3. Remove the battery tray assembly.

4. Disconnect the wiring connector retaining under the hood lamp, if so equipped.

5. Mark the positions of the retaining bolts on the hinges and remove the hood.

6. Remove the radiator upper sight shield, coolant recovery tank, upper and lower radiator hoses, air cleaner, electric fan and shroud, and radiator from the vehicle.

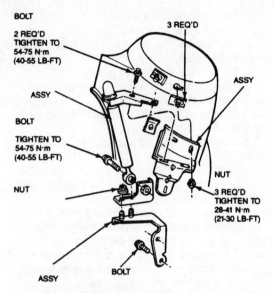

Engine damper and upper bracket—3.0L SHO engine

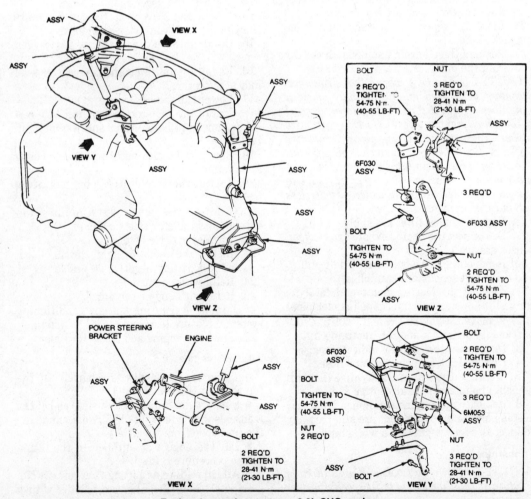

Engine dampening system—3.0L SHO engine

7. Discharge the air conditioning system. Refer to the "Air Conditioning System" in chapter 1 for this procedure. Always plug the disconnected air conditioning lines immediately after removal.

8. Bleed the fuel system. Refer to the "Bleeding Fuel System" section in Chapter 5 for this procedure.

9. Disconnect the fuel inlet and return hoses.

10. Remove the barometric air pressure (BAP) sensor.

11. Remove the engine vibration damper and bracket assembly from the RH side of the engine.

12. Remove the power steering reservoir retaining bolt and place reservoir out of the way.

13. Disconnect the hose to the power steering cooler at the pump, throttle linkage, vacuum hoses, and electrical connectors to the rear of the engine.

14. Loosen the belt tensioner pulley and remove the belt from the air conditioning compressor and the alternator (6 rib). Loosen the belt tensioner pulley and remove the power steering pump belt (4 rib).

15. Remove the lower belt tensioner pulley.

16. Disconnect the cycling switch on top of the suction accumulator/drier.

17. Disconnect the air conditioning line at the dash panel and remove the accumulator and bracket assembly.

18. Remove the alternator assembly. Refer to the "Alternator" removal procedure in this chapter.

19. Disconnect the air conditioning discharge hose, remove the air conditioning compressor, and bracket assembly.

20. Raise the vehicle and support with jackstands.

21. Position a drain pan under oil pan and drain the engine oil.

CAUTION: *The EPA warns that prolonged contact with used engine oil may cause a number of skin disorders, including cancer! You should make every effort to minimize your exposure to used engine oil. Protective gloves should be worn when changing the oil. Wash your hands and any other exposed skin areas as soon as possible after exposure to used engine oil. Soap and water, or waterless hand cleaner should be used.*

22. Remove the oil filter and pull drain pan away from the vehicle.

23. Remove the wheel and tire assemblies.

24. Disconnect the oil level sensor switch, RH lower ball joint, tie rod end, and stabilizer bar.

25. Disconnect the center support bearing bracket and RH CV joint from the transaxle.

26. Disconnect the heated exhaust catalyst-to-engine retaining bolts.

27. Remove the starter motor assembly, lower transaxle-to-engine mounting bolts, engine mount-to-subframe nuts, and crankshaft pulley assembly.

28. Lower the vehicle.

29. Remove the upper transaxle-to-engine mounting bolts.

30. Install the engine lifting eyes.

31. Position the floor jack under the transaxle for support.

32. Position the engine lifting equipment on the lifting eyes.

33. Raise the transaxle assembly slightly.

34. Remove the engine from the vehicle and place on a suitable work stand.

To install:

35. Remove the engine from the workstand and position it in the vehicle.

36. Install the upper transaxle-to-engine bolts.

37. Move the jack out of the way and remove the lifting equipment from the engine.

38. Raise the vehicle and support with jackstands.

39. Install the crankshaft pulley and torque to 113-126 ft. lbs. Install the engine-to-subframe nuts.

40. Install the lower transaxle-to-engine mounting bolts and torque to 25-35 ft. lbs.

41. Install the starter motor, the four exhaust catalyst-to-engine retaining bolts, and the heated exhaust gas oxygen sensor assembly.

42. Connect the center support bearing bracket, RH lower ball joint, tie rod, and stabilizer bar.

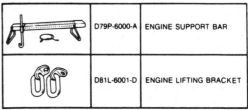

	D79P-6000-A	ENGINE SUPPORT BAR
	D81L-6001-D	ENGINE LIFTING BRACKET

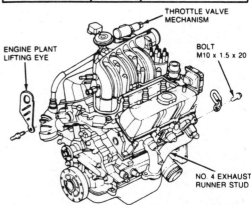

THROTTLE VALVE MECHANISM

ENGINE PLANT LIFTING EYE

BOLT M10 x 1.5 x 20

NO. 4 EXHAUST RUNNER STUD

Engine lifting and support locations—3.0L SHO engine

43. Install the RH CV joint, the wheel and tire assemblies, oil filter, and oil drain plug.

44. Connect the oil sensor and lower the vehicle.

45. Install the air conditioning commpressor and bracket assembly. Torque the bolts to 27-40 ft. lbs.

46. Install the air conditioning discharge hose, accumulator, and cycling switch to the accumulator.

47. Install the alternator assembly and torque the bolts to 36-52 ft. lbs.

48. Install the lower belt tensioner, power steering belt (4 rib), and tighten belt tensioner pulley to 154-198 lbs. for a new belt, and 112-157 lbs. for a used belt.

49. Install the alternator and air conditioning compressor belt (6 rib) and tighten to 220-265 lbs. for a new belt, and 148-192 lbs. for a used belt.

50. Connect the electrical connectors to the wiring harness in the rear of the engine.

51. Connect the heater hoses to heater core, vacuum hoses, throttle linkage, power steering cooler-to-pump hose, and install the power steering reservoir.

52. Install the vibration damper bracket-to-engine for both sides.

53. Install the barometric air pressure (BAP) sensor.

54. Connect the fuel return and inlet hoses.

55. Install the radiator assembly, lower radiator hose, electric fan and shroud assembly, upper radiator hose, and integrated relay controller.

56. Install the air cleaner hose, radiator recovery reservoir, radiator upper sight shield, and oil level indicator tube.

57. Connect the alternator and voltage regulator wiring harness.

58. Install the hood in the same position as previously marked and connect the under hood lamp.

59. Install the battery tray, battery, and connect the battery negative (−) cable.

60. Refill the engine oil and coolant systems.

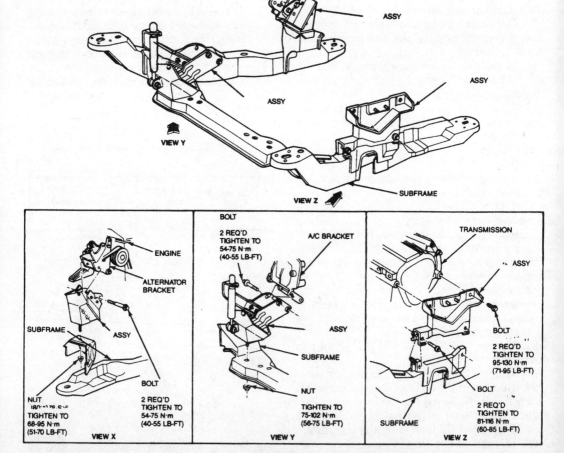

Engine and transaxle mounting—3.0L SHO engine

61. Drain, evacuate, pressure test, and recharge the air conditioning system. Refer to the "Evacuating and Recharging the air conditioning System" procedures in Chapter 1.

62. Start the engine and check for leaks.

Rocker Arm Cover

REMOVAL AND INSTALLATION

2.5L Engine

1. Open and secure the hood.

2. Position protective fender aprons on the fenders.

3. Remove the oil fill cap, rocker arm filler and set them aside.

4. Disconnect the PCV hose and set aside.

5. Disconnect the throttle linkage cable from top of rocker arm cover.

6. Disconnect the speed control cable from top of rocker arm cover, if so equipped.

7. Remove the nine rocker arm cover bolts.

8. Clean both the cylinder head and rocker arm cover mating surfaces (where the gasket contacts).

To install:

9. Coat the gasket contact surfaces of rocker arm cover and UP side of the gasket with Gasket and Seal Contact Adhesive D7AZ-19B508 (ESR-M11P17-A and ESE-M2G52-A) or equivalent. Allow to dry and install gasket in rocker arm cover.

NOTE: *If a rubber gasket is used do not apply sealer.*

10. Install the nine rocker arm cover bolts. Tighten to 6-8 ft. lbs.

11. Connect the speed control cable, if so equipped.

12. Connect the throttle linkage cable.

13. Connect the PCV hose into the rocker arm cover.

14. Install the oil fill cap and the rocker arm filter.

15. Remove the fender covers.

16. Start the engine and run at fast idle. Check for oil leaks.

3.0L Engine

1. Label and disconnect the ignition wires from the spark plugs.

2. Remove the ignition wire separators from the rocker arm cover attaching bolt studs (three places per cover).

3. If the LH rocker arm cover is being removed perform the following:

   a. Remove the oil filler cap.

   b. Disconnect the closure system hose.

4. If the RH rocker arm cover is being removed, perform the following:

   a. Remove the PCV valve.

   b. Disconnect the EGR tube.

   c. Disconnect the heater hose.

5. Remove the (8) rocker arm cover attaching screws and remove cover.

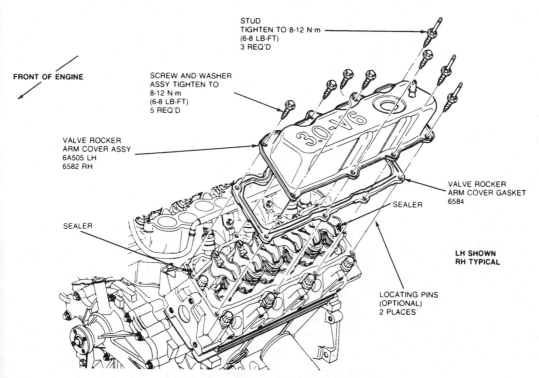

STUD
TIGHTEN TO 8-12 N·m
(6-8 LB-FT)
3 REQ'D

FRONT OF ENGINE

SCREW AND WASHER
ASSY TIGHTEN TO
8-12 N·m
(6-8 LB-FT)
5 REQ'D

VALVE ROCKER
ARM COVER ASSY
6A505 LH
6582 RH

SEALER

VALVE ROCKER
ARM COVER GASKET
6584

SEALER

LH SHOWN
RH TYPICAL

LOCATING PINS
(OPTIONAL)
2 PLACES

Rocker cover mounting—3.0L engine

To install:

NOTE: *Lightly oil all the bolt and stud threads before installation. Using solvent, clean the cylinder head and rocker arm cover mating surfaces to remove all gasket material and dirt.*

6. Apply bead of RTV silicone sealant at the cylinder head to intake manifold rail step (two places per rail). Position a new gasket into place.

7. Position the cover on the cylinder head and install the five attaching bolts and three attaching studs. Note the location of the ignition wire separator clip stud bolts. Tighten attaching bolts to 6-8 ft. lbs.

8. If the LH rocker arm cover is being installed, perform the following:

a. Install the oil fill cap.

b. Connect the PCV closure hose.

9. If the RH rocker arm cover is being installed perform the following:

a. Install the PCV valve.

b. Connect the EGR tube. Tighten to 25-36 ft. lbs.

10. Install the ignition wire separators.

11. Connect the ignition wires to the spark plugs.

12. Start the engine and check for fuel, coolant and oil leaks.

3.8L Engine

1. Label and disconnect the ignition wires from the spark plugs.

2. Remove the ignition wire separators from the rocker arm cover attaching bolt studs (two places per cover).

3. If the LH rocker arm cover is being removed perform the following:

a. Remove the oil filler cap.

b. Disconnect the closure system hose.

4. If RH rocker arm cover is being removed, preform the following:

a. Remove the PCV valve.

b. Disconnect the EGR tube.

c. Disconnect the heater hose.

d. Position the air cleaner assembly aside.

5. Remove the (5) rocker arm cover attaching screws and remove cover.

To install:

NOTE: *Lightly oil all the bolt and stud threads before installation. Using solvent, clean the cylinder head and rocker arm cover mating surfaces to remove all gasket material and dirt.*

6. Apply a bead of RTV silicone sealant at the cylinder head to intake manifold rail step (two places per rail). Position a new gasket into place.

7. Position the cover on the cylinder head and install the three attaching bolts and two attaching studs. Note the location of the ignition wire separator clip stud bolts. Tighten attaching bolts to 72-84 in. lbs.

8. If the LH rocker arm cover is being installed, perform the following:

a. Install the oil fill cap.

b. Connect the PCV closure hose.

9. If the RH rocker arm cover is being installed perform the following:

a. Install the PCV valve.

b. Connect the EGR tube. Tighten to 25-36 ft. lbs.

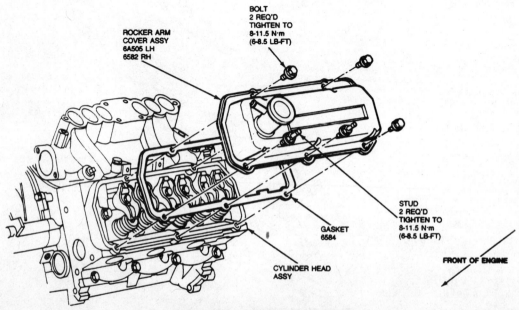

Rocker cover mounting—3.8L engine

10. Install the ignition wire separators.

11. Connect the ignition wires to the spark plugs.

12. Start the engine and check for fuel, coolant and oil leaks.

3.0L SHO Engine

1. Disconnect the negative (−) battery cable.

2. Release the fuel system pressure. Refer to the "Bleeding the Fuel System" procedure in chapter 5.

CAUTION: *The fuel system is under high pressure even when the engine is turned OFF. Disconnecting the fuel lines without releasing the pressure may result in fuel being sprayed out under force. This condition may cause injury or fire.*

3. Disconnect all the vacuum lines and electrical from the intake assembly.

4. Remove the upper intake assembly. Refer to the "Upper Intake" removal and installation procedures in this chapter.

5. Label all spark plug wires for proper reinstallation and disconnect the spark plug wires.

6. If the LH cylinder head cover is being removed.

    a. Remove the oil filler cap.

    b. Remove the coil pack plastic cover.

7. If the RH cylinder head cover is being removed, disconnect the fuel lines after releasing the fuel pressure.

8. Remove the cylinder head cover attaching bolts and remove the cover.

To install:

NOTE: *Lightly oil all of the bolt and stud threads before installation. Using solvent, clean the cylinder head and rocker arm cover sealing surfaces to remove all gasket material and dirt.*

7. Install a new gasket and three spark plug hole gaskets on the cylinder head cover. Position the cover on the cylinder head and install the attaching bolts. Torque the bolts to 8-11 ft. lbs.

8. If installing the LH head cover, install the coil pack plastic cover and the oil filler cap.

9. If installing the RH head cover, connect the fuel lines.

10. Connect the spark plug wires in the same position as they were removed.

11. Install the upper intake assembly, refer to the "Upper Intake Manifold" removal and installation procedures in this chapter.

12. Connect all the vacuum and electrical connectors to the intake manifold.

13. Connect the negative (−) battery cable.

14. Start the engine and check for fuel, coolant, and oil leaks.

Rocker Arms/Shafts

REMOVAL AND INSTALLATION

2.5L & 3.8L Engines

1. Raise the hood and place protective aprons on the fenders.

2. Remove the oil filler cap. Disconnect the PCV hose, the throttle linkage and the speed control cable from the top of the rocker arm cover (if equipped).

3. Remove the rocker arm cover-to-cylinder head bolts and the cover.

4. Remove the rocker arm fulcrum bolts, the fulcrums and the rocker arms. If necessary, remove the pushrods.

NOTE: *When removing the rocker arm assemblies, be sure to keep all of the parts in order for installation purposes.*

5. Using a putty knife, clean the gasket mounting surfaces. Inspect and/or replace any damaged parts.

NOTE: *The following procedure may require the removal of the front timing cover.*

To install:

6. Position the pushrods in the hydraulic lifter.

7. Install the rocker arms, the fulcrums and the bolts onto the valves.

8. Position the crankshaft so that the timing marks, on the crankshaft and the camshaft sprockets, are facing each other (on the center line). Torque the rocker arm fulcrum bolts of the intake valves of cylinders No. 1 and 2 and the exhaust valves of cylinders No. 1 and 3 to 54-90 in. lbs.

9. Turn the crankshaft 1 complete revolution so that the timing marks, on the crankshaft and the camshaft sprockets, are facing opposite each other (on the center line). Torque the rocker arm fulcrum bolts of the intake valves of cylinders No. 3 and 4 and the exhaust valves of cylinders No. 2 and 4 to 54-90 in. lbs.

10. Apply SAE 50 oil to all of the fulcrums, the rocker arms and the pushrods. Torque all of the fulcrum bolts to 19.5-26.5 ft. lbs.

NOTE: *Before torquing the rocker arm fulcrum bolts, be sure that the fulcrums are seated on the cylinder head slots and the pushrods are seated in the rocker arms/tappets.*

11. To check the collapsed lifter gap, perform the following procedures:

    a. Position the crankshaft so that the timing marks, on the crankshaft and the camshaft sprockets, are facing each other (on the center line). Using a feeler gauge, check the tappet gap of the intake valves of cylinders No. 1 and 2 and the exhaust valves of cylinders No. 1 and 3; the tappet gap should be 1.8-4.4mm).

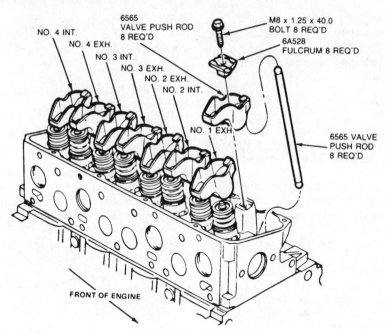

NO. 4 INT.
NO. 4 EXH.
NO. 3 INT.
NO. 3 EXH.
NO. 2 EXH.
NO. 2 INT.
NO. 1 EXH.
6565 VALVE PUSH ROD 8 REQ'D
M8 x 1.25 x 40.0 BOLT 8 REQ'D
6A528 FULCRUM 8 REQ'D
6565 VALVE PUSH ROD 8 REQ'D
FRONT OF ENGINE

Rocker arms—2.5L engine

b. Turn the crankshaft 1 complete revolution so that the timing marks, on the crankshaft and the camshaft sprockets, are facing opposite each other (on the center line). Using a feeler gauge, check the tappet gap of the intake valves of cylinders No. 3 and 4 and the exhaust valves of cylinders No. 2 and 4; the tappet gap should be 1.8-4.4mm.

12. Complete the installation of the remaining components by reversing the removal procedure, use a new gasket and reverse the removal procedures. Start the engine and check for leaks.

3.0L Engine

1. Label and disconnect the ignition wires from the spark plugs.

2. Remove the ignition wire separators from the rocker arm cover mounting bolt studs.

3. To remove the left side rocker arm cover: remove the oil filler cap then disconnect the closure system hose.

4. To remove the right side rocker arm cover: remove the PCV valve, disconnect the EGR tube, then disconnect the heater hoses.

5. Remove the (8) rocker arm covers-to-cylinder head screws and the cover.

6. Remove the rocker arm fulcrum bolts, the fulcrums and the rocker arms. If necessary, remove the pushrods.

NOTE: *When removing the rocker arm assemblies, be sure to keep all of the parts in order for installation purposes.*

7. Using a putty knife, clean the gasket

mounting surfaces. Inspect and/or replace any damaged parts.

8. **To install:** the rocker arm components, first position the pushrods on the tappets. Install the rocker arms, the fulcrums and the bolts onto the valves, but DO NOT tighten the bolts. Using SAE 50 oil, apply it to all of the fulcrums, the rocker arms and the pushrods.

NOTE: *Before torquing the rocker arm fulcrum bolts, be sure that the fulcrums are seated in the cylinder head slots and the pushrods are seated in the rocker arms/tappets.*

9. For each valve, rotate the crankshaft until the tappet rests on the heel (base circle) of the camshaft lobe. Torque the rocker arm fulcrum bolts to 19-25 ft. lbs.

NOTE: *If the original valve components are being installed, a valve clearance check is not required. Valve Clearance: 2.2-4.8mm.*

10. Rotate the crankshaft to place the No. 1 cylinder on TDC of the compression stroke, then allow the lifters to bleed down.

11. Using a feeler gauge, check that the valve clearances of cylinders No. 1, 3 & 6 (intake) and No. 1, 2 & 4 (exhaust) are 2.2-4.8mm.

12. Rotate the crankshaft one complete revolution, positioning the No. 2 cylinder on TDC of the compression stroke, then allow the lifters to bleed down.

13. Using a feeler gauge, check that the valve clearances of cylinders No. 2, 4 & 5 (intake) and No. 3, 5 & 6 (exhaust) are 2.2-4.8mm.

14. To complete the installation, use a new gasket and reverse the removal procedures. Start the engine and check for leaks.

3.0L SHO Engine

The 3.0L SHO engine does not use rocker arm or rocker shafts. The SHO engine is an overhead camshaft engine where the camshaft contacts the top of the valve directly to push it down.

Thermostat

REMOVAL AND INSTALLATION

1. Raise the hood and place protective aprons on the fenders.
2. Disconnect the negative (−) battery cable.
3. Position a drain pan under the radiator, with the engine cool remove the radiator cap, open the draincock and drain the coolant into the drain pan.

> CAUTION: *When draining the coolant, keep in mind that cats and dogs are attracted by the ethylene glycol antifreeze, and are quite likely to drink any that is left in an uncovered container or in puddles on the ground. This will prove fatal in sufficient quantity. Always drain the coolant into a sealable container. Coolant should be reused unless it is contaminated or several years old.*

> NOTE: *Drain the cooling system to a level below the water outlet (thermostat) housing.*

4. On the 2.5L engine, remove the vent plug from the water outlet housing.

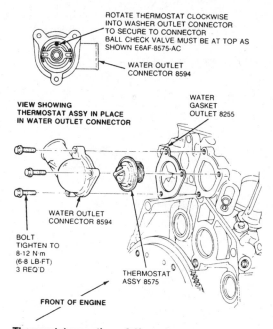

Thermostat mounting—3.0L engine

5. Loosen the upper hose clamp at the radiator. Remove the water outlet housing-to-engine bolts (2 on the 2.5L, 3.0L SHO, 3.8L and 3 on the 3.0L), lift the outlet clear of the engine and remove the thermostat from the housing.
6. Using a putty knife, clean the gasket mounting surfaces.
7. **To install:** use a new gasket, sealant, thermostat and reverse the removal proce-

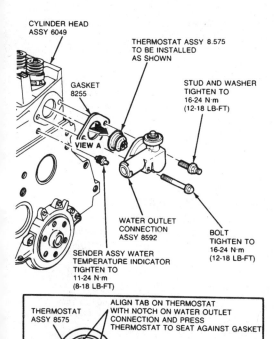

Thermostat mounting—2.5L engine

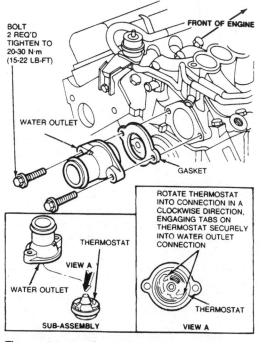

Thermostat mounting—3.8L engine

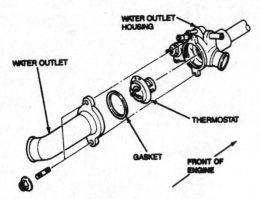

Thermostat mounting—3.0L SHO engine

dures. Torque the water outlet housing-to-engine bolts to;

- 2.5L engine 12-18 ft. lbs.
- 3.0L engine 6-8 ft. lbs.
- 3.8L engine 15-22 ft. lbs.
- 3.0L SHO engine 5-8 ft. lbs.

NOTE: *When installing the thermostat, rotate it clockwise into the water outlet housing. On the 3.0L engine, position the thermostat ball check valve at the top. On the 3.8L engine, rotate the thermostat into connection in a clockwise direction, engaging tabs on thermostat securely into water outlet connection. Check diagram in this section for proper location.*

Intake Manifold

REMOVAL AND INSTALLATION

2.5L Engine

1. Raise and secure the hood. Disconnect the negative (−) battery cable.
2. Place a drain pan under the radiator, remove the radiator cap, open the draincock and drain the cooling system.

CAUTION: *When draining the coolant, keep in mind that cats and dogs are attracted by the ethylene glycol antifreeze, and are quite likely to drink any that is left in an uncovered container or in puddles on the ground. This will prove fatal in sufficient quantity. Always drain the coolant into a sealable container. Coolant should be reused unless it is contaminated or several years old.*

3. Remove the accelerator cable, the air cleaner assembly and the heat stove tube from the heat shield.
4. Label and remove the necessary vacuum lines.
5. Remove the Thermactor belt, the hose below Thermactor pump and the Thermactor pump.
6. Remove the heat shield from the exhaust manifold.

7. Disconnect the Thermactor check valve hose from the tube assembly. Remove the bracket-to-EGR valve nuts.
8. Disconnect the water inlet tube from the intake manifold.
9. Disconnect the EGR tube from the EGR valve.
10. Remove the intake manifold-to-engine bolts and the manifold.
11. Using a putty knife, clean the gasket mounting surfaces.

To install:
12. Replace the manifold and gasket assembly on the engine. Install the 7 bolts and 1 stud into the manifold. The 1 stud goes in the 6th bolt hole.
13. Torque the intake manifold bolts to 15-23 ft. lbs. in sequence. Check diagram in this section for tightening sequence.
14. Connect water inlet tube, EGR tube and bracket, and thermactor check valve.
15. Install the heat shield on the exhaust manifold.
16. Connect the accelerator cable, heat stove tube, and air cleaner.
17. Connect vacuum lines, fill radiator with coolant, and connect negative battery cable.
18. Start engine and check for leaks.

3.0L Engine

1. Disconnect the negative (−) battery cable. Drain the cooling system to a level below the intake manifold.

CAUTION: *When draining the coolant, keep in mind that cats and dogs are attracted by the ethylene glycol antifreeze, and are quite likely to drink any that is left in an uncovered container or in puddles on the ground. This will prove fatal in sufficient quantity. Always drain the coolant into a sealable container. Coolant should be reused unless it is contaminated or several years old.*

2. Refer to the "Throttle Body Removal And Installation" procedures in this section and remove the throttle body from the engine.
3. Reduce the pressure in the fuel system and disconnect the fuel lines. Refer to the "Engine Removal and Installation" procedures for reducing fuel system pressure.
4. Disconnect and remove the fuel injector electrical harness from the engine.
5. Label and disconnect the spark plug wires (for easy installation). Mark and remove the distributor from the engine.
6. Disconnect the upper radiator hose, the water outlet heater hose and the thermostat housing from the engine.
7. Remove the intake manifold-to-engine bolts/studs, the intake manifold; discard the side gaskets and end seals.

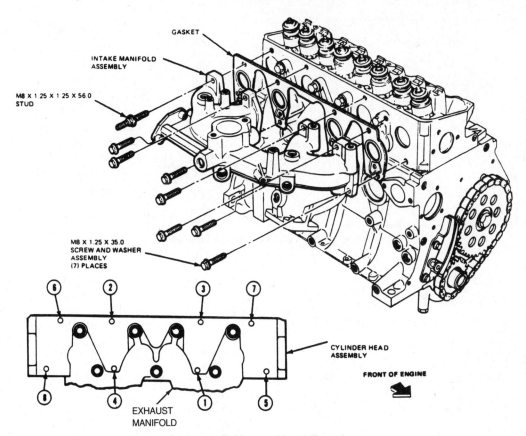

GASKET

INTAKE MANIFOLD
ASSEMBLY

M8 X 1.25 X 1.25 X 56.0
STUD

M8 X 1.25 X 35.0
SCREW AND WASHER
ASSEMBLY
(7) PLACES

CYLINDER HEAD
ASSEMBLY

FRONT OF ENGINE

EXHAUST
MANIFOLD

Intake manifold assembly—2.5L engine

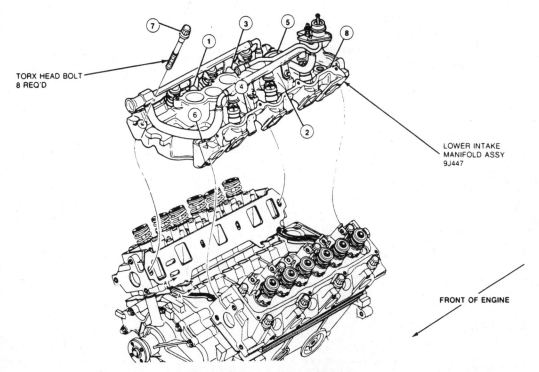

TORX HEAD BOLT
8 REQ'D

LOWER INTAKE
MANIFOLD ASSY
9J447

FRONT OF ENGINE

Intake manifold assembly—3.0L engine

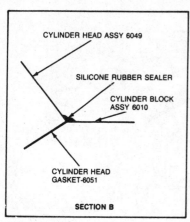

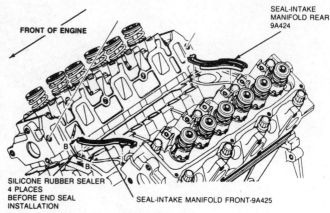

Intake manifold seal locations—3.0L engine

NOTE: *The intake manifold assembly can be removed with the fuel rails and injectors in place.*

8. Using a putty knife, clean the gasket/seal mounting surfaces.

To install:

NOTE: *Lightly oil all attaching bolts and stud threads before installation. When using silicone rubber sealer, let it dry for at least 15 minutes before assembly. The recommended sealer is an RTV sealer or equivalent.*

9. Apply Silicone Rubber Sealer part No. D6AZ-19562-A or equivalent, to the corners of the block and cylinder heads where the intake manifold rests.

10. Install the front and rear intake seals.

11. Position the intake manifold gaskets in place and insert locking tabs over the tabs on the cylinder head gaskets as shown in the diagram.

12. Lower the intake manifold into position on the cylinder block and cylinder heads.

merical sequence shown in the tightening diagram. Tighten bolts in two steps to 11 ft. lbs. and 18 ft. lbs. for the second step.

14. Install thermostat housing and new gasket.

15. Connect PVC line at PVC valve and exhaust manifold.

16. Connect necessary vacuum hoses.

17. Install rocker arm cover, connect heater hoses, coolant bypass hose, and upper radiator hose.

18. Connect fuel lines, air cleaner outlet tube, and fill cooling system with coolant.

19. Connect the negative (−) battery cable, start engine, and check for leaks.

3.8L Engine

1. Position drain pan under radiator and drain coolant. Disconnect negative (−) battery cable.

CAUTION: *When draining the coolant, keep in mind that cats and dogs are attracted by*

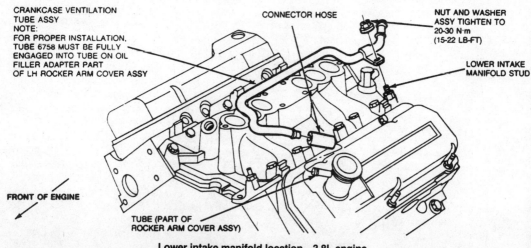

Lower intake manifold location—3.8L engine

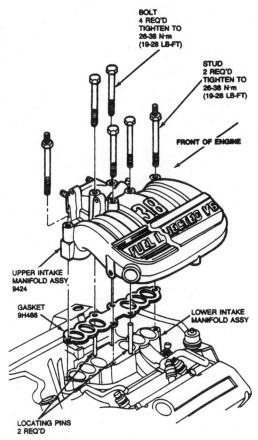

BOLT
4 REQ'D
TIGHTEN TO
26-38 N·m
(19-28 LB-FT)

STUD
2 REQ'D
TIGHTEN TO
26-38 N·m
(19-28 LB-FT)

FRONT OF ENGINE

UPPER INTAKE
MANIFOLD ASSY
9424

GASKET
9H486

LOWER INTAKE
MANIFOLD ASSY

LOCATING PINS
2 REQ'D

Upper intake manifold location—3.8L engine

NOTE: *The lower manifold is sealed with RTV-type sealer. To break the seal, pry on the front of the manifold with a suitable pry bar. Use care to prevent damage to the machined surfaces.*

To Install

NOTE: *Lightly oil all attaching bolts and stud threads before installation. When using silicone rubber sealer, let it dry for at least 15 minutes before assembly. The recommended sealer is an RTV sealer or equivalent.*

10. Clean all mating surfaces with a puddy knife and suitable solvent.

11. Install front and rear intake manifold end seals.

12. Carefully place lower intake manifold into position on cylinder block and cylinder heads.

13. Install manifold bolts and studs in their original locations. Tighten bolts in sequence shown in intake manifold assembly diagram in this section.

14. Torque bolts in three steps: 8 ft. lbs., 15 ft. lbs., and 24 ft. lbs.

15. Install the upper intake manifold and gasket on top of lower manifold.

16. Torque the bolts in three steps just like the lower manifold.

17. Install EGR valve assembly and torque attaching bolts to 15-22 ft. lbs.

18. Install the throttle body and torgue the bolts to 15-22 ft. lbs.

19. Install air conditioning compressor support bracket, if so equipped.

20. Connect all vacuum lines, electrical connectors, and heater hoses.

21. Connect all fuel lines.

22. Connect the speed control cable, if so equipped.

23. Fill the radiator with specified coolant, start engine, and check for leaks.

3.0L SHO Engine

CAUTION: *When draining the coolant, keep in mind that cats and dogs are attracted by the ethylene glycol antifreeze, and are quite likely to drink any that is left in an uncovered container or in puddles on the ground. This will prove fatal in sufficient quantity. Always drain the coolant into a sealable container. Coolant should be reused unless it is contaminated or several years old.*

1. Disconnect the negative (–) battery cable.

2. Partially drain the engine cooling system by placing a suitable drain pan under the radiator drain plug and turning it counterclockwise.

3. Disconnect the electrical connectors and vacuum lines from the intake manifold.

4. Remove the air cleaner tube.

5. Disconnect the coolant lines and cables from the throttle body.

the ethylene glycol antifreeze, and are quite likely to drink any that is left in an uncovered container or in puddles on the ground. This will prove fatal in sufficient quantity. Always drain the coolant into a sealable container. Coolant should be reused unless it is contaminated or several years old.

2. Remove the air cleaner assembly, accelerator cable, transaxle linkage, and thermactor pump supply hose.

3. Release fuel pressure and disconnect fuel lines crossing over valve cover and connecting at fuel rails.

4. Disconnect upper radiator hose, coolant bypass hose, and heater tube at intake manifold.

5. Disconnect vacuum lines and necessary electrical connectors.

6. Remove air conditioning compressor support bracket, if so equipped.

7. Remove throttle body and EGR valve assemblies from upper intake manifold.

8. Remove upper intake manifold bolts and upper intake manifold.

9. Remove lower intake manifold bolts and lower intake manifold.

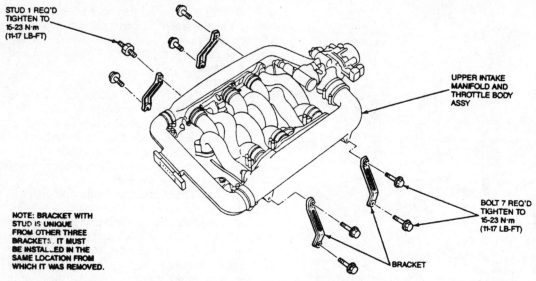

STUD 1 REQ'D
TIGHTEN TO
15-23 N·m
(11-17 LB-FT)

UPPER INTAKE
MANIFOLD AND
THROTTLE BODY
ASSY

NOTE: BRACKET WITH
STUD IS UNIQUE
FROM OTHER THREE
BRACKETS. IT MUST
BE INSTALLED IN THE
SAME LOCATION FROM
WHICH IT WAS REMOVED.

BOLT 7 REQ'D
TIGHTEN TO
15-23 N·m
(11-17 LB-FT)

BRACKET

Intake manifold assembly—3.0L SHO engine

6. Remove the four bolts retaining the upper intake brackets.

7. Loosen the four lower bolts and remove the brackets.

8. Remove the 12 bolts retaining the intake-to-cylinder heads.

9. Remove the intake manifold assembly and gaskets.

To install:

NOTE: *Lightly oil all the attaching bolts and stud threads before installation.*

10. Position a new gasket on the cylinder head.

11. Position the intake manifold on the cylinder head, install the 12 attaching bolts, and torque the bolts to 15-23 ft. lbs.

12. Install the intake manifold brackets and torque to 11-17 ft. lbs.

13. Connect the coolant lines and cables to the throttle body. Connect all the electrical connectors and vacuum lines to the manifold.

14. Install the air cleaner, fill the cooling system, connect the negative (−) battery cable, and start the engine to check for coolant leaks.

Exhaust Manifolds

REMOVAL AND INSTALLATION

2.5L Engine

1. Disconnect the negative (−) battery cable.

2. Disconnect the exhaust pipe-to-exhaust manifold nuts.

3. Remove the heat shield from the exhaust manifold.

4. Disconnect the electrical connector from the EGO sensor.

5. Disconnect the thermactor check valve

hose from the tube assembly. Remove the bracket-to-EGR valve nuts.

6. Remove the 7 exhaust manifold-to-engine bolts and the manifold from the vehicle.

7. Using a putty knife, clean the gasket mounting surfaces.

NOTE: *When installing the exhaust manifold, use the Alignment Stud tools No. T84P-6065-B to align the manifold with the block.*

8. **To install:** use new gaskets and reverse the removal procedures. Torque the exhaust manifold-to-engine bolts (in two steps) to 20-30 ft. lbs., the exhaust manifold-to-exhaust pipe nuts to 25-34 ft. lbs. and the intake manifold-to-engine bolts to 15-23 ft. lbs. Refill the cooling system. Start engine and check for leaks.

3.0L Engine

LEFT SIDE (FRONT)

1. Disconnect the negative (−) battery cable. Remove the oil level indicator support bracket.

2. Disconnect and plug the power steering hoses at the power steering pump.

3. Remove the exhaust manifold-to-exhaust pipe nuts and separate the exhaust pipe from the exhaust manifold.

4. Remove the 6 exhaust manifold-to-cylinder head bolts and the exhaust manifold from the engine.

5. Using a putty knife, clean gasket mounting surfaces. Lightly oil all of the bolt/stud threads prior to installation.

6. **To install:** use new gaskets and reverse the removal procedures. Torque the exhaust manifold-to-engine bolts to 15-22 ft. lbs. and the exhaust manifold-to-exhaust pipe nuts to 16-24 ft. lbs. Refill and bleed the power steering system.

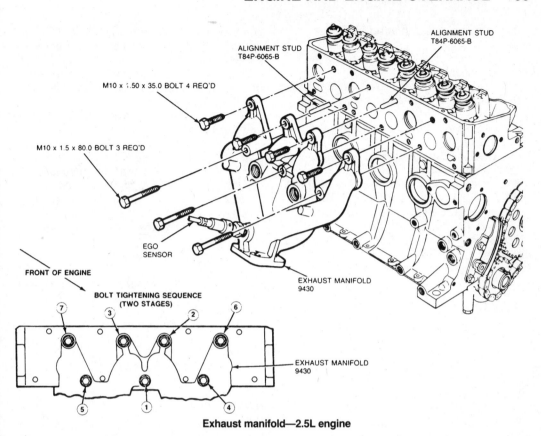

ALIGNMENT STUD
T84P-6065-B

ALIGNMENT STUD
T84P-6065-B

M10 x 1.50 x 35.0 BOLT 4 REQ'D

M10 x 1.5 x 80.0 BOLT 3 REQ'D

EGO
SENSOR

FRONT OF ENGINE

EXHAUST MANIFOLD
9430

BOLT TIGHTENING SEQUENCE
(TWO STAGES)

EXHAUST MANIFOLD
9430

Exhaust manifold—2.5L engine

RIGHT SIDE (REAR)

1. Disconnect the negative (–) battery cable. Remove the heater hose support bracket.

2. Disconnect and plug the heater hoses. Remove the EGR tube from the exhaust manifold; use a back-up wrench on the lower adapter.

3. Remove the exhaust manifold-to-exhaust pipe nuts and separate the pipe from the manifold.

4. Remove the 6 exhaust manifold-to-engine

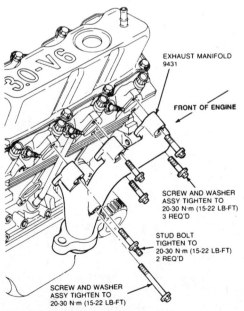

EXHAUST MANIFOLD
9431

FRONT OF ENGINE

SCREW AND WASHER
ASSY TIGHTEN TO
20-30 N·m (15-22 LB-FT)
3 REQ'D

STUD BOLT
TIGHTEN TO
20-30 N·m (15-22 LB-FT)
2 REQ'D

SCREW AND WASHER
ASSY TIGHTEN TO
20-30 N·m (15-22 LB-FT)

Left exhaust manifold—3.0L engine

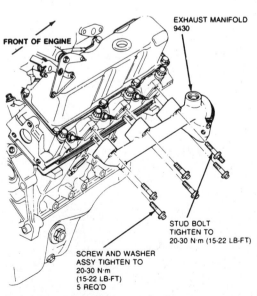

EXHAUST MANIFOLD
9430

FRONT OF ENGINE

STUD BOLT
TIGHTEN TO
20-30 N·m (15-22 LB-FT)

SCREW AND WASHER
ASSY TIGHTEN TO
20-30 N·m
(15-22 LB-FT)
5 REQ'D

Right exhaust manifold—3.0L engine

bolts and the exhaust manifold from the engine.

5. Using a putty knife, clean the gasket mounting surfaces.

NOTE: *Lightly oil all of the bolt and stud threads prior to installation.*

To install:

6. Install the exhaust manifold and new gasket on the engine.

7. Install the 6 manifold bolts in their proper holes. Torque the bolts to 15-22 ft. lbs.

8. Connect the exhaust pipe to the manifold and torque the two bolts to 16-24 ft. lbs.

9. Connect the EGR tube to exhaust manifold and torque to 25-36 ft. lbs.

10. Connect all vacuum lines, fuel lines, and fill cooling system with coolant.

11. Start engine and check for leaks.

3.8L Engine

LEFT SIDE (FRONT)

1. Remove the oil level dipstick tube support bracket.

2. Tag and disconnect the spark plug wires.

3. Raise the vehicle and support safely with jackstands.

4. Remove the manifold-to-exhaust pipe attaching nuts and lower the vehicle.

5. Remove the exhaust manifold retaining bolts and separate the manifold from the cylinder head surface. Discard the gasket and replace with new one.

6. **To install:** lightly oil all bolt and stud threads before installation. Clean the mating

surfaces on the exhaust manifold, cylinder head and exhaust pipe so that they are free of the old gasket material.

7. Position the gasket and exhaust manifold on the cylinder head. Install pilot bolt (lower front bolt hole on No. 5 cylinder).

8. Install the remaining 5 manifold retaining bolts. Torque the bolts 15-22 ft. lbs.

NOTE: *A slight warpage in the exhaust manifold may cause a misalignment between the bolt holes in the head and the manifold. Drill the hole a size bigger to elongate the holes in the exhaust manifold as necessary to correct the misalignment, if apparent. Do not elongate the pilot hole (lower front bolt on No. 5 cylinder).*

9. Raise the vehicle and support safely with jackstands.

10. Connect the exhaust pipe to the manifold. Torque the attaching nuts to 16-24 ft. lbs., and lower the vehicle.

11. Connect the spark plug wires. Install dipstick tube support bracket attaching nut. Tighten to 15-22 ft. lbs.

12. Start the engine and check for exhaust leaks.

RIGHT SIDE (REAR)

1. Remove the air cleaner outlet tube assembly. Disconnect the thermactor hose from the downstream air tube check valve.

2. Tag and disconnect the coil secondary wire from the coil and the wires from spark plugs.

3. Disconnect the EGR tube.

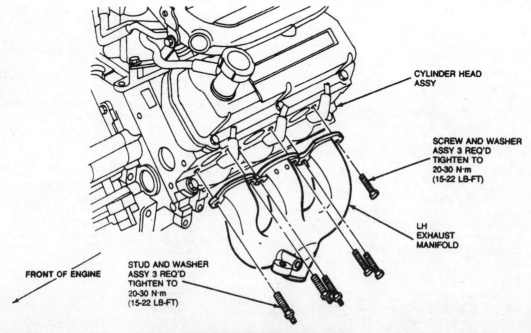

Left exhaust manifold—3.8L engine

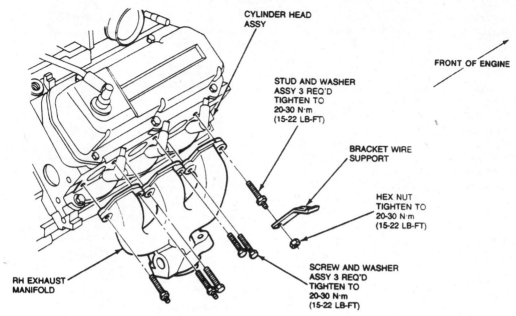

CYLINDER HEAD
ASSY

FRONT OF ENGINE

STUD AND WASHER
ASSY 3 REQ'D
TIGHTEN TO
20-30 N·m
(15-22 LB-FT)

BRACKET WIRE
SUPPORT

HEX NUT
TIGHTEN TO
20-30 N·m
(15-22 LB-FT)

RH EXHAUST
MANIFOLD

SCREW AND WASHER
ASSY 3 REQ'D
TIGHTEN TO
20-30 N·m
(15-22 LB-FT)

Right exhaust manfiold—3.8L engine

4. Raise the vehicle and support safely with jackstands.

5. Remove the transaxle dipstick tube. Remove the thermactor air tube by cutting the tube clamp at the underbody catalyst fitting with a suitable cutting tool.

6. Remove the manifold-to-exhaust pipe attaching nuts.

7. Lower the vehicle.

8. Remove the 6 exhaust manifold-to-engine retaining bolts. Remove the manifold and heat shroud and gasket from the vehicle. Discard the gasket and replace with a new one.

9. Lightly oil all bolt and stud threads before installation. Clean the mating surfaces on the exhaust manifold cylinder head and exhaust pipe so that they are free of the old gasket material.

10. Position the gasket, inner half of the heat shroud and exhaust manifold on cylinder head. Start two attaching bolts to align the manifold with the cylinder head. Install the remaining retaining bolts and torque to 15-22 ft. lbs.

11. Raise the vehicle and support safely with jackstands.

12. Connect the exhaust pipe to manifold. Torque the attaching nuts to 16-24 ft. lbs. Position the thermactor hose to the downstream air tube and clamp tube to the underbody catalyst fitting.

13. Install the transaxle dipstick tube and lower vehicle.

14. Connect the ignition wires to their respective spark plugs and connect coil secondary wire to the coil.

15. Connect the EGR tube. Connect the thermactor hose to the downstream air tube and secure with a clamp. Install the air cleaner outlet tube assembly.

16. Start the engine and check for exhaust leaks.

3.0L SHO Engine

LEFT SIDE (FRONT)

1. Remove the oil level indicator tube support bracket, power steering pump pressure and return hoses, manifold-to-exhaust pipe attaching nuts, and heat shield attaching bolts.

2. Remove the exhaust manifold attaching nuts and the manifold.

3. **To install:** Clean mating surfaces on the exhaust manifold, cylinder head, and exhaust pipe.

4. Position the exhaust manifold on the cylinder head and install the manifold attaching nuts. Torque the nuts to 26-38 ft. lbs.

5. Install the heat shield and attaching bolts. Torque the bolts to 11-17 ft. lbs.

6. Connect the exhaust pipe-to-manifold and torque the nuts to 16-24 ft. lbs.

7. Connect the power steering pump pressure and return hoses.

8. Install the oil level indicator tube support bracket.

RIGHT SIDE (REAR)

CAUTION: *When draining the coolant, keep in mind that cats and dogs are attracted by the ethylene glycol antifreeze, and are quite likely to drink any that is left in an uncovered* container or in puddles on the ground. This will prove fatal in sufficient quantity. Always drain the coolant into a sealable container. Coolant should be reused unless it is contaminated or several years old.

1. Drain the engine cooling system.

2. Remove the upper intake manifold. Refer to the "Intake Manifold" removal and installation procedure in this chapter.

3. Remove the RH cylinder head. Refer to the "Cylinder Head" removal and installation procedures in this chapter.

4. Remove the exhaust-to-manifold attaching nuts and move the pipe out of the way.

5. Remove the exhaust manifold-to-cylinder head attaching nuts and remove the manifold assembly.

To install:

6. Lightly oil all of the bolt and stud threads before installation.

7. Clean the mating surfaces on the exhaust manifold.

8. Install the manifold and attaching nuts on the cylinder head. Torque the nuts to 26-38 ft. lbs.

9. Install the heat shield and torque the attaching bolts to 11-17 ft. lbs.

10. Install the RH cylinder head and exhaust manifold on to the engine. Refer to the "Cylinder Head" installation procedures in this chapter.

11. Start the engine and check for fuel, coolant, and oil leaks.

Air Conditioning Compressor

REMOVAL AND INSTALLATION

1. Discharge the system following the recommended service procedures in Chapter 1. Observe all safety precautions.

2. Disconnect the compressor clutch wires at the field coil connector on the compressor.

3. Loosen and remove the compressor drive belt.

4. Disconnect and plug the hose assemblies from the condenser and suction lines.

5. Remove the four bolts holding the compressor to the side of the engine.

6. Remove the compressor, manifold, and tube assembly from the vehicle.

NOTE: The assembly will not clear the subframe and radiator support if an attempt is made to remove the unit from the bottom of the vehicle. It must be removed from the top.

7. Installation is the reverse of the removal procedure. If the compressor is to be replaced, drain the oil from the removed compressor into a calibrated measuring container. Record the amount of oil (fluid ounces) drained from the

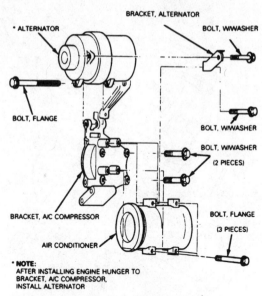

Compressor installation—3.0L SHO engine

old compressor. Fill the new compressor with the measured amount of refrigerant oil only. Discard the old oil. Check the system for proper operation.

Radiator

REMOVAL AND INSTALLATION

1. Place a fluid catch pan under the radiator. With the engine cool, open the radiator draincock and remove the radiator cap, then drain the cooling system.

CAUTION: When draining the coolant, keep in mind that cats and dogs are attracted by the ethylene glycol antifreeze, and are quite likely to drink any that is left in an uncovered container or in puddles on the ground. This will prove fatal in sufficient quantity. Always drain the coolant into a sealable container. Coolant should be reused unless it is contaminated or several years old.

2. Remove the overflow hose from the radiator and the coolant tank.

3. Remove the upper shroud screws, lift the shroud from the lower retaining clips and position it over the fan.

4. Loosen the upper/lower radiator hose clamps, then using a twisting motion, remove the hoses from the radiator.

5. If equipped with an ATX, use the Cooler Line Disconnect tool No. T82L-9500-AH to disconnect the oil cooling lines from the radiator. Be sure to plug the cooling lines to prevent fluid draining from the transaxle.

6. Remove the upper radiator-to-vehicle screws, then tilt the radiator rearward approxi-

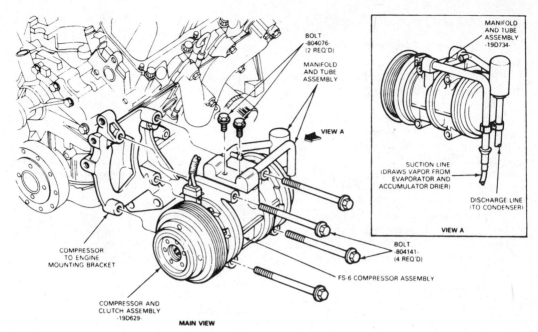

Compressor installation—3.0L engine

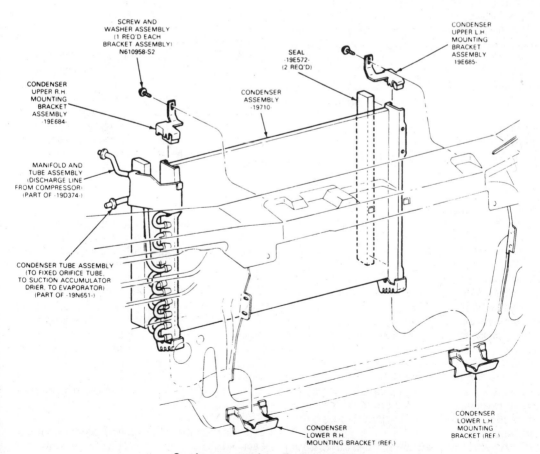

Condenser mounting—Taurus and Sable

mately 25mm, lift it upward (clearing the support and the fan).

7. **To install:** reverse the removal procedures. Torque the upper radiator-to-support bolts to 13-20 ft. lbs., the upper shroud-to-radiator screws to 48-72 in. lbs. and the hose clamps to 20-30 in. lbs.

NOTE: *When installing the radiator, position the molded pins (at the bottom of nylon end tanks) in the slotted holes of the lower support rubber pads.*

8. Install the cooling fluid (to a level of 1½" below the radiator filler neck), start the engine, operate it for 15 minutes and check for leaks.

NOTE: *If installing new cooling fluid, use a 50/50 mixture of water and antifreeze. Be sure to add 2 Cooling System Protector Pellets No. D9AZ-19558-A to the radiator.*

Air Conditioning Condenser
REMOVAL AND INSTALLATION

1. Wearing safety glasses, discharge the refrigerant from the air conditioning system at the service access gauge port valve located on the suction line as described in Chapter 1.

2. Disconnect the refrigerant lines at the fittings on the right side of the radiator.

3. Remove the four bolts attaching the condenser to the radiator support. Remove the condenser from the vehicle.

4. Installation is the reverse of the removal procedure. Leak test, evacuate and charge the system. Check system for proper operation.

Water Pump
REMOVAL AND INSTALLATION
2.5L ENGINE

1. Open the hood, place protection aprons on the fenders and disconnect the negative battery cable.

2. Remove the radiator cap and position a drain pan under the radiator.

CAUTION: *When draining the coolant, keep in mind that cats and dogs are attracted by the ethylene glycol antifreeze, and are quite likely to drink any that is left in an uncovered container or in puddles on the ground. This will prove fatal in sufficient quantity. Always drain the coolant into a sealable container. Coolant should be reused unless it is contaminated or several years old.*

3. Raise and support the front of the vehicle on jackstands. Remove the lower radiator hose from the radiator and drain the coolant into the drain pan.

4. Remove the water pump inlet tube. Loosen the belt tensioner by inserting a ½" flex han-

dle in the square hole of the tensioner, then rotate the tensioner counterclockwise and remove the drive belt from the vehicle.

5. Disconnect the heater hose from the water pump. Remove the three water pump-to-engine block bolts and the pump from the engine.

6. Using a putty knife, clean the gasket mounting surfaces.

To install:

7. Coat the new gasket on both sides with Perfect Seal Sealing Compound part No. B5A-19554-A or equivalent and position on cylinder block.

2. Install the 3 water pump-to-engine bolts. Torque the bolts to 15-22 ft. lbs.

8. Install water pump belt on pulley and adjust tension to specifications.

9. Connect the negative (−) battery cable and fill system with coolant.

10. Start engine and check for leaks.

3.0L Engine

1. Disconnect the negative (−) battery cable and place a suitable drain pan under the radiator draincock.

NOTE: *Drain the system with the engine cool and the heater temperature control set at the maximum heat position. Attach a ⅜" hose to the drain cock so as to direct the coolant into the drain pan.*

CAUTION: *When draining the coolant, keep in mind that cats and dogs are attracted by the ethylene glycol antifreeze, and are quite likely to drink any that is left in an uncovered container or in puddles on the ground. This will prove fatal in sufficient quantity. Always drain the coolant into a sealable container. Coolant should be reused unless it is contaminated or several years old.*

2. Remove the radiator cap, open the drain cock on the radiator and drain the cooling system.

3. Loosen the accessory drive belt idler pulley and remove the drive belts.

4. Remove the idler pulley bracket-to-engine nuts/bolt. Disconnect the heater hose from the water pump.

5. Remove the pulley-to-pump hub bolts. The pulley will remain loose on the hub due to the insufficient clearance between the inner fender and the water pump.

6. Remove the water pump-to-engine bolts, then lift the water pump and pulley out of the vehicle.

7. Using a putty knife, clean the gasket mounting surfaces.

To install:

8. Coat both sides of new gasket with Contact Adhesive part No. D7AZ-19B508-A or equivalent.

9. Install pump-to-engine bolts and torque to 72-96 in. lbs.

10. Install pulley-to-pump bolts and torque to 15-22 ft. lbs.

11. Connect the coolant bypass and heater hoses to the water pump.

12. Install idler bracket, drive belt, and adjust to proper tension.

13. Fill cooling system with coolant and start engine and check for leaks.

3.8L Engine

1. Disconnect the negative (−) battery cable and place a suitable drain pan under the radiator draincock.

NOTE: *Drain the system with the engine cool and the heater temperature control set at the maximum heat position. Attach a ⅜″ hose to the drain cock so as to direct the coolant into the drain pan.*

CAUTION: *When draining the coolant, keep in mind that cats and dogs are attracted by the ethylene glycol antifreeze, and are quite likely to drink any that is left in an uncovered container or in puddles on the ground. This will prove fatal in sufficient quantity. Always drain the coolant into a sealable container. Coolant should be reused unless it is contaminated or several years old.*

2. Remove the radiator cap, open the drain cock on the radiator and drain the cooling system.

3. Remove air cleaner assembly, air intake duct, and fan shroud attaching screws.

4. Remove the fan/clutch assembly and shroud.

5. Loosen accessory drive belt idler and remove the drive belt and water pump pulley.

6. Remove power steering pump mounting bracket attaching bolts, but do not disconnect steering hoses. Just move assembly off to the side.

7. Remove air conditioning compressor front support bracket, leaving compressor in place, if so equipped.

8. Disconnect coolant bypass hose, heater hose, and remove water pump from engine.

To install:

9. Coat both sides of new gasket with Contact Adhesive part No. D7AZ-19B508-A or equivalent.

10. Position water pump on the engine and install the attaching bolts and torque them to 15-22 ft. lbs.

11. Connect cooling bypass hose, heater hose, and radiator lower hose to the water pump.

12. Install the air conditioning compressor front support bracket.

13. Position the power steering pump and

mounting bracket on the water pump and tighten attaching bolts.

14. Install the drive belt and adjust belt tension.

15. Install water pump pulley, fan/clutch, and fan shroud.

16. Fill cooling system with coolant and start engine to check for leaks.

3.0L SHO Engine

1. Position a drain pan under the radiator drain plug and drain the engine coolant.

CAUTION: *When draining the coolant, keep in mind that cats and dogs are attracted by the ethylene glycol antifreeze, and are quite likely to drink any that is left in an uncovered container or in puddles on the ground. This will prove fatal in sufficient quantity. Always drain the coolant into a sealable container. Coolant should be reused unless it is contaminated or several years old.*

2. Disconnect the negative (−) battery cable.

3. Remove the battery and battery tray.

4. Remove the accessory drive belts as follows:

a. **Alternator belt:** loosen the nut in the center of the idler pulley and adjusting screw until the belt can be removed.

b. Remove the alternator belt from the pulleys.

c. **Power steering and air conditioning belt:** loosen the nut on the tensioner counterclockwise until the betl can be removed.

d. Remove the belt off of the pulleys.

5. Remove the three bolts retaining the air conditioning and alternator idler pulley and bracket assembly.

6. Disconnect the electrical connector from the ignition module and ground strap-to-body.

7. Loosen the four screw clamps on the upper intake connector tube and remove the two retaining bolts. Remove the upper intake connector tube and module assembly.

8. Remove the RH tire and wheel, fender apron splash guard, upper timing belt cover, crankshaft pulley, and lower timing belt cover.

9. Remove the bolts from the center timing belt cover and position out of the way.

10. Remove the water pump retaining bolts and water pump.

To install:

11. Clean the gasket mating surfaces on the water pump and cylinder block with a gasket scraper and cleaning solution.

12. Install the water pump-to-cylinder block. Torque the attaching bolts to 12-16 ft. lbs.

13. Install the center timing belt cover, lower timing belt cover, and crankshaft pulley. Torque the pulley bolt to 113-126 ft. lbs.

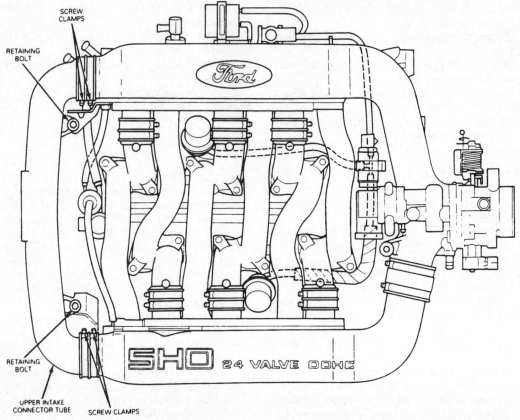

Upper intake connector tube removal—3.0L SHO engine

14. Install the fender apron splash guard and the tire and wheel assembly.

15. Install the upper timing belt cover and upper intake connector tube.

16. Install the two bolts on the upper intake connector tube and torque the bolts to 12-16 ft. lbs.

17. Install the power steering and water pump belt and tighten to 112-157 lbs. for a used belt, and 154-198 lbs for a new belt.

18. Install the air conditioning and alternator idler pulley and bracket assembly.

19. Install the air conditioning and alternator belt and tighten to 148-192 lbs. for a used belt, and 220-265 lbs. for a new belt.

20. Connect the negative (−) battery cable.

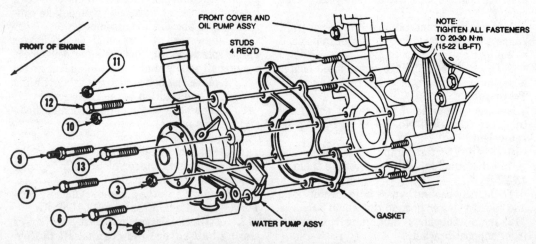

Water pump mounting—3.8L engine

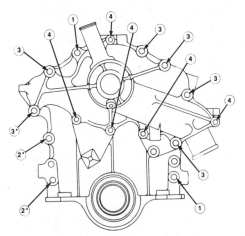

NUMBER	PART NUMBER	SIZE	QTY	N·m	LB-FT
1	N605909-SB	M8 x 1.25 x 42.0	2	20-30	15-22
2	N804113-S8	M8 x 1.25 x 43.5 (LARGE HEX)	2	20-30	15-22
3	N606547-S8	M8 x 1.25 x 70.0	6	20-30	15-22
4	N804168-S8	M6 x 1.0 x 25.0	5	8-12	6-8

NOTE: APPLY PIPE SEALANT D6AZ-19558-A TO THE THREADS OF THESE BOLTS

Water pump mounting—3.0L engine

21. Fill the engine cooling system.
22. Start the engine and check for coolant leaks.

Cylinder Head

REMOVAL AND INSTALLATION

2.5L Engine

1. Disconnect the battery negative (–) cable.
2. Drain the cooling system at lower radiator hose.

CAUTION: *When draining the coolant, keep in mind that cats and dogs are attracted by the ethylene glycol antifreeze, and are quite likely to drink any that is left in an uncovered container or in puddles on the ground. This will prove fatal in sufficient quantity. Always drain the coolant into a sealable container. Coolant should be reused unless it is contaminated or several years old.*

3. Disconnect the heater hose at the fitting located under intake manifold.
4. Disconnect the upper radiator hose at cylinder head.
5. Disconnect the electric cooling fan switch at the plastic connector.
6. Remove the air cleaner assembly.
7. Label, then disconnect the required vacuum hoses.
8. Remove the rocker arm cover.
9. Disconnect all the accessory drive belts.
10. Remove the distributor cap and the spark plug wires as an assembly.
11. Disconnect the EGR tube at the EGR valve.

12. Disconnect the choke cap wire.
13. Release the fuel pressure, disconnect the fuel supply, and return lines at the rubber connectors.
14. Disconnect the accelerator cable and the speed control cable, if so equipped.
15. Raise the vehicle and support with jackstands. Disconnect the exhaust system at exhaust pipe, and hose at tube. Lower the vehicle.
16. Remove the cylinder head bolts.
17. Remove the cylinder head and gasket with exhaust and intake manifolds attached.

WARNING: *DO NOT lay the cylinder head flat. Damage to the spark plugs or the gasket surfaces may result.*

To install:

18. Clean all the gasket material from the mating surfaces on the cylinder head and the block with a puddy knife and proper solvent. Check the cylinder head mating surface for flatness using a straight edge. If the head is warped in excess of 0.25mm, have the cylinder head machined.
19. Match the old gasket to the new one to insure perfect match. Position the cylinder head gasket on the cylinder block using sealer to retain the gasket.

NOTE: *Before installing the cylinder head, thread two Cylinder Head Alignment Studs T84P-6065-A or equivalent through head bolt holes in the gasket and into the block at opposite corners of the block.*

20. Install the cylinder head over Cylinder Head Alignment Studs T84P-6065-A or equivalent onto cylinder block. Start and run down several head bolts until snug. Remove the guide studs and the install cylinder head bolts. Tighten all bolts in sequence in two step to 52-59 ft. lbs., then to 70-76 ft. lbs.
21. Raise the vehicle and support with jackstands.
22. Connect the exhaust system at the exhaust pipe and the hose to the metal tube.
23. Lower the vehicle.
24. Install the Thermactor pump drive belt.

① ③ CHECK DIAGONALLY
② CHECK ACROSS CENTER

Check cylinder head for warpage

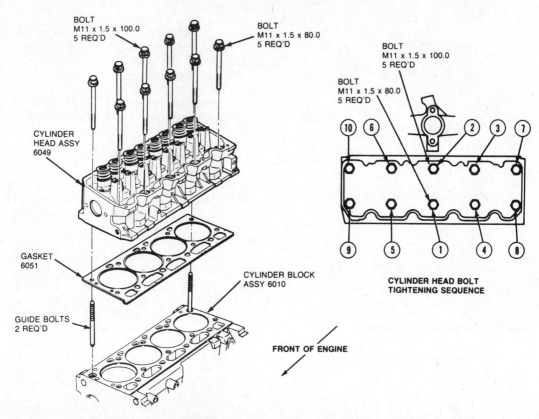

BOLT
M11 x 1.5 x 100.0
5 REQ'D

BOLT
M11 x 1.5 x 80.0
5 REQ'D

BOLT
M11 x 1.5 x 100.0
5 REQ'D

BOLT
M11 x 1.5 x 80.0
5 REQ'D

CYLINDER
HEAD ASSY
6049

GASKET
6051

GUIDE BOLTS
2 REQ'D

CYLINDER BLOCK
ASSY 6010

CYLINDER HEAD BOLT
TIGHTENING SEQUENCE

FRONT OF ENGINE

Cylinder head assembly—2.5L engine

25. Connect the accelerator cable and the speed control cable, if so equipped.

26. Connect the fuel supply and return lines.

27. Connect the choke cap wire.

28. Connect the EGR tube to the EGR valve.

29. Install the distributor cap and the spark plug wires as an assembly.

30. Connect the accessory drive belts.

31. Install the rocker arm cover.

32. Connect the required vacuum hoses.

33. Install the air cleaner assembly.

34. Connect the electric cooling fan switch at connector.

35. Connect the upper radiator hose.

36. Connect the heater hose at the intake manifold.

37. Fill the cooling system.

38. Connect the battery negative (–) cable.

39. Start the engine. Check for vacuum, coolant and oil leaks.

40. After the engine has reached operating temperature, check and, if necessary, add coolant.

3.0L Engine

1. Drain the cooling system after the engine has cooled.

CAUTION: *When draining the coolant, keep in mind that cats and dogs are attracted by the ethylene glycol antifreeze, and are quite likely to drink any that is left in an uncovered container or in puddles on the ground. This will prove fatal in sufficient quantity. Always drain the coolant into a sealable container. Coolant should be reused unless it is contaminated or several years old.*

2. Disconnect the battery negative (–) cable.

3. Remove the air cleaner outlet tube.

4. Remove the intake manifold as outlined earlier in the intake manifold section.

5. Loosen the accessory drive belt idler. Remove the drive belt.

6. If the LH cylinder head is being removed, remove the alternator adjusting arm. If the RH cylinder head is being removed, remove the accessory belt idler.

7. If equipped with power steering, remove the pump mounting brackets attaching bolts. Leaving the hoses connected, place the pump/bracket assembly aside in a position to prevent the fluid from leaking out.

8. If the LH cylinder head is being removed, remove the coil bracket and the dipstick tube. If the RH cylinder head is being removed, remove the grounding strap throttle cable support bracket.

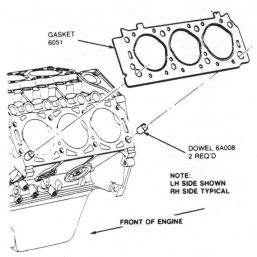

Cylinder head gasket positioning—3.0L engine

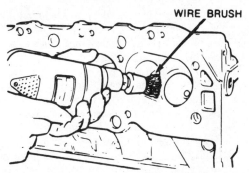

Remove the carbon from cylinder head with a wire brush and electric drill

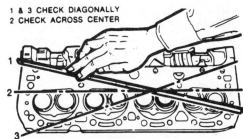

Check the cylinder head for warpage

9. Remove the exhaust manifold(s). Remove the PCV valve and the rocker arm covers.

10. Loosen the rocker arm fulcrum attaching bolts enough to allow the rocker arm to be lifted off the push rod and rotated to one side.

11. Remove the push rods. Identify the position of each rod. The rods should be installed in their original position during assembly.

12. Remove the cylinder head attaching bolts.

13. Remove the cylinder head(s).

14. Remove and discard the old cylinder head gasket(s) after matching them with the new gasket(s).

To install:

NOTE: *Lightly oil all bolt and stud bolt threads before installation except those specifying special sealant.*

15. Clean the cylinder head, intake manifold, rocker arm cover and the cylinder head gasket

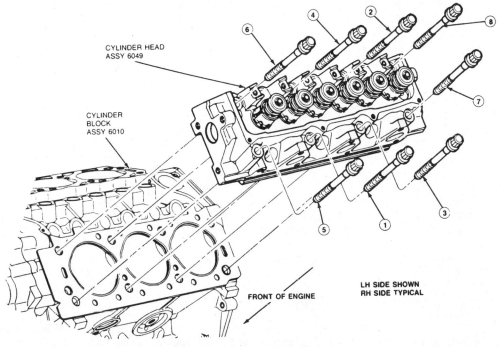

Cylinder head assembly—3.0L engine

surfaces. If the cylinder head was removed for a cylinder head gasket replacement, check the flatness of the cylinder head and block gasket surfaces. If warpage exceeds 0.25mm, have the head machined.

16. Position the new head gasket(s), noting the **UP** designation on the gasket face, on the cylinder block using the dowels for alignment.

NOTE: *Replace the dowels if damaged.*

17. Position the cylinder head(s) on block.

18. Tighten the cylinder head attaching bolts in two tightening steps in the following sequence:

    a. 48-54 ft. lbs.
    b. 63-80 ft. lbs.

NOTE: *When the cylinder head attaching bolts have been tightened using the above procedure, it is not necessary to retighten the bolts after extended engine operation. However, the bolts can be checked for tightness if desired.*

19. Dip each push rod end in Oil Conditioner D9AZ-19579-C or equivalent heavy engine oil. Install the push rods in their original position.

20. For each valve, rotate the crankshaft until the tappet rests on the heel (base circle) of the camshaft lobe, before tightening the fulcrum attaching bolts. Position the rocker arms over the push rods, install the fulcrums, and tighten the fulcrum attaching bolts to 19-29 ft. lbs.

WARNING: *The fulcrums must be fully seated in the cylinder head, and the push rods must be seated in the rocker arm sockets prior to final tightening.*

21. Lubricate all rocker arm assemblies with Oil Conditioner D9AZ-19579-C or equivalent, heavy engine oil.

NOTE: *If the original valve train components are being installed, a valve clearance check is not required. If a component has been replaced, perform a valve clearance check.*

22. Install the exhaust manifold(s).

23. Install the dipstick tube.

24. Install the intake manifold.

25. Position the rocker arm cover and new gasket on the cylinder head and install the attaching bolts. Note the location of spark plug wire routing clip stud bolts. Tighten the attaching bolts to 80-106 in. lbs.

26. Install the spark plugs, if removed.

27. Connect the secondary wires to the spark plugs.

28. If the LH cylinder head is being installed, install the oil fill cap.

29. If equipped with power steering, install the pump mounting and support brackets.

30. Install the PCV valve.

31. Install the throttle body.

32. Install the alternator bracket. Tighten the attaching nuts to 30-40 ft. lbs.

33. Install the accessory drive belt and tighten to specification. Refer to Chapter 1.

34. Connect the battery negative (−) cable.

35. Fill and bleed the cooling system.

WARNING: *This engine has aluminum components and requires a special unique corrosion inhibited coolant formulation to avoid radiator damage.*

36. Start the engine and check for coolant, fuel, oil and exhaust leaks.

37. Check, and if necessary, adjust the transmission throttle linkage and speed control.

38. Install the air cleaner outlet tube duct.

3.8L Engine

1. Position a suitable drain pan under the radiator and drain the cooling system. Disconnect the negative (−) battery cable.

CAUTION: *When draining the coolant, keep in mind that cats and dogs are attracted by the ethylene glycol antifreeze, and are quite likely to drink any that is left in an uncovered container or in puddles on the ground. This will prove fatal in sufficient quantity. Always drain the coolant into a sealable container. Coolant should be reused unless it is contaminated or several years old.*

2. Remove the air cleaner assembly including air intake duct and heat tube.

3. Loosen the accessory drive belt idler and remove the drive belt.

4. If the right side head is being removed, proceed to Step 5. If the left side cylinder head is being removed, perform the following to gain access to the upper intake manifold:

    a. Remove the oil fill cap.

    b. Remove the power steering pump. Leave the hoses connected and place the pump/bracket assembly aside in a position to prevent fluid from leaking out.

    c. If equipped with air conditioning, remove mounting bracket attaching bolts. Leaving the hoses connected, position compressor aside.

    d. Remove the alternator and bracket.

5. To remove the right side cylinder head, perform the following to gain access to the upper intake manifold:

    a. Disconnect the thermactor air control valve or bypass valve hose assembly at the air pump.

    b. Disconnect the thermactor tube support bracket from the rear of cylinder head.

    c. Remove the accessory drive idler.

    d. Remove the thermactor pump pulley and thermactor pump.

    e. Remove the PCV valve.

6. Remove the upper intake manifold.

7. Remove the valve rocker arm cover attaching screws.

8. Remove the injector fuel rail assembly.

9. Remove the lower intake manifold and remove the exhaust manifold(s).

10. Loosen rocker arm fulcrum attaching bolts a sufficient amount to allow rocker arm to be lifted off the push rod and rotate to one side. Remove the push rods. Identify and label the position of each rod as each one is removed. Rods should be installed in their original position during assembly to ensure proper operation.

11. Remove the cylinder head attaching bolts and discard. Do not re-use the old bolts.

12. Remove cylinder head(s) from the engine block surface. Remove and discard old cylinder head gasket(s).

To install:

13. Lightly oil all bolt threads before installation.

14. Clean cylinder head, intake manifold, valve rocker arm cover and cylinder head gasket contact surfaces with a gasket scraper, puddy knife, or equivalent. If cylinder head was removed for a cylinder head gasket replacement, check flatness of cylinder head and block gasket surfaces. If warpage exceeds 0.25mm at any point, have the head or block machined.

15. Position the new head gasket(s) onto cylinder block using dowels for alignment. Position cylinder head(s) onto block.

16. Apply a thin coating of pipe sealant with Teflon® No. D8AZ-19554-A or equivalent to threads of short cylinder head bolts (nearest to the exhaust manifold). Do not apply sealant to the long bolts. Install cylinder head bolts (eight each side).

CAUTION: *Always use new cylinder head bolts to ensure a leak-tight assembly. Torque retention with used bolts can vary, which may result in coolant or compression leakage at the cylinder head mating surface area.*

17. Tighten cylinder head attaching bolts by performing the following 6 step sequence, check sequence diagram in this section:

a. Step 1: 37 ft. lbs.

b. Step 2: 45 ft. lbs.

c. Step 3: 52 ft. lbs.

d. Step 4: 59 ft. lbs.

e. Step 5: Back-off each cylinder head bolt 2-3 turns.

f. Step 6: Repeat Steps 1-4.

NOTE: *When cylinder head attaching bolts have been tightened using the above procedure, it is not necessary to retighten bolts after extended engine operation. However, bolts can be checked for tightness if desired.*

18. Dip each push rod end in oil conditioner D9AZ-19579-C or equivalent heavy engine oil.

19. For each valve, rotate crankshaft until the tappet rests on the heel (base circle) of the cam-

shaft lobe. Torque the fulcrum attaching bolts to 43 in. lbs. maximum.

20. Lubricate all rocker arm assemblies with oil conditioner No. D9AZ-19579-C or equivalent heavy engine oil.

21. Torque the fulcrum bolts a second time to 19-25 ft. lbs. For final tightening, camshaft may be in any position.

NOTE: *If original valve train components are being installed, a valve clearance check is not required. If a component has been replaced, perform a valve clearance check.*

22. Install the exhaust manifold(s), lower intake manifold and injector fuel rail assembly.

23. Position the valve cover(s) and new gasket on cylinder head and install attaching bolts. Note location of spark plug wire routing clip stud bolts. Tighten attaching bolts to 72-96 in. lbs.

24. Install the upper intake manifold and connect the secondary wires to the spark plugs.

25. If the LH cylinder head is being installed, perform the following: install oil fill cap, compressor mounting and support brackets, power steering pump mounting and support brackets and the alternator/support bracket.

26. If the RH cylinder head is being installed, perform the following: install the PCV valve, alternator bracket, thermactor pump and pump pulley, accessory drive idler, thermactor air control valve or air bypass valve hose.

27. Install the accessory drive belt. Attach the thermactor tube(s) support bracket to the rear of the cylinder head. Torque the attaching bolts to 30-40 ft. lbs.

28. Connect the negative (−) battery cable and fill the cooling system.

29. Start the engine and check for leaks.

30. Check and, if necessary, adjust curb idle speed.

31. Install the air cleaner with air intake duct and heat tube.

3.0L SHO Engine

1. Position a drain pan under the radiator drain plug and drain the engine cooling system.

CAUTION: *When draining the coolant, keep in mind that cats and dogs are attracted by the ethylene glycol antifreeze, and are quite likely to drink any that is left in an uncovered container or in puddles on the ground. This will prove fatal in sufficient quantity. Always drain the coolant into a sealable container. Coolant should be reused unless it is contaminated or several years old.*

2. Disconnect the negative (−) battery cable.

3. Remove the air cleaner outlet tube.

4. Remove the upper intake manifold assembly. Refer to the "Upper Intake Manifold" re-

moval and installation procedures in this chapter.

5. Remove the lower intake manifold assembly. Refer to the "Lower Intake Manifold" removal and installation procedure in this chapter.

6. Loosen the accessory drive belt idlers and remove the belts.

7. Remove the upper timing belt cover.

8. Remove the LH idler pulley and bracket assembly.

9. Raise the vehicle and support with jackstands.

10. Remove the RH wheel and tire and fender apron splash guard.

11. Remove the crankshaft damper pulley.

12. Remove the lower timing belt cover.

13. Align the timing marks as shown in the illustration.

14. Release the tension on the timing belt by loosening the tensioner nut and rotating the tensioner with a hex head wrench. When the tensioner is released, tighten the nut.

15. Disconnect the crankshaft sensor wiring assembly, center timing cover, and the timing belt.

NOTE: *The location of the KOA on the timing belt must be installed in the same direction. Refer to the following illustration.*

16. Remove the cylinder head covers. Refer to the "Cylinder Head Cover" removal and installation procedures in this chapter.

17. Remove the camshaft timing pulleys.

18. If the LH cylinder head is being removed, remove the DIS coil bracket and the oil dipstick

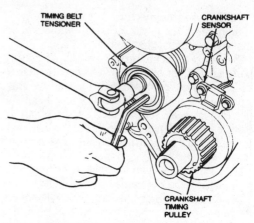

Timing belt tensioner—3.0L SHO engine

tube. If the RH cylinder head is being removed, remove the coolant outlet hose.

19. Remove the exhaust manifold on the LH cylinder head. On the RH cylinder head, the exhaust manifold must be removed with the cylinder head.

20. Remove the eight cylinder head-to-block retaining bolts.

21. Remove the cylinder head assembly.

To install:

22. Lightly oil all of the bolt and stud threads before installation except those specifying special sealant.

23. Clean and remove any foreign materials or oil from the top of the cylinder block and lower surface of the cylinder head.

24. Position a new gasket and the cylinder head on the cylinder block and align with the dowel pins.

NOTE: *Replace the dowel pins if damaged.*

25. Install the eight cylinder head bolts in the proper sequence. Torque the bolts in two steps.

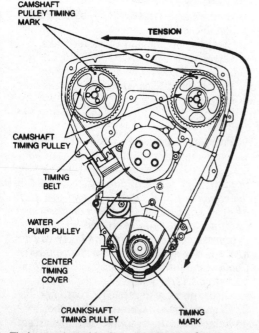

Timing mark positioning—3.0L SHO engine

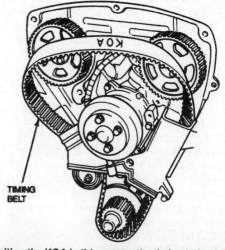

Position the KOA in this way on the timing belt—3.0L SHO engine

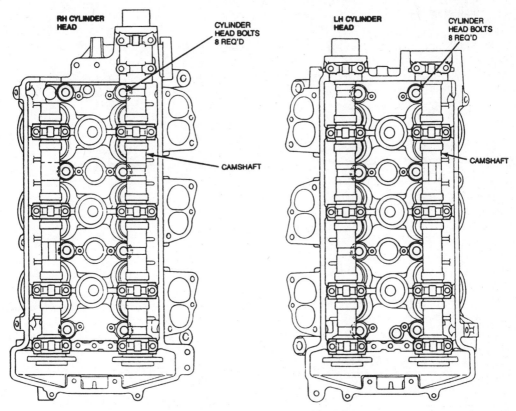

Cylinder head torquing sequence—3.0L SHO engine

a. 1st step: 37-50 ft. lbs.

b. 2nd step: 62-68 ft. lbs.

26. If the LH cylinder head is being installed, install the exhaust manifold, DIS coil bracket, and oil dipstick tube. On the RH cylinder head, install the coolant outlet hose and connect the exhaust catalyst (catalytic converter).

27. Install the upper rear and center rear timing belt covers and camshaft timing pulley in the timed positions.

28. Install the cylinder head covers.

29. Install the timing belt and adjust as follows.

a. Release the tension on the automatic tensioner pulley.

b. Be sure that there is slack between the camshaft and crankshaft pulleys.

c. Using a 14mm socket, turn the automatic tensioner counterclockwise and then release when the timing belt is in position.

30. Connect the crankshaft sensor wiring assembly.

31. Install the lower and center timing belt cover.

32. Raise the vehicle and support with jackstands.

33. Install the fender apron splash guard, wheel and tire, LH idler pulley and bracket, and upper timing cover.

34. Install the power steering and water pump belt. Tighten to 112-157 lbs. for used belts and 154-198 lbs. for new belts.

35. Install the air conditioning and alternator belt. Tighten the belt to 148-192 lbs. for a used belt and 220-265 lbs. for a new belt.

36. Install the lower intake manifold assembly. Refer to the "Lower Intake Manifold" removal and installation procedures in this chapter.

37. Install the upper intake manifold assembly. Refer to the "Upper Intake Manifold" removal and installation procedures in this chapter.

38. Install the air cleaner outlet tube.

39. Connect the negative (−) battery cable.

40. Fill the engine with coolant, start the engine and check for oil, fuel, and coolant leaks.

OVERHAUL

2.5L, 3.0L and 3.8L engine

1. Remove the cylinder head from the car engine (see Cylinder Head Removal and Installation). Place the head on a workbench and remove any manifolds that are still connected. Remove all rocker arm retaining parts and the rocker arms, if still installed or the camshaft (see Camshaft Removal).

2. Turn the cylinder head over so that the

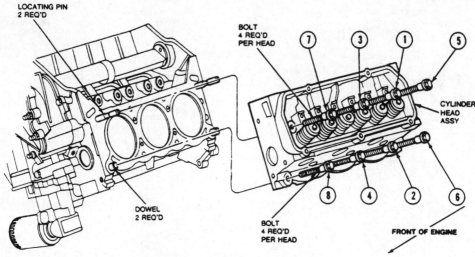

Cylinder head assembly—3.8L engine

mounting surface is facing up and support evenly on wooden blocks.

WARNING: *If you have an aluminum cylinder head, exercise care when cleaning it.*

3. Use a scraper and remove all of the gasket material stuck to the head mounting surface. Mount a wire carbon removal brush in an electric drill and clean away the carbon on the valves and head combustion chambers.

WARNING: *When scraping or decarbonizing the cylinder head take care not to damage or nick the gasket mounting surface.*

4. Number the valve heads with a permanent felt-tip marker for cylinder location.

3.0L SHO Engine

1. Remove the cylinder heads by refering to the "Cylinder Head" removal and installation procedures in this chapter.

2. Place the head on a holding fixture.

NOTE: *The camshaft end play must be inspected before head disassembly. Measure the end play by using a dial indicator while moving the camshaft back and forth. Maximum end play is 0.3mm.*

3. Remove the timing chain tensioner attaching bolts.

4. Uniformly loosen and remove the bearing cap bolts.

CAUTION: *If the bearing cap bolts are not removed uniformly, the camshaft may be damaged.*

5. Remove the valve shim and bucket.

6. Install a valve spring compressor tool part No. T89P-6565-A or equivalent and stand on the cylinder head.

7. Align the spring compressor squarely over the valve retainer. Attach a ½" drive ratchet handle and apply pressure to the valve retainer. Support the valve in the head if necessary to separate the retainer from the valve stem.

8. Remove the valve keepers with a magnet and remove the valve.

RESURFACING

If the cylinder head is warped resurfacing by a machine shop is required. Place a straight-

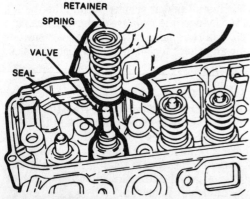

Install valve stem oil seals

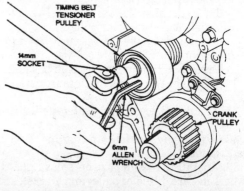

Timing chain tensioner removal—3.0L SHO engine

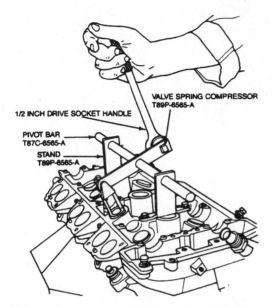

Valve spring compressor and stand—3.0L SHO engine

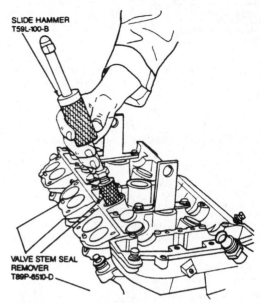

Removing the valve and keepers—3.0L SHO engine

edge across the gasket surface of the head. Using feeler gauges, determine the clearance at the center and along the length between the head and straight-edge. Measure clearance at the center and along the lengths of both diagonals. If warpage exceeds 0.076mm in a 152mm span, or 0.15mm over the total length the cylinder head must be resurfaced.

Valves and Springs

REMOVAL AND INSTALLATION

1. Block the head on its side, or install a pair of head-holding brackets made especially for valve removal.

2. Use a socket slightly larger than the valve stem and keepers, place the socket over the valve stem and gently hit the socket with a plastic hammer to break loose any varnish buildup.

3. Remove the valve keepers, retainer, spring shield and valve spring using a valve spring compressor (the locking C-clamp type is the easiest kind to use).

4. Put the parts in a separate container numbered for the cylinder being worked on. Do not mix them with other parts removed.

5. Remove and discard the valve stem oil seal, a new seal will be used at assembly time.

6. Remove the valve from the cylinder head and place, in order, through numbered holes punched in a stiff piece of cardboard or wooden valve holding stick.

NOTE: *The exhaust valve stems, on some engines, are equipped with small metal caps. Take care not to lose the caps. Make sure to reinstall them at assembly time. Replace any caps that are worn.*

7. Use an electric drill and rotary wire brush to clean the intake and exhaust valve ports, combustion chamber and valve seats. In some cases, the carbon will need to be chipped away. Use a blunt pointed drift for carbon chipping, be careful around the valve seat areas.

8. Use a wire valve guide cleaning brush and safe solvent to clean the valve guides.

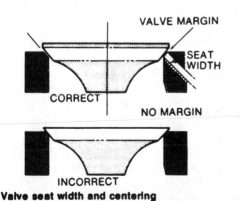

Valve seat width and centering

Reaming the valve seat with a hand reamer

9. Clean the valves with a revolving wire brush. Heavy carbon deposits may be removed with the blunt drift.

NOTE: *When using a wire brush to clean carbon from the valve ports, valves etc., be sure that the deposits are actually removed, rather than burnished.*

10. Wash and clean all valve spring, keepers, retaining caps etc., in safe solvent.

11. Clean the head with a brush and some safe solvent and wipe dry.

12. Check the head for cracks. Cracks in the cylinder head usually start around an exhaust valve seat because it is the hottest part of the combustion chamber. If a crack is suspected but cannot be detected visually have the area checked with dye penetrant or other method by a machine shop.

13. After all cylinder head parts are reasonably clean, check the valve stem-to-guide clearance. If a dial indicator is not on hand, a visual inspection can give you a fairly good idea if the guide, valve stem or both are worn.

14. Insert the valve into the guide until slightly away from the valve seat. Wiggle the valve sideways. A small amount of wobble is normal, excessive wobble means a worn guide or valve stem. If a dial indicator is on hand, mount the indicator so that the stem of the valve is at 90° to the valve stem, as close to the valve guide as possible. Move the valve off the seat, and measure the valve guide-to-stem clearance by rocking the stem back and forth to actuate the dial indicator. Measure the valve stem using a micrometer and compare to specifications to determine whether stem or guide wear is causing excessive clearance.

15. The valve guide, if worn, must be repaired before the valve seats can be resurfaced. Ford supplies valves with oversize stems to fit valve guides that are reamed to oversize for repair. The machine shop will be able to handle the guide reaming for you. In some cases, if the guide is not too badly worn, knurling may be all that is required.

16. Reface, or have the valves and valve seats refaced. The valve seats should be a true 45° angle for the 2.5L and 3.0L engines, and 44.5° angle for the 3.8L engine. Remove only enough material to clean up any pits or grooves. Be sure the valve seat is not too wide or narrow. Use a 60° grinding wheel to remove material from the bottom of the seat for raising and a 30° grinding wheel to remove material from the top of the seat to narrow.

17. After the valves are refaced by machine, hand lap them to the valve seat. Clean the grinding compound off and check the position of face-to-seat contact. Contact should be close to the center of the valve face. If contact is close

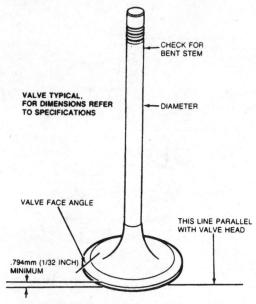

Valve edge minimum

to the top edge of the valve, narrow the seat; if too close to the bottom edge, raise the seat.

18. Valves should be refaced to a true angle of 44° for the 2.5L and 3.0L engines, and 45.8° for the 3.8L engine. Remove only enough metal to clean up the valve face or to correct runout. If the edge of the valve head, after machining, is 0.8mm or less replace the valve. The tip of the valve stem should also be dressed on the valve grinding machine, however, do not remove more than 0.25mm.

19. After all valve and valve seats have been machined, check the remaining valve train parts (springs, retainers, keepers, etc.) for wear. Check the valve springs for straightness and tension.

20. Reassemble the head in the reverse order of disassembly using new valve guide seals and lubricating the valve stems. Check the valve spring installed height, shim or replace as necessary.

CHECKING VALVE SPRINGS

Place the valve spring on a flat surface next to a carpenters square. Measure the height of the spring, and rotate the spring against the edge of the square to measure distortion. If the spring height varies (by comparison) by more than 1.6mm or if the distortion exceeds 1.6mm, replace the spring.

Have the valve springs tested for spring pressure at the installed and compressed (installed height minus valve lift) height using a valve spring tester. Springs should be within one pound, plus or minus each other. Replace spring as necessary.

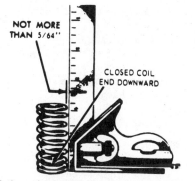

Check the valve spring free length and squareness

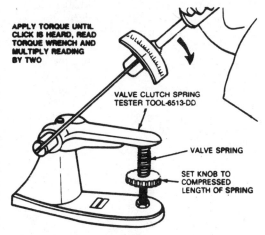

Valve spring pressure tester

VALVE SPRING INSTALLED HEIGHT

After installing the valve spring, measure the distance between the spring mounting pad and the lower edge of the spring retainer. Compare the measurement to specifications. If the installed height is incorrect, add shim washers between the spring mounting pad and the spring. Use only washers designed for valve springs, available at most parts houses.

VALVE STEM OIL SEALS

Most engines are equipped with a positive valve stem seal using a Teflon® insert. Teflon® seals are available for other engines but usually require valve guide machining, consult your automotive machine shop for advice on having positive valve stem oil seals installed.

When installing valve stem oil seals, ensure that a small amount of oil is able to pass the seal to lubricate the valve stems and guide walls; otherwise, excessive wear will occur.

VALVE SEATS

If a valve seat is damaged or burnt and cannot be serviced by refacing, it may be possible to have the seat machined and an insert installed. Consult the automotive machine shop for their advice.

NOTE: *The aluminum heads on V6 engines are equipped with inserts.*

VALVE GUIDES

Worn valve guides can, in most cases, be reamed to accept a valve with an oversized stem. Valve guides that are not excessively worn or distorted may, in some cases, be knurled rather than reamed. However, if the valve stem is worn reaming for an oversized valve stem is the answer since a new valve would be required.

Knurling is a process in which metal is displaced and raised, thereby reducing clearance. Knurling also produces excellent oil control. The possibility of knurling instead of reaming the valve guides should be discussed with a machinist.

Oil Pan

REMOVAL AND INSTALLATION

2.5L Engine

1. Disconnect the battery negative (−) cable.
2. Raise the vehicle and support with jackstands.
3. Drain the oil from the crankcase.

CAUTION: *The EPA warns that prolonged contact with used engine oil may cause a number of skin disorders, including cancer! You should make every effort to minimize your exposure to used engine oil. Protective gloves should be worn when changing the oil. Wash your hands and any other exposed skin areas as soon as possible after exposure to used engine oil. Soap and water, or waterless hand cleaner should be used.*

4. Drain the coolant by removing the lower radiator hose.

CAUTION: *When draining the coolant, keep in mind that cats and dogs are attracted by the ethylene glycol antifreeze, and are quite likely to drink any that is left in an uncovered container or in puddles on the ground. This will prove fatal in sufficient quantity. Always drain the coolant into a sealable container. Coolant should be reused unless it is contaminated or several years old.*

5. Remove the roll restrictor (MTX only).
6. Disconnect the starter cable.
7. Remove the starter.
8. Disconnect the exhaust pipe from the oil pan.
9. Remove the engine coolant tube located at the lower radiator hose, at the water pump and at the tabs on oil pan. Position the air conditioner line off to the side. Remove the oil pan.

To install:

1. Clean both mating surfaces of the oil pan and the cylinder block with Dupont Freon TF® or equivalent.

2. Remove and clean the oil pump pickup tube and screen assembly using a suitable solvent. After cleaning, install the tube and the screen assembly.

3. Insert the oil pan gasket into the groove in the oil pan. Position the oil pan on the engine block and install the oil pan bolts.

4. Install the two oil pan-to-transaxle bolts. Tighten to 30-39 ft.lbs. To align oil pan with transaxle, loosen the bolts one-half turn.

5. Tighten all the oil pan flange bolts to 72-108 in. lbs.

6. Tighten the two oil pan-to-transaxle bolt to 30-39 ft. lbs.

7. Install the exhaust pipe bracket to the oil pan.

8. Install the engine coolant tube and the air conditioning line.

9. Install the starter and cable.

10. Install the roll restrictor (MTX only).

11. Lower the vehicle.

12. Install engine oil and coolant.

13. Connect the battery negative (–)ground cable.

14. Start the engine and check for leaks.

3.0L Engine

1. Disconnect the battery negative (–) cable.

2. Remove the oil level dipstick.

3. Raise the vehicle and support with jackstands.

4. If equipped with a low oil level sensor, remove the retainer clip at the sensor. Remove the electrical connector from the sensor.

5. Drain the oil from the crankcase.

CAUTION: *The EPA warns that prolonged contact with used engine oil may cause a number of skin disorders, including cancer! You should make every effort to minimize your exposure to used engine oil. Protective gloves should be worn when changing the oil. Wash your hands and any other exposed skin*

SPACER 2 REQ'D
6C629

MB X 1.25 X 23.5
SCREW AND WASHER ASSY
HEX HEAD PILOT 11 REQ'D
TIGHTEN TO 20-30 N·m
(15-22 LB-FT)

OIL PAN
ASSY
6675

OIL PAN
ASSY
6675

SECTION A

OIL PAN
GASKET
6710

ESE
M46195-A
SEALER
4 PLACES

CYLINDER
BLOCK ASSY
6010

FRONT OF
ENGINE

FRONT
COVER
6059

Oil pan assembly—2.5L engine

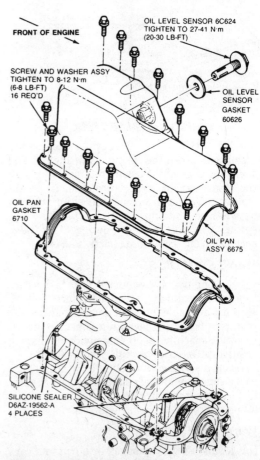

FRONT OF ENGINE

OIL LEVEL SENSOR 6C624
TIGHTEN TO 27-41 N·m
(20-30 LB-FT)

SCREW AND WASHER ASSY
TIGHTEN TO 8-12 N·m
(6-8 LB-FT)
16 REQ'D

OIL LEVEL
SENSOR
GASKET
60626

OIL PAN
GASKET
6710

OIL PAN
ASSY 6675

SILICONE SEALER
D6AZ-19562-A
4 PLACES

Oil pan assembly—3.0L engine

areas as soon as possible after exposure to used engine oil. Soap and water, or waterless hand cleaner should be used.

6. Remove the starter motor.

7. Disconnect the EGO sensor.

8. Remove the catalyst and pipe assembly.

9. Remove the lower engine/flywheel dust cover from the converter housing.

10. Remove the oil pan attaching bolts. Remove the oil pan.

11. Remove the oil pan gasket.

To install:

1. Clean the gasket surfaces on the cylinder block and oil pan.

2. Apply a 4.0-5.0mm bead of Silicone Sealer D6AZ-19562-A or equivalent, to the junction of the rear main bearing cap and the cylinder block and the junction of the front cover assembly and cylinder block.

NOTE: *When using silicone rubber sealer, assembly should occur within 15 minutes after sealer application. After this time, the sealer may start to set-up, and its sealing effectiveness may be reduced.*

3. Locate the oil pan gasket to the oil pan with the bend against the pan surface and secure with the gasket and Seal Contact Adhesive D7AZ-19B508-A (ESR-M11P17-A and ESE-M2G52-A).

4. Position the oil pan onto the cylinder block.

5. Install the oil pan attaching bolts. Tighten to 71-106 in. lbs.

6. Install the lower engine/flywheel dust cover to the converter housing.

7. Install the catalyst and the pipe assembly. Connect the EGO sensor.

8. Install the starter motor.

9. Install the low oil level sensor connector to the sensor and install the retainer clip.

10. Lower the vehicle.

11. Replace the oil level dipstick tube.

12. Connect the battery negative (−) cable.

13. Fill the crankcase with the correct viscosity and amount of engine oil.

14. Start the engine and check for engine oil and exhaust leaks.

3.8L Engine

1. Disconnect the battery negative (−) cable.

2. Raise the vehicle on a hoist and support with jackstands.

3. Drain the engine oil and remove the oil filter.

CAUTION: *The EPA warns that prolonged contact with used engine oil may cause a number of skin disorders, including cancer! You should make every effort to minimize your exposure to used engine oil. Protective gloves should be worn when changing the oil. Wash your hands and any other exposed skin areas as soon as possible after exposure to used engine oil. Soap and water, or waterless hand cleaner should be used.*

4. Remove the catalyst assembly and pipe.

5. Remove the starter motor.

6. Remove the converter housing cover.

7. Remove the bolts retaining the oil pan assembly.

8. Remove the oil pan.

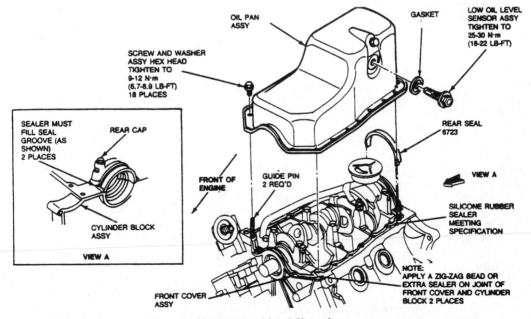

Oil pan assembly—3.8L engine

9. Remove the oil pump pick-up tube and clean with suitable solvent. Reinstall the pick-up tube to the oil pump.

To install:

1. Clean the gasket surfaces on the cylinder block and the oil pan.

NOTE: *When using silicone rubber sealer, assembly should occur within 15 minutes after sealer application. After this time, the sealer may start to set-up, and its sealing effectiveness may be reduced.*

2. Install the oil pan and retaining bolts. Tighten to 71-106 in. lbs.

3. Install the converter assembly, starter motor, and converter housing cover.

4. Lower the vehicle, refill with proper viscosity and amount of motor oil.

5. Connect the battery negative (−) cable and start the engine and check for coolant, oil, and exhaust leaks.

3.0L SHO Engine

1. Disconnect the negative (−) battery cable.

2. Remove the oil level dipstick.

3. Remove the accessory drive belts as outlined in the "Belt" removal and installation procedure in chapter 1.

4. Remove the timing belt and covers as outlined in the "Timing Belt" removal and installation procedures in this chapter.

5. Raise the vehicle and support with jackstands.

6. Remove the electrical connector for the low oil sensor.

7. Drain the oil from the crankcase.

CAUTION: *The EPA warns that prolonged contact with used engine oil may cause a number of skin disorders, including cancer! You should make every effort to minimize your exposure to used engine oil. Protective gloves should be worn when changing the oil. Wash your hands and any other exposed skin areas as soon as possible after exposure to used engine oil. Soap and water, or waterless hand cleaner should be used.*

8. Remove the starter motor.

9. Disconnect the HEGO sensors.

10. Remove the catalytic converter and pipe assembly and move out of the way.

11. Remove the lower engine-to-flywheel dust cover from the converter (bell housing) housing.

12. Remove the ten bolts and four nuts retaining the oil pan-to-engine block.

13. Remove the oil pan.

To install:

1. Clean the gasket surfaces on the cylinder block and oil pan.

2. Locate the oil pan gasket to the oil pan with bend against the pan surface

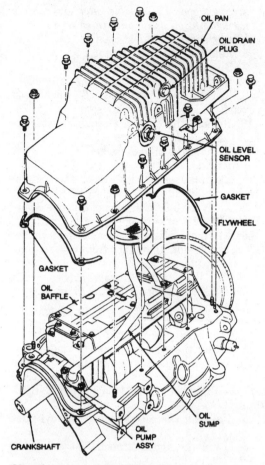

Oil pan removal—3.0L SHO engine

and secure with Gasket and Trim Adhesive part No. D7AZ-19B08-AA or equivalent.

NOTE: *When using silicone rubber sealer, assembly should occur within 15 minutes after the sealer has been applied. After this time, the sealer may start to set-up and it will start to loose its sealing effectiveness.*

3. Position the oil pan on the cylinder block. Install the ten bolts and four nuts and torque to 11-17 ft. lbs.

4. Install the lower engine-to-flywheel dust cover to the converter (bell) housing.

5. Install the catalytic converter, pipe assembly, and HEGO sensor.

6. Install the starter motor assembly.

7. Install the low oil level sensor connector to the sensor.

8. Lower the vehicle.

9. Install the accessory drive belts. Refer to the "Belts" removal and installation procedure in chapter 1.

10. Replace the oil level dipstick and fill the crankcase with the correct viscosity and amount of engine oil.

11. Connect the negative (−) battery cable.

12. Start the engine and check for oil and exhaust leaks.

Oil Pump

REMOVAL AND INSTALLATION

2.5L Engine

1. Refer to the "Oil Pan Removal And Installation" procedures in this section and remove the oil pan.

2. Remove oil pump-to-engine bolts, the oil pump and the intermediate (oil pump) driveshaft.

3. Using a putty knife or equivalent, clean the gasket mounting surfaces.

4. Prime the oil pump by filling the inlet port with engine oil. Rotate the pump shaft until oil flows from the outlet port.

5. If the screen and cover assembly have been removed, replace the gasket. Clean the screen with suitable solvent, then reinstall the screen and cover assembly.

6. Position the intermediate pump driveshaft into the distributor socket.

7. Insert the intermediate pump driveshaft into the oil pump. Install the oil pump and the shaft as an assembly.

CAUTION: *DO NOT attempt to force the pump into position if it will not seat. The shaft has a hexagon shape and may be misaligned with the distributor shaft. To align, remove the oil pump and rotate the intermediate driveshaft into a new position.*

8. Torque the oil pump-to-engine bolts to 15-23 ft. lbs. and the oil pan attaching bolts to 71-106 ft. lbs.

9. To complete the installation, use new gaskets, sealant and reverse the removal procedures. Refill the crankcase. Start engine and check the oil pressure. If oil pressure does not go to specifications within 60 seconds, turn engine OFF and check for problem (oil pan may have to come off again). When oil pressure is normal, operate the engine at fast idle and check for oil leaks.

3.0L and 3.8L Engines

1. Refer to the "Oil Pan Removal And Installation" procedures in this section and remove the oil pan.

2. Remove the oil pump-to-engine bolts, then lift the pump from the engine and withdraw the intermediate (oil pump) driveshaft.

3. Using a putty knife, clean the gasket mounting surfaces.

4. Prime the oil pump by filling either the inlet or the outlet port with engine oil. Rotate the pump shaft to distribute the oil within the oil pump body.

5. Insert the oil pump driveshaft into the

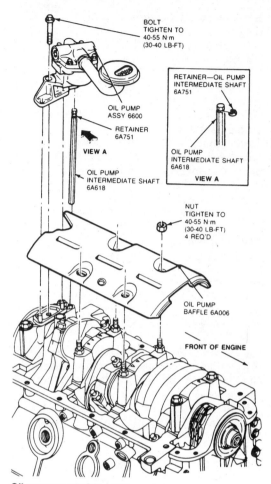

BOLT
TIGHTEN TO
40-55 N·m
(30-40 LB-FT)

OIL PUMP
ASSY 6600

RETAINER
6A751

VIEW A

OIL PUMP
INTERMEDIATE SHAFT
6A618

RETAINER—OIL PUMP
INTERMEDIATE SHAFT
6A751

OIL PUMP
INTERMEDIATE SHAFT
6A618

VIEW A

NUT
TIGHTEN TO
40-55 N·m
(30-40 LB-FT)
4 REQ'D

OIL PUMP
BAFFLE 6A006

FRONT OF ENGINE

Oil pump assembly—3.0L engine

pump with the retainer end facing inward. Place the oil pump in the proper position with a new gasket and install the mounting bolts.

6. Torque the oil pump-to-engine bolts to 30-40 ft. lbs. Clean and install the oil pump inlet tube and screen assembly with a new gasket.

7. To complete the installation, use new gaskets, sealant and reverse the removal procedures. Torque the oil pan-to-engine bolts to 72-96 in. lbs. Refill the crankcase to the proper level with recommended engine oil. Start engine and check the oil pressure. If oil pressure does not go to specifications within 60 seconds, turn the engine OFF and check for a problem (oil pan may have to come off again). When oil pressure is normal, operate the engine at fast idle and check for oil leaks.

3.0L SHO Engine

1. Remove the oil pan assembly. Refer to "Oil Pan" removal and installation procedures in this chapter.

2. The oil pump assembly is located on the

RH (passenger) side or technically the front of the engine.

3. Remove the crankshaft timing belt pulley.

4. Remove the oil sump-to-pump retaining bolts.

5. Remove the oil pump retaining bolts and remove the pump.

6. **To install:** Align the oil pump on the crankshaft and install the retaining bolts. Torque the bolts to 11-17 ft. lbs.

7. Install the oil sump-to-pump retaining bolts and torque to 72-96 in. lbs.

8. Install the crankshaft timing belt and pulley.

9. Install the oil pan assembly.

Front Cover

REMOVAL AND INSTALLATION

2.5L Engine

1. Refer to the "Engine Removal And Installation" procedures in this section and remove the engine and transaxle from the vehicle as an assembly.

2. Remove the dipstick and the accessory drive pulley (if equipped). Remove the crankshaft pulley-to-crankshaft bolt, the washer and the pulley.

3. Remove the 6 front cover-to-engine bolts and pry the top of the front cover away from the block.

NOTE: *The front cover oil seal must be re-moved in order to use the Front Cover Aligner tool No. T84P-6019-C to install the front cover.*

4. Using a putty knife or equivalent, clean the gasket mounting surfaces.

5. **To install:** use a new gasket, sealant, a new oil seal and reverse the removal procedures. Torque the 6 front cover-to-engine bolts to 72-108 in. lbs. and the crankshaft pulley bolt to 140-170 ft. lbs.

3.0L Engine

1. Refer to the "Water Pump Removal And Installation" procedures in this section and remove the water pump.

2. Remove the crankshaft pulley and the damper from the crankshaft.

3. Remove the lower radiator hose from the front cover.

4. Remove the 4 oil pan-to-front cover bolts, the 10 front cover-to-engine bolts and the front cover.

5. Using a putty knife, clean the gasket mounting surfaces.

NOTE: *When the front cover is removed, the oil seal should be replaced.*

6. To install: use new gaskets, sealant and reverse the removal procedures. Torque the 10 front cover-to-engine bolts to 15-22 ft. lbs., the front cover-to-oil pan bolts to 80-106 in. lbs., the water pump-to-front cover bolts to 72-96 in. lbs., the crankshaft damper-to-crankshaft bolt

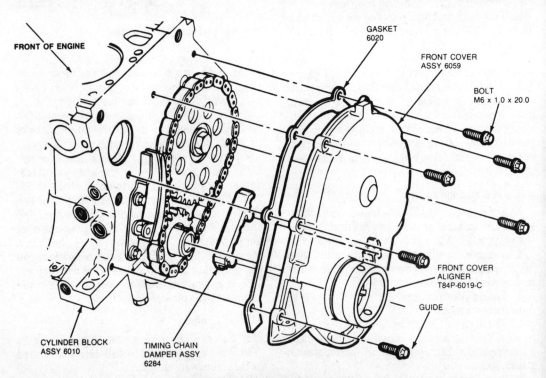

Front cover assembly—2.5L engine

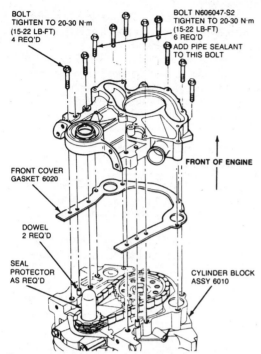

BOLT
TIGHTEN TO 20-30 N·m
(15-22 LB-FT)
4 REQ'D

BOLT N606047-S2
TIGHTEN TO 20-30 N·m
(15-22 LB-FT)
6 REQ'D
ADD PIPE SEALANT
TO THIS BOLT

FRONT OF ENGINE

FRONT COVER
GASKET 6020

DOWEL
2 REQ'D

SEAL
PROTECTOR
AS REQ'D

CYLINDER BLOCK
ASSY 6010

Front cover assembly—3.0L engine

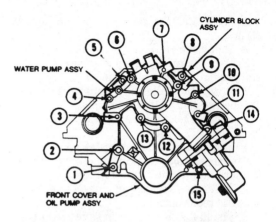

CYLINDER BLOCK
ASSY

WATER PUMP ASSY

FRONT COVER AND
OIL PUMP ASSY

FASTENER AND HOLE NO.	HOLE NO.		FASTENERS	
	WATER PUMP	FRONT COVER	PART NO.	PART NAME
1.		4	N606547	BOLT
2.		2	N606547	BOLT
3.	2	9	N804757	STUD
4.	1	8	N804757	STUD
5.		10	N605787	BOLT
6.	9	15	N605908	BOLT
7.	8	16	N605908	BOLT
8.		11	N605787	BOLT
9.	7	17	N804756	BOLT
10.	6	1	N804757	BOLT
11.	5	7	N804757	STUD
12.	4	13	N605908	BOLT
13.	3	14	N605908	BOLT
14.		6	N804839	BOLT
15.		5	N804841	CAP SCREW
3, 4, 10, 11	2, 1, 6, 5	9, 8 1, 7	N804758	NUT

Water pump & front cover—3.0L engine

to 141-169 ft. lbs., the crankshaft pulley-to-crankshaft damper bolts to 20-28 ft. lbs., the water pump pulley-to-water pump bolts to 15-22 ft. lbs.

3.8L Engine

1. Refer to the "Water Pump Removal And Installation" procedures in this section and remove the water pump.

2. Remove distributor hold down clamp and lift the distributor out of the front cover.

3. Raise the vehicle and support with jackstands.

4. Remove the crankshaft damper and pulley using a crankshaft damper remover tool.

NOTE: *If the crankshaft pulley and the vibration damper have to be separated, mark the damper and pulley so that they may be reassembled in the same position. This is important as the damper and pulley are initially balanced as a unit.*

5. Disconnect the lower radiator hose at the water pump.

6. Remove the oil filter, oil pan attaching bolts, and oil pan, refer to the "Oil Pan Removal" procedure.

7. Lower the vehicle.

8. Remove the 15 front cover and water pump bolts.

CAUTION: *Do not overlook the cover attaching bolt located behind the oil filter adapter. The front cover will break if it is pried upon and all attaching bolts are not removed.*

9. Remove the ignition timing indicator.

10. Remove the front cover and water pump as an assembly.

11. Clean the front cover and cylinder block mating surfaces free of all gasket material and varnish with gasket scraper or equivalent.

To install

1. Lightly oil all the 15 bolt and stud threads before installation.

NOTE: *When removing the front cover assembly, always replace the crankshaft oil seal using a Damper/Front Cover Seal Installer part No. T82L-6316-A.*

2. Install the front cover with new gasket and sealer.

3. Install the ignition timing indicator and 15 attaching bolt and studs. Torque the attaching bolt/studs to 15-22 ft. lbs.

4. Raise the vehicle and support with jackstands.

5. Install the oil pan, oil filter, and oil pan bolts. Refer to the "Oil Pan Installation" procedure.

6. Connect all the coolant hoses and tighten clamps.

7. Install the oil filter.

8. Coat the crankshaft pulley key way and seal journal with clean engine oil.

9. Install the crankshaft damper and bolt. Torque the bolt to 104-132 ft. lbs.

10. Install the crankshaft pulley and torque the bolts to 19-28 ft. lbs.

11. Lower the vehicle and install power steering pump and bracket, air conditioning compressor and bracket, and accessory drive belt.

12. Fill engine with new engine oil that meets viscosity requirements.

13. Install the distributor and line up the timing marks.

14. Fill cooling system with coolant, start engine, and check for leaks.

15. Install the air cleaner and any other vacuum hoses.

3.0L SHO Engine

1. Remove the LH idler pulley and bracket assembly, accessory drive belts, and the RH front wheel assembly.

2. Disconnect the electrical connector from the ignition module.

3. Loosen the four hose clamps and remove the two bolts from the intake manifold connector tube and remove the tube.

4. Remove the upper timing belt cover.

5. Remove the crankshaft damper using a Puller T67L-3600-A or equivalent. Remove the lower timing belt cover.

6. Disconnect the crankshaft sensor wire and move it out of the way.

7. Remove the center timing cover and the pulley from the RH idler pulley.

To install:

1. Install the RH idler pulley, center timing belt cover, and connect the crankshaft sensor wire.

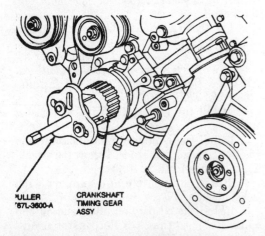

PULLER
T67L-3600-A

CRANKSHAFT
TIMING GEAR
ASSY

Front lower timing cover—3.0L SHO engine

2. Install the lower timing belt cover and the crankshaft damper using a Crank Damper Replacer tool No. T89P-6701-A or equivalent. Torque the center bolt to 113-125 ft. lbs.

3. Install the upper timing belt cover and the intake connector tube.

4. Start the engine and check for oil and coolant leaks.

OIL SEAL REPLACEMENT

2.5L Engine

1. Refer to the "Engine Removal And Installation" procedures in this section, then remove the engine from the vehicle and place it on a workstand.

2. Remove the drive belt(s), the crankshaft pulley bolt/washer and the crankshaft pulley.

3. Using the Damper Removal tool part No. T77F-4220-B1, remove the crankshaft pulley.

4. Using the Front Seal Removal tool part No. T74P-6700-A, remove the front cover oil seal.

5. Coat the new seal with grease. Using the Front Seal Replacer tool part No. T83T-4676-A, install the seal into the cover; drive the seal in until it is fully seated. Check the seal after installation to ensure that the seal spring is properly positioned.

6. To complete the installation, refer to the "Front Cover Installation" procedures. Torque the crankshaft pulley-to-crankshaft bolt to 140-230 ft. lbs.

3.0L Engine

1. Disconnect the negative ($-$) battery cable and loosen the accessory drive belts.

2. Raise and support the front of the vehicle on jackstands, then remove the right side front wheel.

3. Remove the 4 crankshaft pulley-to-damper bolts. Disengage the accessory drive belts and remove the crankshaft pulley.

4. Using the Crankshaft Damper Removal tool part No. T58P-6316-D and the Vibration Damper Removal Adapter tool part No. T82L-6316-B, remove the crankshaft damper from the crankshaft.

5. Using a small pry bar, pry the oil seal from the front cover; be careful not to damage the front cover and the crankshaft.

NOTE: *Before installation; inspect the front cover and shaft seal surface of the crankshaft damper for damage, nicks, burrs or other roughness which may cause the new seal to fail. Sand seal surface with (400-600 grit) paper or replace the components as necessary.*

6. **To install:** lubricate the new seal lip with clean engine oil, then install the seal using the seal installer tool part No. T82L-6316-A and

the front cover seal replacer tool part No. T70P-6B070-A, or their compatible equivalents.

7. Coat the crankshaft damper sealing surface with clean engine oil. Apply RTV to the keyway of the damper prior to installation. Install the damper using the vibration damper seal installer tool part No. T82L-6316-A.

8. To complete the installation, reverse the removal procedures. Torque the crankshaft damper-to-crankshaft bolt to 141-169 ft. lbs., the crankshaft pulley-to-damper bolts to 20-28 ft. lbs.

3.8L Engine

1. Disconnect the negative (−) battery cable.

2. Remove the fan shroud attaching screws and position the shroud back over the fan.

3. Unbolt the fan clutch assembly and remove.

4. Loosen the accessory drive belt idler.

5. Raise the vehicle and support safely on jackstands.

6. Disengage the accessory drive belt and remove crankshaft pulley.

7. Remove the crankshaft damper using the crankshaft Damper Removal tool part No. T58P-6316-D and the Vibration Damper Removal Adapter tool part No. T82L-6316-B.

8. Remove the seal from the front cover with a suitable prying tool. Use care to prevent gouging or scoring the front cover and crankshaft.

NOTE: *Before installation; inspect the front cover and shaft seal surface of the crankshaft damper for damage, nicks, burrs or other roughness which may cause the new seal to fail. Sand seal surface with (400-600 grit) paper or replace the components as necessary.*

9. Lubricate the seal lip with clean engine oil and install the seal using front cover seal replacer tool part No. T70P-6B070-A.

10. Lubricate the seal surface on the damper with clean engine oil. Install damper and pulley assembly. Install the damper attaching bolt and torque to 104-132 ft. lbs.

11. Position accessory drive belt over crankshaft pulley.

12. Lower the vehicle.

13. Check accessory drive belt for proper routing and engagement in the pulleys. Adjust the drive belt tension.

14. Install the fan/clutch assembly and reposition the fan shroud with the attaching screws.

15. Connect the negative (−) battery cable. Start the engine and check for leaks.

3.0L SHO Engine

1. Loosen the accessory drive belts.

2. Remove the RH front wheel.

3. Remove the front damper bolt and the damper from the crankshaft using a Puller part No. T67-3600-A or equivalent.

4. Remove the timing belt as outlined in the "Timing Belt" removal and installation procedure in this chapter.

5. Remove the crankshaft timing gear using a Puller part No. T67-3600-A or equivalent.

6. Remove the crankshaft oil seal using a Seal Puller part No. T78P-3504-N or equivalent.

7. To install: use a Front Seal Replacer tool No. T82L-6816-A or equivalent to install the new seal.

8. Install the timing gear onto the crankshaft.

9. Install the crankshaft damper by using a Crank Damper Replacer tool No. T89P-6701-B or equivalent. Torque the center bolt to 113-126 ft. lbs.

10. Install the accessory drive belts and adjust to proper specifications. Refer to the "Belts" removal and installation procedure in chapter 1.

11. Start the engine, check for oil and coolant leaks.

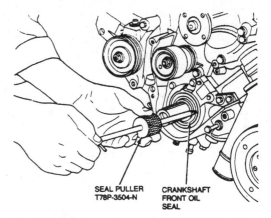

SEAL PULLER
T78P-3504-N

CRANKSHAFT
FRONT OIL
SEAL

Crankshaft timing gear removal—3.0L SHO engine

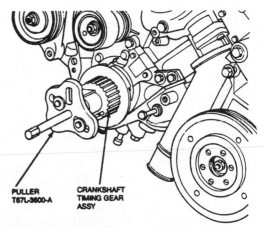

PULLER
T67L-3600-A

CRANKSHAFT
TIMING GEAR
ASSY

Crankshaft oil seal removal—3.0L SHO engine

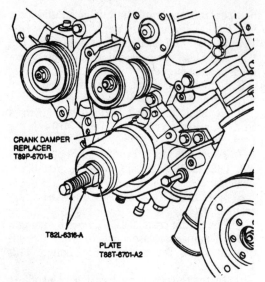

Crankshaft oil seal installation—3.0L SHO engine

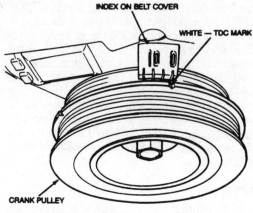

Crankshaft damper timing marks—3.0L SHO engine

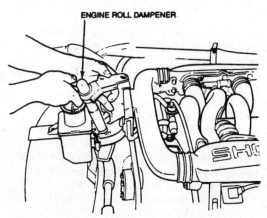

Engine roll damper removal—3.0L SHO engine

Timing Belt

The 3.0L SHO Taurus is the only engine in this book that is equipped with a timing belt and two timing chains. The belt travels from the crankshaft to the LH (front) camshaft gear, across to the RH (rear) camshaft gear, down to the automatic belt tensioner and around again. The belt is made of sythetic rubber and nylon cord. This is a very strong construction, but should be replaced every 60,000 miles with normal driving conditions.

REMOVAL AND INSTALLATION

1. Disconnect the negative (–) battery cable.
2. Set the engine to the TDC (Top Dead Center) on the No. 1 cylinder.

NOTE: *TDC procedure can be performed by removing the spark plug to No. 1 cylinder. With the engine cool, place your finger in the plug hole and rotate the engine until you can feel pressure being forced out of the plug hole. After the pressure starts, move the crankshaft damper to line up the timing mark on the damper with the mark on the timing belt cover.*

3. Disconnect the DIS ignition module connectors and position the wires out of the way.
4. Remove the intake manifold connector tube by loosing the two end clamps and removing the two mounting brackets.
5. Remove the upper timing belt cover and accessory drive belts, refer to the "Belts" removal and installation procedure in chapter 1.
6. Remove the engine roll damper.
7. Raise the vehicle and support with jackstands.

8. Remove the RH front wheel and splash guard assemblies.
9. Remove the crankshaft pulley using Puller tool No. T67L-3600-A or equivalent.
10. Remove the tensioner pulley and bracket for the air conditioning and alternator belt.
11. Remove the center and lower timing belt covers.
12. Release the tension at the automatic tensioner pulley and remove the belt. Check the tensioner release procedure illustration in this section.

To install:

CAUTION: *Before installing a used timing belt, inspect the belt for cracks, wear, and or other damage. Replace the belt if damaged in any way. The timing belt is very cheap compared to the damage that may be caused if the belt fails. Do not allow the timing belt to come in contact with gasoline, oil, water, coolant, or steam. Do not turn the belt inside out or twist the belt. Handle the timing belt as if it is a new born child.*

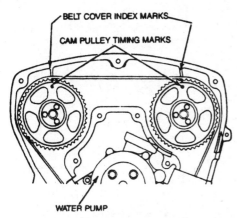

Camshaft pulley timing marks—3.0L SHO engine

1. Raise the vehicle and support with jackstands.

2. Ensure the engine is at TDC on No. 1 cylinder. Check that the camshaft pulley marks line up with the index marks on the upper steel belt cover.

3. Install the timing belt on the crankshaft pulley and route to the camshaft pulleys. The lettering on the belt **KOA** should be readable from the rear of the engine (top of the lettering to the front of the engine). Check the illustration in the "Oil Seal" section in this chapter.

4. Lower the vehicle.

5. Release the tension on the automatic tensioner pulley and install the timing belt over the camshaft pulleys. Make sure that there is a small amount of slack between the camshaft and crank pulleys.

6. Raise the vehicle and support with jackstands.

7. Install the lower and center timing belt covers. Torque the bolts to 60-90 in. lbs.

8. Install the crankshaft pulley using a Crankshaft Seal Installer/Cover Aligner tool No. T88T-6701-A. Install the crankshaft pulley bolt and torque to 71-85 ft. lbs.

9. Install the alternator/air conditioning tensioner pulley and bracket. Torque the bolts to 11-17 ft. lbs.

10. Install the fender apron splash shield and wheel assembly.

11. Lower the vehicle.

12. Rotate the engine two complete revolutions and bring it to TDC of No. 1 cylinder. Make sure that the camshaft pulleys line up with index marks on the belt cover and the crankshaft pulley notch lines up with the index mark on the belt cover. If the marks do not line up, set the engine back to TDC of No.1 cylinder and repeat steps 2-8.

13. Install the upper belt cover, power steering/water pump belt, alternator/air conditioning belt, and the intake manifold connector tube. Torque the manifold bolts to 11-17 ft. lbs.

14. Install the engine roll damper.

15. Connect the electrical connectors to the DIS module and negative (–) battery cable.

16. Start the engine and check for leaks.

Timing Chain

ADJUSTMENT

NOTE: *No adjustments of the timing chain are necessary or possible. The ONLY check to be make is the deflection measurement. If the deflection is beyond specifications, replace the timing chain, the sprockets and/or the tensioners.*

2.5L Engine

1. To check the timing chain deflection, first rotate the crankshaft in the counterclockwise direction (view from the front) to take up the slack.

2. Mark a reference point on the block, then measure the mid-section distance to the timing chain on the left side.

3. Rotate the crankshaft clockwise to take up the slack on the right side of the chain.

4. If the deflection exceeds ½", replace the timing chain and/or the sprockets.

NOTE: *The deflection measurement is the difference between the two measurements.*

5. Check the timing chain tensioner blade for wear depth. If the wear depth exceeds specification, replace the tensioner.

3.0L Engine

1. Refer to the "Rocker Arm Removal And Installation" procedures in this section and remove the left side valve cover.

2. Loosen the exhaust valve fulcrum bolt of the No. 5 cylinder and rotate the rocker to one side.

3. Using a dial indicator, install it onto the pushrod.

4. Rotate the crankshaft until the No. 1 cylinder is at the TDC of the compression stroke.

NOTE: *The damper pulley timing mark should be on the TDC of the timing plate. This operation will take the slack from the right side of the timing chain.*

5. Using the dial indicator, set the dial on zero.

6. Slowly turn the crankshaft counterclockwise until the slightest movement on the dial indicator is observed, then inspect the position of the damper pulley with the timing plate.

7. If the reading on the timing plate exceeds 6°, replace the timing chain and the sprockets.

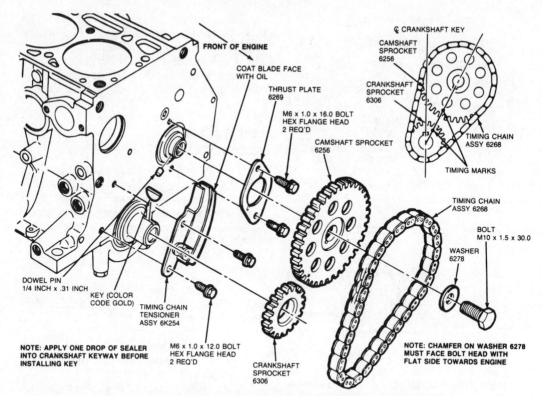

Timing chain & sprockets—2.5L engine

REMOVAL AND INSTALLATION

2.5L Engine

1. Refer to the "Engine Removal And Installation" procedures in this section and remove the engine and secure it to a workstand.

2. Refer to the "Front Cover Removal And Installation" procedures in this section and remove the front cover.

3. Rotate the crankshaft until the timing marks of the crankshaft and the camshaft sprockets are aligned.

4. Remove the camshaft sprocket bolt and washer, then slide the camshaft sprocket, the timing chain and the crankshaft sprocket off as an assembly.

5. Inspect and/or replace the parts as necessary.

6. **To install:** slide the sprockets/timing chain assembly onto the camshaft and crankshaft, as an assembly, with timing marks aligned. Torque the camshaft sprocket-to-camshaft bolt to 41-56 ft. lbs. Oil the timing chain, the sprockets and the tensioner after installation.

7. Apply oil resistant sealer to a new front cover gasket and position gasket onto the front cover.

8. Using the Front Cover Aligner tool part No. T84P-6019-C, position it onto the end of

the crankshaft, ensuring that the crank key is aligned with the keyway in the tool. Bolt the front cover to the engine. Tighten all the attaching bolts to 15-22 ft. lbs. Remove the front cover aligner tool.

9. Lubricate the hub of the crankshaft pulley with Polyethylene Grease to prevent damage to the seal during installation and initial engine start. Install crankshaft pulley.

10. To complete the installation, reverse the removal procedures. Torque the crankshaft pulley bolt to 140-170 ft. lbs. Refill the cooling system. Start the engine and check for leaks.

3.0L Engine

1. Refer to the "Front Cover Removal And Installation" procedures in this section and remove the front cover.

2. Rotate the crankshaft until the No. 1 piston is at the TDC of it's compression stroke and the timing marks are aligned.

4. Remove the camshaft sprocket-to-camshaft bolt and washer, then slide the sprockets and timing chain forward to remove them as an assembly.

5. Inspect the timing chain and sprockets for excessive wear; replace them, if necessary.

6. Using a putty knife, clean the gasket mounting surfaces.

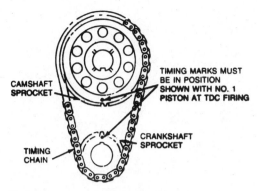

Timing marks—3.0L and 3.8L engine

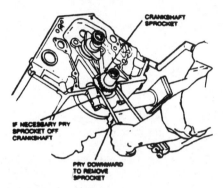

Removing the crankshaft sprocket

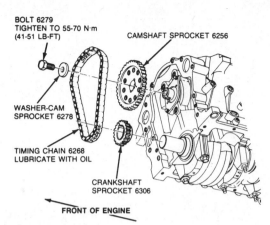

Timing chain and sprocket assembly—3.0L engine

7. Apply oil to the timing chain and sprockets after installation.

NOTE: *The camshaft bolt has a drilled oil passage in it for timing chain lubrication. If the bolt is damaged do not replace it with a standard bolt.*

8. Apply a bead of RTV sealant on the gap at the cylinder block.

9. Apply an oil resistant sealer part No. B5A-19554-A, or equivalent, to a new front gasket and position the gasket onto the front cover.

10. Position the front cover on the engine taking care not to damage the front seal. Make sure the cover is installed over the alignment dowels.

NOTE: *When installing the front cover onto the engine, make sure that the oil pan seal is not dislodged.*

11. If necessary, replace the front cover seal using the Seal Installation tool part No. T70P-6B070-A.

12. To complete the installation, reverse the removal procedures. Torque the camshaft sprocket-to-camshaft bolt to 40-51 ft. lbs., the front cover-to-engine bolts to 15-22 ft. lbs., the water pump-to-front cover bolts to 72-96 in. lbs., the damper-to-crankshaft bolt to 141-169 ft. lbs. and the damper pulley-to-damper bolts to 20-28 ft. lbs.

13. Refill the crankcase with the recommended oil.

14. Refill the cooling system. Start the engine and check for leaks.

3.8L Engine

1. Refer to the "Front Cover Removal And Installation" procedures in this section and remove the front cover.

2. Rotate the crankshaft until the No. 1 piston is at the TDC of it's compression stroke and the timing marks are aligned.

3. Remove the camshaft bolt and washer from end of the camshaft.

4. Remove the distributor drive gear.

5. Remove the camshaft sprocket, crankshaft sprocket, and timing chain as an assembly

NOTE: *If the crankshaft sprocket is difficult to remove, pry the sprocket off the shaft using a pair of pry bars positioned on both sides of the sprocket.*

5. **To install:** clean all gasket surfaces on the front cover and cylinder block.

6. When the front cover is off, replace the front cover seal using the Seal Installation tool part No. T70P-6B070-A.

7. Install the camshaft sprocket, crankshaft, and timing chain as an assembly.

8. Line up the timing marks so that the key and the timing mark on the camshaft sprocket is at the 6 o'clock position and the key and the timing mark on the crankshaft sprocket is at the 12 o'clock position.

9. To complete the installation, reverse the removal procedures. Torque the camshaft sprocket-to-camshaft bolt to 54-67 ft. lbs., the front cover-to-engine bolts to 15-22 ft. lbs., the water pump-to-front cover bolts to 72-96 in. lbs., the damper-to-crankshaft bolt to 104-132 ft. lbs. and the damper pulley-to-damper bolts to 19-28 ft. lbs.

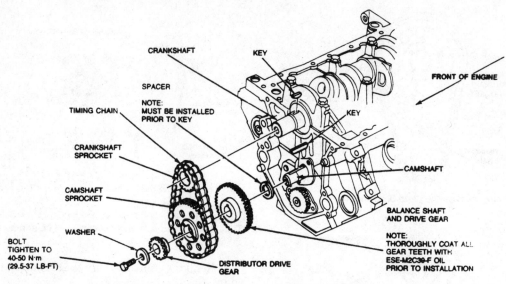

CRANKSHAFT

KEY

FRONT OF ENGINE

SPACER

NOTE:
MUST BE INSTALLED
PRIOR TO KEY

TIMING CHAIN

KEY

CRANKSHAFT
SPROCKET

CAMSHAFT

CAMSHAFT
SPROCKET

BALANCE SHAFT
AND DRIVE GEAR

NOTE:
THOROUGHLY COAT ALL
GEAR TEETH WITH
ESE-M2C39-F OIL
PRIOR TO INSTALLATION

WASHER

BOLT
TIGHTEN TO
40-50 N·m
(29.5-37 LB-FT)

DISTRIBUTOR DRIVE
GEAR

Timing chain and sprocket assembly—3.8L engine

3.0L SHO Engine

1. Disconnect the negative (–) battery cable.
2. Set the engine to the TDC (top dead center) on the No. 1 cylinder.

NOTE: *TDC procedure can be performed by removing the spark plug to No. 1 cylinder. With the engine cool, place your finger in the plug hole and rotate the engine until you can feel pressure being forced out of the plug hole. After the pressure starts, move the crankshaft damper to line up the timing mark on the damper with the mark on the timing belt cover.*

3. Remove the intake manifold connector tube. Refer to the "Upper Intake Manifold" removal and installation procedure in this chapter.
4. Remove the cylinder head covers as out-lined in the "Cylinder Head Cover" removal and installation procedures in this chapter.
5. Remove the four camshaft timing chain tensioner mounting bolts.
6. Remove the two cam sprocket-to-camshaft bolts for each one of the two camshafts.
7. Carefully slid the cam sprocket off the camshafts and remove the sprockets and chain as an assembly.

To install:

1. With the sprockets and chain on a flat surface, install the chain over the sprockets. Align the white painted link of the chain with the timing marks on the two sprockets. Check the following illustration.
2. Align the timing marks on the chain sprocket(s) with the camshaft and install the spockets and chain as an assembly. Torque the four retaining bolts to 10-13 ft. lbs. (14-18 Nm).

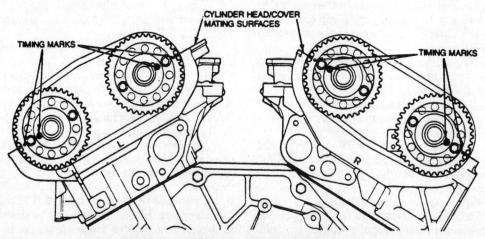

CYLINDER HEAD/COVER
MATING SURFACES

TIMING MARKS

TIMING MARKS

L

R

Camshaft sprockets and chain timing marks—3.0L SHO engines

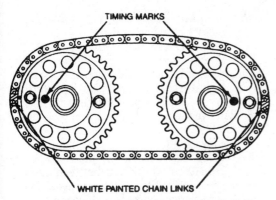

Camshaft sprocket timing marks—3.0L SHO engine

3. Rotate the camshafts approximately 60 degrees counterclockwise. Set the chain tensioner between the sprockets and install the four attaching bolts. Torque the bolts to 11-14 ft. lbs.

4. Install a new gasket and the cylinder head cover. Torque the bolts to 7-12 ft. lbs.

5. Install the intake manifold connector assembly as outlined in the "Upper Intake Manifold" removal and installation procedures in this chapter.

Camshaft

REMOVAL AND INSTALLATION

2.5L Engine

CAUTION: *When draining the coolant, keep in mind that cats and dogs are attracted by the ethylene glycol antifreeze, and are quite likely to drink any that is left in an uncovered container or in puddles on the ground. This will prove fatal in sufficient quantity. Always drain the coolant into a sealable container. Coolant should be reused unless it is contaminated or several years old.*

1. Refer to the "Engine Removal And Installation" procedures in this section, then remove the engine and place it on a workstand.

2. Refer to the "Timing Chain Removal And Installation" procedures in this section and remove the timing chain with the camshaft sprocket.

3. Remove the cylinder head.

4. Using a magnet, remove the hydraulic tappets and keep them in order so that they can be installed in their original positions. If the tappets are stuck in the bores by excessive varnish, etc., use a Hydraulic Tappet Puller to remove the tappets.

6. Remove the oil pan.

7. To check the camshaft end play, install the camshaft sprocket to the camshaft and perform the following procedures:

   a. Push the camshaft toward the rear of the engine and install a dial indicator tool No. 4201-C, so that the indicator point is on the camshaft sprocket mounting bolt.

   b. Zero the dial indicator. Position a large screwdriver between the camshaft sprocket and the block.

   c. Pull the camshaft forward and release it. Compare the dial indicator reading with the camshaft end play specification of 0.23mm.

   d. If the camshaft end play is over the amount specified, replace the thrust plate.

8. Remove the camshaft sprocket and the camshaft thrust plate.

9. Carefully remove the camshaft by pulling it toward the front of the engine. Use caution to avoid damaging the bearings, journals and lobes.

10. Using a putty knife, clean the gasket mounting surfaces.

11. Clean the oil pump inlet tube screen, the oil pan and the cylinder block gasket surfaces. Prime the oil pump by filling the inlet opening with oil and rotate the pump shaft until oil emerges from the outlet tube. Install the oil pump, the oil pump inlet tube screen and the oil pan.

To install

1. Lubricate the camshaft lobes and journals with heavy engine oil, SAE 50 weight. Carefully slide camshaft through bearings into the cylinder block. Be very careful not to damage the cam bearings.

2. Install the thrust plate and torque the bolts to 72-108 in. lbs.

3. Install the timing chain and sprockets as an assemble.

4. Install the front timing cover and bolts. Torque the bolts to 15-22 ft. lbs.

5. Install the accessory drive belts and pulleys.

6. Lubricate all the tappet bores with SAE 50 weight engine oil and install the tappets.

7. Install the cylinder head and a new gasket, refer to the "Cylinder head" section in this chapter.

8. Install the engine, refer to the "Engine Removal and Installation" for procedure.

9. Position No.1 piston at TDC after compression stroke. Position the distributor in the block with the rotor at No. 1 firing position on the distributor cap. Tighten the hold down.

10. Fill the cooling system. Fill the engine with the proper oil.

11. Start the engine and check for leaks.

3.0L Engine

1. Refer to the "Engine Removal And Installation" procedures in this section, then remove the engine and place it on a workstand.

2. Ensure the cooling system, the fuel system and the crankcase have been drained.

CAUTION: *When draining the coolant, keep in mind that cats and dogs are attracted by the ethylene glycol antifreeze, and are quite likely to drink any that is left in an uncovered container or in puddles on the ground. This will prove fatal in sufficient quantity. Always drain the coolant into a sealable container. Coolant should be reused unless it is contaminated or several years old.*

3. Remove the idler pulley and bracket assembly. Remove the drive and accessory belts. Remove the water pump.

4. Remove the crankshaft pulley and damper, using a crankshaft damper pulling tool. Remove the lower radiator hose. Remove 4 the oil pan-to-front cover bolts, the 10 front cover-to-engine bolts and the front cover from the engine.

5. Label and remove the spark plug wires and the rocker arm covers. Loosen the rocker arm fulcrum nuts and turn them to the side to expose the pushrods. Remove the pushrods and mark them to install in their original positions.

6. Using a magnet, remove the hydraulic tappets and keep them in order so that they can be installed in their original positions. If the tappets are stuck in the bores by excessive varnish, use the Hydraulic Tappet Puller tool part No. T70L-6500-A, to remove the tappets.

7. To check the camshaft end play, perform the following procedures:

a. Push the camshaft toward the rear of the engine and install a Dial Indicator tool No. 4201-C, so that the indicator point is on the camshaft sprocket bolt. Zero the dial indicator.

b. Using a medium pry bar, position it between the camshaft sprocket and the block.

NOTE: *When applying pressure to the cam-*

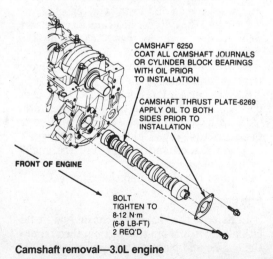

CAMSHAFT 6250
COAT ALL CAMSHAFT JOURNALS
OR CYLINDER BLOCK BEARINGS
WITH OIL PRIOR
TO INSTALLATION

CAMSHAFT THRUST PLATE-6269
APPLY OIL TO BOTH
SIDES PRIOR TO
INSTALLATION

FRONT OF ENGINE

BOLT
TIGHTEN TO
8-12 N·m
(6-8 LB-FT)
2 REQ'D

Camshaft removal—3.0L engine

shaft sprocket, be careful not to break the powdered metal camshaft sprocket.

c. Pry the camshaft forward and release it. Compare the dial indicator reading with the camshaft end play specification of 0.23mm.

d. If the camshaft end play is over the amount specified, replace the thrust plate.

8. Remove the timing chain and sprockets as an assembly.

9. Remove the camshaft thrust plate. Carefully remove the camshaft by putting a long bolt the same size as the camshaft end bolt in the camshaft and pulling it slowly to avoid damaging the bearings, journals and lobes.

To install:

1. Using a putty knife, clean the gasket mounting surfaces.

2. **To install:** use new gaskets, sealant, lubricate the internal parts with SAE 50 weight oil.

3. Carefully slide the camshaft through the bearing in the cylinder block.

4. Install the thrust plate and torque bolts to 72-96 in. lbs.

5. Install the front cover, refer to "Front Timing Cover" section in this chapter.

6. Lubricate the tappets and tappet bores with heavy engine oil, SAE 50 weight. Install the tappets to their original bores.

7. Install the intake manifold, rocker arms, and valve covers, refer to the "Intake Manifold" section for procedure.

8. Install accessory drive belts and pulleys. Adjust to specifications.

9. Install the engine, refer to the "Engine Removal and Installation" for the procedures.

10. Fill the cooling system. Fill the crankcase with proper viscosity and weight oil.

11. Start the engine and check for fuel, vacuum, and coolant leaks. Check and adjust ignition timing.

Torque the camshaft thrust plate-to-engine bolts to 72-96 in. lbs., the front cover-to-engine bolts to 15-22 ft. lbs., the water pump-to-front cover bolts to 72-96 in. lbs., the crankshaft damper-to-crankshaft bolt to 141-169 ft. lbs. and the crankshaft pulley-to-damper bolts to 20-28 ft. lbs.

3.0L SHO Engine

The SHO (Super High Output) engine is equipped with dual overhead cams (DOHC) per cylinder head. This adds up to four camshafts, four camshaft sprockets, two timing chains, one timing belt, and thirty-two valves. With this arrangement, the engine does not have to be removed to replace the camshafts or related parts.

1. Disconnect the negative (−) battery cable.

2. Set the engine to TDC (top dead center) on the No. 1 cylinder.

NOTE: *TDC procedure can be performed by removing the spark plug to No. 1 cylinder. With the engine cool, place your finger in the plug hole and rotate the engine until you can feel pressure being forced out of the plug hole. After the pressure starts, move the crankshaft damper to line up the timing mark on the damper with the mark on the timing belt cover.*

3. Remove the intake manifold assembly as outlined in the "Intake Manifold" removal and installation procedures in this chapter.

4. Remove the timing belt and covers as outlined in the "Timing Belt" removal and installation in this chapter.

5. Remove the cylinder head covers.

6. Note the positions of the camshaft dowel pins and remove the camshaft pulleys.

7. Remove the upper rear timing belt cover and loosen the camshaft bearing caps.

CAUTION: *If the camshaft bearing caps are not uniformly loosened, the camshaft may be damaged.*

8. Remove the camshaft bearing caps. Note the positions for installation.

9. Remove the four camshaft chain tensioner mounting bolts and remove the camshafts together with the chain and tensioner.

10. Discard the camshaft oil seal.

11. Remove the chain sprockets from the camshaft.

To install:

1. Align the timing marks on the chain

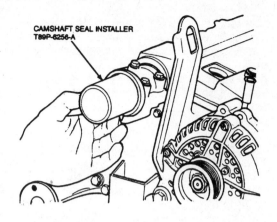

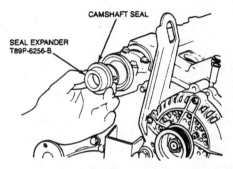

Camshaft seal installation

sprockets with the camshaft and install the sprockets. Torque the bolts to 10-13 ft. lbs.

2. Install the chain over the camshaft sprockets. Align the white painted link with the timing marks on the sprockets. Refer to the

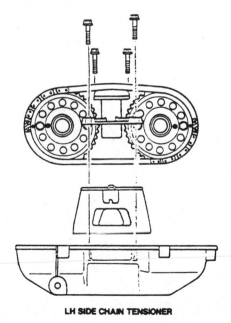

LH SIDE CHAIN TENSIONER

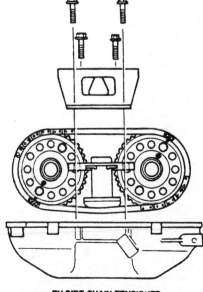

RH SIDE CHAIN TENSIONER

Timing chain tensioner location—3.0L SHO engine

camshaft and sprocket timing marks illustration in the timing chain section.

3. Apply a thin coat of engine oil to the camshaft journals, lobes, and caps. Rotate the camshafts approximately 60 degrees counterclockwise. Set the chain tensioner between the sprockets and position the camshafts on the cylinder heads.

NOTE: *The LH and RH chain tensioners are not interchangeable. They should be marked for proper installation.*

4. Install the bearing caps to 2 through 5. Loosely install the bearing ataching bolts, but do not tighten.

NOTE: *The arrows on the bearing caps should face to the front of the engine when installed.*

5. Apply Silicone Sealer D6AZ-19579C or equivalent to the outer diameter of the camshaft seal seating area of the cylinder head.

6. Install the camshaft seal with a Camshaft Seal Expander tool No. T89P-6265-B and a Camshaft Seal Replacer tool No. T89P-6265-A or equivalent.

7. Apply a 2.5mm bead of Silicone Sealer or equivalent to the No. 1 bearing cap and install the bearing cap. Loosely install the bolts.

8. Tighten the bearing caps in a two sequence step method. Torque the bolts in the second step to 12-16 ft. lbs. Refer to the following torque sequence illustration.

9. Install the chain tensioner and the four attaching bolts. Torque the bolts to 11-14 ft. lbs.

10. Rotate the camshafts 60 degrees and check for proper alignment of the timing marks. The marks on the camshaft sprockets should align with the cylinder head cover mating surface as shown in the illustration of the camshaft timing marks.

11. Set the Camshaft Positioning tool No. T89P-6256-C or equivalent on the camshafts to ensure the correct positioning.

12. Install the camshaft pulleys ensuring that they are aligned with the dowel pins properly. Torque the bolts to 15-18 ft. lbs.

13. Install the timing belt and covers as outlined in the "Timing Belt" section in this chapter.

14. Install the cylinder head covers and torque the bolts to 7-12 ft. lbs.

CAUTION: *Do not over tighten the cylinder head cover bolts. The cast aluminum cover may crack or the gasket may split causing a severe oil leak.*

15. Install the intake manifold assembly as outlined in the "Intake Manifold" section in this chapter.

16. Connect the negative (−) battery cable. Start the engine and check for oil leaks.

CHECKING CAMSHAFT

Degrease the camshaft using safe solvent, clean all oil grooves. Visually inspect the cam lobes and bearing journals for excessive wear. If a lobe is questionable, check all lobes and journals with a micrometer.

Measure the lobes from nose to base and again at 90°. The lift is determined by subtracting the second measurement from the first. If all exhaust lobes and all intake lobes are not identical, the camshaft must be reground or replaced. Measure the bearing journals and compare to specifications. If a journal is worn there

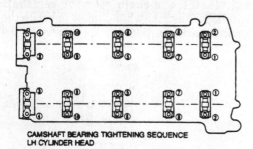

CAMSHAFT BEARING TIGHTENING SEQUENCE
LH CYLINDER HEAD

← FRONT OF →
ENGINE

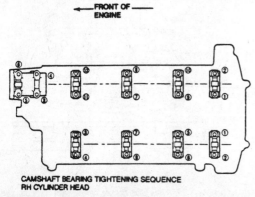

CAMSHAFT BEARING TIGHTENING SEQUENCE
RH CYLINDER HEAD

Camshaft torquing sequence in two steps—3.0L SHO engine

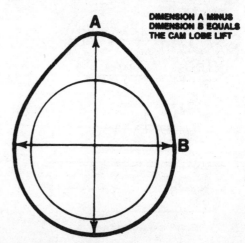

DIMENSION A MINUS
DIMENSION B EQUALS
THE CAM LOBE LIFT

A

B

Measuring camshaft lift

is a good chance that the cam bearings are worn too, requiring replacement.

If the lobes and journals appear intact, place the front and rear cam journals in V-blocks and rest a dial indicator on the center journal. Rotate the camshaft to check for straightness, if deviation exceeds 0.025mm, replace the camshaft.

Camshaft Bearings

The camshaft bearings are available prefinished to size and require no reaming for standard and 0.38mm undersize journal diameters.

REMOVAL AND INSTALLATION

2.5L, 3.0L, and 3.8L engines

1. Remove the engine as outlined in the "Engine Assembly" removal and installation procedures in this chapter. Place the engine on work stand and remove the camshaft, refer to the "Camshaft Removal and Installation" procedure. Remove the crankshaft and the rear bearing bore plug.

2. Remove the camshaft bearing with Camshaft Bearing Set part No. T65L-6250-A or equivalent.

3. Select the proper size expanding collet and backup nut and assemble on the expanding mandrel. With the expanding collet collapsed, install the collet assembly in the camshaft bearing. Tighten the backup nut on the expanding mandrel until the collet fits the camshaft bearing.

4. Assemble the puller screw and extension, if necessary, and install it on the expanding mandrel. Wrap a cloth around the threads of the puller screw to protect the bearing or journal. Tighten the puller nut against the thrust bearing and the pulling plate to remove the camshaft bearing. Hold the end of the puller screw to prevent it from turning.

5. Repeat Step 4 for each bearing. To remove the front bearing, install the puller from rear of block.

To install:

1. Position the new bearings at the bearing bores and press them in place. Center the pulling plate and the puller screw to avoid damage to the bearing. Failure to use the correct expanding collet can cause severe bearing damage.

NOTE: *Align the oil holes in the bearings and install below the front face of the cylinder block. Check the oil passage for obstructions by squirting oil into the opening in the cylinder block and observing the flow through the oil hole at the rear camshaft bearing.*

2. Install the new bearing bore plug in the rear of the block.

3. Install the camshaft, flywheel and related parts. Do not check the connecting rod and main bearing clearance as part of camshaft bearing replacement. Install the engine, refer to the "Engine Removal and Installation" procedure.

3.0L SHO Engine

1. The engine does NOT have to be removed to replace the camshaft bearings.

2. Remove the intake manifold, cylinder head covers, timing belt and covers, and camshafts. **Detailed procedures can be found in the "Camshaft" removal and installation section in this chapter.**

CAUTION: *If the camshaft bearing caps are not uniformly loosened, camshaft damage may result.*

3. Remove the camshaft.

4. Remove the lower bearing halves.

5. **To install:** place the lower bearing halfs in their respective saddles. Lightly oil the bearings, camshaft journals, and lobes.

6. Position the two camshafts and chain assemblies in the lower bearing saddles and align the camshaft timing marks with the chain and head casting marks.

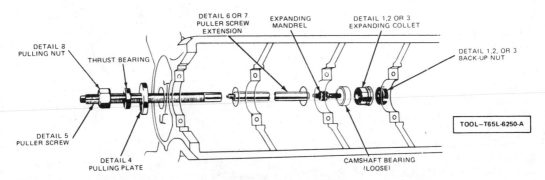

Camshaft bearing installation

7. Install the chain tensioner and the four attaching bolts. Torque the bolts to 11-14 ft. lbs.

8. Install the bearing caps and bolts to their respective bearing journals. Refer to the tightening sequence illustration in the "Camshaft" removal and installation section in this section.

9. Hand tighten all of the bolts until they have seated. Torque the bearing cap bolts in sequence and in a two step method. Torque the bearing caps to 12-16 ft. lbs. Do not tighten one cap completely until the remainder of the caps have been seated.

10. Install the timing belt, pulleys, and covers.

11. Install the cylinder head covers and intake manifold.

12. Start the engine and check for oil leaks.

Pistons and Connecting Rods

REMOVAL AND INSTALLATION

NOTE: *Although, in most cases, the pistons and connecting rods can be removed from the engine (after the cylinder head and oil pan are removed) while the engine is still in the car, it is far easier to remove the engine from the car. If removing pistons with the engine still installed, disconnect the radiator hoses, automatic transmission cooler lines and radiator shroud. Unbolt front mounts before jacking up the engine. Block the engine in position with wooden blocks between the mounts.*

1. Remove the engine from the car. Remove cylinder head(s), oil pan and front cover (if necessary).

2. Because the top piston ring does not travel to the very top of the cylinder bore, a ridge is built up between the end of the travel and the top of the cylinder. Pushing the piston and connecting rod assembly past the ridge is difficult and may cause damage to the piston. If new rings are installed and the ridge has not been removed, ring breakage and piston damage can occur when the ridge is encountered at engine speed.

3. Turn the crankshaft to position the piston at the bottom of the cylinder bore. Cover the top of the piston with a rag. Install a cylinder ridge reamer part No. T64L-6011-EA in the bore and follow the manufacturer's instructions to remove the ridge. Use caution. Avoid cutting too deeply or into the ring travel area. Remove the rag and medal cuttings from the top of the piston. Remove the ridge from all cylinders.

4. Check the edges of the connecting rod and bearing cap for numbers or matchmarks, if none are present mark the rod and cap numerically and in sequence from front to back of engine. The numbers or marks not only tell from which cylinder the piston came from but also ensures that the rod caps are installed in the correct matching position.

5. Turn the crankshaft until the connecting rod is at the bottom of the travel. Remove the two attaching nuts and the bearing cap. Take two pieces of rubber tubing and cover the rod bolts to prevent crank or cylinder scoring. Use a wooden hammer handle to help push the piston and rod up and out of the cylinder. Reinstall the rod cap in proper position. Remove all pistons and connecting rods. Inspect cylinder walls and deglaze or hone using a cylinder hone set part No. T73L-6011-A or equivalent.

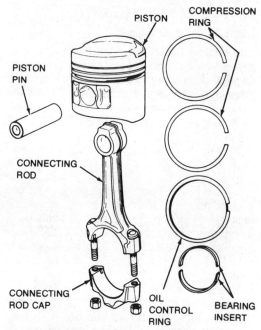

Piston and connecting rod assembly

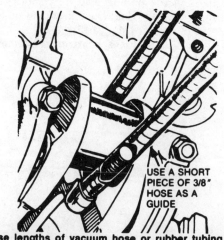

Use lengths of vacuum hose or rubber tubing to protect the crankshaft journals and cylinder walls during installation

RING COMPRESSOR

Install the piston using a ring compressor

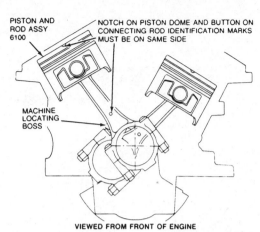

PISTON AND ROD ASSY 6100

NOTCH ON PISTON DOME AND BUTTON ON CONNECTING ROD IDENTIFICATION MARKS MUST BE ON SAME SIDE

MACHINE LOCATING BOSS

VIEWED FROM FRONT OF ENGINE

Piston and connecting rod positioning—3.0L engine

To install:

1. Lubricate each piston, rod bearing, and cylinder wall with heavy weight engine oil.

2. Take the bearing nuts and cap off connecting rod. Install rubber hoses over the connecting rod bolts to protect the block and crankshaft journal.

3. Install a ring compressor over the piston,

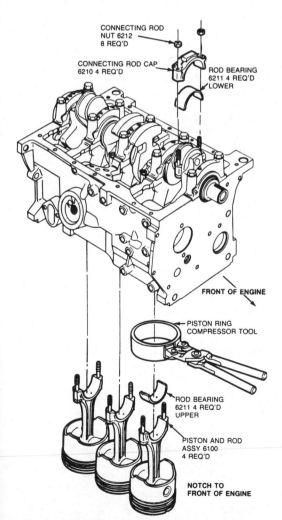

CONNECTING ROD NUT 6212 8 REQ'D

CONNECTING ROD CAP 6210 4 REQ'D

ROD BEARING 6211 4 REQ'D LOWER

FRONT OF ENGINE

PISTON RING COMPRESSOR TOOL

ROD BEARING 6211 4 REQ'D UPPER

PISTON AND ROD ASSY 6100 4 REQ'D

NOTCH TO FRONT OF ENGINE

Piston and connecting rod assembly—2.5L engine

position piston with the mark toward front of engine and carefully install.

4. Position the connecting rod with bearing insert over the crank journal. Install the rod cap with bearing in proper position. Secure with rod nuts and torque to the proper specifications. Install all of the rod and piston assemblies.

CLEANING AND INSPECTION

1. Use a piston ring expander and remove the rings from the piston.

2. Clean the ring grooves using piston ring groove cleaner part No. D81L-6002-D or equivalent. Exercise care to avoid cutting too deeply.

3. Clean all varnish and carbon from the piston with a safe solvent. Do not use a wire brush or caustic solution on the pistons.

4. Inspect the pistons for scuffing, scoring, cracks, pitting or excessive ring groove wear. If wear is evident, the piston must be replaced.

5. Have the piston and connecting rod assembly checked by a machine shop for correct alignment, piston pin wear and piston diameter. If the piston has collapsed, it will have to be replace or knurled to restore original diameter. Connecting rod bushing replacement, piston pin fitting and piston changing can be handled by the machine shop.

CYLINDER BORE

Check the cylinder bore for wear using a telescope gauge and a micrometer, measure the cylinder bore diameter perpendicular to the piston pin at a point 63.5mm below the top of the engine block. Measure the piston skirt perpendicular to the piston pin. The difference between the two measurements is the piston clearance. If the clearance is within specifications, finish honing or glaze breaking is all that is required. If clearance is excessive a slightly oversize piston may be required. If greatly oversize, the en-

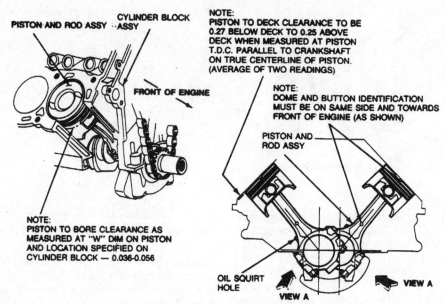

NOTE:
PISTON TO DECK CLEARANCE TO BE 0.27 BELOW DECK TO 0.25 ABOVE DECK WHEN MEASURED AT PISTON T.D.C. PARALLEL TO CRANKSHAFT ON TRUE CENTERLINE OF PISTON. (AVERAGE OF TWO READINGS)

NOTE:
DOME AND BUTTON IDENTIFICATION MUST BE ON SAME SIDE AND TOWARDS FRONT OF ENGINE (AS SHOWN)

NOTE:
PISTON TO BORE CLEARANCE AS MEASURED AT "W" DIM ON PISTON AND LOCATION SPECIFIED ON CYLINDER BLOCK — 0.036-0.056

Crankshaft and bearing assembly—3.8L engine

gine will have to be bored and oversized pistons installed.

FITTING AND POSITIONING PISTON RINGS

1. Take the new piston rings and compress one at a time into the cylinder that they will be used in. Press the ring about 25mm below the top of the cylinder block using an inverted piston.

2. Use a feeler gauge and measure the distance between the ends of the ring. This is called measuring the ring end gap. Compare the reading to the one called for in the specifications table. If the measurement is too small, when the engine heats up the ring ends will butt together and cause damage. File the ends of the ring with a fine file to obtain necessary clearance.

NOTE: *If inadequate ring end gap is utilized, ring breakage will result.*

3. Inspect the ring grooves on the piston for excessive wear or taper. If necessary, have the grooves recut for use with a standard ring and spacer. The machine shop can handle the job for you.

4. Check the ring grooves by rolling the new piston ring around the groove to check for burrs or carbon deposits. If any are found, remove with a fine file. Hold the ring in the groove and measure side clearance with a feeler gauge. If the clearance is excessive, spacer(s) will have to be added.

NOTE: *Always add spacers above the piston ring.*

5. Install the ring on the piston, lower oil ring first. Use a ring installing tool (piston ring

expander) on the compression rings. Consult the instruction sheet that comes with the rings to be sure they are installed with the correct side up. A mark on the ring usually faces upward.

6. When installing oil rings, first, install the expanding ring in the groove. Hold the ends of the ring butted together (they must not overlap) and install the bottom rail (scraper) with the end about 25mm away from the butted end of the control ring. Install the top rail about 25mm away from the butted end of the control but on the opposite side from the lower rail. Be careful not to scrap the piston when installing oil control rings.

7. Install the two compression rings. The lower ring first.

8. Consult the illustration for ring positioning, arrange the rings as shown, install a ring compressor and insert the piston and rod assembly into the engine.

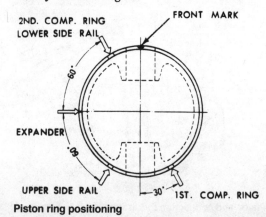

Piston ring positioning

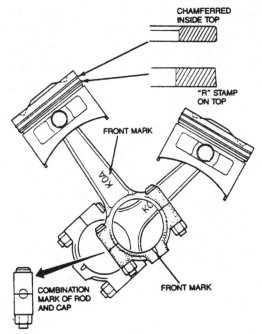

CHAMFERRED INSIDE TOP

"R" STAMP ON TOP

FRONT MARK

COMBINATION MARK OF ROD AND CAP

FRONT MARK

Piston, ring, and connecting rod positioning—3.0L SHO engine

Crankshaft

REMOVAL AND INSTALLATION

2.5L Engine

1. With the engine removed from the vehicle and placed on a work stand, remove the oil level dipstick. Refer to the "Engine Assembly" removal and installation procedures in this chapter.

2. Remove the accessory drive pulley, if so equipped. Remove the crankshaft pulley attaching bolts and washer.

3. Remove the cylinder front cover and the air conditioning idler pulley assembly, if so equipped. Remove cover assembly.

4. Check the timing chain deflection. Remove the timing chain and sprockets.

5. Invert the engine on work stand. Remove the flywheel and the rear seal cover. Remove the oil pan and gasket. Remove the oil pump inlet and the oil pump assembly.

6. Ensure all bearing caps (main and connecting rod) are marked so they can be installed in their original positions. Turn the crankshaft until the connecting rod from which the cap is being removed is up. Remove the connecting rod cap. Install rubber hose onto the connecting rod bolts to prevent journal damage. Push the connecting rod and piston assembly up in the cylinder and install the cap and nuts in their original positions. Repeat the procedure for the remaining connecting rod assemblies.

7. Remove the main bearing caps.

8. Carefully lift crankshaft out of block so upper thrust bearing surfaces are not damaged. WARNING: *Handle the crankshaft with care to avoid possible fracture or damage to the finished surfaces.*

To install:

NOTE: *If the bearings are to be reused they should be identified to ensure that they are installed in their original position.*

1. Remove the main bearing inserts from the block and bearing caps.

2. Remove the connecting rod bearing inserts from connecting rods and caps.

3. Install a new rear oil seal in the rear seal cover.

4. Apply a thin coat of Ford Polyethylene Grease D0AZ-19584-A (ESR-M1C159-A or ESB-M1C93-A) or equivalent, to the rear crankshaft surface. Do not apply sealer to the area forward of oil sealer groove. Inspect all the machined surfaces on the crankshaft for nicks, scratches or scores which could cause premature bearing wear.

5. If the crankshaft main bearing journals have been refinished to a definite undersize, install the correct undersize bearings, usually 0.25mm, 0.50mm, 0.80mm undersize. Ensure the bearing inserts and bearing bores are clean. Foreign material under the inserts will distort the bearing and cause a failure.

6. Place the upper main bearing inserts in position in the bores with the tang fitted in the slot provided. NOTE: *Lubricate the bearing surfaces with Oil Conditioner part No. D9AZ-19579-CF or equivalent. Conditioner is needed for lubrication at initial start up.*

7. Install the lower main bearings inserts in the bearing caps.

8. Carefully lower the crankshaft into place.

9. Check the clearance of each main bearing. Select fit the bearings for proper clearance.

10. After the bearings have been fitted, apply a light coat of Oil Conditioner to journals and bearings. Install all the bearing caps and torque to proper specifications. NOTE: *The main bearing cap must be installed in their original positions.*

11. Align the upper thrust bearing.

12. Check the crankshaft end play, using a dial indicator mounted on the front of the engine.

13. If the end play exceeds specification, replace the upper thrust bearing. If the end play is less than the specification, inspect the thrust bearing faces for damage, dirt or improper alignment. Install the thrust bearing and align the faces. Check the end play.

14. Install the new bearing inserts in the con-

necting rods and caps. Install rubber hoses on the rod bolts to prevent crankshaft journal damage. Check the clearance of each bearing using a piece of Plastigage®, refer to the "Bearing Oil Clearance" in this section.

15. If the bearing clearances are to specification, apply a light coat of Oil Conditioner part No. D9AZ-19579-CF to the journals and bearings.

16. Turn the crankshaft throw to the bottom of the stroke. Push the piston all the way down until the rod bearings seat on the crankshaft journal.

17. Install the connecting rod cap and nuts. Torque the nuts to specifications

18. After the piston and connecting rod assemblies have been installed, check all the connecting-rod-crankshaft journal clearances using a piece of Plastigage®, refer to the "Bearing Oil Clearance" in this section.

19. Turn the engine on the work stand so the front end is up. Install the timing chain, sprockets, timing chain tensioner, front cover, oil seal and the crankshaft pulley.

20. Clean the oil pan, oil pump and the oil pump screen assembly.

21. Prime the oil pump by filling the inlet opening with oil and rotating the pump shaft until oil emerges from the outlet opening. Install the oil pump.

22. Position the flywheel on the crankshaft. Apply Pipe Sealant with Teflon D8AZ-19554-A (ESG-M4G194-A and ESR-M18P7-A) or equivalent oil resistant sealer to the flywheel attaching bolts. Torque to specification.

NOTE: *On the flywheel (MTX only) locate clutch disc and install pressure plate.*

23. Turn the engine on the work stand so the engine is in the normal upright position. Install the oil level dipstick. Install the accessory drive pulley, if so equipped. Install and adjust the drive belt and the accessory belts to specification.

24. Install either the MTX transmission clutch assembly or the ATX torque converter.

25. Install the oil pan.

26. Remove the engine from work stand. Install the engine in the vehicle.

3.0L Engine

1. With the engine removed from the vehicle and placed on a workstand, refer to the "Engine Assembly" removal and installation procedures

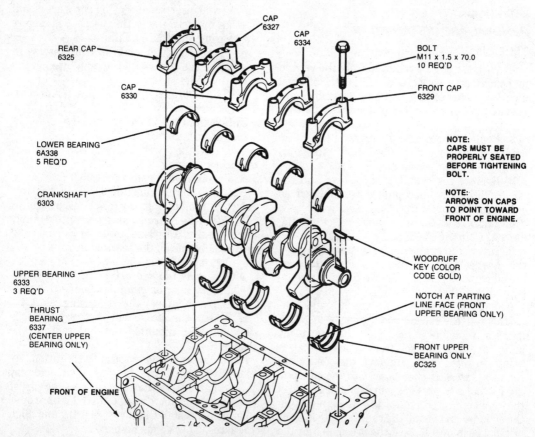

Crankshaft and bearing assembly—2.5L engine

in this chapter. Loosen the idler pulley and the alternator belt adjusting bolt.

2. Remove the oil pan and gasket.

3. Remove the front cover assembly.

4. Check the timing chain deflection. Remove the timing chain and sprockets.

5. Invert the engine on the workstand. Remove the flywheel. Remove the oil pump inlet and the oil pump assembly.

6. Ensure all bearing caps (main and connecting rod) are marked so that they can be installed in their original positions. Turn the crankshaft until the connecting rod from which the cap is being removed is up. Remove the connecting rod cap. Push the connecting rod and piston assembly up in the cylinder. Repeat the procedure for the remaining connecting rod assemblies.

7. Remove the main bearing caps.

8. Carefully lift the crankshaft out of the block so that the upper thrust bearing surfaces are not damaged.

To install:

NOTE: *If the bearings are to be reused they should be identified to ensure that they are installed in their original positions.*

1. Remove the main bearing inserts from the block and bearing caps.

2. Remove the connecting rod bearing inserts from the connecting rods and caps.

3. Inspect all the machined surfaces on the crankshaft for nicks, scratches, scores, etc., which could cause premature bearing wear.

4. If the crankshaft main bearing journals have been refinished to a definite undersize, install the correct undersize bearings, usually in 0.25mm, 0.50mm, 0.80mm undersize.

WARNING: *Ensure the bearing inserts and the bearing bores are clean. Foreign material under the inserts will distort the bearing and cause a failure.*

5. Place the upper main bearing inserts in position in the bores with the tang fitted in the slot provided.

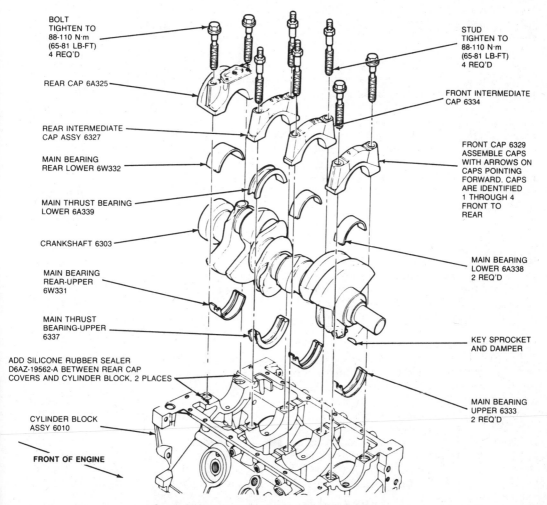

Crankshaft and bearing assembly—3.0L engine

6. Install the lower main bearing inserts in the bearing caps.

7. Carefully lower the crankshaft into place.

8. Check the clearance of each main bearing. Select fit the bearings for proper clearance.

9. After the bearings have been fitted, apply a light coat of Oil Conditioner part No. D9AZ-19578-CO or heavy engine oil, SAE 50 weight, to the journals bearings and rear seal surface. Install all the bearing caps. Apply RTV to the gap between the rear main bearing and the block. Take care to keep RTV from the parting surfaces between the block and the cap.

NOTE: *Ensure the main bearing caps are installed in their original positions and orientation.*

10. Lubricate the journal with Oil Conditioner or heavy engine oil 50 SAE weight. Install the thrust bearing cap with the bolts finger-tight. Pry the crankshaft forward against the thrust surface of the upper half of the bearing. Hold the crankshaft cap to the rear. This will align the thrust surfaces of both halves of the bearing to be positioned properly. Retain the forward pressure on the crankshaft. Tighten the cap bolts to 65-81 ft. lbs.

11. Check the crankshaft end play with a dial indicator mounted on the front of the engine.

12. If the end play exceeds specification, replace the upper and lower thrust bearings. If the end play is less than specification, inspect the thrust bearing faces for damage, dirt or improper alignment. Install the thrust bearing and align the faces. Recheck the end play.

13. Install the new bearing inserts in the connecting rods and caps. Check the clearance of each bearing by using a piece of Plastigage®, refer to the "Bearing Oil Clearance" section in this chapter.

14. If the bearing clearances are to specification, apply a light coat of Oil Conditioner part No. D9AZ-19579-C or heavy engine oil, SAE 50 weight, to the journals and bearings.

15. Turn the crankshaft throw to the bottom of the stroke. Push the piston all the way down until the rod bearings seat on the crankshaft journal.

16. Install the connecting rod cap.

17. After the piston and connecting rod assemblies have been installed, check all the connecting rod crankshaft journal clearances using a piece of Plastigage®, refer to the "Bearing Oil Clearance" in this section.

18. Turn the engine on the work stand so that the front end is up. Install the timing chain, sprockets, front cover, new oil seal and crankshaft pulley. Turn the engine on the work stand so that the rear end is up. Install the rear oil seal.

19. Clean the oil pan, oil pump and the oil pump screen assembly.

20. Prime the oil pump by filling the inlet opening with oil and rotating the pump shaft until the oil emerges from the outlet opening. Install the oil pump, baffle and oil pan.

21. Position the flywheel on the crankshaft. Tighten to 54-64 ft lbs.

22. Turn the engine on work stand so that the engine is in the normal upright position. Install the accessory drive pulley. Install and adjust the accessory drive belts to specification.

23. Install the ATX torque converter.

24. Remove the engine from the work stand. Install the engine in the vehicle.

3.8L Engine

NOTE: *If the bearings are to be reused they should be identified to ensure that they are installed in their original positions.*

1. Remove the engine from the vehicle and mount on a suitable workstand. Refer to the "Engine Assembly" removal and installation procedures in this chapter.

2. Remove the oil pan and oil pickup tube.

3. Remove the front cover and water pump as an assembly.

4. Remove the distributor drive gear, timing chain assembly, and flywheel.

5. Remove the connecting rod bearing nuts and caps. Identify each bearing cap to insure that they are installed in their original positions. Push the pistons up into the cylinder and put pieces of rubber hose on the connecting rod bolts so the crankshaft journals do not get damaged.

6. Inspect all the machined surfaces on the crankshaft for nicks, scratches, scores, etc., which could cause premature bearing wear.

WARNING: *Because the engine crankshaft incorporates deep rolling of the main journal fillets, journal refinishing is limited to 0.25mm undersize. Further refinishing may result in fatigue failure of the crankshaft.*

Ensure the bearing inserts and the bearing bores are clean. Foreign material under the inserts will distort the bearing and cause a failure.

7. Remove the main bearing caps and identify each bearing cap to insure that they are installed in their original positions.

8. Carefully lift the crankshaft out of the block to prevent damage to bearing surfaces.

To install:

1. Make sure all crankshaft bearing journals and bearing caps are clean. Contaminants under a bearing will cause distortion. Contaminants on the bearing surface will cause damage to the bearing journals.

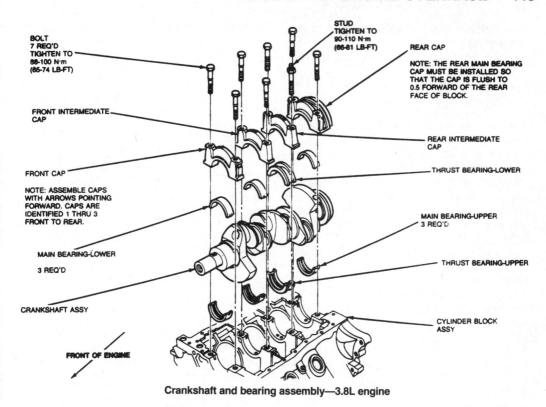

Crankshaft and bearing assembly—3.8L engine

2. If the crankshaft journals have been refinished to a definite undersize, make sure the proper undersize is being used.

3. Install the used main bearings to their original positions. If using new ones, install the tabs on the bearings into the slots in the cap and the block.

4. Carefully lower crankshaft into position in the cylinder block. Be careful not to damage the thrust bearing surfaces.

5. Apply a 3mm bead of Silicone Sealer part No. D6AZ-19562-A or equivalent to the rear main bearing cap-to-cylinder block parting line.

6. Lubricate the bearing surfaces and journals with Oil Conditioner part No. D9AZ-19579-CF or equivalent heavy engine oil 50 SAE weight.

7. Install the main bearing caps in the proper direction. Torque the bolts to the proper specifications, 65-81 ft. lbs.

8. If the end play exceeds specification, replace the upper and lower thrust bearings. If the end play is less than specification, inspect the thrust bearing faces for damage, dirt or improper alignment. Install the thrust bearing and align the faces. Recheck the end play.

9. Install the used connecting rod bearings to their original positions. If using new ones, install the tabs on the bearings into the slots in the cap and the rod.

10. Rotate the crankshaft as necessary to bring each throw to the lowest point of travel. Pull the piston downward until the connecting rod seats on the crank throw. Install the rod caps and torque to specification, 31-36 ft. lbs.

11. Install the timing chain assembly, distributor gear, oil pan, rear cover and flywheel, and spark plugs.

12. Install the engine in the vehicle.

3.0L SHO Engine

The engine does not have to be removed to replace the crankshaft. But the job will be much easier if the engine is removed from the vehicle. The following procedures describe the removal procedure when the engine remains in the vehicle. If your wish to remove the engine assembly, refer to the "Engine Assembly" removal and installation procedures in this chapter.

1. Disconnect the negative (−) battery cable.

2. Raise the vehicle and support with jackstands.

3. Remove the sub-frame assembly as outlined below.

    a. Install the Engine Support Tool No. D87L-6000-A or equivalent to the existing engine lifting eyes.

    b. Remove the front wheels and tire assemblies.

    c. Support the steering gear with wire

from the tie rod end to coil spring to hold the steering gear in position.

d. Disconnect the exhaust system at the flex coupling and drop it down.

e. Remove the two nuts attaching the steering gear to No. 2 crossmember.

f. Remove the attaching nuts from the RH front engine mount and RH rear engine mount-to-sub-frame.

g. Remove the stabilizer bar link attachment at the through bolts at the sub-frame.

h. Support the sub-frame with adjustable jacks at the sub-frame body mount location points.

i. Remove the four body mount attaching bolts.

j. With an assistant, lower the adjustable jacks and allow the sub-frame to lower. Rotate the front of the sub-frame down and pick up the rear of the sub-frame off of the exhaust pipe. Work the sub-frame rearward until it can be lowered down past the exhaust pipe.

4. Remove the transaxle assembly. Refer to the "Transaxle MTX" removal and installation procedure in chapter 7.

5. Remove the clutch cover, disc and frywheel assemblies.

6. Remove the oil pan as outlined in the "Oil Pan" removal and installation procedures in this chapter.

7. Remove the oil baffle plate and oil pick-up tube.

8. Remove the oil seal carrier.

9. Remove the oil pump and the main bearing support beam.

10. Remove the connecting rod nuts, rod caps, and note the cap position for installation.

11. Loosen the main bearing bolts. Note the numerical order and that numbers on the caps point forward. Loosen the caps uniformly from the innermost bearing outward.

12. Remove all the bearing caps but one. With an assistant, support the crankshaft and re-

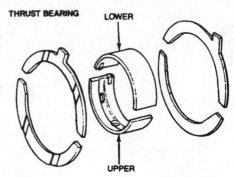

Thrust bearing positioning—3.0L SHO engine

move the remaining bearing cap. Lower the crankshaft out of the engine.

To install:

1. Inspect the bearing journals and bearing faces for any damage prior to assembly.

2. Press the bearing upper halves into the cylinder block. Make sure the bearing is fully installed in the bearing seat.

3. Lubricate the bearing surfaces and journals with assembly lube or heavy weight engine oil. Install the bearings into the lower main caps.

4. With an assistant, install the crankshaft into the cylinder block and loosely install the No. 1 and 4 bearing caps.

NOTE: *The arrows on the bearing caps always face forward (towards passenger fender). The numbers on the bearing caps go from No. 1 to 4, from front to rear.*

5. Install the upper thrust bearings on the front and rear on the No. 3 bearing journal by moving the crankshaft back and forth.

NOTE: *The oil groove on the thrust bearing should face the crankshaft.*

6. Install the lower thrust bearing the with No. 3 main cap. Install the No. 2 main cap.

7. Apply a coat of engine oil to the bearing cap bolts and tighten in sequence shown in the following illustration.

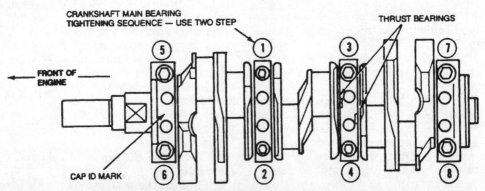

Crankshaft main bearing cap torquing sequence—3.0L SHO engine

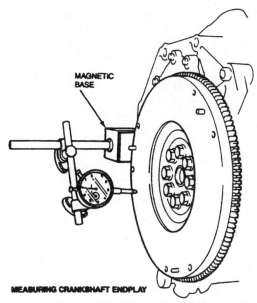

Checking crankshaft endplay—3.0L SHO engine

8. Torque the main bearing caps in a two step sequence, the first step to 36-51 ft. lbs., and the second step to 58-64 ft. lbs.

9. Check to make sure the crankshaft turns freely.

10. Check the crankshaft end play by installing a dial indicator to the end on the crankshaft flywheel. The measurement should be between 0.02-0.22mm. If this measurement is NOT within specifications, the thrust bearing will have to be sized.

11. Install the connecting rod and piston assemblies using a piston ring compressor. Install the connecting rod bearing caps and nuts. Torque the nuts in a two step method to 22-26 ft. lbs., and to 33-36 ft. lbs. for the second step.

12. Install the main bearing support bean and torque the nuts to 11-17 ft. lbs.

13. Install the oil seal carrier with a new gasket. Torque the bolts to 55-82 in. lbs.

14. Install the oil pump with a new gasket and torque the bolts to 11-17 ft. lbs.

15. Replace the front crankshaft oil seal. Refer to the "Front Oil Seal" removal and installation procedures in this chapter.

16. Install a new rear crankshaft oil seal by using a Seal Starter tool No. T81P-6701-A and a Seal Installer tool No. T89P-6701-C or equivalent.

17. Install the oil pickup with a new gasket and torque the bolts to 60-90 in. lbs. and to 15-24 ft. lbs. for the pickup nuts.

18. Clean the oil pan sealing surfaces. Apply a 5mm bead of Silicone Sealer No. D6AZ-19562-B or equivalent to the sealing surface. Install a new pan end gasket and install the oil pan to the block. Torque the oil pan bolts to 11-17 ft. lbs.

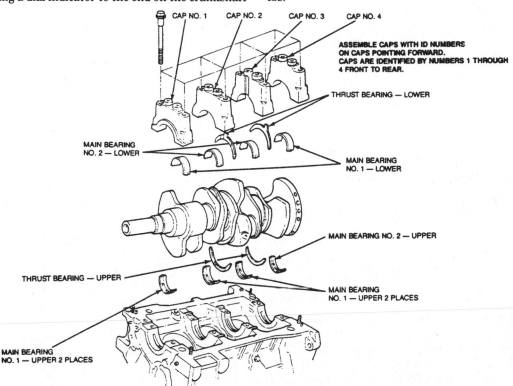

Crankshaft and bearing assembly—3.0L SHO engine

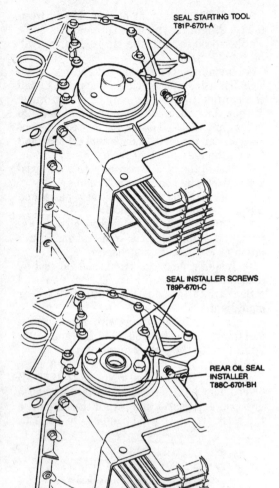

Installing the rear crankshaft main seal—3.0L SHO engine

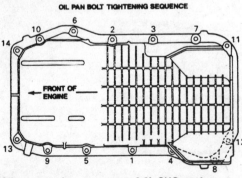

Oil pan torquing sequence—3.0L SHO engine

19. Install the flywheel and torque the bolts in a three step method.

1. 29-43 ft. lbs.
2. 43-48 ft. lbs.
3. 51-58 ft. lbs.

20. Align the clutch disc and pressure plate on to the flywheel. Torque the clutch assembly-to-flywheel attaching bolts to 12-24 ft. lbs.

21. Install the transaxle, sub-frame, and lower the vehicle.

22. Fill the engine with specified engine oil. Connect the negative (−) battery cable, and start the engine and check for leaks.

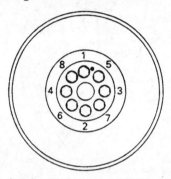

Flywheel torquing sequence—3.0L SHO engine

BEARING OIL CLEARANCE

Remove the cap from the bearing to be checked. Using a clean, dry rag, thoroughly clean all oil from the crankshaft journal and bearing insert.

NOTE: *Plastigage® is soluble in oil, therefore, oil on the journal or bearing could result in erroneous readings.*

Place a piece of Plastigage® along the full width of the bearing insert, reinstall cap, and torque to specifications.

NOTE: *Specifications are given in the engine specifications earlier in this chapter.*

Remove the bearing cap, and determine bearing clearance by comparing width of the bearing insert, reinstall cap, and torque to specifications.

NOTE: *Do not rotate crankshaft with Plastigage® installed. If the bearing insert and journal appear intact, and are within tolerances, no further main bearing service is required. If the bearing or journal appear defec-*

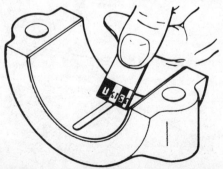

Measure the Plastigage® to determine bearing clearance

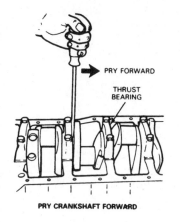
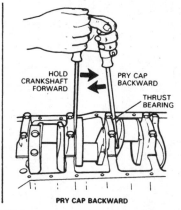
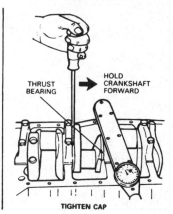

Aligning the thrust bearing—3.0L engine

tive, cause of failure should be determined before replacement.

CRANKSHAFT ENDPLAY/CONNECTING ROD SIDE PLAY

Place a pry bar between a main bearing cap and crankshaft casting taking care not to damage any journals. Pry backward and forward, measure the distance between the thrust bearing and crankshaft with a feeler gauge. Compare reading with specifications, 0.10-0.20mm. If too great a clearance is determined, a main bearing with a larger thrust surface or crank machining may be required. Check with an automotive machine shop for their advice.

Connecting rod clearance between the rod and crank throw casting can be checked with a feeler gauge. Pry the rod carefully on one side as far as possible and measure the distance on the other side of the rod. Check the crankshaft and connecting rod specification table.

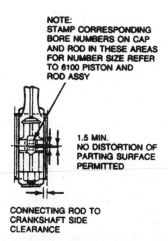

NOTE:
STAMP CORRESPONDING BORE NUMBERS ON CAP AND ROD IN THESE AREAS FOR NUMBER SIZE REFER TO 6100 PISTON AND ROD ASSY

1.5 MIN.
NO DISTORTION OF PARTING SURFACE PERMITTED

CONNECTING ROD TO CRANKSHAFT SIDE CLEARANCE

Connecting rod to crankshaft side clearance

CRANKSHAFT REPAIRS

If a journal is damaged on the crankshaft, repair is possible by having the crankshaft machined to a standard undersize.

In most cases, however, since the engine must be removed from the car and disassembled, some thought should be given to replacing the damaged crankshaft with a reground shaft kit. A reground crankshaft kit contains the necessary main and rod bearings for installation. The shaft has been ground and polished to undersize specifications and will usually hold up well if installed correctly.

Rear Main Bearing Oil Seal
REMOVAL AND INSTALLATION
2.5L Engine

1. Remove the transaxle.
2. Remove the flywheel.
3. Remove the rear cover plate.
4. With a sharp awl, punch a hole into the seal metal surface between the lip and retainer. Screw in threaded end of Slide Hammer T77L-9533-B or equivalent. Remove the seal.
NOTE: *Use caution to avoid damaging the oil seal surface.*
To install:
NOTE: *Inspect the crankshaft flange seal area for any damage which may cause the seal to leak. If damage is evident, service the crankshaft flange or replace the crankshaft as necessary.*
1. Coat the crankshaft seal area and the seal lip with engine oil.
2. Using Seal Installer T81P-6701-A or equivalent, install the rear seal.
3. Install the rear cover plate and two dowels.

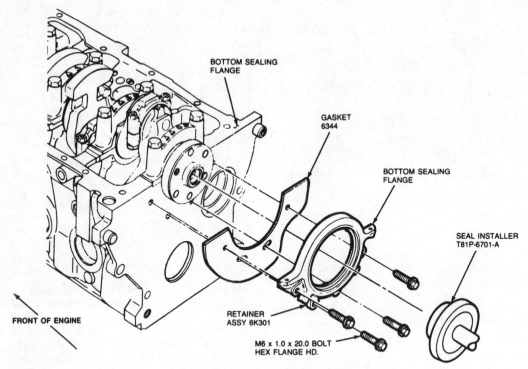

Rear main bearing oil seal—2.5L engine

4. Install the flywheel. Tighten attaching bolts to 54-64 ft. lbs.

5. Install the transaxle.

3.0L Engine

1. Using a sharp awl, punch one hole into the seal metal surface between the lip and block.

2. Screw in the threaded end of Slide Hammer Tool T77L-9533-B or equivalent.

3. Use the slide hammer to remove seal. Use caution to avoid scratching or damaging oil seal surface.

NOTE: *Use caution to avoid damaging the oil seal surface.*

To install:

NOTE: *Inspect the crankshaft flange seal*

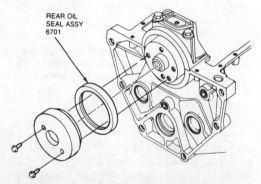

Rear main bearing oil seal—3.0L engine

area for any damage which may cause the seal to leak. If damage is evident, service the crankshaft flange or replace the crankshaft as necessary.

1. Coat the crankshaft seal area and the seal lip with engine oil.

2. Position the seal on the Rear Main Seal Installer T82L-6701-A or equivalent.

3. Position the tool and seal to rear of engine.

4. Alternate the bolt tightening to seat the seal properly. (Two bolts are supplied with Rear Main Seal Installer T82L-6701-A. The engine flywheel bolts may be used if necessary.

3.8L Engine

1. Remove the transaxle.

2. Remove the flywheel.

3. Remove the rear cover plate.

4. With a sharp awl, punch a hole into the seal metal surface between the lip and retainer. Screw in threaded end of Slide Hammer T77L-9533-B or equivalent. Remove the seal.

NOTE: *Use caution to avoid damaging the oil seal surface.*

To install:

NOTE: *Inspect the crankshaft flange seal area for any damage which may cause the seal to leak. If damage is evident, service the crankshaft flange or replace the crankshaft as necessary.*

1. Coat the crankshaft seal area and the seal lip with engine oil.

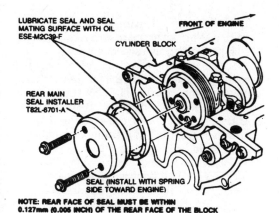

LUBRICATE SEAL AND SEAL
MATING SURFACE WITH OIL
ESE-M2C39-F

FRONT OF ENGINE

CYLINDER BLOCK

REAR MAIN
SEAL INSTALLER
T82L-6701-A

REAR MAIN
SEAL INSTALLER
T82L-6701-A

SEAL (INSTALL WITH SPRING
SIDE TOWARD ENGINE)

NOTE: REAR FACE OF SEAL MUST BE WITHIN
0.127mm (0.005 INCH) OF THE REAR FACE OF THE BLOCK

Rear main bearing oil seal—3.8L engine

2. Position the Rear Main Seal Installer part No. T81L-6701-A or equivalent. Position the tool and seal to the rear of the engine. Tighten the installer bolts to seat the seal evenly.

3. Install the flywheel, cover plate, and transaxle.

3.0L SHO Engine

1. Disconnect the negative (−) battery cable.

2. Remove the transaxle assembly as outlined in the "Transaxle MTX" removal and installation procedures in chapter 7.

3. Remove the oil pan assembly as outlined in the "Oil Pan" removal and installation procedures in this chapter.

4. Remove the nine oil seal carrier-to-cylinder block and the seal carrier.

5. **To install:** install the oil seal carrier with a new gasket. Install the attaching bolts and torque to 55-82 in. lbs.

6. Install the oil pan and transaxle assemblies. Fill the engine with the specified engine oil. Start the engine and check for oil leaks.

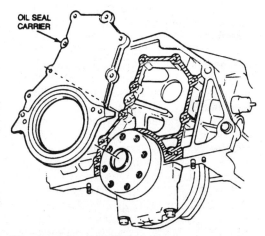

OIL SEAL
CARRIER

Oil seal carrier—3.0L SHO engine

COMPLETING THE REBUILDING PROCESS

Fill the oil pump with oil, to prevent cavitating (sucking air) on initial engine start up. Install the oil pump and the pickup tube on the engine. Coat the oil pan gasket as necessary, and install the gasket and the oil pan. Mount the flywheel and the crankshaft vibration damper or pulley on the crankshaft.

NOTE: *Always use new bolts when installing the flywheel. Inspect the clutch shaft pilot bushing in the crankshaft. If the bushing is excessively worn, remove it with an expanding puller and a slide hammer, and tap a new bushing into place.*

Position the engine, cylinder head side up. Lubricate the lifters, and install them into their bores. Install the cylinder head, and torque it as specified. Insert the pushrods (where applicable), and install the rocker shaft(s) (if so equipped) or position the rocker.

Install the intake and exhaust manifolds, the carburetor(s), the distributor and spark plugs. Mount all accessories and install the engine in the car. Fill the radiator with coolant, and the crankcase with high quality engine oil.

BREAK-IN PROCEDURE

Start the engine, and allow it to run at low speed for a few minutes, while checking for leaks. Stop the engine, check the oil level, and fill as necessary. Restart the engine, and fill the cooling system to capacity. Check and adjust the ignition timing. Run the engine at low to medium speed (800-2,500 rpm) for approximately ½ hour, and retorque the cylinder head bolts. Road test the car, and check again for leaks.

NOTE: *Some gasket manufacturers recommend not retorquing the cylinder head(s) due to the composition of the head gasket. Follow the directions in the gasket set.*

Flywheel/Flex Plate
REMOVAL AND INSTALLATION

1. Remove the transaxle.

2. Remove the flywheel/flex plate attaching bolts and the flywheel.

3. The rear cover plate can be removed (manual transmission only).

To install:

NOTE: *All major rotating components including the flex plate/flywheel are individually balance to zero. Engine assembly balancing is not required. Balance weights should NOT be installed on new flywheels.*

1. Install the rear cover plate, if removed.

2. Position the flywheel on the crankshaft and install the attaching bolts. Tighten the at-

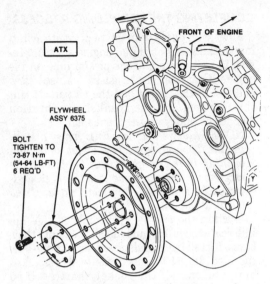

Flywheel/Flexplate assembly—3.0L engine

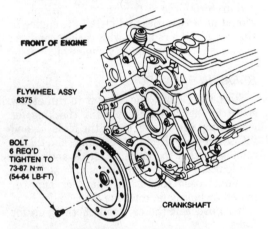

Flywheel/flexplate assembly—3.8L engine

taching bolts to 54-64 ft. lbs., using the standard cross-tightening sequence.

EXHAUST SYSTEM

Safety Precautions

For a number of reasons, exhaust system work can be the most dangerous type of work you can do on your car. Always observe the following precautions:

• Support the car extra securely. Not only will you often be working directly under it, but you'll frequently be using a lot of force, say, heavy hammer blows, to dislodge rusted parts. This can cause a car that's improperly supported to shift and possibly fall.

• Wear goggles. Exhaust system parts are always rusty. Metal chips can be dislodged, even when you're only turning rusted bolts. Attempting to pry pipes apart with a chisel makes the chips fly even more frequently.

• If you're using a cutting torch, keep it a great distance from either the fuel tank or lines. Stop what you're doing and feel the temperature of the fuel bearing pipes on the tank frequently. Even slight heat can expand and/or vaporize fuel, resulting in accumulated vapor, or even a liquid leak, near your torch.

• Watch where your hammer blows fall and make sure you hit squarely. You could easily tap a brake or fuel line when you hit an exhaust system part with a glancing blow. Inspect all lines and hoses in the area where you've been working.

CAUTION: *Be very careful when working on or near the catalytic converter. External temperatures can reach 1,500°F (816°C) and more, causing severe burns. Removal or installation should be performed only on a cold exhaust system.*

Special Tools

A number of special exhaust system tools can be rented from auto supply houses or local stores that rent special equipment. A common one is a tail pipe expander, designed to enable you to join pipes of identical diameter.

It may also be quite helpful to use solvents designed to loosen rusted bolts or flanges. Soaking rusted parts the night before you do the job can speed the work of freeing rusted parts considerably. Remember that these solvents are often flammable. Apply only to parts after they are cool!

Inspect inlet pipes, outlet pipes and mufflers for cracked joints, broken welds and corrosion damage that would result in a leaking exhaust system. It is normal for a certain amount of moisture and staining to be present around the muffler seams. The presence of soot, light surface rust or moisture does not indicate a faulty muffler. Inspect the clamps, brackets and insulators for cracks and stripped or badly corroded bolt threads. When flat joints are loosened and/or disconnected to replace a shield pipe or muffler, replace the bolts and flange nuts if there is reasonable doubt that its service life is limited.

The exhaust system, including brush shields, must be free of leaks, binding, grounding and excessive vibrations. These conditions are usually caused by loose or broken flange bolts, shields, brackets or pipes. If any of these conditions exist, check the exhaust system components and alignment. Align or replace as necessary. Brush shields are positioned on the underside of the catalytic converter and should be free from bends which would bring any part of

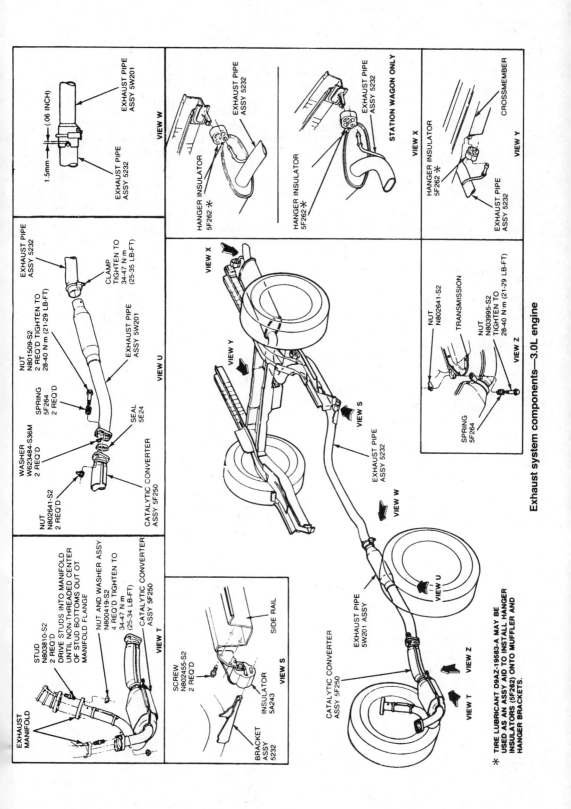

EXHAUST PIPE
ASSY 5W201

1.5mm

(.06 INCH)

EXHAUST PIPE
ASSY 5232

VIEW W

HANGER INSULATOR
5F262 *

EXHAUST PIPE
ASSY 5232

EXHAUST PIPE
ASSY 5232

HANGER INSULATOR
5F262 *

STATION WAGON ONLY

VIEW X

HANGER INSULATOR
5F262 *

CROSSMEMBER

EXHAUST PIPE
ASSY 5232

VIEW Y

EXHAUST PIPE
ASSY 5232

CLAMP
TIGHTEN TO
34-47 N·m
(25-35 LB-FT)

NUT
N801509-S2
2 REQ'D TIGHTEN TO
28-40 N·m (21-29 LB-FT)

EXHAUST PIPE
ASSY 5W201

SPRING
5F264
2 REQ'D

WASHER
W623484-S36M
2 REQ'D

SEAL
5E24

NUT
N802641-S2
2 REQ'D

CATALYTIC CONVERTER
ASSY 5F250

VIEW U

NUT
N802641-S2

TRANSMISSION

NUT
N803995-S2
TIGHTEN TO
28-40 N·m (21-29 LB-FT)

VIEW Z

SPRING
5F264

VIEW X

VIEW Y

VIEW S

EXHAUST PIPE
ASSY 5232

VIEW W

EXHAUST PIPE
ASSY 5232

VIEW U

CATALYTIC CONVERTER
ASSY 5F250

EXHAUST PIPE
5W201 ASSY

VIEW T   **VIEW Z**

STUD
N803810-S2
2 REQ'D

DRIVE STUDS INTO MANIFOLD
UNTIL NON-THREADED CENTER
OF STUD BOTTOMS OUT OT
MANIFOLD FLANGE

NUT AND WASHER ASSY
N800419-S2
4 REQ'D TIGHTEN TO
34-47 N·m
(25-34 LB-FT)

CATALYTIC CONVERTER
ASSY 5F250

VIEW T

EXHAUST
MANIFOLD

SCREW
N802455-S2
2 REQ'D

INSULATOR
5A243

SIDE RAIL

BRACKET
ASSY
5232

VIEW S

Exhaust system components—3.0L engine

* TIRE LUBRICANT D9AZ-19583-A MAY BE
USED AS AN ASSY AID TO INSTALL HANGER
INSULATORS (5F262) ONTO MUFFLER AND
HANGER BRACKETS.

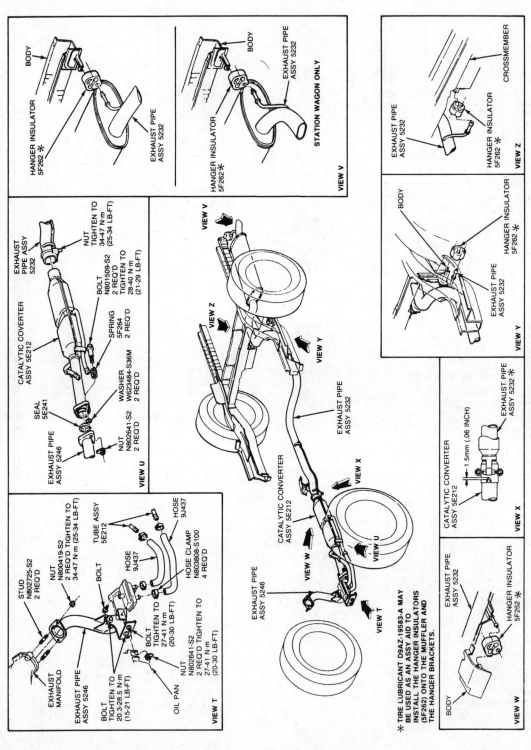

BODY

HANGER INSULATOR
5F262 *

EXHAUST PIPE
ASSY 5232

BODY

EXHAUST PIPE
ASSY 5232

HANGER INSULATOR
5F262 *

STATION WAGON ONLY

VIEW V

CROSSMEMBER

EXHAUST PIPE
ASSY 5232

HANGER INSULATOR
5F262 *

VIEW Z

CATALYTIC COVERTER
ASSY 5E212

EXHAUST
PIPE ASSY
5232

NUT
TIGHTEN TO
34-47 N·m
(25-34 LB-FT)

BOLT
N801509-S2
2 REQ'D
TIGHTEN TO
28-40 N·m
(21-29 LB-FT)

SPRING
5F264
2 REQ'D

SEAL
5E241

WASHER
W623484-S36M
2 REQ'D

EXHAUST PIPE
ASSY 5246

NUT
N802641-S2
2 REQ'D

VIEW U

VIEW V

VIEW Z

VIEW Y

EXHAUST PIPE
ASSY 5232

CATALYTIC CONVERTER
ASSY 5E212

EXHAUST PIPE
ASSY 5246

VIEW X

VIEW U

VIEW W

VIEW T

BODY

EXHAUST PIPE
ASSY 5232

HANGER INSULATOR
5F262 *

VIEW Y

STUD
N802725-S2
2 REQ'D

NUT
N800419-S2
2 REQ'D TIGHTEN TO
34-47 N·m (25-34 LB-FT)

BOLT

HOSE
9J437

HOSE
9J437

TUBE ASSY
5E212

HOSE CLAMP
N800808-S100
4 REQ'D

EXHAUST
MANIFOLD

EXHAUST PIPE
ASSY 5246

BOLT
TIGHTEN TO
20.3-28.5 N·m
(15-21 LB-FT)

BOLT
TIGHTEN TO
27-41 N·m
(20-30 LB-FT)

NUT
N802641-S2
2 REQ'D TIGHTEN TO
27-41 N·m
(20-30 LB-FT)

OIL PAN

VIEW T

* TIRE LUBRICANT D9AZ-19583-A MAY
BE USED AS AN ASSY AID TO
INSTALL THE HANGER INSULATORS
(5F262) ONTO THE MUFFLER AND
THE HANGER BRACKETS.

CATALYTIC CONVERTER
ASSY 5E212

1.5mm (.06 INCH)

EXHAUST PIPE
ASSY 5232 *

VIEW X

EXHAUST PIPE
ASSY 5232

HANGER INSULATOR
5F262 *

BODY

VIEW W

Exhaust system components—2.5L engine

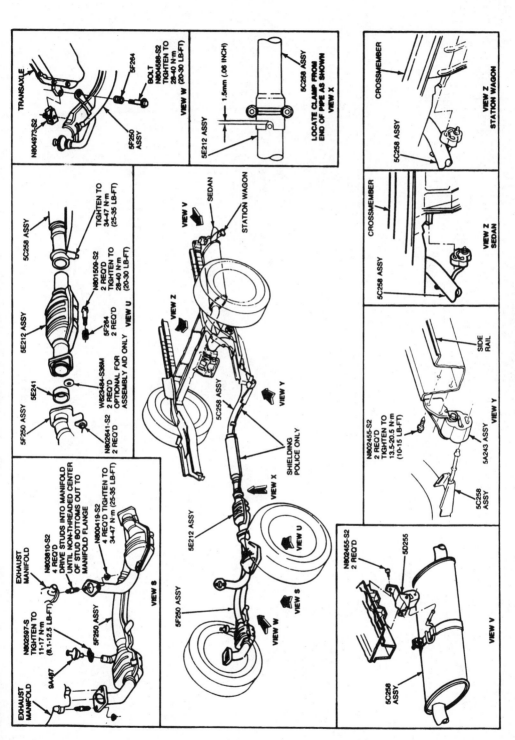

Exhaust system components—3.8L Taurus/Sable

TRANSAXLE

J-NUT
N804973-S2

5F250
ASSY

SPRING
5F264

BOLT
N804588-S2
TIGHTEN TO
28-40 N·m
(21-30 LB-FT)

VIEW S

VIEW U

PIPE
5E212

0.0
1.5

5C258 ASSY

LOCATE CLAMP FROM
END OF PIPE AS SHOWN

VIEW T

5F262

MUFFLER
5C258
ASSY

BODY

VIEW U

BOLT
N802455-S2
2 REQ'D
TIGHTEN TO
13.5-20.5 N·m
(10-15 LB-FT)

SIDE
RAIL

5A243

5C258
ASSY

VIEW V

BODY

PIPE
5C258

5F262

VIEW W

VIEW U

VIEW W

VIEW V

PIPE ASSY
5C258

CATALYTIC
CONVERTER
5E212 ASSY

PIPE ASSY
5F250

VIEW T

VIEW X

VIEW Y

VIEW S

VIEW Y

STUD
N803810-S2
4 REQ'D
DRIVE STUDS INTO MANIFOLD UNTIL
NON THREADED CENTER OF STUD
BOTTOMS OUT TO MANIFOLD FLANGE

NUT
N800419-S2
4 REQ'D
TIGHTEN TO
34-47 N·m
(25-35 LB-FT)

EXHAUST
MANIFOLD

5F250 ASSY

VIEW Y

EXHAUST
MANIFOLD

N802597-S
TIGHTEN TO
11-17 N·m
(8-12 LB-FT)

CONVERTER ASSY
5C258 ASSY

NUT
TIGHTEN TO
34-47 N·m
(25-35 LB-FT)

BOLT
N801509-S2
2 REQ'D
TIGHTEN TO
28-40 N·m
(20-30 LB-FT)

5E212

SPRING
5F264
2 REQ'D

WASHER
W623484-S36M
2 REQ'D
OPTIONAL FOR
ASSEMBLY AID ONLY

5E241

NUT
N802641-S2
2 REQ'D

VIEW X

Exhaust system components—3.8L Continental

the shield in contact with the catalytic converter or muffler. The shield should also be clear of any combustible material such as dried grass or leaves.

Coat all of the exhaust connections and bolt threads with anti-seize compound to prevent corrosion from making the next disassembly difficult.

REMOVAL AND INSTALLATION

2.5L Engine

1. Raise the vehicle and support on jackstands.
2. Remove the U-bolt assembly and the rubber insulators from the hanger brackets and remove the muffler assembly. Slide the muffler assembly toward the rear of the car to disconnect it from the converter.
3. Replace parts as needed.
4. Position the muffler assembly under the car and slide it forward onto the converter outlet pipe. Check that the slot in the muffler and the tab on the converter are fully engaged.
5. Install the rubber insulators on the hanger assemblies. Install the U-bolt and tighten. Be careful not to over-tighten the U-bolt.
6. Check the system for leaks. Lower the vehicle.

3.0L and 3.0L SHO Engines

1. Raise the vehicle and support on jackstands.
2. Remove the U-bolt assembly and the rubber insulators from the hanger brackets and remove the muffler assembly. Slide the muffler assembly toward the rear of the car to disconnect it from the resonator.
3. Replace parts as needed.
4. Position the muffler assembly under the car and slide it forward onto the converter outlet pipe. Check that the slot in the muffler and the tab on the converter are fully engaged.
5. Install the rubber insulators on the hanger assemblies. Install the U-bolt and tighten. Be careful not to over-tighten the U-bolts.
6. Check the system for leaks. Lower the vehicle.

3.8L Engine

1. Raise the vehicle and support on jackstands.
2. Remove the U-bolt assembly and the rubber insulators from the hanger brackets and remove the muffler assembly. Slide the muffler

assembly toward the rear of the car to disconnect it from the resonator.
3. Replace parts as needed.
4. Position the muffler assembly under the car and slide it forward onto the converter outlet pipe. Check that the slot in the muffler and the tab on the converter are fully engaged.
5. Install the rubber insulators on the hanger assemblies. Install the U-bolt and tighten. Be careful not to over-tighten the U-bolts.
6. Check the system for leaks. Lower the vehicle.

Catalytic Converter and/or Pipe Assembly

REMOVAL AND INSTALLATION

2.5L Engine

1. Raise the vehicle and support on jackstands.
2. Remove the front catalytic converter flange fasteners at the flex joint and discard the flex joint gasket, remove the rear U-bolt connection.
3. Separate the catalytic converter inlet and outlet connections. Remove the converter.
4. Install the converter to the muffler. Install a new flex joint gasket.
5. Install the converter and muffler assembly to the inlet pipe/flex joint. Connect the air hoses and position the U-bolt.
6. Align the exhaust system into position and, starting at the front of the system, tighten all the nuts and bolts.
7. Check the system for leaks. Lower the vehicle.

3.0L and 3.8L Engines

1. Raise the vehicle and support on jackstands.
2. Remove the front and rear catalytic converter flange fasteners, and the bolt and spring attachments at the transmission.
3. Separate the catalytic converter inlet and outlet connections. Remove the converter.
4. Loosely install the converter to the resonator.
5. Install the converter and resonator assembly to the manifold connection. Install the bolt and spring to the converter and the transmission.
6. Align the exhaust system into position and, starting at the front of the system, tighten all the nuts and bolts.
7. Check the system for leaks. Lower the vehicle.

Emission Controls

EMISSION CONTROLS

There are three basic sources of automotive pollution in the modern internal combustion engine. They are the crankcase with its accompanying blow-by vapors, the fuel system with its evaporation of unburned gasoline and the combustion chambers with their resulting exhaust emissions. Pollution arising from the incomplete combustion of fuel generally falls into three categories: hydrocarbons (HC) (unburned fuel), carbon monoxide (CO) and oxides of nitrogen (NOx).

The engines are equipped with an air pump system, positive crankcase ventilation, exhaust gas recirculation, electronic ignition, catalytic converter, thermostatically controlled air cleaner, or an evaporative emissions system depending on the model. Electronic engine controls are used on various engines, depending on model and year.

The belt driven air pump injects clean air either into the exhaust manifold, or downstream into the catalytic converter, depending on engine conditions. The oxygen contained in the injected air, supports continued combustion of the hot carbon monoxide (CO) and hydrocarbon (HC) gases, reducing their release into the atmosphere.

No external PCV valve is necessary on the Taurus/Sable and Continental PCV system. Instead, an internal baffle and an orifice control the flow of crankcase gases.

The back pressure modulated EGR valve is mounted next to the upper intake manifold. Vacuum applied to the EGR diaphragm raises the pindle valve from its seat, allowing hot exhaust gases to be drawn into the intake manifold with the intake charge. The exhaust gases reduce peak combustion temperature; lower temperatures reduce the formation of oxides of nitrogen (NOx).

The dual brick catalytic converter is mounted in the exhaust system, ahead of the muffler. Catalytic converters use noble metals (platinum, palladium, and rhodium) and great heat — 1,200°F (650°C) — to catalytically oxidize HC and CO gases into H_2O and CO_2. The Thermactor system is used as a fresh air (and therefore, oxygen) supply.

The thermostatically controlled air cleaner housing is able to draw fresh air from two sources: cool air from outside the car (behind the grille), or warm air obtained from a heat stove encircling the exhaust manifold. A warm air supply is desirable during cold engine operation. Because it promotes better atomization of the air/fuel mixture, while cool air promotes better combustion in a hot engine.

Instead of venting gasoline vapors from the carburetor float bowl or fuel tank into the atmosphere, an evaporative emission system captures the vapors and stores them in a charcoal filled canister, located ahead of the left front wheel arch. When the engine is running, a purge control solenoid allows fresh air to be drawn through the canister. The fresh air and vapors are then routed to the carburetor or fuel injection system, to be mixed with the intake charge.

Thermactor Air Pump System
OPERATION

A typical air injection system consists of an air supply pump and centrifugal filter, an air bypass valve, check valve, air manifold and air hoses.

Simply, the air pump injects air into the engine which reduces the hydrocarbon and carbon monoxide content of exhaust gases by continuing the combustion of the unburned gases after they leave the combustion chamber. Fresh air mixed with the hot exhaust gases promotes further oxidation of both the hydrocarbons and carbon monoxide, thereby reducing their concentration and converting some of them into harmless carbon dioxide and water.

The Taurus/Sable and Continental (except 3.0L SHO) use an 11 cubic inch Thermactor Air Supply Pump. Air for the system is cleaned by means of a remote filter attached to the air inlet nipple.

To prevent excessive pressure, the air pump is equipped with a pressure relief valve.

The air pump has sealed bearings which are lubricated for the life of the unit, and preset rotor vane adjust bearing clearances, which do not require any periodic adjustments.

The air supply from the pump is controlled by the air by-pass valve, sometimes a dump valve. During deceleration, the air by-pass valve opens, momentarily diverting the air supply into the atmosphere, thus preventing backfires within the exhaust system.

A check valve is incorporated in the air inlet side of the air manifold. It purpose is to prevent the exhaust gases from backing up into the system. The valve is especially important in the event of drive belt failure and during deceleration, when the air by-pass valve is dumping the air supply. The air manifold channels the air from the pump into the exhaust thus completing the cycle of the Thermactor system.

Air Pump

REMOVAL AND INSTALLATION

2.5L and 3.8L Engines

1. The thermactor pump is mounted on the right rear (passenger side) of the engine

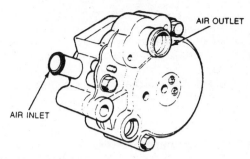

Thermactor (air) pump

2. Loosen the drive belt tensioner and remove the belt.

3. Loosen the hose clamps on the air inlet and outlet. Remove the two hoses and move out of the way.

4. Remove the two pump bolts.

5. Remove the air pump from the vehicle.

6. **To install:** position the pump into the brackets, install the two bolts and torgue to 15-22 ft. lbs.

7. Install the drive belt and adjust to specifications.

3.0L Engine

1. The thermactor (air) pump is mounted on the right rear (passenger side) of the engine underneath the alternator.

2. Loosen the alternator and drive belt tensioners and remove the belts

3. Remove the alternator wire connectors, attaching bolts, and alternator.

4. Loosen the hose clamps on the air inlet and outlet. Remove the two hoses and move out of the way.

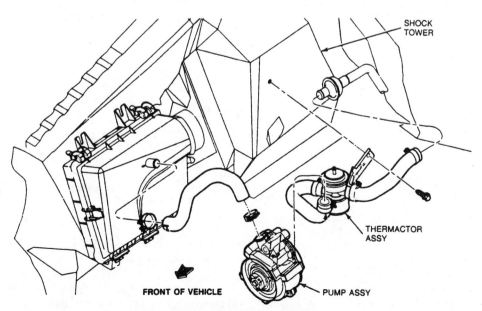

Thermactor (air) pump location

5. Remove the two pump bolts.

6. Remove the air pump from the vehicle.

7. **To install:** position the pump into the brackets, install the two bolts and torque to 15-22 ft. lbs.

8. Install the alternator, wire connectors, and tighten the two attaching bolts.

9. Install the drive belt first and then the alternator belt and adjust to specifications.

COMBINATION AIR BYPASS AIR CONTROL VALVE

The combination air bypass/air control valve combines the functions of the air bypass valve and air control valve into a single unit. Both the valves are normally closed.

Functional Test

1. Disconnect the two hoses that go to the engine or converter (outlet **A** and outlet **B**, see the illustration).

2. Disconnect and plug the vacuum line at port **D**.

3. With the engine operating at 1,500 rpm, air flow should be coming out of the bypass vents.

4. Reconnect the vacuum line to port **D**. Disconnect and plug the vacuum line to port **S**. Make sure vacuum is present at vacuum port **D**.

5. Operate the engine at 1,500 rpm, air flow should be detected at outlet B. No air flow should be at outlet **A**.

6. Use a hand vacuum pump and apply 8-10 in.Hg to port S. With the engine operating at 1,500 rpm, air flow should be noted coming out of outlet **A**.

7. Replace the combination valve if any of the tests indicate a problem.

CHECK VALVE

The check valve is a one way valve. Pressure at the inlet allows air to flow past a viton disc.

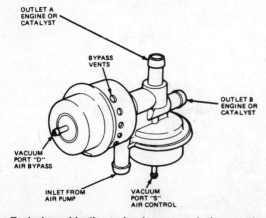

Typical combination valve bypass and air control valve

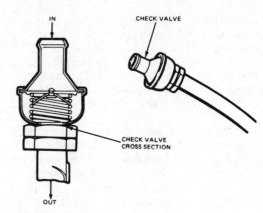

Typical air check valve

Vacuum at the outlet causes the reed to open, effecting one-way air flow in reed type valves. Air is prevented from passing through the valve if pressure at the outlet side of the valve is positive.

Functional Test

1. With the engine not running, disconnect the air supply at the pump side of the valve.

2. Blow through the check valve, toward the manifold, then attempt to suck back through the valve. Air should pass in the direction of the exhaust manifold only. Replace the valve if air flows both ways.

Positive Crankcase Ventilation
SYSTEM OPERATION

A small amount of the fuel/air mixture in each cylinder escapes from the combustion chamber around the piston rings and enters the engine's crankcase, above the oil level. Since this material has been cooled by the lubricating oil and metal parts well below burning temperature, it is only partially burned and constitutes a large source of pollution. The PCV system allows outside air to be drawn into the crankcase and to sweep this material back into the intake passages of the engine to be reburned before it either dirties the oil or escaped to the outside air. An internal baffle and an orifice control the flow of crankcase gases.

Exhaust Emission Control

All engines are equipped with a single muffler, a single catalytic converter and connecting pipes. The converter is of the dual brick type which uses both a three way catalyst and a conventional oxidation catalyst.

CONVERTER
REMOVAL AND INSTALLATION

1. Jack up the car and safely support it on jackstands. Refer to the "Exhaust System" section at the end of chapter 3.
2. Remove the front and rear converter mounting bolts. Separate the flange connections and remove the converter.
3. **To install:** align the flanges, install new gaskets and install the attaching bolts.
4. Align the exhaust system so that it won't rattle, and tighten the mounting bolts.
5. Remove the car from the jackstands.

Thermostatically Controlled Air Cleaner (Inlet Air Temperature System)

The air cleaner assembly intake duct is attached to a cold air intake as well as a heat shroud that surrounds the exhaust manifold. Air flow from these two sources is controlled by a door in the intake duct operated by a vacuum motor. The vacuum motor is controlled by a thermal sensor and a vacuum control system.

The Taurus/Sable equipped with the 2.5L engines have Inlet Air Temperature systems for cold weather operation. The Taurus/Sable and Continental 3.0L, 3.0L SHO, and 3.8L engines are not equipped with Inlet Air Temperature systems.

The thermal sensor is attached to the air valve actuating lever, along with the vacuum motor lever, both of which control the position of the air valve to supply either heated air from the exhaust manifold or cooler air from the engine compartment.

During the warm-up period, when the under-the-hood temperatures are low, the thermal sensor doesn't exert enough tension on the air valve actuating lever to close (heat off) the air valve. Thus, the throttle body receives heated air from around the exhaust manifold.

As the temperature of the air entering the air cleaner approaches approximately 110°F (43°C), the thermal sensor begins to push on the air valve actuating lever and overcome the spring tension which holds the air valve in the open (heat on) position. The air valve begins to move to the closed (heat off position, allowing only under-the-hood air to enter the air cleaner.

The air valve in the air cleaner will also open, regardless of the air temperature, during heavy acceleration to obtain maximum airflow through the air cleaner. The extreme decrease in intake manifold vacuum during heavy acceleration permits the vacuum motor to override the thermostatic control. This opens the system to both heated air and air from the engine compartment.

HEATED AIR INTAKE TEST

1. With the engine completely cold, look inside the cold air duct and make sure that the valve plate is fully in the up position (closing the cold air duct).
2. Start the engine and bring it to operating temperature.
3. Stop the engine and look inside the cold air duct again. The valve plate should be down, allowing an opening from the cold air duct into the air cleaner.
4. If the unit appears to be malfunctioning, remove it and examine it to make sure that the springs are not broken or disconnected, and re-

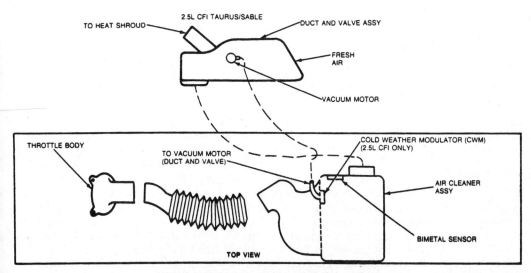

Inlet air temperature system—2.5L Taurus/Sable

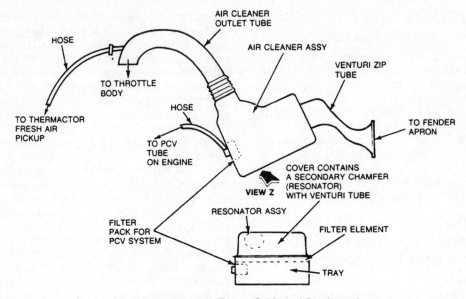

Inlet air system—3.8L Taurus/Sable and Continental

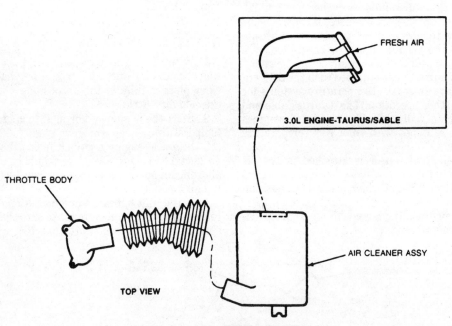

Inlet air system—3.0L Taurus/Sable

place the thermostat if all other parts appear intact and properly connected.

Evaporative Emission Controls

Changes in atmospheric temperature cause fuel tanks to breathe, that is, the air within the tank expands and contracts with outside temperature changes. As the temperature rises, air escapes through the tank vent tube or the vent in the tank cap. The air which escapes contains gasoline vapors. In a similar manner, the gaso-

line which fills the carburetor float bowl expands when the engine is stopped. Engine heat causes this expansion. The vapors escape through the carburetor and air cleaner.

The Evaporative Emission Control System provides a sealed fuel system with the capability to store and condense fuel vapors. The system has three parts: a fill control vent system; a vapor vent and storage system; and a pressure and vacuum relief system (special fill cap).

The fill control vent system is a modification to the fuel tank. It uses an air space within the tank which is 10-12% of the tank's volume. The air space is sufficient to provide for the thermal expansion of the fuel. The space also serves as part of the in-tank vapor vent system.

The in-tank vent system consists of the air space previously described and a vapor separator assembly. The separator assembly is mounted on the top of the fuel tank and is secured by a cam lockring, similar to the one which secures the fuel sending unit. Foam material fills the vapor separator assembly. The foam material separates raw fuel and vapors, thus retarding the entrance of fuel into the vapor line.

The sealed filler cap has a pressure vacuum relief valve. Under normal operating conditions, the filler cap operates as a check valve, allowing air to enter the tank to replace the fuel consumed. At the same time, it prevents vapors from escaping through the cap. In case of excessive pressure within the tank, the filler cap valve opens to relieve the pressure.

Because the filler cap is sealed, fuel vapors have but one place through which they may escape — the vapor separator assembly at the top of the fuel tank. The vapors pass through the foam material and continue through a single vapor line which leads to a canister in the engine compartment. The canister is filled with activated charcoal.

Another vapor line runs from the top of the carburetor float chamber to the charcoal canister.

As the fuel vapors (hydrocarbons) enter the charcoal canister, they are absorbed by the charcoal. The air is dispelled through the open bottom of the charcoal canister, leaving the hydrocarbons trapped within the charcoal. When the engine is started, vacuum causes fresh air to be drawn into the canister from its open bottom. The fresh air passes through the charcoal picking up the hydrocarbons which are trapped there and feeding them into the carburetor for burning with the fuel mixture.

Exhaust Gas Recirculation (EGR)

The Exhaust Gas Recirculation System is designed to introduce small amounts of exhaust gas into the combustion cycle. Re-introducing the exhaust gas helps reduce the generation of nitrous oxides (NOx). The amount of exhaust gases re-introduced and the timing of the cycle varies as to engine speed, altitude, engine vacuum and exhaust system.

Funtional Test

The EEC-IV is controlled by the ECA (Electronic Control Assembly) or processor assembly brain. The MPU controls the EGR valve opera-

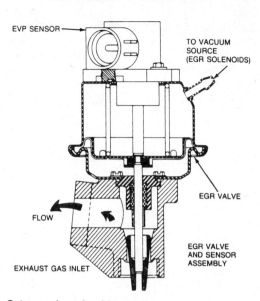

EVP SENSOR

TO VACUUM SOURCE (EGR SOLENOIDS)

EGR VALVE

FLOW

EGR VALVE AND SENSOR ASSEMBLY

EXHAUST GAS INLET

Cutaway view of a side entry type EGR valve

tions. If there is a malfunction in the EGR valve, special testing equipment is needed. This equipment is expensive and is not practical to purchase for limited use. Refer to a qualified technician for tests that are needed for this system.

HOW TO DETERMINE VEHICLE CALIBRATION

The vehicle calibration label is located on one of the following, under side of the hood, engine valve cover, radiator support bracket, or fan shroud. The calibration label contains information such as engine displacement, vehicle model year, emission calibration, and other important information needed when servicing your vehicle. The information on the label is very important when ordering parts.

EGR MAINTENANCE REMINDER SYSTEM

Some models are equipped with an EGR Maintenance Reminder System that consists of a mileage sensor module, an instrument panel warning light and associated wiring harness. The system provides a visual warning to indicate EGR service at 30,000 miles. The sensor is an blue plastic box mounted on the dash panel in the passenger's compartment forward of the glove box. After performing the required service, the warning light is reset by installing a new sensor.

Electronic Engine Control

The EEC-IV system is similar to other Ford engine control systems in that the center of the system is a microprocessor called an electronic control assembly (ECA). This assembly receives data from the sensors, switches, relays and other electronic components, then issues commands to control engine functions. The electronic control assembly is calibrated to optimize emissions, fuel economy and driveability. The electronic control assembly in the EEC-IV system is a microprocessor like other EEC systems, but the calibration modules are located within the electronic control assembly instead of being attached to the outside, as in previous models. The harness connectors are edge type connectors which provide a more positive connection and allow probing from the rear while connected. The electronic control assembly is usually mounted in the passenger compartment under the front section of the center console on the Taurus/Sable. The Continental's electronic control assembly is usually mounted under the right (passenger side) kick paned. The EEC-IV system does not control the pulse air injection or the upshift lamp. The system does control the fuel injectors for air fuel mixture, spark timing, deceleration fuel cut-off, EGR function, curb and fast idle speed, evapo-

Attached to all 1988 production engines is an Engine Code Information Label containing among other pertinent data— the engine calibration number. The size and shape of the decal is dependent upon the engine displacement. To determine the engine calibration, look at Step 1A. You **do not** have to refer to the Vehicle Emission decal for calibration numbers as in prior years.

1   DETERMINE ENGINE DISPLACEMENT FROM VEHICLE EMISSION CONTROL INFORMATION DECAL**
—ENTER IN BLANK "A" OF EXAMPLE SHOWN BELOW.

2   DETERMINE VEHICLE MODEL YEAR FROM VEHICLE EMISSION CONTROL INFORMATION DECAL**
—ENTER LAST DIGIT IN BLANK "B." SEE EXAMPLE BELOW.

3   DETERMINE CALIBRATION BASE NUMBER FROM ENGINE CODE INFORMATION LABEL
—ENTER NUMBERS AND LETTERS IN BLANK "C."

4   DETERMINE REVISION LEVEL FROM ENGINE CODE INFORMATION LABEL*
—ENTER IN BLANK "D."

(A)   (B) (C)   (D)
EXAMPLE: ENGINE: 1.6L CALIBRATION 5—03F—R00

* Located on engine valve cover.

** Located on engine valve cover, radiator support bracket, underside of hood or fan shroud.

How to determine vehicle calibration

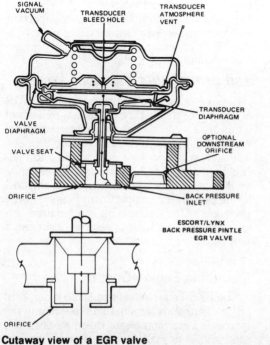

Cutaway view of a EGR valve

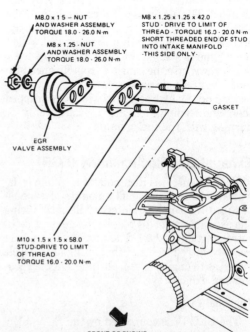

Typical EGR valve installation

rative emission purge, air condition cut-off during wide open throttle, cold engine start and enrichment, electric fuel pump and self test engine diagnostics.

Distributorless Ignition System (DIS)

The DIS ignition system eliminates the distributor by using a multiple coil arrangement. Each coil fires two spark plugs at the same time. The spark plugs are paired so that as one fires during the compression cycle the other fires during the exhaust stroke.

The DIS system is new for the 1989 Taurus equipped with the 3.0L SHO (Super High Output) engine. This system incorporates a crankshaft and camshaft sensor that are digital output Hall Effect devices that responds to a rotating metallic vane mounted on the crankshaft damper and the camshaft end cap. A coil pack consisting of three coils receives information from the DIS module to fire two spark plugs at the same time. The EEC-IV processor is basically the same as the processor on most late model Ford vehicles. The EEC processor determines spark angle using the PIP (Profile Ignition Pickup) signal to establish base timing.

SYSTEM COMPONENTS

Air Bypass Solenoid Valve

The air bypass solenoid is used to control engine idle speed. This component is operated by the electronic control assembly (ECA). The function of the valve is to allow air to pass around the throttle plates in order to control cold engine fast idle, no touch start, dashpot operation, over temperature idle boost and engine idle load correction. The electrical signal to the solenoid should be one volt or less, with all accessories off. Applying twelve volts to the solenoid will cause a neutral idle speed change greater than 1,000 rpm. The air bypass solenoid is located on top of the upper intake manifold on the EFI 3.0L and 3.8L engines. The CFI 2.5L engine does not have an air bypass solenoid.

Air Charge Temperature Sensor

The air charge temperature sensor (ACT) provides the electronic fuel injection system with the correct air/fuel mixture information. This sensor is used as both a density corrector to calculate air flow and to proportion cold enrichment fuel flow. This sensor is similar in construction to the engine coolant temperature sensor. The sensor is located in the engine cylinder runner of the intake manifold.

Engine Coolant Temperature Sensor (Dual)

The engine coolant temperature sensor (ECT) provides the electronic control assembly (ECA) the coolant temperature data. The switch is closed in the normal operating temperature range. The ECT sensor is located in the cooling passage of the intake manifold. The Defects in the switch are diagnosed as part of the ECU system.

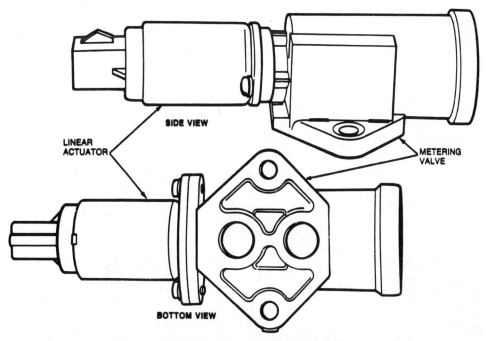

SIDE VIEW

LINEAR
ACTUATOR

METERING
VALVE

BOTTOM VIEW

Air bypass valve—3.0L and 3.8L engine

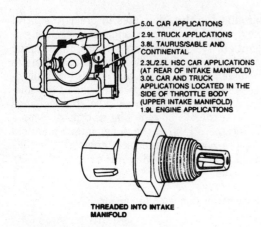

THREADED INTO INTAKE MANIFOLD

5.0L CAR APPLICATIONS
2.9L TRUCK APPLICATIONS
3.8L TAURUS/SABLE AND CONTINENTAL
2.3L/2.5L HSC CAR APPLICATIONS (AT REAR OF INTAKE MANIFOLD)
3.0L CAR AND TRUCK APPLICATIONS LOCATED IN THE SIDE OF THROTTLE BODY (UPPER INTAKE MANIFOLD)
1.9L ENGINE APPLICATIONS

Air charge temperature sensor

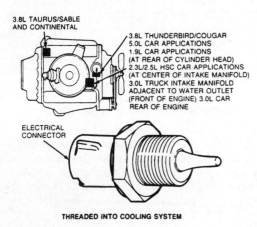

3.8L TAURUS/SABLE AND CONTINENTAL

3.8L THUNDERBIRD/COUGAR
5.0L CAR APPLICATIONS
1.9L CAR APPLICATIONS (AT REAR OF CYLINDER HEAD)
2.3L/2.5L HSC CAR APPLICATIONS (AT CENTER OF INTAKE MANIFOLD)
3.0L TRUCK INTAKE MANIFOLD ADJACENT TO WATER OUTLET (FRONT OF ENGINE) 3.0L CAR REAR OF ENGINE

ELECTRICAL CONNECTOR

THREADED INTO COOLING SYSTEM

Coolant temperature sensor (dual)

DC Motor/Idle Speed Control Actuator (DC-ISCA)

On vehicles equipped, the DC motor/idle speed control actuator is mounted to the fuel charging assembly (upper intake manifold). This component controls the idle speed, including such functions as high cam rpm, anti-diesel shut off, dashpot and prepositioning the engine fuel charging assembly for restart. This control actuator is driven by the EEC-IV system, which includes an integral idle tracking switch.

Electronic Control Assembly (EFI/CFI)

The center of the EEC-IV system is a microprocessor called the electronic control assembly (ECA). This component receives data from a number of sensors and other electronic components. The ECA contains a specific calibration for optimizing emissions, fuel economy and driveability. Based on data received and programmed into the ECA memory, the electronic control assembly generates output signals to control various relays, solenoids and other actuators. The electronic control assembly that is used in the EEC-IV system, utilizes a calibration module that is located inside itself.

Engine Coolant Temperature Sensor (Single)

This component detects the temperature of the engine coolant and relays the information to the electronic control assembly. The sensor is located by the heater outlet fitting or in a cooling passage on the engine, depending upon the particular type vehicle. The function of the sensor is to modify ignition timing, control EGR flow and regulate the air/fuel mixture. On vehicles equipped with the electronic instrument cluster, the sensor is also used to control the coolant temperature indicator.

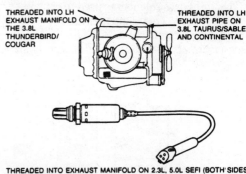

THREADED INTO LH EXHAUST MANIFOLD ON THE 3.8L THUNDERBIRD/COUGAR

THREADED INTO LH EXHAUST PIPE ON 3.8L TAURUS/SABLE AND CONTINENTAL

THREADED INTO EXHAUST MANIFOLD ON 2.3L, 5.0L SEFI (BOTH SIDES)
THREADED INTO CROSSOVER BOSS TUBULAR RUNNER ON 1.9L EFI
THREADED INTO EXHAUST MANIFOLD ON 1.9L, 5.0L TRUCK
THREADED INTO CENTER REAR OF EXHAUST MANIFOLD ON 2.3L HSC
THREADED INTO Y-PIPE JUNCTURE OF CATALYST INLET ON 3.0L EFI

Heated exhaust gas oxygen sensor

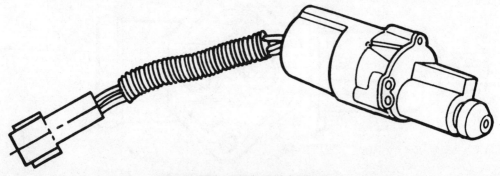

IC motor-idle speed control actuator

Heated Exhaust Gas Oxygen Sensor (HEGO)

The exhaust gas oxygen sensor supplies the electronic control assembly with a signal which indicates either a rich or lean mixture condition, during the engine operation. This sensor is located on and screwed into the exhaust manifold.

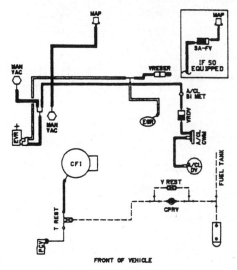

Vacuum hose routing—1987 2.5L engine

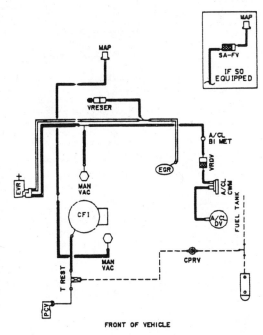

Vacuum hose routing—1986 2.5L engine

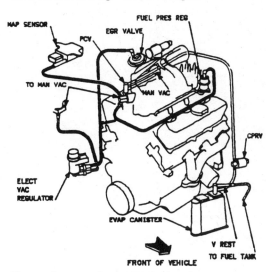

Vacuum hose routing—1987 3.0L engine

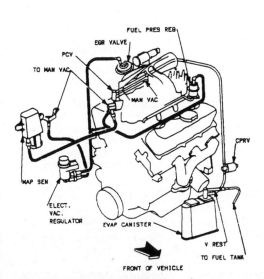

Vacuum hose routing—1986 3.0L engine

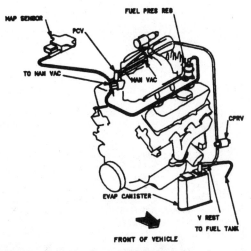

Vacuum hose routing—1988 3.0L engine

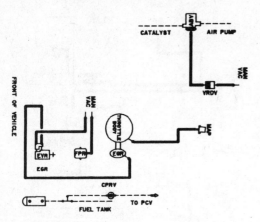

Vacuum hose routing—1988 3.8L engine

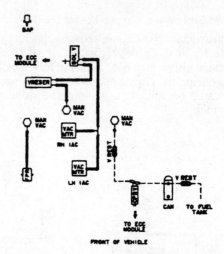

Vacuum hose routing—3.0L SHO engine (49 states and Canada)

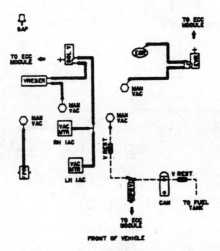

Vacuum hose routing—3.0L SHO engine (California)

Troubleshooting the Thermactor System

Condition	Possible Source	Resolution
• Excessive Belt Noise	• Loose belt	• Tighten to specification CAUTION: *Do not use a pry bar to move the air pump.*
	• Seized pump	• Replace pump.
	• Loose pulley	• Replace pulley and/or pump if damaged. Tighten bolts to specification 130–180 in. lbs.
	• Loose or broken mounting brackets or bolts	• Replace parts as required and tighten bolts to specification.
• Excessive Mechanical Clicking	• Over-tightened mounting bolt	• Tighten to 25 ft. lbs.
	• Excessive flash on the air pump adjusting arm boss.	• Remove flash from the boss.
	• Distorted adjusting arm.	• Replace adjusting arm.
• Excessive Thermactor System Noise (Putt-Putt, Whirling or Hissing)	• Leak in hose	• Locate source of leak using soap solution, and replace hoses as necessary.
	• Loose, pinched or kinked hose	• Reassemble, straighten, or replace hose and clamps as required.

Troubleshooting the EGR System

Conditon	Possible Source	Resolution
• Excessive Thermactor System Noise (Putt-Putt, Whirling or Hissing) (cont.)	• Hose touching other engine parts • Bypass valve inoperative • Check valve inoperative • Pump mounting fasteners loose • Restricted or bent pump outlet fitting • Air dumping through bypass valve (at idle only)	• Adjust hose to prevent contact with other engine parts. • Test the valve. • Test the valve. • Tighten fasteners to specification. • Inspect fitting, and remove any flash blocking the air passage way. Replace bent fittings. • On many vehicles, the thermactor system has been designed to dump air at idle to prevent overheating the catalyst. This condition is normal. Determine that the noise persists at higher speeds before proceeding further.
• Excessive Pump Noise (Chirps, Squeaks and Ticks)	• Insufficient break-in or worn or damaged pump	• Check the thermactor system for wear or damage and make any necessary corrections.
• Rough Idle and/or Stalling	• EGR valve receiving vacuum at idle, vacuum hoses misrouted • EGR valve not closing fully or stuck open • EGR valve gasket blown, or valve attachment loose. • EGR valve air bleeds plugged	• Check EGR valve vacuum hose routing. Correct as required. Check vacuum supply at idle with engine at operating temperature. • Remove EGR valve to inspect for proper closing and seating of valve components. Clean or replace valve as required. • Check EGR valve attaching bolts for tightness. Inspect gasket. Tighten valve or replace gasket as required. • Check to see if valve holds vacuum with engine off. If so, replace valve.
• Rough running, surge, hesitation and general poor performance at part throttle when engine is cold	• EGR valve receiving vacuum. Vacuum hoses misrouted. • EGR valve not closing fully or stuck open • EGR valve gasket blown, or valve attachment loose. • EGR valve air bleeds plugged (back pressure-type valve only)	• Check EGR valve vacuum hose routing. Correct as required. • Remove EGR valve to inspect for proper closing and seating of valve components. Clean or replace valve as required. • Check EGR valve attaching bolts for tightness. Inspect gasket. Tighten valve or replace gasket as required. • Check to see if valve holds vacuum with engine off. If so, replace valve.
• Rough running, surge, hesitation, and general poor performance at part-throttle when engine is hot or cold.	Excessive EGR due to: • EGR valve stuck wide open	• Remove EGR valve to inspect for proper freedom of movement of valve components. Clean or replace as required.
• Engine stalls on deceleration	• EGR valve sticking open or not closing fully	• Remove EGR valve to inspect for proper closing and seating of valve components. Clean or replace as required.
• Part-throttle engine detonation	Insufficient EGR due to: • EGR valve stuck closed	• Check EGR valve for freedom of operation by pressing and releasing valve diaphragm to stroke the valve mechanism. Clean or replace valve if not operating smoothly.

Troubleshooting the EGR System (cont.)

Conditon	Possible Source	Resolution
• Part-throttle engine detonation (cont.)	• Leaky valve diaphragm not actuating valve	• Check valve by applying vacuum. (Back pressure-type valves only—block tailpipe with drive socket of outside diameter approximately $1/16''$ less than inside diameter of tailpipe. DO NOT BLOCK FULLY. Idle engine while applying vacuum to valve. DO NOT RUN ENGINE FASTER THAN IDLE OR FOR PROLONGED PERIODS OF TIME. BE SURE TO REMOVE SOCKET FROM TAILPIPE AT END OF THIS TEST. IF THESE PRECAUTIONS ARE NOT OBSERVED, ENGINE AND/OR EXHAUST SYSTEM DAMAGE COULD OCCUR.) If valve leaks vacuum, replace it.
	• Vacuum restricted to EGR valve	• Check vacuum hoses, fittings, routing, and supply for blockage.
• Part-throttle engine detonation (cont'd).	• EGR disconnected	• Check connections and reconnect as required.
	• Load control valve venting	• Check for proper functioning. Vacuum should be present at load control valve vacuum port to EGR valve. Replace if damaged.
	• EGR passages blocked.	• Check EGR passages for restrictions and blockage.
	• Insufficient exhaust back pressure (back pressure EGR valve only)	• Check for exhaust leaks ahead of muffler/catalyst or for blown-out muffler/catalyst. Also check for blockage to EGR valve. Service or replace all damaged components.
	• Vacuum hose leaking (cracked, split, broken, loose connections)	• Check all vacuum hoses for breaks and all connections for proper fit. Service or replace as required.

(NOTE: *Detonation can also be due to carburetor or ignition malfunction.*)

• Abnormally low power at wide open throttle.	• Load control valve not venting	• Check for proper functioning. Vacuum should not be present at vacuum port to EGR valve at wide-open throttle or heavy load. If vacuum is present, replace damaged valve.
• Engine starts but stalls immediately thereafter when cold	• EGR valve receiving vacuum, vacuum hoses misrouted	• Check EGR valve hose routing. Correct as required.
	• EGR valve not closing fully	• Remove EGR valve to inspect for proper closing and seating of valve components. Clean or replace as required.

(NOTE: *Stalling can also be due to carburetor malfunction.*)

• Engine hard to start, or no start condition	• EGR valve receiving vacuum. Vacuum hoses misrouted	• Check EGR valve hose routing. Correct as required.
	• EGR valve stuck open	• Remove EGR valve to inspect for proper closing and seating of valve components. Clean or replace as required.
• Poor Fuel Economy	EGR related if: • Caused by detonation or other symptom of restricted or no EGR flow	• See Resolution for part-throttle engine detonation condition.

Fuel System

5

GENERAL FUEL SYSTEM SERVICE

CAUTION: *Do not smoke or carry lighted tobacco or open flame of any type when working on or near any fuel related component. Highly flammable mixtures are always present and may be ignited, resulting in possible personal injury.*

Before servicing any components of the fuel system, perform the following procedure for releasing the fuel system pressure. Both the CFI (central fuel infection) and EFI (electronic fuel injection) fuel injection systems may be under pressure even when the engine is not running.

BLEEDING THE FUEL SYSTEM

NOTE: *The pressure in the fuel can be released by using the valve provided on the fuel rail assembly. Remove the air cleaner and attach an EFI and CFI fuel pressure gauge part No. T80L-9974-B or equivalent to the fuel diagnostic (pressure relief) valve on the fuel rail assembly.*

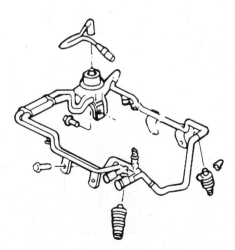

Fuel pressure relief valve—3.0L and 3.8L engine

2.5L Engine Central Fuel Injection (CFI)

1. On the left side of the luggage compartment, disconnect the electrical connector from the inertia switch.
2. Using the ignition switch, crank the engine for 15 seconds to reduce the pressure in the fuel system.
3. To pressurize the fuel system, perform the following procedures:
    a. Reconnect the electrical connector to the inertia switch.
    b. Start the engine and check for leaks.

3.0L and 3.8L Engines
Electronic Fuel Injection (EFI)

1. Remove the fuel tank cap and the air filter.
2. Disconnect the negative (−) battery cable.
3. Using the Fuel Pressure Gauge tool No. T80L-9974-A, connect it to the pressure relief valve (remove the valve cap) on the fuel injection manifold.
4. Open the pressure relief valve and reduce the fuel pressure.
5. To pressurize the fuel system, perform the following:
    a. Tighten the pressure relief valve and remove the pressure gauge.
    b. Reinstall the negative (−) battery cable.
    c. Start the engine and check for leaks.

Electric Fuel Pump

The electric fuel pump is located in the fuel tank and is a part of the fuel gauge sending unit. The EFI and CFI fuel pump use a pump relay that is controlled by the electronic engine control (EEC) module, which provides power to the fuel pump under various operating conditions.

REMOVAL AND INSTALLATION

1. Position the vehicle on a level surface.
2. Refer to "Bleeding the Fuel System" pro-

cedures in this section and reduce the pressure in the fuel system.

3. Remove the fuel from the fuel tank by pumping it out through the filler neck. Take precautions to avoid the risk of fire when handling gasoline.

4. Raise and support the rear of the vehicle on jackstands. Remove the fuel filler tube (neck).

5. Support the fuel tank, with a suitable jack, and remove the fuel tank straps. Lower the fuel tank slightly, then remove the fuel lines using fuel lines removal tool part No. D87L-9280-A — ⅜" or D87L-9280-B — ½", the electrical connectors, and the vent lines.

6. Remove the fuel tank and place it on a workbench. Clean any dirt from around the fuel pump attaching flange.

7. Using a brass drift and a hammer, turn the fuel pump locking ring counterclockwise and remove it.

8. Remove the fuel pump assembly from the fuel tank and discard the flange gasket.

9. **To install:** perform the following procedures:

   a. Using Multi-purpose Long Life Lubricant C1AZ-19590 or equivalent, coat the new O-ring and install it in the fuel ring groove.

   b. Install the fuel pump and sender assembly carefully to ensure that the filter is not damaged.

   c. Secure the unit with the locking ring by rotating the ring clockwise using a fuel tank sender wrench part No. D84P-9275-A or equivalent until the ring stops.

   d. Support the tank on a jack and place assembly close to the mounts.

	2.5L CFI	3.0L EFI	3.8L EFI
Engine Running	90-120 kPa (13-17 psi)	210-310 kPa (30-45 psi)	210-310 kPa (30-45 psi)
Ignition On Engine Off	90-120 kPa (13-16 psi)	240-310 kPa (35-45 psi)	240-310 kPa (35-45 psi)

Fuel pump specifications

e. Connect the fuel and vent lines and the electrical connector.

f. Install the straps and tighten.

g. Lower the vehicle.

h. Refill the fuel tank.

i. Start the engine and check for fuel leaks.

Functional Test

1. Check fuel pump pressure at the pressure relief valve on the fuel rail using a pressure gauge part No. T80L-9974-B or equivalent. If the pressure is below specifications, replace the pump/sender assembly.

2. If the pressure is within specifications, check the power supply to the pump . Lower the tank enough to disconnect the electrical connector, refer to the "Electric Fuel Pump" section. With a 12V test light, touch the positive terminal on the connector. If the light does not work, check the wires, pump relay, and inertia switch. Replace if inoperative. If the light does light, check the ground terminal at the electrical connector. Using the 12V test light, connect the one end to the ground terminal and the other to the power terminal. If the tester lights, replace the fuel pump.

INERTIA SWITCH

A safety inertia switch is installed to shut off the electric fuel pump in case of collision. The switch is located on the left hand side (driver's side) of the car, behind the rear most seat side trim panel, or inside the rear quarter shock tower access door. If the pump shuts off, or if the vehicle has been hit and will not start, check for leaks first then reset the switch. The switch is reset by pushing down on the button provided.

Functional Test

Pull the electrical connector off of the inertia switch. Using a 12V test light, turn the ignition

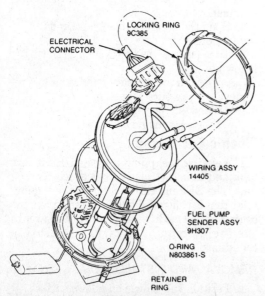

LOCKING RING 9C385

ELECTRICAL CONNECTOR

WIRING ASSY 14405

FUEL PUMP SENDER ASSY 9H307

O-RING N803861-S

RETAINER RING

Fuel pump and sender assembly

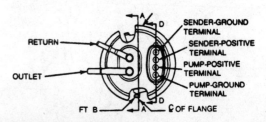

RETURN

OUTLET

SENDER-GROUND TERMINAL

SENDER-POSITIVE TERMINAL

PUMP-POSITIVE TERMINAL

PUMP-GROUND TERMINAL

FT B

℄ OF FLANGE

Fuel pump terminals

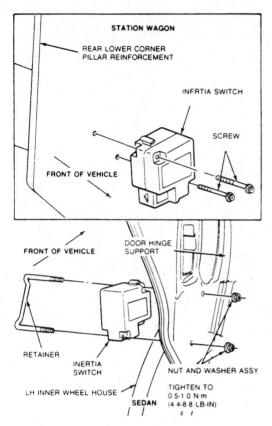

Inertia switch location

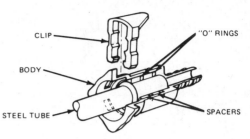

Push connect fittings with hairpin clip

ing of dust is present, clean the fitting before disassembly.

2. Remove the hairpin type clip from the fitting. This is done (using hands only) by spreading the two clip legs about 3mm each to disengage the body and pushing the legs into the fitting. Complete removal is accomplished by lightly pulling from the triangular end of the clip and working it clear of the tube and fitting.

NOTE: *Do not use any tools.*

3. Grasp the fitting and hose assembly and pull in an axial direction to remove the fitting from the steel tube. Adhesion between sealing surfaces may occur. A slight twist of the fitting may be required to break this adhesion and permit effortless removal.

4. When the fitting is removed from the tube end, inspect clip to ensure it has not been damaged. If damaged, replace the clip. If undamaged, immediately reinstall the clip, insert the clip into any two adjacent openings with the triangular portion pointing away from the fitting opening. Install the clip to fully engage the body (legs of hairpin clip locked on outside of body). Piloting with an index finger is necessary.

5. Before installing the fitting on the tube, wipe the tube end with a clean cloth. Inspect the inside of the fitting to ensure it is free of dirt and/or obstructions.

6. To reinstall the fitting onto the tube, lubricate the sealing O-rings with clean engine oil, align the fitting and tube axially and push the fitting onto the tube end. When the fitting is engaged, a definite click will be heard. Pull on the fitting to ensure it is fully engaged.

½" and ¼" Fittings (Duck Bill Clip)

The fitting consists of a body, spacers, O-rings and a duck bill retaining clip. The clip maintains the fitting to the steel tube juncture. When disassembly is required for service, one of the two following methods are to be followed:

¼" FITTINGS

To disengage the tube from the fitting, align the slot on the push connect disassembly Tool T82L-9500-AH or equivalent with either tab on the clip (90° from slots on side of fitting) and insert the tool. This disengages the duck bill from

to the ON position. Ground the light to the medal body and connect the other end to the power lead of the connector. If the tester lights, check the ground wire. Connect one tester lead to the power lead and the other to the ground lead. If the tester lights, the inertia switch is inoperative. If the tester does not light, check the wiring harness and pump relay.

Push Connect Fittings

Push connect fittings are designed with two different retaining clips. The fittings used with 8mm diameter tubing use a hairpin clip. The fittings used with 6mm and 12.7mm diameter tubing use a "duck bill" clip. Each type of fitting requires different procedures for service.

Push connect fitting disassembly must be accomplished prior to fuel component removal (filter, pump, etc.) except for the fuel tank where removal is necessary for access to the push connects.

REMOVAL AND INSTALLATION

⁵⁄₁₆" Fittings (Hairpin Clip)

1. Inspect the internal portion of the fitting for dirt accumulation. If more than a light coat-

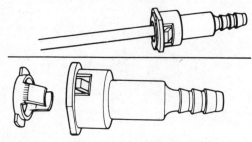

Push connect fittings with duck bill clip

the tube. Holding the tool and the tube with one hand, pull fitting away from the tube.

NOTE: *Only moderate effort is required if the tube has been properly disengaged. Use hands only. After disassembly, inspect and clean the tube sealing surface. Also inspect the inside of the fitting for damage to the retaining clip. If the retaining clip appears to be damaged, replace it.*

Some fuel tubes have a secondary bead which aligns with the outer surface of the clip. These beads can make tool insertion difficult. If there is extreme difficulty, use the disassembly method following.

½" FITTING AND ALTERNATE METHOD FOR ¼" FITTING

This method of disassembly disengages the retaining clip from the fitting body.

Use a pair of narrow pliers, (6" [153mm] locking pliers are ideal). The pliers must have a jaw width of 5mm or less.

Align the jaws of the pliers with the openings in the side of the fitting case and compress the portion of the retaining clip that engages the

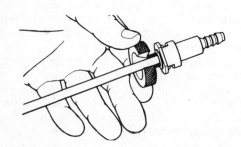

Removing push connect with tool

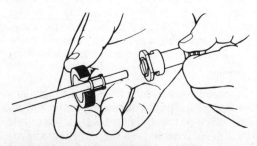

Pulling off push connect fitting

fitting case. This disengages the retaining clip from the case (often one side of the clip will disengage before the other. It is necessary to disengage the clip from both openings). Pull the fitting off the tube.

NOTE: *Only moderate effort is required if the retaining clip has been properly disengaged. Use hands only.*

The retaining clip will remain on the tube. Disengage the clip from the tube bead and remove. Replace the retaining clip if it appears to be damaged.

NOTE: *Slight ovality of the ring of the clip will usually occur. If there are no visible cracks and the ring will pinch back to its circular configuration, it is not damaged. If there is any doubt, replace the clip.*

Install the clip into the body by inserting one of the retaining clip serrated edges on the duck bill portion into one of the window openings. Push on the other side until the clip snaps into place. Lubricate the O-rings with clean engine oil and slide the fuel line back into the clip.

2.5L ENGINE CENTRAL FUEL INJECTION (CFI) SYSTEM

The Ford Central Fuel Injection (CFI) System is a single point, pulse time modulated injection system. Fuel is metered into the air intake stream according to engine demands by one or two solenoid injection valves, mounted in a throttle body on the intake manifold. Fuel is supplied from the fuel tank by a single low-pressure pump. The fuel is filtered, and sent to the air throttle body where a regulator keeps the fuel delivery pressure at a constant 39 psi (269 kPa) on high-pressure systems, or 14.5 psi (100kPa) on low-pressure systems. One or two injector nozzles are mounted vertically above the throttle plates and connected in parallel with the fuel pressure regulator. Excess fuel supplied by the pump but not needed by the engine is returned to the fuel tank by a steel fuel return line.

CFI FUEL DELIVERY SYSTEM

Fuel Charging Assembly

The fuel charging assembly controls air/fuel ratio. It consists of a typical carburetor throttle body. It has one or two bores without venturis. The throttle shaft and valves control engine air flow based on driver demand. The throttle body attaches to the intake manifold mounting pad.

A throttle position sensor is attached to the throttle shaft. It includes a potentiometer (or rheostat) that electrically senses throttle opening. A throttle kicker solenoid fastens opposite

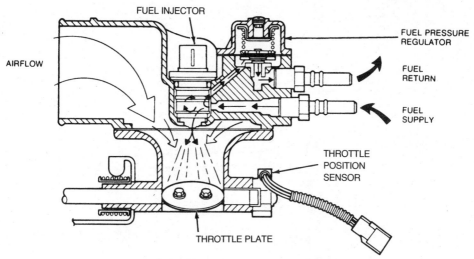

Central fuel injection—2.5L engine

the throttle position sensor. During air conditioning operation, the solenoid extends to slightly increase engine idle speed.

Cold engine speed is controlled by an automatic kick-down vacuum motor. There is also an all-electric, bimetal coil spring which controls cold idle speed. The bimetal electric coil operates like a conventional carburetor choke coil, but the electronic fuel injection system uses no choke. Fuel enrichment for cold starts is controlled by the computer and injectors.

Fuel Pressure Regulator

The fuel pressure regulator controls critical injector fuel pressure. The regulator receives fuel from the electric fuel pump and then adjusts the fuel pressure for uniform fuel injection. The regulator sets fuel pressure at 39 psi on high pressure systems, or 14.5 psi on low pressure systems.

Fuel Manifold

The fuel manifold (or fuel rail) evenly distributes fuel to each injector. Its main purpose is to equalize the fuel flow. One end of the fuel rail contains a relief valve for testing fuel pressure during engine operation.

Fuel Injectors

The fuel injectors are electromechanical devices. The electrical solenoid operates a pindle or ball metering valve which always travels the same distance from closed to open to closed. Injection is controlled by varying the length of time the valve is open.

The computer, based on voltage inputs from the crank position sensor, operates each injector solenoid two times per engine revolution. When the injector metering valve unseats, fuel

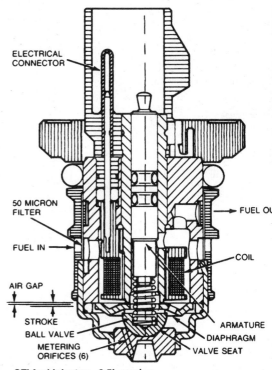

CFI fuel injector—2.5L engine

is sprayed in a fine mist into the intake manifold. The computer varies fuel enrichment based on voltage inputs from the exhaust gas oxygen sensor, barometric pressure sensor, manifold absolute pressure sensor, etc., by calculating how long to hold the injectors open. The longer the injectors remain open, the richer the mixture. This injector ON time is called pulse duration.

ITEM	PART NO.	PART NAME
1.	9C531-A	Spring—engine idle speed-up control actuator
2.	9G542-A	Lever—carb. transmission linkage
3.	9E551-A	Ball—carb. throttle lever
4.	9D549-A	Lever—carb. idle speed-up control
5.	9B569-A	Spring—carb. throttle return
6.	9583-AA	Lever—carb. throttle
7.	9C834-A	Bearing—throttle control linkage
8.	9E951-A	Shaft—air intake charge throttle
9.	9E950-A	Plate—air intake charge throttle
10.	903076-S100	Screw—M4 × 7 × 8.0
11.	384755-S2	Screw—M4.2 × 1.41 × 15.9 (self tapping)
12.	9S555-A	Bracket—engine throttle positioner
13.	9N825-A	Actuator Assy—throttle control
14.	9F553-A	Plate—engine air distribution
15.	N603253-S100	Screw—M5 × 8 × 14.0
16.	6B608-B	Tube—carb. emission inlet
17.	9F681-A	Connector—quick connect fuel injection (⁵⁄₁₆ × ¼ NPTF)
18.	87021-S100	O-ring—20.4 ID × 1.78 wide
19.	9D920-A	Spring—fuel pressure reg. valve
20.	87049-S100	O-ring—18.6 ID × 3.50 wide
21.	9C976-A	Retainer—fuel injector
22.	N603078-S100	Screw—M4 × 7 × 12.0
23.	9F593-A	Injector assy—fuel
24.	9D911-B	Cover—fuel pressure regulator
25.	383191-S	Plug—expansion
26.	N603245-S100	Screw—M4 × 7 × 16.0
27.	9D932-A	Screw—fuel pressure regulator adjusting
28.	9D923	Cup and spring assy—fuel pressure regulator
29.	9D919	Diaphragm assy—fuel pressure regulator
30.	9D909-A	Tube—fuel press reg. outlet
31.	9C974-B	Body assy—fuel charging main
32.	9C973-A	Body—fuel charging main
33.	9C983-B	Gasket—fuel charging body
34.	N800885-S	Screw—M4 × .7 × 22.0
35.	9B989-B	Potentiometer assy—carburetor throttle
36.	N603256-S100	Screw—M5 × .8 × 25.0
37.	9C981-A	Body—fuel charging throttle
39.	NN800545-S52	Screw—M5 × .8 × 19.0
40.	N603257-S100	Screw—M5 × 8 × 30.0
41.	9F791-A	Seal—fuel charging shaft
42.	9F525-AA	Screen—fuel inlet

CFI fuel injection components—2.5L engine

Fuel Charging Assembly

REMOVAL AND INSTALLATION

1. Remove the air cleaner.

2. Release pressure from the fuel system at the diagnostic (pressure relief) valve on the fuel charging assembly by carefully depressing the pin and discharging fuel into the throttle body.

3. Disconnect the throttle cable and transmission throttle valve lever.

4. Disconnect fuel, vacuum and electrical connections.

NOTE: *Either the multi or single ten pin connectors may be used on the system. To disconnect electrical ten pin connectors, push in or squeeze on the right side lower locking tab while pulling up on the connection. Multi connectors disconnect by pulling apart. The ISC (Idle Speed Control) connector tab must be moved out while pulling apart.*

5. Remove fuel charging assembly retaining nuts, then, remove fuel charging assembly.

6. Remove mounting gasket from intake manifold. Always use a new gasket for installation.

To install:

1. Clean gasket mounting surfaces of spacer and fuel charging assembly.

2. Place spacer between two new gaskets and place spacer and gaskets on the intake manifold. Position the charging assembly on the spacer and gasket.

3. Secure fuel charging assembly with attaching nuts.

NOTE: *To prevent leakage, distortion or damage to the fuel charging assembly body flange, snug the nuts; then, alternately tighten each nut in a criss-cross pattern. Tighten to 10 ft. lbs.*

4. Connect the fuel line, electrical connectors, throttle cable and all emission lines.

5. Start the engine, check for leaks. Adjust engine idle speed if necessary. Refer to the Engine/Emission Control Decal for idle speed specifications.

DISASSEMBLY

To prevent damage to the throttle plates, the fuel charging assembly should be placed on a work stand during disassembly and assembly procedures. If a proper stand is not available, use four bolts $5/16'' \times 2\frac{1}{2}''$ as legs. Install nuts on the bolts above and below the throttle body. The following is a step-by-step sequence of operations for completely overhauling the fuel charging assembly. Most components may be serviced without a complete disassembly of the fuel charging assembly. To replace individual components follow only the applicable steps.

NOTE: *Use a separate container for the com-*

ponent parts of each sub-assembly to insure proper assembly. The automatic transmission throttle valve lever must be adjusted whenever the fuel charging assembly is removed for service or replacement.

1. Remove the air cleaner stud. The air cleaner stud must be removed to separate the fuel charging assembly from the throttle body.

2. Turn the fuel charging assembly over and remove four screws from the bottom of the throttle body.

3. Separate the throttle body from the main body. Set the throttle body aside.

4. Carefully remove and discard the gasket.

NOTE: *If scraping is necessary, be careful not damage the gasket surfaces of the main body and throttle body.*

5. Remove the three pressure regulator retaining screws.

6. Remove the pressure regulator. Inspect the condition of the gasket and O-ring.

7. Remove the fuel injector by removing the hold-down retainer and screw. Carefully pull the injector out of the fuel charging assembly.

NOTE: *Each injector has a small O-ring at its top. If the O-ring does not come out with the injector, carefully pick the O-ring out of the cavity in the throttle body.*

8. Remove the fuel fittings and filter screen from the fuel inlet channel.

9. Loosen, DO NOT REMOVE, the wiring harness retaining screw with multi connector; with the single ten-pin connector loosen the two retaining screws.

10. Remove fuel diagnostic valve assembly.

11. Note the position of index mark on choke cap housing.

12. Remove three retaining ring screws.

13. Remove choke cap retaining ring, choke cap, and gasket, if so equipped.

14. Remove thermostat lever screw, and lever, if so equipped.

15. Remove fast idle cam assembly, is so equipped.

16. Remove fast idle control rod positioner, if so equipped.

17. Hold control diaphragm cover tightly in position, while removing two retaining screws, if so equipped.

18. Carefully, remove cover, spring, and pull-down control diaphragm, if so equipped.

19. Remove fast idle retaining nut, if so equipped.

20. Remove throttle position sensor connector bracket retaining screw.

21. Remove throttle position sensor retaining screws and slide throttle position sensor off the throttle shaft.

22. If CFI assembly is equipped with a throttle positioner, remove the throttle positioner

retaining screw, and remove the throttle positioner. If the CFI assembly is equipped with an ISC DC Motor, remove the motor.

ASSEMBLY

1. Install fuel pressure diagnostic (pressure relief) valve and cap. Tighten valve to 48-84 in. lbs. Tighten cap to 5-10 in. lbs.

2. Lubricate new O-rings with clean engine oil and install on each injector.

3. Install the injector in the appropriate location in the fuel charging assembly. Use a light twisting, pushing motion to install the injectors.

4. With injectors installed, install injector retainer into position.

5. Install injector retainer screw, and tighten to 18-22 in. lbs.

6. Install injector wiring harness in upper body.

7. Snap the electrical connectors into position on injector.

8. Lubricate new fuel pressure regulator O-ring with light engine oil. Install O-ring and new gasket on regulator.

9. Install pressure regulator in upper body. Tighten retaining screws to 27-35 in. lbs.

10. Depending upon CFI assembly, install either the throttle positioner, or the ISC DC Motor.

11. Hold throttle position sensor so wire faces up.

12. Slide throttle position sensor on throttle shaft.

13. Rotate throttle position sensor clockwise until aligned with screw holes on throttle body. Install retaining screws and tighten to 11-16 in. lbs.

14. Install throttle position wiring harness bracket retaining screw. Tighten screw to 18-22 in. lbs.

15. Install E-clip, fast idle lever and spring, fast idle adjustment lever and fast idle retaining nut, if so equipped.

16. Tighten fast idle retaining nut to 16-20 in. lbs., if so equipped.

17. Install new fuel charging gasket on upper body. Be sure gasket is positioned over bosses. Place throttle body in position on upper body.

18. Install four upper body to throttle body retaining screws. Tighten to 38-44 in. lbs.

19. Install air cleaner stud. Tighten stud to 70-95 in. lbs.

Throttle Valve (TV) Linkage Adjustment

The TV linkage must be adjusted after service has been performed on the CFI system. The transaxle may not shift properly causing damage to the transaxle.

1. Locate the Self-test connector and Self-test (STI) input Connector in the engine compartment. The two connectors are located next to each other near the dash panel on the passenger side of the vehicle.

2. Connect a jumper wire between the STI connector and the signal return ground on the Self-test connector.

3. Turn the ignition key to the RUN position. DO NOT START THE ENGINE. The ISC plunger will retract. Wait until the plunger is fully retracted, approximately 10 seconds.

4. Loosen the bolt on the sliding trunnion block on the TV control rod assembly one turn minimum. Remove any corrosion from the control rod and trunnion so that the rod slides freely.

5. Apply the emergency brake and block the drive wheels. Place the shift selector in the PARK position. Start the engine and idle.

6. Rotate the TV control lever up using one finger and light force, to ensure that the TV control lever is against its internal idle stop.

7. While holding in place, tighten the bolt on the trunnion block to 48-84 in. lbs.

8. Turn the key to OFF position and remove jumper wire.

3.0L ENGINE ELECTRONIC FUEL INJECTION (EFI) SYSTEM

The EFI fuel subsystem include a high pressure (30-45 psi) tank mounted electric fuel pump, fuel charging manifold, pressure regulator, fuel filter and both solid and flexible fuel lines. The fuel charging manifold includes six electronically controlled fuel injectors, each mounted directly above an intake port in the lower intake manifold. The Electronic Engine Control computer outputs a command to the fuel injectors to meter the appropriate quantity of fuel.

The fuel pressure regulator maintains a constant pressure drop across the injector nozzles. The regulator is referenced to intake manifold vacuum and is connected parallel to the fuel injectors and positioned on the far end of the fuel rail. Any excess fuel supplied by the pump passes through the regulator and is returned to the fuel tank via a return line.

The fuel pressure regulator is a diaphragm operated relief valve in which one side of the diaphragm senses fuel pressure and the other side senses manifold vacuum. Normal fuel pressure is established by a spring preload applied to the diaphragm. Control of the fuel system is maintained through the EEC (Electronic Engine Control) power relay and the EEC IV control unit, although electrical power is routed through the fuel pump relay and an inertia

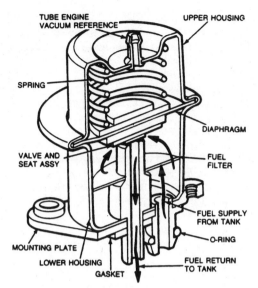

Fuel pressure regulator—3.0L and 3.8L engines

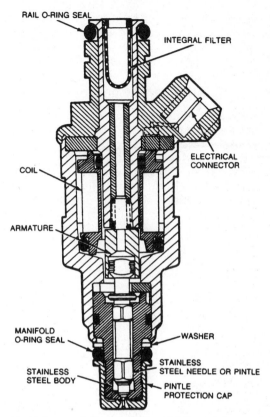

Fuel injector—3.0L, 3.0L SHO and 3.8L engines

switch. The fuel pump relay is normally located on a bracket somewhere above the Electronic Control Assembly (ECA) and the Inertia Switch is located in the trunk. Tank-mounted pumps can be either high or low-pressure, depending on the model.

The inertia switch opens the power circuit to the fuel pump in the event of a collision. Once tripped, the switch must be reset manually by pushing the reset button on the assembly. Check that the inertia switch is reset before diagnosing power supply problems to the fuel pump circuit.

Fuel Injectors

The fuel injectors used with the EFI system are electromechanical (solenoid) type designed to meter and atomize fuel delivered to the intake ports of the engine. The injectors are mounted in the lower intake manifold and positioned so that their spray nozzles direct the fuel charge in front of the intake valves. The injector body consists of a solenoid actuated pindle and needle valve assembly. The control unit sends an electrical impulse that activates the solenoid, causing the pindle to move inward off the seat and allow the fuel to flow. The amount of fuel delivered is controlled by the length of time the injector is energized (pulse width), since the fuel flow orifice is fixed and the fuel pressure drop across the injector tip is constant. Correct atomization is achieved by contouring the pindle at the point where the fuel enters the pindle chamber.

NOTE: *Exercise care when handling fuel injectors during service. Be careful not to lose the pindle cap and replace O-rings to assure a*

tight seal. Never apply direct battery voltage to test a fuel injector.

The injectors receive high pressure fuel from the fuel manifold (fuel rail) assembly. The complete assembly includes a single, preformed tube with six injector connectors, mounting flange for the pressure regulator, mounting attachments to locate the manifold and provide the fuel injector retainers and a Schrader® quick-disconnect fitting used to perform fuel pressure tests.

The fuel manifold is normally removed with fuel injectors and pressure regulator attached. Fuel injector electrical connectors are plastic and have locking tabs that must be released when disconnecting the wiring harness.

AIR SUBSYSTEM

The air subsystem components include the air cleaner assembly, air flow (vane) meter, throttle air bypass valve and air ducts that connect the air system to the throttle body assembly. The throttle body regulates the air flow to the engine through a single butterfly-type throttle plate controlled by conventional accelerator linkage. The throttle body has an idle adjustment screw (throttle air bypass valve) to set the throttle plate position, a PCV fresh air source upstream of the throttle plate, individual vacuum taps for PCV and control signals and a throttle position sensor that provides a voltage signal for the EEC-IV control unit.

Throttle Air Bypass Valve

The throttle air bypass valve is an electro-mechanical (solenoid) device whose operation is controlled by the EEC IV control unit. A variable air metering valve controls both cold and warm idle air flow in response to commands from the control unit. The valve operates by bypassing a regulated amount of air around the throttle plate; the higher the voltage signal from the control unit, the more air is bypassed through the valve. In this manner, additional air can be added to the fuel mixture without moving the throttle plate. At curb idle, the valve provides smooth idle for various engine coolant temperatures, compensates for A/C load and compensates for transaxle load and no-load conditions. The valve also provides fast idle for start-up, replacing the fast idle cam, throttle kicker and anti-dieseling solenoid common to previous models.

There are no curb idle or fast idle adjustments. As in curb idle operation, the fast idle

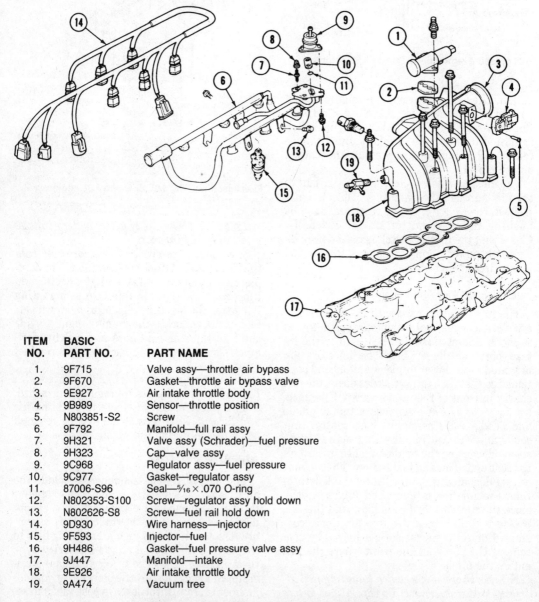

ITEM NO.	BASIC PART NO.	PART NAME
1.	9F715	Valve assy—throttle air bypass
2.	9F670	Gasket—throttle air bypass valve
3.	9E927	Air intake throttle body
4.	9B989	Sensor—throttle position
5.	N803851-S2	Screw
6.	9F792	Manifold—full rail assy
7.	9H321	Valve assy (Schrader)—fuel pressure
8.	9H323	Cap—valve assy
9.	9C968	Regulator assy—fuel pressure
10.	9C977	Gasket—regulator assy
11.	87006-S96	Seal—5/16 × .070 O-ring
12.	N802353-S100	Screw—regulator assy hold down
13.	N802626-S8	Screw—fuel rail hold down
14.	9D930	Wire harness—injector
15.	9F593	Injector—fuel
16.	9H486	Gasket—fuel pressure valve assy
17.	9J447	Manifold—intake
18.	9E926	Air intake throttle body
19.	9A474	Vacuum tree

Electronic fuel injection components—3.0L engine

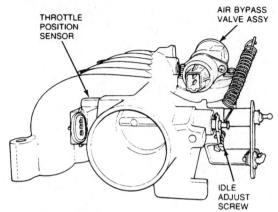

Throttle body assembly—3.0L engine

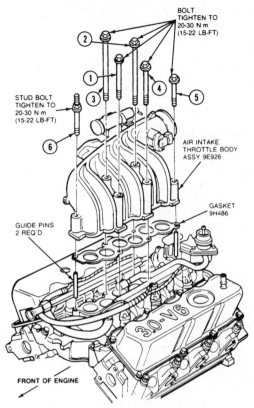

Fuel charging assembly—3.0L engine

speed is proportional to engine coolant temperature. Fast idle kick-down will occur when the throttle is kicked. A time-out feature in the ECA will also automatically kick-down fast idle to curb idle after a time period of approximately 15-25 seconds; after coolant has reached approximately 71°C (160°F). The signal duty cycle from the ECA to the valve will be at 100% (maximum current) during the crank to provide maximum air flow to allow no touch starting at any time (engine cold or hot).

Fuel Charging Assembly

REMOVAL AND INSTALLATION

1. With the ignition OFF, disconnect the negative (−) battery cable.
2. Remove the fuel cap and release the pressure at the pressure relief valve on the fuel rail assembly using a Fuel Pressure Gauge part No. T80L-9974-B.
3. Disconnect electrical connectors at air bypass valve, throttle position sensor, EGR sensor and air charge temperature sensor (ACT).
4. Disconnect the fuel supply and return lines using a Fuel Line Disconnect Tool part No. D87L-9280-A or equivalent.
5. Disconnect the wiring connectors from the fuel injectors.
6. Remove snow/ice shield to expose throttle linkage. Disconnect throttle cable from ball stud.
7. Remove the engine air cleaner outlet tube between air cleaner and air throttle body by loosening the two clamps.
8. Disconnect and remove the accelerator and speed control cables, if so equipped, from the throttle lever.
9. Remove the transaxle TV (throttle valve) linkage from the throttle lever (automatic only).

10. Loosen bolt which retains A/C line at the upper rear of the upper manifold and disengage retainer.
11. Remove the six retaining bolts and lift air intake throttle body assembly from the lower intake manifold assembly.
12. Clean and inspect mounting faces of the lower and upper intake manifold.

To install:

1. Position new gasket on lower intake mounting face. The use of alignment studs may be helpful.
2. Install upper intake manifold and throttle

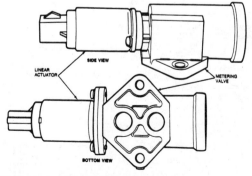

Air bypass valve—3.0L and 3.8L engines

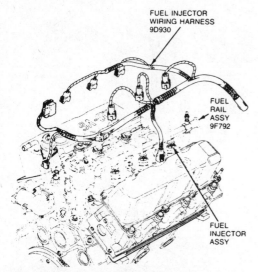

Fuel injector wiring harness—3.0L engine

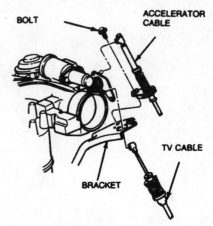

Throttle linkage—3.0L engine

body assembly to lower manifold making sure gasket remains in place (if alignment studs aren't used). Align EGR tube in valve.

3. Install six upper intake manifold retaining bolts. Tighten to 15-22 ft. lbs. in sequence as shown in the fuel charging assembly diagram in this section.

4. Engage A/C line retainer cup and tighten bolt to specification.

5. Tighten EGR tube and flare fitting. Tighten lower retainer nut at the exhaust manifold.

6. Install canister purge line to fitting.

7. Connect PCV vacuum hose to bottom of

upper manifold and PCV closure hose to throttle body.

8. Connect vacuum lines to vacuum tree, EGR valve, and fuel pressure regulator.

9. Connect throttle cable to throttle body and install snow/ice shield.

10. Connect electrical connector at air bypass valve, TPS sensor, EGR sensor, and ACT sensor.

11. Install the fuel cap, start the engine and idle, and check for vacuum, fuel, or coolant leaks.

12. **Important:** The transaxle TV (throttle valve) linkage has to be readjusted after the fuel charging assembly has been serviced:

 a. With the ignition key OFF and shift selector in PARK.

 b. Reset the automatic transaxle TV linkage by holding the ratchet in the released position and pushing the cable fitting toward the accelerator control bracket.

 c. At the throttle body, reset the TV cable by rotating the throttle linkage to wide-open throttle position by hand and release.

NOTE: *If lower intake manifold was removed, fill and bleed the cooling system.*

Fuel Manifold and Injectors
REMOVAL AND INSTALLATION

1. Remove the air intake/throttle body assembly as previously described. Be sure to depressurize the fuel system before disconnecting any fuel lines.

2. Carefully disconnect the wiring harness from the fuel injectors.

3. Disconnect the vacuum line from the fuel pressure regulator.

4. Remove the four fuel injector manifold retaining bolts, two on each side.

5. Carefully disengage the fuel rail assembly from the fuel injectors by lifting and gently rocking the rail.

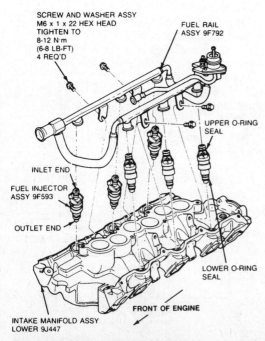

Fuel rail assembly—3.0L engine

6. Remove the fuel injectors from the intake manifold by lifting while gently rocking from side to side. Place all removed components on a clean surface to prevent contamination by dirt or grease.

CAUTION: *Injectors and fuel rail must be handles with extreme care to prevent damage to sealing areas and sensitive fuel metering orifices.*

To install:

1. Inspect the injector O-rings for deterioration or damage and install new O-rings, if required (two per injector).

2. Make sure the injector caps are clean and free from contamination or damage.

3. Lubricate all O-rings with clean engine oil, then install the injectors in the fuel rail using a light twisting/pushing motion.

4. Carefully install the fuel rail assembly and injectors into the lower intake manifold, one side at a time, pushing down on the fuel rail to make sure the O-rings are seated.

5. Hold the fuel rail assembly in place and install the retaining bolts finger tight. Tighten the retaining bolts to 72-84 in. lbs.

6. Connect the fuel supply and return lines.

7. Connect the fuel injector wiring harness at the injectors.

8. Connect the vacuum line to the fuel pressure regulator.

9. Install the air intake/throttle body as previously described.

10. Start the engine and check for fuel, vacuum, and coolant leaks.

Fuel Pressure Regulator

REMOVAL AND INSTALLATION

1. Depressurize the fuel system by connecting a Fuel Pressure Gauge part No. T80L-9974-B or equivalent to the pressure relief valve on the fuel rail assembly.

2. Remove the vacuum line at the pressure regulator.

3. Remove the three Allen retaining screws from the regulator housing.

4. Remove the pressure regulator assembly, gasket and O-ring. Discard the gasket and check the O-ring for signs of cracks or deterioration.

5. Clean the gasket mating surfaces. If scraping is necessary, be careful not to damage the fuel pressure regulator or supply line gasket mating surfaces.

6. Lubricate the pressure regulator O-ring with with light engine oil. Do not use silicone grease; it will clog the injectors.

7. Install the O-ring and a new gasket on the pressure regulator.

8. Install the pressure regulator on the fuel manifold and tighten the retaining screws to 27-40 in. lbs.

9. Install the vacuum line at the pressure regulator. Build up fuel pressure by turning the ignition switch on and off at least six times, leaving the ignition on for at least five seconds each time. Check for fuel leaks.

Throttle Position (TP) Sensor

REMOVAL AND INSTALLATION

1. Disconnect the TP sensor from wiring harness

2. Scribe a reference mark across the edge of the sensor and to the throttle body to ensure correct position during installation.

3. Remove the two TP sensor retaining screws and sensor.

4. **To install:** place the TP sensor in the same position as it was removed. Install the two retaining screws and torque to 11-16 in. lbs.

3.8L ENGINE ELECTRONIC FUEL INJECTION (EFI) SYSTEM

The EFI fuel subsystem include a high pressure (30-45 psi) tank mounted electric fuel pump, fuel charging manifold, pressure regulator, fuel filter and both solid and flexible fuel lines. The fuel charging manifold includes six electronically controlled fuel injectors, each mounted directly above an intake port in the lower intake manifold. The Electronic Engine Control computer outputs a command to the fuel injectors to meter the appropriate quantity of fuel.

The fuel pressure regulator maintains a constant pressure drop across the injector nozzles. The regulator is referenced to intake manifold vacuum and is connected parallel to the fuel injectors and positioned on the far end of the fuel rail. Any excess fuel supplied by the pump passes through the regulator and is returned to the fuel tank via a return line.

The fuel pressure regulator is a diaphragm operated relief valve in which one side of the diaphragm senses fuel pressure and the other side senses manifold vacuum. Normal fuel pressure is established by a spring preload applied to the diaphragm. Control of the fuel system is maintained through the EEC (Electronic Engine Control) power relay and the EEC IV control unit, although electrical power is routed through the fuel pump relay and an inertia switch. The fuel pump relay is normally located on a bracket somewhere above the Electronic Control Assembly (ECA) and the Inertia Switch is located in the trunk. Tank-mounted pumps can be either high or low-pressure, depending on the model.

The inertia switch opens the power circuit to the fuel pump in the event of a collision. Once tripped, the switch must be reset manually by pushing the reset button on the assembly. Check that the inertia switch is reset before diagnosing power supply problems to the fuel pump circuit.

Fuel Injectors

The fuel injectors used with the EFI system are electromechanical (solenoid) type designed to meter and atomize fuel delivered to the intake ports of the engine. The injectors are mounted in the lower intake manifold and positioned so that their spray nozzles direct the fuel charge in front of the intake valves. The injector body consists of a solenoid actuated pindle and needle valve assembly. The control unit sends an electrical impulse that activates the solenoid, causing the pindle to move inward off the seat and allow the fuel to flow. The amount of fuel delivered is controlled by the length of time the injector is energized (pulse width), since the fuel flow orifice is fixed and the fuel pressure drop across the injector tip is constant. Correct atomization is achieved by contouring the pindle at the point where the fuel enters the pindle chamber.

NOTE: *Exercise care when handling fuel injectors during service. Be careful not to lose the pindle cap and replace O-rings to assure a tight seal. Never apply direct battery voltage to test a fuel injector.*

The injectors receive high pressure fuel from the fuel manifold (fuel rail) assembly. The complete assembly includes a single, preformed tube with six injector connectors, mounting flange for the pressure regulator, mounting attachments to locate the manifold and provide the fuel injector retainers and a Schrader® quick-disconnect fitting used to perform fuel pressure tests.

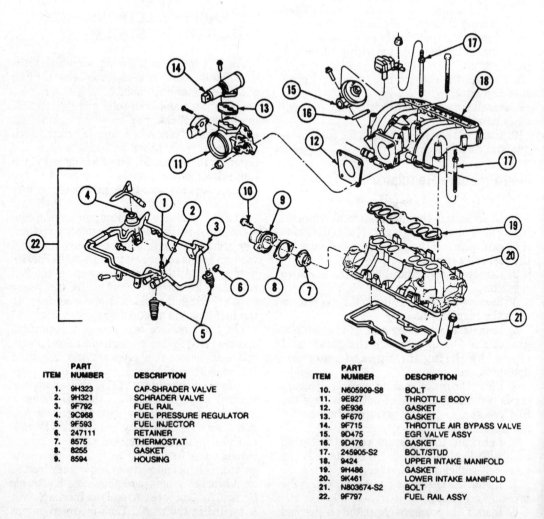

ITEM	PART NUMBER	DESCRIPTION
1.	9H323	CAP-SHRADER VALVE
2.	9H321	SCHRADER VALVE
3.	9F792	FUEL RAIL
4.	9C968	FUEL PRESSURE REGULATOR
5.	9F593	FUEL INJECTOR
6.	247111	RETAINER
7.	8575	THERMOSTAT
8.	8255	GASKET
9.	8594	HOUSING

ITEM	PART NUMBER	DESCRIPTION
10.	N605909-S8	BOLT
11.	9E927	THROTTLE BODY
12.	9E936	GASKET
13.	9F670	GASKET
14.	9F715	THROTTLE AIR BYPASS VALVE
15.	9D475	EGR VALVE ASSY
16.	9D476	GASKET
17.	245905-S2	BOLT/STUD
18.	9424	UPPER INTAKE MANIFOLD
19.	9H486	GASKET
20.	9K461	LOWER INTAKE MANIFOLD
21.	N803674-S2	BOLT
22.	9F797	FUEL RAIL ASSY

Electronic fuel injection (EFI) components—3.8L engine

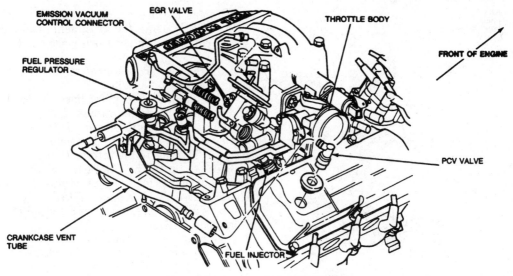

EMISSION VACUUM CONTROL CONNECTOR

EGR VALVE

THROTTLE BODY

FRONT OF ENGINE

FUEL PRESSURE REGULATOR

PCV VALVE

CRANKCASE VENT TUBE

FUEL INJECTOR

Throttle body assembly—3.8L engine

The fuel manifold is normally removed with fuel injectors and pressure regulator attached. Fuel injector electrical connectors are plastic and have locking tabs that must be released when disconnecting the wiring harness.

AIR SUBSYSTEM

The air subsystem components include the air cleaner assembly, air flow (vane) meter, throttle air bypass valve and air ducts that connect the air system to the throttle body assembly. The throttle body regulates the air flow to the engine through a single butterfly-type throttle plate controlled by conventional accelerator linkage. The throttle body has an idle adjustment screw (throttle air bypass valve) to set the throttle plate position, a PCV fresh air source upstream of the throttle plate, individual vacuum taps for PCV and control signals and a throttle position sensor that provides a voltage signal for the EEC-IV control unit.

Throttle Air Bypass Valve

The throttle air bypass valve is an electro-mechanical (solenoid) device whose operation is controlled by the EEC IV control unit. A variable air metering valve controls both cold and warm idle air flow in response to commands from the control unit. The valve operates by bypassing a regulated amount of air around the throttle plate; the higher the voltage signal from the control unit, the more air is bypassed through the valve. In this manner, additional air can be added to the fuel mixture without moving the throttle plate. At curb idle, the valve provides smooth idle for various engine coolant temperatures, compensates for A/C load and compensates for transaxle load and no-load conditions. The valve also provides fast idle for start-up, replacing the fast idle cam, throttle kicker and anti-dieseling solenoid common to previous models.

There are no curb idle or fast idle adjustments. As in curb idle operation, the fast idle speed is proportional to engine coolant temperature. Fast idle kick-down will occur when the throttle is kicked. A time-out feature in the ECA will also automatically kick-down fast idle to curb idle after a time period of approximately 15-25 seconds; after coolant has reached approximately 71°C (160°F). The signal duty cycle from the ECA to the valve will be at 100% (maximum current) during the crank to provide maximum air flow to allow no touch starting at any time (engine cold or hot).

Fuel Charging Assembly
REMOVAL AND INSTALLATION

1. Disconnect the battery negative (−) cable.
2. Drain cooling system
3. Remove the fuel cap at the tank.
4. Release the fuel pressure by attaching a Fuel Pressure Gauge part No. T80L-9974-B or equivalent to the pressure relief valve on the fuel rail assembly.
5. Disconnect the electrical connectors at the air bypass valve, throttle position sensor, and EGR position sensor.
6. Disconnect the throttle linkage at the throttle ball and transaxle linkage from the throttle body.

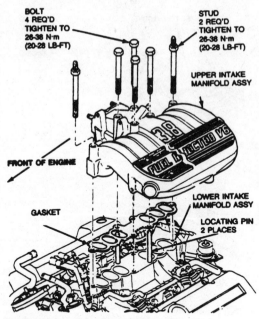

Fuel charging assembly—3.8L engine

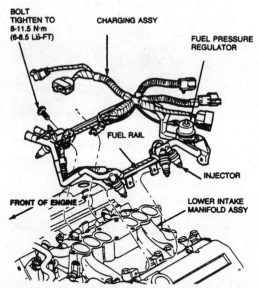

Fuel injection wiring harness and fuel rail assembly—3.8L engine

7. Position the throttle and speed control linkage out of the way.

8. Disconnect the upper intake manifold vacuum fittings at the vacuum tree.

9. Remove the six upper intake manifold retaining bolts.

10. Remove the upper intake and throttle body assembly from the lower intake.

To install:

1. Clean and inspect the mounting surfaces of the upper and lower intake manifolds. Be careful not to damage the mounting surfaces.

2. Install the new gasket and upper intake into position using the alignment studs. If alignment studs are not used, make sure the gasket stays in place.

3. Install the six manifold retaining bolts and torque to 20-28 ft. lbs.

4. Install the canister purge lines, PCV hose, and vacuum lines to the vacuum tree.

5. Install the throttle and speed control, if so equipped, to the upper intake manifold. Connect the TV cable to the throttle body.

6. **Important:** The transaxle TV (throttle valve) linkage has to be readjusted after the fuel charging assembly has been serviced

a. With the ignition key OFF and shift selector in PARK

b. Reset the automatic transaxle TV linkage by holding the ratchet in the released position and pushing the cable fitting toward the accelerator control bracket.

c. At the throttle body, reset the TV cable by rotating the throttle linkage to wide-open throttle position by hand and release.

7. Refill the engine with coolant. Start the engine and check for fuel, vacuum, and coolant leaks.

Fuel (Rail) Manifold and Injectors
REMOVAL AND INSTALLATION

1. Remove the air intake/throttle body assembly as previously described. Be sure to depressurize the fuel system before disconnecting any fuel lines.

2. Carefully disconnect the wiring harness from the fuel injectors.

3. Disconnect the vacuum line from the fuel pressure regulator.

4. Remove the four fuel injector (rail) manifold retaining bolts, two on each side.

5. Carefully disengage the fuel rail assembly from the fuel injectors by lifting and gently rocking the rail.

6. Remove the fuel injectors from the intake manifold by lifting while gently rocking from side to side. Place all removed components on a clean surface to prevent contamination by dirt or grease.

CAUTION: *Injectors and fuel rail must be handles with extreme care to prevent damage to sealing areas and sensitive fuel metering orifices.*

To install:

1. Inspect the injector O-rings for deterioration or damage and install new O-rings, if required (two per injector).

2. Make sure the injector caps are clean and free from contamination or damage.

3. Lubricate all O-rings with clean engine oil,

then install the injectors in the fuel rail using a light twisting/pushing motion.

4. Carefully install the fuel rail assembly and injectors into the lower intake manifold, one side at a time, pushing down on the fuel rail to make sure the O-rings are seated.

5. Hold the fuel rail assembly in place and install the retaining bolts finger tight. Tighten the retaining bolts to 72-84 in. lbs.

6. Connect the fuel supply and return lines.

7. Connect the fuel injector wiring harness at the injectors.

8. Connect the vacuum line to the fuel pressure regulator.

9. Install the air intake/throttle body as previously described.

10. Start the engine and check for fuel, vacuum, and coolant leaks.

Fuel Pressure Regulator

REMOVAL AND INSTALLATION

1. Depressurize the fuel system by connecting a Fuel Pressure Gauge part No. T80L-9974-B or equivalent to the pressure relief valve on the fuel rail assembly.

2. Remove the vacuum line at the pressure regulator.

3. Remove the three Allen retaining screws from the regulator housing.

4. Remove the pressure regulator assembly, gasket and O-ring. Discard the gasket and check the O-ring for signs of cracks or deterioration.

5. Clean the gasket mating surfaces. If scraping is necessary, be careful not to damage the fuel pressure regulator or supply line gasket mating surfaces.

6. Lubricate the pressure regulator O-ring with with light engine oil. Do not use silicone grease; it will clog the injectors.

7. Install the O-ring and a new gasket on the pressure regulator.

8. Install the pressure regulator on the fuel manifold and tighten the retaining screws to 27-40 in. lbs.

9. Install the vacuum line at the pressure regulator. Build up fuel pressure by turning the ignition switch on and off at least six times, leaving the ignition on for at least five seconds each time. Check for fuel leaks.

Throttle Position (TP) Sensor

REMOVAL AND INSTALLATION

1. Disconnect the TP sensor from wiring harness

2. Scribe a reference mark across the edge of the sensor and to the throttle body to ensure correct position during installation.

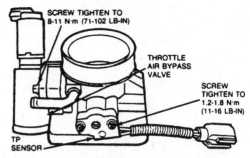

Throttle position sensor—3.0L and 3.8L engines

3. Remove the two TP sensor retaining screws and sensor.

4. **To install:** place the TP sensor in the same position as it was removed. Install the two retaining screws and torque to 11-16 in. lbs.

3.0L SHO SEQUENTIAL ELECTRONIC FUEL INJECTION (SEFI)

The Sequential Electronic Fuel Injection system is classified as a multi-point, pulse time, speed density control fuel injection system. The fuel is metered into the intake manifold port in sequence in accordance with the engine demand through the six injectors mounted on a tuned intake manifold. The Electronic Engine Control (EEC) computer outputs a command to the fuel injectors to meter the appropriate quantity of fuel. The remainder of the fuel system is basically the same as the EFI system installed on the 3.0L and 3.8L engines.

The SEFI fuel subsystem include a high pressure (30-45 psi) tank mounted electric fuel pump, fuel charging manifold, pressure regulator, fuel filter and both solid and flexible fuel lines.

The fuel pressure regulator maintains a constant pressure drop across the injector nozzles. The regulator is referenced to intake manifold vacuum and is connected parallel to the fuel injectors and positioned on the far end of the fuel rail. Any excess fuel supplied by the pump passes through the regulator and is returned to the fuel tank via a return line.

The fuel pressure regulator is a diaphragm operated relief valve in which one side of the diaphragm senses fuel pressure and the other side senses manifold vacuum. Normal fuel pressure is established by a spring preload applied to the diaphragm. Control of the fuel system is maintained through the EEC (Electronic Engine Control) power relay and the EEC IV control unit, although electrical power is routed

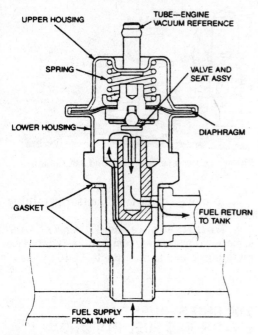

Fuel pressure regulator—3.0L SHO engine

through the fuel pump relay and an inertia switch. The fuel pump relay is normally located on a bracket somewhere above the Electronic Control Assembly (ECA) and the Inertia Switch is located in the trunk. Tank mounted pumps can be either high or low pressure, depending on the model.

Fuel Injectors

The fuel injectors used with the SEFI system are electromechanical (solenoid) type designed to meter and atomize fuel delivered to the intake ports of the engine. The injectors are mounted in the lower intake manifold and positioned so that their spray nozzles direct the fuel charge in front of the intake valves. The injector body consists of a solenoid actuated pindle and needle valve assembly. The control unit sends an electrical impulse that activates the solenoid, causing the pindle to move inward off the seat and allow the fuel to flow. The amount of fuel delivered is controlled by the length of time the injector is energized (pulse width), since the fuel flow orifice is fixed and the fuel pressure drop across the injector tip is constant. Correct atomization is achieved by contouring the pindle at the point where the fuel enters the pindle chamber.

NOTE: *Exercise care when handling fuel injectors during service. Be careful not to lose the pindle cap and replace O-rings to assure a tight seal. Never apply direct battery voltage to test a fuel injector.*

The injectors receive high pressure fuel from the fuel manifold (fuel rail) assembly. The complete assembly includes a single, preformed tube with six injector connectors, mounting flange for the pressure regulator, mounting attachments to locate the manifold and provide the fuel injector retainers and a Schrader® quick-disconnect fitting used to perform fuel pressure tests.

The fuel manifold is normally removed with fuel injectors and pressure regulator attached. Fuel injector electrical connectors are plastic and have locking tabs that must be released when disconnecting the wiring harness.

AIR SUBSYSTEM

The air subsystem components include the air cleaner assembly, air flow (vane) meter, throttle air bypass valve and air ducts that connect the air system to the throttle body assembly. The throttle body regulates the air flow to the engine through a single butterfly-type throttle plate controlled by conventional accelerator linkage. The throttle body has an idle adjustment screw (throttle air bypass valve) to set the throttle plate position, a PCV fresh air source upstream of the throttle plate, individual vacuum taps for PCV and control signals, and a throttle position sensor that provides a voltage signal for the EEC-IV control unit.

Throttle Air Bypass Valve

The throttle air bypass valve is an electro-mechanical (solenoid) device whose operation is controlled by the EEC IV control unit. A variable air metering valve controls both cold and warm idle air flow in response to commands from the control unit. The valve operates by bypassing a regulated amount of air around the throttle plate; the higher the voltage signal

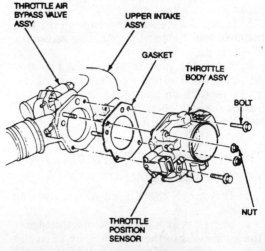

Throttle body assembly—3.0L SHO engine

from the control unit, the more air is bypassed through the valve. In this manner, additional air can be added to the fuel mixture without moving the throttle plate. At curb idle, the valve provides smooth idle for various engine coolant temperatures, compensates for A/C load and compensates for transaxle load and no-load conditions. The valve also provides fast idle for start-up, replacing the fast idle cam, throttle kicker and anti-dieseling solenoid common to previous models.

There are no curb idle or fast idle adjustments. As in curb idle operation, the fast idle speed is proportional to engine coolant temperature. Fast idle kick-down will occur when the throttle is kicked. A time-out feature in the ECA will also automatically kick-down fast idle to curb idle after a time period of approximately 15-25 seconds; after coolant has reached approximately 71°C (160°F). The signal duty cycle from the ECA to the valve will be at 100% (maximum current) during the crank to provide maximum air flow to allow no touch starting at any time (engine cold or hot).

Fuel Charging Assembly (Throttle Body, Upper and Lower Manifolds)

REMOVAL AND INSTALLATION

NOTE: *The fuel charging assembly consists of the air throttle body, and the upper and lower intake manifolds. Prior to service or removal of the fuel charging assembly, the following procedures must be taken.*

a. Open the hood and install protective fender covers.

b. Disconnect the negative (–) battery cable.

c. Remove the fuel cap at the tank.

d. Release the fuel pressure from the fuel system. Depressurize the fuel system by connecting a Fuel Pressure Gauge part No. T80L-9974-B or equivalent to the pressure relief valve on the fuel rail assembly.

1. Remove the intake air boot from the throttle body and airflow sensor and disconnect the throttle cable.

2. Disconnect the vacuum and electrical connectors from the throttle body.

3. Disconnect the coolant bypass hoses at the throttle body.

CAUTION: *The cooling system may be under pressure. Release the pressure at the radiator cap before removing the hoses. Also, allow the engine to cool down before performing any service.*

4. Disconnect the EGR pipe from the EGR valve, if so equipped.

5. Remove the eight bolts at the intake manifold support brackets and remove the brackets.

6. Remove the bolt retaining the coolant hose bracket and disconnect the PCV hoses, if so equipped.

7. Remove the intake and throttle body assembly.

To install:

1. Clean and inspect the manifold mounting surfaces.

2. Position new intake manifold gaskets and install the manifold assembly onto the cylinder heads.

3. Install the 12 intake-to-head attaching bolts and torque to 11-17 ft. lbs.

4. Install the intake manifold support brackets and coolant hose bracket.

5. Connect all the coolant and vacuum hoses.

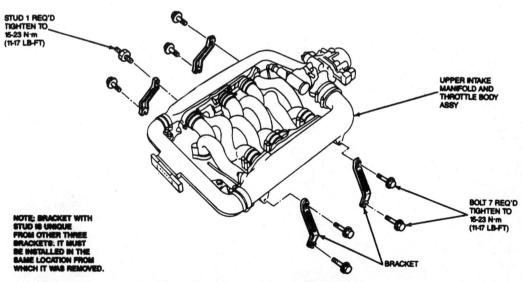

STUD 1 REQ'D TIGHTEN TO 15-23 N·m (11-17 LB-FT)

UPPER INTAKE MANIFOLD AND THROTTLE BODY ASSY

BOLT 7 REQ'D TIGHTEN TO 15-23 N·m (11-17 LB-FT)

NOTE: BRACKET WITH STUD IS UNIQUE FROM OTHER THREE BRACKETS; IT MUST BE INSTALLED IN THE SAME LOCATION FROM WHICH IT WAS REMOVED.

BRACKET

Intake manifold brackets—3.0L SHO engine

6. Connect the electrical connectors at the DIS module, vacuum switching valve, throttle position sensor, and the air bypass valve.

7. Install the throttle cable and intake air boot.

8. Connect the negative (−) battery cable. Start the engine and check for fuel and coolant leaks.

Fuel (Rail) Supply Manifold
REMOVAL AND INSTALLATION

1. Disconnect the negative (−) battery cable.

2. The pressure in the fuel can be released by using the valve provided on the fuel rail assembly. Install a fuel pressure gauge part No. T80L-9974-B or equivalent to the fuel diagnostic (pressure relief) Shrader® valve on the fuel rail assembly. Release the pressure slowly to prevent fuel spills.

3. Remove the upper intake and throttle

body assembly. Refer to the "Fuel Charging Assembly" removal and installation procedures in this section.

4. Disconnect the fuel supply and return lines.

5. Disconnect the vacuum hoses from the fuel pressure regulator.

6. Remove the four fuel rail-to-manifold attaching bolts.

7. Carefully lift the fuel rail assembly off the fuel injectors and remove the fuel rail.

8. **To install:** Position the fuel rail onto the fuel injectors, tighten the four retaining bolts, connect the two fuel lines, and install the pressure regulator connections.

9. Install the upper intake and throttle body assembly. Refer to the "Fuel Charging Assembly" installation in this section.

10. Connect the negative (−) battery cable.

11. Start the vehicle and check for fuel and coolant leaks.

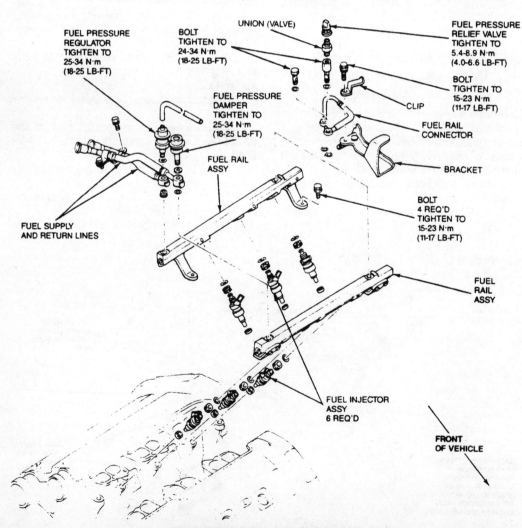

Fuel rail assemblies—3.0L SHO engine

CHILTON'S
FUEL ECONOMY
& TUNE-UP TIPS

Tune-up • Spark Plug Diagnosis • Emission Controls

Fuel System • Cooling System • Tires and Wheels

General Maintenance

CHILTON'S FUEL ECONOMY & TUNE-UP TIPS

Fuel economy is important to everyone, no matter what kind of vehicle you drive. The maintenance-minded motorist can save both money and fuel using these tips and the periodic maintenance and tune-up procedures in this Repair and Tune-Up Guide.

There are more than 130,000,000 cars and trucks registered for private use in the United States. Each travels an average of 10-12,000 miles per year, and, and in total they consume close to 70 billion gallons of fuel each year. This represents nearly ⅔ of the oil imported by the United States each year. The Federal government's goal is to reduce consumption 10% by 1985. A variety of methods are either already in use or under serious consideration, and they all affect you driving and the cars you will drive. In addition to "down-sizing", the auto industry is using or investigating the use of electronic fuel delivery, electronic engine controls and alternative engines for use in smaller and lighter vehicles, among other alternatives to meet the federally mandated Corporate Average Fuel Economy (CAFE) of 27.5 mpg by 1985. The government, for its part, is considering rationing, mandatory driving curtailments and tax increases on motor vehicle fuel in an effort to reduce consumption. The government's goal of a 10% reduction could be realized — and further government regulation avoided — if every private vehicle could use just 1 less gallon of fuel per week.

How Much Can You Save?

Tests have proven that almost anyone can make at least a 10% reduction in fuel consumption through regular maintenance and tune-ups. When a major manufacturer of spark plugs sur-

TUNE-UP

1. Check the cylinder compression to be sure the engine will really benefit from a tune-up and that it is capable of producing good fuel economy. A tune-up will be wasted on an engine in poor mechanical condition.

2. Replace spark plugs regularly. New spark plugs alone can increase fuel economy 3%.

3. Be sure the spark plugs are the correct type (heat range) for your vehicle. See the Tune-Up Specifications.

Heat range refers to the spark plug's ability to conduct heat away from the firing end. It must conduct the heat away in an even pattern to avoid becoming a source of pre-ignition, yet it must also operate hot enough to burn off conductive deposits that could cause misfiring.

The heat range is usually indicated by a number on the spark plug, part of the manufacturer's designation for each individual spark plug. The numbers in bold-face indicate the heat range in each manufacturer's identification system.

Periodically, check the spark plugs to be sure they are firing efficiently. They are excellent indicators of the internal condition of your engine.

Manufacturer	Typical Designation
AC	R **45** TS
Bosch (old)	WA **145** T30
Bosch (new)	HR **8** Y
Champion	RBL **15** Y
Fram/Autolite	4**15**
Mopar	P-**62** PR
Motorcraft	BRF-**42**
NGK	BP **5** ES-15
Nippondenso	W **16** EP
Prestolite	14GR **5** 2A

On AC, Bosch (new), Champion, Fram/Autolite, Mopar, Motorcraft and Prestolite, a higher number indicates a hotter plug. On Bosch (old), NGK and Nippondenso, a higher number indicates a colder plug.

4. Make sure the spark plugs are properly gapped. See the Tune-Up Specifications in this book.

5. Be sure the spark plugs are firing efficiently. The illustrations on the next 2 pages show you how to "read" the firing end of the spark plug.

6. Check the ignition timing and set it to specifications. Tests show that almost all cars have incorrect ignition timing by more than 2°.

veyed over 6,000 cars nationwide, they found that a tune-up, on cars that needed one, increased fuel economy over 11%. Replacing worn plugs alone, accounted for a 3% increase. The same test also revealed that 8 out of every 10 vehicles will have some maintenance deficiency that will directly affect fuel economy, emissions or performance. Most of this mileage-robbing neglect could be prevented with regular maintenance.

Modern engines require that all of the functioning systems operate properly for maximum efficiency. A malfunction anywhere wastes fuel. You can keep your vehicle running as efficiently and economically as possible, by being aware of your vehicle's operating and performance characteristics. If your vehicle suddenly develops performance or fuel economy problems it could be due to one or more of the following:

PROBLEM	POSSIBLE CAUSE
Engine Idles Rough	Ignition timing, idle mixture, vacuum leak or something amiss in the emission control system.
Hesitates on Acceleration	Dirty carburetor or fuel filter, improper accelerator pump setting, ignition timing or fouled spark plugs.
Starts Hard or Fails to Start	Worn spark plugs, improperly set automatic choke, ice (or water) in fuel system.
Stalls Frequently	Automatic choke improperly adjusted and possible dirty air filter or fuel filter.
Performs Sluggishly	Worn spark plugs, dirty fuel or air filter, ignition timing or automatic choke out of adjustment.

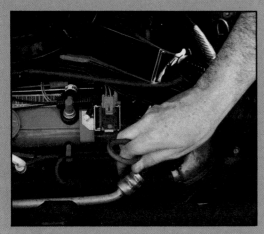

Check spark plug wires on conventional point type ignition for cracks by bending them in a loop around your finger.

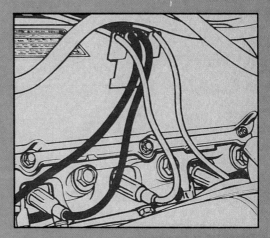

Be sure that spark plug wires leading to adjacent cylinders do not run too close together. (Photo courtesy Champion Spark Plug Co.)

7. If your vehicle does not have electronic ignition, check the points, rotor and cap as specified.

8. Check the spark plug wires (used with conventional point-type ignitions) for cracks and burned or broken insulation by bending them in a loop around your finger. Cracked wires decrease fuel efficiency by failing to deliver full voltage to the spark plugs. One misfiring spark plug can cost you as much as 2 mpg.

9. Check the routing of the plug wires. Misfiring can be the result of spark plug leads to adjacent cylinders running parallel to each other and too close together. One wire tends to pick up voltage from the other causing it to fire "out of time".

10. Check all electrical and ignition circuits for voltage drop and resistance.

11. Check the distributor mechanical and/or vacuum advance mechanisms for proper functioning. The vacuum advance can be checked by twisting the distributor plate in the opposite direction of rotation. It should spring back when released.

12. Check and adjust the valve clearance on engines with mechanical lifters. The clearance should be slightly loose rather than too tight.

SPARK PLUG DIAGNOSIS

Normal

APPEARANCE: This plug is typical of one operating normally. The insulator nose varies from a light tan to grayish color with slight electrode wear. The presence of slight deposits is normal on used plugs and will have no adverse effect on engine performance. The spark plug heat range is correct for the engine and the engine is running normally.

CAUSE: Properly running engine.

RECOMMENDATION: Before reinstalling this plug, the electrodes should be cleaned and filed square. Set the gap to specifications. If the plug has been in service for more than 10-12,000 miles, the entire set should probably be replaced with a fresh set of the same heat range.

Oil Deposits

APPEARANCE: The firing end of the plug is covered with a wet, oily coating.

CAUSE: The problem is poor oil control. On high mileage engines, oil is leaking past the rings or valve guides into the combustion chamber. A common cause is also a plugged PCV valve, and a ruptured fuel pump diaphragm can also cause this condition. Oil fouled plugs such as these are often found in new or recently overhauled engines, before normal oil control is achieved, and can be cleaned and reinstalled.

RECOMMENDATION: A hotter spark plug may temporarily relieve the problem, but the engine is probably in need of work.

Incorrect Heat Range

APPEARANCE: The effects of high temperature on a spark plug are indicated by clean white, often blistered insulator. This can also be accompanied by excessive wear of the electrode, and the absence of deposits.

CAUSE: Check for the correct spark plug heat range. A plug which is too hot for the engine can result in overheating. A car operated mostly at high speeds can require a colder plug. Also check ignition timing, cooling system level, fuel mixture and leaking intake manifold.

RECOMMENDATION: If all ignition and engine adjustments are known to be correct, and no other malfunction exists, install spark plugs one heat range colder.

Photos Courtesy Fram Corporation

Carbon Deposits

APPEARANCE: Carbon fouling is easily identified by the presence of dry, soft, black, sooty deposits.

CAUSE: Changing the heat range can often lead to carbon fouling, as can prolonged slow, stop-and-start driving. If the heat range is correct, carbon fouling can be attributed to a rich fuel mixture, sticking choke, clogged air cleaner, worn breaker points, retarded timing or low compression. If only one or two plugs are carbon fouled, check for corroded or cracked wires on the affected plugs. Also look for cracks in the distributor cap between the towers of affected cylinders.

RECOMMENDATION: After the problem is corrected, these plugs can be cleaned and reinstalled if not worn severely.

MMT Fouled

APPEARANCE: Spark plugs fouled by MMT (Methycyclopentadienyl Maganese Tricarbonyl) have reddish, rusty appearance on the insulator and side electrode.

CAUSE: MMT is an anti-knock additive in gasoline used to replace lead. During the combustion process, the MMT leaves a reddish deposit on the insulator and side electrode.

RECOMMENDATION: No engine malfunction is indicated and the deposits will not affect plug performance any more than lead deposits (see Ash Deposits). MMT fouled plugs can be cleaned, regapped and reinstalled.

High Speed Glazing

APPEARANCE: Glazing appears as shiny coating on the plug, either yellow or tan in color.

CAUSE: During hard, fast acceleration, plug temperatures rise suddenly. Deposits from normal combustion have no chance to fluff-off; instead, they melt on the insulator forming an electrically conductive coating which causes misfiring.

RECOMMENDATION: Glazed plugs are not easily cleaned. They should be replaced with a fresh set of plugs of the correct heat range. If the condition recurs, using plugs with a heat range one step colder may cure the problem.

Ash (Lead) Deposits

APPEARANCE: Ash deposits are characterized by light brown or white colored deposits crusted on the side or center electrodes. In some cases it may give the plug a rusty appearance.

CAUSE: Ash deposits are normally derived from oil or fuel additives burned during normal combustion. Normally they are harmless, though excessive amounts can cause misfiring. If deposits are excessive in short mileage, the valve guides may be worn.

RECOMMENDATION: Ash-fouled plugs can be cleaned, gapped and reinstalled.

Detonation

APPEARANCE: Detonation is usually characterized by a broken plug insulator.

CAUSE: A portion of the fuel charge will begin to burn spontaneously, from the increased heat following ignition. The explosion that results applies extreme pressure to engine components, frequently damaging spark plugs and pistons.

Detonation can result by over-advanced ignition timing, inferior gasoline (low octane) lean air/fuel mixture, poor carburetion, engine lugging or an increase in compression ratio due to combustion chamber deposits or engine modification.

RECOMMENDATION: Replace the plugs after correcting the problem.

Photos Courtesy Champion Spark Plug Co.

EMISSION CONTROLS

13. Be aware of the general condition of the emission control system. It contributes to reduced pollution and should be serviced regularly to maintain efficient engine operation.

14. Check all vacuum lines for dried, cracked or brittle conditions. Something as simple as a leaking vacuum hose can cause poor performance and loss of economy.

15. Avoid tampering with the emission control system. Attempting to improve fuel econ-

FUEL SYSTEM

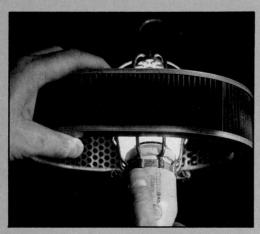 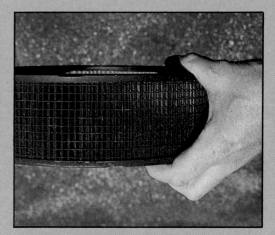

Check the air filter with a light behind it. If you can see light through the filter it can be reused.

Extremely clogged filters should be discarded and replaced with a new one.

18. Replace the air filter regularly. A dirty air filter richens the air/fuel mixture and can increase fuel consumption as much as 10%. Tests show that ⅓ of all vehicles have air filters in need of replacement.

19. Replace the fuel filter at least as often as recommended.

20. Set the idle speed and carburetor mixture to specifications.

21. Check the automatic choke. A sticking or malfunctioning choke wastes gas.

22. During the summer months, adjust the automatic choke for a leaner mixture which will produce faster engine warm-ups.

COOLING SYSTEM

29. Be sure all accessory drive belts are in good condition. Check for cracks or wear.

30. Adjust all accessory drive belts to proper tension.

31. Check all hoses for swollen areas, worn spots, or loose clamps.

32. Check coolant level in the radiator or expansion tank.

33. Be sure the thermostat is operating properly. A stuck thermostat delays engine warm-up and a cold engine uses nearly twice as much fuel as a warm engine.

34. Drain and replace the engine coolant at least as often as recommended. Rust and scale

TIRES & WHEELS

38. Check the tire pressure often with a pencil type gauge. Tests by a major tire manufacturer show that 90% of all vehicles have at least 1 tire improperly inflated. Better mileage can be achieved by over-inflating tires, but never exceed the maximum inflation pressure on the side of the tire.

39. If possible, install radial tires. Radial tires deliver as much as ½ mpg more than bias belted tires.

40. Avoid installing super-wide tires. They only create extra rolling resistance and decrease fuel mileage. Stick to the manufacturer's recommendations.

41. Have the wheels properly balanced.

omy by tampering with emission controls is more likely to worsen fuel economy than improve it. Emission control changes on modern engines are not readily reversible.

16. Clean (or replace) the EGR valve and lines as recommended.

17. Be sure that all vacuum lines and hoses are reconnected properly after working under the hood. An unconnected or misrouted vacuum line can wreak havoc with engine performance.

---

23. Check for fuel leaks at the carburetor, fuel pump, fuel lines and fuel tank. Be sure all lines and connections are tight.

24. Periodically check the tightness of the carburetor and intake manifold attaching nuts and bolts. These are a common place for vacuum leaks to occur.

25. Clean the carburetor periodically and lubricate the linkage.

26. The condition of the tailpipe can be an excellent indicator of proper engine combustion. After a long drive at highway speeds, the inside of the tailpipe should be a light grey in color. Black or soot on the insides indicates an overly rich mixture.

27. Check the fuel pump pressure. The fuel pump may be supplying more fuel than the engine needs.

28. Use the proper grade of gasoline for your engine. Don't try to compensate for knocking or "pinging" by advancing the ignition timing. This practice will only increase plug temperature and the chances of detonation or pre-ignition with relatively little performance gain.

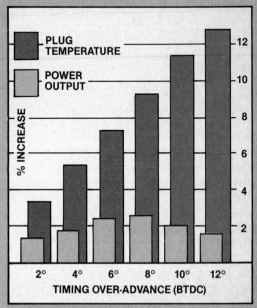

Increasing ignition timing past the specified setting results in a drastic increase in spark plug temperature with increased chance of detonation or preignition. Performance increase is considerably less. (Photo courtesy Champion Spark Plug Co.)

---

that form in the engine should be flushed out to allow the engine to operate at peak efficiency.

35. Clean the radiator of debris that can decrease cooling efficiency.

36. Install a flex-type or electric cooling fan, if you don't have a clutch type fan. Flex fans use curved plastic blades to push more air at low speeds when more cooling is needed; at high speeds the blades flatten out for less resistance. Electric fans only run when the engine temperature reaches a predetermined level.

37. Check the radiator cap for a worn or cracked gasket. If the cap does not seal properly, the cooling system will not function properly.

---

42. Be sure the front end is correctly aligned. A misaligned front end actually has wheels going in differed directions. The increased drag can reduce fuel economy by .3 mpg.

43. Correctly adjust the wheel bearings. Wheel bearings that are adjusted too tight increase rolling resistance.

Check tire pressures regularly with a reliable pocket type gauge. Be sure to check the pressure on a cold tire.

GENERAL MAINTENANCE

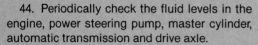

Check the fluid levels (particularly engine oil) on a regular basis. Be sure to check the oil for grit, water or other contamination.

A vacuum gauge is another excellent indicator of internal engine condition and can also be installed in the dash as a mileage indicator.

44. Periodically check the fluid levels in the engine, power steering pump, master cylinder, automatic transmission and drive axle.

45. Change the oil at the recommended interval and change the filter at every oil change. Dirty oil is thick and causes extra friction between moving parts, cutting efficiency and increasing wear. A worn engine requires more frequent tune-ups and gets progressively worse fuel economy. In general, use the lightest viscosity oil for the driving conditions you will encounter.

46. Use the recommended viscosity fluids in the transmission and axle.

47. Be sure the battery is fully charged for fast starts. A slow starting engine wastes fuel.

48. Be sure battery terminals are clean and tight.

49. Check the battery electrolyte level and add distilled water if necessary.

50. Check the exhaust system for crushed pipes, blockages and leaks.

51. Adjust the brakes. Dragging brakes or brakes that are not releasing create increased drag on the engine.

52. Install a vacuum gauge or miles-per-gallon gauge. These gauges visually indicate engine vacuum in the intake manifold. High vacuum = good mileage and low vacuum = poorer mileage. The gauge can also be an excellent indicator of internal engine conditions.

53. Be sure the clutch is properly adjusted. A slipping clutch wastes fuel.

54. Check and periodically lubricate the heat control valve in the exhaust manifold. A sticking or inoperative valve prevents engine warm-up and wastes gas.

55. Keep accurate records to check fuel economy over a period of time. A sudden drop in fuel economy may signal a need for tune-up or other maintenance.

Fuel Injectors

REMOVAL AND INSTALLATION

1. Disconnect the negative (–) battery cable.
2. The pressure in the fuel can be released by using the valve provided on the fuel rail assembly. Install a fuel pressure gauge part No. T80L-9974-B or equivalent to the fuel diagnostic (pressure relief) Shrader® valve on the fuel rail assembly. Release the pressure slowly to prevent fuel spills.
3. Remove the intake manifold as outlined in

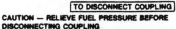

TO DISCONNECT COUPLING

CAUTION — RELIEVE FUEL PRESSURE BEFORE DISCONNECTING COUPLING

CLIP

① REMOVE CLIP FROM COUPLING

USE SPECIFIED TOOL OR EQUIVALENT

TOOL:
D87L-9280-A — 3/8 INCH
D87L-9280-B — 1/2 INCH

CAGE OPENING

② FIT TOOL TO COUPLING SO THAT TOOL CAN ENTER CAGE OPENING TO RELEASE THE GARTER SPRING.

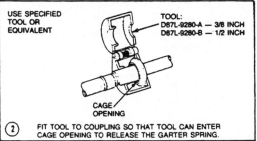

PUSH TOOL INTO CAGE OPENING

NOTE: SPECIFIED TOOL WILL FIT AROUND RUBBER COVERED FUEL LINE.

③ PUSH THE TOOL INTO THE CAGE OPENING TO RELEASE THE FEMALE FITTING FROM THE GARTER SPRING

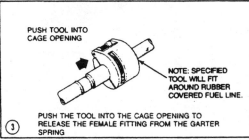

④ PULL THE COUPLING MALE AND FEMALE FITTINGS APART

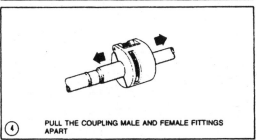

⑤ REMOVE THE TOOL FROM THE DISCONNECTED SPRING LOCK COUPLING

TO CONNECT COUPLING

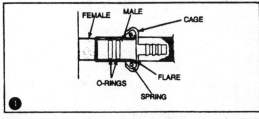

FEMALE   MALE   CAGE

O-RINGS   FLARE

SPRING

①

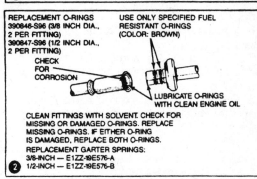

REPLACEMENT O-RINGS 390846-S96 (3/8 INCH DIA., 2 PER FITTING) 390847-S96 (1/2 INCH DIA., 2 PER FITTING)

USE ONLY SPECIFIED FUEL RESISTANT O-RINGS (COLOR: BROWN)

CHECK FOR CORROSION

LUBRICATE O-RINGS WITH CLEAN ENGINE OIL

CLEAN FITTINGS WITH SOLVENT. CHECK FOR MISSING OR DAMAGED O-RINGS. REPLACE MISSING O-RINGS. IF EITHER O-RING IS DAMAGED, REPLACE BOTH O-RINGS.
REPLACEMENT GARTER SPRINGS:
3/8-INCH — E1ZZ-19E576-A
1/2-INCH — E1ZZ-19E576-B

②

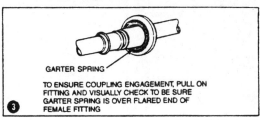

GARTER SPRING

TO ENSURE COUPLING ENGAGEMENT, PULL ON FITTING AND VISUALLY CHECK TO BE SURE GARTER SPRING IS OVER FLARED END OF FEMALE FITTING

③

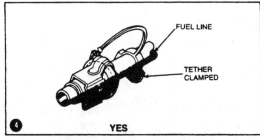

FUEL LINE

TETHER CLAMPED

④   YES

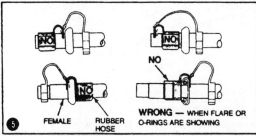

NO   NO

NO

WRONG — WHEN FLARE OR O-RINGS ARE SHOWING

⑤   FEMALE   RUBBER HOSE

Fuel line disconnects—3.0L SHO engine

the "Fuel Charging Assembly" removal and installation procedures in this section.

4. Disconnect the electrical connectors at the fuel injectors.

5. Remove the four fuel rail retaining bolts.

6. Raise and slightly rotate the fuel rail assembly and remove the injectors.

To install:

1. Inspect the injector O-ring seals and insulators for damage or deterioration. Replace if necessary.

2. Lubricate the O-rings with light grade engine oil.

3. Install the injectors in the fuel rail. Lightly twist and push the injectors into position.

4. Install the fuel rail and injectors into the cylinder head.

5. Install the fuel rail retaining bolts and torque to 11-17 ft. lbs.

6. Connect the electrical connectors at the injectors.

7. Install the intake manifold as outlined in the "Fuel Charging Assembly" procedures in this section.

8. Connect the negative (−) battery cable. Start the engine and check for coolant and fuel leaks.

FUEL TANK

CAUTION: *Do not smoke or carry lighted tobacco or open flame of any type when working on or near any fuel related component. Highly flammable mixtures are always present and may be ignited, resulting in possible personal injury.*

Before servicing any components of the fuel system, perform the following procedure for releasing the fuel system pressure. Both the CFI (central fuel infection) and EFI (electronic fuel injection) fuel injection systems may be under pressure even when the engine is not running.

Before servicing any components of the fuel system, perform the following procedure for releasing the fuel system pressure. Both the CFI (central) and EFI (electronic) fuel injection systems may be under pressure even when the engine is not running.

1. Remove the fuel filler cap.

2. Release the fuel pressure by attaching a Fuel Pressure Gauge part No. T80L-9974-B or equivalent to the pressure relief valve on the fuel rail assembly.

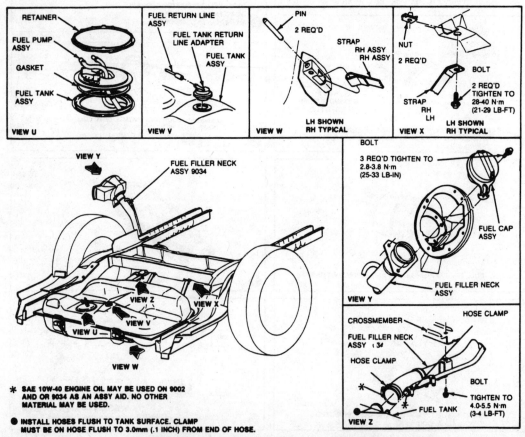

* SAE 10W-40 ENGINE OIL MAY BE USED ON 9002 AND OR 9034 AS AN ASSY AID. NO OTHER MATERIAL MAY BE USED.

● INSTALL HOSES FLUSH TO TANK SURFACE. CLAMP MUST BE ON HOSE FLUSH TO 3.0mm (.1 INCH) FROM END OF HOSE.

Fuel tank removal—Taurus/Sable and Continental

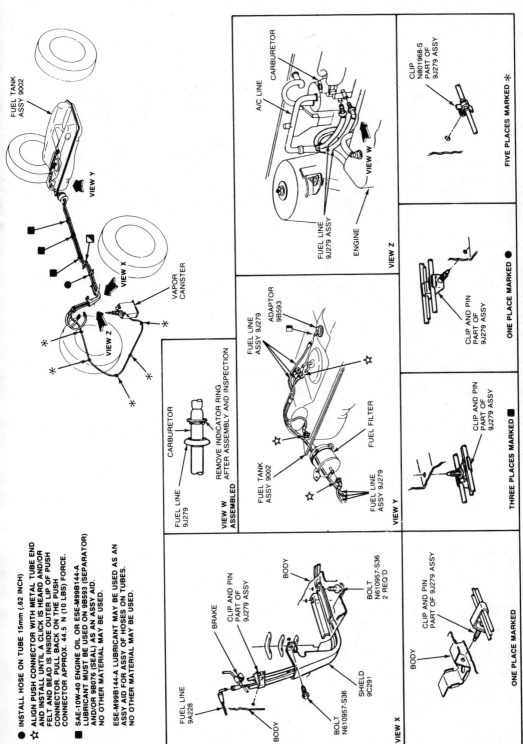

- INSTALL HOSE ON TUBE 15mm (.62 INCH)

☆ ALIGN PUSH CONNECTOR WITH METAL TUBE END AND INSTALL UNTIL A CLICK IS HEARD AND/OR FELT AND BEAD IS INSIDE OUTER LIP OF PUSH CONNECTOR. PULL BACK ON THE PUSH CONNECTOR APPROX. 44.5 N (10 LBS) FORCE.

SAE-10W-40 ENGINE OIL OR ESE-M99B144-A LUBRICANT MUST BE USED ON 9B593 (SEPARATOR) AND/OR 9B076 (SEAL) AS AN ASSY AID. NO OTHER MATERIAL MAY BE USED.

ESE-M99B144-A LUBRICANT MAY BE USED AS AN ASSY AID FOR ASSY OF HOSES ON TUBES. NO OTHER MATERIAL MAY BE USED.

FUEL TANK ASSY 9002

VIEW Y

VIEW X

VAPOR CANISTER

VIEW Z

CARBURETOR

A/C LINE

FUEL LINE 9J279 ASSY

ENGINE

VIEW W

VIEW Z

CLIP N801968-S PART OF 9J279 ASSY

FIVE PLACES MARKED ✳

FUEL LINE ASSY 9J279

ADAPTOR 9B593

FUEL TANK ASSY 9002

FUEL FILTER

FUEL LINE ASSY 9J279

VIEW Y

CLIP AND PIN PART OF 9J279 ASSY

ONE PLACE MARKED ●

CLIP AND PIN PART OF 9J279 ASSY

FUEL LINE 9J279

CARBURETOR

REMOVE INDICATOR RING AFTER ASSEMBLY AND INSPECTION

VIEW W ASSEMBLED

CLIP AND PIN PART OF 9J279 ASSY

THREE PLACES MARKED ■

FUEL LINE 9A228

BODY

BODY

BOLT N610957-S36

BRAKE

CLIP AND PIN PART OF 9J279 ASSY

BODY

BOLT N610957-S36 2 REQ'D

SHIELD 9C291

VIEW X

BODY

CLIP AND PIN PART OF 9J279 ASSY

ONE PLACE MARKED

Fuel tank and lines—2.5L engine, 3.0L engine similar

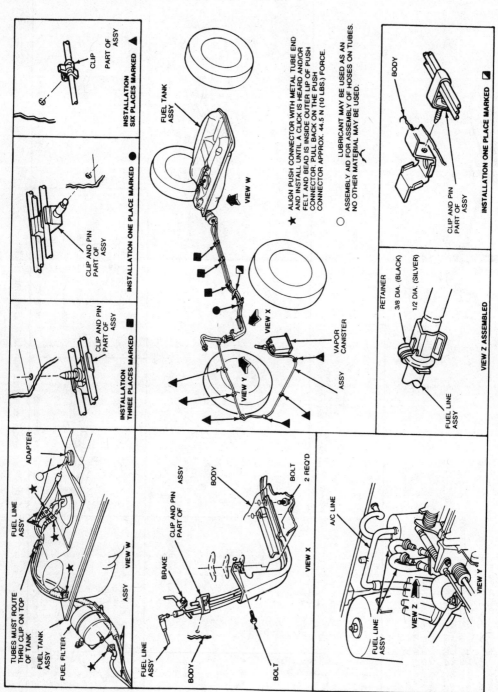

INSTALLATION SIX PLACES MARKED ▲

CLIP
PART OF ASSY

INSTALLATION ONE PLACE MARKED ●

CLIP AND PIN
PART OF ASSY

INSTALLATION THREE PLACES MARKED ■

CLIP AND PIN
PART OF ASSY

FUEL TANK ASSY

VIEW W

VIEW X

VIEW Y

VAPOR CANISTER

ASSY

★ ALIGN PUSH CONNECTOR WITH METAL TUBE END AND INSTALL UNTIL A CLICK IS HEARD AND/OR FELT AND BEAD IS INSIDE OUTER LIP OF PUSH CONNECTOR. PULL BACK ON THE PUSH CONNECTOR APPROX. 44.5 N (10 LBS.) FORCE.

○ LUBRICANT MAY BE USED AS AN ASSEMBLY AID FOR ASSEMBLY OF HOSES ON TUBES. NO OTHER MATERIAL MAY BE USED.

BODY

INSTALLATION ONE PLACE MARKED ◤

CLIP AND PIN
PART OF ASSY

RETAINER
3/8 DIA. (BLACK)
1/2 DIA. (SILVER)

FUEL LINE ASSY

VIEW Z ASSEMBLED

TUBES MUST ROUTE THRU CLIP ON TOP OF TANK
FUEL TANK ASSY
FUEL FILTER
ADAPTER
FUEL LINE ASSY
ASSY   VIEW W

FUEL LINE ASSY
BRAKE
CLIP AND PIN PART OF ASSY
BODY
BOLT
BODY
BOLT
2 REQ'D
VIEW X

A/C LINE
FUEL LINE ASSY
VIEW Z
VIEW Y

Fuel tank and lines—Continental

3. Leave the pressure out slowly to prevent the fuel from being ejected under pressure.

REMOVAL AND INSTALLATION

CAUTION: *Have the tank as empty as possible. No smoking or open flame while working on the fuel system.*

1. Disconnect the negative (–) battery cable from the battery.

NOTE: *The fuel tank has to be drained before any service can be performed. The fuel injected Taurus/Sable and Continental have reservoirs inside the tank to maintain fuel near the fuel pickup during cornering and under low fuel conditions. The reservoir can block the siphon hose from reaching the bottom of the tank. This situation can be overcome with a few repeated attempts using different hose positions.*

2. Raise the rear of the car and safely support it on jackstands.

3. Remove the two mounting bolts at the top rear of the tank while supporting the tank on a piece of wood and a floor jack.

4. Disconnect the gas fill and breather lines from the tank. Disconnect the fuel feed, return and breather lines from the front of the tank, plug these lines Refer to "Push Connect Fitting" removal earlier in this chapter. Use extreme caution not to damage the plastic fuel connections.

5. Lower and remove the gas tank.

To install:

1. Before proceeding check the following:

a. Leak check the pump/sendor unit.

b. Make sure the fuel vapor separator valve is installed completely in the tank.

c. Make all the required fuel line, fuel return line, and electrical connections before the tank is installed.

2. Place the fuel tank in its proper position in the vehicle.

3. Place the tank straps around the tank and start attaching nut and bolts.

4. Tighten the strap bolts to 21-29 ft. lbs.

Troubleshooting Basic Fuel System Problems

Problem	Cause	Solution
Engine cranks, but won't start (or is hard to start) when cold	• Empty fuel tank • Incorrect starting procedure • Defective fuel pump • No fuel in carburetor • Clogged fuel filter • Engine flooded • Defective choke	• Check for fuel in tank • Follow correct procedure • Check pump output • Check for fuel in the carburetor • Replace fuel filter • Wait 15 minutes; try again • Check choke plate
Engine cranks, but is hard to start (or does not start) when hot— (presence of fuel is assumed)	• Defective choke	• Check choke plate
Rough idle or engine runs rough	• Dirt or moisture in fuel • Clogged air filter • Faulty fuel pump	• Replace fuel filter • Replace air filter • Check fuel pump output
Engine stalls or hesitates on acceleration	• Dirt or moisture in the fuel • Dirty carburetor • Defective fuel pump • Incorrect float level, defective accelerator pump	• Replace fuel filter • Clean the carburetor • Check fuel pump output • Check carburetor
Poor gas mileage	• Clogged air filter • Dirty carburetor • Defective choke, faulty carburetor adjustment	• Replace air filter • Clean carburetor • Check carburetor
Engine is flooded (won't start accompanied by smell of raw fuel)	• Improperly adjusted choke or carburetor	• Wait 15 minutes and try again, without pumping gas pedal • If it won't start, check carburetor

Chassis Electrical

UNDERSTANDING AND TROUBLESHOOTING ELECTRICAL SYSTEMS

At the rate which both import and domestic manufacturers are incorporating electronic control systems into their production lines, it won't be long before every new vehicle is equipped with one or more on-board computer, like the EEC-IV unit installed on the car. These electronic components (with no moving parts) should theoretically last the life of the vehicle, provided nothing external happens to damage the circuits or memory chips.

While it is true that electronic components should never wear out, in the real world malfunctions do occur. It is also true that any computer-based system is extremely sensitive to electrical voltages and cannot tolerate careless or haphazard testing or service procedures. An inexperienced individual can literally do major damage looking for a minor problem by using the wrong kind of test equipment or connecting test leads or connectors with the ignition switch ON. When selecting test equipment, make sure the manufacturers instructions state that the tester is compatible with whatever type of electronic control system is being serviced. Read all instructions carefully and double check all test points before installing probes or making any test connections.

The following section outlines basic diagnosis techniques for dealing with computerized automotive control systems. Along with a general explanation of the various types of test equipment available to aid in servicing modern electronic automotive systems, basic repair techniques for wiring harnesses and connectors is given. Read the basic information before attempting any repairs or testing on any computerized system, to provide the background of information necessary to avoid the most common and obvious mistakes that can cost both time and money. Although the replacement and testing procedures are simple in themselves, the systems are not, and unless one has a thorough understanding of all components and their function within a particular computerized control system, the logical test sequence that these systems demand cannot be followed. Minor malfunctions can make a big difference, so it is important to know how each component affects the operation of the overall electronic system to find the ultimate cause of a problem without replacing good components unnecessarily. It is not enough to use the correct test equipment; the test equipment must be used correctly.

Safety Precautions

CAUTION: *Whenever working on or around any computer based microprocessor control system, always observe these general precautions to prevent the possibility of personal injury or damage to electronic components.*

• Never install or remove battery cables with the key ON or the engine running. Jumper cables should be connected with the key OFF to avoid power surges that can damage electronic control units. Engines equipped with computer controlled systems should avoid both giving and getting jump starts due to the possibility of serious damage to components from arcing in the engine compartment when connections are made with the ignition ON.

• Always remove the battery cables before charging the battery. Never use a high output charger on an installed battery or attempt to use any type of "hot shot" (24 volt) starting aid.

• Exercise care when inserting test probes into connectors to insure good connections without damaging the connector or spreading the pins. Always probe connectors from the rear (wire) side, NOT the pin side, to avoid accidental shorting of terminals during test procedures.

• Never remove or attach wiring harness

connectors with the ignition switch ON, especially to an electronic control unit.

• Do not drop any components during service procedures and never apply 12 volts directly to any component (like a solenoid or relay) unless instructed specifically to do so. Some component electrical windings are designed to safely handle only 4 or 5 volts and can be destroyed in seconds if 12 volts are applied directly to the connector.

• Remove the electronic control unit if the vehicle is to be placed in an environment where temperatures exceed approximately 176°F (80°C), such as a paint spray booth or when arc or gas welding near the control unit location in the car.

ORGANIZED TROUBLESHOOTING

When diagnosing a specific problem, organized troubleshooting is a must. The complexity of a modern automobile demands that you approach any problem in a logical, organized manner. There are certain troubleshooting techniques that are standard:

1. Establish when the problem occurs. Does the problem appear only under certain conditions? Were there any noises, odors, or other unusual symptoms?

2. Isolate the problem area. To do this, make some simple tests and observations; then eliminate the systems that are working properly. Check for obvious problems such as broken wires, dirty connections or split or disconnected vacuum hoses. Always check the obvious before assuming something complicated is the cause.

3. Test for problems systematically to determine the cause once the problem area is isolated. Are all the components functioning properly? Is there power going to electrical switches and motors? Is there vacuum at vacuum switches and/or actuators? Is there a mechanical problem such as bent linkage or loose mounting screws? Doing careful, systematic checks will often turn up most causes on the first inspection without wasting time checking components that have little or no relationship to the problem.

4. Test all repairs after the work is done to make sure that the problem is fixed. Some causes can be traced to more than one component, so a careful verification of repair work is important to pick up additional malfunctions that may cause a problem to reappear or a different problem to arise. A blown fuse, for example, is a simple problem that may require more than another fuse to repair. If you don't look for a problem that caused a fuse to blow, for example, a shorted wire may go undetected.

Experience has shown that most problems tend to be the result of a fairly simple and obvious cause, such as loose or corroded connectors or air leaks in the intake system; making careful inspection of components during testing essential to quick and accurate troubleshooting. Special, hand held computerized testers designed specifically for diagnosing the EEC-IV system are available from a variety of aftermarket sources, as well as from the vehicle manufacturer, but care should be taken that any test equipment being used is designed to diagnose that particular computer controlled system accurately without damaging the control unit (ECU) or components being tested.

NOTE: *Pinpointing the exact cause of trouble in an electrical system can sometimes only be accomplished by the use of special test equipment. The following describes commonly used test equipment and explains how to put it to best use in diagnosis. In addition to the information covered below, the manufacturer's instructions booklet provided with the tester should be read and clearly understood before attempting any test procedures.*

TEST EQUIPMENT

Jumper Wires

Jumper wires are simple, yet extremely valuable, pieces of test equipment. Jumper wires are merely wires that are used to bypass sections of a circuit. The simplest type of jumper wire is merely a length of multi-strand wire with an alligator clip at each end. Jumper wires are usually fabricated from lengths of standard automotive wire and whatever type of connector (alligator clip, spade connector or pin connector) that is required for the particular vehicle being tested. The well equipped tool box will have several different styles of jumper wires in several different lengths. Some jumper wires are made with three or more terminals coming from a common splice for special purpose testing. In cramped, hard-to-reach areas it is advisable to have insulated boots over the jumper wire terminals in order to prevent accidental grounding, sparks, and possible fire, especially when testing fuel system components.

Jumper wires are used primarily to locate open electrical circuits, on either the ground (–) side of the circuit or on the hot (+) side. If an electrical component fails to operate, connect the jumper wire between the component and a good ground. If the component operates only with the jumper installed, the ground circuit is open. If the ground circuit is good, but the component does not operate, the circuit between the power feed and component is open. You can sometimes connect the jumper wire directly from the battery to the hot terminal of the component, but first make sure the component uses 12 volts in operation. Some electrical components, such as fuel injectors, are designed to operate on about 4 volts and running 12 volts directly to the injector terminals can burn out the wiring. By inserting an inline fuseholder between a set of test leads, a fused jumper wire can be used for bypassing open circuits. Use a 5 amp fuse to provide protection against voltage spikes. When in doubt, use a voltmeter to check the voltage input to the component and measure how much voltage is being applied normally. By moving the jumper wire successively back from the lamp toward the power source, you can isolate the area of the circuit where the open is located. When the component stops functioning, or the power is cut off, the open is in the segment of wire between the jumper and the point previously tested.

CAUTION: *Never use jumpers made from wire that is of lighter gauge than used in the circuit under test. If the jumper wire is of too small gauge, it may overheat and possibly melt. Never use jumpers to bypass high resistance loads (such as motors) in a circuit. Bypassing resistances, in effect, creates a short circuit which may, in turn, cause damage and fire. Never use a jumper for anything other than temporary bypassing of components in a circuit.*

12 Volt Test Light

The 12 volt test light is used to check circuits and components while electrical current is flowing through them. It is used for voltage and ground tests. Twelve volt test lights come in different styles but all have three main parts; a ground clip, a probe, and a light. The most commonly used 12 volt test lights have pick-type probes. To use a 12 volt test light, connect the ground clip to a good ground and probe wherever necessary with the pick. The pick should be sharp so that it can penetrate wire insulation to make contact with the wire, without making a large hole in the insulation. The wrap-around light is handy in hard to reach areas or where it is difficult to support a wire to push a probe pick into it. To use the wrap around light, hook the wire to probed with the hook and pull the trigger. A small pick will be forced through the wire insulation into the wire core.

CAUTION: *Do not use a test light to probe electronic ignition spark plug or coil wires. Never use a pick-type test light to probe wiring on computer controlled systems unless specifically instructed to do so. Any wire insulation that is pierced by the test light probe should be taped and sealed with silicone after testing.*

Like the jumper wire, the 12 volt test light is used to isolate opens in circuits. But, whereas the jumper wire is used to bypass the open to operate the load, the 12 volt test light is used to locate the presence of voltage in a circuit. If the test light glows, you know that there is power up to that point; if the 12 volt test light does not glow when its probe is inserted into the wire or connector, you know that there is an open circuit (no power). Move the test light in successive steps back toward the power source until the light in the handle does glow. When it does glow, the open is between the probe and point previously probed.

NOTE: *The test light does not detect that 12 volts (or any particular amount of voltage) is present; it only detects that some voltage is present. It is advisable before using the test light to touch its terminals across the battery posts to make sure the light is operating properly.*

Self-Powered Test Light

The self-powered test light usually contains a 1.5 volt penlight battery. One type of self-powered test light is similar in design to the 12 volt test light. This type has both the battery and the light in the handle and pick-type probe tip. The second type has the light toward the open tip, so that the light illuminates the contact point. The self-powered test light is dual purpose piece of test equipment. It can be used to test for either open or short circuits when power is isolated from the circuit (continuity test). A powered test light should not be used on any computer controlled system or component unless specifically instructed to do so. Many engine sensors can be destroyed by even this small amount of voltage applied directly to the terminals.

Open Circuit Testing

To use the self-powered test light to check for open circuits, first isolate the circuit from the vehicle's 12 volt power source by disconnecting the battery or wiring harness connector. Connect the test light ground clip to a good ground and probe sections of the circuit sequentially with the test light. (start from either end of the circuit). If the light is out, the open is between the probe and the circuit ground. If the light is on, the open is between the probe and end of the circuit toward the power source.

Short Circuit Testing

By isolating the circuit both from power and from ground, and using a self-powered test light, you can check for shorts to ground in the circuit. Isolate the circuit from power and ground. Connect the test light ground clip to a good ground and probe any easy-to-reach test point in the circuit. If the light comes on, there is a short somewhere in the circuit. To isolate the short, probe a test point at either end of the isolated circuit (the light should be on). Leave the test light probe connected and open connectors, switches, remove parts, etc., sequentially, until the light goes out. When the light goes out, the short is between the last circuit component opened and the previous circuit opened.

NOTE: *The 1.5 volt battery in the test light does not provide much current. A weak battery may not provide enough power to illuminate the test light even when a complete circuit is made (especially if there are high resistances in the circuit). Always make sure that the test battery is strong. To check the battery, briefly touch the ground clip to the probe; if the light glows brightly the battery is strong enough for testing. Never use a self-powered test light to perform checks for opens or shorts when power is applied to the electrical system under test. The 12 volt vehicle power will quickly burn out the 1.5 volt light bulb in the test light.*

Voltmeter

A voltmeter is used to measure voltage at any point in a circuit, or to measure the voltage drop across any part of a circuit. It can also be used to check continuity in a wire or circuit by indicating current flow from one end to the other. Voltmeters usually have various scales on the meter dial and a selector switch to allow the selection of different voltages. The voltmeter has a positive and a negative lead. To avoid damage to the meter, always connect the negative lead to the negative (–) side of the circuit (to ground or nearest the ground side of the circuit) and connect the positive lead to the positive (+) side of the circuit (to the power source or the nearest power source). Note that the negative voltmeter lead will always be black and that the positive voltmeter will always be some color other than black (usually red). Depending on how the voltmeter is connected into the circuit, it has several uses.

A voltmeter can be connected either in parallel or in series with a circuit and it has a very high resistance to current flow. When connected in parallel, only a small amount of current will flow through the voltmeter current path; the rest will flow through the normal circuit current path and the circuit will work normally. When the voltmeter is connected in series with a circuit, only a small amount of current can flow through the circuit. The circuit will not work properly, but the voltmeter reading will show if the circuit is complete or not.

Available Voltage Measurement

Set the voltmeter selector switch to the 20V position and connect the meter negative lead to the negative (–) post of the battery. Connect the positive meter lead to the positive (+) post of the battery and turn the ignition switch ON to provide a load. Read the voltage on the meter or digital display. A well charged battery should register over 12 volts. If the meter reads below 11.5 volts, the battery power may be insufficient to operate the electrical system properly. This test determines voltage available from the battery and should be the first step in any electrical trouble diagnosis procedure. Many electrical problems, especially on computer controlled systems, can be caused by a low state of charge in the battery. Excessive corrosion at the battery cable terminals can cause a poor contact that will prevent proper charging and full battery current flow.

Normal battery voltage is 12 volts when fully charged. When the battery is supplying current to one or more circuits it is said to be "under load". When everything is off the electrical system is under a "no-load" condition. A fully charged battery may show about 12.5 volts at no load; will drop to 12 volts under medium load; and will drop even lower under heavy load. If the battery is partially discharged the voltage decrease under heavy load may be excessive, even though the battery shows 12 volts or more at no load. When allowed to discharge further, the battery's available voltage under load will decrease more severely. For this reason, it is important that the battery be fully charged during all testing procedures to avoid errors in diagnosis and incorrect test results.

Voltage Drop

When current flows through a resistance, the voltage beyond the resistance is reduced (the larger the current, the greater the reduction in voltage). When no current is flowing, there is no voltage drop because there is no current flow. All points in the circuit which are connected to the power source are at the same voltage as the power source. The total voltage drop always equals the total source voltage. In a long circuit with many connectors, a series of small, unwanted voltage drops due to corrosion at the connectors can add up to a total loss of voltage which impairs the operation of the normal loads in the circuit.

INDIRECT COMPUTATION OF VOLTAGE DROPS

1. Set the voltmeter selector switch to the 20 volt position.
2. Connect the meter negative lead to a good ground.
3. Probe all resistances in the circuit with the positive meter lead.
4. Operate the circuit in all modes and observe the voltage readings.

DIRECT MEASUREMENT OF VOLTAGE DROPS

1. Set the voltmeter switch to the 20 volt position.

2. Connect the voltmeter negative lead to the ground side of the resistance load to be measured.

3. Connect the positive lead to the positive side of the resistance or load to be measured.

4. Read the voltage drop directly on the 20 volt scale.

Too high a voltage indicates too high a resistance. If, for example, a blower motor runs too slowly, you can determine if there is too high a resistance in the resistor pack. By taking voltage drop readings in all parts of the circuit, you can isolate the problem. Too low a voltage drop indicates too low a resistance. If, for example, a blower motor runs too fast in the MED and/or LOW position, the problem can be isolated in the resistor pack by taking voltage drop readings in all parts of the circuit to locate a possibly shorted resistor. The maximum allowable voltage drop under load is critical, especially if there is more than one high resistance problem in a circuit because all voltage drops are cumulative. A small drop is normal due to the resistance of the conductors.

HIGH RESISTANCE TESTING

1. Set the voltmeter selector switch to the 4 volt position.

2. Connect the voltmeter positive lead to the positive (+) post of the battery.

3. Turn on the headlights and heater blower to provide a load.

4. Probe various points in the circuit with the negative voltmeter lead.

5. Read the voltage drop on the 4 volt scale. Some average maximum allowable voltage drops are:

FUSE PANEL – 7 volts
IGNITION SWITCH – 5volts
HEADLIGHT SWITCH – 7 volts
IGNITION COIL (+) – 5 volts
ANY OTHER LOAD – 1.3 volts
NOTE: *Voltage drops are all measured while a load is operating; without current flow, there will be no voltage drop.*

Ohmmeter

The ohmmeter is designed to read resistance (ohms) in a circuit or component. Although there are several different styles of ohmmeters, all will usually have a selector switch which permits the measurement of different ranges of resistance (usually the selector switch allows the multiplication of the meter reading by 10, 100, 1000, and 10,000). A calibration knob allows the meter to be set at zero for accurate measurement. Since all ohmmeters are powered by an internal battery (usually 9 volts), the ohmmeter can be used as a self-powered test light. When the ohmmeter is connected, current from the ohmmeter flows through the circuit or component being tested. Since the ohmmeter's internal resistance and voltage are known values, the amount of current flow through the meter depends on the resistance of the circuit or component being tested.

The ohmmeter can be used to perform continuity test for opens or shorts (either by observation of the meter needle or as a self-powered test light), and to read actual resistance in a circuit. It should be noted that the ohmmeter is used to check the resistance of a component or wire while there is no voltage applied to the circuit. Current flow from an outside voltage source (such as the vehicle battery) can damage the ohmmeter, so the circuit or component should be isolated from the vehicle electrical system before any testing is done. Since the ohmmeter uses its own voltage source, either lead can be connected to any test point.

NOTE: *When checking diodes or other solid state components, the ohmmeter leads can only be connected one way in order to measure current flow in a single direction. Make sure the positive (+) and negative (–) terminal connections are as described in the test procedures to verify the one-way diode operation.*

In using the meter for making continuity checks, do not be concerned with the actual resistance readings. Zero resistance, or any resistance readings, indicate continuity in the circuit. Infinite resistance indicates an open in the circuit. A high resistance reading where there should be none indicates a problem in the circuit. Checks for short circuits are made in the same manner as checks for open circuits except that the circuit must be isolated from both power and normal ground. Infinite resistance indicates no continuity to ground, while zero resistance indicates a dead short to ground.

RESISTANCE MEASUREMENT

The batteries in an ohmmeter will weaken with age and temperature, so the ohmmeter must be calibrated or "zeroed" before taking measurements. To zero the meter, place the selector switch in its lowest range and touch the two ohmmeter leads together. Turn the calibration knob until the meter needle is exactly on zero.

NOTE: *All analog (needle) type ohmmeters must be zeroed before use, but some digital ohmmeter models are automatically calibrated when the switch is turned on. Self-calibrating digital ohmmeters do not have an adjusting knob, but its a good idea to check for a zero readout before use by touching the leads together. All computer controlled systems require the use of a digital ohmmeter with at least 10 megohms impedance for testing. Before any test procedures are attempted, make sure the ohmmeter used is compatible with the electrical system or damage to the onboard computer could result.*

To measure resistance, first isolate the circuit from the vehicle power source by disconnecting the battery cables or the harness connector. Make sure the key is OFF when disconnecting any components or the battery. Where necessary, also isolate at least one side of the circuit to be checked to avoid reading parallel resistances. Parallel circuit resistances will always give a lower reading than the actual resistance of either of the branches. When measuring the resistance of parallel circuits, the total resistance will always be lower than the smallest resistance in the circuit. Connect the meter leads to both sides of the circuit (wire or component) and read the actual measured ohms on the meter scale. Make sure the selector switch is set to the proper ohm scale for the circuit being tested to avoid misreading the ohmmeter test value.

CAUTION: *Never use an ohmmeter with power applied to the circuit. Like the self-powered test light, the ohmmeter is designed to operate on its own power supply. The normal 12 volt automotive electrical system current could damage the meter.*

Ammeters

An ammeter measures the amount of current flowing through a circuit in units called amperes or amps. Amperes are units of electron flow which indicate how fast the electrons are flowing through the circuit. Since Ohms Law dictates that current flow in a circuit is equal to the circuit voltage divided by the total circuit resistance, increasing voltage also increases the current level (amps). Likewise, any decrease in resistance will increase the amount of amps in a circuit. At normal operating voltage, most circuits have a characteristic amount of amperes, called "current draw" which can be measured using an ammeter. By referring to a specified current draw rating, measuring the amperes, and comparing the two values, one can determine what is happening within the circuit to aid in diagnosis. An open circuit, for example, will not allow any current to flow so the ammeter reading will be zero. More current flows through a heavily loaded circuit or when the charging system is operating.

An ammeter is always connected in series with the circuit being tested. All of the current that normally flows through the circuit must also flow through the ammeter; if there is any other path for the current to follow, the ammeter reading will not be accurate. The ammeter itself has very little resistance to current flow and therefore will not affect the circuit, but it will measure current draw only when the circuit is closed and electricity is flowing. Excessive current draw can blow fuses and drain the battery, while a reduced current draw can cause motors to run slowly, lights to dim and other components to not operate properly. The ammeter can help diagnose these conditions by locating the cause of the high or low reading.

Multimeters

Different combinations of test meters can be built into a single unit designed for specific tests. Some of the more common combination test devices are known as Volt/Amp testers, Tach/Dwell meters, or Digital Multimeters. The Volt/Amp tester is used for charging system, starting system or battery tests and consists of a voltmeter, an ammeter and a variable resistance carbon pile. The voltmeter will usually have at least two ranges for use with 6, 12 and 24 volt systems. The ammeter also has more than one range for testing various levels of battery loads and starter current draw and the carbon pile can be adjusted to offer different amounts of resistance. The Volt/Amp tester has heavy leads to carry large amounts of current and many later models have an inductive ammeter pickup that clamps around the wire to simplify test connections. On some models, the ammeter also has a zero-center scale to allow testing of charging and starting systems without switching leads or polarity. A digital multimeter is a voltmeter, ammeter and ohmmeter combined in an instrument which gives a digital readout. These are often used when testing solid state circuits because of their high input impedance (usually 10 megohms or more).

The tach/dwell meter combines a tachometer and a dwell (cam angle) meter and is a specialized kind of voltmeter. The tachometer scale is marked to show engine speed in rpm and the dwell scale is marked to show degrees of distributor shaft rotation. In most electronic ignition systems, dwell is determined by the control unit, but the dwell meter can also be used to check the duty cycle (operation) of some electronic engine control systems. Some tach/dwell meters are powered by an internal battery, while others take their power from the car battery in use. The battery powered testers usually require calibration much like an ohmmeter before testing.

Special Test Equipment

A variety of diagnostic tools are available to help troubleshoot and repair computerized engine control systems. The most sophisticated of these devices are the console type engine analyzers that usually occupy a garage service bay, but there are several types of aftermarket electronic testers available that will allow quick circuit tests of the engine control system by plugging directly into a special connector located in the engine compartment or under the dashboard. Several tool and equipment manufacturers offer simple, hand held testers that measure various circuit voltage levels on command to check all system components for proper operation. Although these testers usually cost about $300–500, consider that the average computer control unit (or ECM) can cost just as much and the money saved by not replacing perfectly good sensors or components in an attempt to correct a problem could justify the purchase price of a special diagnostic tester the first time it's used.

These computerized testers can allow quick and easy test measurements while the engine is operating or while the car is being driven. In addition, the on-board computer memory can be read to access any stored trouble codes; in effect allowing the computer to tell you where it hurts and aid trouble diagnosis by pinpointing exactly which circuit or component is malfunctioning. In the same manner, repairs can be tested to make sure the problem has been corrected. The biggest advantage these special testers have is their relatively easy hookups that minimize or eliminate the chances of making the wrong connections and getting false voltage readings or damaging the computer accidentally.

NOTE: *It should be remembered that these testers check voltage levels in circuits; they don't detect mechanical problems or failed components if the circuit voltage falls within the preprogrammed limits stored in the tester PROM unit. Also, most of the hand held testes are designed to work only on one or two systems made by a specific manufacturer.*

A variety of aftermarket testers are available to help diagnose different computerized control systems. Owatonna Tool Company (OTC), for example, markets a device called the OTC Monitor which plugs directly into the assembly line diagnostic link (ALDL). The OTC tester makes diagnosis a simple matter of pressing the correct buttons and, by changing the internal PROM or inserting a different diagnosis cartridge, it will work on any model from full size to subcompact, over a wide range of years. An adapter is supplied with the tester to allow connection to all types of ALDL links, regardless of the number of pin terminals used. By inserting an updated PROM into the OTC tester, it can be easily updated to diagnose any new modifications of computerized control systems.

Wiring Harnesses

The average automobile contains about ½ mile of wiring, with hundreds of individual connections. To protect the many wires from damage and to keep them from becoming a confusing tangle, they are organized into bundles, enclosed in plastic or taped together and called wire harnesses. Different wiring harnesses serve different parts of the vehicle. Individual wires are color coded to help trace them through a harness where sections are hidden from view.

A loose or corroded connection or a replacement wire that is too small for the circuit will add extra resistance and an additional voltage drop to the circuit. A ten percent voltage drop can result in slow or erratic motor operation, for example, even though the circuit is complete. Automotive wiring or circuit conductors can be in any one of three forms:

1. Single strand wire
2. Multi-strand wire
3. Printed circuitry

Single strand wire has a solid metal core and is usually used inside such components as alternators, motors, relays and other devices. Multi-strand wire has a core made of many small strands of wire twisted together into a single conductor. Most of the wiring in an automotive electrical system is made up of multi-strand wire, either as a single conductor or grouped together in a harness. All wiring is color coded on the insulator, either as a solid color or as a colored wire with an identification stripe. A printed circuit is a thin film of copper or other conductor that is printed on an insulator backing. Occasionally, a printed circuit is sandwiched between two sheets of plastic for more protection and flexibility. A complete printed circuit, consisting of conductors, insulating material and connectors for lamps or other components is called a printed circuit board. Printed circuitry is used in place of individual wires or harnesses in places where space is limited, such as behind instrument panels.

Wire Gauge

Since computer controlled automotive electrical systems are very sensitive to changes in resistance, the selection of properly sized wires is critical when systems are repaired. The wire gauge number is an expression of the cross section area of the conductor. The most common system for expressing wire size is the American Wire Gauge (AWG) system.

Wire cross section area is measured in circular mils. A mil is $\frac{1}{1000}$ in. (0.001 in.); a circular mil is the area of a circle one mil in diameter. For example, a conductor $\frac{1}{4}$ in. in diameter is 0.250 in. or 250 mils. The circular mil cross section area of the wire is 250 squared (250^2) or 62,500 circular mils. Imported car models usually use metric wire gauge designations, which is simply the cross section area of the conductor in square millimeters (mm^2).

Gauge numbers are assigned to conductors of various cross section areas. As gauge number increases, area decreases and the conductor becomes smaller. A 5 gauge conductor is smaller than a 1 gauge conductor and a 10 gauge is smaller than a 5 gauge. As the cross section area of a conductor decreases, resistance increases and so does the gauge number. A conductor with a higher gauge number will carry less current than a conductor with a lower gauge number.

NOTE: *Gauge wire size refers to the size of the conductor, not the size of the complete wire. It is possible to have two wires of the same gauge with different diameters because one may have thicker insulation than the other.*

12 volt automotive electrical systems generally use 10, 12, 14, 16 and 18 gauge wire. Main power distribution circuits and larger accessories usually use 10 and 12 gauge wire. Battery cables are usually 4 or 6 gauge, although 1 and 2 gauge wires are occasionally used. Wire length must also be considered when making repairs to a circuit. As conductor length increases, so does resistance. An 18 gauge wire, for example, can carry a 10 amp load for 10 feet without excessive voltage drop; however if a 15 foot wire is required for the same 10 amp load, it must be a 16 gauge wire.

An electrical schematic shows the electrical current paths when a circuit is operating properly. It is essential to understand how a circuit works before trying to figure out why it doesn't. Schematics break the entire electrical system down into individual circuits and show only one particular circuit. In a schematic, no attempt is made to represent wiring and components as they physically appear on the vehicle; switches and other components are shown as simply as possible. Face views of harness connectors show the cavity or terminal locations in all multi-pin connectors to help locate test points.

If you need to backprobe a connector while it is on the component, the order of the terminals must be mentally reversed. The wire color code can help in this situation, as well as a keyway, lock tab or other reference mark.

NOTE: *Wiring diagrams are not included in this book. As cars and trucks have become more complex and available with longer op-tion lists, wiring diagrams have grown in size and complexity. It has become almost impossible to provide a readable reproduction of a wiring diagram in a book this size. Information on ordering wiring diagrams from the vehicle manufacturer can be found in the owner's manual.*

WIRING REPAIR

Soldering is a quick, efficient method of joining metals permanently. Everyone who has the occasion to make wiring repairs should know how to solder. Electrical connections that are soldered are far less likely to come apart and will conduct electricity much better than connections that are only "pig-tailed" together. The most popular (and preferred) method of soldering is with an electrical soldering gun. Soldering irons are available in many sizes and wattage ratings. Irons with higher wattage ratings deliver higher temperatures and recover lost heat faster. A small soldering iron rated for no more than 50 watts is recommended, especially on electrical systems where excess heat can damage the components being soldered.

There are three ingredients necessary for successful soldering; proper flux, good solder and sufficient heat. A soldering flux is necessary to clean the metal of tarnish, prepare it for soldering and to enable the solder to spread into tiny crevices. When soldering, always use a resin flux or resin core solder which is non-corrosive and will not attract moisture once the job is finished. Other types of flux (acid core) will leave a residue that will attract moisture and cause the wires to corrode. Tin is a unique metal with a low melting point. In a molten state, it dissolves and alloys easily with many metals. Solder is made by mixing tin with lead. The most common proportions are 40/60, 50/50 and 60/40, with the percentage of tin listed first. Low priced solders usually contain less tin, making them very difficult for a beginner to use because more heat is required to melt the solder. A common solder is 40/60 which is well suited for all-around general use, but 60/40 melts easier, has more tin for a better joint and is preferred for electrical work.

Soldering Techniques

Successful soldering requires that the metals to be joined be heated to a temperature that will melt the solder – usually 360–460°F (182–238°C). Contrary to popular belief, the purpose of the soldering iron is not to melt the solder itself, but to heat the parts being soldered to a temperature high enough to melt the solder when it is touched to the work. Melting flux-cored solder on the soldering iron will usually destroy the effectiveness of the flux.

NOTE: *Soldering tips are made of copper for good heat conductivity, but must be "tinned" regularly for quick transference of heat to the project and to prevent the solder from sticking to the iron. To "tin" the iron, simply heat it and touch the flux-cored solder to the tip; the solder will flow over the hot tip. Wipe the excess off with a clean rag, but be careful as the iron will be hot.*

After some use, the tip may become pitted. If so, simply dress the tip smooth with a smooth file and "tin" the tip again. An old saying holds that "metals well cleaned are half soldered." Flux-cored solder will remove oxides, but rust, bits of insulation and oil or grease must be removed with a wire brush or emery cloth. For maximum strength in soldered parts, the joint must start off clean and tight. Weak joints will result in gaps too wide for the solder to bridge.

If a separate soldering flux is used, it should be brushed or swabbed on only those areas that are to be soldered. Most solders contain a core of flux and separate fluxing is unnecessary. Hold the work to be soldered firmly. It is best to solder on a wooden board, because a metal vise will only rob the piece to be soldered of heat and make it difficult to melt the solder. Hold the soldering tip with the broadest face against the work to be soldered. Apply solder under the tip close to the work, using enough solder to give a heavy film between the iron and the piece being soldered, while moving slowly and making sure the solder melts properly. Keep the work level or the solder will run to the lowest part and favor the thicker parts, because these require more heat to melt the solder. If the soldering tip overheats (the solder coating on the face of the tip burns up), it should be retinned. Once the soldering is completed, let the soldered joint stand until cool. Tape and seal all soldered wire splices after the repair has cooled.

Wire Harness and Connectors

The on-board computer (ECM) wire harness electrically connects the control unit to the various solenoids, switches and sensors used by the control system. Most connectors in the engine compartment or otherwise exposed to the elements are protected against moisture and dirt which could create oxidation and deposits on the terminals. This protection is important because of the very low voltage and current levels used by the computer and sensors. All connectors have a lock which secures the male and female terminals together, with a secondary lock holding the seal and terminal into the connector. Both terminal locks must be released when disconnecting ECM connectors.

These special connectors are weather-proof and all repairs require the use of a special terminal and the tool required to service it. This tool is used to remove the pin and sleeve terminals. If removal is attempted with an ordinary pick, there is a good chance that the terminal will be bent or deformed. Unlike standard blade type terminals, these terminals cannot be straightened once they are bent. Make certain that the connectors are properly seated and all of the sealing rings in place when connecting leads. On some models, a hinge-type flap provides a backup or secondary locking feature for the terminals. Most secondary locks are used to improve the connector reliability by retaining the terminals if the small terminal lock tangs are not positioned properly.

Molded-on connectors require complete replacement of the connection. This means splicing a new connector assembly into the harness. All splices in on-board computer systems should be soldered to insure proper contact. Use care when probing the connections or replacing terminals in them as it is possible to short between opposite terminals. If this happens to the wrong terminal pair, it is possible to damage certain components. Always use jumper wires between connectors for circuit checking and never probe through weatherproof seals.

Open circuits are often difficult to locate by sight because corrosion or terminal misalignment are hidden by the connectors. Merely wiggling a connector on a sensor or in the wiring harness may correct the open circuit condition. This should always be considered when an open circuit or a failed sensor is indicated. Intermittent problems may also be caused by oxidized or loose connections. When using a circuit tester for diagnosis, always probe connections from the wire side. Be careful not to damage sealed connectors with test probes.

All wiring harnesses should be replaced with identical parts, using the same gauge wire and connectors. When signal wires are spliced into a harness, use wire with high temperature insulation only. With the low voltage and current levels found in the system, it is important that the best possible connection at all wire splices be made by soldering the splices together. It is seldom necessary to replace a complete harness. If replacement is necessary, pay close attention to insure proper harness routing. Secure the harness with suitable plastic wire clamps to prevent vibrations from causing the harness to wear in spots or contact any hot components.

NOTE: *Weatherproof connectors cannot be replaced with standard connectors. Instructions are provided with replacement connector and terminal packages. Some wire harnesses have mounting indicators (usually pieces of colored tape) to mark where the harness is to be secured.*

In making wiring repairs, it's important that you always replace damaged wires with wires that are the same gauge as the wire being replaced. The heavier the wire, the smaller the gauge number. Wires are color-coded to aid in identification and whenever possible the same color coded wire should be used for replacement. A wire stripping and crimping tool is necessary to install solderless terminal connectors. Test all crimps by pulling on the wires; it should not be possible to pull the wires out of a good crimp.

Wires which are open, exposed or otherwise damaged are repaired by simple splicing. Where possible, if the wiring harness is accessible and the damaged place in the wire can be located, it is best to open the harness and check for all possible damage. In an inaccessible harness, the wire must be bypassed with a new insert, usually taped to the outside of the old harness.

When replacing fusible links, be sure to use fusible link wire, NOT ordinary automotive wire. Make sure the fusible segment is of the same gauge and construction as the one being replaced and double the stripped end when crimping the terminal connector for a good contact. The melted (open) fusible link segment of the wiring harness should be cut off as close to the harness as possible, then a new segment spliced in as described. In the case of a damaged fusible link that feeds two harness wires, the harness connections should be replaced with two fusible link wires so that each circuit will have its own separate protection.

NOTE: *Most of the problems caused in the wiring harness are due to bad ground connections. Always check all vehicle ground connections for corrosion or looseness before performing any power feed checks to eliminate the chance of a bad ground affecting the circuit.*

Repairing Hard Shell Connectors

Unlike molded connectors, the terminal contacts in hard shell connectors can be replaced. Weatherproof hard-shell connectors with the leads molded into the shell have non-replacable terminal ends. Replacement usually involves the use of a special terminal removal tool that depress the locking tangs (barbs) on the connector terminal and allow the connector to be removed from the rear of the shell. The connector shell should be replaced if it shows any evidence of burning, melting, cracks, or breaks. Replace individual terminals that are burnt, corroded, distorted or loose.

NOTE: *The insulation crimp must be tight to prevent the insulation from sliding back on the wire when the wire is pulled. The insulation must be visibly compressed under the crimp tabs, and the ends of the crimp should be turned in for a firm grip on the insulation.*

The wire crimp must be made with all wire strands inside the crimp. The terminal must be fully compressed on the wire strands with the ends of the crimp tabs turned in to make a firm grip on the wire. Check all connections with an ohmmeter to insure a good contact. There should be no measurable resistance between the wire and the terminal when connected.

Mechanical Test Equipment

Vacuum Gauge

Most gauges are graduated in inches of mercury (in.Hg), although a device called a manometer reads vacuum in inches of water (in. H_2O). The normal vacuum reading usually varies between 18 and 22 in.Hg at sea level. To test engine vacuum, the vacuum gauge must be connected to a source of manifold vacuum. Many engines have a plug in the intake manifold which can be removed and replaced with an adapter fitting. Connect the vacuum gauge to the fitting with a suitable rubber hose or, if no manifold plug is available, connect the vacuum gauge to any device using manifold vacuum, such as EGR valves, etc. The vacuum gauge can be used to determine if enough vacuum is reaching a component to allow its actuation.

Hand Vacuum Pump

Small, hand-held vacuum pumps come in a variety of designs. Most have a built-in vacuum gauge and allow the component to be tested without removing it from the vehicle. Operate the pump lever or plunger to apply the correct amount of vacuum required for the test specified in the diagnosis routines. The level of vacuum in inches of Mercury (in.Hg) is indicated on the pump gauge. For some testing, an additional vacuum gauge may be necessary.

Intake manifold vacuum is used to operate various systems and devices on late model vehicles. To correctly diagnose and solve problems in vacuum control systems, a vacuum source is necessary for testing. In some cases, vacuum can be taken from the intake manifold when the engine is running, but vacuum is normally provided by a hand vacuum pump. These hand vacuum pumps have a built-in vacuum gauge that allow testing while the device is still attached to the component. For some tests, an additional vacuum gauge may be necessary.

HEATER AND AIR CONDITIONING

NOTE: *For charging, discharging and basic maintenance of the Air conditioning system, please refer to Chapter 1.*

Heater Core

REMOVAL AND INSTALLATION

Taurus/Sable

1. Disconnect the negative (–) battery cable.
2. Remove the four screws retaining the steering column opening cover and remove cover.
3. Remove the sound insulator under the glove box by removing the two pushnuts secur-ing the insulator to studs on the climate control case.
4. Remove all steering column trim shrouds.
5. Remove the column retaining bolts and re-move the steering column.
6. Remove the screws retaining the lower LH and radio finish panels and remove the panels by snapping out.
7. Remove the seven instrument cluster fin-ish panel retaining screws, one jam nut behind headlight switch, and one screw behind the clock. Remove the finish panel.
8.. Lower the fuse panel on the hinge to al-low access to the speedometer cable.
9. The instrument panel can be removed with the cluster still in place.

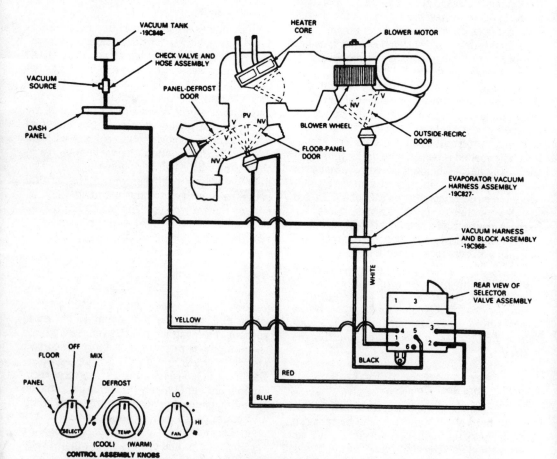

FUNCTION — SELECTOR KNOB POSITION	OUTSIDE — RECIRC. DOOR	PANEL — FLOOR DOOR		PANEL — DEFROST DOOR	BLOWER MOTOR
		FULL FLOOR	PANEL/FLOOR		
PANEL	NV	NV	NV	V	ON
FLOOR	NV	V	V	NV	ON
OFF	V	V	V	V	OFF
MIX	NV	NV	V	NV	ON
DEFROST	NV	NV	NV	NV	ON
VACUUM HOSE COLOR CODE	WHITE	RED·BLUE	BLUE	YELLOW	—

V = VACUUM; NV = NO VACUUM (ATMOSPHERE ONLY)

Heater system vacuum schematic and selector test positions—Taurus/Sable

10. Remove the glove compartment assembly.

11. Disconnect all electrical connectors at main wire loom. Disengage the rubber grommet from dash panel and push wire and connectors into instrument panel area.

12. Remove RH and LH speaker opening covers by snapping out with screwdriver.

13. Remove the two lower instrument panel-to-cowl side retaining screws.

14. Remove the one instrument panel brace retaining screw (under the radio area).

15. Remove the three panel upper retaining screws and place the instrument on the front seat. Always use a seat cover so the instrument panel does not damage the seat.

CAUTION: *16.*

Drain the engine coolant.

CAUTION: *When draining the coolant, keep*

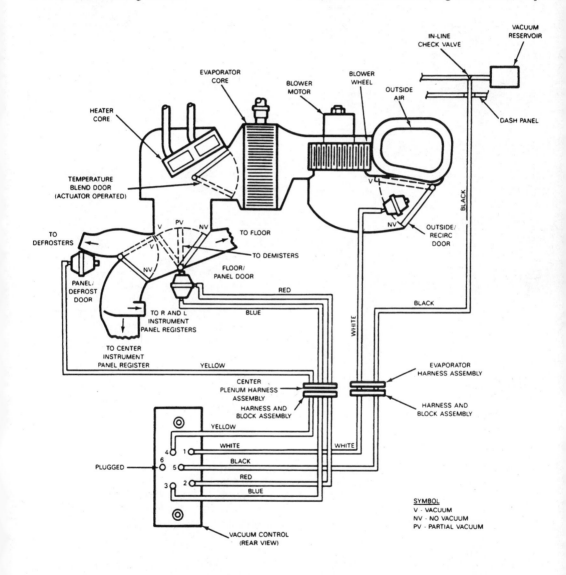

VACUUM PORT	FUNCTION	SELECTION						
		OFF	MAX A/C (RECIRC)	VENT	PANEL-FLOOR	FLOOR	FLOOR-DEFROST	DEFROST
1	OUTSIDE - RECIRC	V	V	NV	NV	NV	NV	NV
2	FULL FLOOR	NV	NV	NV	NA	V	NA	NV
3	FLOOR - PANEL (PARTIAL)	NV	NA	NV	PV	V	PV	NV
4	PANEL - DEFROST	NV	V	V	V	NV	NV	NV
5	SOURCE	V	V	V	V	V	V	V
6	PLUGGED	:	-	-	-	-	-	-

Heater system vacuum schematic and selector test positions—Continental

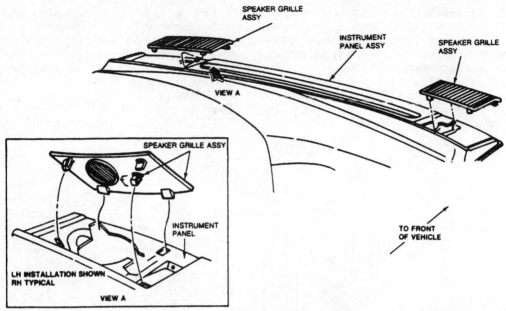

Speaker grill removal—Taurus/Sable

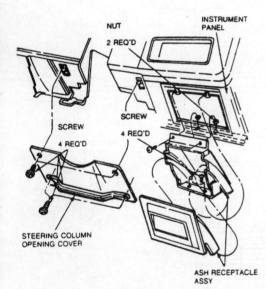

Radio removal—Taurus/Sable

in mind that cats and dogs are attracted by the ethylene glycol antifreeze, and are quite likely to drink any that is left in an uncovered container or in puddles on the ground. This will prove fatal in sufficient quantity. Always drain the coolant into a sealable container. Coolant should be reused unless it is contaminated or several years old.

NOTE: *If equipped with Air Conditioning, the system has to be discharged before heater core can be serviced. Refer to the "Air Condi-*

tioning System" in chapter 1 for the proper procedure.

17. Remove the screws attaching the brackets to the top cowl top panel. Pull the heater assembly away from the dash panel.

18. Remove the vacuum source line from the heater core tube seal. Remove the seal from the heater core tubes.

19. Remove the heater core access cover attaching screws. Remove the access cover from the heater case. Remove the heater core and seal from the heater case.

To install:

1. Push the instrument wiring harness through the dash panel into engine compartment and install grommet in dash panel.

2. Connect the speedometer cable to the speedometer head.

3. Position the instrument panel through the hole in the steering column reinforcement. Install the three upper panel retaining screws. Torque to 12-20 in. lbs.

4. Install the two lower panel-to-side cowl retaining screws. Torque to 60-96 in. lbs.

5. Install the brace-to-lower panel retaining screws under the radio.

6. Install the radio speaker grills, connect the panel wiring connectors, and connect all vacuum hoses.

7. Connect the A/C and heater control cables and radio antenna cable.

8. Swing the glove compartment assembly back into place and install by depressing side tabs on the housing.

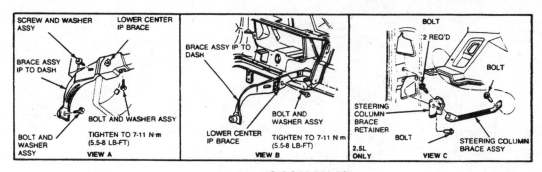

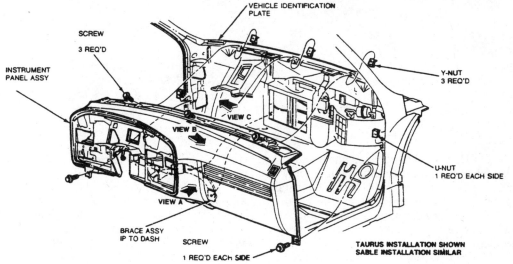

Instrument panel removal—Taurus/Sable

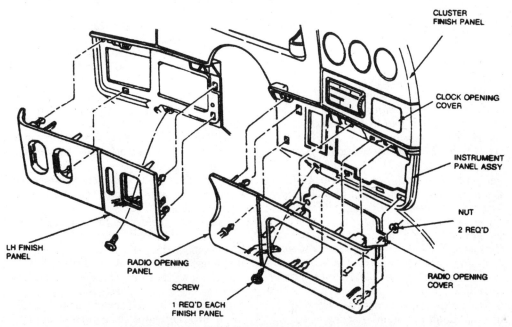

Instrument panel finish panel removal—Taurus/Sable

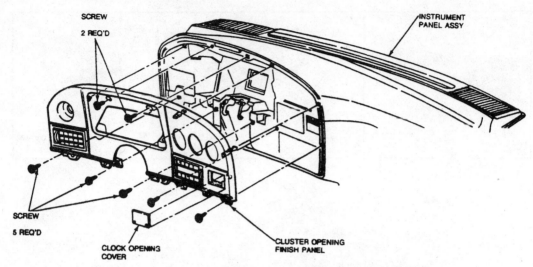

Instrument cluster finish panel removal—Taurus/Sable

9. Install instrument cluster finish panel in position and install the eight retaining screws.

10. Snap in the lower radio panel and install the retaining screws.

11. Raise steering column in position and install four retaining screws at the support bracket.

12. Connect all the electrical connectors for the column switches.

13. Install the column trim panels, sound insulators, and climate control case.

14. Fill the cooling system with proper antifreeze and start engine and check for leaks.

15. Don't go anywhere, if you have Air Conditioning, the system will have to be evacuated and recharged. Refer to the "Air Conditioning System" section in chapter 1.

Continental

1. Disconnect the negative (−) battery cable.

2. Drain the engine coolant.

CAUTION: *When draining the coolant, keep in mind that cats and dogs are attracted by the ethylene glycol antifreeze, and are quite likely to drink any that is left in an uncovered container or in puddles on the ground. This will prove fatal in sufficient quantity. Always drain the coolant into a sealable container. Coolant should be reused unless it is contaminated or several years old.*

NOTE: *If equipped with Air Conditioning, the system has to be discharged before heater core can be serviced. Refer to the "Air Conditioning System" in chapter 1 for the proper procedure.*

3. Discharge the A/C system, refer to "Air Conditioning System" in chapter 1.

4. Remove the four screws retaining the

steering column opening cover and remove cover.

5. Remove the one screw retaining the tilt/wheel lever and remove the lever.

6. Remove the key lock cylinder by pushing a small allen wrench into groove located beneath lock cylinder. Place the key into the lock and pull the cylinder out of the column.

7. Remove the steering column shroud, steering column pad, and disconnect the horn electrical connector from the pad.

8. Remove the 15mm bolt retaining steering wheel and remove the wheel.

9. Remove the PRNDL cable from steering column.

10. Disconnect all electrical connectors, hood, and brake release cables.

11. Remove the three plastic retainers on each side that hold the LH and RH lower close out panels.

12. Disconnect the ignition switch and remove the lower shaft universal joint retention nuts.

13. Remove the four steering column retaining nuts, lower the steering column, and transmission shift cable.

14. Disconnect the two vacuum hoses and all electrical connectors and remove the column from the vehicle.

15. Remove the center finish panel by snapping out the five clips.

16. Remove the LH and RH finish panels and disconnect the electrical connectors.

17. Remove the radio, storage bin, and disconnect the electrical connectors.

18. Remove the AC control, cluster reinforcement bracket, and four cluster retaining screws.

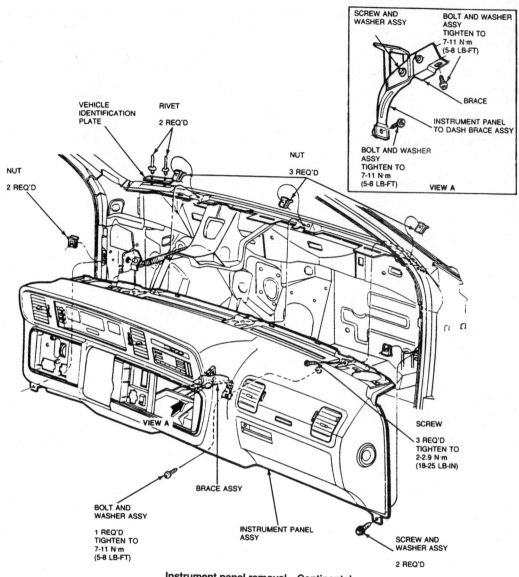

Instrument panel removal—Continental

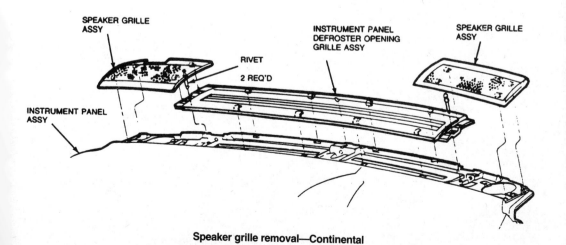

Speaker grille removal—Continental

19. Remove the four glove compartment assembly.

20. Remove the speaker and defrost grilles.

21. Under the hood, disconnect all electrical connectors at the main wire loom and feed them through the hole into the instrument panel area.

22. Remove the RH and LH cowl trim panels

23. Remove the three screws at instrument panel, one on each end and middle.

24. Remove the three upper instrument panel retaining screws, carefully lower the panel, and disconnect the electrical connectors.

25. Disconnect the heater hoses from the core assembly.

26. Discharge A/C system, disconnect the liquid line and accumulator from the evaporator core, and cap open refrigerant lines.

27. Remove the floor register to back seat, housing-to-dash panel attaching nuts, and the top cowl support brackets.

28. Carefully pull evaporator assembly away from the dash panel and remove from the vehicle.

29. Remove the vacuum source line from the heater core.

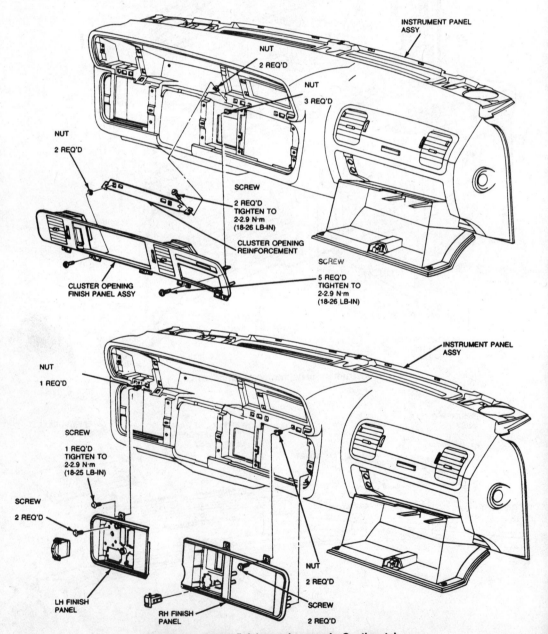

Instrument cluster finish panel removal—Continental

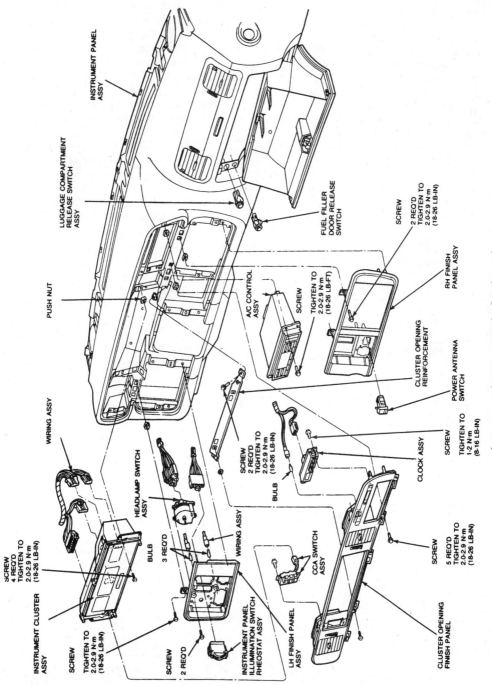

Instrument cluster removal—Continental

30. Remove the four heater core access cover attaching screws and remove access cover and seal. Lift the core and seals out of the evaporator case.

To install:

1. Install the heater core and seal in the evaporator assembly. Tighten the four cover attaching bolts.

2. Install Caulking Cord part No. D9AZ-19560-A or equivalent to seal evaporator case against leakage along the cut line.

3. Install the blend door actuator in housing and tighten the three screws.

4. Install the evaporator housing-to-dash panel attaching bolts and tighten.

5. Connect all vacuum and electrical connections to the evaporator case.

6. Install the rear seat heater duct, all panel brackets, and pull wiring harness through dash panel.

7. Install the instrument panel in place and install the upper and lower attaching bolts. Torque to 15-20 ft. lbs.

8. Install all bracket bolts, pull all wiring through instrument panel, and install the lower then the upper finish panels.

9. Install the steering column, column wiring, and trim panels.

10. Install the radio and trim panels.

11. Install the speaker and defrost grilles.

12. Connect all heater and A/C hoses, fill the cooling system, and evacuate, leak-test, and recharge the A/C system.

13. Start the engine and check for leaks and proper heater and A/C operations.

Control Assembly

REMOVAL AND INSTALLATION

Taurus/Sable

1. Disconnect the battery negative (−) cable.

2. Remove the instrument cluster finish

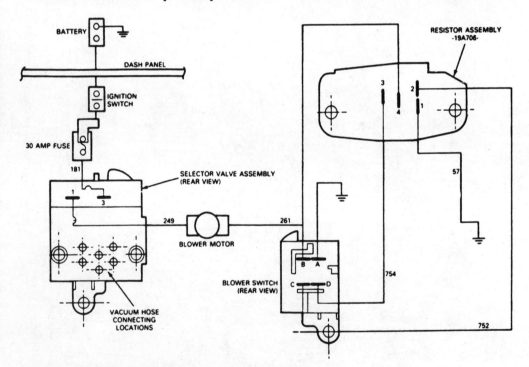

MODE SELECTOR SWITCH						
TERMINAL	AMPS	PANEL	FLOOR	OFF	MIX	DEF
3-BATTERY 1-BLOWER	30	1 · 3	1 · 3	NONE	1 · 3	1 · 3

BLOWER SWITCH		
POSITION	CIRCUIT MAKE	AMPS
1. LOW	B	—
2. MED. 1	B · D	20
3. MED 2	B · C · D	25
4 HIGH	B · A · C	35

CIRCUIT NO.	WIRE COLOR	WIRE GAUGE
57	BLACK	12
754	LT. GREEN w/WHITE HASH	14
752	YELLOW w/RED DOT	14
2611	ORANGE w/BLACK STRIPE	12
261	ORANGE w/BLACK STRIPE	12
181	BROWN w/ORANGE STRIPE	12

Heater system electrical schematic and continuity test information—Taurus/Sable

panel, the four control assembly attaching screws, and disconnect the vacuum and electrical harness from the control assembly.

3. Remove the control assembly from the vehicle.

4. To install the control assembly, reverse the order of removal.

Continental

1. Disconnect the negative (–) battery cable.

2. Remove the instrument cluster finish panel by grasping lower LH corner and pulling away in a clockwise direction.

3. Remove the four Torx® head screws retaining the control assembly.

4. Disconnect the two electrical harness connectors and vacuum harness retaining nuts.

5. To install the control assembly, reverse the order of removal.

Temperature Control (Function) Cable

REMOVAL AND INSTALLATION

Taurus/Sable Only

1. Disconnect the negative (–) battery cable.

2. Remove the instrument cluster finish panel retaining screws. Remove the finish panel.

3. Rotate the temperature control knob to the cool position. Disconnect the temperature control cable housing end retainer from the heater case bracket.

4. Disconnect the cable wire from the temperature door crank arm.

5. Remove the screws attaching the control assembly to the instrument panel. Pull the control assembly away from the instrument panel.

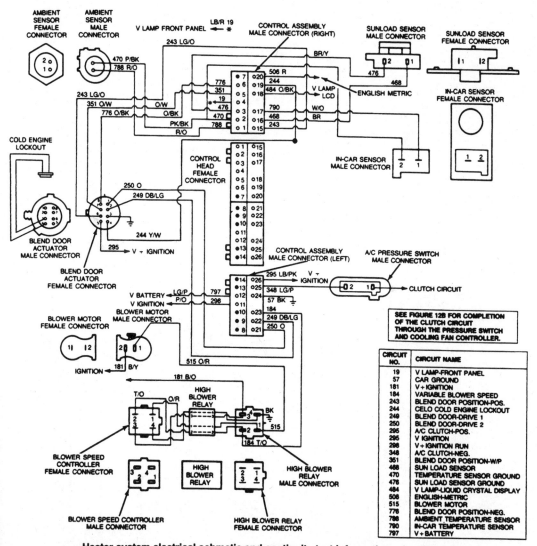

Heater system electrical schmatic and continuity test information—Continental

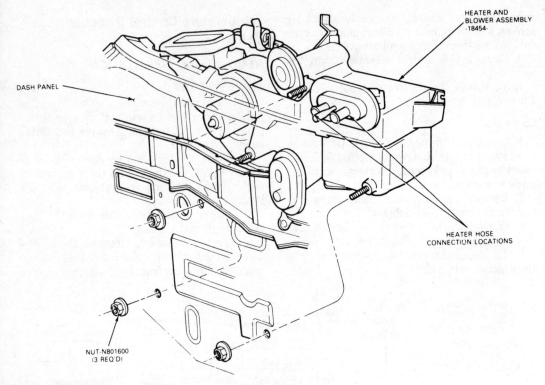

DASH PANEL

HEATER AND
BLOWER ASSEMBLY
·18454·

HEATER HOSE
CONNECTION LOCATIONS

NUT·N801600
(3 REQ'D)

Heater case assembly

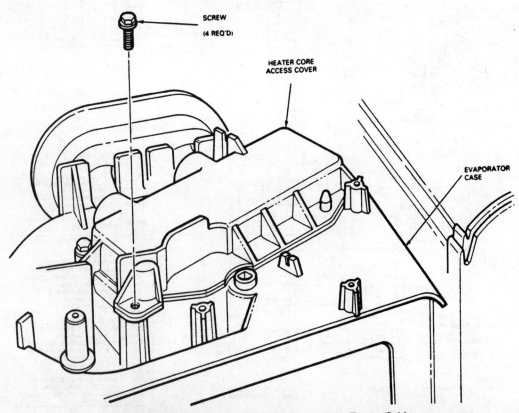

SCREW

(4 REQ'D)

HEATER CORE
ACCESS COVER

EVAPORATOR
CASE

Heater core access cover and attaching screws—Taurus/Sable

REMOVAL

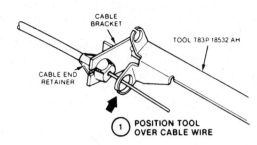

CABLE BRACKET

TOOL T83P 18532 AH

CABLE END RETAINER

1 POSITION TOOL OVER CABLE WIRE

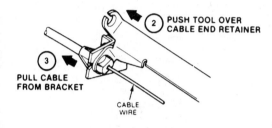

2 PUSH TOOL OVER CABLE END RETAINER

3 PULL CABLE FROM BRACKET

CABLE WIRE

INSTALLATION

1 PUSH CABLE END RETAINER INTO BRACKET UNTIL LATCHED WITH BRACKET

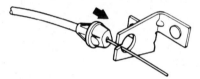

Temperature control cable attachments

6. Disconnect the cable housing end retainer from the control assembly and cable wire from the temperature control lever arm.

7. Remove the cable assembly from the vehicle through the control assembly opening in the instrument panel.

8. Installation is the reverse of the removal procedure.

CABLE PRE-SET AND SELF-ADJUSTMENT

Before Installation

1. Insert the blade of a small pocket knife of equivalent into the wire and loop (crank arm end) of the function or temperature control cable.

2. Hold the self-adjusting cable attaching clip with a suitable tool and slide it down the shaft (away from the end loop) approximately 25mm.

3. Install the cable assembly and move the temperature control lever to the top of the slot (temperature cable to warm and function to defrost) to position the self adjusting clip. Check for proper control operation.

After Installation

1. Move the control lever (temperature) to the cool position and function to the off position.

2. Hold the crank arm firmly in position, insert the blade of a small pocket knife or equivalent into the wire loop and pull the cable wire end through the self-adjusting clip until there is

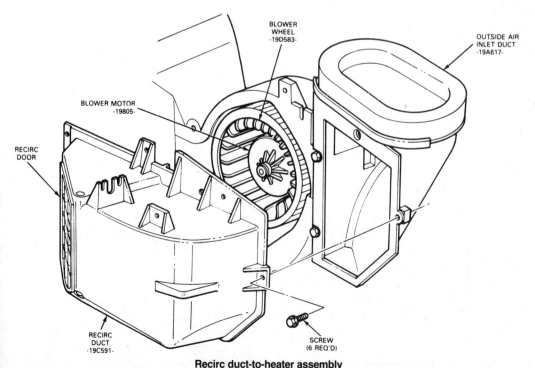

BLOWER WHEEL -19D583-

OUTSIDE AIR INLET DUCT -19A617-

BLOWER MOTOR -19805-

RECIRC DOOR

RECIRC DUCT -19C591-

SCREW (6 REQ'D)

Recirc duct-to-heater assembly

a space about 25mm between the clip and the wire end loop.

3. Force the control lever(s) to the top of the slot (temperature cable to the warm position and function to the defrost) to position the self-adjusting clip and check for proper control operation.

Heater Blower

REMOVAL AND INSTALLATION

1. Open the glove box door, release the retainers and lower the door.

2. Remove the recirc duct support bracket-to-cowl screw, the vacuum line-to-vacuum motor hose and the recirc duct-to-heater assembly screws.

3. Remove the recirc duct-to-heater assembly duct, then lower the recirc duct from between the instrument panel and the heater case.

4. Disconnect the heater motor electrical connector.

5. Remove the heater motor wheel clip and the heater wheel.

6. Remove the heater motor-to-mounting

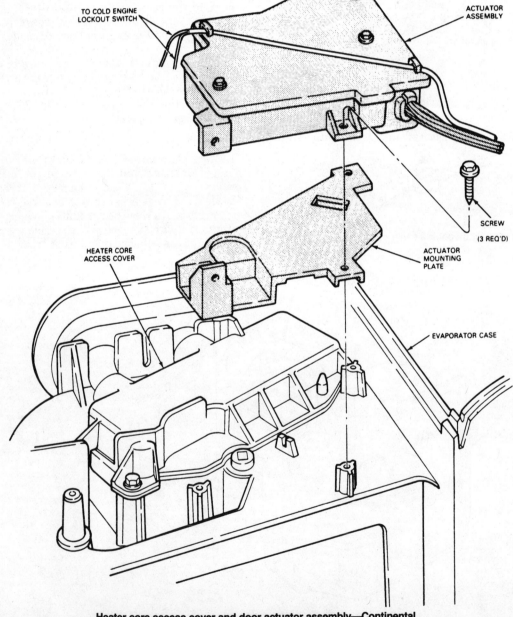

Heater core access cover and door actuator assembly—Continental

plate screws and heater motor from the evaporator case.

To install:

1. Install blower motor electrical lead through the evaporator case.

2. Position the motor in the case and install the four screws.

3. Install the blower wheel and tighten a new retaining nut.

4. Connect the electric and vacuum leads and install the recirc duct assembly.

Evaporator Case

NOTE: *In order to remove the evaporator core the evaporator case must be removed first. Refer to the "Heater Core" removal procedure in this section.*

REMOVAL AND INSTALLATION

1. Disconnect the negative (−) battery cable.

2. Drain the cooling system. Discharge the refrigerant from the A/C system.

CAUTION: *When draining the coolant, keep in mind that cats and dogs are attracted by the ethylene glycol antifreeze, and are quite likely to drink any that is left in an uncovered container or in puddles on the ground. This will prove fatal in sufficient quantity. Always drain the coolant into a sealable container. Coolant should be reused unless it is contaminated or several years old.*

3. Disconnect the heater hoses from the heater core. Disconnect the vacuum supply hose from the inline vacuum check valve in the engine compartment.

4. Disconnect the liquid line and the accumulator from the evaporator core at the dash

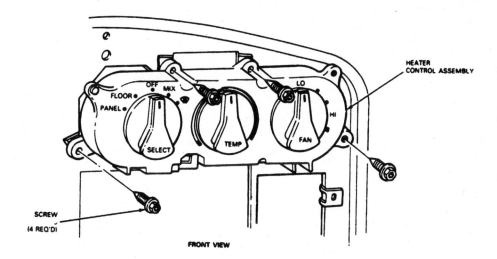

FRONT VIEW

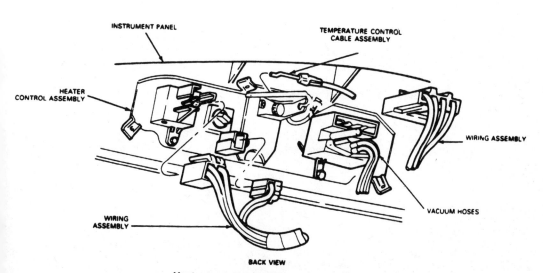

BACK VIEW

Heater control assembly—Taurus/Sable

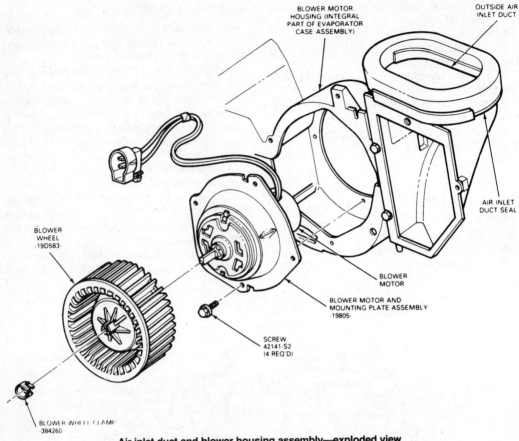

BLOWER MOTOR
HOUSING (INTEGRAL
PART OF EVAPORATOR
CASE ASSEMBLY)

OUTSIDE AIR
INLET DUCT

AIR INLET
DUCT SEAL

BLOWER
WHEEL
·19D583·

BLOWER
MOTOR

BLOWER MOTOR AND
MOUNTING PLATE ASSEMBLY
·19805·

SCREW
42141-S2
(4 REQ'D)

BLOWER WHEEL CLAMP
·384260·

Air inlet duct and blower housing assembly—exploded view

panel. Cap all refrigerant lines to prevent the entrance of dirt and moisture.

5. Remove the instrument panel as outlined in this section under heater core. Remove the screw holding the instrument panel shake brace to the evaporator case. Remove the shake brace.

6. Remove the floor register from the bottom of the evaporator case.

7. Remove the retaining nuts attaching the evaporator case to the dash panel in the engine compartment.

8. Remove the support brackets to the cowl top panel.

9. Remove the evaporator case away from the dash panel and remove it from the vehicle.

10. Installation is the reverse of the removal procedure. Leak test, evacuate and charge the A/C system.

Evaporator Core

REMOVAL AND INSTALLATION

1. Remove the evaporator case as outlined earlier. Disconnect and remove the vacuum harness from the vacuum motor.

2. Remove the recirc duct screws from the evaporator. Remove the duct.

3. Remove the air inlet duct from the evaporator case. Remove the support bracket from the evaporator case.

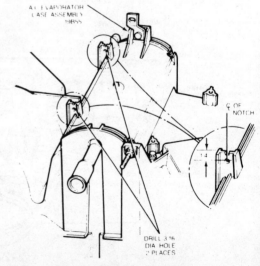

A/C EVAPORATOR
CASE ASSEMBLY
·19855·

€ OF
NOTCH

DRILL 3/16
DIA HOLE
2 PLACES

Drilling holes in evaporator case tabs

4. Remove the molded seals from the evaporator core tubes.

5. Drill a $^3/_{16}$" hole in each of the two upright tabs on top of the evaporator case. (Check the illustration in this section for drill locations)

6. Using a hot knife or a small saw blade, cut the top of the evaporator case on the raised outlines.

7. Fold the cutout cover back from the opening and lift the evaporator core from the case.

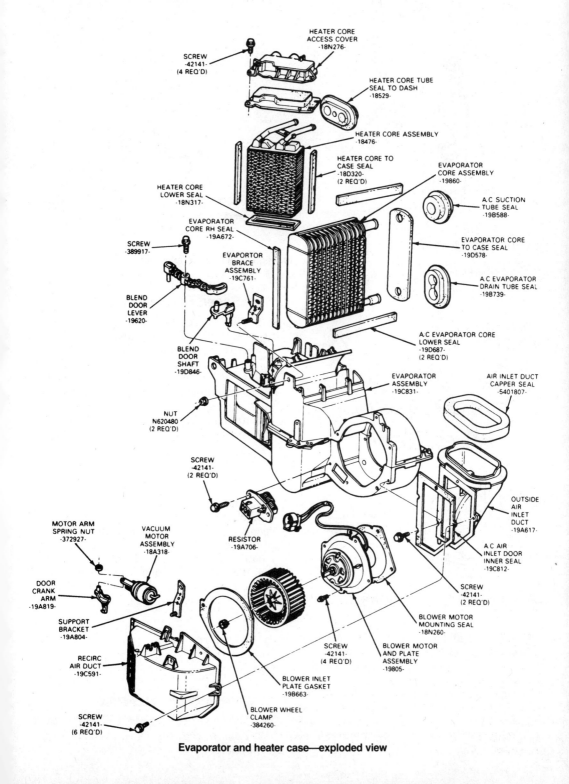

Evaporator and heater case—exploded view

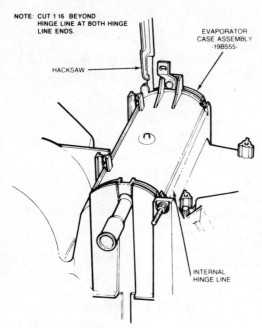

NOTE: CUT 1 16 BEYOND HINGE LINE AT BOTH HINGE LINE ENDS.

HACKSAW

EVAPORATOR CASE ASSEMBLY -19B555-

INTERNAL HINGE LINE

Cutting the evaporator case

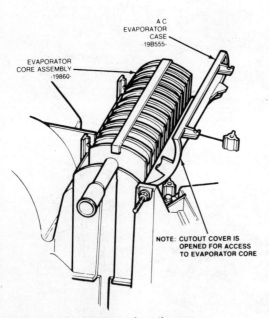

A C EVAPORATOR CASE -19B555-

EVAPORATOR CORE ASSEMBLY -19860-

NOTE: CUTOUT COVER IS OPENED FOR ACCESS TO EVAPORATOR CORE

Removing the evaporator from the case

8. When installing, transfer the foam core seals to the new evaporator core. Install spring nut on each of the two upright tabs and adjacent to the holes drilled in the front flange.

9. Install rope sealer D9AZ-19560-A or equivalent to seal the evaporator case against leakage along the cut line. The remainder of installation is the reverse of the removal procedure.

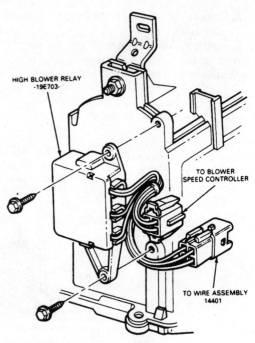

HIGH BLOWER RELAY -19E703-

TO BLOWER SPEED CONTROLLER

TO WIRE ASSEMBLY 14401

High speed blower relay—Continental

High Speed Blower Relay

The function of the high speed blower relay is to convert low current signals from the electronic control assembly to a high current, variable ground feed to the blower motor.

CAUTION: *The system should not be operated with the blower motor disconnected. Damage may occur to the electronic blower speed controller if the cooling air is not provided by the blower motor.*

REMOVAL AND INSTALLATION

1. Disconnect the negative (−) battery cable.
2. Disengage the glove compartment door stops and allow door to hang by the hinge.
3. Working through the glove compartment opening, disconnect the two electrical snap-like connectors and remove the relay from the mounting bracket on top of the evaporator case.
4. **To install:** reverse the removal procedures. Turn ignition ON and check for proper operation.

SOUND SYSTEMS

Radio

REMOVAL AND INSTALLATION

1. Disconnect the negative (−) battery cable.
2. Remove the trim panel-to-center instrument panel.

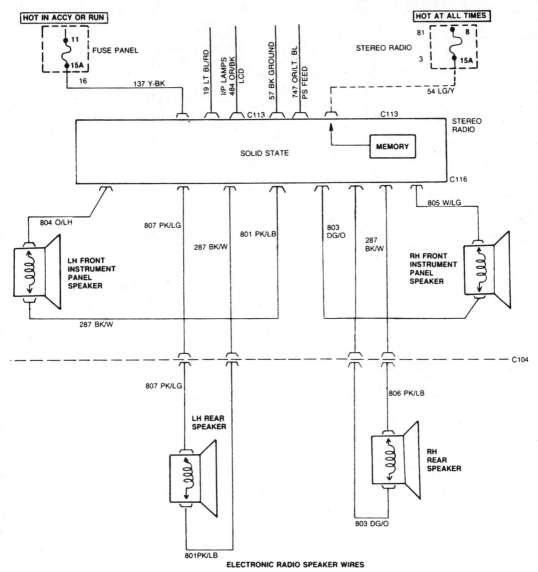

Electronic radio wiring diagram

3. Remove the radio/bracket-to-instrument panel screws.

4. Push the radio toward the front, then raise the rear of the radio slightly so that the rear support bracket clears the clip in the instrument panel. Slowly, pull the radio from the instrument panel.

5. Disconnect the electrical connectors and the antenna cable from the radio.

6. **To install:** reverse the removal procedures. Torque the radio/bracket-to-instrument panel screws to 14-16 in. lbs. Test the radio for operation.

Compact Disc Player (Continental)

REMOVAL AND INSTALLATION

1. Disconnect the negative (−) battery cable.

2. Remove the radio/CD player trim panel

3. Remove the four attaching screws and slide out the radio and CD player as an assembly. Disconnect the wiring and antenna connectors from the rear of the radio.

4. Remove the CD player attaching screws and separate from the radio.

5. **To install: reverse the removal procedures.**

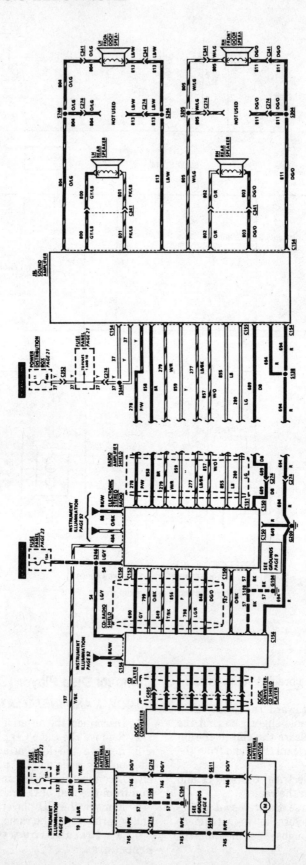

Electronic premium sound system wiring schematic—Continental

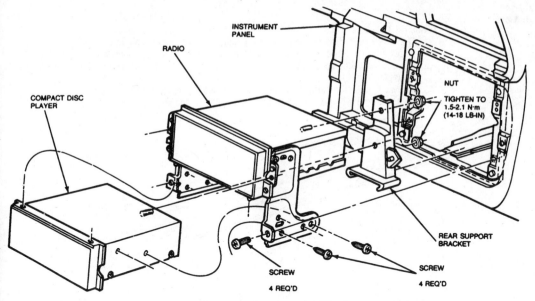

Premium sound system with CD player

WINDSHIELD WIPERS

Wiper Arm Assembly

REMOVAL AND INSTALLATION

1. Raise the blade end of the arm off the windshield and move the slide latch away from the pivot shaft.

2. The wiper arm should not be unlocked and can now be pulled off of the pivot shaft.

3. **To install:** position the auxiliary arm (if so equipped) over the pivot pin, hold it down and push the main arm head over the pivot shaft. Make sure the pivot shaft is in the park position.

4. Hold the main arm head on the pivot shaft while raising the blade end of the wiper arm and push the slide latch into the lock under the pivot shaft. Lower the blade to the windshield.

NOTE: *If the blade does not touch the windshield, the slide latch is not completely in place.*

ARM AND BLADE ADJUSTMENT

1. With the arm and blade assemblies removed from the pivot shafts turn on the wiper switch and allow the motor to move the pivot shaft three or four cycles, and then turn off the wiper switch. This will place the pivot shafts in the park position.

2. Install the arm and blade assemblies on the pivot shafts to the correct distance between the windshield lower molding or weatherstrip and the blade saddle centerline.

Windshield Wiper Switch

REMOVAL AND INSTALLATION

Front

The front windshield wiper switch is a part of the combination switch, which is mounted to the steering column. Refer to the "Combination Switch Removal And Installation" procedures in "Chapter 8" and remove the combination switch from the steering column. To install, reverse the removal procedures.

Rear – Station Wagon

1. Disconnect the negative (−) battery cable.

2. Remove the finish panel-to-instrument panel screws, then rock the upper edge toward the driver seat.

3. Disconnect the electrical connector from the rear washer switch.

4. Remove the washer switch from the instrument panel.

NOTE: *On the Sable model, the switch is retained by two screws.*

5. To install, reverse the removal procedures.

Windshield Wiper Motor

REMOVAL AND INSTALLATION

Front

1. Disconnect the negative (−) battery cable.

2. Disconnect the electrical connector from the motor.

3. Remove the left side wiper arm.

Tridon

Blade replacement
1. Cycle arm and blade assembly to a position on the windshield where removal of blade assembly can be performed without difficulty. Turn ignition key off at desired position.
2. To remove blade assembly from wiper arm, press on spring lock and pull blade assembly from pin (View A).
3. To install, push the blade assembly on the pin so that the spring lock engages the pin (View A). Be sure the blade assembly is securely attached to pin.

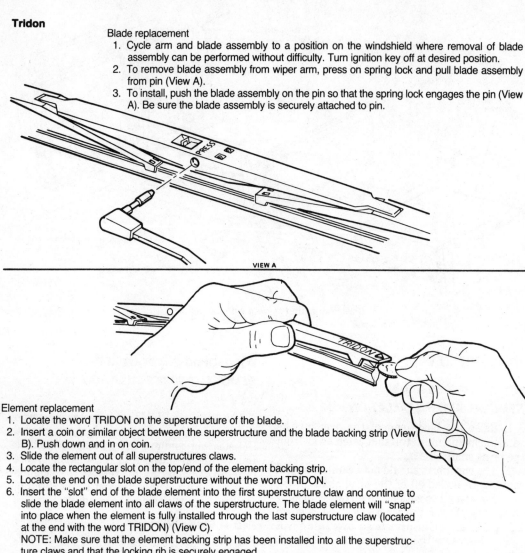

VIEW A

Element replacement
1. Locate the word TRIDON on the superstructure of the blade.
2. Insert a coin or similar object between the superstructure and the blade backing strip (View B). Push down and in on coin.
3. Slide the element out of all superstructures claws.
4. Locate the rectangular slot on the top/end of the element backing strip.
5. Locate the end on the blade superstructure without the word TRIDON.
6. Insert the "slot" end of the blade element into the first superstructure claw and continue to slide the blade element into all claws of the superstructure. The blade element will "snap" into place when the element is fully installed through the last superstructure claw (located at the end with the word TRIDON) (View C).
   NOTE: Make sure that the element backing strip has been installed into all the superstructure claws and that the locking rib is securely engaged.

VIEW B

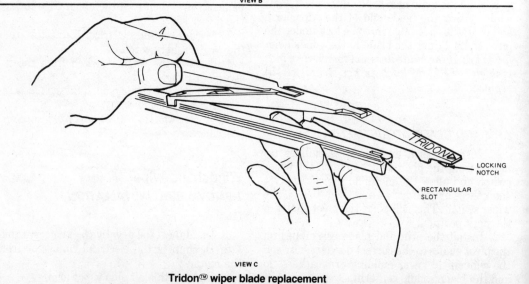

LOCKING
NOTCH

RECTANGULAR
SLOT

VIEW C

Tridon™ wiper blade replacement

Trico

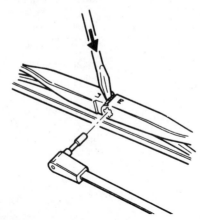

Blade replacement
1. Cycle arm and blade assembly to up position on the windshield where re-moval of blade assembly can be performed without difficulty. Turn ignition key off at desired position.
2. To remove blade assembly, insert screwdriver in slot, push down on spring lock and pull blade assembly from pin (View A).
3. To install, push the blade assembly on the pin so that the spring lock en-gages the pin (View A). Be sure the blade assembly is securely attached to pin.

VIEW A

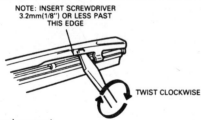

NOTE: INSERT SCREWDRIVER
3.2mm(1/8") OR LESS PAST
THIS EDGE

TWIST CLOCKWISE

Element replacement
1. Insert screwdriver between the edge of the super structure and the blade backing drip (View B). Twist screwdriver slowly until element clears one side of the super structure claw.
2. Slide the element out of all the super structure claws.

VIEW B

4. Insert element into one side of the end claws (View D) and with a rocking motion push element upward until it snaps in (View E).

VIEW D

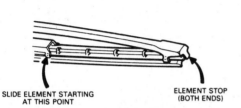

SLIDE ELEMENT STARTING
AT THIS POINT

ELEMENT STOP
(BOTH ENDS)

3. Slide the element into the super structure claws, starting with second set from either end (View C) and continue to slide the blade element into all the super structure claws to the element stop (View C).

VIEW C

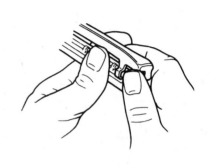

VIEW E

Trico™ wiper blade replacement

4. On the passenger side, lift the water shield cover from the cowl.

5. Remove the linkage-to-operating arm clip. NOTE: *When removing the retaining clip, lift up the locking tab and pull the clip away from the pin.*

6. Remove the motor/bracket-to-cowl bolts and the assembly from the vehicle.

7. **To install:** reverse the removal procedures. Torque the motor/bracket-to-cowl bolts to 60-85 in. lbs.

Rear – Station Wagon

1. Disconnect the negative (–) battery cable.

2. Remove the wiper arm/blade assembly from the rear wiper motor.

3. Remove the rear motor pivot shaft-to-glass nut/spacers.

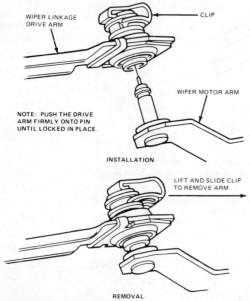

Wiper linkage clip removal

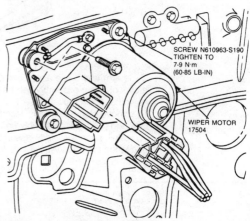

Wiper motor removal—front

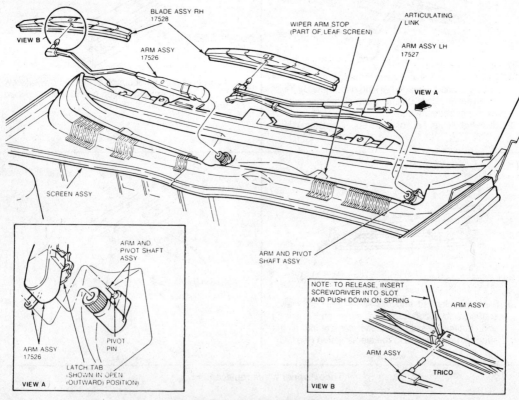

Wiper arm and blade assembly

4. Disconnect the electrical connector from the rear wiper motor.

NOTE: *When removing the electrical connector, pull on the connector and not the wire.*

5. Remove the motor-to-handle nut and the motor from the vehicle.

6. **To install:** reverse the removal procedures. Torque the motor-to-handle nut to 48-72 in. lbs. and the wiper motor-to-glass nut to 11-14 ft. lbs.

INSTRUMENTS AND SWITCHES

Instrument Cluster
Taurus/Sable
REMOVAL AND INSTALLATION
Except Electronic Instrument Cluster

1. Disconnect the negative (−) battery cable.
2. Drop the fuse panel (on its hinges), to pro-

Front

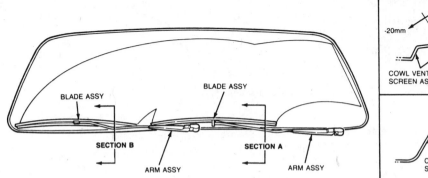
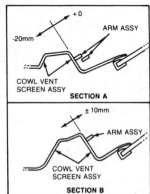

Rear

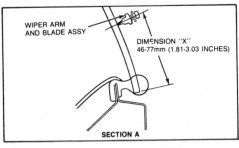

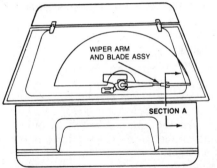

Wiper blade and arm positioning

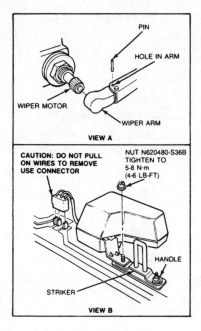

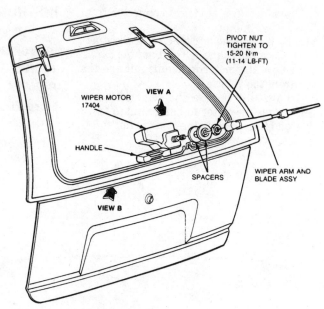

Wiper motor removal—rear

vide access to the speedometer cable latch attachment. Disconnect the speedometer cable by disengaging the cable latch from the speedometer head and pulling the cable away from the speedometer.

3. Remove the instrument panel finish screws and the instrument finish panel.

4. Remove the steering column shroud.

NOTE: *On Sable models equipped with a tachometer cluster, remove the lower trim panel screws and the trim panel from the vehicle.*

5. Remove the mask/lens-to-instrument panel screws and the mask/lens from the vehicle.

NOTE: *On Sable models equipped with a tachometer cluster, remove the lower floodlight bulb and socket assemblies from the vehicle.*

6. Lift the main dial assembly from the backing plate.

NOTE: *The speedometer, tachometer and gauges are mounted to the main dial and some effort may be required to pull the quick-connect electrical terminals from the clip.*

CAUTION: *Position the vehicle on a flat surface, block the wheels, and apply emergency brake to prevent movement when the gear shift selector is out of position.*

7. On column shift vehicles, remove the transmission selector indicator-to-main dial (PRNDL or PRN D D1) screws and the indicator from the vehicle.

8. Remove the instrument cluster-to-instrument panel screws and the instrument cluster from the vehicle.

9. To install, reverse the removal procedures.

Electronic Instrument Cluster

1. Disconnect the negative (−) battery cable. Remove the two lower panel trim covers.

CAUTION: *Position the vehicle on a flat surface, block the wheels, and apply emergency brake to prevent movement when the gear shift selector is out of position.*

2. Remove the steering column cover and disconnect the transmission selector indicator cable from the steering column.

3. Remove the cluster trim panel and disconnect the electrical connector to the switch module.

4. Remove the four cluster mounting screws and pull the bottom of the cluster out towards the steering wheel.

5. Disconnect the three cluster connectors, from behind the cluster assembly.

6. Swing the bottom of the cluster out to clear the top of the crash pad and then remove the cluster assembly from the vehicle.

7. Installation is the reverse order of the removal procedure.

Continental

CAUTION: *Position the vehicle on a flat surface, block the wheels, and apply emergency brake to prevent movement when the gear shift selector is out of position.*

1. Turn the ignition switch to unlock the shift lever and move the lever down to the bottom position.

2. Tilt the steering column down as far as possible.

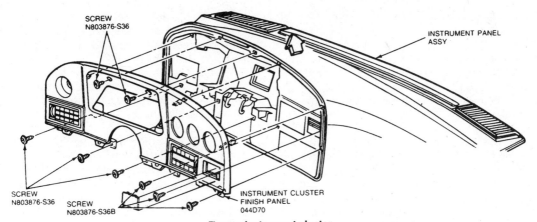

SCREW
N803876-S36

INSTRUMENT PANEL
ASSY

SCREW
N803876-S36

SCREW
N803876-S36B

INSTRUMENT CLUSTER
FINISH PANEL
044D70

Taurus instrument cluster

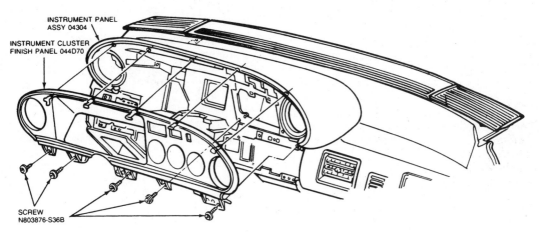

INSTRUMENT PANEL
ASSY 04304

INSTRUMENT CLUSTER
FINISH PANEL 044D70

SCREW
N803876-S36B

Sable instrument cluster

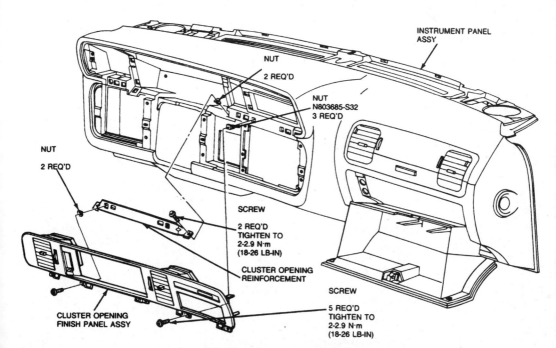

INSTRUMENT PANEL
ASSY

NUT

2 REQ'D

NUT
N803685-S32
3 REQ'D

NUT

2 REQ'D

SCREW

2 REQ'D
TIGHTEN TO
2-2.9 N·m
(18-26 LB-IN)

CLUSTER OPENING
REINFORCEMENT

CLUSTER OPENING
FINISH PANEL ASSY

SCREW

5 REQ'D
TIGHTEN TO
2-2.9 N·m
(18-26 LB-IN)

Continental instrument panel

3. Remove the two lower cluster finish panel screws. Remove the five Torx® screws below instrument cluster. Gently pry the cluster panel away from instrument panel.

4. Disconnect the switch assembly connected to the cluster.

5. Remove the two Torx® screws below the cluster and move the medal reinforcement strip out of the way.

6. Remove the lower steering column shroud, tilt lever, and gap cover from under the cluster.

7. Remove the four Torx® screws mounting cluster to the instrument panel.

8. Tilt the cluster toward the rear of the vehicle. Undo the two snaps beneath the cluster retaining the PRNDL assembly in the cluster.

9. Place a clean cloth on the steering column to prevent scratches. Tilt the cluster toward the rear of vehicle and pull slightly out of cavity.

10. Reach around the cluster and disconnect the electrical connectors, pull the cluster out instrument cavity, and place the cluster on a clean cloth so the face does not get damaged.

11. **To install:** reverse the removal procedures. Also, Check the instrument cluster illustration in this section if problems occur.

Headlight Switch
REMOVAL AND INSTALLATION
Taurus/Sable

1. Disconnect the negative (−) battery cable. On the Taurus models, remove the headlight switch knob.

2. On the Taurus models, remove the bezel retaining nut and remove the bezel. On the Sable models, remove the lower left finish panel from the instrument panel.

3. On the Taurus models, remove the instrument cluster finish panel and remove the two screws retaining the headlamp switch to the instrument panel. Pull the switch out of the instrument panel and disconnect the electrical connector. Remove the switch from the vehicle.

4. On the Sable models, remove the two screws retaining the headlight switch to the finish panel, disconnect the electrical connector and remove the switch from the vehicle.

5. Installation is the reverse order of the removal procedure.

Continental

1. Pull off headlamp switch knob.

2. Remove the outer finish panel and moulding above finish panel.

3. Remove the inner finish panel screws and finish panel.

4. Disconnect the electrical connectors from the rear of the dimmer and switch.

5. To install, reverse the order of the removal procedure.

Clock
REMOVAL AND INSTALLATION

1. Using a 90° bent scriber, dental pick or similar hardened tool, insert the bent end of the

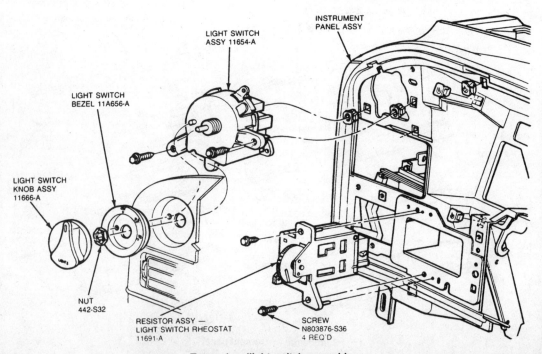

LIGHT SWITCH ASSY 11654-A

INSTRUMENT PANEL ASSY

LIGHT SWITCH BEZEL 11A656-A

LIGHT SWITCH KNOB ASSY 11666-A

NUT 442-S32

RESISTOR ASSY — LIGHT SWITCH RHEOSTAT 11691-A

SCREW N803876-S36 4 REQ'D

Taurus headlight switch assembly

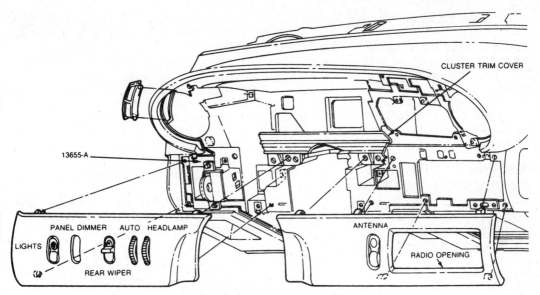

Sable headlight switch assembly

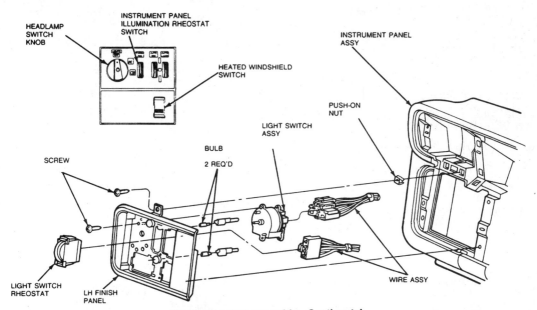

Headlight switch assembly—Continental

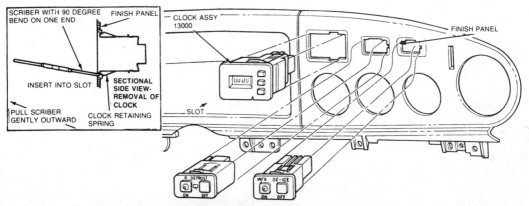

Clock removal and installation

tool into the slot at the bottom center of the clock.

2. Gently pull the scriber tool outward until the bottom clock retaining spring releases.

3. Grasp the clock and pull it outward to remove.

4. Disconnect the electrical connector.

5. **To install:** connect the electrical connector and snap the clock back into position.

Speedometer Cable
REMOVAL AND INSTALLATION

NOTE: *The mechanical (analog) speedometers use a speedometer cable. The electronic (digital) speedometers have no cable.*

1. Remove the instrument cluster, refer to the "Instrument Cluster" removal and installation procedures in this section.

2. Pull the speedometer cable from the casing. If the cable is broken, disconnect the casing from the transaxle and remove the broken piece from the transaxle end.

3. Lubricate the new cable with graphite lubricant. Feed the cable into the casing from the instrument panel end.

4. Attach the cable to the speedometer. Install the cluster.

Ignition Switch
REMOVAL AND INSTALLATION

All Models

1. Disconnect the negative (–) battery cable.

2. Rotate the ignition lock cylinder to the RUN position and depress lock cylinder retaining pin through the access hole in the shroud with a ⅛" diameter punch.

3. Remove the lock cylinder. On vehicle with tilt columns, remove the tilt release lever by removing one socket head capscrew.

4. Remove the instrument panel lower cover, steering column shroud, and steering column support bracket.

5. Disconnect the switch electrical connector.

6. Remove the lock actuator cover plate by removing one tamper resistant Torx® head bolt.

NOTE: *The lock actuator assembly will slide freely out of the lock cylinder housing when the ignition switch is removed.*

7. Remove the ignition switch and cover by removing the two tamper resistant Torx® head bolts

To install:

1. Make sure that the ignition switch is in the RUN position by rotating the driveshaft clockwise to start position and release.

2. Install the lock actuator assembly to a depth of 11.5-13.5mm from the bottom of the housing.

3. Install the ignition switch, switch cover attaching bolts, and lock cylinder.

4. Rotate the ignition lock cylinder to the LOCK position and measure the depth of the actuator assembly in step 2.

5. Install the lock actuator cover plate with the tamper resistant Torx® head bolt and torque to 30-48 in. lbs.

6. Install the ignition switch electrical connector.

7. Connect the negative (–) battery cable. Check the ignition switch, shift selector, and tilt release for proper operation.

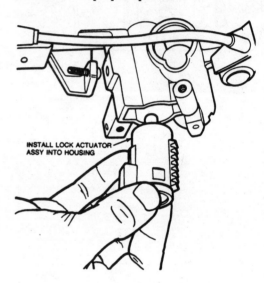

INSTALL LOCK ACTUATOR ASSY INTO HOUSING

Depth Measurement

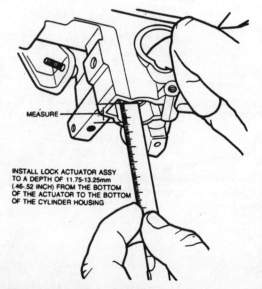

MEASURE

INSTALL LOCK ACTUATOR ASSY TO A DEPTH OF 11.75-13.25mm (.46-.52 INCH) FROM THE BOTTOM OF THE ACTUATOR TO THE BOTTOM OF THE CYLINDER HOUSING

Lock actuator depth measurement

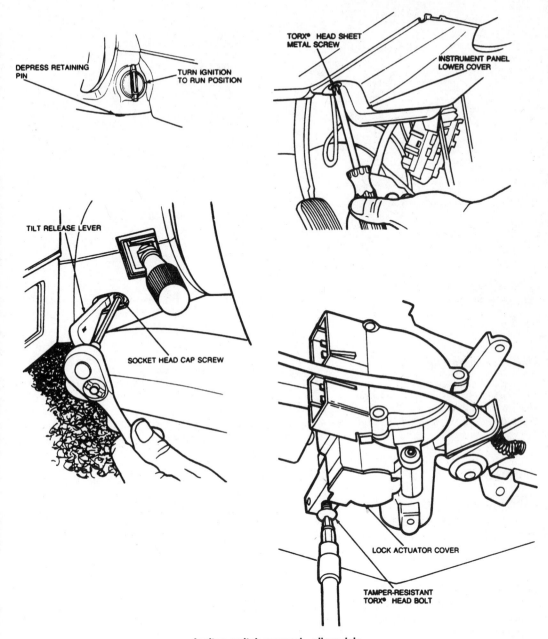

Igniton switch removal—all models

8. If the switch does not operate properly, the lock actuator has to be readjusted.

Multi-Function Switch
Turn-Signal, Headlight Dimmer, Hazard Flasher

REMOVAL AND INSTALLATION

1. Disconnect the negative (–) battery cable.
2. If the vehicle is equipped with a tilt column, place the wheel in its lowest position and remove the tilt lever.

3. Remove the ignition lock cylinder. Refer to the "Ignition Switch" removal and installation procedure in this section.
4. Remove the steering column shroud.
5. Remove the wiring harness retainer and electrical connectors.
6. Remove the two self tapping screws and the multi-switch assembly from the steering column.
7. **To install:** position the switch on the column and install the two attaching screws, connect the harness connectors, install the lock cyl-

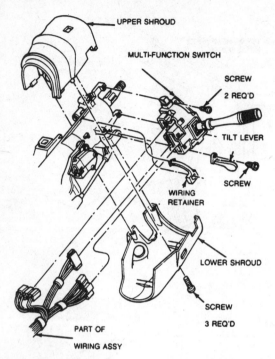

Multi-function switch

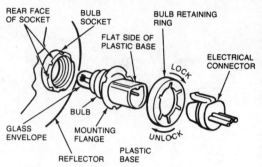

Headlamp bulb replacement

inder, install the column shroud, connect the battery negative (−) battery cable, and start the vehicle and check the switches operation.

LIGHTING

Headlights

All Taurus/Sable and Continental models are equipped with flush mount headlights. The bulb may be replaced without removing the lens and body assembly.

BULB REPLACEMENT

CAUTION: *The replaceable Halogen head-lamp bulb contains gas under pressure. The bulb may shatter if the glass envelope is scratched or the bulb is dropped. Handle the bulb carefully. Grasp the bulb ONLY by its plastic base. Avoid touching the glass enve-lope because the finger prints from your hand may cause the bulb to burst when turned on. Keep the bulb out of the reach of children.*

1. Check to see that the headlight switch is in the OFF position.
2. Raise the hood and locate the bulb in-stalled in the rear of the headlight body.
3. Remove the electrical connector from the bulb by grasping the wires firmly and snapping the connector rearward.
4. Remove the bulb retaining ring by rotat-ing it counterclockwise (when viewed from the

rear) about ⅛ of a turn, then slide the ring off the plastic base.

NOTE: *Keep the bulb retaining ring, it will be reused with the new bulb.*

5. Carefully remove the headlight bulb from its socket in the reflector by gently pulling it straight backward out of the socket. DO NOT rotate the bulb during removal.

To install:

6. With the flat side of the plastic base of the bulb facing upward, insert the glass envelope of the bulb into the socket. Turn the base slightly to the left or right, if necessary to align the grooves in the forward part of the plastic base with the corresponding locating tabs inside the socket. When the grooves are aligned, push the bulb firmly into the socket until the mounting flange on the base contacts the rear face of the socket.

7. Slip the bulb retaining ring over the rear of the plastic base against the mounting flange. Lock the ring into the socket by rotating the ring counterclockwise. A stop will be felt when the retaining ring is fully engaged.

8. Push the electrical connector into the rear of the plastic until it snaps and locks into position.

9. Turn the headlights on and check for proper operation.

Parking/Front Turn Signal Combination
REMOVAL AND INSTALLATION

The parking and turn signal lights share the same dual filament bulb.

Taurus

1. Using the access hole in the radiator sup-port, rotate the bulb socket counterclockwise to disengage it from the light housing and remove the bulb.

2. **To install:** reverse the removal proce-dure. Rotate the bulb socket clockwise to en-gage the socket into the housing.

Sable

1. Remove the two screws attaching the parking lamp assembly and pull it forward.

2. Remove the bulb socket by twisting and then remove the bulb.

3. Install the bulb in the socket, and install the socket in the lamp assembly by twisting.

4. Position the parking lamp in place and install the screws.

Continental

1. Remove the two sockets by twisting counterclockwise.

2. Remove the two nuts from the attaching studs at the back of the lamp assembly.

3. Pull the lamp out from the fender.

4. Install the bulb in the assembly, position the assembly in the fender, and install the two nuts and attaching studs and tighten.

Side Marker Lamp

REMOVAL AND INSTALLATION

Taurus

1. Remove one nut and washer from the attaching stud at the top of the lamp assembly.

2. Rotate the top outboard until the stud tip has cleared the slot in the housing.

3. Lift the lamp to clear the two lower tabs (on the headlamp) from the headlamp housing.

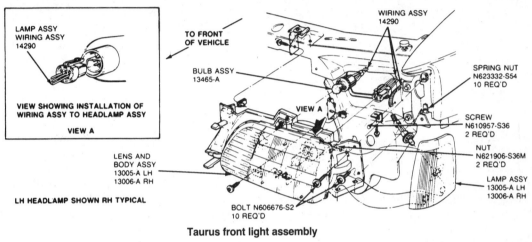

Taurus front light assembly

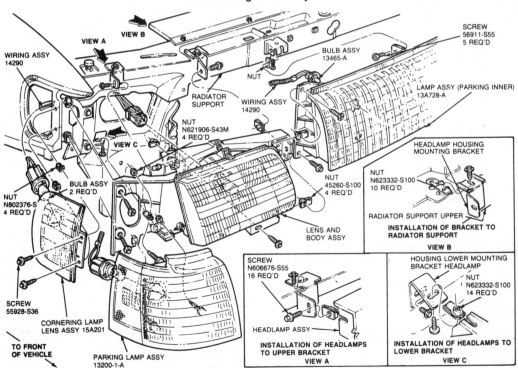

Sable front light assembly

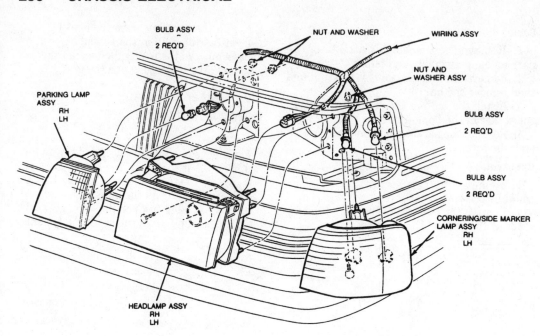

Front lighter assembly—Continental

4. Remove the bulb socket by twisting it counterclockwise and pull the bulb from the socket.

To install:

5. Install the bulb into the socket, and install the socket by twisting it counterclockwise.

6. Position the lamp in place by lowering the two tabs on the lamp into the two slots on the headlamp housing.

7. Rotate the lamp inboard to allow the stud to enter the upper slot in the housing.

8. Install the nut and washer to the attaching stud, and secure them.

Cornering Lamp

REMOVAL AND INSTALLATION

Sable

1. Remove the two screws attaching the parking lamp assembly and pull it forward.

2. Remove the bulb socket by twisting and then remove the bulb.

3. Remove the two screws attaching the cornering lamp assembly and lift it out.

4. Remove the bulb by twisting it counterclockwise.

To install:

5. Install the bulb, and install the socket by turning it clockwise.

6. Position the cornering light back in place, and install the two screws.

7. Install the parking lamp bulb in the socket, and install the socket in the lamp assembly by twisting.

8. Position the parking lamp in place and install the screws.

Rear Turn Signal, Brake and Parking Lights

REMOVAL AND INSTALLATION

All Models

1. Bulbs can be serviced from the inside of the luggage compartment by removing the luggage compartment rear trim panel, if so equipped.

2. Remove the socket(s) from the lamp body and replace the bulb(s).

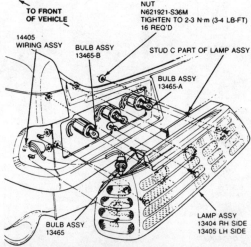

LH SHOWN RH SYMMETRICALLY OPPOSITE

Taurus rear lamp assembly

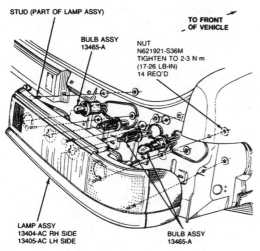

Sable rear lamp assembly

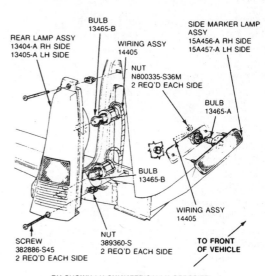

Taurus/Sable station wagon rear lamp assembly

3. Install the socket(s) in the lamp body and install the trim panel.

TRAILER WIRING

Wiring the car for towing is fairly easy. There are a number of good wiring kits available and these should be used, rather than trying to design your own. All trailers will need brake lights and turn signals as well as tail lights and side marker lights. Most states require extra marker lights for overly wide trailers. Also, most states have recently required back-up lights for trailers, and most trailer manufacturers have been building trailers with back-up lights for several years.

Additionally, some Class I, most Class II and just about all Class III trailers will have electric brakes.

Add to this number an accessories wire, to operate trailer internal equipment or to charge the trailer's battery, and you can have as many as seven wires in the harness.

Determine the equipment on your trailer and buy the wiring kit necessary. The kit will contain all the wires needed, plus a plug adapter set which included the female plug, mounted on

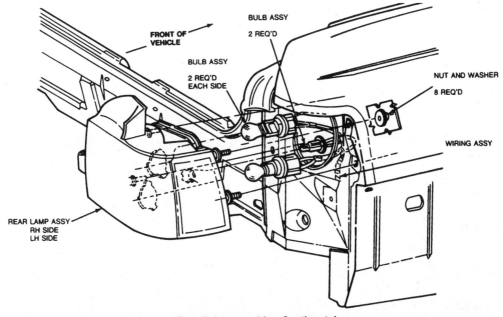

Rear light assembly—Continental

the bumper or hitch, and the male plug, wired into, or plugged into the trailer harness.

When installing the kit, follow the manufacturer's instructions. The color coding of the wires is standard throughout the industry.

One point to note: some domestic vehicles, and most imported vehicles, have separate turn signals. On most domestic vehicles, the brake lights and rear turn signals operate with the same bulb. For those vehicles with separate turn signals, you can purchase an isolation unit so that the brake lights won't blink whenever the turn signals are operated, or, you can go to your local electronics supply house and buy four diodes to wire in series with the brake and turn signal bulbs. Diodes will isolate the brake and turn signals. The choice is yours. The isolation units are simple and quick to install, but far more expensive than the diodes. The diodes, however, require more work to install properly, since they require the cutting of each bulb's wire and soldering in place of the diode.

One final point, the best kits are those with a spring loaded cover on the vehicle mounted socket. This cover prevents dirt and moisture from corroding the terminals. Never let the vehicle socket hang loosely; always mount it securely to the bumper or hitch.

CIRCUIT PROTECTION

Circuit breakers

Circuit breakers operate when a circuit overload exceeds its rated amperage. Once operated, they automatically reset after a certain period of time.

There are two kinds of circuit breaker, as previously mentioned, one type will reset itself. The second will not reset itself until the problem in the circuit has been repaired.

Turn Signal and Hazard Flasher

The turn signal unit is located on the LH side of the instrument panel. The combination turn signal and hazard flasher can be removed by pressing the plastic retaining clip and pulling straight rearward. On the Taurus/Sable models, one phillips® head screw has to be removed from the retaining bracket.

Fuse Panel

The fuse panel is located below and to the left of the steering column.

Fuses are a one-time circuit protection. If a circuit is overloaded or shorts, the fuse will blow thus protecting the circuit. A fuse will continue to blow until the circuit is repaired.

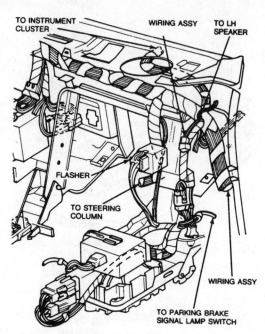

Flasher unit location—Continental

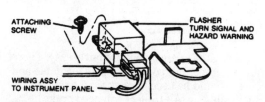

Flasher unit location—Taurus/Sable

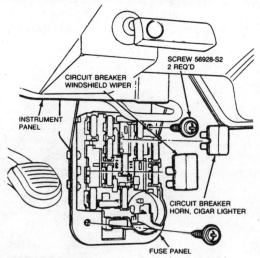

Fuse panel location

High Current Fuse Panel
Continental

The Continental does not use any fuse links. They have been replaced by a high current fuse panel. The panel is located in the engine compartment on the LH fender apron.

CAUTION: *Always disconnect the negative (−) battery cable before servicing the high current fuses. It is recommended that a qualified technician replace these fuses.*

Circuit Breakers

The circuits protected by circuit breakers and fusible links are show in the following chart.

Fuse Link (Taurus/Sable)

The fuse link is a short length of special, Hypalon (high temperature) insulated wire, integral with the engine compartment wiring harness and should not be confused with standard wire. It is several wire gauges smaller than the circuit which it protects. Under no circumstances should a fuse link replacement repair be made using a length of standard wire cut

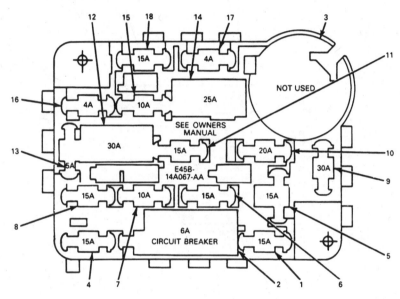

Cavity Number	Fuse Rating	Color	Circuit Protected	Cavity Number	Fuse Rating	Color	Circuit Protected
1	15 Amp	Lt. Blue	Stoplamps, Hazard Warning Lamps, Speed Control, Air Suspension	8	15 Amp	Lt. Blue	Glove Compartment Lamp, Engine Compartment Lamp, Courtesy Lamps, Keyless Entry Module, Power Mirrors, Vanity Lamps, Roof Module, Anti-Theft Relay, Air Suspension, Luggage Compartment Lamp, Radio, Heated Windshield Switch
2	6.0 Amp Circuit Breaker		Windshield Wiper Governor, Windshield Wiper Switch and Motor, Windshield Washer Motor, Windshield Fluid Level Switch				
3	Spare		Not Used	9	30 Amp	Lt. Green	Blower Motor, Blower Speed Controller
4	15 Amp	Lt. Blue	Tail Lamps, Parking Lamps, Side Marker Lamps, License Lamps, Headlamp Switch, Illuminated Entry, Coach Lamps, EATC Stowage Lamps, Ash Receptacle Lamps, Control Lamps on Warning, Auto Lamp Relay Power Feed	10	20 Amp	Yellow	Horns, Fuel Filler Door, Speed Control
				11	15 Amp	Lt. Blue	Radio, Premium Sound Amplifier, Power Antenna Motor
				12	30 Amp	Lt. Green	Cigar Lighters
5	15 Amp	Lt. Blue	Heated Backlite Switch, Electronic Flasher, Steering Rate Sensor, Roof Console, Air Suspension, Day/Night Mirror, Back-Up Lamps, EATC Control Head, Cluster Control Buttons, Variable Assist Power Steering Module, Keyless Entry Module	13	5 Amp	Tan	Instrument Panel Illumination, Clock, Compass, PRNDL, Liquid Crystal Radio Display, Climate Control Head
				14	25 Amp	Natural	Flash-to-Pass (High Beam)
				15	10 Amp	Red	Rear Running Lamps, Trailer Tow
6	15 Amp	Lt. Blue	Electronic Chime, Decklid Release, Overhead Console, Anti-Theft Module, Reading Lamps, Cluster Control Buttons, Daytime Display Lamps, Outside Temperature Display Module	16	4 Amp	Pink	Electronic Cluster, EATC Control Switch, Message Center
				17	4 Amp	Pink	EATC Compressor Clutch, EATC Blend Door Actuator, Power Window Relay, Blower Motor Speed Relay, Enhanced Illumination Module
7	10 Amp	Red	Heated Rear View Mirrors	18	15 Amp	Lt. Blue	Warning Lamps, Flash-to-Pass Relay, Lamp Out Warning, Window Safety Relay, Keyless Entry Module, Decklid Pulldown, Seat Control, Recliner, Power Door Locks

Fuse panel circuit locations—Continental

Fuse Value Amps	Color Code
4	Pink
5	Tan
10	Red
15	Light Blue
20	Yellow
25	Natural
30	Light Green

Fuse amperage values

from bulk stock or from another wiring harness.

To repair any blown fuse link use the following procedure:

1. Determine which circuit is damaged, its location and the cause of the open fuse link. If the damaged fuse link is one of three fed by a common No. 10 or 12 gauge feed wire, determine the specific affected circuit.

2. Disconnect the negative (−) battery cable.

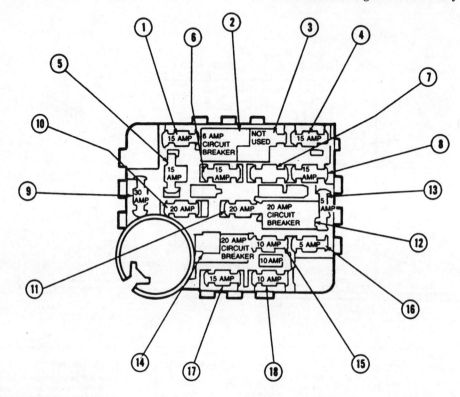

CAVITY NUMBER	CIRCUIT PROTECTED
1	HI-MOUNT STOPLAMP, STOPLAMPS, FRONT AND REAR TURN SIGNALS, INSTRUMENT PANEL TURN INDICATOR LAMPS
2	WINDSHIELD WIPER MOTOR, INTERMITTENT WIPER MODULE, WINDSHIELD WASHER MOTOR
3	NOT USED
4	FRONT PARK, SIDE MARKER AND TAIL LAMPS, "HEADLAMPS-ON" WARNING BUZZER/CHIME, FRONT LASER LAMP (SABLE).
5	ELECTRONIC CLUSTER, HEATED BACKLIGHT SWITCH, ELECTRONIC FLASHER, BACKUP LAMPS, HEATED E G O , ILLUMINATED/KEYLESS ENTRY MODULE
6	REAR WINDOW WIPER AND WASHER MOTORS (WAGONS), DIAGNOSTIC WARNING LAMP MODULE, WARNING CHIME, HEADLAMP SWITCH ILLUMINATION (SABLE), CLOCK ILLUMINATION, RADIO ILLUMINATION, EATC CONTROL ILLUMINATION, POWER WINDOW RELAY
7	NOT USED
8	CLOCK, RADIO MEMORY, GLOVE COMPT. LAMP, LUGGAGE COMPT. LAMP, INST. PANEL COURTESY LAMPS, INTERIOR LAMPS, ILLUMINATED/KEYLESS ENTRY MODULE, POWER MIRRORS

CAVITY NUMBER	CIRCUIT PROTECTED
9	BLOWER MOTOR, BLOWER SPEED CONTROLLER (EATC)
10	FLASH-TO-PASS, HIGH BEAM HEADLAMPS AND INDICATOR LAMP
11	RADIO, PREMIUM SOUND AMPLIFIER, POWER ANTENNA MOTOR
12	CIGAR LIGHTERS, HORN RELAY, HORNS
13	CLUSTER ILLUMINATION, RADIO DISPLAY, ASH TRAY ILLUM., EATC CONTROL DISPLAY, HEATED BACKLIGHT SWITCH ILLUM., HEATED WINDSHIELD SWITCH ILLUM., REAR WIPER SWITCH ILLUM., HEADLAMP SWITCH ILLUM., CLOCK DISPLAY, P R N D L ILLUMINATION
14	NOT USED
15	LICENSE LAMPS, SIDE MARKER AND TAIL LAMPS
16	ELECTRONIC CLUSTER EATC CONTROL SWITCH
17	EATC COMPRESSOR CLUTCH, EATC BLEND DOOR ACTUATOR, A/C COMPRESSOR CLUTCH
18	AUTOLAMP MODULE, CLUSTER WARNING LAMPS, LOW OIL LEVEL RELAY, BUZZER/CHIME

Fuse panel circuit locations—Taurus/Sable

3. Cut the damaged fuse link from the wiring harness and discard it. If the fuse link is one of three circuits fed by a single feed wire, cut it out of the harness at each splice end and discard it.

4. Identify and procure the proper fuse link and butt connectors for attaching the fuse link to the harness.

5. To repair any fuse link in a 3-link group with one feed:

a. After cutting the open link out of the harness, cut each of the remaining undamaged fuse links close to the feed wire weld.

b. Strip approximately 13mm of insulation from the detached ends of the two good fuse links, Then insert two wire ends into one end of a butt connector and carefully push one stripped end of the replacement fuse link into the same end of the butt connector and crimp all three firmly together.

NOTE: *Care must be taken when fitting the three fuse links into the butt connector as the internal diameter is a snug fit for three wires. Make sure to use a proper crimping tool. Pliers, side cutter, etc. will not apply the proper crimp to retain the wires and withstand a pull test.*

c. After crimping the butt connector to the three fuse links, cut the weld portion from the feed wire and strip approximately 13mm of insulation from the cut end. Insert the stripped end into the open end of the butt connector and crimp very firmly.

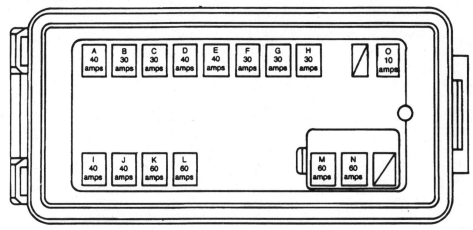

CAVITY	FUSE RATING	COLOR	CIRCUIT PROTECTED
A	40 AMP	GREEN	AIR SUSPENSION MOTOR
B	30 AMP	PINK	AIR SUSPENSION MODULE
C	30 AMP	PINK	ANTI-LOCK MODULE
D	40 AMP	GREEN	ANTI-LOCK MOTOR
E	40 AMP	GREEN	REAR WINDOW DEFROST
F	30 AMP	PINK	IGNITION COIL (TFI)
G	30 AMP	PINK	ELECTRONIC ENGINE CONTROL
H	30 AMP	PINK	FUSE PANEL
I	40 AMP	GREEN	POWER WINDOWS, POWER LUMBAR, KEYLESS/ POWER LOCKS, POWER DECKLID, POWER SEATS
J	40 AMP	GREEN	FUSE PANEL
K	60 AMP	YELLOW	HEADLAMP SWITCH, CORNERING LAMPS
L	60 AMP	YELLOW	COOLING FAN MOTOR
M	60 AMP	YELLOW	IGNITION SWITCH FEED
N	60 AMP	YELLOW	IGNITION SWITCH FEED/BLOWER MOTOR
O	10" AMP	RED	HEGO

High-current fuse panel—Continental

Circuit(s)	Circuit Protection and Rating	Location
Ignition coil, Ignition Module, Cooling Fan Controller	20 Gauge Fuse Link	Left Hand Shock Tower
Battery Feed to Ignition Switch and Fuse Panel	16 Gauge Fuse Link	Left Hand Shock Tower
Battery Feed to Headlamp Switch and Fuse Panel	16 Gauge Fuse Link	Left Hand Shock Tower
Power Windows, Power Seats, Power Door Locks	20 AMP Circuit Breaker	Battery Terminal-Starter Motor Relay
Station Wagon Rear Window Wiper/Washer	4.5 AMP Circuit Breaker	Taurus — I/P Brace Left Side of Steering Column Sable — Left Hand I/P End Panel

Circuit protection locations

d. To attach the remaining end of the replacement fuse link, strip approximately 13mm of insulation from the wire end of the circuit from which the blown fuse link was removed, and firmly crimp a butt connector or equivalent to the stripped wire. Then, insert the end of the replacement link into the other end of the butt connector and crimp firmly.

e. Using resin core solder with a consistency of 60 percent tin and 40 percent lead, solder the connectors and the wires at the repairs and insulate with electrical tape.

6. To replace any fuse link on a single circuit in a harness, cut out the damaged portion, strip approximately 13mm of insulation from the two wire ends and attach the appropriate replacement fuse link to the stripped wire ends

REMOVE EXISTING VINYL TUBE SHIELDING
REINSTALL OVER FUSE LINK BEFORE CRIMPING
FUSE LINK TO WIRE ENDS

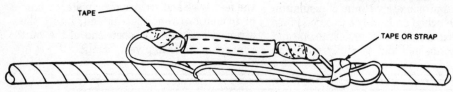

TAPE

TAPE OR STRAP

TYPICAL REPAIR USING THE SPECIAL #17 GA. (9.00" LONG-YELLOW) FUSE LINK REQUIRED FOR THE AIR/COND. CIRCUITS

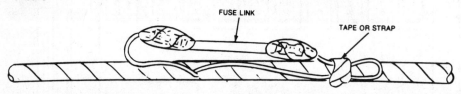

FUSE LINK

TAPE OR STRAP

TYPICAL REPAIR FOR ANY IN-LINE FUSE LINK USING THE SPECIFIED GAUGE FUSE LINK FOR THE SPECIFIC CIRCUIT

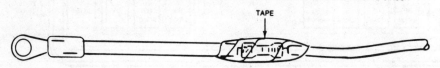

TAPE

TYPICAL REPAIR USING THE EYELET TERMINAL FUSE LINK OF THE SPECIFIED GAUGE FOR ATTACHMENT TO A CIRCUIT WIRE END

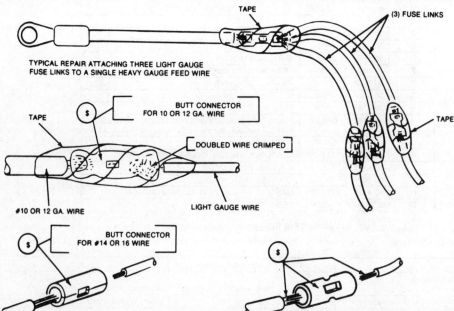

TAPE

(3) FUSE LINKS

TYPICAL REPAIR ATTACHING THREE LIGHT GAUGE
FUSE LINKS TO A SINGLE HEAVY GAUGE FEED WIRE

TAPE

BUTT CONNECTOR
FOR 10 OR 12 GA. WIRE

DOUBLED WIRE CRIMPED

TAPE

#10 OR 12 GA. WIRE

LIGHT GAUGE WIRE

BUTT CONNECTOR
FOR #14 OR 16 WIRE

FUSIBLE LINK REPAIR PROCEDURE

General fuse link repair procedures

with two proper size butt connectors. Solder the connectors and wires and insulate with tape.

7. To repair any fuse link which has an eyelet terminal on one end such as the charging circuit, cut off the open fuse link behind the weld, strip approximately 13mm of insulation from the cut end and attach the appropriate new eyelet fuse link to the cut stripped wire with an appropriate size butt connector. Solder the connectors and wires at the repair and insulate with tape.

8. Connect the negative (−) battery cable to the battery and test the system for proper operation.

NOTE: *Do not mistake a resistor wire for a fuse link. The resistor wire is generally longer and has print stating, "Resistor-don't cut or splice".*

When attaching a single No. 16, 17, 18 or 20 gauge fuse link to a heavy gauge wire, always double the stripped wire end of the fuse link before inserting and crimping it into the butt connector for positive wire retention.

Troubleshooting Basic Lighting Problems

Problem	Cause	Solution
Lights		
One or more lights don't work, but others do	• Defective bulb(s) • Blown fuse(s) • Dirty fuse clips or light sockets • Poor ground circuit	• Replace bulb(s) • Replace fuse(s) • Clean connections • Run ground wire from light socket housing to car frame
Lights burn out quickly	• Incorrect voltage regulator setting or defective regulator • Poor battery/alternator connections	• Replace voltage regulator • Check battery/alternator connections
Lights go dim	• Low/discharged battery • Alternator not charging • Corroded sockets or connections • Low voltage output	• Check battery • Check drive belt tension; repair or replace alternator • Clean bulb and socket contacts and connections • Replace voltage regulator
Lights flicker	• Loose connection • Poor ground • Circuit breaker operating (short circuit)	• Tighten all connections • Run ground wire from light housing to car frame • Check connections and look for bare wires
Lights "flare"—Some flare is normal on acceleration—if excessive, see "Lights Burn Out Quickly"	• High voltage setting	• Replace voltage regulator
Lights glare—approaching drivers are blinded	• Lights adjusted too high • Rear springs or shocks sagging • Rear tires soft	• Have headlights aimed • Check rear springs/shocks • Check/correct rear tire pressure
Turn Signals		
Turn signals don't work in either direction	• Blown fuse • Defective flasher • Loose connection	• Replace fuse • Replace flasher • Check/tighten all connections
Right (or left) turn signal only won't work	• Bulb burned out • Right (or left) indicator bulb burned out • Short circuit	• Replace bulb • Check/replace indicator bulb • Check/repair wiring
Flasher rate too slow or too fast	• Incorrect wattage bulb • Incorrect flasher	• Flasher bulb • Replace flasher (use a variable load flasher if you pull a trailer)
Indicator lights do not flash (burn steadily)	• Burned out bulb • Defective flasher	• Replace bulb • Replace flasher
Indicator lights do not light at all	• Burned out indicator bulb • Defective flasher	• Replace indicator bulb • Replace flasher

Troubleshooting Basic Turn Signal and Flasher Problems

Most problems in the turn signals or flasher system, can be reduced to defective flashers or bulbs, which are easily replaced. Occasionally, problems in the turn signals are traced to the switch in the steering column, which will require professional service.

F = Front   R = Rear   ● = Lights off   o = Lights on

Problem		Solution
Turn signals light, but do not flash		• Replace the flasher
No turn signals light on either side		• Check the fuse. Replace if defective. • Check the flasher by substitution • Check for open circuit, short circuit or poor ground
Both turn signals on one side don't work		• Check for bad bulbs • Check for bad ground in both housings
One turn signal light on one side doesn't work		• Check and/or replace bulb • Check for corrosion in socket. Clean contacts. • Check for poor ground at socket
Turn signal flashes too fast or too slow		• Check any bulb on the side flashing too fast. A heavy-duty bulb is probably installed in place of a regular bulb. • Check the bulb flashing too slow. A standard bulb was probably installed in place of a heavy-duty bulb. • Check for loose connections or corrosion at the bulb socket
Indicator lights don't work in either direction		• Check if the turn signals are working • Check the dash indicator lights • Check the flasher by substitution

One indicator light doesn't light		• On systems with 1 dash indicator: See if the lights work on the same side. Often the filaments have been reversed in systems combining stoplights with taillights and turn signals.
		  Check the flasher by substitution
		• On systems with 2 indicators: Check the bulbs on the same side
		  Check the indicator light bulb
		  Check the flasher by substitution

Troubleshooting Basic Dash Gauge Problems

Problem	Cause	Solution
Coolant Temperature Gauge		
Gauge reads erratically or not at all	• Loose or dirty connections • Defective sending unit	• Clean/tighten connections • Bi-metal gauge: remove the wire from the sending unit. Ground the wire for an instant. If the gauge registers, replace the sending unit.
	• Defective gauge	• Magnetic gauge: disconnect the wire at the sending unit. With ignition ON gauge should register COLD. Ground the wire; gauge should register HOT.
Ammeter Gauge—Turn Headlights ON (do not start engine). Note reaction		
Ammeter shows charge Ammeter shows discharge Ammeter does not move	• Connections reversed on gauge • Ammeter is OK • Loose connections or faulty wiring • Defective gauge	• Reinstall connections • Nothing • Check/correct wiring • Replace gauge
Oil Pressure Gauge		
Gauge does not register or is inaccurate	• On mechanical gauge, Bourdon tube may be bent or kinked	• Check tube for kinks or bends preventing oil from reaching the gauge
	• Low oil pressure	• Remove sending unit. Idle the engine briefly. If no oil flows from sending unit hole, problem is in engine.
	• Defective gauge	• Remove the wire from the sending unit and ground it for an instant with the ignition ON. A good gauge will go to the top of the scale.
	• Defective wiring	• Check the wiring to the gauge. If it's OK and the gauge doesn't register when grounded, replace the gauge.
	• Defective sending unit	• If the wiring is OK and the gauge functions when grounded, replace the sending unit
All Gauges		
All gauges do not operate	• Blown fuse • Defective instrument regulator	• Replace fuse • Replace instrument voltage regulator
All gauges read low or erratically	• Defective or dirty instrument voltage regulator	• Clean contacts or replace
All gauges pegged	• Loss of ground between instrument voltage regulator and car • Defective instrument regulator	• Check ground • Replace regulator
Warning Lights		
Light(s) do not come on when ignition is ON, but engine is not started	• Defective bulb • Defective wire	• Replace bulb • Check wire from light to sending unit
	• Defective sending unit	• Disconnect the wire from the sending unit and ground it. Replace the sending unit if the light comes on with the ignition ON.
Light comes on with engine running	• Problem in individual system • Defective sending unit	• Check system • Check sending unit (see above)

Troubleshooting the Heater

Problem	Cause	Solution
Blower motor will not turn at any speed	• Blown fuse • Loose connection • Defective ground • Faulty switch • Faulty motor • Faulty resistor	• Replace fuse • Inspect and tighten • Clean and tighten • Replace switch • Replace motor • Replace resistor
Blower motor turns at one speed only	• Faulty switch • Faulty resistor	• Replace switch • Replace resistor
Blower motor turns but does not circulate air	• Intake blocked • Fan not secured to the motor shaft	• Clean intake • Tighten security
Heater will not heat	• Coolant does not reach proper temperature • Heater core blocked internally • Heater core air-bound • Blend-air door not in proper position	• Check and replace thermostat if necessary • Flush or replace core if necessary • Purge air from core • Adjust cable
Heater will not defrost	• Control cable adjustment incorrect • Defroster hose damaged	• Adjust control cable • Replace defroster hose

Troubleshooting Basic Windshield Wiper Problems

Problem	Cause	Solution
Electric Wipers		
Wipers do not operate— Wiper motor heats up or hums	• Internal motor defect • Bent or damaged linkage • Arms improperly installed on linking pivots	• Replace motor • Repair or replace linkage • Position linkage in park and reinstall wiper arms
Wipers do not operate— No current to motor	• Fuse or circuit breaker blown • Loose, open or broken wiring • Defective switch • Defective or corroded terminals • No ground circuit for motor or switch	• Replace fuse or circuit breaker • Repair wiring and connections • Replace switch • Replace or clean terminals • Repair ground circuits
Wipers do not operate— Motor runs	• Linkage disconnected or broken	• Connect wiper linkage or replace broken linkage
Vacuum Wipers		
Wipers do not operate	• Control switch or cable inoperative • Loss of engine vacuum to wiper motor (broken hoses, low engine vacuum, defective vacuum/fuel pump) • Linkage broken or disconnected • Defective wiper motor	• Repair or replace switch or cable • Check vacuum lines, engine vacuum and fuel pump • Repair linkage • Replace wiper motor
Wipers stop on engine acceleration	• Leaking vacuum hoses • Dry windshield • Oversize wiper blades • Defective vacuum/fuel pump	• Repair or replace hoses • Wet windshield with washers • Replace with proper size wiper blades • Replace pump

TRANSAXLE

Identification

Your Taurus/Sable and Continental uses a front wheel drive transmission called a transaxle. The transaxle may either be manual or automatic.

A 5-speed fully synchronized manual transaxle is available on the 2.5L and 3.0L SHO Taurus/Sable models. An internally gated shift mechanism and a single rail shift linkage eliminate the need for periodic shift linkage adjustments. The MTX transaxle is designed to use Type F or Dexron®II automatic transmission fluid as a lubricant. Never use gear oil (GL) in the place of Type F or Dexron®II.

Two automatic transaxle units are available on the Taurus/Sable models, the ATX (automatic transaxle) model which is used with the 2.5L engine, and the AXOD (automatic transaxle overdrive) which is used with the 3.0L and 3.8L engine. The Continental is equipped with the AXOD transaxle.

The ATX automatic transaxle is a 3-speed unit. A unique feature is a patented split path torque converter. The engine torque in second and third gears is divided, so that part of the engine torque is transmitted hydrokinetically through the torque converter, and part is transmitted mechanically by direct connection of the engine and transaxle. In the third gear, 93% of the torque is transmitted mechanically, making the ATX highly efficient. Torque splitting is accomplished through a splitter gear set. A conventional compound gear set is also used.

Only one band is used in the ATX. In service fluid additions, or fluid changes may be made with **Motorcraft Type H** automatic transmission fluid.

The AXOD automatic transaxle is a 4-speed unit. This unit has two planetary gear sets and a combination planetary/differential gear set.

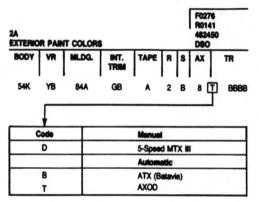

Code	Manual
D	5-Speed MTX III
	Automatic
B	ATX (Batavia)
T	AXOD

Transmission identification via the door post label

Four multiple plate clutches, two band assemblies, and two one-way clutches act together for proper operation of the planetary gear sets.

A lockup torque converter is coupled to the engine crankshaft and transmits engine power to the gear train by means of a drive link assembly (chain) that connects the drive and the driven sprockets. The application of the converter clutch is controlled through an electronic control integrated in the on-board EEC-IV system computer. These controls, along with the hydraulic controls in the valve body, operate a piston plate clutch in the torque converter to provide improved fuel economy by eliminating converter slip when applied.

In service fluid additions, or fluid changes may be made with **Motorcraft Type H** automatic transmission fluid.

Halfshafts

The front wheel drive halfshafts use constant velocity (CV) joints at both its inboard (differential) and outboard (wheel) ends of the vehicle. The CV-joints are connected by an interconnecting shaft. The interconnecting shafts (LH

Troubleshooting the Manual Transmission and Transfer Case

Problem	Cause	Solution
Transmission shifts hard	• Clutch adjustment incorrect • Clutch linkage or cable binding • Shift rail binding	• Adjust clutch • Lubricate or repair as necessary • Check for mispositioned selector arm roll pin, loose cover bolts, worn shift rail bores, worn shift rail, distorted oil seal, or extension housing not aligned with case. Repair as necessary.
	• Internal bind in transmission caused by shift forks, selector plates, or synchronizer assemblies • Clutch housing misalignment • Incorrect lubricant • Block rings and/or cone seats worn	• Remove, dissemble and inspect transmission. Replace worn or damaged components as necessary. • Check runout at rear face of clutch housing • Drain and refill transmission • Blocking ring to gear clutch tooth face clearance must be 0.030 inch or greater. If clearance is correct it may still be necessary to inspect blocking rings and cone seats for excessive wear. Repair as necessary.
Gear clash when shifting from one gear to another	• Clutch adjustment incorrect • Clutch linkage or cable binding • Clutch housing misalignment • Lubricant level low or incorrect lubricant • Gearshift components, or synchronizer assemblies worn or damaged	• Adjust clutch • Lubricate or repair as necessary • Check runout at rear of clutch housing • Drain and refill transmission and check for lubricant leaks if level was low. Repair as necessary. • Remove, disassemble and inspect transmission. Replace worn or damaged components as necessary.
Transmission noisy	• Lubricant level low or incorrect lubricant • Clutch housing-to-engine, or transmission-to-clutch housing bolts loose • Dirt, chips, foreign material in transmission • Gearshift mechanism, transmission gears, or bearing components worn or damaged • Clutch housing misalignment	• Drain and refill transmission. If lubricant level was low, check for leaks and repair as necessary. • Check and correct bolt torque as necessary • Drain, flush, and refill transmission • Remove, disassemble and inspect transmission. Replace worn or damaged components as necessary. • Check runout at rear face of clutch housing
Jumps out of gear	• Clutch housing misalignment • Gearshift lever loose • Offset lever nylon insert worn or lever attaching nut loose • Gearshift mechanism, shift forks, selector plates, interlock plate, selector arm, shift rail, detent plugs, springs or shift cover worn or damaged • Clutch shaft or roller bearings worn or damaged	• Check runout at rear face of clutch housing • Check lever for worn fork. Tighten loose attaching bolts. • Remove gearshift lever and check for loose offset lever nut or worn insert. Repair or replace as necessary. • Remove, disassemble and inspect transmission cover assembly. Replace worn or damaged components as necessary. • Replace clutch shaft or roller bearings as necessary

Troubleshooting the Manual Transmission and Transfer Case (cont.)

Problem	Cause	Solution
Jumps out of gear (cont.)	• Gear teeth worn or tapered, synchronizer assemblies worn or damaged, excessive end play caused by worn thrust washers or output shaft gears	• Remove, disassemble, and inspect transmission. Replace worn or damaged components as necessary.
	• Pilot bushing worn	• Replace pilot bushing
Will not shift into one gear	• Gearshift selector plates, interlock plate, or selector arm, worn, damaged, or incorrectly assembled	• Remove, disassemble, and inspect transmission cover assembly. Repair or replace components as necessary.
	• Shift rail detent plunger worn, spring broken, or plug loose	• Tighten plug or replace worn or damaged components as necessary
	• Gearshift lever worn or damaged	• Replace gearshift lever
	• Synchronizer sleeves or hubs, damaged or worn	• Remove, disassemble and inspect transmission. Replace worn or damaged components.
Locked in one gear—cannot be shifted out	• Shift rail(s) worn or broken, shifter fork bent, setscrew loose, center detent plug missing or worn	• Inspect and replace worn or damaged parts
	• Broken gear teeth on countershaft gear, clutch shaft, or reverse idler gear	• Inspect and replace damaged part
	Gearshift lever broken or worn, shift mechanism in cover incorrectly assembled or broken, worn damaged gear train components	• Disassemble transmission. Replace damaged parts or assemble correctly.
Transfer case difficult to shift or will not shift into desired range	• Vehicle speed too great to permit shifting	• Stop vehicle and shift into desired range. Or reduce speed to 3–4 km/h (2–3 mph) before attempting to shift.
	• If vehicle was operated for extended period in 4H mode on dry paved surface, driveline torque load may cause difficult shifting	• Stop vehicle, shift transmission to neutral, shift transfer case to 2H mode and operate vehicle in 2H on dry paved surfaces
	• Transfer case external shift linkage binding	• Lubricate or repair or replace linkage, or tighten loose components as necessary
	• Insufficient or incorrect lubricant	• Drain and refill to edge of fill hole with SAE 85W-90 gear lubricant only
	• Internal components binding, worn, or damaged	• Disassemble unit and replace worn or damaged components as necessary
Transfer case noisy in all drive modes	• Insufficient or incorrect lubricant	• Drain and refill to edge of fill hole with SAE 85W-90 gear lubricant only. Check for leaks and repair if necessary. Note: If unit is still noisy after drain and refill, disassembly and inspection may be required to locate source of noise.
Noisy in—or jumps out of four wheel drive low range	• Transfer case not completely engaged in 4L position	• Stop vehicle, shift transfer case in Neutral, then shift back into 4L position
	• Shift linkage loose or binding	• Tighten, lubricate, or repair linkage as necessary
	• Shift fork cracked, inserts worn, or fork is binding on shift rail	• Disassemble unit and repair as necessary
Lubricant leaking from output shaft seals or from vent	• Transfer case overfilled	• Drain to correct level
	• Vent closed or restricted	• Clear or replace vent if necessary

Troubleshooting the Manual Transmission and Transfer Case (cont.)

Problem	Cause	Solution
Lubricant leaking from output shaft seals or from vent (cont.)	• Output shaft seals damaged or installed incorrectly	• Replace seals. Be sure seal lip faces interior of case when installed. Also be sure yoke seal surfaces are not scored or nicked. Remove scores, nicks with fine sandpaper or replace yoke(s) if necessary.
Abnormal tire wear	• Extended operation on dry hard surface (paved) roads in 4H range	• Operate in 2H on hard surface (paved) roads

and RH) are splined at both ends and are retained in the inboard and outboard CV-joints by circlips.

The CV-joints are lube-for-life with a special CV-joint grease and require no periodic lubrication. The CV-joint boots, however, should be periodically inspected and replaced immediately when grease leakage is evident. Continued operation would result in the destruction of the CV-joints, in turn big bucks.

The halfshaft design is similar for both the automatic and the manual transaxle applications. However, close attention should be given to the service procedures as there are significant differences in design that affect disassembly and assembly. Halfshaft removal procedures also differ, however, between automatic and manual transaxles. Halfshaft removal is accomplished (on the AXOD and MTX units) by applying a load on the back face of the inboard constant velocity (CV) joint assembly. On the ATX units, the right link shaft assembly must be removed from the transaxle in order to remove the left halfshaft assembly. Performing this procedure in any other manner could result in damage to the left inboard CV-joint.

REMOVAL

NOTE: *Special tools are required for removing, installing and servicing halfshafts. They are listed by descriptive name (Ford part number). Front Hub Installer Adapter (T81P1104A), Wheel Bolt Adapters (T81P1104B or T83P1104BH), CV-joint Separator (T81P3514A), Front Hub Installer/Remover (T81P1104C), Shipping Plug Tool (T81P1177B), Dust Deflector Installer CV-joint (T83P3425AH), Differential Rotator (T81P4026A).*

It is necessary to have on hand new hub nuts and new lower control arm to steering knuckle attaching nuts and bolts. Once removed, these parts must not be reused. The torque holding ability is destroyed during removal.

1. Remove the wheel covers and loosen the front hub nut, then, the wheel lug nuts.

NOTE: *The hub retaining nut is torqued to*

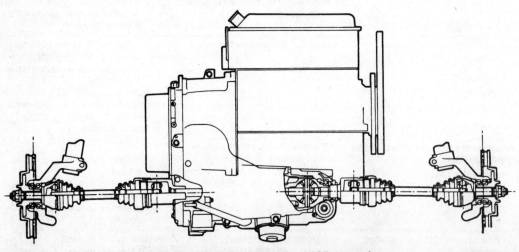

CV joint and halfshaft assembly—AXOD transaxle

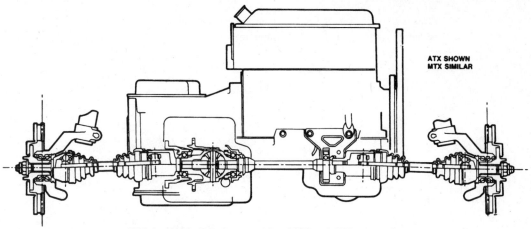

CV joint and halfshaft assembly—MTX and ATX transaxles

180-200 ft. lbs. and will require considerable force to remove it.

2. Jack up the front of the car and safely support it on jackstands.

3. Remove the tire and wheel assembly. Remove and discard the front hub nut. Save the washers.

4. Remove the ball joint-to-steering knuckle nut. Using a punch and a hammer, drive the bolt from the steering knuckle; discard the bolt/nut.

5. Using a medium pry bar, separate the ball joint from the steering knuckle.

NOTE: *Position the end of the pry bar outside of the bushing pocket to avoid damaging the bushing. Use care to prevent damage to the ball joint boot.*

6. Remove the stabilizer bar link from the stabilizer bar.

NOTE: *The following procedures differ for the right and left shafts depending on the application. Refer to the appropriate vehicles below depending on the vehicle you are working on.*

Halfshaft/link shaft – ATX and MTX, right side

7. Remove the bearing support-to-bracket bolts, then slide the shaft out of the transaxle.

8. Using a piece of wire, support the end of the shaft from a convenient underbody component.

NOTE: *DO NOT allow the shaft to hang unsupported, for damage to the outboard CV-joint may occur.*

9. Separate the outboard CV-joint from the hub using the front hub remover tool part No. T81P-1104-C, the metric adapters tools part No. T83-P-1104-BH, T86-1104-Al and T81P-1104-A.

NOTE: *NEVER use a hammer to separate the outboard CV-joint stub shaft from the hub; damage to the CV-joint threads and internal components may result. The right side link shaft and halfshaft assembly is removed as a complete unit.*

AXOD, right and left; MTX, left

10. Place CV-joint puller tool part No. T86-3514-A1 between the CV-joint and transaxle

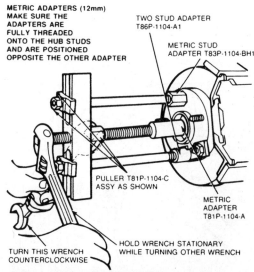

PRY BAR
DO NOT ALLOW PRY BAR TO DAMAGE BALL JOINT BOOT

CONTROL ARM BALL JOINT

NOTE: EXERCISE CARE NOT TO DAMAGE OR CUT BALL JOINT BOOT. PRY BAR MUST NOT CONTACT LOWER ARM.

Separating the ball joint from the knuckle

METRIC ADAPTERS (12mm) MAKE SURE THE ADAPTERS ARE FULLY THREADED ONTO THE HUB STUDS AND ARE POSITIONED OPPOSITE THE OTHER ADAPTER

TWO STUD ADAPTER T86P-1104-A1

METRIC STUD ADAPTER T83P-1104-BH1

PULLER T81P-1104-C ASSY AS SHOWN

METRIC ADAPTER T81P-1104-A

HOLD WRENCH STATIONARY WHILE TURNING OTHER WRENCH

TURN THIS WRENCH COUNTERCLOCKWISE

Separating the outboard shaft from the hub

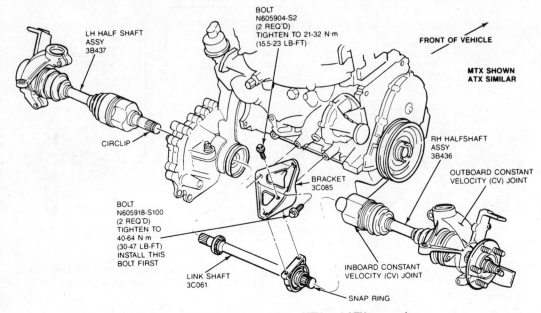

BOLT
N605904-S2
(2 REQ'D)
TIGHTEN TO 21-32 N·m
(15.5-23 LB-FT)

FRONT OF VEHICLE

MTX SHOWN
ATX SIMILAR

LH HALF SHAFT
ASSY
3B437

CIRCLIP

RH HALFSHAFT
ASSY
3B436

OUTBOARD CONSTANT
VELOCITY (CV) JOINT

BRACKET
3C085

BOLT
N605918-S100
(2 REQ'D)
TIGHTEN TO
40-64 N·m
(30-47 LB-FT)
INSTALL THIS
BOLT FIRST

LINK SHAFT
3C061

INBOARD CONSTANT
VELOCITY (CV) JOINT

SNAP RING

Halfshaft and Linkshaft assemblies—MTX and ATX transaxles

case. Turn the steering hub and/or wire the strut assembly out of the way.

11. Assemble the screw extension tool part No. T86P-3514-A2 into the CV-Joint puller and hand tighten. Assemble the screw impact slide hammer tool part No. D79-100-A onto the extension and remove the CV-joint.

12. Support the end of the shaft by suspending it from a convenient underbody component with a piece of wire.

NOTE: *DO NOT allow the shaft to hang unsupported, damage to the outboard CV-joint may occur.*

13. Separate the outboard CV-joint from the hub using the front hub remover tool part No. T81P-1104-C, the metric adapters tools part

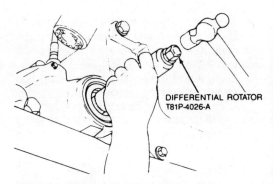

DIFFERENTIAL ROTATOR
T81P-4026-A

Using the differential rotator tool

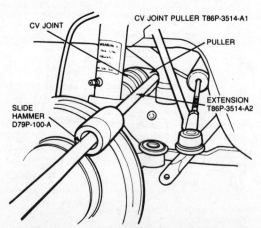

CV JOINT

CV JOINT PULLER T86P-3514-A1

PULLER

SLIDE
HAMMER
D79P-100-A

EXTENSION
T86P-3514-A2

Tool positioning for inboard CV joint removal

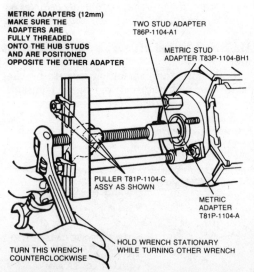

METRIC ADAPTERS (12mm)
MAKE SURE THE
ADAPTERS ARE
FULLY THREADED
ONTO THE HUB STUDS
AND ARE POSITIONED
OPPOSITE THE OTHER ADAPTER

TWO STUD ADAPTER
T86P-1104-A1

METRIC STUD
ADAPTER T83P-1104-BH1

PULLER T81P-1104-C
ASSY AS SHOWN

METRIC
ADAPTER
T81P-1104-A

TURN THIS WRENCH
COUNTERCLOCKWISE

HOLD WRENCH STATIONARY
WHILE TURNING OTHER WRENCH

Outboard CV joint removal

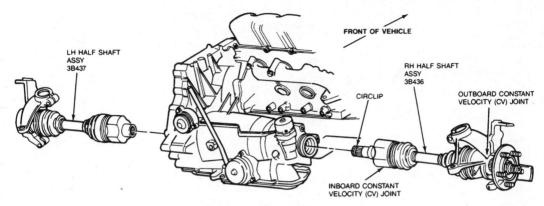

Halfshaft assembly—AXOD transaxle

No. T83-P-1104-BH, T86P-1104-Al and T81P-1104-A.

NOTE: *Never use a hammer to separate the outboard CV-joint stub shaft from the hub. Damage to the CV-joint threads and internal components may result.*

14. Remove the halfshaft assembly from the vehicle.

ATX, left side

NOTE: *Due to the ATX case configuration, the right side halfshaft assembly MUST be removed first.*

15. Remove the right hand halfshaft assembly (from the transaxle) and support it on a wire.

16. Insert the differential rotator tool part No. T81P-4026-A into the transaxle and drive the left side inboard CV-joint assembly from the transaxle.

17. Support the end of the shaft by suspending it from a convenient underbody component with a piece of wire. DO NOT allow the shaft to hang unsupported, for damage to the outboard CV-joint may occur.

18. Using the front hub removal tool part No. T81P-1104-C, the metric adapter tools part No. T83-P-1104-BH, T86P-1104-A1 and T81P-1104-A, separate the outboard CV-joint from the hub.

NOTE: *Never use a hammer to separate the outboard CV-joint stub shaft from the hub. Damage to the CV-joint threads and internal components may result.*

19. Remove the halfshaft assembly from the vehicle.

INSTALLATION

1. Install a new circlip on the inboard CV-joint stub shaft and or link shaft. Align the splines of the inboard CV-joint stub shaft with the splines in the differential. Push the CV-joint into the differential until the circlip seats

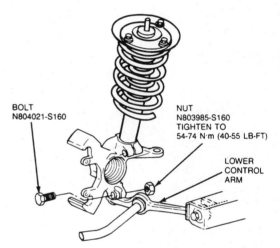

Lower control arm bolt installation

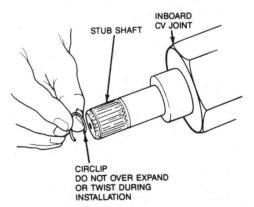

Circlip installation

on the side gear. Some force may be necessary to seat.

2. Lubricate the stub shaft splines with chassis grease. Carefully align the splines of the outboard CV-joint stub shaft with the splines in the front wheel hub.

3. Push the shaft into the hub as far as possible.

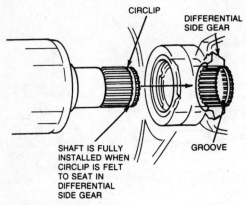

Inboard driveshaft installation

CIRCLIP

DIFFERENTIAL
SIDE GEAR

SHAFT IS FULLY
INSTALLED WHEN
CIRCLIP IS FELT
TO SEAT IN
DIFFERENTIAL
SIDE GEAR

GROOVE

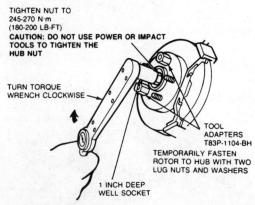

TIGHTEN NUT TO
245-270 N·m
(180-200 LB-FT)
CAUTION: DO NOT USE POWER OR IMPACT
TOOLS TO TIGHTEN THE
HUB NUT

TURN TORQUE
WRENCH CLOCKWISE

TOOL
ADAPTERS
T83P-1104-BH

TEMPORARILY FASTEN
ROTOR TO HUB WITH TWO
LUG NUTS AND WASHERS

1 INCH DEEP
WELL SOCKET

Outer halfshaft nut tightening

4. Install the hub nut and washer and a new hub retaining nut. Manually thread the retainer nut onto the CV-joint as far as possible.

5. Connect the control arm to the steering knuckle and install a new mounting bolt and nut. Torque to 40-55 ft. lbs.

6. Connect the stabilizer bar link to the stabilizer bar. Torque to 35-48 ft. lbs.

7. Install the tire and wheel assembly.

8. Lower the car to the ground. Tighten the wheel nuts to 80-105 ft. lbs.

9. Tighten the center hub nut to 180-200 ft. lbs.

10. Fill the transaxle to the proper level with the specified lubricant. Please refer to Chapter 1.

Outboard CV-joint and Boot

Disassembly

NOTE: *The CV-joint components are matched during manufacturing and therefore cannot be interchanged with components from another CV-joint. Extreme care should be taken not to mix or substitute components between CV-joints.*

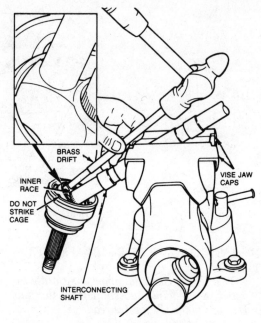

BRASS
DRIFT

INNER
RACE

DO NOT
STRIKE
CAGE

VISE JAW
CAPS

INTERCONNECTING
SHAFT

Removing outer CV joint from halfshaft

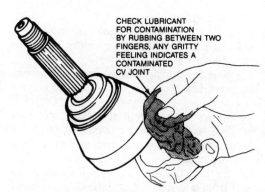

CHECK LUBRICANT
FOR CONTAMINATION
BY RUBBING BETWEEN TWO
FINGERS, ANY GRITTY
FEELING INDICATES A
CONTAMINATED
CV JOINT

Checking CV joint grease for contamination

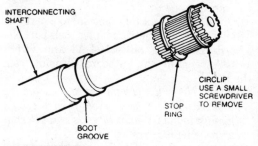

INTERCONNECTING
SHAFT

CIRCLIP
USE A SMALL
SCREWDRIVER
TO REMOVE

STOP
RING

BOOT
GROOVE

Circlip positioning

1. Clamp the halfshaft in a vise that is equipped with soft jaw covers. Do not allow the vise jaws to contact the boot or boot clamp.

2. Cut the large boot clamp with a pair of side cutters and peel the clamp away from the boot. Roll the boot back over the shaft after the clamp has been removed.

3. Check the grease for contamination by rubbing some between two fingers. If the grease feels gritty, it is contaminated and the joint will have to be disassembled, cleaned and inspected. If the grease is not contaminated and the CV-joints were operating satisfactorily, repack them with grease and install a new boot, or reinstall the old boot with a new clamp.

4. If disassembly is required, clamp the interconnecting shaft in a soft jawed vise with the CV-joint pointing downward so that the inner bearing race is exposed.

5. Use a brass drift and hammer, give a sharp tap to the inner bearing race to dislodge the internal snapring and separate the CV-joint from the interconnecting shaft. Take care to secure the CV-joint so that it does not drop on the ground after separation. Remove the clamp and boot from the shaft.

6. Remove and discard the circlip at the end

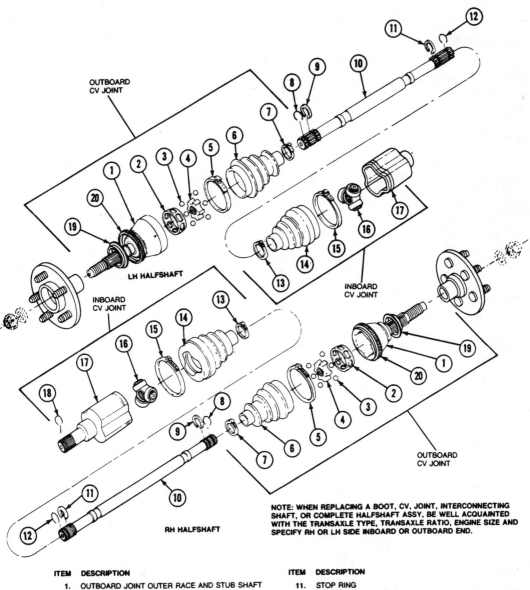

NOTE: WHEN REPLACING A BOOT, CV, JOINT, INTERCONNECTING SHAFT, OR COMPLETE HALFSHAFT ASSY, BE WELL ACQUAINTED WITH THE TRANSAXLE TYPE, TRANSAXLE RATIO, ENGINE SIZE AND SPECIFY RH OR LH SIDE INBOARD OR OUTBOARD END.

ITEM	DESCRIPTION	ITEM	DESCRIPTION
1.	OUTBOARD JOINT OUTER RACE AND STUB SHAFT	11.	STOP RING
2.	BALL CAGE	12.	CIRCLIP
3.	BALLS (SIX)	13.	BOOT CLAMP (SMALL)
4.	OUTBOARD JOINT INNER RACE	14.	BOOT
5.	BOOT CLAMP (LARGE)	15.	BOOT CLAMP (LARGE)
6.	BOOT	16.	INBOARD JOINT TRIPOD ASSY
7.	BOOT CLAMP (SMALL)	17.	INBOARD JOINT OUTER RACE AND STUB SHAFT
8.	CIRCLIP	18.	CIRCLIP
9.	STOP RING	19.	DUST SEAL
10.	INTERCONNECTING SHAFT	20.	SPEED INDICATOR RING (ANTI-LOCK BRAKES)

Halfshaft disassembled view

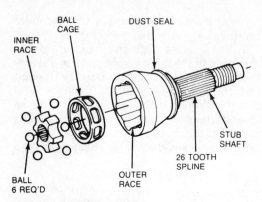

Outboard CV joint assembly

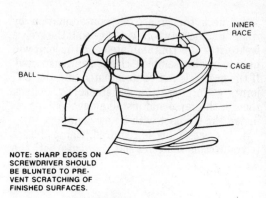

NOTE: SHARP EDGES ON SCREWDRIVER SHOULD BE BLUNTED TO PREVENT SCRATCHING OF FINISHED SURFACES.

of the interconnecting shaft. The stop ring, located just below the circlip should be removed and replaced only if damaged or worn.

7. Clean the interconnecting shaft splines and install a circlip, and stop ring if removed.

8. Clamp the CV-joint stub shaft in a vise with the outer face facing up. Care should be taken not to damage the dust seal.

9. Press down on the inner race until it tilts enough to allow removal of the ball.

NOTE: *A tight assembly can be tilted by tapping the inner race with a wooden dowel and hammer. DO NOT hit the cage.*

10. With the cage sufficiently tilted, remove the ball from the cage. Repeat this step until all six balls are removed.

NOTE: *If the balls are tight in the cage, and a tool is used to pry them out, make sure it is dull! Any scratching or other damage to the bearing cage or inner race spheres will destroy the CV-joint once you get it operating again.*

11. Pivot the cage and inner race assembly until it is straight up and down in the outer race. Align the cage windows with the outer cage lands while pivoting the bearing cage.

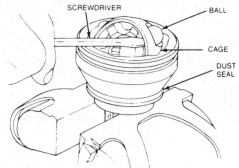

Removing the cage balls from the cage

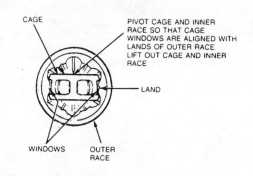

PIVOT CAGE AND INNER RACE SO THAT CAGE WINDOWS ARE ALIGNED WITH LANDS OF OUTER RACE. LIFT OUT CAGE AND INNER RACE

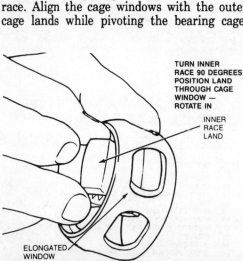

TURN INNER RACE 90 DEGREES POSITION LAND THROUGH CAGE WINDOW — ROTATE IN

Removing the inner race land from the cage

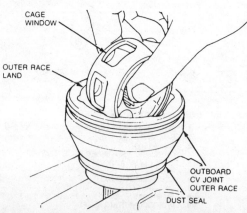

Remvoing the cage from the outer race land

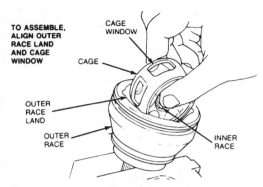

Cage race and outer race land assembly

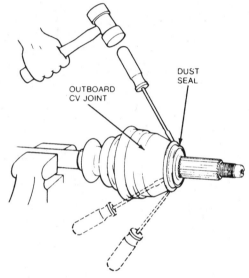

Dust seal removal

With the cage pivoted and aligned, lift the assembly from the outer race. Check the removing cage balls from cage illustration in this section.

12. Rotate the inner race up and out of the cage as follows: Pivot the inner race until it is straight up and down in the cage. Align one of the inner race lands with one of the elongated windows and position the race through the window. Rotate the inner race up and out of the cage.

ASSEMBLY

NOTE: *The CV-joint components are matched during manufacturing and therefore cannot be interchanged with components from another CV-joint. Extreme care should be taken not to mix or substitute components between CV-joints. Use only Constant Velocity Joint Grease Ford Spec. No. E2FZ-19590-A or equivalent.*

1. Apply a light coating of grease on the inner

and outer ball races. Install the inner race in the bearing cage.

2. Install the inner race and cage assemble into the outer race.

3. Install the assembly vertically and pivot it 90° into position.

4. Align the bearing cage and inner race with the outer race. Tilt the inner race and cage and install a ball. Repeat this step until all six balls are installed.

5. Examine the halfshaft. The left and right interconnecting shafts are not the same end for end. The outboard end is shorter from end of the shaft to the end of the boot groove than the inboard end. Take a measurement to ensure correct installation of the inboard and outboard CV-joints.

6. If removed, install the CV-joint boot after removing the stop ring. Ensure the boot is seated in its groove and clamp in position using crimping pliers.

NOTE: *Most original equipment boot clamps are made of steel and require a special crimping plier to install, however on replacement boots often a plastic clamp is used and doesn't require special tools. Whichever type you use, tighten the clamp securely, but not to the point where the clamp bridge is cut or the boot is damaged.*

7. If removed, install the stop ring. If it wasn't removed, ensure the stop ring is properly seated in its groove.

8. Install a new circlip (usually supplied in the boot kit), in the groove nearest the end of the shaft. To install the circlip correctly, start one end in the groove and work the circlip over the shaft end and into the groove.

9. Pack the CV-joint and boot with the grease supplied in the joint or boot kit. The CV-joint and boot should be packed with about 90 grams of grease. Use only Constant Velocity Joint Grease Ford Spec. No. E2FZ-19590-A or equivalent.

10. With the boot peeled back, position the

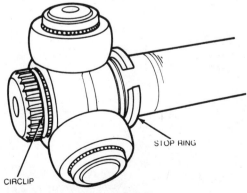

Circlip and stopring positioning

HALFSHAFT ASSEMBLED LENGTHS

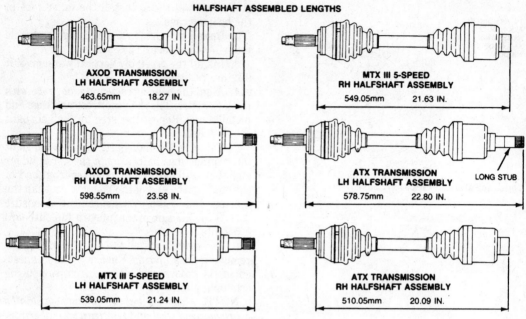

AXOD TRANSMISSION
LH HALFSHAFT ASSEMBLY
463.65mm   18.27 IN.

MTX III 5-SPEED
RH HALFSHAFT ASSEMBLY
549.05mm   21.63 IN.

AXOD TRANSMISSION
RH HALFSHAFT ASSEMBLY
598.55mm   23.58 IN.

ATX TRANSMISSION
LH HALFSHAFT ASSEMBLY
578.75mm   22.80 IN.

LONG STUB

MTX III 5-SPEED
LH HALFSHAFT ASSEMBLY
539.05mm   21.24 IN.

ATX TRANSMISSION
RH HALFSHAFT ASSEMBLY
510.05mm   20.09 IN.

Halfshaft overall length dimensions

CV-joint on the shaft and tap into position using a plastic tipped hammer. The CV-joint is fully seated when the snapring locks into the groove cut into the CV-joint inner bearing race. Check for seating by attempting to pull the joint away from the shaft.

11. Remove all excess grease from the CV-joint external surface and position the boot over the joint.

12. Before installing the boot clamp, make sure all air pressure that may have built up in the boot is removed. Pry up on the boot lip to allow the air to escape. Install the boot clamp.

Outboard CV-joint Dust Seal
DISASSEMBLY

The dust shield on the outside end of the CV-joint is removed by using a light hammer and

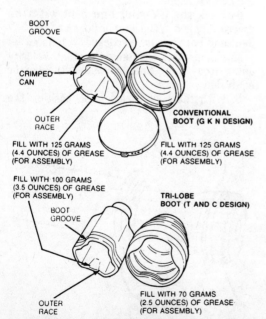

BOOT GROOVE

CRIMPED CAN

OUTER RACE

CONVENTIONAL BOOT (G K N DESIGN)

FILL WITH 125 GRAMS
(4.4 OUNCES) OF GREASE
(FOR ASSEMBLY)

FILL WITH 125 GRAMS
(4.4 OUNCES) OF GREASE
(FOR ASSEMBLY)

FILL WITH 100 GRAMS
(3.5 OUNCES) OF GREASE
(FOR ASSEMBLY)

TRI-LOBE BOOT (T AND C DESIGN)

BOOT GROOVE

OUTER RACE

FILL WITH 70 GRAMS
(2.5 OUNCES) OF GREASE
(FOR ASSEMBLY)

Conventional and Tri-lobe style CV joints

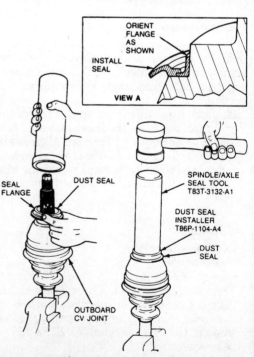

ORIENT FLANGE AS SHOWN

INSTALL SEAL

VIEW A

SEAL FLANGE

DUST SEAL

OUTBOARD CV JOINT

SPINDLE/AXLE SEAL TOOL T83T-3132-A1

DUST SEAL INSTALLER T86P-1104-A4

DUST SEAL

Dust seal installation

drift and tapping lightly around the seal until it becomes free.

ASSEMBLY

Install the dust shield with the flange facing outboard. Special Tools T83T-3132-A1 and T86P-1104-A4 or equivalent (Spindle/Axle Tool and Dust Seal Installer) are necessary to drive the seal into position.

Inboard CV-Joint

Two different types of inboard CV-joints and boots are used. The conventional style uses a crimped can on the large end. The tri-lobe style CV-joint does not require a crimped can on the large end.

NOTE: *Although the designs are similar, there is no interchangeability of parts between the two designs. The CV-joint tripod, outer race, boot and interconnecting shaft are unique for each style.*

DISASSEMBLY

1. Cut and remove both boot clamps and slide the boot back on the shaft.

2. Slide the outer race off of the tripod.

3. Check the grease for contamination by rubbing some between two fingers. If the grease feels gritty, it is contaminated and the joint will have to be disassembled, cleaned and inspected. If the grease is not contaminated and the CV-joints were operating satisfactorily, repack them with grease and install a new boot, or re-install the old boot with a new clamp.

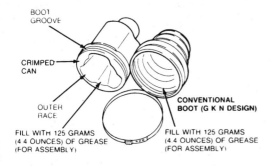

FILL WITH 125 GRAMS
(4 4 OUNCES) OF GREASE
(FOR ASSEMBLY)

BOOT GROOVE

CRIMPED CAN

OUTER RACE

CONVENTIONAL BOOT (G K N DESIGN)

FILL WITH 125 GRAMS
(4 4 OUNCES) OF GREASE
(FOR ASSEMBLY)

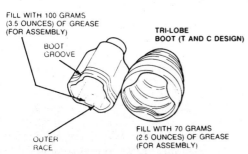

FILL WITH 100 GRAMS
(3.5 OUNCES) OF GREASE
(FOR ASSEMBLY)

BOOT GROOVE

TRI-LOBE BOOT (T AND C DESIGN)

OUTER RACE

FILL WITH 70 GRAMS
(2 5 OUNCES) OF GREASE
(FOR ASSEMBLY)

Inboard CV joint and boot grease capacity

4. Move the stop ring back on the shaft using snapring pliers.

5. Move the tripod assembly back on the shaft to allow access to the circlip.

6. Remove the circlip from the shaft.

7. Remove the tripod assembly from the shaft. Remove the boot if necessary.

8. Check the CV shaft diagrams in this section.

ASSEMBLY

1. Install the CV-joint boot on the shaft, if removed during disassembly. Ensure the boot is seated in its groove and clamp in position using crimping pliers.

NOTE: *Most original equipment boot clamps are made of steel and require a special crimping plier to install, however on replacement boots often a plastic clamp is used and doesn't require special tools. Whichever type you use, tighten the clamp securely, but not to the point where the clamp bridge is cut or the boot is damaged.*

2. Install the tripod assembly on the shaft with the chamfered side toward the stop ring.

3. Install a new circlip on the shaft.

4. Compress the circlip and slide the tripod assembly forward over the circlip to expose the stop ring groove.

5. Move the stop ring into the groove using snapring pliers, ensuring it is fully seated in the groove.

6. Pack the CV-joint outer race and boot with the grease supplied in the joint or boot kit. The CV-joint outer race and boot should be packed with grease as shown in the illustration. Use only Constant Velocity Joint Grease Ford Spec. No. E2FZ-19590-A or equivalent.

7. Install the outer race over the tripod assembly and position the boot over the outer race ensuring the boot is properly seated in its groove.

8. Remove all excess grease from the CV-joint external surface and position the boot over the joint. Move the CV-joint in and out, as necessary, to adjust the overall length as shown in the illustration.

9. Before installing the boot clamp, make sure all air pressure that may have built up in the boot is removed. Pry up on the boot lip to allow the air to escape.

10. Seat the boot in the groove and clamp into position using crimping pliers.

NOTE: *All vehicles require a reusable low profile large clamp on the right inboard CV-joint.*

11. Install the clamp as follows:

   a. With the boot seated in the groove, place the clamp over the boot.

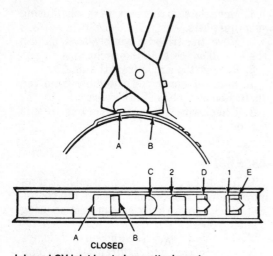

Inboard CV joint boot clamp attachment

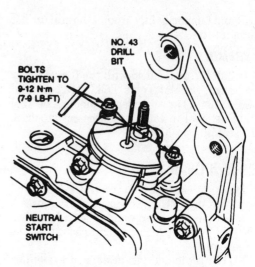

Neutral start switch adjustment—AXOD and ATX transaxles

b. Engage hook **C** in the window.

c. Place pincer jaws in the closing hooks **A** and **B**.

d. Secure the clamp by drawing the closing hooks together. When the windows are near **2** are above the locking hooks **D** and **E** the spring tab will press the windows over the locking hooks and engage the clamp.

12. Install a new circlip in the groove nearest the end of the shaft by starting one end in the groove and working the circlip over the stub shaft end and into the groove.

Neutral Start and Backup Switch AXOD and ATX

The neutral start and backup switch are one unit mounted on the top left end of the transaxle. The neutral start portion of the switch allows electrical current to travel to the ignition system when the shift selector is in PARK or

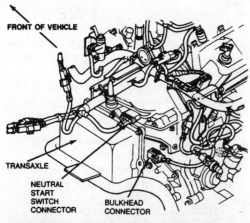

Neutral start and back-up switch location—AXOD and ATX transaxles

NEUTRAL only. The vehicle will not start when the selector is in any other gear. The backup portion operates the rear backup lamps when selector is in the REVERSE gear.

REMOVAL AND INSTALLATION

1. Place the shift selector in the PARK position and apply the emergency brake.

2. Disconnect the negative (-) battery cable.

3. Disconnect the neutral start switch electrical connector and remove the shift control lever on top of the switch.

4. Remove the two neutral switch attaching bolts and remove the switch.

5. **To install:** reverse the removal procedures and adjust linkage.

6. **Neutral Switch Adjustment:** Loosely install the two switch attaching bolts and washers, insert a No. 43 drill bit through the hole provided in the switch, and torque the two attaching bolts to 84-108 in. lbs. Check the neutral start switch illustration in this section.

Backup Lamp Switch MTX 5-speed

REMOVAL AND INSTALLATION

1. The backup lamp switch is located on the top left side of the transaxle.

2. Disconnect the negative (-) battery cable.

3. Disconnect the switch electrical connector.

4. Using a 22mm wrench, remove the switch.

5. **To install:** apply Pipe Sealant with Teflon® part No. D8AZ-19554-A or equivalent to the threads of the switch. Turn the switch into the transaxle case clockwise and torque to 14-18 ft. lbs, and connect the electrical connector.

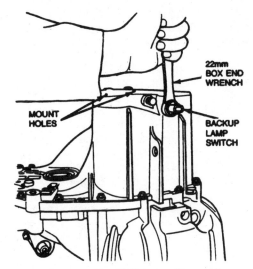

Back-up lamp switch—MTX 5-speed transaxle

6. There is no adjustment needed on the backup lamp switch.

MANUAL TRANSAXLE

REMOVAL

1. Disconnect the negative (−) battery cable and drain the transaxle lubricant into a suitable container.

2. Wedge a wood block approximately 178mm long under the clutch pedal to hold the pedal up slightly beyond its normal position.

3. Grasp the clutch cable and pull forward, disconnecting it from the clutch release shaft assembly. Remove the clutch casing from the rib on the top surface of the transaxle case.

4. Using a 13mm socket, remove the two top transaxle-to-engine mounting bolts. Using a 10mm socket, remove the air cleaner.

5. Raise and safely support the car with jack

stands. Remove the front stabilizer bar to control arm attaching nut and washer (driver side). Discard the attaching nut. Remove the two front stabilizer bar mounting brackets. Discard the bolts.

6. Using a 15mm socket, remove the nut and bolt that secures the lower control arm ball joint to the steering knuckle assembly. Refer to the illustrations in the "Halfshaft Removal" section in this chapter. Discard the nut and bolt. Repeat this procedure on the opposite side.

7. Using a large pry bar, pry the lower control arm away from the knuckle.

WARNING: *Exercise care not to damage or cut the ball joint boot. Pry bar must not contact the lower arm. Repeat this procedure on the opposite side.*

8. Using a large pry bar, pry the left inboard CV-joint assembly from the transaxle.

NOTE: *Install shipping plugs (T81P-1177-B or equivalent). Two plugs are required (one for each seal). Remove the inboard CV-joint from the transaxle by grasping the left hand steering knuckle and swinging the knuckle and halfshaft outward from the transaxle.*

CAUTION: *Exercise care when using a pry bar to remove the CV-joint assembly. If you're not careful, damage to the differential oil seal may result.*

9. If the CV-joint assembly cannot be pried from the transaxle, insert Differential Rotator Tool part No. (T81P-4026-A or equivalent), through the left side and tap the joint out. Tool can be used from either side of transaxle.

10. Wire the halfshaft assembly in a near level position to prevent damage to the assembly during the remaining operations. Repeat this procedure on the opposite side.

11. Remove the backup lamp switch connector from the transaxle back-up lamp switch.

12. Using a 13mm deep socket, remove the three starter mounting stud bolts.

13. Remove the 6mm shift mechanism-to-shift shaft attaching nut and bolt and control

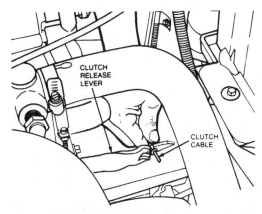

Removing the clutch cable

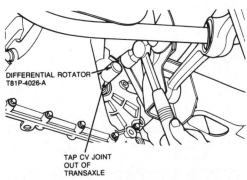

Using the differential rotator tool

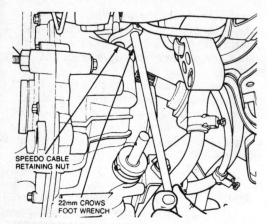

Speedometer cable removal from the transaxle

selector indicator switch arm. Remove from the shift shaft.

14. Remove the 10mm and 12mm bolts attaching the shift cable and bracket assembly to the transaxle.

15. Using a 22mm crows foot wrench, remove the speedometer cable from the transaxle.

16. Using a 13mm socket, remove the two stiffener brace attaching bolts from the lower position of the clutch housing.

17. Remove the subframe assembly.

18. Position a suitable jack under the transaxle.

19. Using a 13mm socket, remove the lower engine-to-transaxle attaching bolts

20. Lower the transaxle support jack.

21. Remove the transaxle from the rear face of the engine and lower it from the vehicle.

CAUTION: *The clutch driven disc contains asbestos, which has been determined to be a cancer causing agent. Never clean clutch surfaces with compressed air! Avoid inhaling any dust from any clutch surface! When cleaning clutch surfaces, use a commercially available brake cleaning fluid.*

To install:

WARNING: *Do not attempt to start the engine before installing the CV-joints. Differential side gear damage could result.*

1. Place a suitable jack under the transaxle and raise it into position. Engage the input shaft spline into the clutch disc and work the transaxle onto the dowel sleeves (pins).

NOTE: *Make sure that the transaxle assembly is flush with the rear face of the engine prior to installation of the attaching bolts.*

2. Using a 13mm socket, install the lower engine-to-transaxle attaching bolts. Tighten the bolts to 28-31 ft. lbs.

3. Using a 22mm crowfoot wrench, install the speedometer cable. Be careful not to cross-thread the cable nut!

4. Install the 10mm and 12mm bolts attaching the shift cable and bracket to the transaxle. Tighten the 10mm bolts to 16-22 ft. lbs. Tighten the 12mm bolts to 22-35 ft. lbs.

5. Install the 6mm bolts attaching the shift mechanism-to-shift shaft. Tighten the bolt to 7-10 ft. lbs.

6. Using a 13mm socket, install the two bolts that attach the stiffener brace to the lower portion of the clutch housing. Tighten the bolts to 15-21 ft. lbs.

7. Using a 13mm deep-well socket, install the three starter stud bolts. Tighten the bolts to 30-40 ft. lbs.

8. Install the backup lamp switch connector to the transaxle switch.

9. Remove the seal plugs and install the inner CV-joints into the transaxle.

10. Install two 10mm center bearing to the bracket on the right side halfshaft.

11. Before going any further please observe the following points:

• New circlips must be installed on both inner joints prior to installation.

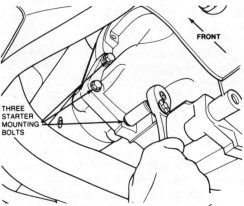

Starter bolt installation

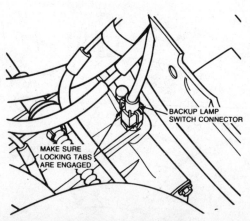

Backup lamp switch connector location

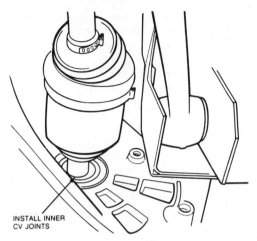

INSTALL INNER
CV JOINTS

CV joint installation

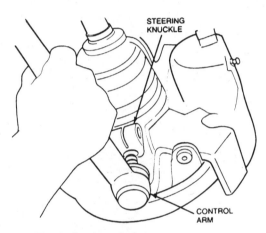

STEERING
KNUCKLE

CONTROL
ARM

Installing the lower control arm

• Be careful when inserting the shaft into the transaxle to avoid damage to the oil seals.

• Be certain that both joints are fully seated in the transaxle. Lightly pry outward to confirm that the retaining rings are seated. If the rings are not seated, the joint will move out of the transaxle.

12. Attach the sub-frame and the lower ball joint to the steering knuckle, taking care not to damage or cut the ball joint boot. Insert a new service pinch bolt (part No. N7801305-S100) and attach a new nut (part No. N801308). Tighten the nut to 37-44 ft. lbs. DO NOT tighten the bolt!

13. Fill the transaxle with either Type F or Dexron®II transmission fluid.

14. Using a 13mm socket, install the top transaxle-to-engine mounting bolts. Tighten the bolts to 28-31 ft. lbs.

15. Connect the clutch cable to the clutch release shaft assembly.

16. Remove the wood block from under the clutch pedal.

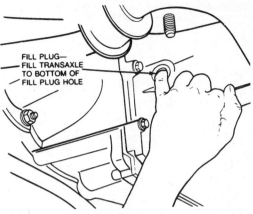

FILL PLUG—
FILL TRANSAXLE
TO BOTTOM OF
FILL PLUG HOLE

Checking the transaxle fluid level

NOTE: *Before starting the engine, set the handbrake and pump the clutch pedal a minimum of two times to ensure proper clutch adjustment.*

Manual Transaxle Overhaul

GEAR SET REMOVAL

1. Using a drift in the input shift shaft hole, shift the transaxle into NEUTRAL. Pull or push the shaft into the center detent position (NEUTRAL). The shift shaft will rotate slightly from side-to-side when positioned in NEUTRAL.

2. Remove the two shipping Plugs T81P-1177-B or equivalent from the transaxle and drain the transmission fluid.

NOTE: *Place the transaxle on a bench with the clutch housing face down to aid draining and service. If case half is being replaced, use a 22mm box end wrench to remove the backup lamp switch assembly.*

3. Using a 13mm socket wrench, remove the reverse idler shaft retaining bolt.

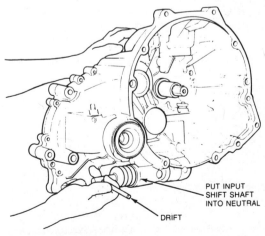

PUT INPUT
SHIFT SHAFT
INTO NEUTRAL

DRIFT

Shift shaft positioning

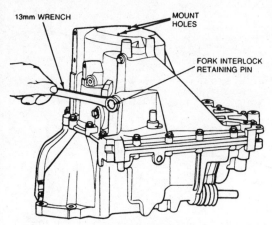

Interlock sleeve retaining pin removal

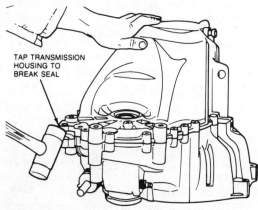

Separating the case halves

4. Using a 8mm socket wrench, loosen the detent plunger retaining screw in the transmission case.

5. Using a 13mm wrench, remove the shift fork interlock sleeve retaining pin.

6. Using a ⅜″ extension bar and ratchet, remove the fill plug.

7. Using a 10mm socket wrench, remove the 15 clutch housing-to-transmission case attaching bolts.

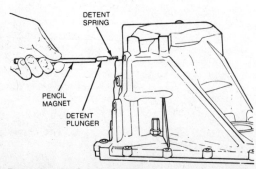

Removing the detent plunger

8. Using a plastic tipped hammer, tap the transmission case to break the seal between the case halves.

9. Separate the case halves.

NOTE: *Do not insert pry bars or screwdrivers between the case halves. Be careful not to drop the bearing cup or shims from the transmission case housing.*

10. Remove the detent plunger retaining screw. Then, using a pencil magnet, remove the detent spring and the detent plunger.

11. Remove the case magnet.

12. Using a small prybar, remove the C-clip retaining ring from the 5th relay lever pivot pin. Remove the 5th gear shift relay lever.

13. Lift the reverse idler shaft and reverse idler gear from the case.

14. Using a 4mm punch, drive the roll pin from the shift lever shaft.

15. Using a small prybar, gently pry on the shaft lever shaft so that the hole in the shaft is exposed.

WARNING: *Be careful not to damage the main shaft gear teeth or pedestal when prying with the prybar.*

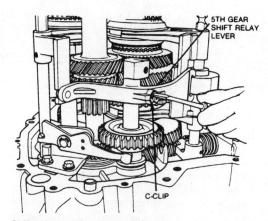

Shift relay rod lever removal

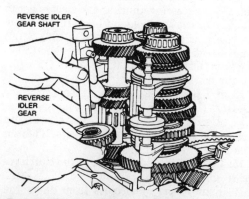

Reverse idler shaft and gear removal

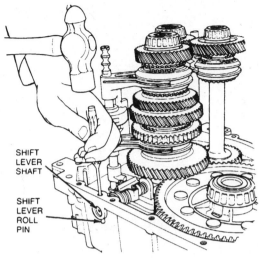

Shift lever shaft roll pin

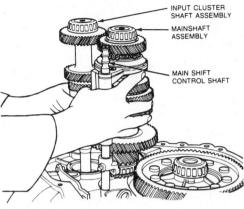

Mainshaft removal

retaining reverse shift relay lever support bracket assembly.

GEAR SET INSTALLATION

NOTE: *Prior to installation, thoroughly clean all parts and inspect their condition. Lightly oil the bores with Type F or Dexron®II transmission fluid or equivalent.*

1. Using a 10mm socket, install reverse relay lever support bracket assembly to the case with two bolts. Tighten bolts to 72-84 in. lbs.

2. Place the differential and the final drive gear assembly into the clutch housing case. Align the differential gears for later installation of the halfshafts.

3. Install the 5th gear shaft assembly and the fork shaft assembly in the case.

WARNING: *Be careful not to damage the 5th gear shaft oil funnel.*

4. Position the main shift control shaft assembly so that the shift forks engage their respective slots in the synchronizer sleeves on the main shaft assembly.

5. Bring the main shaft assembly into mesh with the input Cluster shaft assembly. Holding

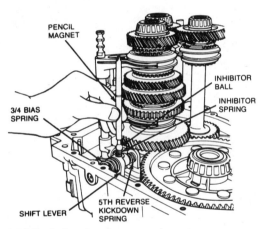

Inhibitor ball and spring removal

16. Hold a rag over the hole in the lever to prevent the ball and the 5th inhibitor spring from shooting out and remove the shift lever shaft.

17. Remove the inhibitor ball and spring from the hole in the shift lever using a pencil magnet. Then, remove the shift lever, 5th/reverse kickdown spring, and 3-4 bias spring.

18. Remove the main shaft assembly, input cluster shaft assembly and the main shift control shaft assembly as one unit.

NOTE: *Be careful not to drop bearings or gears (slip fit).*

19. Remove the 5th gear shaft assembly and 5th gear fork assembly from their bores in the case.

NOTE: *Be careful not to drop bearings or gear (slip fit).*

20. Lift the differential and final drive gear assembly from the clutch housing case.

21. Using a 10mm socket, remove two bolts

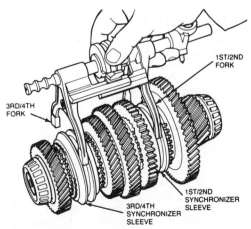

Main shift control assembly

MTX DISASSEMBLED VIEW

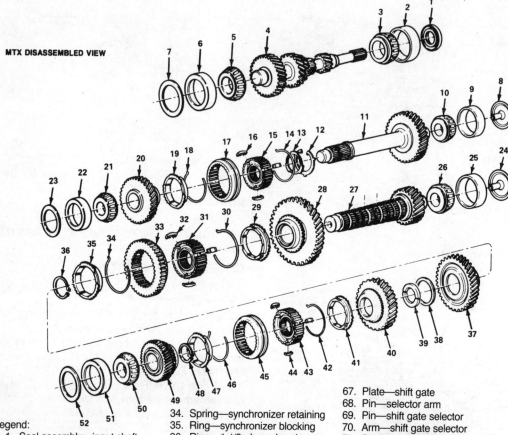

Legend:

1. Seal assembly—input shaft
2. Cup—roller bearing
3. Bearing—input shaft front
4. Shaft—input cluster
5. Bearing input shaft rear
6. Cup—roller bearing
7. Shim—bearing preload
8. Funnel—5th gear
9. Cup—roller bearing
10. Bearing—5th gear shaft—front
11. Shaft—5th gear drive
12. Retainer—synchronizer insert
13. Spacer—synchronizer retaining
14. Spring—synchronizer retaining
15. Hub—5th synchronizer
16. Insert—synchronizer hub 5th
17. Sleeve—5th synchronizer
18. Spring—synchronizer retaining
19. Ring—synchronizer blocking
20. Gear—5th speed
21. Bearing—5th gear shaft—rear
22. Cup—roller bearing
23. Shim—bearing preload
24. Funnel—mainshaft
25. Cup—roller bearing
26. Bearing—mainshaft front
27. Shaft—main
28. Gear—1st speed
29. Ring—synchronizer blocking
30. Spring—synchronizer retaining
31. Hub—1st/2nd synchronizer
32. Insert—synchronizer hub 1st/2nd
33. Gear—reverse sliding

34. Spring—synchronizer retaining
35. Ring—synchronizer blocking
36. Ring—1st/2nd synchronizer
    retaining
37. Gear—2nd speed
38. Ring—2nd/3rd thrust washer
    retaining
39. Washer—2nd/3rd thrust
40. Gear—3rd speed
41. Ring—synchronizer blocking
42. Spring—synchronizer retaining
43. Hub—3rd/4th synchronizer
44. Insert—synchronizer hub 3rd/4th
45. Sleeve—3rd/4th synchronizer
46. Spring—synchronizer retaining
47. Ring—synchronizer blocking
48. Ring—3rd/4th synchronizer
49. Gear—4th speed
50. Bearing—main shaft rear
51. Cup—roller bearing
52. Shim—bearing preload
53. Case—clutch housing
54. Switch assembly backup lamps
55. Lever—reverse relay
56. Pin—reverse relay lever pivot
57. Ring—external retaining
58. Pin—shift gate selector
59. Lever—shift
60. Ball—10.319 mm
61. Spring—5th/reverse inhibitor
62. Spring—3rd/4th shift bias
63. Shaft—shift lever
64. Pin—shift lever
65. Seal—shift lever shaft
66. Bolts—shift gate attaching

67. Plate—shift gate
68. Pin—selector arm
69. Pin—shift gate selector
70. Arm—shift gate selector
71. Shaft—input shift
72. Plunger—shift shaft detent
73. Spring—shift shaft detent
74. Seal—assembly—shift shaft—oil
75. Boot—shift shaft
76. Block—trans input fork control shaft
77. Spring pin—reverse relay lever
    actuating
78. Shaft—main shift fork control
79. Fork—1st/2nd
80. Sleeve—fork interlock
81. Pin—spring
82. Arm—fork selector
83. Fork—3rd/4th
84. Lever—5th shift relay
85. Pin—reverse shift relay lever
86. Pin—5th relay lever pivot
87. Ring—external retaining
88. Fork—5th
89. Fork—5th fork retaining
90. Shaft—5th fork control
91. Shaft—reverse idler gear
92. Bushing—reverse idler gear
93. Gear—reverse idler
94. Magnet—case
95. Case—transaxle
96. Vent assembly
97. Plug—fill
98. Bolt—reverse shaft retaining
99. Screw—detent plunger
    retaining
100. Plunger—shift shaft detent
101. Spring—shift shaft detent

Gearset exploded view—MTX transaxle

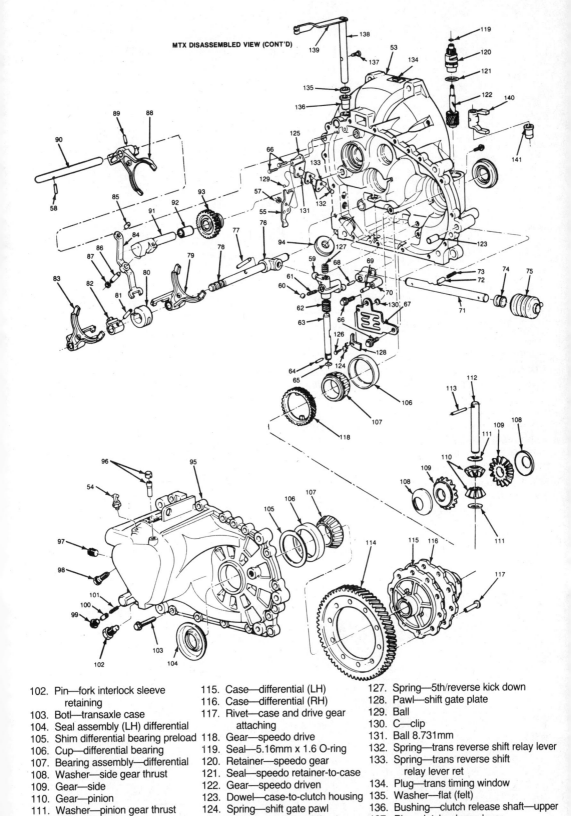

MTX DISASSEMBLED VIEW (CONT'D)

102. Pin—fork interlock sleeve retaining
103. Botl—transaxle case
104. Seal assembly (LH) differential
105. Shim differential bearing preload
106. Cup—differential bearing
107. Bearing assembly—differential
108. Washer—side gear thrust
109. Gear—side
110. Gear—pinion
111. Washer—pinion gear thrust
112. Shaft—pinion gear
113. Pin—pinion gear shaft retaining
114. Gear—final drive

115. Case—differential (LH)
116. Case—differential (RH)
117. Rivet—case and drive gear attaching
118. Gear—speedo drive
119. Seal—5.16mm x 1.6 O-ring
120. Retainer—speedo gear
121. Seal—speedo retainer-to-case
122. Gear—speedo driven
123. Dowel—case-to-clutch housing
124. Spring—shift gate pawl
125. Bracket—reverse shift relay lever support
126. Pin—reverse lockout pawl pivot

127. Spring—5th/reverse kick down
128. Pawl—shift gate plate
129. Ball
130. C—clip
131. Ball 8.731mm
132. Spring—trans reverse shift relay lever
133. Spring—trans reverse shift relay lever ret
134. Plug—trans timing window
135. Washer—flat (felt)
136. Bushing—clutch release shaft—upper
137. Pin—clutch release lever
138. Shaft—clutch release
139. Lever—clutch release

Exploded view of the MTX transaxle

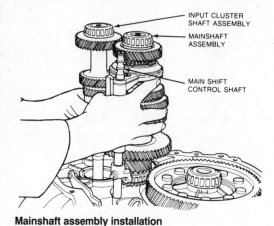

Mainshaft assembly installation

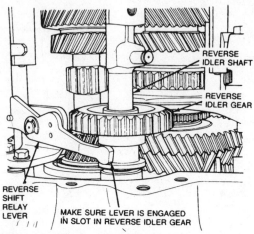

Reverse idler gear installation

the three shafts (input cluster shaft, main shaft and the main shift control shaft) in their respective working positions, lower them into their bores in the clutch housing case as one unit.

NOTE: *When performing this operation care must be taken to avoid movement of the 3rd/4th synchronizer sleeve. This could result in over travel of the synchronizing sleeve to hub, allowing inserts to pop out of position.*

Be careful not to damage the input shaft oil seal or main shaft oil funnel.

6. Position the shift lever, 3-4 bias spring and 5th/reverse kickdown spring in their working positions (with one shift leverball located in the socket of the input shift gate selector plate arm assembly and the other in the socket of the main shift control shaft block). Install the spring and ball in the 5th and reverse inhibitor sift lever hole. Slide the shift lever shaft (notch down) through the shift lever. Then using a small drift, depress the inhibitor ball and spring and tap the shift shaft through the shift lever and the 5th gear kickdown spring and then tap into its bore in the clutch housing.

7. Align the shift shaft roll pin hole with the case bore and tap the roll pin in slightly below the case mating surface.

8. Verify that the selector pin is in the neutral gate of the control selector plate and the finger of the fork selector arm is partially engaged with the 1st/2nd fork and partially engaged with the 3rd/4th fork.

9. Position reverse idler gear over bore in clutch housing while engaging reverse shift relay lever in the slot of the gear. Slide the reverse idler shaft through the gear and into its bore. Make sure the lever is engaged in slot in gear.

10. Install the magnet in its pocket in the clutch housing case.

11. Install the 5th shift relay lever onto the reverse idler shaft, aligning it with the fork interlock sleeve and 5th gear fork slot and install the retaining ring (C-clip).

12. Verify that the gasket surfaces of the transmission case and clutch housing are perfectly clean and free of burrs or nicks. Apply a 1.5mm wide bead of Gasket Eliminator E1FZ-19562-A (ESP-M4G228) or equivalent RTV to the clutch housing.

13. Install the detent spring and plunger in

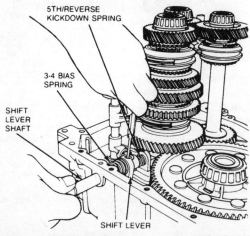

Shift lever shaft installation

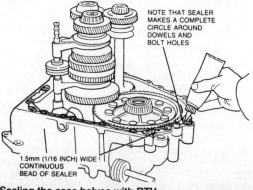

Sealing the case halves with RTV

their bore in the case. Carefully lower the transmission case over the clutch housing, then using a punch, depress the spring and plunger. Gently move the transmission case until the shift control shaft, main shaft, input cluster shaft and 5th gear shaft align with their respective bores in the transmission case.

14. Gently slide the transmission case over the dowels and flush onto the clutch housing case. Make sure that the case does not bind on the magnet.

15. Apply Pipe Sealant with Teflon D8AZ-19554-A or equivalent to the threads of the interlock sleeve retaining pin, in a clockwise direction. Use a drift to align the slot in the interlock sleeve with the hole in the transaxle case and install the retaining pin. Using a 13mm socket tighten to 12-15 ft. lbs.

NOTE: *If the hole in the case does not align with the slot in the interlock sleeve, remove the case half and check for proper installation of the interlock sleeve.*

16. Using a 10mm socket and torque wrench, install the 15 transmission case-to-clutch housing bolts. Tighten to 13-17 ft. lbs.

17. Use a drift to align the bore in the reverse idler shaft with the retaining screw hole in the transmission case.

18. Install the reverse idler shaft retaining bolt. Tighten to 16-20 ft. lbs.

19. Apply Pipe Sealant with Teflon (D8AZ-19554-A or equivalent) to the threads of the backup lamp switch in a clockwise direction and install. Using a 22mm box end wrench tighten to 12-15 ft. lbs.

20. Apply Pipe Sealant with Teflon (D8AZ-19554-A or equivalent) to the threads of the detent plunger retaining screw. Install the retaining screw using a 8mm socket and torque wrench. Tighten to 72-96 in. lbs.

21. Tap the differential seal into the transmission case with Differential Seal Installer T81P-1177-A or equivalent.

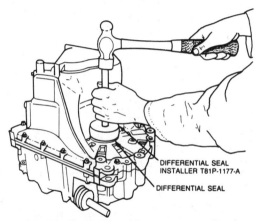

DIFFERENTIAL SEAL INSTALLER T81P-1177-A

DIFFERENTIAL SEAL

Installing the differential seal

22. Place the transaxle upright and position a drift through the hole in the input shift shaft. Shift the transaxle into and out of all gears to verify proper installation.

NOTE: *The transaxle will not shift directly into REVERSE from 5th gear. The fill plug should be attached to the transaxle and installed after the transaxle has been installed in the vehicle and fluid has been added.*

MAINSHAFT DISASSEMBLY

1. Remove the slip fit bearing on the 4th speed gear end of the shaft. Label the bearing for proper installation.

2. Remove the 4th speed gear and synchronizer blocker ring.

NOTE: *Tag the blocker ring for proper installation.*

3. Remove the 3rd/4th synchronizer retaining ring. Slide the 3rd/4th synchronizer assembly, blocker ring and 3rd speed gear from the shaft.

NOTE: *Tag the blocker ring from proper installation.*

4. Remove the 2nd/3rd thrust washer retaining ring and the two piece thrust washer.

5. Remove the 2nd speed gear and its blocker ring.

NOTE: *Tag the blocker ring for proper installation.*

6. Remove the 1st/2nd synchronizer retaining ring. Slide the 1st/2nd synchronizer assembly, blocker ring and 1st speed gear off the shaft.

NOTE: *Tag the blocker ring for proper installation.*

7. Remove the tapered roller bearing from the pinion end of the main shaft using a socket or extension and Pinion Bearing Cone Remover part No. D79L-4621-A or equivalent and an arbor press. Label the bearing.

NOTE: *This bearing does not have to be removed to disassemble the main shaft only to replace if damaged.*

SYNCHRONIZER DISASSEMBLY AND ASSEMBLY

NOTE: *Prior to disassembly note position of index marks.*

To disassemble the synchronizer assembly, remove the synchronizer springs with a small screwdriver. do not compress the springs more than is necessary. Remove the three hub inserts. Slide the hub and sleeve apart.

When assembling the synchronizers, some points must be noted:

1. Side the sleeve over the hub. The index marks must be aligned.

2. Place the three inserts into their slots. Place the tab on the synchronizer spring into

**SYNCHRONIZER ASSEMBLY
1ST/2ND AND 3RD/4TH (TYPICAL)**

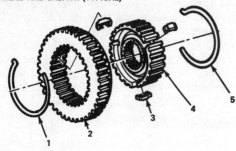

Legend:
1. Spring—synchronizer retainer
2. Gear and synchronizer sleeve
3. Inserts—synchronizer hub
4. Hub—synchronizer
5. Spring—synchronizer retainer

Exploded view of the synchronizer assembly

the groove of one of the inserts and snap the spring into place.

Place the tab of the other spring into the same insert (on the other side of the synchronizer assembly) and rotate the spring in the opposite direction and snap into place.

NOTE: *When assembling synchronizers, notice that the sleeve and the hub have an ex-*

5TH SYNCHRONIZER ASSEMBLY

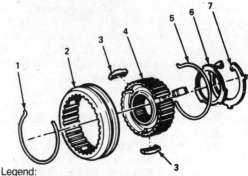

Legend:
1. Spring—synchronizer retainer
2. Gear and synchronizer sleeve
3. Inserts—synchronizer hub
4. Hub—synchronizer
5. Spring—synchronizer retainer
6. Spacer—synchronizer insert retaining
7. Retainer—5th synchronizer insert
NOTE: The 5th synchronizer is positioned on shaft so that plastic spacer and retainer is next to 5th drive gear

Exploded view of the synchronizer assembly

tremely close fit and must be held square to prevent jamming. (Do not force the sleeve onto the hub).

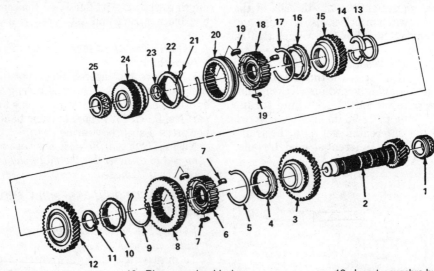

Legend
1. Bearing—mainshaft front
2. Shaft—main
3. Gear—1st speed
4. Ring—synchro blocker
5. Spring—synchronizer
6. Hub—1st/2nd synchro
7. Insert—synchro hub 1st/2nd
8. Gear—reverse sliding
9. Spring—synchronizer
10. Ring—synchro blocker
11. Ring—1st/2nd synchro retaining
12. Gear—2nd speed
13. Ring—2nd/3rd thrust washer retaining
14. Washer—2nd/3rd gear thrust
15. Gear—3rd speed
16. Ring—synchro blocker
17. Spring—synchronizer
18. Hub—3rd/4th synchro
19. Insert—synchro hub 3rd/4th
20. Sleeve—3rd/4th synchro
21. Spring—synchronizer
22. Ring—synchro retaining
23. Ring—retaining
24. Gear—4th speed
25. Bearing—mainshaft rear

Exploded view of the mainshaft assembly

MAIN SHAFT ASSEMBLY ASSEMBLY

NOTE: *Prior to assembly of the main shaft, thoroughly clean all parts and inspect their condition. Lightly oil the gear bores and other parts with Type F or DEXRON®II transmission fluid.*

1. Install the bearing on the pinion end of the shaft using a 27mm socket and an arbor press.

2. Slide the 1st speed gear and tagged blocker ring onto the main shaft. slide the 1st/2nd synchronizer assembly into place, making sure the shift fork groove on the reverse sliding gear faces the 1st speed gear.

NOTE: *When installing the synchronizer, align the three grooves in the 1st gear blocker ring with the synchronizer inserts. This allows the synchronizer assembly to seat properly in the blocker ring.*

3. Install the synchronizer retaining ring.

4. Install the tagged 2nd speed blocker ring and the 2nd speed gear.

NOTE: *When install the synchronizer, align the three grooves in the 2nd gear blocker ring with the synchronizer inserts. This allows the synchronizer assembly to seat properly in the blocker ring.*

5. Install the thrust washer halves into the groove on the main shaft and then the retaining ring around the thrust washer halves.

6. Slide the 3rd speed gear onto the shaft followed by the tagged 3rd gear synchronizer blocker ring and the 3rd/4th gear synchronizer assembly.

NOTE: *When installing the synchronizer, align the three grooves in the 3rd gear blocker ring with the synchronizer inserts. This allows the synchronizer assembly to seat properly in the blocker ring.*

7. Install the synchronizer retaining ring.

8. Install the tagged 4th gear blocker ring and the 4th speed gear.

NOTE: *When install the synchronizer, align the three grooves in the 4th gear blocker ring with the synchronizer inserts. This allows the synchronizer assembly to seat properly in the blocker ring.*

9. Install the slip fit bearing on the 4th gear end of the shaft.

NOTE: *Make sure bearings are seated against the shoulder of the main shaft. Make sure bearings are placed on the proper end, as labeled during disassembly. Rotate each gear on the shaft to check for binding or roughness. Make sure that the synchronizer sleeves are in NEUTRAL position.*

5TH GEAR SHAFT DISASSEMBLY

1. Remove the slip fit bearing from the 5th gear end of the shaft and label it for proper installation.

2. Remove the 5th gear and blocking ring.

3. Remove the 5th gear synchronizer assembly.

4. Remove the press fit bearing from the pinion end of the shaft, using Pinion Bearing Cone Remover D79L-4621-A or equivalent.

5TH GEAR SHAFT ASSEMBLY

NOTE: *Prior to assembly, thoroughly clean all parts and inspect their condition. Lightly oil the gear bore with either Type F or DEXRON®II transmission fluid.*

1. Press the bearing onto the pinion gear end of the 5th gear shaft.

2. Install the 5th synchronizer assembly with the plastic insert retainer facing the pinion gear.

3. Install the 5th gear and blocking ring.

4. Install the slip fit bearing on the 5th gear end of the shaft.

CLUTCH HOUSING DISASSEMBLY

1. Using a 10mm socket wrench, remove the two control selector plate attaching bolts and remove the plate from the case.

2. With the input shift shaft in the center detent position, using a drift, drive the spring pin through the selector plate arm assembly and through the input shift shaft into the recess in the clutch housing case.

3. Remove the shift shaft boot. Using a drift, rotate the input shift shaft 90°, depressing the detent notches inside the housing and pull input shift shaft out. Remove the input shift shaft selector plate arm assembly and the spring pin.

4. Using a pencil magnet, remove the input shift shaft detent plunger and spring and label for proper installation.

5. Using Sector Shaft Seal Tool part No. T77F-7288-A and Impact Slide Hammer T50T-100-A or equivalent, remove the transmission input shift shaft oil seal assembly.

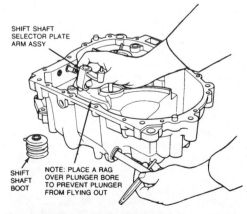

SHIFT SHAFT SELECTOR PLATE ARM ASSY

SHIFT SHAFT BOOT

NOTE: PLACE A RAG OVER PLUNGER BORE TO PREVENT PLUNGER FROM FLYING OUT

Removing the shift shaft selector plate arm

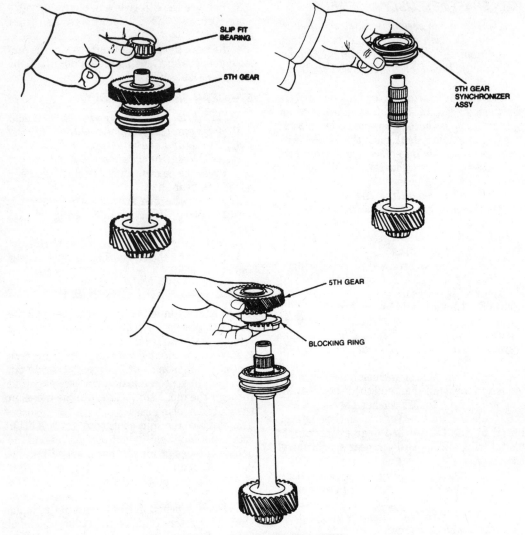

5th gear shaft disassembly—MTX

CLUTCH HOUSING ASSEMBLY

NOTE: *Prior to assembly, thoroughly clean all parts and inspect their condition. Lightly oil all parts and inspect their condition. Lightly oil all parts and bore with Type F or DEXRON®II transmission fluid.*

1. Grease the seal lip of the new shift shaft oil seal. Using Sector Shaft Seal Tool part No. T77F-7288-A and Impact Slide Hammer T50T0100-A or equivalent, install a new shift shaft oil seal assembly.

2. Install the input shift shaft detent spring and plunger in the clutch housing case.

3. Using a small drift, force the spring and plunger down into its bore while sliding the input shift shaft into its bore and over the plunger.

WARNING: *Be careful not to cut the shift shaft oil seal when inserting the shaft.*

4. Install the selector plate arm in its working position and slide the shaft through the selector plate arm. Align the hole in the selector

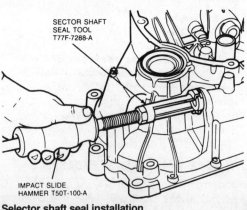

Selector shaft seal installation

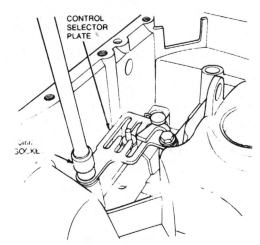

CONTROL
SELECTOR
PLATE

Control selector plate installation

plate arm with the hole in the shaft and install the roll pin. Install the input shift shaft boot.

NOTE: *Be sure notches in the shift shaft face the detent plunger.*

5. Install the control selector plate. Using a 10mm socket wrench, tighten the attaching bolts to 72-96 in. lbs., (pin in selector arm must ride in cut-out of gate in the selector plate). Move input shift shaft through the selector plate positions to make sure EVERYTHING works properly.

MAIN SHIFT CONTROL SHAFT DISASSEMBLY

1. Rotate the 3rd/4th shift fork on the shaft until the notch in the fork is located over the interlock sleeve. Rotate the 1st/2nd shift fork on the shaft until the notch in the fork is located over the shift fork selector arm finger. With the forks in position, slide 3rd/4th and interlock sleeve off the shaft.

2. Using a 5mm punch, remove the selector arm retaining pin.

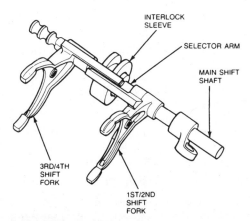

INTERLOCK
SLEEVE

SELECTOR ARM

MAIN SHIFT
SHAFT

3RD/4TH
SHIFT
FORK

1ST/2ND
SHIFT
FORK

Main control shaft assembly

3. Remove the shift fork selector arm and 1st/2nd shift fork from the shaft.

4. Using a 5mm punch, remove the fork control block retaining pin. Remove the fork control block from the shift control shaft.

MAIN SHIFT CONTROL SHAFT ASSEMBLY

NOTE: *Prior to assembly of the main shaft control shaft, thoroughly clean all parts and inspect their condition. Lightly oil all parts with Type F or DEXRON®II transmission fluid.*

1. Slide the fork control block onto the shift control shaft. Align the hole in the block with the hole in the shaft and install the fork CONTROL block pin using a 5mm punch.

NOTE: *With the pin installed in control block, off-set must point towards end of shaft.*

2. Install the 1st/2nd shift fork and the selector arm on the shaft.

NOTE: *The 1st/2nd shift fork is thinner than the 3rd/4th shift fork.*

3. Align the hold in the shift fork selector arm with the hold in the shaft and install the retaining pin.

4. Position the slot in the 1st/2nd fork over the fork selector arm finger. Slide the 3rd/4th fork and interlock sleeve onto the main shift control shaft. Align the slot in the interlock sleeve with the spline on the shift fork selector arm and slide the sleeve and 3rd/4th fork into position.

NOTE: *When assembled, the forks should be aligned.*

5TH GEAR SHIFT CONTROL DISASSEMBLY

1. Using a 5mm punch, remove the roll pin.
2. Slide the fork from the shaft.

5TH GEAR SHIFT CONTROL ASSEMBLY

1. Holding the shaft with the hole on the left, install the 5th gear shift fork so that the protruding arm is pointing toward the long end of the shaft.

2. Install the roll pin.

REVERSE SHIFT RELAY LEVER AND BRACKET DISASSEMBLY

1. Using a small screwdriver, remove the C-clip retaining ring from the reverse shift relay support bracket.

2. Slide the reverse shift relay lever off the support shaft and remove the steel ball and springs between them.

REVERSE SHIFT RELAY LEVER AND BRACKET ASSEMBLY

1. Place the ball in the pocket provided in the support bracket.

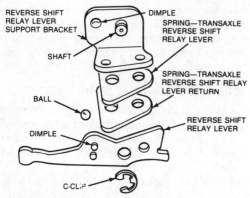

Reverse shift relay lever assembly

2. Slide the reverse relay lever onto the support bracket pin.

NOTE: *Make sure the lever is installed so that the bend in the lever is towards the bracket. Align the ball with dimples on reverse shift relay lever.*

3. Install C-clip onto reverse shift lever support bracket shaft to retain reverse shift relay lever.

SELECTOR CONTROL PLATE DISASSEMBLY

1. Using a small screwdriver, remove the C-clip retaining reverse lock out pawl pivot pin to shift gate plate.

2. Remove the reverse lock out pawl, pin and spring from shift gate plate.

SELECTOR CONTROL PLATE ASSEMBLY

1. Install the reverse lock out pawl, pin and spring.

NOTE: *Make sure the lower leg of the spring rests against the shift gate plate and the upper leg of the spring rests against the reverse lock out pawl. Also make sure spring is against shoulder of reverse lock out pivot pin and does not interfere with pin seating against reverse lock out pawl.*

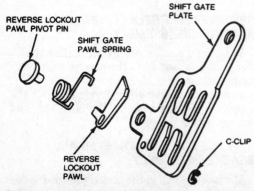

Selector control plate assembly

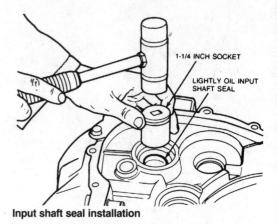

Input shaft seal installation

2. Install C-clip to reverse lock out pawl pivot pin.

INPUT CLUSTER SHAFT SEAL ASSEMBLY REMOVAL

1. Using Input Shaft Seal Remover T77F-7050-A or equivalent and a hammer, remove the input shaft seal, working from outside the case.

2. Position the remover against the seal by placing it in the slot cut in the case.

INPUT CLUSTER SHAFT SEAL ASSEMBLY INSTALLATION

To install, lightly oil the input shaft seal and using a 32mm socket and hammer, tap into place.

INPUT CUSTER SHAFT BEARINGS REMOVAL

NOTE: *Inspect the bearings and replace them only if worn or damaged.*

Remove the bearing cone and roller assemblies using Pinion Bearing Cone Remover/Installer part No. D79L-4621-A or equivalent and an arbor press. Label bearings for proper installation.

INPUT CUSTER SHAFT BEARINGS INSTALLATION

NOTE: *Prior to installation of the bearings, thoroughly clean the bearing and inspect their condition. Lightly oil the bearings with Type F or DEXRON®II transmission fluid.*

Using Pinion Bearing Cone Remover/Installer part No. D79L-4621-A or equivalent and an arbor press, install the bearing on the shaft. Make sure the bearings are pressed on the proper end as labeled during disassembly.

SPEEDOMETER DRIVE GEAR REMOVAL

1. Using a 7mm socket, remove the retaining screw from the speedometer driven gear retainer assembly.

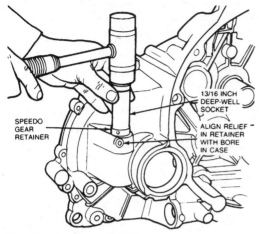

SPEEDO
GEAR
RETAINER

13/16 INCH
DEEP-WELL
SOCKET

ALIGN RELIEF
IN RETAINER
WITH BORE
IN CASE

Speedometer gear installation

2. Using a screwdriver, pry on the speedometer retainer to remove both the speedometer gear and retainer assembly from the clutch housing case bore.

SPEEDOMETER DRIVE GEAR INSTALLATION

NOTE: *Prior to install, clean all speedometer gear parts and the retainer's bore in the case. Inspect all parts.*

1. Lightly grease the (25mm x 2.6mm) O-ring seal on the speedometer driven gear retainer.

2. Align the relief in the retainer with the attaching screw bore and using a 21mm deep-well socket, tap the assembly into its bore.

3. Using a 7mm socket and torque wrench, tighten the retaining screw to 12-24 in. lbs.

SPEEDOMETER DRIVE GEAR DISASSEMBLY AND ASSEMBLY

1. Carefully remove the O-ring seal from the stem end of the speedometer driven gear.

2. Slide the speedometer driven gear from the retainer.

3. Carefully remove the O-ring seal from its groove in the retainer.

NOTE: *Prior to assembly of the speedometer driven gear, clean all parts thoroughly. Inspect all parts and replace if damaged. Lightly grease the O-ring on the retainer.*

4. To assembly the speedometer driven gear, reverse Steps 1, 2, and 3.

CLUTCH

The transmission and clutch are employed to vary the relationship between engine speed and the speed of the wheels so that adequate engine power can be produced under all circumstances.

The clutch allows engine torque to be applied to the transmission input shaft gradually, due to mechanical slippage. The car can, consequently, be started smoothly from a full stop.

The transmission changes the ratio between the rotating speeds of the engine and the wheels by the use of gears. The lower gears allow full engine power to be applied to the rear wheels during acceleration at low speeds.

The clutch driven plate is a thin disc, the center of which is splined to the transmission input shaft. Both sides of the disc are covered with a layer of material which is similar to brake lining and which is capable of allowing slippage without roughness or excessive noise.

The clutch cover is bolted to the engine flywheel and incorporates a diaphragm spring which provides the pressure to engage the clutch. The cover also houses the pressure plate. The driven disc is sandwiched between the pressure plate and the smooth surface of the flywheel when the clutch pedal is released, thus forcing it to turn at the same speed as the engine crankshaft.

The transmission contains a mainshaft which passes all the way through the transmission, from the clutch to the final drive gear in the transaxle. This shaft is separated at one point, so that front and rear portions can turn at different speeds.

Power is transmitted by a countershaft in the lower gears and reverse. The gears of the countershaft mesh with gears on the mainshaft, allowing power to be carried from one to the other. All the countershaft gears are integral with that shaft, while several of the mainshaft gears can either rotate independently of the shaft or be locked to it. Shifting from one gear to the next causes one of the gear to be freed from rotating with the shaft, and locks another to it. Gears are locked and unlocked by internal dog clutches which slide between the center of the gear and the shaft. The forward gears usually employ synchronizers: friction members which smoothly bring gear and shaft to the same speed before the toothed dog clutches are engaged.

The clutch is operating properly if:

1. It will stall the engine when released with the vehicle held stationary.

2. The shift lever can be moved freely between first and reverse gears when the vehicle is stationary and the clutch disengaged.

Adjustments

FREE PLAY ADJUSTMENT

The free play in the clutch is adjusted by a built in mechanism that allows the clutch con-

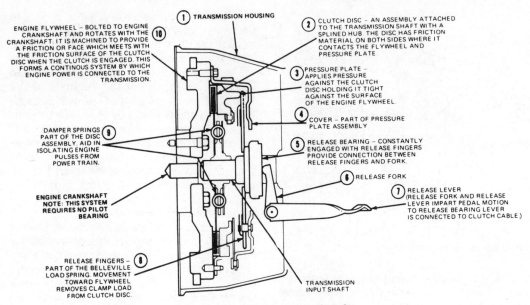

ENGINE FLYWHEEL – BOLTED TO ENGINE CRANKSHAFT AND ROTATES WITH THE CRANKSHAFT. IT IS MACHINED TO PROVIDE A FRICTION OR FACE WHICH MEETS WITH THE FRICTION SURFACE OF THE CLUTCH DISC WHEN THE CLUTCH IS ENGAGED. THIS FORMS A CONTINOUS SYSTEM BY WHICH ENGINE POWER IS CONNECTED TO THE TRANSMISSION.

① TRANSMISSION HOUSING

② CLUTCH DISC – AN ASSEMBLY ATTACHED TO THE TRANSMISSION SHAFT WITH A SPLINED HUB. THE DISC HAS FRICTION MATERIAL ON BOTH SIDES WHERE IT CONTACTS THE FLYWHEEL AND PRESSURE PLATE

③ PRESSURE PLATE – APPLIES PRESSURE AGAINST THE CLUTCH DISC HOLDING IT TIGHT AGAINST THE SURFACE OF THE ENGINE FLYWHEEL.

④ COVER – PART OF PRESSURE PLATE ASSEMBLY

⑤ RELEASE BEARING – CONSTANTLY ENGAGED WITH RELEASE FINGERS PROVIDE CONNECTION BETWEEN RELEASE FINGERS AND FORK.

⑥ RELEASE FORK

⑦ RELEASE LEVER (RELEASE FORK AND RELEASE LEVER IMPART PEDAL MOTION TO RELEASE BEARING LEVER IS CONNECTED TO CLUTCH CABLE)

⑨ DAMPER SPRINGS PART OF THE DISC ASSEMBLY. AID IN ISOLATING ENGINE PULSES FROM POWER TRAIN.

ENGINE CRANKSHAFT NOTE: THIS SYSTEM REQUIRES NO PILOT BEARING

⑧ RELEASE FINGERS – PART OF THE BELLEVILLE LOAD SPRING. MOVEMENT TOWARD FLYWHEEL REMOVES CLAMP LOAD FROM CLUTCH DISC.

TRANSMISSION INPUT SHAFT

Operation of the clutch components

trols to be self-adjusted during normal operation.

The self-adjusting feature should be checked every 5000 miles. This is accomplished by insuring that the clutch pedal travels to the top of its upward position. Grasp the clutch pedal with your hand or put your foot under the clutch pedal. pull up on the pedal until it stops. Very little effort is required (about 10 lbs.). During the application of upward pressure, a click may be heard which means an adjustment was necessary and has been accomplished.

Clutch Cable
REMOVAL AND INSTALLATION

WARNING: *The clutch pedal must be lifted to disengage the adjusting mechanism during cable installation. Failure to do so will re-*

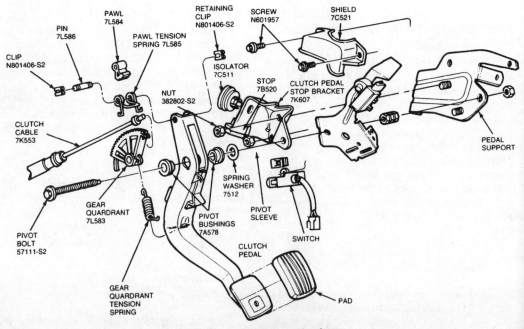

PAWL 7L584

PIN 7L586

PAWL TENSION SPRING 7L585

CLIP N801406-S2

RETAINING CLIP N801406-S2

SCREW N601957

SHIELD 7C521

ISOLATOR 7C511

NUT 382802-S2

STOP 7B520

CLUTCH PEDAL STOP BRACKET 7K607

CLUTCH CABLE 7K553

GEAR QUARDRANT 7L583

SPRING WASHER 7512

PIVOT SLEEVE

PEDAL SUPPORT

PIVOT BOLT 57111-S2

PIVOT BUSHINGS 7A578

SWITCH

CLUTCH PEDAL

GEAR QUARDRANT TENSION SPRING

PAD

Self-adjusting clutch mechanism

sult in damage to the self-adjuster mechanism.

1. From under the hood, use a pair of pliers and grasp the extended tip of the clutch cable (on top of transaxle). Unhook the clutch cable from the clutch throwout bearing release lever.

2. From inside the car, remove the fresh air duct next to the clutch pedal (non-air conditioned cars). Remove the shield from the brake pedal support bracket.

3. Lift up on the clutch pedal to release the adjusting pawl. Rotate the adjustment gear quadrant forward. Unhook the clutch cable from the gear quadrant. Swing the quadrant to the rear.

4. Pull the clutch cable out from between the clutch pedal and the gear quadrant and from the isolator on the gear quadrant.

5. From under the hood, pull the clutch cable through the firewall and remove it from the car.

6. From under the hood, insert the clutch cable through the firewall into the drivers compartment.

7. Push the clutch cable through the isolator on the pedal stop bracket and through the recess between the clutch pedal and the adjusting gear quadrant.

8. Lift the clutch pedal to release the pawl and rotate the gear quadrant forward. Hook the clutch cable to the gear quadrant.

9. Install the fresh air duct. Install the shield on the brake pedal support.

10. Secure the clutch pedal in the up position. Use a piece of wire, tape, etc.

11. From under the hood, hook the cable to the clutch throwout bearing release lever.

12. Unfasten the clutch pedal and adjust the clutch by operating the clutch pedal several times. Pull up on the pedal to make sure it is reaching the maximum upward position.

Pressure Plate and Clutch Disc
REMOVAL AND INSTALLATION

CAUTION: *Whenever servicing a clutch component, always wear a chemical respirator or particle mask. The clutch driven disc contains asbestos, which has been determined to be a cancer causing agent. Never clean clutch surfaces with compressed air! Avoid inhaling any dust from any clutch surface! When cleaning clutch surfaces, use a commercially available brake cleaning fluid.*

1. Remove the transaxle, refer to the previous "Transaxle Removal and Installation" procedure.

2. Mark the pressure plate assembly and the flywheel so that they may be assembled in the same position if the original pressure plate is to be reused.

3. Loosen the attaching bolts one turn at a time, in sequence, until spring pressure is relieved.

4. Support the pressure plate and clutch disc and remove the bolts. Remove the pressure plate and disc.

5. Inspect the flywheel, clutch disc, pressure plate, throwout bearing and the clutch fork for

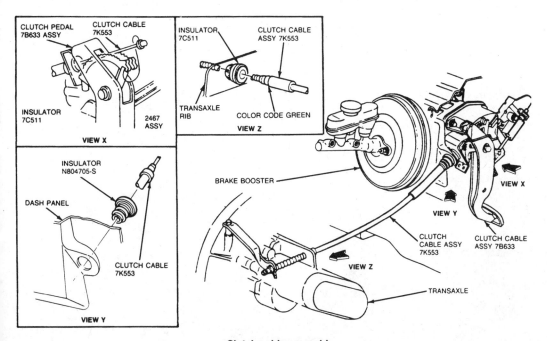

Clutch cable assembly

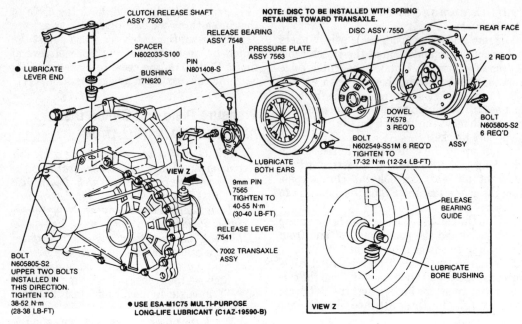

CLUTCH RELEASE SHAFT ASSY 7503

NOTE: DISC TO BE INSTALLED WITH SPRING RETAINER TOWARD TRANSAXLE.

REAR FACE

RELEASE BEARING ASSY 7548

DISC ASSY 7550

SPACER N802033-S100

PRESSURE PLATE ASSY 7563

PIN N801408-S

2 REQ'D

● **LUBRICATE LEVER END**

BUSHING 7N620

DOWEL 7K578 3 REQ'D

BOLT N605805-S2 6 REQ'D

BOLT N602549-S51M 6 REQ'D TIGHTEN TO 17-32 N·m (12-24 LB-FT)

ASSY

VIEW Z

LUBRICATE BOTH EARS

9mm PIN 7565 TIGHTEN TO 40-55 N·m (30-40 LB-FT)

RELEASE LEVER 7541

RELEASE BEARING GUIDE

7002 TRANSAXLE ASSY

BOLT N605805-S2 UPPER TWO BOLTS INSTALLED IN THIS DIRECTION. TIGHTEN TO 38-52 N·m (28-38 LB-FT)

LUBRICATE BORE BUSHING

● **USE ESA-M1C75 MULTI-PURPOSE LONG-LIFE LUBRICANT (C1AZ-19590-B)**

VIEW Z

Clutch disc, pressure plate and release bearing

wear. If the flywheel shows any sign of overheating (blue discoloration), or if it is badly scored or grooved, it should be refaced or replaced. Replace any other parts that are worn.

6. Clean the pressure plate (if it is to be reused) and the flywheel surfaces thoroughly. Position the clutch disc and pressure plate into the installed position.

NOTE: *The clutch disc must be assembled so that the flatter side is toward the flywheel.*

Align the match marks on the pressure plate and flywheel (when reusing the original pressure plate). Support the clutch disc and pressure plate with a dummy shaft or clutch aligning tool part No. T81P-7550-A.

7. Install the pressure plate to flywheel bolts. Tighten them gradually in a criss-cross pattern. Remove the aligning tool. Mounting bolt torque is 12-24 ft. lbs.

8. Lubricate the release bearing and install it on the throwout fork.

9. Install the transaxle.

Clutch Pedal Assembly
REMOVAL AND INSTALLATION

1. Prop the clutch pedal up to disengage the automatic clutch adjuster using tape or a piece of wire.

2. Remove the air cleaner assembly to gain access to the clutch cable.

3. Grasp the extended tip of the clutch cable with a pair of pliers and unlock the cable from the release lever. Do not grasp the wire strand portion of the inner cable because the strands may be damaged causing cable failure.

4. Position the clutch shield away from the mounting plate.

5. Pull the cable out through the recess between the pedal and gear quadrant.

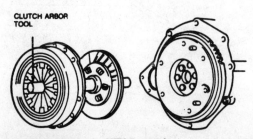

CLUTCH ARBOR TOOL

Clutch aligning tool—MTX 5-speed

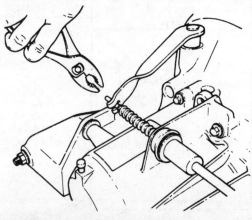

Clutch cable removal—MTX 5-speed

6. Unseat the cable from the insulator at the clutch pedal stop bracket. Disconnect the clutch switches.

7. Remove the mounting plate and the clutch pedal assembly from the brake pedal support by removing the two nuts from the brake booster

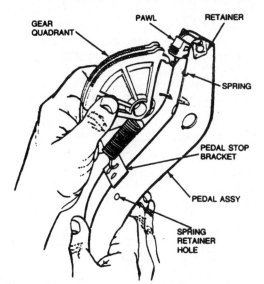

Quadrant gear, pawl, and spring positioning

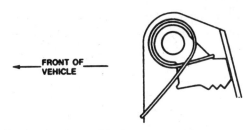

Pawl and spring positioning

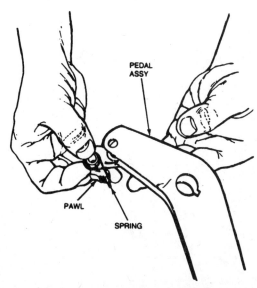

Pawl spring in pedal assembly positioning

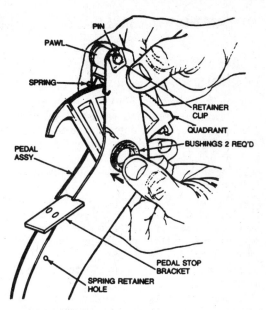

Bushing and quadrant positioning

studs and two screws from the pedal support.

8. Remove the pedal stop bracket-to-mounting and remove the pedal.

To install:

1. Lubricate the quadrant pivot bore, pawl pivot bore, quadrant pivot pin, and quadrant pivot sleeve.

2. Insert the pawl, spring, and the pivot pin into the clutch pedal and secure the retainer clip.

3. Assemble the gear quadrant spring to the gear quadrant.

4. Install the two bushings and pivot sleeve into clutch pedal.

5. Place the bolt through the pivot sleeve and torque to 25-30 ft. lbs.

6. Position the assembly on the mounting plate and install the three nuts, torque to 15-25 ft. lbs.

7. Secure the clutch pedal assembly and mounting plate to the brake booster studs and brake pedal support.

8. Pull the clutch cable through the insulator and gear quadrant. Hook the cable into the gear quadrant.

9. Install the clutch switch electrical connectors, clutch shield, and make sure all the fasteners are torqued properly.

10. Using a piece of wire or tape, secure the clutch pedal in its upright position. Hook the clutch cable into the release lever in the engine compartment.

11. Adjust the clutch by depressing the clutch pedal up against its stop several times. Install the air cleaner and start engine to check clutch operation.

AUTOMATIC TRANSAXLE

Transmission Fluid and Filter

DRAIN AND REFILL

In normal service it should not be necessary or required to drain and refill the AT fluid. However, under severe operation or dusty conditions the fluid should be changed every 20 months or 20,000 miles.

1. Raise the car and safely support it on jackstands.

2. Place a suitable drain pan underneath the transaxle oil pan. Loosen the oil pan mounting bolts and allow the fluid to drain until it reaches the level of the pan flange. Remove the attaching bolts, leaving one end attached so that the pan will tip and the rest of the fluid will drain.

3. Remove the oil pan. Thoroughly clean the pan. Remove the old gasket. Make sure that the gasket mounting surfaces are clean.

4. Remove the transmission filter screen retaining bolt. Remove the screen.

5. Install a new filter screen and O-ring. Place a new gasket on the pan and install the pan to the transmission. Torque the transaxle pan to 15-19 ft. lbs.

6. Fill the transmission to the correct level. Remove the jackstands and lower the car to the ground.

TRANSAXLE FLUID CONDITION

Pull the transmission dipstick out. Observe the color and odor of the transmission fluid. The color should be red not brown or black. An odor can sometimes indicate an overheating condition, clutch disc or band failure.

Wipe the dipstick with a clean white rag. Examine the stain on the rag for specks of solids (metal or dirt) and for signs of contaminates (antifreeze, gum or varnish condition).

If examination shows evidence of metal specks or antifreeze contamination transaxle removal and inspection may be necessary.

THROTTLE VALVE CONTROL LINKAGE ATX TRANSAXLE

The Throttle Valve (TV) Control Linkage System consists of a lever on the throttle body of the injection unit, linkage shaft assembly, mounting bracket assembly, control rod assembly, a control lever on the transaxle and a lever return spring.

The coupling lever follows the movement of throttle lever and has an adjustment screw that is used for setting TV linkage adjustment when a line pressure gauge is used. If a pressure gauge is not available, a manual adjustment can be made.

A number of shift troubles can occur if the throttle valve linkage is not in adjustment. Some are:

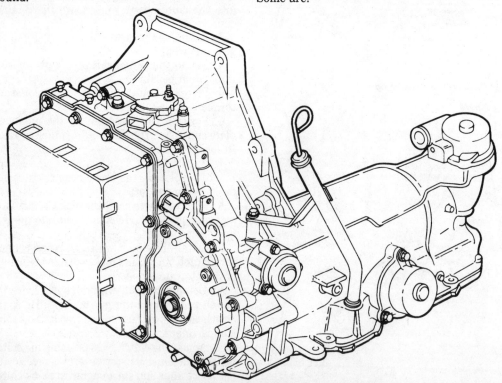

Automatic transaxle assembly—AXOD shown, ATX similar

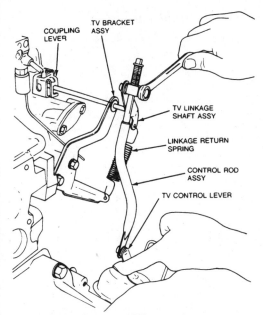

COUPLING LEVER

TV BRACKET ASSY

TV LINKAGE SHAFT ASSY

LINKAGE RETURN SPRING

CONTROL ROD ASSY

TV CONTROL LEVER

Throttle valve linkage—ATX transaxle

1. **Symptom:** Excessively early and/or soft upshift with or without slip-bump feel. No forced downshift (kickdown) function at appropriate speeds.

Cause: TV control linkage is set too short.

Remedy: Adjust linkage.

2. **Symptom:** Extremely delayed or harsh upshifts and harsh idle engagement.

Cause: TV control linkage is set too long.

Remedy: Adjust linkage.

3. **Symptom:** Harsh idle engagement after the engine is warmed up. Shift clunk when throttle is backed off after full or heavy throttle acceleration. Harsh coasting downshifts (automatic 3-2, 2-1 shift in D range). Delayed upshift at light acceleration.

Cause: Interference due to hoses, wires, etc. prevents return of TV control rod or TV linkage shaft. Excessive friction caused by binding grommets prevents the TV control linkage to return to its proper location.

Remedy: Correct the interference area, check for bent or twisted rods, levers. or damaged grommets. Repair or replace whatever is necessary. Check and adjust linkage is necessary.

4. **Symptom:** Erratic/delayed upshifts, possibly no kickdown, harsh engagement.

Cause: Clamping bolt on trunnion at the upper end of the TV control rod is loose.

Remedy: Reset TV control linkage.

5. **Symptom:** No upshift and harsh engagements.

Cause: TV control rod is disconnected or the linkage return spring is broken or disconnected.

Remedy: Reconnect TV control rod, check and replace the connecting grommet if necessary, reconnect or replace the TV return spring.

LINKAGE ADJUSTMENT

The TV control linkage is adjusted at the sliding trunnion block.

1. Operate the engine until normal operating temperature is reached. Adjust the curb idle speed to specification as shown on the under hood decal.

2. After the curb idle speed has been set, shut off the engine. Make sure the choke is completely opened. Check the throttle lever to make sure it is against the hot engine curb idle stop.

3. Set the coupling lever adjustment screw at its approximate midrange. Make sure the TV linkage shaft assembly is fully seated upward into the coupling lever.

CAUTION: *If adjustment of the linkage is necessary, allow the EGR valve to cool so you won't get burned.*

4. **To adjust:** loosen the bolt on the sliding block on the TV control rod a minimum of one turn. Clean any dirt or corrosion from the control rod, free-up the trunnion block so that it will slide freely on the control rod.

5. Rotate the transaxle TV control lever up using a finger and light force, to insure that the TV control lever is against its internal stop. With reducing the pressure on the control lever, tighten the bolt on the trunnion block.

6. Check the throttle lever to be sure it is still against the hot idle stop. If not, repeat the adjustment steps.

TRANSMISSION CONTROL LEVER ADJUSTMENT

1. Position the selector lever in Drive against the rear stop.

2. Raise the car and support it safely on jackstands. Loosen the manual lever to control lever nut.

3. Move the transmission lever to the Drive position, second detent from the rear most position. Tighten the attaching nut. Check the operation of the transmission in each selector position. Readjust if necessary. Lower the car.

SHIFT LEVER CABLE REMOVAL AND INSTALLATION

1. Remove the shift knob, locknut, console, bezel assembly, control cable clip and cable retaining pin.

2. Disengage the rubber grommet from the floor pan by pushing it into the engine compartment.

3. Raise the car and safely support it on jackstands.

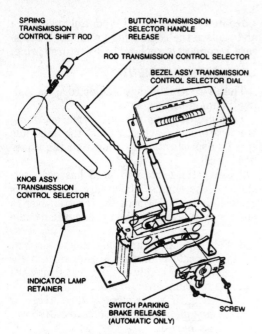

SPRING TRANSMISSION CONTROL SHIFT ROD

BUTTON-TRANSMISSION SELECTOR HANDLE RELEASE

ROD TRANSMISSION CONTROL SELECTOR

BEZEL ASSY TRANSMISSION CONTROL SELECTOR DIAL

KNOB ASSY TRANSMISSSION CONTROL SELECTOR

INDICATOR LAMP RETAINER

SWITCH PARKING BRAKE RELEASE (AUTOMATIC ONLY)

SCREW

Floor mounted shift selector

4. Remove the retaining nut and control cable assembly from the transmission lever.

5. Remove the control cable bracket bolts. Pull the cable through the floor.

6. To install the cable, feed the round end through the floor board. Press the rubber grommet into its mounting hole.

7. Position the control cable assembly in the selector lever housing and install the spring clip.

8. Install the bushing and control cable assembly on the selector lever and housing assembly shaft and secure it with the retaining pin.

9. Install the bezel assembly, console, locknut and shift knob.

10. Position the selector lever in the Drive position. The selector lever must be held in this position while attaching the other end of the control cable.

11. Position the control cable bracket on the retainer bracket and secure the tow mounting bolts.

12. Shift the control lever into the second detent from full rearward (Drive position).

13. Place the cable end on the transmission lever stud. Align the flats on the stud with the slot in the cable. Make sure the transmission selector lever has not moved from the second detent position and tighten the retaining nut.

14. Lower the car to the ground. Check the operation of the transmission selector in all positions. Make sure the neutral safety switch is operating properly. The engine should start only in Park or Neutral position.

Automatic Transaxle
REMOVAL AND INSTALLATION

1. Disconnect the battery negative (-) cable. Remove the air cleaner, the hoses and the tubes.

2. Using a screwdriver, place it in the shift cable/bracket assembly slot, to keep the assembly from moving, then remove the assembly-to-transaxle bolt and the assembly from the transaxle.

3. Disconnect the electrical connector from the neutral safety switch and the electrical bulkhead connector from the rear of the transaxle.

4. Disconnect the throttle valve cable from the throttle body lever and the throttle valve-to-transaxle bolt. Pull the throttle valve cable Up and disconnect it from the TV link.

NOTE: *Pulling too hard on the throttle valve cable may bend the internal TV bracket.*

5. On the left side, remove the engine support-to-strut nut/bolt. Remove the top torque converter housing-to-engine bolts.

6. Attach the engine support (3-bar system) hooks to the engine lifting points, tighten the hooks to slowly lift the engine.

7. Raise and support the front of the vehicle on jackstands. Remove the front tires.

8. Remove the tie rod-to-steering knuckle cotter pin and castle nut, then separate the tie rod end from the steering knuckle.

9. Remove the lower control arm ball joint-to-steering knuckle cotter pin and castle nut,

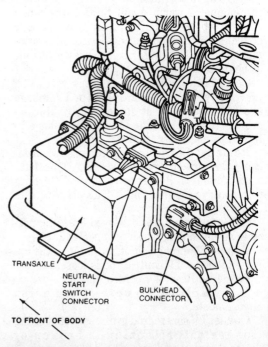

TRANSAXLE

NEUTRAL START SWITCH CONNECTOR

BULKHEAD CONNECTOR

TO FRONT OF BODY

Electrical connector disconnect points

then separate the ball joint from the steering knuckle.

10. Remove the stabilizer bar-to-control arm nuts.

11. Remove the rack/pinion-to-subframe nuts/bolts and the engine mount-to-subframe nuts. Using a piece of wire, support the steering gear from the tie rod end to the coil spring to hold the steering gear in position.

12. Disconnect the electrical connector from the oxygen sensor.

13. Remove the exhaust pipe-to-exhaust manifold nuts and the rear portion of the convertor pipe-to-exhaust pipe.

14. Using an assistant, lower the adjustable jacks and allow the subframe to lower. Rotate the front of the subframe down and pick up the rear of the subframe off the exhaust pipe. Work the subframe rearward until it can be lowered past the exhaust pipe.

15. Remove the subframe-to-chassis bolts. Remove the left side engine support mount-to-subframe nuts/bolts and lower the subframe.

16. Position a transmission jack under the transaxle oil pan. Remove the vehicle speed sensor from the transaxle.

NOTE: *Vehicles equipped with electronic instrument clusters do not use a speedometer cable.*

17. On the left side, remove the engine support-to-transaxle bolts. Remove the engine support-to-chassis bolts and the support.

18. Remove the separator plate-to-transaxle bolt and the starter-to-transaxle bolts, then position the starter out of the way. Remove the separator plate.

19. Using a ½" drive ratchet and a 22mm deep socket on the crankshaft pulley bolt, rotate the crankshaft to align the torque converter bolts with the starter drive hole. As the torque converter-to-flywheel nuts are exposed, remove them.

20. Disconnect and plug the oil cooler lines from the transaxle.

21. To remove the halfshafts on the AXOD (Automatic Overdrive Transaxle), perform the following procedures:

a. Screw the extension tool No. T86P-3514-A2, or equivalent, into the CV-Joint puller tool No. T86P-3514-A1 and install the slide hammer tool No. D79P-100-A onto the extension.

b. Position the puller behind the inboard CV-joint and pull the CV-joint from the transaxle; DO NOT pry against the case.

22. To remove the halfshafts on the ATX (Automatic Transaxle), perform the following procedures:

a. On the right side, remove the link shaft bearing support-to-bracket bolts.

b. While supporting the bearing support, slide the link shaft from the transaxle.

c. Using a wire, support the link shaft.

d. Using the driver tool part. No. T81P-4026-A, or equivalent, insert it into the transaxle to drive the left hand inboard CV-joint assembly from the transaxle.

e. Using a length of wire, support the halfshaft.

NOTE: *DO NOT allow the shaft to hang unsupported, for damage may result to the outboard CV-joint.*

23. Remove the lower torque converter housing-to-engine bolts. Separate the transmission from the engine and carefully lower it out of the vehicle.

To install:

1. Before installing the transaxle, the oil

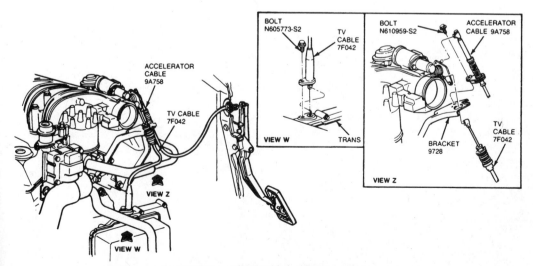

Accelerator and TV cables—AXOD transaxle

cooler, lines, and torque converter must be flushed using the torque converter cleaner part No. 014-00028.

2. Install the transaxle in the vehicle and align the torque converter with the four flywheel studs. Install the four nuts and torque to 23-39 ft. lbs.

3. Install the transaxle-to-engine bolts and torque to 41-50 ft. lbs.

4. Install the torque converter cover to the lower housing.

5. Install the starter and attaching bolts and torque to 30-40 ft. lbs.

6. Install the starter support bracket, starter cable, the transaxle cooler lines, and shift cable bracket and bolts.

7. Connect the speedometer and neutral start switch.

8. Install the sub-frame and retaining bolts. Torque the bolts to 40-50 ft. lbs.

9. Install the insulator-to-engine bolts and nuts and tighten.

10. Install the left front spash shield.

11. Install new circlips on the left and right CV-joint steel shafts, Carefully install the halfshafts in the transaxle aligning the splines of the CV-joint with the splines in the differential.

12. Install the right halfshaft axle support and tighten the bolts.

13. Position the rack-and-pinion onto the mounting surface, install the mounting bolts, and tighten.

14. Install the stabilizer bar retaining nuts and tighten.

15. Install the lower control arm in the spindle and torque the new bolts to 33-44 ft. lbs.

16. Attach the tie rod ends to the spindle and torque the nuts to 23-35 ft. lbs.

NOTE: *Torque the tie rod end nuts to the minimum specified torque, continue torqueing to the nearest cotter pin slot and stop. Always install a new cotter pin and bend over.*

17. Reconnect the engine exhaust air hose and catalytic converter inlet pipe.

18. Install the two wheels and tighten the lug nuts.

19. Remove the engine support bar from the support areas.

20. Install the power steering support brackets and the TV linkage.

21. Fill the transaxle with Type H automatic transmission fluid as outlined in the "Transmission Fluid and Filter" drain and filter procedures.

22. Adjust the TV linkage as outlined in the "Linkage Adjustment" section.

Differential Halfshaft Seals
REMOVAL AND INSTALLATION
MTX 5-speed

1. Raise the vehicle and support with jackstands.

2. Remove the halfshaft that has the leaking

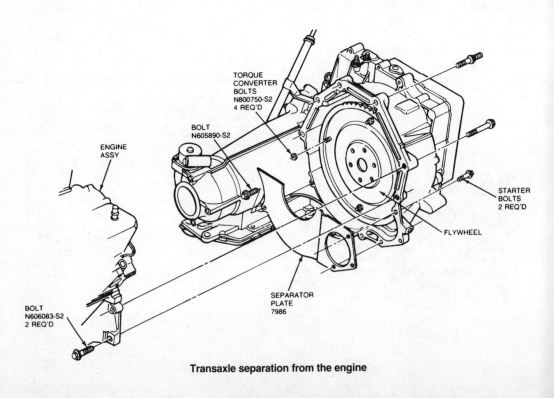

Transaxle separation from the engine

seal. Refer to the "Halfshaft" removal and installation section in this chapter.

3. Using a suitable pry bar, pry the old seal out of the housing.

4. Install the new seal using a differential seal replacer tool part No. T81P-1177-A.

5. Lubricate the seal with Type F or Dextron II®. Install the halfshaft and start engine to check for leaks.

ATX and AXOD

1. Raise the vehicle and support with jackstands.

2. Remove the halfshaft that has the leaking seal. Refer to the "Halfshaft" removal and installation section in this chapter.

3. Remove the six bearing retainer bolts and remove the bearing retainer.

4. Remove the old seal from the bearing retainer using a suitable drift.

5. Install the differential seal in the bearing retainer and case using a Seal Replacer tool part No. T81P-1177-A or equivalent.

6. Install a new retainer gasket and install the bearing retainer in the transaxle.

7. Install the bearing retainer bolts and torque to 15-19 ft. lbs.

8. Lubricate the seal with automatic transmission fluid (Type H) and install the halfshaft.

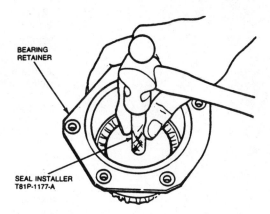

Halfshaft seal installation—ATX and AXOD

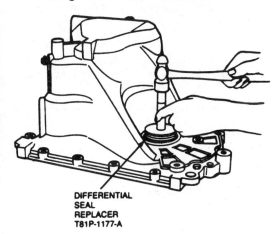

Differential halfshaft seal replacement—MTX 5-speed

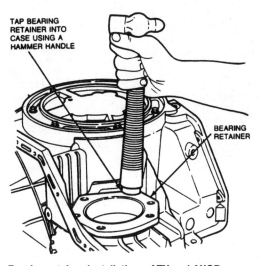

Bearing retainer installation—ATX and AXOD

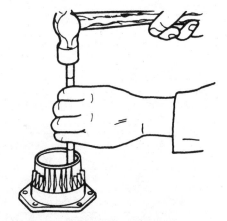

Halfshaft seal removal—ATX and AXOD

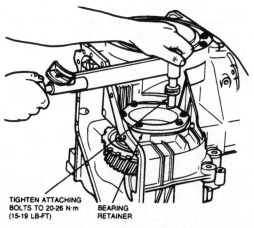

Halfshaft bearing retainer torque—ATX and AXOD

Troubleshooting Basic Clutch Problems

Problem	Cause
Excessive clutch noise	Throwout bearing noises are more audible at the lower end of pedal travel. The usual causes are: • Riding the clutch • Too little pedal free-play • Lack of bearing lubrication A bad clutch shaft pilot bearing will make a high pitched squeal, when the clutch is disengaged and the transmission is in gear or within the first 2″ of pedal travel. The bearing must be replaced. Noise from the clutch linkage is a clicking or snapping that can be heard or felt as the pedal is moved completely up or down. This usually requires lubrication. Transmitted engine noises are amplified by the clutch housing and heard in the passenger compartment. They are usually the result of insufficient pedal free-play and can be changed by manipulating the clutch pedal.
Clutch slips (the car does not move as it should when the clutch is engaged)	This is usually most noticeable when pulling away from a standing start. A severe test is to start the engine, apply the brakes, shift into high gear and SLOWLY release the clutch pedal. A healthy clutch will stall the engine. If it slips it may be due to: • A worn pressure plate or clutch plate • Oil soaked clutch plate • Insufficient pedal free-play
Clutch drags or fails to release	The clutch disc and some transmission gears spin briefly after clutch disengagement. Under normal conditions in average temperatures, 3 seconds is maximum spin-time. Failure to release properly can be caused by: • Too light transmission lubricant or low lubricant level • Improperly adjusted clutch linkage
Low clutch life	Low clutch life is usually a result of poor driving habits or heavy duty use. Riding the clutch, pulling heavy loads, holding the car on a grade with the clutch instead of the brakes and rapid clutch engagement all contribute to low clutch life.

Transmission Fluid Indications

The appearance and odor of the transmission fluid can give valuable clues to the overall condition of the transmission. Always note the appearance of the fluid when you check the fluid level or change the fluid. Rub a small amount of fluid between your fingers to feel for grit and smell the fluid on the dipstick.

If the fluid appears:	It indicates:
Clear and red colored	• Normal operation
Discolored (extremely dark red or brownish) or smells burned	• Band or clutch pack failure, usually caused by an overheated transmission. Hauling very heavy loads with insufficient power or failure to change the fluid, often result in overheating. Do not confuse this appearance with newer fluids that have a darker red color and a strong odor (though not a burned odor).
Foamy or aerated (light in color and full of bubbles)	• The level is too high (gear train is churning oil) • An internal air leak (air is mixing with the fluid). Have the transmission checked professionally.
Solid residue in the fluid	• Defective bands, clutch pack or bearings. Bits of band material or metal abrasives are clinging to the dipstick. Have the transmission checked professionally.
Varnish coating on the dipstick	• The transmission fluid is overheating

Lockup Torque Converter Service Diagnosis

Problem	Cause	Solution

No lockup	• Faulty oil pump
	• Sticking governor valve
	• Valve body malfunction
	    (a) Stuck switch valve
	    (b) Stuck lockup valve
	    (c) Stuck fail-safe valve
	• Failed locking clutch
	• Leaking turbine hub seal
	• Faulty input shaft or seal ring
		• Replace oil pump
		• Repair or replace as necessary
		• Repair or replace valve body or its
		   internal components as neces-
		   sary
		
		• Replace torque converter
		• Replace torque converter
		• Repair or replace as necessary

Will not unlock	• Sticking governor valve
	• Valve body malfunction
	    (a) Stuck switch valve
	    (b) Stuck lockup valve
	    (c) Stuck fail-safe valve
		• Repair or replace as necessary
		• Repair or replace valve body or its
		   internal components as neces-
		   sary

Stays locked up at too low a speed
   in direct
	• Sticking governor valve
	• Valve body malfunction
	    (a) Stuck switch valve
	    (b) Stuck lockup valve
	    (c) Stuck fail-safe valve
		• Repair or replace as necessary
		• Repair or replace valve body or its
		   internal components as neces-
		   sary

Locks up or drags in low or second	• Faulty oil pump
	• Valve body malfunction
	    (a) Stuck switch valve
	    (b) Stuck fail-safe valve
		• Replace oil pump
		• Repair or replace valve body or its
		   internal components as neces-
		   sary

Sluggish or stalls in reverse	• Faulty oil pump
	• Plugged cooler, cooler lines or
	   fittings
	• Valve body malfunction
	    (a) Stuck switch valve
	    (b) Faulty input shaft or seal
	       ring
		• Replace oil pump as necessary
		• Flush or replace cooler and flush
		   lines and fittings
		• Repair or replace valve body or its
		   internal components as neces-
		   sary

Loud chatter during lockup engage- ment (cold)	• Faulty torque converter • Failed locking clutch • Leaking turbine hub seal	• Replace torque converter • Replace torque converter • Replace torque converter

Vibration or shudder during lockup
   engagement
	• Faulty oil pump
	
	• Valve body malfunction
	
	• Faulty torque converter
	• Engine needs tune-up
		• Repair or replace oil pump as nec-
		   essary
		• Repair or replace valve body or its
		   internal components as neces-
		   sary
		• Replace torque converter
		• Tune engine

Vibration after lockup engagement	• Faulty torque converter • Exhaust system strikes underbody • Engine needs tune-up • Throttle linkage misadjusted	• Replace torque converter • Align exhaust system • Tune engine • Adjust throttle linkage

Vibration when revved in neutral
Overheating: oil blows out of dip
   stick tube or pump seal
	• Torque converter out of balance
	• Plugged cooler, cooler lines or fit-
	   tings
	• Stuck switch valve
		• Replace torque converter
		• Flush or replace cooler and flush
		   lines and fittings
		• Repair switch valve in valve body
		   or replace valve body

Shudder after lockup engagement	• Faulty oil pump
	• Plugged cooler, cooler lines or
	   fittings
	• Valve body malfunction
	
	• Faulty torque converter
	• Fail locking clutch
	• Exhaust system strikes underbody
	• Engine needs tune-up
	• Throttle linkage misadjusted
		• Replace oil pump
		• Flush or replace cooler and flush
		   lines and fittings
		• Repair or replace valve body or its
		   internal components as neces-
		   sary
		• Replace torque converter
		• Replace torque converter
		• Align exhaust system
		• Tune engine
		• Adjust throttle linkage

Troubleshooting Basic Automatic Transmission Problems

Problem	Cause	Solution
Fluid leakage	• Defective pan gasket	• Replace gasket or tighten pan bolts
	• Loose filler tube	• Tighten tube nut
	• Loose extension housing to transmission case	• Tighten bolts
	• Converter housing area leakage	• Have transmission checked professionally
Fluid flows out the oil filler tube	• High fluid level	• Check and correct fluid level
	• Breather vent clogged	• Open breather vent
	• Clogged oil filter or screen	• Replace filter or clean screen (change fluid also)
	• Internal fluid leakage	• Have transmission checked professionally
Transmission overheats (this is usually accompanied by a strong burned odor to the fluid)	• Low fluid level	• Check and correct fluid level
	• Fluid cooler lines clogged	• Drain and refill transmission. If this doesn't cure the problem, have cooler lines cleared or replaced.
	• Heavy pulling or hauling with insufficient cooling	• Install a transmission oil cooler
	• Faulty oil pump, internal slippage	• Have transmission checked professionally
Buzzing or whining noise	• Low fluid level	• Check and correct fluid level
	• Defective torque converter, scored gears	• Have transmission checked professionally
No forward or reverse gears or slippage in one or more gears	• Low fluid level	• Check and correct fluid level
	• Defective vacuum or linkage controls, internal clutch or band failure	• Have unit checked professionally
Delayed or erratic shift	• Low fluid level	• Check and correct fluid level
	• Broken vacuum lines	• Repair or replace lines
	• Internal malfunction	• Have transmission checked professionally

Suspension and Steering

8 ⊘

FRONT SUSPENSION

CAUTION: *When servicing the front suspension, brake shoes contain asbestos which has been determined to be a cancer causing agent. Never clean the brake surfaces with compressed air! Avoid inhaling any dust from any brake surface! When cleaning brake surfaces, use a commercially available brake cleaning fluid.*

Your car has fully independent four-wheel suspension. Because wheel movements are controlled independently, the suspension provides exceptional road-hugging and ride comfort advantages.

Your car is equipped with a MacPherson strut front suspension. The strut acts upon a cast steering knuckle, which pivots on a ball joint mounted on a forged lower control arm. A stabilizer bar, which also acts as a locating link, is standard equipment. To maintain good directional stability, negative scrub radius is designed into the suspension geometry. This means that an imaginary line extended from the strut intersects the ground outside the tire patch. Caster and camber are present and nonadjustable. The front suspension fittings are "lubed-for-life"; no grease fittings are provided.

The front suspension fasteners for the lower

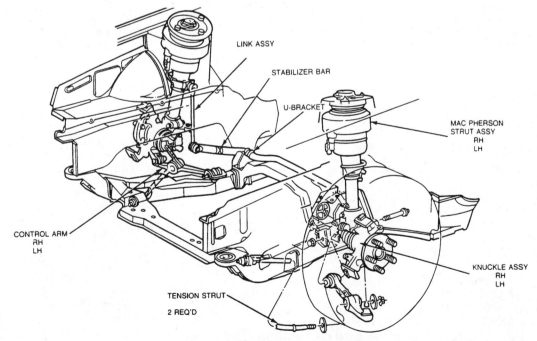

Front suspension assembly—Continental

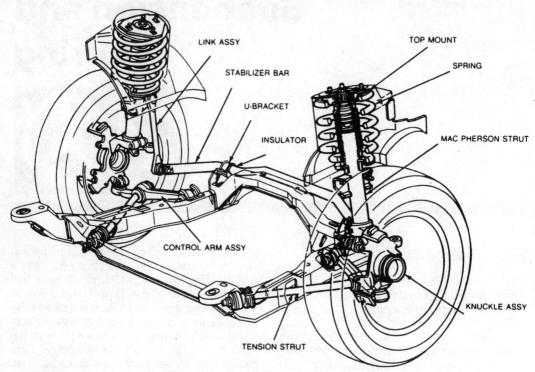

Front suspension assembly—Taurus/Sable

arm, tie rod and shock struts require only one wrench for loosening and tightening making them easier to work on.

The front strut is attached to a shear type upper mount to reduce engine, transaxle noise, vibration and harshness. The strut spring is contained between an offset lower spring seat fixed to the strut body and a rotating upper seat attached to the upper mount. The offset spring seat reduces friction in the strut to improve ride and decrease wear. The hydraulic damping (shock) system for the front strut has twin tubes with a single acting piston attached to the rod.

Component Serviceability

The following components may be replaced individually or as components:
- Shock Absorber Struts (MacPherson)
- Strut Upper Mounts
- Coil Springs
- Ball Joints
- Lower Control Arm Bushing
- Forged Lower Control Arm
- Steering Knuckle
- Stabilizer Bar: The stabilizer bar is replaceable and contains the body mounting bushings. The stabilizer bar to lower arm insulator is replaceable as is the stabilizer bar to body bushing.

MacPherson Strut

REMOVAL AND INSTALLATION

Taurus/Sable

1. Place the ignition switch to the OFF position and the steering column in the unlocked position.

2. Remove the hub nut. Loosen the strut-to-fender apron nuts; DO NOT remove the nuts.

3. Raise and support the front of the vehicle on jackstands. Remove the wheels.

NOTE: *When raising the vehicle, DO NOT lift it by using the lower control arms.*

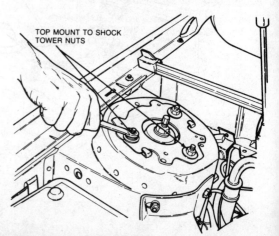

Upper strut mounting nuts

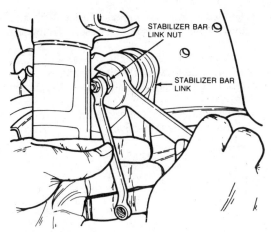

Stabilizer bar link connection

4. Remove the brake caliper (support it on a wire) and the rotor.

5. At the tie rod end, remove the cotter pin and the castle nut.

6. Using the tie rod end remover tool No. 3290-C and the tie rod remover adapter tool No. T81P-3504-W, separate the tie rod from the steering knuckle.

7. Remove the stabilizer bar link nut and the link from the strut.

8. Remove the lower arm-to-steering knuckle pinch bolt and nut; it may be necessary to use a drift punch to remove the bolt. Using a small pry bar, spread the knuckle-to-lower arm pinch joint and remove the lower arm from the steering knuckle.

9. Remove the halfshaft from the hub and support it on a wire.

NOTE: *When removing the halfshaft, DO NOT allow it to move outward for the tripod CV-joint could separate from the internal parts, causing failure of the joint.*

10. Remove the strut-to-steering knuckle pinch bolt. Using a small pry bar, spread the pinch bolt joint and separate the strut from the steering knuckle. Remove the steering knuckle/hub assembly from the strut assembly.

11. Remove the strut-to-fender apron nuts and the strut assembly from the vehicle.

To install:

1. Install the strut assembly into position and install the three top mount-to-shock tower nuts.

2. Install the steering knuckle and hub assembly to the shock absorber strut.

3. Install a new shock absorber strut-to-steering knuckle pinch bolt and nut. Tighten the nut to 70-95 ft. lbs.

4. Install the halfshaft into the hub.

5. Install the lower arm to the steering knuckle and install a new pinch bolt and nut. Tighten to 40-55 ft. lbs.

6. Install the stabilizer bar link to the strut and install a stabilizer bar link nut. Tighten the nut to 35-48 ft. lbs.

7. Install the tie rod end onto the knuckle.

8. Install a new tie rod end slotted nut. Tighten the nut to 23-35 ft. lbs.

9. Install a new slotted nut retaining cotter pin.

10. Install the brake rotor, then install the brake caliper.

11. Install the wheels.

12. Tighten the three top mount-to-shock tower nuts to 22-32 ft. lbs.

13. Lower the vehicle and tighten the hub nut to 180-200 ft. lbs.

14. Depress the brake pedal several times before moving the vehicle.

15. Check wheel alignment.

Continental

The Continental uses MacPherson struts both front and rear. The struts use an integral air spring and two stage damping mechanism. The two stage damping is achieved by varying the effective piston orifice area with an externally mounted electronic rotary actuator. The front struts are mounted to the body through a high precision ball bearing and rubber mount system. The ball bearing provides a very smooth highly durable pivot for strut/wheel assembly. The top is mounted to the fender apron by three attaching studs and the bottom is mounted to the lower control arm and steering knuckle.

CAUTION: *All the vehicles are equipped with gas-pressurized shock absorbers which will extend unassisted. Do not apply heat or flame to the shock strut during removal.*

The electrical power supply to the air suspension system must be shut OFF prior to hoisting, jacking, or towing an air suspension vehicle. This can be accomplished by disconnecting the battery negative (-) cable or turning OFF the power switch located in the luggage compartment on the left side. Failure to do so may result in unexpected inflation or deflation of the air springs which may result in shifting of the vehicle during these operations.

REMOVAL

1. Turn OFF the air suspension switch (located in left side of the luggage compartment. Also check switch location diagram in this section.

2. Turn the ignition switch to the OFF position and place the column in the unlocked position.

3. Remove the plastic cover from the shock

tower to expose the upper mounting nuts and the dual damping actuator.

4. Remove the two actuator retaining screws, located on top of the strut tower, and lift off the actuator.

5. Remove the hub nut.

6. Loosen, but do not remove the three top mount-to-shock tower nuts.

7. Raise the vehicle and support with jackstands, remove the tire assembly, and remove the brake line bracket from the strut.

8. Disconnect the height sensor link from the ball stud pin at the lower control arm. Check height sensor link disconnect diagram in this section.

9. Disconnect air line and electrical connector from the solenoid valve.

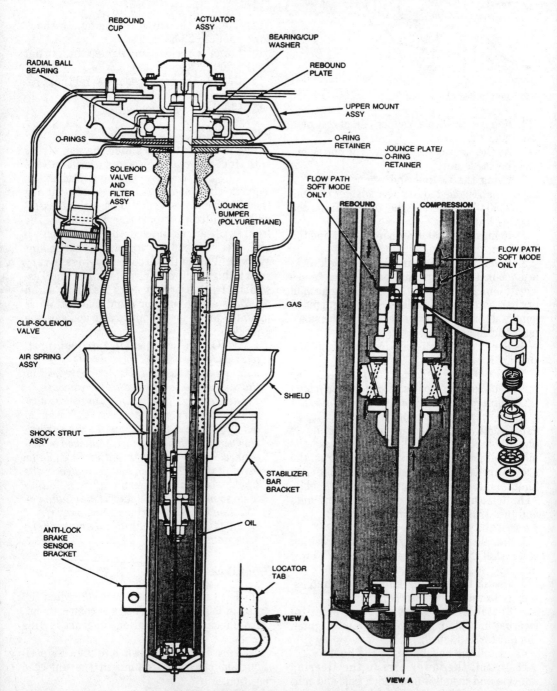

MacPherson strut assembly—Continental

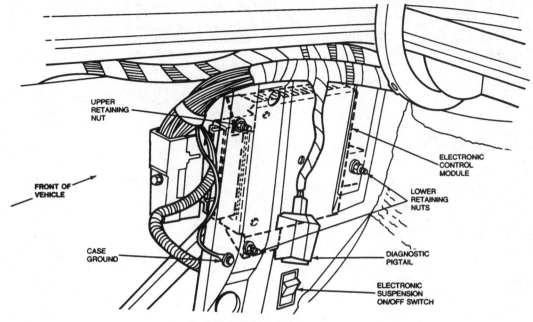

Electronic suspension ON/OFF switch located in the LH luggage compartment—Continental

10. Move the brake caliper and wire out of the way.

11. Remove the brake rotor, the cotter pin from the tie rod end stud, and the slotted nut.

12. Using a tie rod end remover tool part No. 3290-D and a tie rod end remover adapter tool part No. T81P-3504-W or equivalent.

13. Remove the tie rod from the steering knuckle.

14. Remove the stabilizer bar link nut and link from the strut.

15. Remove and discard the lower arm-to-steering knuckle pinch bolt and nut. (A drift punch may be used to remove the bolt). Use a

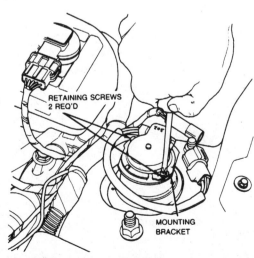

Actuator assembly—Continental

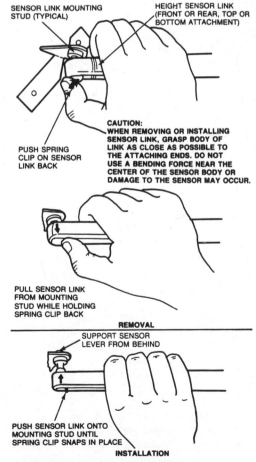

Height sensor link disconnect—Continental

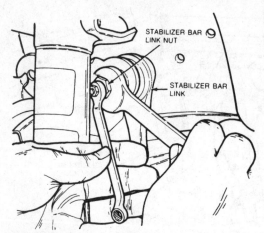

STABILIZER BAR
LINK NUT

STABILIZER BAR
LINK

Stabilizer bar link nut removal—Continental

pry bar to slightly spread the knuckle-to-lower arm pinch joint and remove the lower arm from the steering knuckle.

16. Press the halfshaft from the hub. Refer to the "Halfshaft" section in chapter 7.

CAUTION: *Do not allow the halfshaft to move outboard. Over-extension of the tripod CV joint could result in separation of the internal parts, causing failure of the joint.*

17. Remove the shock absorber strut-to-steering knuckle pinch bolt using a pry bar to slightly spread the pinch joint.

18. Remove the steering knuckle and hub assembly from the shock absorber strut.

19. Remove the three top mount-to-shock tower nuts and remove the strut and air spring assembly from the vehicle.

To install:

1. Install the strut and air spring assembly and the three top mount-to-shock tower nuts, leave the nuts loose.

2. Install steering knuckle and hub assembly to the shock absorber strut.

3. Install a new shock absorber strut-to-steering knuckle pinch bolt. Torque the bolt to 70-95 ft. lbs.

4. Install the halfshaft into the hub, the lower arm to steering knuckle, and install a new pinch bolt and nut. Torque the bolt to 40-55 ft. lbs.

5. Install the stabilizer bar link to the strut, stabilizer bar link nut, and torque to 55-75 ft. lbs.

6. Install the tie rod end onto the steering knuckle, new rod end slotted nut with steering wheel in the straight ahead position, and torque the nut to 23-35 ft. lbs.

7. Install a new slotted nut retaining cotter pin, brake rotor, and brake caliper.

8. Connect the electrical connectors for the solenoid valve.

9. Connect the air line to the solenoid valve.

10. Install the height sensor link on the ball stud pin on the control arm.

11. Install the brake line bracket, the wheel assembly, and torque the three top mount-to-shock tower nuts to 22-32 ft. lbs.

12. Install the dual damping, plastic shock tower cover, and fill the air spring prior to fully lowering the vehicle by turning ON the switch located in the left side of the luggage compartment.

13. Lower the vehicle and torque the hub nut to 180-200 ft. lbs.

14. Pump the brake pedal a few times before moving the vehicle.

STRUT OVERHAUL

Taurus/Sable

The following procedure is performed with the strut assembly removed from the car. A MacPherson Strut compression tool is required for the disassembly of the strut, a cage type tool such as the part No. D85P-7181-A or equivalent is required.

CAUTION: *Never attempt to disassemble the spring or top mount without first compressing the spring using the strut compressor tool No. D85P-7178-A or equivalent.*

1. Compress the spring with the coil spring

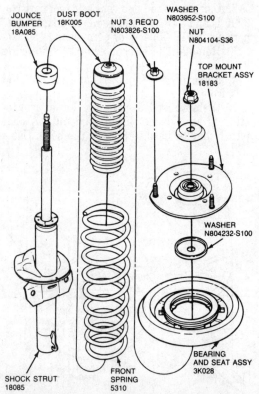

JOUNCE
BUMPER
18A085

DUST BOOT
18K005

NUT 3 REQ'D
N803826-S100

WASHER
N803952-S100

NUT
N804104-S36

TOP MOUNT
BRACKET ASSY
18183

WASHER
N804232-S100

BEARING
AND SEAT ASSY
3K028

SHOCK STRUT
18085

FRONT
SPRING
5310

Exploded view of the front Macpherson strut assembly

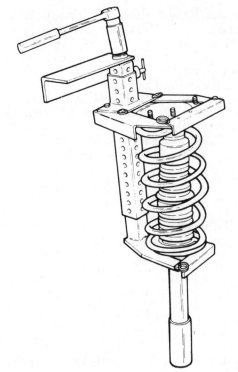

Compressing the coil spring with a strut compression tool

compressor part No. D85P-7178-A or equivalent.

2. Place a 10mm box wrench on top of the shock strut shaft and hold while removing the top shaft mounting nut with a 21mm 6-point crow foot wrench and ratchet.

WARNING: *It is important that the mounting nut be turned and the rod held still to prevent fracture of the rod at the base of the hex.*

3. Loosen the spring compressor tool, then remove the top mounting bracket assembly, bearing plate assembly and spring.

To assemble:

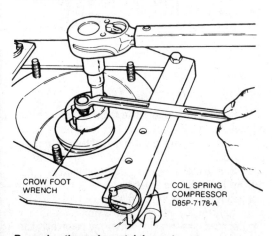

CROW FOOT
WRENCH

COIL SPRING
COMPRESSOR
D85P-7178-A

Removing the spring retaining nut

Warning: *Ensure that the correct assembly sequence and proper positioning of the bearing and seat assembly are followed. The bearing and seat assembly is press-fit onto the upper mount. The mount washers must be installed with orientation.*

4. Install the spring compressor tool part No. D85P-7178-A or equivalent.

5. Install the spring, bearing plate assembly, lower washer and top mount bracket assembly.

6. Compress the spring with the coil spring compressor tool.

7. Install the upper washer and nut on the shock strut shaft.

8. Place a 10mm box end wrench on the top of the shock strut shaft and hold while tightening the top shaft mounting nut with a 21mm 6-point crow foot wrench and a ratchet.

9. The strut assembly may now be installed in the vehicle.

Continental

The strut and air spring assemblies must be replaced as an assembly. The strut is not serviceable. Replace only the damaged assembly. It is not necessary to replace in pairs. The upper mount and bearing assembly, solenoid, and actuator can be and replaced separately.

Ball Joints

The ball joint is a part of the lower control arm and cannot be replaced. If the ball joint is bad, the control arm must be replaced.

INSPECTION

1. Raise and support the front of the vehicle on jackstands.

NOTE: *DO NOT raise or support the vehicle on the front control arms.*

2. Have an assistant grasp the lower edge of the tires and move the assembly in and out.

3. As the wheel is being moved, observe the control arm-to-steering knuckle ball joint for movement; movement indicates a worn out ball joint.

4. If ball joint movement is present, replace the lower control arm.

REMOVAL AND INSTALLATION

1. Refer to the "Lower Control Arm Removal And Installation" procedures in this chapter and remove the control arm from the vehicle.

2. **To install:** use a new control arm and reverse the removal procedures.

Stabilizer Bar

REMOVAL AND INSTALLATION

1. Raise and support the front of the vehicle on jackstands.

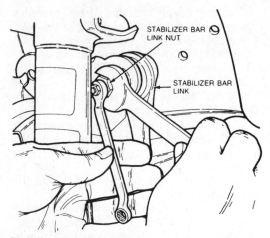

Stabilizer bar link removal

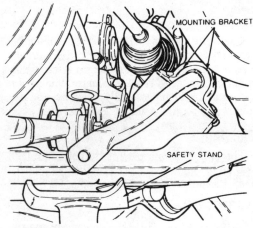

Stabilizer bar mounting brackets

NOTE: *DO NOT raise or support the vehicle on the front control arms.*

2. Remove the stabilizer bar link-to-stabilizer bar nut, the stabilizer bar link-to-strut nut and the link from the vehicle.

3. Remove the steering gear-to-subframe nuts and move the gear off the subframe.

4. Position another set of jackstands under the subframe and remove the rear subframe-to-frame bolts. Lower the subframe rear to obtain access to the stabilizer bar brackets.

5. Remove the stabilizer bar U-bracket bolts and the stabilizer bar from the vehicle.

NOTE: *When removing the stabilizer bar, replace the insulators and the U-bracket bolts with new ones.*

To install:

6. Clean the stabilizer bar around the area of the insulator bushings.

7. Lubricate the inside diameter of the bushings with grease part No. E25Y-19553-A or equivalent.

8. Install the new insulators onto the stabilizer bar and position them into their approximate position.

9. Install the U-brackets onto the insulators, install new bolts and tighten to 21-32 ft. lbs.

10. Raise the subframe and install new subframe-to-body attaching bolts. Position the steering gear onto the subframe and install the retaining nuts. Tighten to 85-100 ft. lbs.

11. Install new nuts and secure the link assembly to the stabilizer bar and shock strut. Tighten to 35-48 ft. lbs.

12. Remove the jackstands and lower the vehicle.

Tension Struts

REMOVAL AND INSTALLATION

1. Refer to the "Lower Control Arm Removal And Installation" procedures in this section and remove the control arm from the vehicle.

2. Remove the tension strut-to-subframe nut, washer and insulator, then pull the tension strut rearward to remove it from the vehicle.

3. Remove the insulator from the tension strut.

NOTE: *When installing the tension strut, use a new insulator, washer and nut.*

4. **To install:** reverse the removal procedures. Torque the tension strut-to-subframe nut to 70-95 ft. lbs.; the control arm-to-frame nut/bolt to 70-95 ft. lbs. the control arm-to-steering knuckle nut/bolt to 40-55 ft. lbs.; the tension strut-to-control arm nut to 70-95 ft. lbs.; and the wheel lug nuts to 80-105 ft. lbs. Check and/or adjust the front wheel alignment.

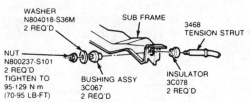

Tension strut attachment

Lower Control Arm

REMOVAL AND INSTALLATION

1. Raise and support the front of the vehicle on jackstands. Remove the tire assembly. Position the steering column in the unlocked position.

2. Remove the tension strut-to-control arm nut and the dished washer.

3. Remove and discard the control arm-to-steering knuckle pinch bolt. Using a small pry bar, spread the pinch joint and separate the control arm from the steering knuckle.

NOTE: *When separating the control arm from the steering knuckle, DO NOT use a hammer. Be careful not to damage the bolt seal.*

4. Remove the control arm-to-frame nut/bolt, then the control arm from the frame and the tension strut.

WARNING: *DO NOT allow the halfshaft to move outward or the tripod CV-joint could separate from the internal parts, causing failure of the joint.*

5. **To install:** use a new pinch nut/bolt and reverse the removal procedures. Torque the control arm-to-frame nut/bolt to 70-95 ft. lbs.; the control arm-to-steering knuckle nut/bolt to 40-55 ft. lbs.; the tension strut-to-control arm nut to 70-95 ft. lbs.; and the wheel lug nuts to 80-105 ft. lbs. Check the front end alignment.

Front Axle Hub And Bearings

Front wheel bearings are located in the front knuckle, not the rotor. The bearings are protected by inner and outer grease seals and an additional inner grease shield immediately inboard of the inner grease seal. The wheel hub is installed with an interference fit to the constant velocity universal joint outer race shaft. The hub nut and washer are installed and tightened to 180-200 ft. lbs. The rotor fits loosely on the hub assembly and is secured when the wheel and wheel nuts are installed.

The front wheel bearings have a set-right design that requires no scheduled maintenance. The bearing design relies on component stack-up and deformation/torque at assembly to determine bearing setting. Therefore, bearings cannot be adjusted. In addition to maintaining bearing adjustment, the hub nut torque of 180-200 ft. lbs., restricts bearing/hub relative movement and maintains axial position of the hub. Die to the importance of the hub nut torque/tension relationship, certain precautions must be taken during service.

REMOVAL AND INSTALLATION

CAUTION: *When servicing the front suspension, brake shoes contain asbestos which has been determined to be a cancer causing agent. Never clean the brake surfaces with compressed air! Avoid inhaling any dust from any brake surface! When cleaning brake surfaces, use a commercially available brake cleaning fluid.*

1. Remove the wheelcover/hub cover from the wheel and tire assembly and loosen the lug nuts.

2. Remove the hub retaining nut and washer by applying sufficient torque to the nut to overcome the prevailing torque feature of the crimp in the nut collar. Do not use an impact type tool to remove the hub nut. The hub nut must be discarded after removal.

3. Loosen the three strut top mount to apron nuts.

4. Raise and support the vehicle safely. Remove the wheel and tire assembly.

5. Remove the brake caliper by removing the caliper locating pins and rotating the caliper off of the rotor, starting from the lower end of the caliper and lifting upward. Lift the caliper off the rotor and hang it free of the rotor. Do not allow the caliper assembly to hang from the brake hose. Support the caliper assembly with a length of wire.

6. Remove the rotor from the hub by pulling it off the hub bolts. If the rotor is difficult to remove from the hub, strike the rotor sharply between the studs with a rubber or plastic hammer.

NOTE: *If the rotor will not pull off, apply a suitable penetrating fluid to the inboard and outboard rotor hub mating surfaces. Install a 3 jaw puller and remove the rotor by pulling on the rotor outside diameter and pushing on the hub center. If excessive force is required, check the rotor for lateral runout prior to installation.*

7. The lateral runout must be checked with the nuts clamping the stamped section of the rotor. Remove the rotor splash shield.

8. Disconnect the lower control arm and tie rod from the steering knuckle. Loosen the strut pinch bolt, but do not remove the strut.

9. Install hub remover/installer tool part No.

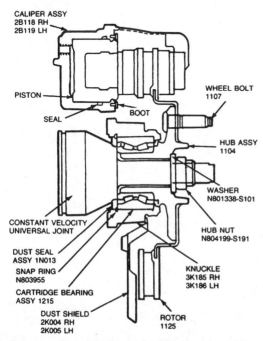

CALIPER ASSY
2B118 RH
2B119 LH

PISTON

SEAL

BOOT

WHEEL BOLT
1107

HUB ASSY
1104

WASHER
N801338-S101

CONSTANT VELOCITY
UNIVERSAL JOINT

DUST SEAL
ASSY 1N013

SNAP RING
N803955

CARTRIDGE BEARING
ASSY 1215

DUST SHIELD
2K004 RH
2K005 LH

HUB NUT
N804199-S191

KNUCKLE
3K185 RH
3K186 LH

ROTOR
1125

Cut-away view of the front wheel bearing assembly

T81P-1104-A with T81P-1104-C and hub knuckle adapters T83P-1104-BH1 and T86P-1104-A1 or equivalent.

10. Remove the hub, bearing and knuckle assembly by pushing out the constant velocity joint outer shaft until it is free of assembly. Wire the halfshaft to the body to maintain a level position.

11. Remove the strut bolt and slide the hub/bearings/knuckle assembly off the strut using spindle carrier lever tool part No. T85M-3206-A or equivalent. Carefully remove the support wire and carry the hub/bearing/knuckle assembly to a suitable workbench.

12. On the bench, install front hub puller D80L-1002-L and shaft protector D80L-625-1 or equivalent, with the jaws of the puller on the knuckle bosses and remove the hub.

NOTE: *Be sure the shaft protector is centered, clears the bearing ID and rests on the end face of the hub journal.*

13. Remove the snapring, which retains the bearing in the knuckle assembly, with the snapring pliers and discard.

14. Using a suitable hydraulic press, place the front bearing spacer part No. T86P-1104-A2 or equivalent step side up on the press plate and position the knuckle (outboard side up) on the spacer.

15. Install bearing remover part No. T83P-1104-AH2 or equivalent centered on the bearing inner race and press the bearing out of the knuckle. Discard the old bearing.

16. Remove the halfshaft and place it in a suitable vise.

17. Remove the bearing dust seal by equally tapping on the outer edge with a light duty hammer and a suitable tool. Discard the dust seal.

To Install:

18. Remove all foreign material from the knuckle bearing bore and hub bearing journal to ensure the correct seating of a new bearing.

NOTE: *If the hub bearing journal is scored or damaged, replace the hub. Do not attempt to service a bad hub. The front wheel bearings are of a cartridge design and are pre-greased, sealed and require no schedule maintenance. The bearings are preset and cannot be adjusted. If a bearing is disassembled for any reason, it must be replaced as a unit. No individual service seals, roller or races are available.*

19. Place the front bearing spacer part No. T86P-1104-A2 or equivalent step side down on a press plate and position the knuckle (outboard side down) on a spacer. Position a new bearing in the inboard side of the knuckle.

20. Install the bearing installer T86P-1104-A3 or equivalent (undercut side facing the bearing) on the bearing outer race and press bearing into the knuckle.

METRIC ADAPTERS (12mm) MAKE SURE THE ADAPTERS ARE FULLY THREADED ONTO THE HUB STUDS AND ARE POSITIONED OPPOSITE THE OTHER ADAPTER

TWO STUD ADAPTER T86P-1104-A1

METRIC STUD ADAPTER T83P-1104-BH1

PULLER T81P-1104-C ASSY AS SHOWN

METRIC ADAPTER T81P-1104-A

TURN THIS WRENCH COUNTERCLOCKWISE

HOLD WRENCH STATIONARY WHILE TURNING OTHER WRENCH

Removing the hub with special tools shown

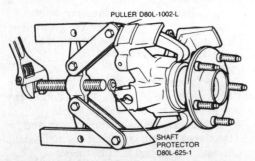

PULLER D80L-1002-L

SHAFT PROTECTOR D80L-625-1

Removing the hub from the knuckle

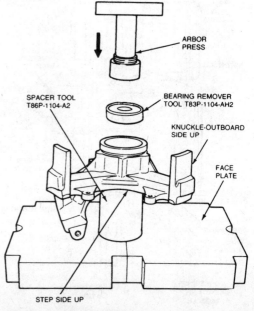

ARBOR PRESS

SPACER TOOL T86P-1104-A2

BEARING REMOVER TOOL T83P-1104-AH2

KNUCKLE-OUTBOARD SIDE UP

FACE PLATE

STEP SIDE UP

Pressing bearing from hub

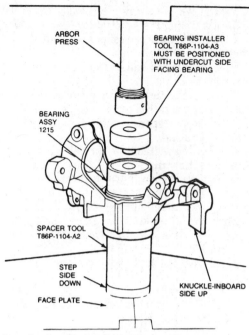

Pressing bearing into knuckle

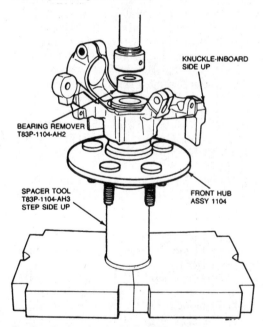

Seating the bearing in the knuckle

21. Check that the bearing seats completely against the shoulder of the knuckle bore. The bearing installer must be installed as indicated above to prevent bearing damage during installation.

22. Install a new snapring in the knuckle groove with a suitable pair of snapring pliers. Place the front bearing spacer part No. T86P-1104-A2 or equivalent on the arbor press plate and position the hub on the tool with the lugs

facing downward. Position the knuckle assembly (outboard side down) on the hub barrel.

23. Place bearing remover part No. T83P-1104-AH2 or equivalent flat side down, centered on the inner race of the bearing and press down on the tool until the bearing is fully seated onto the hub. Check that the hub rotates freely in the knuckle after installation.

24. Prior to the hub/bearing/knuckle installation, replace the bearing dust seal on the outboard CV-joint with a new seal from the bearing kit.

25. Install the dust seal, ensuring the seal flange faces outboard toward the bearing. Use drive tube T83P-3132-A1 and front bearing dust seal installer T86P-1104-A4 or equivalent.

26. Suspend the hub/bearing/knuckle assembly on the vehicle with a wire and attach the strut loosely to the knuckle. Lubricate the CV-joint stub shaft splines with a SAE 30 weight motor oil and insert the shaft onto the hub splines as far as possible using hand pressure only. Check that the splines are properly engaged.

27. Temporarily fasten the rotor to hub with washers and two wheel lug nuts. Insert a steel rod into the rotor diameter and rotate it clockwise to contact the knuckle.

28. Install the hub nut washer and new hub nut. Rotate the nut clockwise to seat the CV-joint. Tighten the nut to 180-200 ft. lbs. and do not use power or impact tools to install the hub nut. Remove the steel rod, washers and lug nuts.

29. Install the disc brake caliper over the ro-

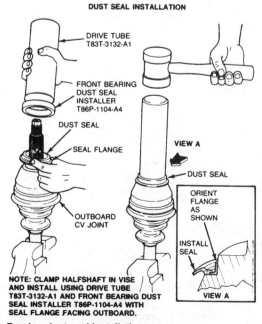

Bearing dust seal installation

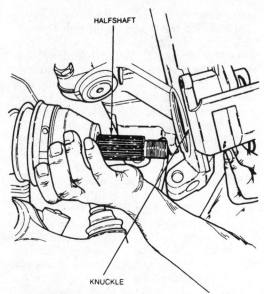

HALFSHAFT

KNUCKLE

Installing halfshaft into knuckle

tor. Be sure the outer brake shoe spring hook is seated under the upper arm of the knuckle.

30. Complete installation of the front suspension components. Install the wheel and tire assembly, tighten the lug nuts finger tight. Lower the vehicle and block the wheels to prevent the vehicle from moving. Tighten the lug nuts to 80-105 ft. lbs.

NOTE: *Replacement lug nuts or studs must be of the same type and size as those being replaced.*

31. Tighten the hub nut to 180-200 ft. lbs. Install the wheel cover or hub cover. Lower the vehicle completely to the ground and remove wheel blocks. Road test the vehicle and check to see if the vehicle is operating properly.

Upper Mount and Bearing Assembly

REMOVAL AND INSTALLATION

CAUTION: *When servicing the front suspension, brake shoes contain asbestos which has been determined to be a cancer causing agent. Never clean the brake surfaces with compressed air! Avoid inhaling any dust from any brake surface! When cleaning brake surfaces, use a commercially available brake cleaning fluid.*

Taurus/Sable

1. Place the ignition switch to the OFF position and the steering column in the unlocked position.

2. Remove the hub nut. Loosen the strut-to-fender apron nuts; DO NOT remove the nuts.

3. Raise and support the front of the vehicle on jackstands. Remove the wheels.

NOTE: *When raising the vehicle, DO NOT lift it by using the lower control arms.*

4. Remove the brake caliper (support it on a wire) and the rotor.

5. At the tie rod end, remove the cotter pin and the castle nut.

6. Using the tie rod end remover tool No. 3290-C and the tie rod remover adapter tool No. T81P-3504-W, separate the tie rod from the steering knuckle.

7. Remove the stabilizer bar link nut and the link from the strut.

8. Remove the lower arm-to-steering knuckle pinch bolt and nut; it may be necessary to use a drift punch to remove the bolt. Using a small pry bar, spread the knuckle-to-lower arm pinch joint and remove the lower arm from the steering knuckle.

9. Remove the halfshaft from the hub and support it on a wire.

NOTE: *When removing the halfshaft, DO NOT allow it to move outward for the tripod CV-joint could separate from the internal parts, causing failure of the joint.*

10. Remove the strut-to-steering knuckle pinch bolt. Using a small pry bar, spread the pinch bolt joint and separate the strut from the steering knuckle. Remove the steering knuckle/hub assembly from the strut assembly.

11. Remove the strut-to-fender apron nuts and the strut assembly from the vehicle.

CAUTION: *Never attempt to disassemble the spring or top mount without first compressing the spring using a Universal MacPherson Strut Spring Compressor D85P-7178-A or a Rotunda Spring Compressor 086-00029 or equivalent.*

12. Place a 10mm box-end wrench on top of the shock strut shaft and hold while removing the top shaft mounting nut with a 21mm 6-point crow foot wrench and ratchet.

13. Loosen the MacPherson Strut Spring Compressor slowly. Remove the top mount bracket assembly, bearing plate, and spring.

NOTE: *When servicing the shock absorber strut, check the spring insulator for damage before assembly. If the outer metal splash shield is bent or damaged, it must be bent back carefully so that it does not touch the locator tabs on the bearing and seal assembly.*

14. **To install:** place the MacPherson Strut Spring Compressor on the base of the strut.

15. Install the upper mount and bearing assembly on top of the strut and tighten the spring compressor far enough to install the shaft mounting nut.

16. Install the washer and nut on the shock strut shaft and tighten with the 10mm box-end and the 21mm 6-point crow foot wrench and ratchet.

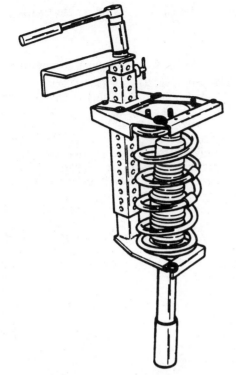

Compressing the strut with a MacPherson strut compressor—MUST BE USED

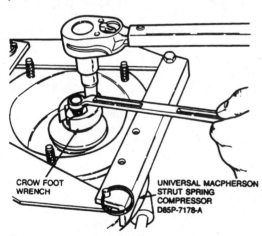

CROW FOOT WRENCH

UNIVERSAL MACPHERSON STRUT SPRING COMPRESSOR D85P-7178-A

Removing the spring retainer nut

17. Refer to the "MacPherson Strut" installation procedure in this section.

Continental

CAUTION: *When servicing the front suspension, brake shoes contain asbestos which has been determined to be a cancer causing agent. Never clean the brake surfaces with compressed air! Avoid inhaling any dust from any brake surface! When cleaning brake surfaces, use a commercially available brake cleaning fluid.*

1. Turn OFF the air suspension switch (lo-cated in left side of the luggage compartment. Also check switch location diagram in this section.

2. Turn the ignition switch to the OFF position and place the column in the unlocked position.

3. Remove the plastic cover from the shock tower to expose the upper mounting nuts and the dual damping actuator.

4. Remove the two actuator retaining screws, located on top of the strut tower, and lift off the actuator.

5. Remove the hub nut.

6. Loosen, but do not remove the three top mount-to-shock tower nuts.

7. Raise the vehicle and support with jackstands, remove the tire assembly, and remove the brake line bracket from the strut.

8. Disconnect the height sensor link from the ball stud pin at the lower control arm. Check height sensor link disconnect diagram in this section.

9. Disconnect the air line and electrical connector from the solenoid valve.

10. Move the brake caliper and wire out of the way. Do not hang by the brake hose.

11. Remove the brake rotor, the cotter pin from the tie rod end stud, and the slotted nut.

12. Using a tie rod end remover tool part No. 3290-D and a tie rod end remover adapter tool part No. T81P-3504-W or equivalent.

13. Remove the tie rod from the steering knuckle.

14. Remove the stabilizer bar link nut and link from the strut.

15. Remove and discard the lower arm-to-steering knuckle pinch bolt and nut. (A drift punch may be used to remove the bolt). Use a pry bar to slightly spread the knuckle-to-lower arm pinch joint and remove the lower arm from the steering knuckle.

16. Press the halfshaft from the hub. Refer to the "Halfshaft" section in chapter 7.

CAUTION: *Do not allow the halfshaft to move outboard. Over-extension of the tripod CV joint could result in separation of the internal parts, causing failure of the joint.*

17. Remove the shock absorber strut-to-steering knuckle pinch bolt using a pry bar to slightly spread the pinch joint.

18. Remove the steering knuckle and hub assembly from the shock absorber strut.

19. Remove the three top mount-to-shock tower nuts and remove the strut and air spring assembly from the vehicle.

20. Bleed the air out of the air spring assembly as follows.

    a. Remove the solenoid clip

    b. Rotate the solenoid counterclockwise to the first stop.

CAUTION: *Do not fully release the solenoid until the air is completely bled from the air spring.*

c. After the air is fully bled from the system, rotate the solenoid counterclockwise to the third stop and remove the solenoid from the housing.

d. Inspect the solenoid O-ring. Replace it if there is any signs of damage.

21. Place the actuator mounting bracket (rebound cup) loosely in a vise by the flats.

22. Remove the nut and rebound cup, upper mount and bearing assembly, and the O-ring retainer plate. Replace the O-ring if necessary.

23. **To install:** place the O-ring, retainer plate, upper mount, and rebound cup on top of the air spring assembly.

24. Start the nut on the strut shaft.

25. Hold the rebound cup loosely in a vise and torque the nut to 35-50 ft. lbs.

26. Install the solenoid.

27. Install the air spring and strut assembly in the vehicle. Refer to the "Continental Mac-Pherson Strut" installation procedure in this section.

Front Wheel Alignment

ADJUSTMENT

CAUTION: *When servicing the front suspension, brake shoes contain asbestos which has been determined to be a cancer causing agent. Never clean the brake surfaces with compressed air! Avoid inhaling any dust from any brake surface! When cleaning brake surfaces, use a commercially available brake cleaning fluid.*

Caster and Camber

Caster and camber angles are preset at the factory and can only be adjusted by extensive upper strut modifications and are not included in this publication. Measurement procedures that follow are for diagnostic purposes.

Caster measurements must be made on the left hand side by turning the left wheel through the prescribed angle of the sweep and on the right hand side by turning the right wheel through the prescribed angle of sweep.

When using the alignment equipment designed to measure the caster on both the right hand and left hand side, turning only one wheel will result in a significant error in the caster angle for the opposite side.

Toe-In Angle

The toe-in is controlled by adjusting the tie rod ends. To adjust the toe-in setting, loosen the tie rod jam nuts. Rotate the tie rod as required to adjust the toe-in into specifications.

Once the toe-in is set, re-tighten the tie rod jam nuts.

Ride Height Setup and Measuring (Continental)

The ride height is set at the factory and is NOT adjustable on the Taurus/Sable models.

However, the ride height is adjustable on the Continental models. The Continental is equipped with an air suspension that is electronically controlled through an electronic control module. The proper suspension height must be obtained before the alignment procedure can be performed.

The Do-it-Yourself mechanic should not attempt to perform any wheel alignment procedures. Expensive alignment tools are needed and would not be cost efficient to purchase these tools. The wheel alignment should be performed by a certified alignment technician using the proper alignment tools.

1. Position the vehicle on the alignment rack.

2. The vehicle should be measured only after the Service Bay Diagnostic Auto Mode has successfully been completed and the STAR tester displays a code "12".

3. Remove the STAR tester and turn the suspension switch to the OFF position located in the left side of the luggage compartment.

4. Measure the front suspension "C" dimension shown in the suspension height illustration. The front ride height "C" is the vertical difference between the lower arm inner pivot attachment height minus the outer pivot height.

5. Measure the rear suspension "D" dimension as shown in the suspension height illustration. This measurement is the difference between the rear lower arm and the outer pivot height.

6. The suspension heights for the top of the trim band are.

a. "C" Dimension: 43.6mm
b. "D" Dimension: −9.3mm

If the suspension heights are not within the following tolerances, the ride height adjustment is required.

c. "C" Dimension: ± 10mm
d. "D" Dimension: + 10mm/-5mm

7. If adjustment to the front ride height is required, it should be performed by replacing the height sensor link according to the suspension height chart. When removing the link, carefully separate it from the ball stud with a wide-blade screwdriver. Each incremental link change changes the ride height approximately 6mm.

8. Loosen the rear height sensor adjustment by loosening and repositioning the height sensor lever adjustment screw.

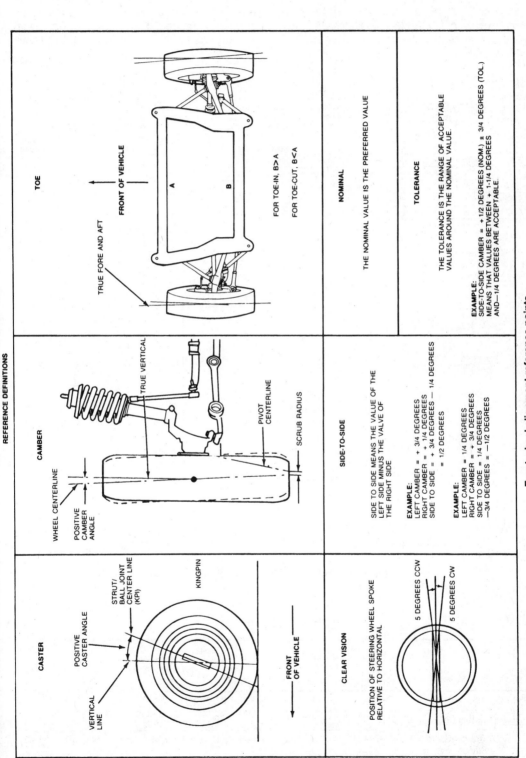

Front wheel alignment reference points

REAR SUSPENSION

Taurus/Sable Sedan

Your car features a strut type independent rear suspension. Each side has a shock absorber (strut), lower control (transverse) arm, tension strut, forged spindle, and a coil spring mounted on the strut itself.

The lower control (transverse) arm and the tension strut provide lateral and longitudinal control. The shock strut counters backing forces and provides the necessary suspension damping. The coil is mounted on the shock

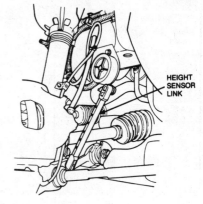

Link Part Number		Height Sensor Link Change	Front Ride Height Affect With Respect To The Nominal Link
LH Front	**RH Front**		
E80F-3C111-CA	E80F-3C111-GA	Plus One (Green)	+6mm (+0.24 IN)
E80F-3C111-BA	E80F-3C111-FA	Minus One (Red)	-6mm (-0.24 IN)
E80F-3C111-JA	E80F-3C111-KA	Nominal (Blue)	-0-
E80F-3C111-DA	E80F-3C111-HA	Plus Two (Yellow)	+12mm (+0.47 IN)
E80F-3C111-AA	E80F-3C111-EA	Minus Two (White)	-12mm (-0.47 IN)

Suspension ride height chart

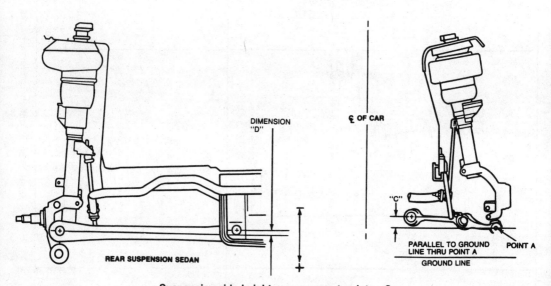

Suspension ride height measurement points—Continental

Wheel Alignment

Year	Model	Caster		Camber		Toe-in (in.)	Wheel Turning Angle (deg.)
		Range (deg.)	Preferred Setting (deg.)	Range (deg.)	Preferred Setting (deg.)		
1986–89	Taurus Sedan	3P–6P	4P	1¹⁄₁₀N–¹⁄₁₀P	½N	⁷⁄₃₂N–¹⁄₃₂P	18.25
	Sable Sedan	2⅞P–5⅞P	3⅞P	1¹⁄₁₀N–¹⁄₁₀P	½N	⁷⁄₃₂N–¹⁄₃₂P	18.25
	Taurus/Sable Station Wagon	2¹³⁄₁₆P–5¹³⁄₁₆P	3¹³⁄₁₆P	1¹⁄₃₂N–⁵⁄₃₂P	⁷⁄₁₆N	⁷⁄₃₂N–¹⁄₃₂P	18.25
	Continental	4P–5⅝P	4¹³⁄₁₆P	Front 1½N–⁵⁄₁₆N	Front ⅞N	Front 2¹⁄₃₂N–¹⁄₁₆P	18.21

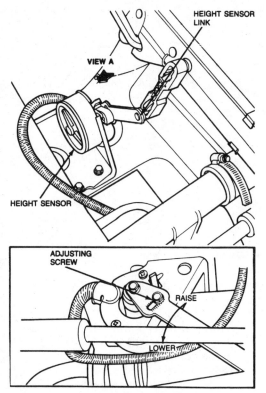

Ride height sensor link—Continental

Taurus/Sable Station Wagon

The suspension used on the station wagons consists of five major components; the upper and lower control arms, shock absorber, two piece cast spindle tension strut and a coil spring mounted between the lower suspension arm and the body crossmember.

The shock absorber assembly is attached to the body side panel by a rubber insulated top mount assembly and nut and to the lower suspension arm by two studs pressed into a bar-pin mounted in a rubber bushing. The upper suspension arms are attached to the spindle and the crossmember. The lower suspension arm attaches to the underbody and the spindle. A coil spring is located between the lower suspension arm and the body crossmember inboard of the shock absorber. A tension strut attaches the underbody and the lower suspension arm.

Continental

The Continental utilizes a MacPherson strut independent rear air suspension. The components consist of a shock absorber and air spring assembly, two parallel control arms per side, a tension strut, cast spindle, and shock strut mounted stabilizer.

The rear shock strut and air spring assembly is a dual dampening hydraulic strut. the shock strut is mounted at the top by three studs which retain the top mount of the strut to the inner body side panel. The lower end of the assembly is attached to the spindle with a pinch clamp and bolt that goes through a locator tab welded to the strut. Two stamped control arms

strut assembly and acts as a metal to metal jounce stop in case of heavy bottoming (going over bumps with weight in the back).

The unique independent rear suspension provides exceptional road hugging ability and adds to ride comfort.

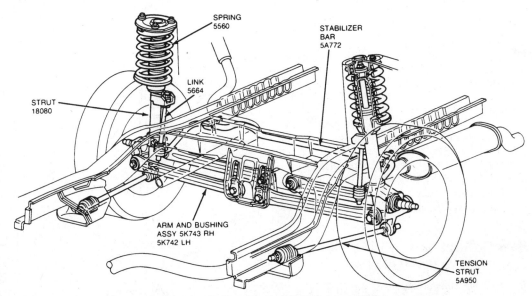

Rear suspension—Taurus/Sable sedan models

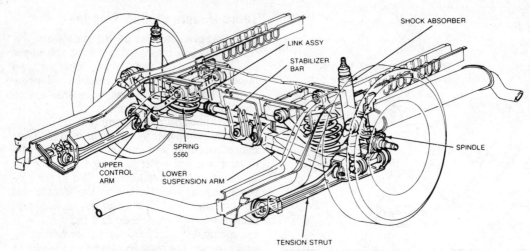

Rear suspension—Taurus/Sable station wagon models

attach to the underbody and spindle. A counterbalancing torsion spring neutralizes side load on the strut rod for smoother suspension travel.

COMPONENT DESCRIPTION AND SERVICABILITY

● Rear Coil Spring: Controls the suspension travel, provides ride height control and acts as a metal to metal jounce stop. The coil springs are replaceable, however the upper spring insulator must be replace at the same time.

● Lower Control (Transverse) Arm: Controls the side to side movement of each wheel and has the lower coil spring seat built in. The lower control arm is replaceable, however the control arm bushings are not. If the bushings are worn the control arm must be replaced.

● Shock Absorber Strut: Counters the braking forces and provides the necessary damping action to rear suspension travel caused by road conditions. The assembly is not repairable and must be replaced as a unit. The upper mounting may be serviced separately.

● Tension Strut: Controls the fore and aft wheel movement and holds the rear toe-in adjustment. The tension strut may be replaced as an assembly. Mounting bushings may be replaced separately , but new ones should be installed if the tension strut is replaced.

● Wheel Spindle: The one piece forged spindle attached to the lower arm, tension strut, shock strut and brake assembly. The rear wheel is mounted on the spindle. It may be replaced as a unit.

Rear Coil Spring

REMOVAL AND INSTALLATION

Taurus/Sable Station Wagon

1. Jack up the rear of the car and safely support it on jackstands. The jackstand location should be on the frame pads slightly in front of the rear wheels.

2. Place a floor jack or small hydraulic jack under the rear control arm. Raise the control arm to its normal height with the jack, do not lift the car frame from the jackstands.

3. Remove the tire and wheel assembly.

4. Remove the bracket retaining the brake hose to the body.

5. Remove the stabilizer bar U-bracket from the lower suspension arm.

6. Remove the nuts attaching the shock absorber to the lower suspension arm.

7. Remove the parking brake cable and clip from the lower suspension arm.

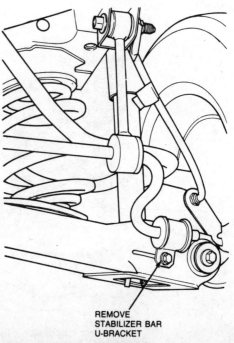

REMOVE
STABILIZER BAR
U-BRACKET

Rear stabilizer bracket location

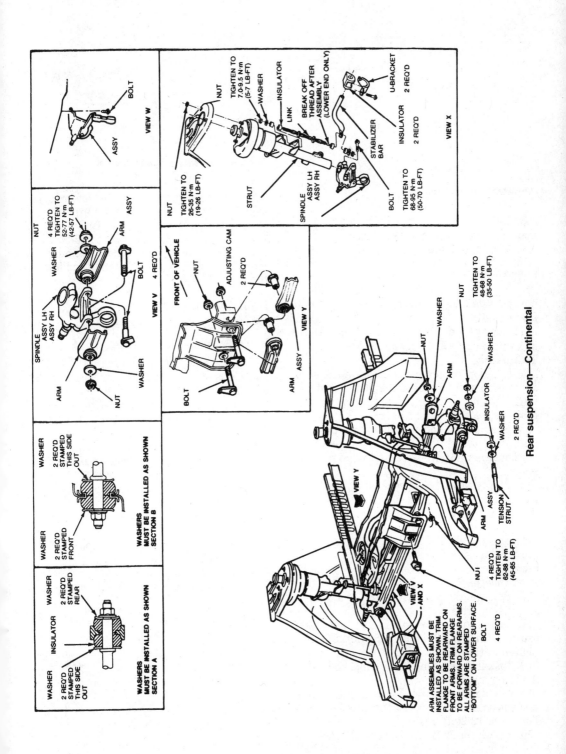

VIEW W

BOLT

ASSY

NUT

TIGHTEN TO
7.0-9.5 N·m
(5-7 LB-FT)

WASHER

INSULATOR

LINK

BREAK OFF
THREAD AFTER
ASSEMBLY
(LOWER END ONLY)

U-BRACKET

2 REQ'D

INSULATOR

2 REQ'D

STABILIZER
BAR

VIEW X

NUT

TIGHTEN TO
26-35 N·m
(19-26 LB-FT)

STRUT

SPINDLE
ASSY LH
ASSY RH

BOLT

TIGHTEN TO
68-95 N·m
(50-70 LB-FT)

NUT

4 REQ'D
TIGHTEN TO
52-77 N·m
(42-57 LB-FT)

WASHER

ARM
ASSY

BOLT

4 REQ'D

SPINDLE
ASSY LH
ASSY RH

ARM

WASHER

NUT

VIEW V

FRONT OF VEHICLE

NUT

ADJUSTING CAM

2 REQ'D

ARM
ASSY

VIEW Y

BOLT

WASHER

2 REQ'D
STAMPED
THIS SIDE
OUT

WASHER

2 REQ'D
STAMPED
FRONT

**WASHERS
MUST BE INSTALLED AS SHOWN
SECTION B**

WASHER

2 REQ'D
STAMPED
THIS SIDE
OUT

INSULATOR

WASHER

2 REQ'D
STAMPED
REAR

**WASHERS
MUST BE INSTALLED AS SHOWN
SECTION A**

NUT

WASHER

ARM

TIGHTEN TO
48-68 N·m
(35-50 LB-FT)

NUT

WASHER

INSULATOR

WASHER

2 REQ'D

ARM
ASSY

TENSION
STRUT

NUT

4 REQ'D
TIGHTEN TO
62-88 N·m
(45-65 LB-FT)

VIEW V
AND X

BOLT

4 REQ'D

VIEW Y

ARM ASSEMBLIES MUST BE
INSTALLED AS SHOWN. TRIM
FLANGE TO BE REARWARD ON
FRONT ARMS. TRIM FLANGE
TO BE FORWARD ON REARARMS.
ALL ARMS ARE STAMPED
"BOTTOM" ON LOWER SURFACE.

Rear suspension—Continental

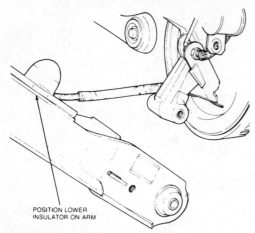

POSITION LOWER
INSULATOR ON ARM

Lower spring insulator

8. Remove the nut and bolt attaching the tension strut to the lower suspension arm.

9. Wire the spindle and upper suspension arms to the body to prevent them from dropping down.

10. Remove the nut, bolt, washer and adjusting cam retaining the lower suspension arm to the spindle.

11. Slowly lower the suspension arm with the jack until the spring can be removed.

To Install:

12. Position the lower insulator on the lower suspension arm and press the insulator downward into place. Check that the insulator is properly seated!

13. Position the upper insulator on the top of the spring. Install the spring on the lower suspension arm making sure the spring is properly seated.

14. Slowly raise the suspension arm with the jack and guide the upper spring insulator onto the upper spring seat on the underbody.

15. Position the spindle in the lower suspension arm and install a new bolt, nut, washer and the existing cam. Install the bolt with the head toward the front of the vehicle. DO NOT tighten at this time!

16. Remove the wire from the spindle and suspension arms.

17. Install the tension strut in the lower suspension arm using a new bolt and nut. DO NOT tighten at this time!

18. Install the parking brake cable and clip to the lower suspension arm.

19. Position the shock absorber on the lower suspension arm and install the two new nuts. Torque to 12-20 ft. lbs.

20. Install the stabilizer bar and U-bracket to the lower suspension arm using a new bolt. Torque to 20-30 ft. lbs.

21. Install the brake hose bracket to the body. Torque the bolt to 8-12 ft. lbs.

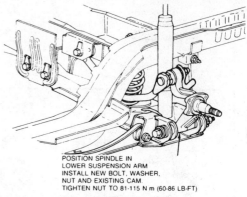

POSITION SPINDLE IN
LOWER SUSPENSION ARM
INSTALL NEW BOLT, WASHER,
NUT AND EXISTING CAM.
TIGHTEN NUT TO 81-115 N m (60-86 LB-FT)

Lower suspension spindle mounting

22. Using a floor jack, raise the lower suspension arm to normal curb height. torque the arm to spindle nut to 60-68 ft. lbs. Torque the tension strut to body bracket bolt to 40-55 ft. lbs.

23. Install the tire and wheel assembly. Remove the car from the jackstands and lower to the ground.

Rear Shock Absorber

REMOVAL AND INSTALLATION

Taurus/Sable Station Wagon

1. Raise and support the rear of the vehicle on jackstands. Remove the rear wheel and tire assembly.

2. Position a jackstand under the lower suspension arm and remove the two nuts retaining the shock absorber to lower suspension arm.

CAUTION: *The lower suspension arm must be supported before removal of the upper or lower shock absorber fasteners.*

3. From inside the vehicle, remove the rear access panels.

4.Remove the top shock absorber attaching nut using a crow foot wrench and a ratchet while holding the shock absorber shaft with an open end wrench.

WARNING: *If the shock is to be reused, DO NOT grip the shaft with pliers or vise grips as*

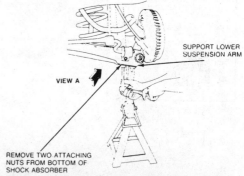

SUPPORT LOWER
SUSPENSION ARM

VIEW A

REMOVE TWO ATTACHING
NUTS FROM BOTTOM OF
SHOCK ABSORBER

Lower shock absorber attaching nuts

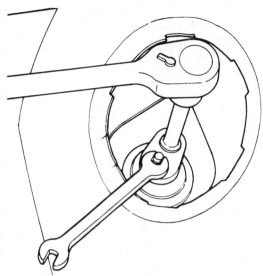

Upper shock absorber attaching nut

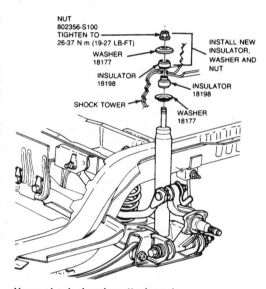

NUT
802356-S100
TIGHTEN TO
26-37 N·m (19-27 LB-FT)
WASHER
18177
INSTALL NEW
INSULATOR,
WASHER AND
NUT
INSULATOR
18198
INSULATOR
18198
SHOCK TOWER
WASHER
18177

Upper shock absorber attachments

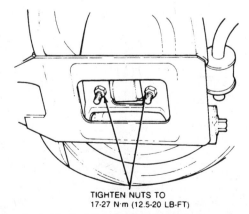

TIGHTEN NUTS TO
17-27 N·m (12.5-20 LB-FT)

Lower shock absorber attaching nuts

this will damage the shaft surface finish and result in severe oil leakage.

5. Remove the washer and rubber insulator from the shock.

6. Remove the shock absorber from the vehicle.

NOTE: *The shocks are gas filled and will require an effort to collapse the shock in order to remove the shock absorber from the lower arm.*

To install:

7. Install a new washer and insulator on the upper shock absorber rod.

8. Position the upper part of the shock absorber into the shock tower opening in the body and push slowly on the lower part of the shock absorber until the mounting studs are lined up with the mounting holes in the lower suspension arm.

9. Install the new lower attaching nuts, but DO NOT torque at this time.

10. Install a new insulator, washer and nut on the top of the shock absorber. torque the nut to 19-27 ft. lbs.

11. Torque the two lower attaching nuts to 12-20 ft. lbs.

12. Install the tire and wheel assembly. Remove the car from the jackstands and lower to the ground.

MacPherson Strut

REMOVAL

Taurus/Sable Sedan

1. Raise and support the rear of the vehicle on jackstands. Remove the rear tires.

NOTE: *DO NOT raise or support the vehicle using the tension struts.*

2. Raise the rear lid and loosen (do not remove) the upper strut-to-body nuts.

3. Remove the brake differential control valve-to-control arm bolt. Using a wire, secure the control arm to the body to ensure proper support leaving 152mm clearance to aid in the strut removal.

4. Remove the brake hose-to-strut bracket clip and move the hose out of the way.

5. If equipped, remove the stabilizer bar U-bracket from the vehicle.

6. If equipped, remove the stabilizer bar-to-stabilizer link nut, washer and insulator, then separate the stabilizer bar from the link.

NOTE: *When removing the strut, be sure that the rear brake flex hose is not stretched or the steel brake tube is not bent.*

7. Remove the tension strut-to-spindle nut, washer and insulator. Move the spindle rearward to separate it from the tension strut.

8. Remove the shock strut-to-spindle pinch bolt. If necessary, use a medium pry bar, spread

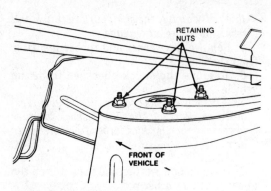

Upper strut mounting nuts

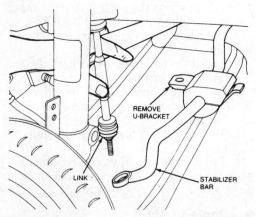

Stabilizer bar link

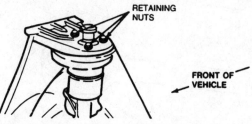

Three upper shock strut-to-body bolts—Continental

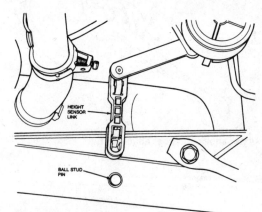

Disconnect height sensor—Continental

the strut-to-spindle pinch joint to remove the strut.

9. Lower the jackstand and separate the shock strut from the spindle.

10. Support the shock strut, then remove the upper strut-to-body nuts.

11. Remove the strut from the vehicle.

12. Remove the nut, washer and insulator attaching the link to the shock strut and remove the link.

Continental

1. Turn OFF the air suspension switch located in the left side of the luggage compartment. Check the illustration in the "Front MacPherson Strut" section in this chapter.

2. Disconnect the electrical connector for the dual dampening actuator located in the luggage compartment.

3. Loosen, but do not remove the three nuts retaining the upper shock strut-to-body.

4. Raise the rear of vehicle and support with jackstands.

5. Remove the wheel and tire assembly.

6. Disconnect the air line and electrical connector from the solenoid valve.

7. Disconnect the brake hose retainer, wire

retainer, and parking brake cable to the caliper.

8. Disconnect the height sensor link from the ball stud pin on the lower suspension arm.

9. Remove the caliper assembly from the spindle and hang out of the way by a wire affixed to the body. Do not hang from the brake hose or kink the parking brake hose.

10. Bleed the air spring as follows.

   a. Remove the solenoid clip

   b. Rotate the solenoid counterclockwise to the first stop.

   c. Pull the solenoid straight out slowly to the second stop to bleed the air from the system.

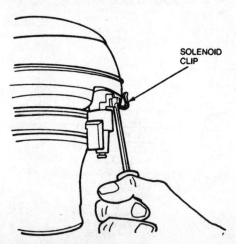

Remove the solenoid clip

CAUTION: *Do not fully release the solenoid until the air is completely bled from the air spring.*

   d. After the air is bleed out of the system, rotate the solenoid to the third stop and remove the solenoid.

11. Mark the position of the notch on the toe adjustment cam.

12. Remove the nut from the inboard bushing on the lower suspension arm.

13. Install a Torsion Spring Remover tool part No. T88P-5310-A or equivalent on the arm. Pry up the tool and arm using a ¾" drive ratchet to relieve the pressure on the pivot bolt.

14. Repeat step 13 for the opposite arm.

15. Remove the torsion spring, stabilizer U-

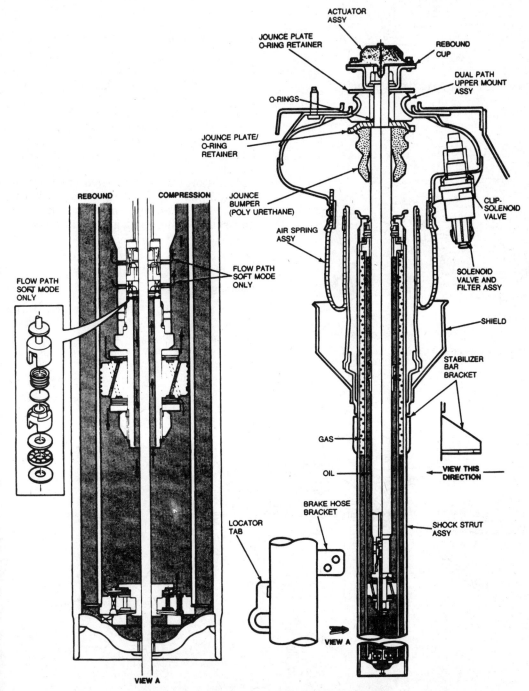

Shock strut and air spring assembly—Continental

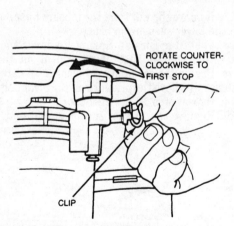

Rotate the solenoid to the first stop

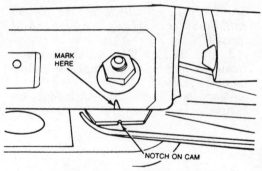

Mark the notch on the toe adjuster—Continental

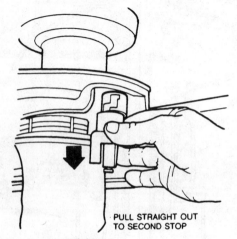

Full solenoid straight out

bracket from body, and nut and insulator attaching stabilizer bar-to-link. Separate the stabilizer bar from the link.

16. Remove the nut, washer, and insulator retaining the tension strut to the spindle.

17. Remove the shock strut-to-spindle pinch bolt and slightly spread the strut from the spindle.

18. Remove the spindle from the arms attached. From inside the luggage compartment, remove the three upper mount-to-body nuts, and remove the strut assembly from the vehicle.

INSTALLATION

Taurus/Sable Sedan

1. Position the stabilizer bar link in the shock strut bracket. Install the insulator, washer and nut. torque to 6-12 ft. lbs.

2. Install the strut assembly into position

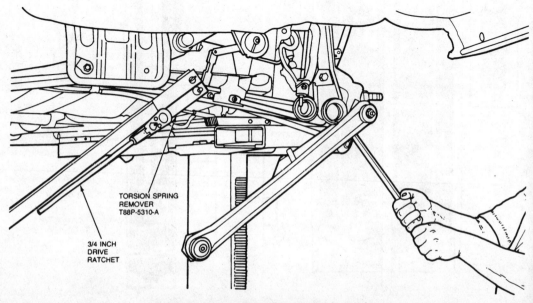

Releasing lower suspension arm torsion spring

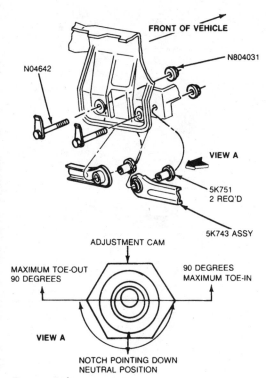

FRONT OF VEHICLE

N804031

N04642

VIEW A

5K751
2 REQ'D

5K743 ASSY

ADJUSTMENT CAM

MAXIMUM TOE-OUT
90 DEGREES

90 DEGREES
MAXIMUM TOE-IN

VIEW A

NOTCH POINTING DOWN
NEUTRAL POSITION

Rear control arm

and install the three top mount-to-shock tower nuts. Do Not tighten at this time.

3. Partially raise the vehicle. Install the shock strut into the spindle pinch bolt.

4. Install a new pinch bolt into the spindle and through the shock strut bracket. torque the nut to 52-81 ft. lbs.

5. Move the spindle rearward and install the tension strut into the spindle. Install the insulator, washer and nut on the tension strut. Torque the nut to 52-74 ft. lbs.

6. Position the link into the stabilizer bar. Install the insulator, washer and nut on the link. torque to 6-12 ft. lbs.

7. Position the stabilizer bar U-bracket on the body. Install the bolt and torque to 26-30 ft. lbs.

8. Install the brake hose to shock strut bracket.

9. Install the brake control differential valve on the control arm and remove the retaining wire.

10. Torque the two top mount-to-body nuts to 19-26 ft. lbs.

11. Install the wheel and tire assembly and lower the vehicle.

Continental

1. Install the solenoid valve on the air spring.

2. Install the strut assembly in the vehicle

and the three attaching nuts to the upper strut mount. Do not tighten at this time.

3. Connect the spindle, suspension arms, and tension strut to the shock strut.

4. Install the stabilizer bar with washer and retaining nut.

5. Install the stabilizer bar U-bracket to the body.

6. Install the torsion spring to the suspension arms.

7. Position the inboard bushing using the Torsion Spring Remover tool part No. T88P-5310-A or equivalent and install the bolt.

8. Repeat step 7 for the opposite arm.

9. Install the nut to the inboard bushing on the suspension arm. Do not tighten at this time.

10. Set the toe adjustment cam to the alignment mark previously made.

11. Install the caliper on the spindle, the height sensor link to the ball stud, all wire retainers, and parking brake cable retainers.

12. Install the brake hose retainer at the bracket, parking brake cable to the caliper, and connect the electrical and air connectors to the solenoid valve.

13. Install the wheel and tire assembly and lower the vehicle partially.

14. Torque the three upper mount-to-body retaining nuts to 19-26 ft. lbs.

CAUTION: *Lowering the vehicle with a deflated air spring may damage the air spring.*

15. Connect the electrical connectors to the dual dampening actuator in the luggage compartment and turn ON the air suspension switch.

16. The vehicle should have a 4-wheel alignment performed by a certified alignment technican.

STRUT OVERHAUL

The following procedure is performed with the strut assembly removed from the car. A MacPherson Strut compression tool is required for the disassembly of the strut, a cage type tool such as the No. D85P-7181-A or equivalent is required.

CAUTION: *Never attempt to disassemble the spring or top mount without first compressing the spring using the strut compressor tool No. D85P-7178-A or equivalent. If a strut spring compressor is not used, the assembly will fly apart by the force of the spring tension!*

NOTE: *Before compressing the spring, mark the location of the insulator to the top mount using a grease pencil.*

Taurus/Sable Sedan

1. Compress the spring with the coil spring compressor D85P-7178-A or equivalent.

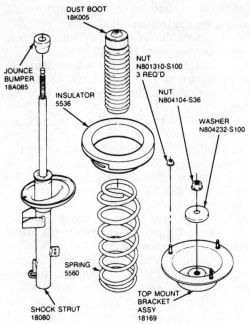

Exploded view of the rear Macpherson strut assembly

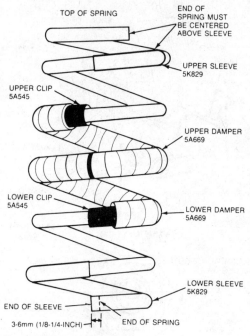

Rear spring components

2. Place a 10mm box wrench on top of the shock strut shaft and hold while removing the top shaft mounting nut with a 21mm 6-point crowfoot wrench and ratchet.

WARNING: *It is important that the mounting nut be turned and the rod held still to prevent fracture of the rod at the base of the hex.*

3. Loosen the spring compressor tool, then remove the top mounting bracket assembly, bearing plate assembly and spring.

To assemble:

Warning: *Ensure that the correct assembly sequence and proper positioning of the bearing and seat assembly are followed. The bearing and seat assembly is press-fit onto the up-*

per mount. The mount washers must be installed with orientation.

4. Inspect the spring to ensure the dampers, sleeves and clips are properly positioned.

5. Install the spring compressor tool No. D85P-7178-A or equivalent.

6. Install the spring, bearing plate assembly, lower washer and top mount bracket assembly.

7. Compress the spring with the coil spring compressor tool. Be certain the spring is properly located in the upper and lower spring seats and that the mount washers are oriented correctly.

8. Install the upper washer and nut on the shock strut shaft.

9. Place a 10mm box end wrench on the top of the shock strut shaft and hold while tightening the top shaft mounting nut with a 21mm 6-

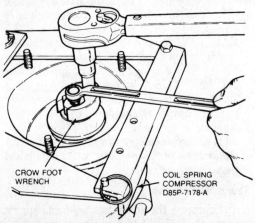

Removing the spring retaining nut

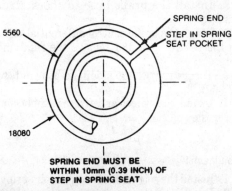

Spring seat dimensions

point crowfoot wrench and a ratchet. Torque the nut to 35-50 ft. lbs.

10. The strut assembly may now be installed in the vehicle. Refer to the "Rear MacPherson Strut" installation section in this chapter.

Continental

The shock strut and air spring is one unit and has to be replaced as such. The solenoid and actuator may be replaced as separate units. Refer to "Continental MacPherson Strut" removal and installation procedures to remove the solenoid and actuator.

Rear Control Arms

REMOVAL AND INSTALLATION

1. Raise and support the rear of the vehicle on jackstands. Remove the rear tires.

NOTE: *DO NOT raise or support the vehicle using the tension struts.*

2. From the left side of the rear control arm, disconnect the brake proportioning valve.

3. From the front of the control arms, disconnect the parking brake cable.

4. Remove the control arm-to-spindle bolt, washer and nut.

5. Remove the control arm-to-body nut/bolt and the arm from the vehicle.

NOTE: *When installing new control arms, be sure that the offset is facing upwards; the arms are stamped with "Bottom" on the lower edge. The flange edge of the right side rear arm stamping MUST face the front of the vehicle; the other three MUST face the rear of the vehicle.*

6. **To install:** position the arm (cam where required) at the center of the vehicle (insert the bolts but do not tighten) and reverse the removal procedures. Torque the control arm-to-spindle bolts to 52-74 ft. lbs. and the control arm-to-body nuts to 52-74 ft. lbs. Check the rear wheel alignment.

Stabilizer Bar/Link

REMOVAL AND INSTALLATION

1. Raise and support the rear of the vehicle on jackstands. Remove the rear tires.

NOTE: *DO NOT raise or support the vehicle using the tension struts.*

2. Remove the stabilizer bar-to-link (both sides) nuts, washers and insulators.

3. Remove the stabilizer bar U-bracket-to-body bolts and the stabilizer bar from the vehicle.

4. Remove the stabilizer link-to-shock strut bracket nut, washer and insulator; inspect the condition of the insulators and replace them if necessary.

5. **To install:** reverse the removal procedures. Torque the stabilizer link-to-shock strut bracket nut to 6-12 ft. lbs.; the stabilizer bar U-bracket-to-body bolts to 25-39 ft. lbs.; and the stabilizer bar-to-link nuts to 6-12 ft. lbs.

Rear Tension Strut

REMOVAL AND INSTALLATION

1. Raise and support the rear of the vehicle on jackstands. Remove the rear tires.

NOTE: *DO NOT raise or support the vehicle using the tension struts.*

2. Loosen, but DO NOT remove the upper shock strut-to-body nuts.

3. Remove the tension strut-to-spindle nut and the tension strut-to-body nut.

4. Move the spindle rearward and remove the tension strut from the vehicle.

NOTE: *The tension strut bushings at the front and the rear are different; the rear bushings have indentations in them.*

5. **To install:** use new tension strut washers/bushings and reverse the removal procedures. Torque the tension strut-to-spindle nut to 52-74 ft. lbs. and the tension strut-to-body bracket nut 52-74 ft. lbs.

Rear Wheel Alignment

Year	Model	Caster		Camber		Toe-in (in.)
		Range (deg)	Preferred Setting (deg)	Range (deg)	Preferred Setting (deg)	
1986	Taurus/Sable Station Wagon	—	—	−1⅝N−¼P	−¹⁵⁄₁₆N	¹⁄₁₆N−³⁄₁₆P
1987–89	Taurus/Sable Station Wagon	—	—	−1⁵⁄₁₆N−¹⁄₁₆P	−⅝N	¹⁄₁₆N−³⁄₁₆P
1986–89	Taurus/Sable Sedan	—	—	−1⅝N−¼P	−¹⁵⁄₁₆N	¹⁄₁₆N−³⁄₁₆P
1988–89	Continental	—	—	−2N−⅝P	−1⁵⁄₁₆N	¹⁄₃₂N−⁷⁄₃₂P

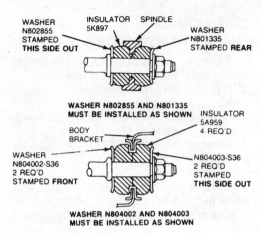

WASHER N802855 AND N801335
MUST BE INSTALLED AS SHOWN

WASHER N804002 AND N804003
MUST BE INSTALLED AS SHOWN

Tension strut bushings

Rear Wheel Bearings

CAUTION: *When servicing the rear wheel bearings, brake shoes contain asbestos which has been determined to be a cancer causing agent. Never clean the brake surfaces with compressed air! Avoid inhaling any dust from any brake surface! When cleaning brake surfaces, use a commercially available brake cleaning fluid.*

ADJUSTMENT

The following procedure should be performed whenever the wheel is excessively loose on the spindle or it does not rotate freely.

NOTE: *The rear wheel uses a tapered roller bearing which may feel loose when properly adjusted; this feel should be considered normal.*

1. Raise and support the rear of the vehicle on jackstands.

2. Remove the wheelcover or the ornament and nut covers. Remove the hub grease cap.

NOTE: *If the vehicle is equipped with styled steel or aluminum wheels, the wheels must be removed to remove the dust cover.*

3. Remove the cotter pin and the nut retainer.

4. Back off the hub nut one full turn.

5. While rotating the hub/drum assembly, torque the adjusting nut to 17-25 ft. lbs. Back off the adjusting nut ½ turn, then retighten it to 10-15 in.lbs.

6. Position the nut retainer over the adjusting nut so that the slots are in line with cotter pin hole (without rotating the adjusting nut).

7. Install the cotter pin and bend the ends around the retainer flange.

8. Check the hub rotation. If the hub rotates freely, install the grease cap. If not, check the bearings for damage and replace as necessary.

9. Install the wheel and tire assembly, then

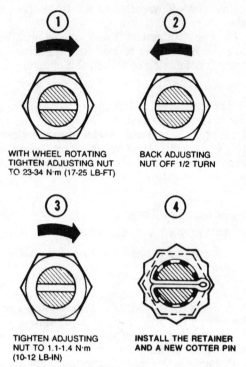

Rear wheel bearing adjustment

lower the vehicle and torque the lug nuts to 80-105 ft. lbs.

REMOVAL

CAUTION: *When servicing the rear wheel bearings, brake shoes contain asbestos which has been determined to be a cancer causing agent. Never clean the brake surfaces with compressed air! Avoid inhaling any dust from any brake surface! When cleaning brake surfaces, use a commercially available brake cleaning fluid.*

1. Raise the vehicle and support it safely. Remove the wheel from the hub and drum.

2. Remove the grease cap from the hub, making sure not to damage the cap. Remove the cotter pin, nut retainer, adjusting nut and keyed

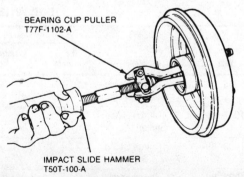

Removing bearing cups with slide hammer

flat washer from the spindle. Discard the cotter pin.

3. Pull the hub and drum assembly off the spindle being careful not to drop the outer bearing assembly. Remove the outer bearing assembly.

4. Using seal remover 1175-AC or equivalent, remove and discard the grease seal. Remove the inner bearing assembly from the hub.

5. Wipe all grease from the spindle and inside the hub. Cover the spindle with a clean cloth and vacuum all the loose dirt from the brake assembly. Carefully remove the cloth to prevent the dust from falling on the spindle.

6. Clean both bearing assemblies and cups using a suitable solvent. Inspect the bearing assemblies and cups for excessive wear, scratches, pits or other damage. Replace all worn or damaged parts as required.

NOTE: *Allow the solvent to dry before repacking bearings. DO NOT spin dry the bearing with compressed air! Replace bearing cups and races as an assembly, don't mix-match parts.*

7. If the cups (outer race) are to be replaced, remove them with a slide hammer T50T-100-A and Bearing Cup Puller T77F-1102-A or equivalent.

INSTALLATION

1. If the inner or outer bearing cups (outer race) were removed, install replacement cups using Drive Handle T80T-4000-W and Bearing Cup Replacers T73F-1217-A and T77F-1217-B or equivalent.

WARNING: *DO NOT use the cone and roller assembly to install the cup as this will cause damage to the bearing cup, and cone and roller assembly.*

Support the drum hub on a wood block to prevent damage. Be certain the cups (outer race) are properly seated in the hub.

2. Make sure all bearing and spindle surfaces are clean.

3. Using a bearing packer, pack the bearing assemblies with Multi-Purpose Long-Life Lu-

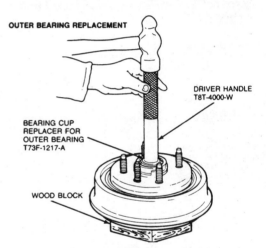

Driving the outer bearing cup into the hub

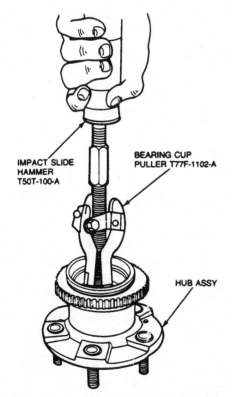

Removing bearing cups with slid hammer—Continental

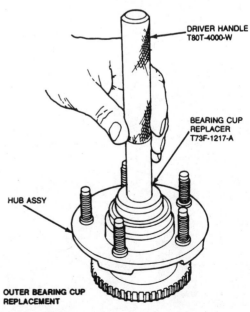

Driving outer bearing into hub—Continental

bricant C1AZ-19590-B or equivalent. If a bearing packer is not available, work in as much grease as possible between the rollers and cages. Grease the cup surfaces.

4. Place the inner bearing cone and roller assembly in the inner cup. Apply a light film of grease to the lips of a new grease seal and install the seal with Rear Hub Seal Replacer T56T-4676-B or equivalent. Be sure the retainer flange is seated all the way around.

5. Apply a light film of grease on the spindle shaft bearing surfaces.

6. Install the hub and drum assembly on the spindle. Keep the hub centered on the spindle to prevent damage to the grease seal and the spindle threads.

7. Install the outer bearing assembly and keyed flat washer on the spindle. Install the adjusting nut finger tight.

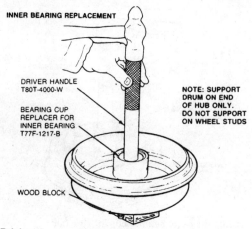

INNER BEARING REPLACEMENT

DRIVER HANDLE T80T-4000-W

BEARING CUP REPLACER FOR INNER BEARING T77F-1217-B

NOTE: SUPPORT DRUM ON END OF HUB ONLY. DO NOT SUPPORT ON WHEEL STUDS

WOOD BLOCK

Driving the inner bearing cup into the hub

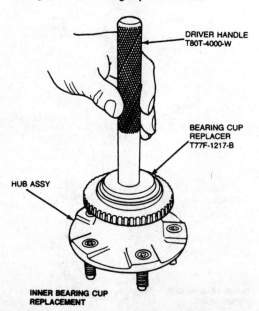

DRIVER HANDLE T80T-4000-W

BEARING CUP REPLACER T77F-1217-B

HUB ASSY

INNER BEARING CUP REPLACEMENT

Driving outer bearing cup into hub—Continental

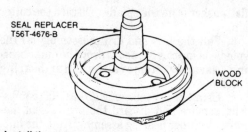

SEAL REPLACER T56T-4676-B

WOOD BLOCK

Install the rear grease seal

8. Follow the procedures shown under "Wheel Bearing Adjustment" above.

Rear End Alignment

Rear toe is adjustable but requires special equipment and procedures. If you suspect an alignment problem have it checked by a qualified repair shop.

STEERING

Your Taurus/Sable and Continental is equipped with power rack and pinion steering and gives you precise steering control. The increased use of aluminum and the use of a one piece valve sleeve make this a very light steering gear configuration.

Lightweight, sturdy bushings are used to mount the steering, these are long lasting and lend to quieter gear operation. The steering also features lifetime lubricated outer tie rod ends, eliminating the need for scheduled maintenance.

The steering column geometry uses a double universal joint shaft system and separate column support brackets for improved energy absorbing capabilities.

Steering Wheel

REMOVAL AND INSTALLATION

1. Disconnect the negative (−) battery cable. Position the steering wheel so that the wheels are in the straight-forward position.

2. From the rear of the steering wheel, remove the steering wheel-to-horn pad screws.

3. Disconnect the horn pad electrical connectors. If equipped with cruise control, disconnect the electrical connector from the slip ring terminal.

4. Remove and discard the steering wheel-to-steering column nut.

5. Firmly grasp the steering wheel and pull it from the steering column. **DO NOT use a steering wheel puller!**

To install:

6. Position the steering wheel on the end of the steering wheel shaft. Align the mark on the

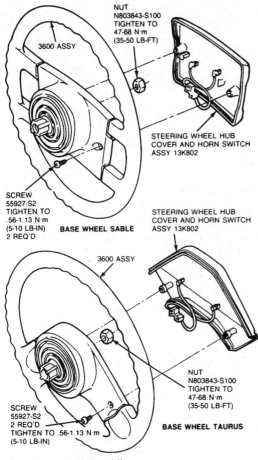

NUT
N803843-S100
TIGHTEN TO
47-68 N·m
(35-50 LB-FT)

3600 ASSY

STEERING WHEEL HUB
COVER AND HORN SWITCH
ASSY 13K802

SCREW
55927-S2
TIGHTEN TO
.56-1.13 N·m
(5-10 LB-IN)
2 REQ'D

BASE WHEEL SABLE

STEERING WHEEL HUB
COVER AND HORN SWITCH
ASSY 13K802

3600 ASSY

NUT
N803843-S100
TIGHTEN TO
47-68 N·m
(35-50 LB-FT)

SCREW
55927-S2
2 REQ'D
TIGHTEN TO .56-1.13 N·m
(5-10 LB-IN)

BASE WHEEL TAURUS

Steering wheel assemblies

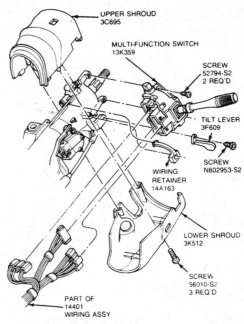

UPPER SHROUD
3C695

MULTI-FUNCTION SWITCH
13K359

SCREW
52794-S2
2 REQ'D

TILT LEVER
3F609

SCREW
N802953-S2

WIRING
RETAINER
14A163

LOWER SHROUD
3K512

SCREW
56010-S2
3 REQ'D

PART OF
14401
WIRING ASSY

Combination switch assembly

steering wheel with the mark on the shaft to ensure the straight-ahead steering wheel position corresponds with the straight-ahead position of the front wheels.

WARNING: *The combination switch lever must be in the neutral position before installing the steering wheel or damage to the switch cam may result!*

7. Install a new steering wheel nut. Torque the nut to 35-55 ft. lbs.

8. Connect negative (−) battery cable. Check the steering column for proper operation.

Combination Switch

The combination switch is mounted on the steering column and consists of the following switches: turn signal, cornering lights, hazard warning, headlight dimmer, headlight flash-to-pass, windshield washer and windshield wiper.

REMOVAL AND INSTALLATION

1. Refer to the "Steering Wheel Removal And Installation" procedures in this chapter and remove the steering wheel.

2. If equipped with a tilt-steering column, position the steering wheel in the lowest position and remove the tilt lever.

3. Remove the ignition lock cylinder from the steering column.

4. Remove the upper/lower shroud-to-steering column screws and the shrouds from the steering column.

5. Remove the electrical harness-to-steering column retainer and disconnect the electrical connectors from the steering column.

6. Remove the combination switch-to-steering column screws and the switch from the steering column.

7. **To install:** reverse the removal procedures. Torque the combination switch-to-steering column screws to 18-27 in. lbs., the shroud-to-steering column screws 6-10 in. lbs., the steering wheel-to-steering column nut to 35-55 ft. lbs., and the tilt lever-to-steering column screw to 6-8.5 in. lbs.

Ignition Lock/Switch

REMOVAL AND INSTALLATION

1. Disconnect the negative (−) battery cable.

2. Turn the ignition lock cylinder to the **RUN** position.

3. Using a 3mm diameter punch, insert it through the access hole in the bottom of the lower steering column shroud, depress the retaining pin and remove the ignition lock cylinder.

4. If equipped with a tilt steering column, re-

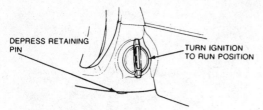

Ignition switch lock removal

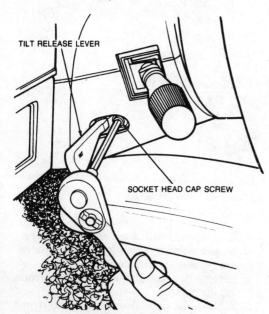

Tilt release lever removal

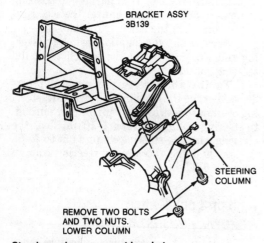

Steering column support bracket

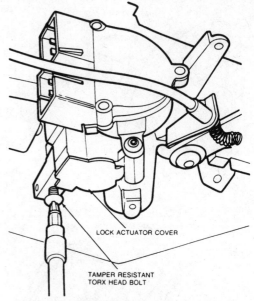

Lock actuator cover plate removal

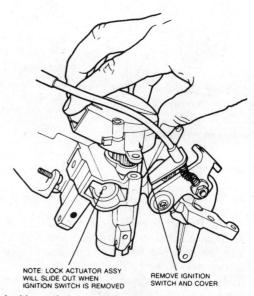

Ignition switch assembly removal

move the tilt lever-to-steering column screw and the tilt lever.

5. Remove the lower instrument panel cover Torx® screws and the cover.

6. Using a Phillips head screw driver, remove the upper/lower steering column shrouds.

7. Remove the steering column-to-support bracket nuts/bolts and lower the steering column.

8. Disconnect the electrical harness connector from the ignition switch.

9. Using the Torx® Driver tool No. D83L-2100-A, remove the ignition lock actuator cover plate Torx® head bolt and the cover plate.

10. Using the driver tool No. D83L-2100-A, or equivalent, remove the ignition switch-to-actuator assembly Torx® head bolts and the cover assembly from the actuator assembly, then slide the lock actuator from the actuator assembly.

11. **To install** the ignition switch-to-actuator assembly, perform the following procedures:

a. Position the ignition switch in the RUN position.

NOTE: *To position the ignition switch in the RUN position, turn the switch drive shaft fully clockwise to the START position and release it.*

b. Using a small ruler, insert the lock actuator into the actuator assembly to a depth of 11.75-13.25mm.

c. While holding the lock actuator at the proper depth, install the ignition switch.

d. Using new tamper-resistant Torx® head bolts, torque the ignition switch-to-actuator assembly bolts to 30-48 in. lbs.

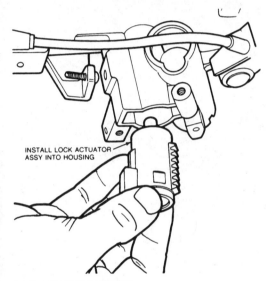

INSTALL LOCK ACTUATOR ASSY INTO HOUSING

Lock cylinder installation

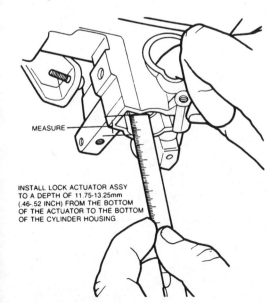

MEASURE

INSTALL LOCK ACTUATOR ASSY TO A DEPTH OF 11.75-13.25mm (.46-.52 INCH) FROM THE BOTTOM OF THE ACTUATOR TO THE BOTTOM OF THE CYLINDER HOUSING

Depth measurement

12. **To install** the lock cylinder, perform the following procedures:

a. While measuring the lock actuator, turn the ignition switch to the Lock position and install it, the depth should be 23.5-25.5mm; if this specification is not met, repeat the lock actuator installation.

b. Using a new tamper-resistant Torx® head bolt, torque the cover-to-lock actuator assembly bolt to 30-48 in. lbs.

13. Check the operation of the ignition lock cylinder; if the operation is OK, remove the ignition lock cylinder.

14. To complete the installation, reverse the removal procedures and reinstall the ignition lock cylinder. Torque the steering column support bracket-to-instrument panel nuts/bolts to 15-25 ft. lbs., the shroud-to-steering column screws to 6-10 in. lbs., and the tilt release lever-to-steering column screw to 6.5-8.5 ft. lbs.

Steering Column
REMOVAL AND INSTALLATION

NOTE: *All the steering column components are assembled with fasteners. They are designed with a thread locking system to prevent loosening due to vibrations associated with normal vehicle operations. The original fastener must be used in their respective locations.*

1. Disconnect the negative (−) battery cable.

2. Remove the steering column cover from the lower portion of the instrument panel by removing the four self-tapping screws.

3. Remove the tilt release lever and retaining screw.

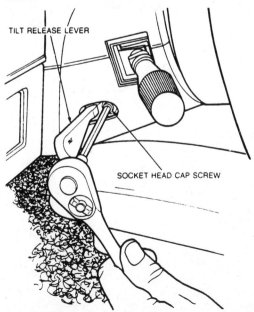

TILT RELEASE LEVER

SOCKET HEAD CAP SCREW

Tilt lever removal

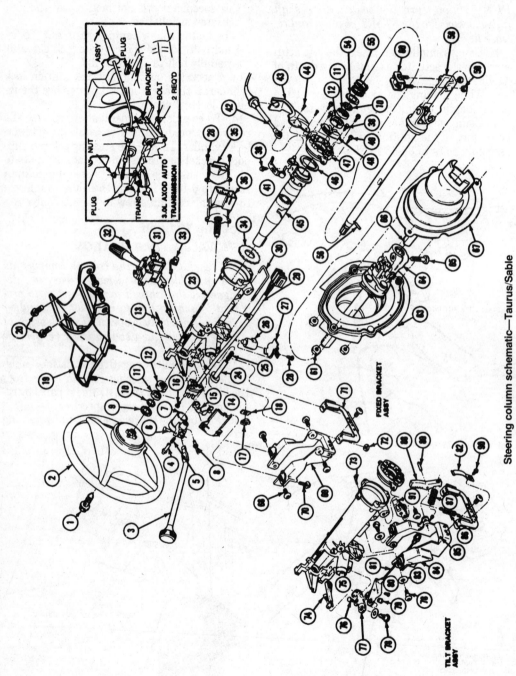

Steering column schematic—Taurus/Sable

4. Remove the ignition lock cylinder. Refer to the "Ignition Lock/Switch" removal and installation section in this chapter.

5. Remove the lower column shroud, horn pad from the steering wheel, and disconnect the PRNDL cable from the lock cylinder housing.

6. Remove the PRNDL cable from the retaining hook on the bottom of the lock cylinder housing.

7. Disconnect the speed control wiring from the main harness. Remove the multi-function switch wiring harness.

8. Remove the multi-switch.

9. Disconnect the key warning buzzer, ignition switch, and angular speed sensor wiring connectors.

10. Disconnect the steering shaft from the intermediate shaft by removing the two nuts and one U-clamp.

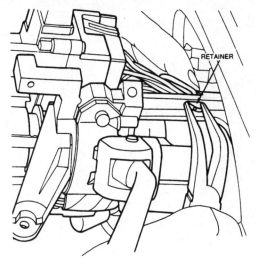

Multi-function switch harness removal

ITEM	PART NO.	DESCRIPTION	ITEM	PART NO.	DESCRIPTION
1	N805167	Bolt	45.	3K521	Tube and Bearing Assy.
2.	3600	Wheel	46.	3C708	Washer
3.	7202	Shift Lever	47.	3E738	Retainer
4.	7361	Plunger	48.	2B623	Parking Brake Rel. Switch
5.	7B071	Spring	49.	N804130	3 Screw Attach Retainer to Column
6.	7G357	Pin	54.	3D672	Spacer
7.	7228	Socket	55.	3C874	Spring
8.	380096	Rivet	56.	3E718	Pin
9.	3D640	Spacer	58.	3E729	Shaft Assy.
10.	3L539	Ring	59.	N620457	Nut — 2 Req'd.
11.	3517	Bearing Assy.	60.	3C088	Plate Assy.
12.	3518	Sleeve	61.	N804795-S2	Nut — 3 Req'd.
13.	3F643	Rivet Serviced	63.	3E735	Boot
*14.	3A673	Cover	64.		Intermediate Shaft
15.	3F643	Insert Serviced	65.	N803942	Bolt
16.	N804445-S2	Screw	66.		Steering Gear Input Shaft
17.	3F579	Retainer	67.	3E735	Boot
18.	3E700	Bearing	68.	N804086	Torx® Bolt — 5 Req'd. Also 2 Req'd.
19.		Not Used	69.	3E660	Fixed Bracket Assy.
20.	N605905	Bolt — 4 Req'd.	70.	N804140	Screw/Washer Assy. — 2 Req'd.
21.		Not Used	71.	3B632	Bracket
22.		Not Used	72.	N621939	Nut — 2 Req'd.
23.	3F643	Housing Assy.	73.	3F643	Pin Serviced
*24.	3F531	Key Release Knob	74.	N802953	Screw
*25.	3E696	Spring	75.	3F609	Handle Shank Assy.
26.	3E723	Actuator Assy.	76.	N804087	Bolt
27.	3E745	Actuator Cover	77.	3D544	Bracket
28.	N804089	Bolt — 3 Req'd.	78.	N804068	Bolt
29.	9C899	Brush Assy.	79.	N804084	Nut
*30.	3F528	Key Release Lever	80.	390345	Screw
31.	13K359	Turn Signal	81.	3F700	Bracket/Cable Assy.
32.	52794	Screw — 2 Req'd.	82.	3D655	Spring
33.	14A163	Wire Retainer	83.	N804085	Washer — 3 Req'd.
*34.	3K618	Bearing	. 84.	3E660	Tilt Bracket Assy.
35.		Not Used	85.	3D656	Bumper
36.	11572	Ignition Switch	86.	3D655	Spring
38.	N804444-S2	Screw — 3 Req'd.	87.	3D655	Spring
41.	2B624	Actuator	88.	3B662	Lever
42.	7E395	Cable	89.	N804090	Pin
43.	7E364	Bracket	90.	N804409	Screw — 7 Req'd.
44.	N605771	Screw — 2 Req'd.	91.	3F716	Locator

*Floor Shift only.

Multi-function switch harness removal

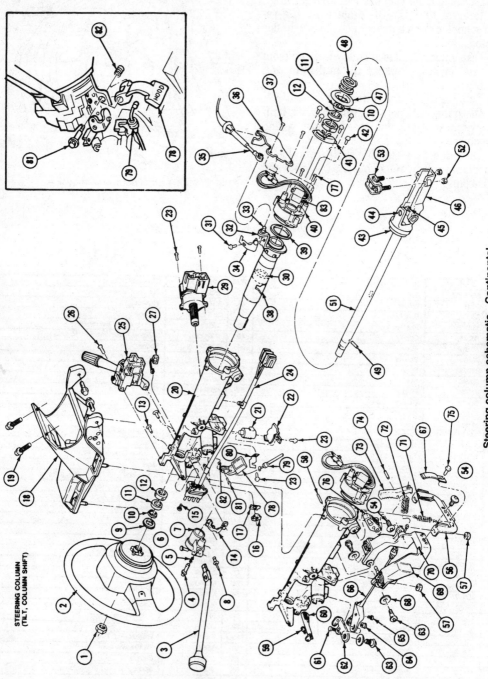

STEERING COLUMN
(TILT, COLUMN SHIFT)

Steering column schematic—Continental

11. Remove the vacuum hoses from the parking brake release switch and the hood release cable grommet from the column bracket.

12. Unbolt the four column assembly retaining nuts while supporting the column.

13. After removing the four nuts, the column should be supported on the rear two studs by push-on clips and must be lowered by forcing the column downward. These clips are factory assembly aids and do NOT have to be replaced.

14. Carefully lower the steering column assembly and remove it from the vehicle.

To install:

1. Carefully raise the steering column assembly into the vehicle and align the four mounting holes over the support studs.

2. Hand start the four retaining bolts, center the column, and torque the bolts to 15-25 ft. lbs.

3. Install the vacuum hoses to the parking brake release switch.

4. **Column Shift:** Attach the shift cable bracket to the lock cylinder housing and torque the screws to 5-7 ft. lbs. Snap the shift cable into selector pivot ball.

5. Apply grease to the vee-shaped steering shaft yoke. Connect the steering shaft to the intermediate shaft with the one U-clamp and two

ITEM	PART NO.	DESCRIPTION	ITEM	PART NO.	DESCRIPTION
1.	N803843	Nut	42.	N804130	Screw — Attach Retainer to Col., 3 Req'd.
2.	3600	Wheel	43.	3B250	Yoke
3.	7202	Shift Lever	44.	4869	Bearing
4.	7361	Plunger	45.	3D661	Pin
5.	7B071	Spring	46.	3A325	Yoke
6.	7G357	Pin	47.	3C131	Ring
7.	7228	Socket	48.	3C674	Spring
8.	380098	Rivet	49.	3E718	Pin
9.	3D640	Spacer	51.	3E729	Shaft Assy.
10.	3L539	Ring	52.	N620467	Nut, 2 Req'd.
11.	3517	Bearing Assy.	53.	3C088	Plate Assy.
12.	3518	Sleeve	54.	N804086	TORX® Bolt, 2 Req'd.
13.	N804096	Rivet, 2 Req'd.	56.	3B632	Bracket
14.	7A216	Insert	57.	N802811	Nut, 4 Req'd.
15.	N804445	Screw	58.	3E718	Pin
16.	3F579	Retainer	59.	N802953	Screw
17.	3E700	Bearing	60.	3F609	Handle Shank Assy.
18.	3B139	Support Bracket Assy.	61.	N804087	Bolt
19.	N801662	Bolt, 4 Req'd.	62.	3D544	Bracket
20.	3F643	Housing Assy.	63.	N804088	Bolt, 2 Req'd.
21.	3E723	Actuator Assy.	64.	N804084	Nut
22.	3E745	Actuator Cover	65.	390345	Screw
23.	N804089	Bolt, 4 Req'd.	66.	3F700	Bracket Cable Assy.
24.	9C899	Brush Assy.	67.	3D655	Spring
25.	13K359	Turn Signal	68.	N804085	Washer, 3 Req'd.
26.	52794	Screw, 2 Req'd.	69.	3B140	Tilt Bracket Assy.
27.	14A163	Wire Retainer	70.	3D656	Bumper
29.	11572	Ignition Switch Assy.	71.	3D655	Spring
30.	3K618	Bearing	72.	3D655	Spring
31.	N611133	Screw, 3 Req'd.	73.	3B662	Lever
32.	7302	Arm Assy.	74.	N804090	Pin
33.	7F031	Pin	75.	N804409	Screw, 7 Req'd.
34.	2B624	Actuator	76.	3F716	Locator
35.	7E395	Cable	77.	N611133	Screw, 2 Req'd.
36.	7E364	Bracket	78.	16B974	Hood Release Handle
37.	N605771	Screw, 2 Req'd.	79.	16C656	Hood Release Cable Assy.
38.	3K521	Tube and Bearing Assy.	80.	16C730	Hood Release Cable Bracket
39.	3C708	Washer	81.	N804924	Shoulder Bolt
40.	3E738	Retainer	82.	N-800354	Nut
41.	2B623	Parking Brake Rel. Sw.	83.	18B015	Sensor Assy.

Steering column schematic—Continental

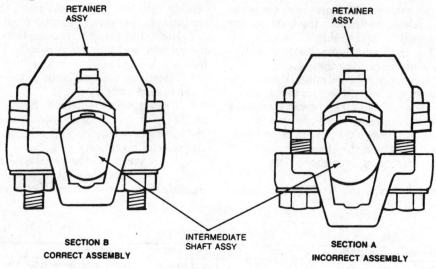

SECTION B
CORRECT ASSEMBLY

INTERMEDIATE
SHAFT ASSY

SECTION A
INCORRECT ASSEMBLY

Intermediate shaft positioning

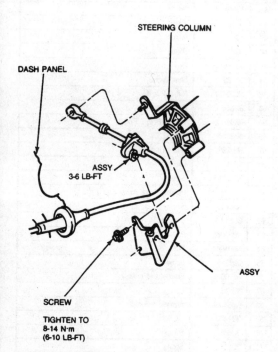

Shift cable instllation—Column shift

hex nuts. Make sure that the vee-angle of the intermediate shaft fits correctly into the vee-angle of the mating steering column yoke. Torque the nuts to 15-25 ft. lbs.

CAUTION: *If the vee-angle on the intermediate shaft is mis-aligned to the column yoke, and the retainer is tightened to specifications, the retainer plate will be bent, and then MUST be replaced.*

6. Install the main harness to the ignition switch, warning buzzer, and to the multi-func-

tion switch. Torque the multi-function attaching screws to 18-26 in. lbs.

7. Install the steering sensor wire connector to the sensor lead connector (Continental Only).

8. Connect the wiring harness to the steering wheel horn pad and install it to the steering column shaft.

9. Slip the hood release handle through the shroud and install the retaining screws.

10. Install the ignition lock cylinder. Install the steering column cover from the lower portion of the instrument panel with the four screws.

11. Install the tilt release lever with one socket head capscrews and torque to 6.5-9.0 ft. lbs.

12. Connect the battery negative (−) cable.

13. Check the steering column functions and adjust if necessary.

Tie Rod End

REMOVAL AND INSTALLATION

1. Raise and support the front of the vehicle on jackstands.

2. Remove the discard the cotter pin and the nut from the tie rod end ball stud.

3. Using the tie rod remover tool No. TOOL-3290-C, or equivalent, separate the tie rod end from the steering knuckle.

4. While holding the tie rod end, loosen the tie rod jam nut.

5. Note the depth of the tie rod end-to-tie rod, then remove the tie rod end from the tie rod.

6. **To install:** reverse the removal procedures. Torque the tie rod-to-steering knuckle nut to 36 ft. lbs. and the tie rod end-to-tie rod

nut to 35-50 ft. lbs. Check and/or adjust the toe-in. Have a certified alignment mechanic perform the alignment adjustments.

Power Steering Gear

The Taurus/Sable power steering gear is an integral rack and pinion type where fluid is pumped into the steering gear assembly under high pressure. The gear and valve housing are incorporated into one cast aluminum die casting. When the steering is turned, resistance of the vehicle cause a torsion bar to deflect. This deflection changes the position of the valve spool and sleeve ports, directing fluid to the appropriate end of the power cylinder. When the stops applying steering force, the valve is forced back to a centered position by the torsion bar.

The Continental is equipped with basically the same power steering gear as the Taurus/Sable. The difference is that the Continental is equipped with a Variable Assist Power Steering (VAPS) system. The system consists of a microprocessor-based module, power rack and pinion assembly, an actuator valve assembly, and high pressure pump and hoses. When the vehicle is traveling at a slow speed, the fluid flow is pumped into the primary circuit by an electri-cally controlled actuator valve. When the speed increases, the actuator valve gradually opens increasing the amount of fluid to the secondary circuit which provides increased steering control.

REMOVAL AND INSTALLATION

Taurus/Sable

1. From inside the vehicle, remove the steering shaft weather boot-to-dash panel nuts.
2. Remove the intermediate shaft-to-steering column shaft bolts and set the weather boot aside. Remove the steering gear input shaft pinch bolt and the intermediate shaft.
3. Raise and support the front of the vehicle on jackstands.
4. Remove the left front wheel and the heat shield, then cut the bundling strap lines from the steering gear.
5. Remove the tie rod ends from the steering knuckles. Refer to the "Tie Rod End" removal and installation procedures in this section.
6. Position a drain pan under the vehicle, then disconnect the pressure and return hoses from the steering gear and drain the fluid.
NOTE: *The pressure and return hoses are located on the front of the valve housing.*

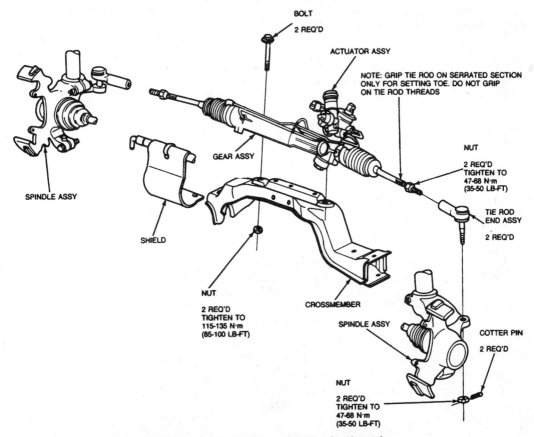

Power rack and pinion assembly—Continental

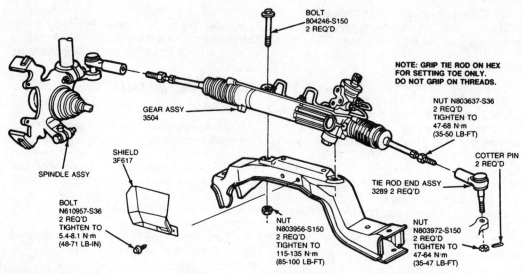

Power rack and pinion assembly

7. Remove the steering gear-to-chassis nuts.
NOTE: *The steering gear bolts are pressed into the housing; no attempt should be made to remove them.*

8. While pushing the weather boot into the vehicle, lift the steering gear from the mounting holes, rotate the gear (so that the input shaft will pass between the brake booster and the floorpan) and work it through the left fender apron opening.
NOTE: *If the steering gear appears to be stuck, check the right side tie rod to ensure that it is not caught on anything.*

To install:
1. To install, use new plastic seals on the hydraulic line fittings.
2. Insert the steering gear through the left fender apron. Rotate the input shaft forward to completely clear the fender apron opening.
3. Align the steering gear bolts in the bolt holes and torque to 84-100 ft. lbs.
4. Lower the vehicle, install the hydraulic pressure and return lines, and torque the pressure line to 20-25 ft. lbs.
5. Secure the pressure and return lines to the transfer tube by a bundling strap or equiva-

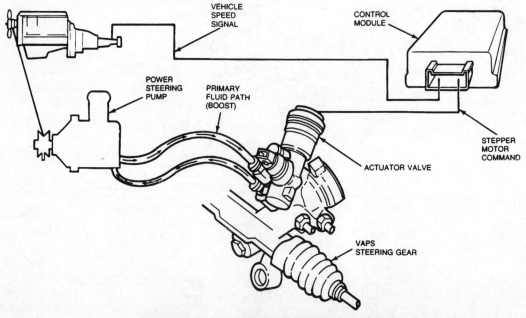

Variable assist power steering (VAPS) system—Continental

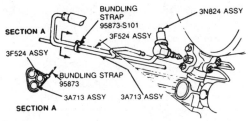

Steering gear pressure and return lines

lent. Check the steering gear pressure and return line illustration in the removal procedure.

6. Install the heat shield, tie rod end-to-spin-
dles, and torque the castle nuts to 35 ft. lbs. Install and bent over a new cotter pin.

7. Install the wheel and lower vehicle.

8. From inside the vehicle, pull the weather
boot end out of the vehicle and install it over the
valve housing.

9. Install the intermediate shaft-to-input
shaft and install the weather boot to floorpan.

10. Install the intermediate shaft to the steering column shaft.

11. Fill the power steering system with Type
F automatic transmission fluid. Start the engine and check for leaks.

12. Bleed the system by turning the steering
from stop-right to stop-left at least three times
and then check fluid level again.

13. Have a qualified wheel alignment technician set the toe-in.

ADJUSTMENT

The power steering gear preload adjustment
must be performed with the steering gear removed from the vehicle.

1. Refer to the "Power Steering Gear" removal And installation procedures in this chapter and remove the power steering gear from
the vehicle.

2. Mount the steering gear in a holding fixture tool No. T57L-500-B, or equivalent.

NOTE: *If the steering gear mounting holes
in the holding fixture are too small, drill the
holes larger using a ⁹⁄₁₆" drill bit.*

3. DO NOT remove the external pressure
lines from the steering gear unless they are
leaking or damaged. If they are removed, they
must be replaced with new ones.

4. Using the pinion shaft torque adjuster
tool No. T86P-3504-K, or equivalent, position it
on the input shaft and rotate the shaft (twice),
from lock-to-lock, to drain the power steering
fluid.

5. Using the pinion housing yoke locknut
wrench tool No. T86P-3504-E, or equivalent,
loosen the yoke plug locknut and the yoke plug.

6. Position the steering gear in the center of
it's travel and torque the yoke plug to 45-50 in.

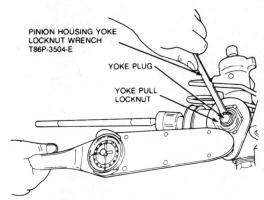

Loosening the yoke plug locknut

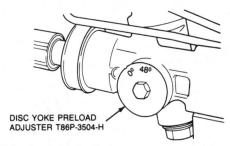

Disk yoke preload adjuster

lbs., be sure to clean the yoke plug threads before torquing.

7. Mark the position of the 0 degree mark on
the steering gear housing. Using the disc-yoke
preload adjuster tool No. T86P-3504-H, back
off the adjuster to align the 48° mark with the
0° mark.

8. Using the pinion housing yoke locknut
wrench to hold the yoke plug, torque the yoke
plug locknut to 40-50 ft. lbs.

NOTE: *When torquing the yoke plug locknut, DO NOT allow the yoke plug to move.*

9. Install the steering gear. Refill the power
steering reservoir, bleed the system and check
for leaks.

Power Steering Pump

REMOVAL AND INSTALLATION

2.5L Engine

1. Disconnect the negative (–) battery cable.

2. Remove the radiator overflow bottle to
gain access to the three bolts attaching the pulley to the pump.

3. Mark the pulley-to-hub positions with
grease pencil for reassembly to maintain
balance.

4. Using a ½" drive ratchet, insert it into the
square hole of the drive belt tensioner pulley,
rotate the pulley clockwise and remove the
drive belt.

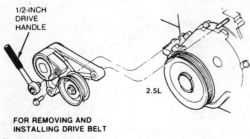

FOR REMOVING AND
INSTALLING DRIVE BELT

Removing drive belt

5. Remove the three bolts from the pulley.

3. Position a drain pan under the vehicle, disconnect the power steering pump fluid lines and drain the fluid into the pan.

4. Using the hub puller tool No. T69L-10300-B, or equivalent, remove the pulley from the power steering pump.

5. Remove the pump-to-bracket bolts and the pump from the vehicle.

6. **To install:** reverse the removal procedures.

7. Using the steering pump pulley replacer tool No. T65P-3A733-C, or equivalent, press the pump pulley onto the shaft so that the pulley is flush with the pump shaft within ± 0.25mm.

NOTE: *When installing the pump pulley, the small diameter tool threads must be fully engaged in the pump shaft.*

8. Fill the pump reservoir with power steering fluid, bleed the system and check for leaks.

3.0L Engine

1. Disconnect the negative (–) battery cable.

2. Loosen the idler pulley and remove the power steering belt.

3. Remove the pulley from the pump hub and the return line from the pump.

4. Back off the pressure line nut until the line separates from the pump.

5. Remove the pump-to-bracket bolts and the pump from the vehicle.

6. **To install:** reverse the removal procedures. Torque the pump-to-bracket bolts to 30-45 ft. lbs. Refill the power steering pump reservoir, bleed the system and check for leaks.

3.8L Engine

1. Disconnect the negative (–) battery cable.

2. Loosen the tensioner assembly, rotate the pulley clockwise, and remove the belt from the power steering pump.

3. Position a drain pan under pump and disconnect the pressure and return lines.

4. Remove the pulley from the shaft using a Steering Pump Pulley tool No. T69L-10300-B or equivalent.

5. Remove the three bolts retaining the pump-to-bracket and remove the pump.

6. **To install:** reverse the removal procedures. Torque the pump-to-bracket bolts to 30-45 ft. lbs. Refill the power steering pump reservoir, bleed the system and check for leaks.

NOTE: *The small diameter threads must be fully engaged on the pump shaft before pressing on the pulley. Hold the screw head and turn the nut to install the pulley. Install the pulley face flush with the pump shaft within ± 0.25mm.*

3.0L SHO Engine

1. Disconnect the negative (–) battery cable.

2. Remove the engine damper strut and power steering belt.

3. Raise the vehicle and support with jackstands.

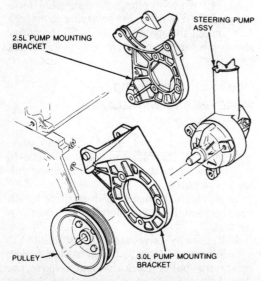

STEERING PUMP ASSY

2.5L PUMP MOUNTING BRACKET

PULLEY

3.0L PUMP MOUNTING BRACKET

Power steering pump mounting brackets

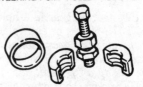

Cll STEERING PUMP PULLEY REMOVER T69L-10300-B

35.05mm (1 3/8 INCH) HUB DIAMETER PULLEYS

Cll STEERING PUMP PULLEY
REPLACER T65P-3A733-C

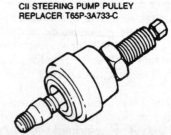

35.05mm (1 3/8 INCH) HUB DIAMETR PULLEYS

Steering pump pulley tools

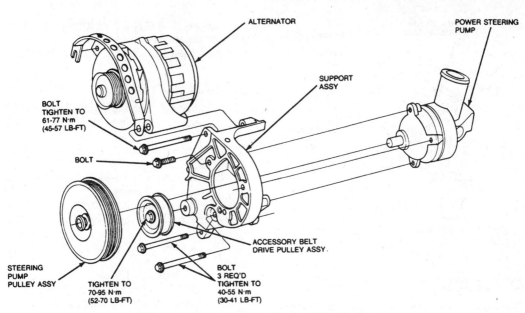

ALTERNATOR

POWER STEERING PUMP

SUPPORT ASSY

BOLT TIGHTEN TO 61-77 N·m (45-57 LB-FT)

BOLT

ACCESSORY BELT DRIVE PULLEY ASSY

STEERING PUMP PULLEY ASSY

TIGHTEN TO 70-95 N·m (52-70 LB-FT)

BOLT 3 REQ'D TIGHTEN TO 40-55 N·m (30-41 LB-FT)

Power steering pump mounting bracket—Continental

4. Remove the right front wheel and tire assembly.

5. Position a jack under the engine and remove the right rear engine mount as outlined below.

    a. Remove the lower damper bolt from the right side of the engine.

    b. Place a jack and wood block in a suitable place under the engine.

    c. Remove the nuts attaching roll damper-to-engine mount and remove the damper.

    d. Raise the engine with a jack to unload the insulator (engine mount).

    e. Remove the two through bolts and remove the insulator.

6. Remove the power steering pump pulley.

7. Position a suitable drain pan under the pump and remove the pressure and return lines from the pump.

8. Remove the four pump retaining bolts (three in front, one in rear) and remove the pump.

To install:

1. Position the pump and install the four retaining bolts.

2. Install the pressure and return lines and the pulley to the pump.

3. Install the right rear engine mount and remove the jack.

    a. Attach the insulator-to-engine bracket with the two through bolts. Torque the bolts to 40-55 ft. lbs.

    b. Lower the engine down onto the frame.

    c. Install the nuts attaching the right front and right rear insulators to the frame. Torque the bolts to 50-70 ft. lbs.

    d. Install the roll damper and torque the nuts to 40-55 ft. lbs.

    e. Remove the jack and lower the vehicle.

    f. Install the bolt attaching the right engine damper-to-engine and torque the bolts to 40-55 ft. lbs.

4. Install the right front wheel and tire assembly.

5. Lower the vehicle and install the accessory drive belt over the pulleys.

6. Install the engine damper strut.

7. Connect the negative (−) battery cable. Fill the power steering reservoir with Type F or Dexron®II automatic transmission fluid.

8. Bleed the system by turning the steering from stop-right to stop-left at least three times and then check fluid level again.

9. Start the engine and check for fluid leaks.

Remote Power Steering Reservoir (3.0L SHO only)

REMOVAL AND INSTALLATION

1. Loosen the inlet and outlet hose clamps.

2. Remove the hoses and allow the fluid to drain into a suitable drain pan.

3. Remove the reservoir from the attachments.

4. **To install:** position the reservoir onto the attachments, install the hoses and torque the clamps to 13-17 in. lbs.

5. Fill the reservoir to the proper level with Type F or Dexron®II.

6. Bleed the system by turning the steering

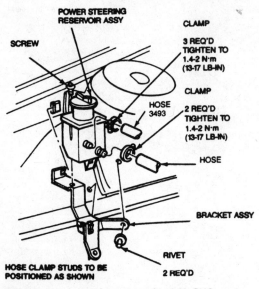

POWER STEERING
RESERVOIR ASSY

SCREW

CLAMP

3 REQ'D
TIGHTEN TO
1.4-2 N·m
(13-17 LB-IN)

CLAMP

HOSE
3493

2 REQ'D
TIGHTEN TO
1.4-2 N·m
(13-17 LB-IN)

HOSE

BRACKET ASSY

RIVET

HOSE CLAMP STUDS TO BE
POSITIONED AS SHOWN

2 REQ'D

Remote power steering reservoir—3.0L SHO engine
(only)

from stop-right to stop-left at least three times
and then check fluid level again.

7. Start the engine and check for leaks.

SYSTEM BLEEDING

1. Using power steering pump fluid, fill the
power steering reservoir to the maximum fill
line.

2. Run the engine until it reaches normal operating temperature.

3. Turn the steering wheel from the left-stop
to right-stop several times.

NOTE: *When turning the steering wheel, do
not hold it in the far left or right positions too
long.*

4. Check and/or refill the power steering
system.

5. If air remains in the system, it must be
purged by performing the following procedures:

   a. Remove the power steering pump dipstick cap assembly.

Troubleshooting Basic Steering and Suspension Problems

Problem	Cause	Solution
Hard steering (steering wheel is hard to turn)	• Low or uneven tire pressure • Loose power steering pump drive belt • Low or incorrect power steering fluid • Incorrect front end alignment • Defective power steering pump • Bent or poorly lubricated front end parts	• Inflate tires to correct pressure • Adjust belt • Add fluid as necessary • Have front end alignment checked/ adjusted • Check pump • Lubricate and/or replace defective parts
Loose steering (too much play in the steering wheel)	• Loose wheel bearings • Loose or worn steering linkage • Faulty shocks • Worn ball joints	• Adjust wheel bearings • Replace worn parts • Replace shocks • Replace ball joints
Car veers or wanders (car pulls to one side with hands off the steering wheel)	• Incorrect tire pressure • Improper front end alignment • Loose wheel bearings • Loose or bent front end components • Faulty shocks	• Inflate tires to correct pressure • Have front end alignment checked/ adjusted • Adjust wheel bearings • Replace worn components • Replace shocks
Wheel oscillation or vibration transmitted through steering wheel	• Improper tire pressures • Tires out of balance • Loose wheel bearings • Improper front end alignment • Worn or bent front end components	• Inflate tires to correct pressure • Have tires balanced • Adjust wheel bearings • Have front end alignment checked/ adjusted • Replace worn parts
Uneven tire wear	• Incorrect tire pressure • Front end out of alignment • Tires out of balance	• Inflate tires to correct pressure • Have front end alignment checked/ adjusted • Have tires balanced

b. Using type F automatic transmission fluid, fill the reservoir to the COLD FULL mark on the pump dipstick.

c. Disconnect the ignition coil wire. Raise and support the front of the vehicle on jackstands.

d. Using the starter motor, crank the engine, then check the fluid level; do not turn the steering wheel at this time.

e. Check and/or refill the pump reservoir. Using the starter motor, crank the engine and cycle the steering wheel from lock-to-lock, then recheck the fluid level.

f. Using the vacuum tester tool No. 021-00014, or equivalent, press the rubber stopper into the pump reservoir. Install the coil wire and start the engine.

g. Apply 15 in.Hg to the pump reservoir for at least three minutes (engine idling).

NOTE: *As the air is being purged from the system, the vacuum will fall off; be sure to maintain adequate vacuum with the vacuum source.*

h. Release and remove the vacuum source. Check and/or refill the power steering pump reservoir to the Cold Full mark.

i. With the engine idling, connect 15 in.Hg to the pump reservoir. Every 30 seconds for approx. 5 min., turn the steering wheel from lock-to-lock; DO NOT hold the steering wheel in the lock position.

NOTE: *When bleeding the power steering system, be sure to maintain adequate vacuum.*

j. Release the vacuum, remove the vacuum equipment and add fluid, if necessary.

k. Start the engine, cycle the steering wheel and check for oil leaks.

Troubleshooting the Steering Column

Problem	Cause	Solution
Will not lock	• Lockbolt spring broken or defective	• Replace lock bolt spring
High effort (required to turn ignition key and lock cylinder)	• Lock cylinder defective	• Replace lock cylinder
	• Ignition switch defective	• Replace ignition switch
	• Rack preload spring broken or deformed	• Replace preload spring
	• Burr on lock sector, lock rack, housing, support or remote rod coupling	• Remove burr
	• Bent sector shaft	• Replace shaft
	• Defective lock rack	• Replace lock rack
	• Remote rod bent, deformed	• Replace rod
	• Ignition switch mounting bracket bent	• Straighten or replace
	• Distorted coupling slot in lock rack (tilt column)	• Replace lock rack
Will stick in "start"	• Remote rod deformed	• Straighten or replace
	• Ignition switch mounting bracket bent	• Straighten or replace
Key cannot be removed in "off-lock"	• Ignition switch is not adjusted correctly	• Adjust switch
	• Defective lock cylinder	• Replace lock cylinder
Lock cylinder can be removed without depressing retainer	• Lock cylinder with defective retainer	• Replace lock cylinder
	• Burr over retainer slot in housing cover or on cylinder retainer	• Remove burr
High effort on lock cylinder between "off" and "off-lock"	• Distorted lock rack	• Replace lock rack
	• Burr on tang of shift gate (automatic column)	• Remove burr
	• Gearshift linkage not adjusted	• Adjust linkage
Noise in column	• One click when in "off-lock" position and the steering wheel is moved (all except automatic column)	• Normal—lock bolt is seating
	• Coupling bolts not tightened	• Tighten pinch bolts
	• Lack of grease on bearings or bearing surfaces	• Lubricate with chassis grease

Troubleshooting the Steering Column (cont.)

Problem	Cause	Solution
Noise in column (cont.)	• Upper shaft bearing worn or broken	• Replace bearing assembly
	• Lower shaft bearing worn or broken	• Replace bearing. Check shaft and replace if scored.
	• Column not correctly aligned	• Align column
	• Coupling pulled apart	• Replace coupling
	• Broken coupling lower joint	• Repair or replace joint and align column
	• Steering shaft snap ring not seated	• Replace ring. Check for proper seating in groove.
	• Shroud loose on shift bowl. Housing loose on jacket—will be noticed with ignition in "off-lock" and when torque is applied to steering wheel.	• Position shroud over lugs on shift bowl. Tighten mounting screws.
High steering shaft effort	• Column misaligned	• Align column
	• Defective upper or lower bearing	• Replace as required
	• Tight steering shaft universal joint	• Repair or replace
	• Flash on I.D. of shift tube at plastic joint (tilt column only)	• Replace shift tube
	• Upper or lower bearing seized	• Replace bearings
Lash in mounted column assembly	• Column mounting bracket bolts loose	• Tighten bolts
	• Broken weld nuts on column jacket	• Replace column jacket
	• Column capsule bracket sheared	• Replace bracket assembly
Lash in mounted column assembly (cont.)	• Column bracket to column jacket mounting bolts loose	• Tighten to specified torque
	• Loose lock shoes in housing (tilt column only)	• Replace shoes
	• Loose pivot pins (tilt column only)	• Replace pivot pins and support
	• Loose lock shoe pin (tilt column only)	• Replace pin and housing
	• Loose support screws (tilt column only)	• Tighten screws
Housing loose (tilt column only)	• Excessive clearance between holes in support or housing and pivot pin diameters	• Replace pivot pins and support
	• Housing support-screws loose	• Tighten screws
Steering wheel loose—every other tilt position (tilt column only)	• Loose fit between lock shoe and lock shoe pivot pin	• Replace lock shoes and pivot pin
Steering column not locking in any tilt position (tilt column only)	• Lock shoe seized on pivot pin	• Replace lock shoes and pin
	• Lock shoe grooves have burrs or are filled with foreign material	• Clean or replace lock shoes
	• Lock shoe springs weak or broken	• Replace springs
Noise when tilting column (tilt column only)	• Upper tilt bumpers worn	• Replace tilt bumper
	• Tilt spring rubbing in housing	• Lubricate with chassis grease
One click when in "off-lock" position and the steering wheel is moved	• Seating of lock bolt	• None. Click is normal characteristic sound produced by lock bolt as it seats.
High shift effort (automatic and tilt column only)	• Column not correctly aligned	• Align column
	• Lower bearing not aligned correctly	• Assemble correctly
	• Lack of grease on seal or lower bearing areas	• Lubricate with chassis grease
Improper transmission shifting—automatic and tilt column only	• Sheared shift tube joint	• Replace shift tube
	• Improper transmission gearshift linkage adjustment	• Adjust linkage
	• Loose lower shift lever	• Replace shift tube

Troubleshooting the Turn Signal Switch

Problem	Cause	Solution
Turn signal will not cancel	• Loose switch mounting screws • Switch or anchor bosses broken • Broken, missing or out of position detent, or cancelling spring	• Tighten screws • Replace switch • Reposition springs or replace switch as required
Turn signal difficult to operate	• Turn signal lever loose • Switch yoke broken or distorted • Loose or misplaced springs • Foreign parts and/or materials in switch • Switch mounted loosely	• Tighten mounting screws • Replace switch • Reposition springs or replace switch • Remove foreign parts and/or material • Tighten mounting screws
Turn signal will not indicate lane change	• Broken lane change pressure pad or spring hanger • Broken, missing or misplaced lane change spring • Jammed wires	• Replace switch • Replace or reposition as required • Loosen mounting screws, reposition wires and retighten screws
Turn signal will not stay in turn position	• Foreign material or loose parts impeding movement of switch yoke • Defective switch	• Remove material and/or parts • Replace switch
Hazard switch cannot be pulled out	• Foreign material between hazard support cancelling leg and yoke	• Remove foreign material. No foreign material impeding function of hazard switch—replace turn signal switch.
No turn signal lights	• Inoperative turn signal flasher • Defective or blown fuse • Loose chassis to column harness connector • Disconnect column to chassis connector. Connect new switch to chassis and operate switch by hand. If vehicle lights now operate normally, signal switch is inoperative • If vehicle lights do not operate, check chassis wiring for opens, grounds, etc.	• Replace turn signal flasher • Replace fuse • Connect securely • Replace signal switch • Repair chassis wiring as required
Instrument panel turn indicator lights on but not flashing	• Burned out or damaged front or rear turn signal bulb • If vehicle lights do not operate, check light sockets for high resistance connections, the chassis wiring for opens, grounds, etc. • Inoperative flasher • Loose chassis to column harness connection • Inoperative turn signal switch • To determine if turn signal switch is defective, substitute new switch into circuit and operate switch by hand. If the vehicle's lights operate normally, signal switch is inoperative.	• Replace bulb • Repair chassis wiring as required • Replace flasher • Connect securely • Replace turn signal switch • Replace turn signal switch
Stop light not on when turn indicated	• Loose column to chassis connection • Disconnect column to chassis connector. Connect new switch into system without removing old.	• Connect securely • Replace signal switch

Troubleshooting the Turn Signal Switch (cont.)

Problem	Cause	Solution
Stop light not on when turn indicated (cont.)	Operate switch by hand. If brake lights work with switch in the turn position, signal switch is defective.	
	• If brake lights do not work, check connector to stop light sockets for grounds, opens, etc.	• Repair connector to stop light circuits using service manual as guide
Turn indicator panel lights not flashing	• Burned out bulbs • High resistance to ground at bulb socket • Opens, ground in wiring harness from front turn signal bulb socket to indicator lights	• Replace bulbs • Replace socket • Locate and repair as required
Turn signal lights flash very slowly	• High resistance ground at light sockets • Incorrect capacity turn signal flasher or bulb • If flashing rate is still extremely slow, check chassis wiring harness from the connector to light sockets for high resistance • Loose chassis to column harness connection • Disconnect column to chassis connector. Connect new switch into system without removing old. Operate switch by hand. If flashing occurs at normal rate, the signal switch is defective.	• Repair high resistance grounds at light sockets • Replace turn signal flasher or bulb • Locate and repair as required • Connect securely • Replace turn signal switch
Hazard signal lights will not flash—turn signal functions normally	• Blow fuse • Inoperative hazard warning flasher • Loose chassis-to-column harness connection • Disconnect column to chassis connector. Connect new switch into system without removing old. Depress the hazard warning lights. If they now work normally, turn signal switch is defective. • If lights do not flash, check wiring harness "K" lead for open between hazard flasher and connector. If open, fuse block is defective	• Replace fuse • Replace hazard warning flasher in fuse panel • Conect securely • Replace turn signal switch • Repair or replace brown wire or connector as required

Troubleshooting the Ignition Switch

Problem	Cause	Solution
Ignition switch electrically inoperative	• Loose or defective switch connector • Feed wire open (fusible link) • Defective ignition switch	• Tighten or replace connector • Repair or replace • Replace ignition switch
Engine will not crank	• Ignition switch not adjusted properly	• Adjust switch
Ignition switch wil not actuate mechanically	• Defective ignition switch • Defective lock sector • Defective remote rod	• Replace switch • Replace lock sector • Replace remote rod
Ignition switch cannot be adjusted correctly	• Remote rod deformed	• Repair, straighten or replace

Troubleshooting the Power Steering Gear

Problem	Cause	Solution
Hissing noise in steering gear	• There is some noise in all power steering systems. One of the most common is a hissing sound most evident at standstill parking. There is no relationship between this noise and performance of the steering. Hiss may be expected when steering wheel is at end of travel or when slowly turning at standstill.	• Slight hiss is normal and in no way affects steering. Do not replace valve unless hiss is extremely objectionable. A replacement valve will also exhibit slight noise and is not always a cure. Investigate clearance around flexible coupling rivets. Be sure steering shaft and gear are aligned so flexible coupling rotates in a flat plane and is not distorted as shaft rotates. Any metal-to-metal contacts through flexible coupling will transmit valve hiss into passenger compartment through the steering column.
Rattle or chuckle noise in steering gear	• Gear loose on frame	• Check gear-to-frame mounting screws. Tighten screws to 88 N·m (65 foot pounds) torque.
	• Steering linkage looseness	• Check linkage pivot points for wear. Replace if necessary.
	• Pressure hose touching other parts of car	• Adjust hose position. Do not bend tubing by hand.
	• Loose pitman shaft over center adjustment **NOTE:** A slight rattle may occur on turns because of increased clearance off the "high point." This is normal and clearance must not be reduced below specified limits to eliminate this slight rattle.	• Adjust to specifications
	• Loose pitman arm	• Tighten pitman arm nut to specifications
Squawk noise in steering gear when turning or recovering from a turn	• Damper O-ring on valve spool cut	• Replace damper O-ring
Poor return of steering wheel to center	• Tires not properly inflated	• Inflate to specified pressure
	• Lack of lubrication in linkage and ball joints	• Lube linkage and ball joints
	• Lower coupling flange rubbing against steering gear adjuster plug	• Loosen pinch bolt and assemble properly
	• Steering gear to column misalignment	• Align steering column
	• Improper front wheel alignment	• Check and adjust as necessary
	• Steering linkage binding	• Replace pivots
	• Ball joints binding	• Replace ball joints
	• Steering wheel rubbing against housing	• Align housing
	• Tight or frozen steering shaft bearings	• Replace bearings
	• Sticking or plugged valve spool	• Remove and clean or replace valve
	• Steering gear adjustments over specifications	• Check adjustment with gear out of car. Adjust as required.
	• Kink in return hose	• Replace hose
Car leads to one side or the other (keep in mind road condition and wind. Test car in both directions on flat road)	• Front end misaligned	• Adjust to specifications
	• Unbalanced steering gear valve **NOTE:** If this is cause, steering effort will be very light in direction of lead and normal or heavier in opposite direction	• Replace valve

Troubleshooting the Power Steering Gear (cont.)

Problem	Cause	Solution
Momentary increase in effort when turning wheel fast to right or left	• Low oil level • Pump belt slipping • High internal leakage	• Add power steering fluid as required • Tighten or replace belt • Check pump pressure. (See pressure test)
Steering wheel surges or jerks when turning with engine running especially during parking	• Low oil level • Loose pump belt • Steering linkage hitting engine oil pan at full turn • Insufficient pump pressure • Pump flow control valve sticking	• Fill as required • Adjust tension to specification • Correct clearance • Check pump pressure. (See pressure test). Replace relief valve if defective. • Inspect for varnish or damage, replace if necessary
Excessive wheel kickback or loose steering	• Air in system • Steering gear loose on frame • Steering linkage joints worn enough to be loose • Worn poppet valve • Loose thrust bearing preload adjustment • Excessive overcenter lash	• Add oil to pump reservoir and bleed by operating steering. Check hose connectors for proper torque and adjust as required. • Tighten attaching screws to specified torque • Replace loose pivots • Replace poppet valve • Adjust to specification with gear out of vehicle • Adjust to specification with gear out of car
Hard steering or lack of assist	• Loose pump belt • Low oil level **NOTE:** Low oil level will also result in excessive pump noise • Steering gear to column misalignment • Lower coupling flange rubbing against steering gear adjuster plug • Tires not properly inflated	• Adjust belt tension to specification • Fill to proper level. If excessively low, check all lines and joints for evidence of external leakage. Tighten loose connectors. • Align steering column • Loosen pinch bolt and assemble properly • Inflate to recommended pressure
Foamy milky power steering fluid, low fluid level and possible low pressure	• Air in the fluid, and loss of fluid due to internal pump leakage causing overflow	• Check for leak and correct. Bleed system. Extremely cold temperatures will cause system aeriation should the oil level be low. If oil level is correct and pump still foams, remove pump from vehicle and separate reservoir from housing. Check welsh plug and housing for cracks. If plug is loose or housing is cracked, replace housing.
Low pressure due to steering pump	• Flow control valve stuck or inoperative • Pressure plate not flat against cam ring	• Remove burrs or dirt or replace. Flush system. • Correct
Low pressure due to steering gear	• Pressure loss in cylinder due to worn piston ring or badly worn housing bore • Leakage at valve rings, valve body-to-worm seal	• Remove gear from car for disassembly and inspection of ring and housing bore • Remove gear from car for disassembly and replace seals

Troubleshooting the Power Steering Pump

Problem	Cause	Solution
Chirp noise in steering pump	• Loose belt	• Adjust belt tension to specification
Belt squeal (particularly noticeable at full wheel travel and stand still parking)	• Loose belt	• Adjust belt tension to specification
Growl noise in steering pump	• Excessive back pressure in hoses or steering gear caused by restriction	• Locate restriction and correct. Replace part if necessary.
Growl noise in steering pump (particularly noticeable at stand still parking)	• Scored pressure plates, thrust plate or rotor • Extreme wear of cam ring	• Replace parts and flush system • Replace parts
Groan noise in steering pump	• Low oil level • Air in the oil. Poor pressure hose connection.	• Fill reservoir to proper level • Tighten connector to specified torque. Bleed system by operating steering from right to left—full turn.
Rattle noise in steering pump	• Vanes not installed properly • Vanes sticking in rotor slots	• Install properly • Free up by removing burrs, varnish, or dirt
Swish noise in steering pump	• Defective flow control valve	• Replace part
Whine noise in steering pump	• Pump shaft bearing scored	• Replace housing and shaft. Flush system.
Hard steering or lack of assist	• Loose pump belt • Low oil level in reservoir **NOTE:** Low oil level will also result in excessive pump noise • Steering gear to column misalignment • Lower coupling flange rubbing against steering gear adjuster plug • Tires not properly inflated	• Adjust belt tension to specification • Fill to proper level. If excessively low, check all lines and joints for evidence of external leakage. Tighten loose connectors. • Align steering column • Loosen pinch bolt and assemble properly • Inflate to recommended pressure
Foaming milky power steering fluid, low fluid level and possible low pressure	• Air in the fluid, and loss of fluid due to internal pump leakage causing overflow	• Check for leaks and correct. Bleed system. Extremely cold temperatures will cause system aeriation should the oil level be low. If oil level is correct and pump still foams, remove pump from vehicle and separate reservoir from body. Check welsh plug and body for cracks. If plug is loose or body is cracked, replace body.
Low pump pressure	• Flow control valve stuck or inoperative • Pressure plate not flat against cam ring	• Remove burrs or dirt or replace. Flush system. • Correct
Momentary increase in effort when turning wheel fast to right or left	• Low oil level in pump • Pump belt slipping • High internal leakage	• Add power steering fluid as required • Tighten or replace belt • Check pump pressure. (See pressure test)
Steering wheel surges or jerks when turning with engine running especially during parking	• Low oil level • Loose pump belt • Steering linkage hitting engine oil pan at full turn • Insufficient pump pressure	• Fill as required • Adjust tension to specification • Correct clearance • Check pump pressure. (See pressure test). Replace flow control valve if defective.

Troubleshooting the Power Steering Pump (cont.)

Problem	Cause	Solution
Steering wheel surges or jerks when turning with engine running especially during parking (cont.)	· Sticking flow control valve	· Inspect for varnish or damage, replace if necessary
Excessive wheel kickback or loose steering	· Air in system	· Add oil to pump reservoir and bleed by operating steering. Check hose connectors for proper torque and adjust as required.
Low pump pressure	· Extreme wear of cam ring · Scored pressure plate, thrust plate, or rotor · Vanes not installed properly · Vanes sticking in rotor slots · Cracked or broken thrust or pressure plate	· Replace parts. Flush system. · Replace parts. Flush system. · Install properly · Freeup by removing burrs, varnish, or dirt · Replace part

BRAKE SYSTEM
Understanding the Brakes Hydraulic System
BASIC OPERATING PRINCIPLES

Hydraulic systems are used to actuate the brakes of all modern automobiles. The system transports the power required to force the frictional surfaces of the braking system together from the pedal to the individual brake units at each wheel. A hydraulic system is used for two reasons. First, fluid under pressure can be carried to all parts of an automobile by small hoses, some of which are flexible, without taking up a significant amount of room or posing routing problems. Second, a great mechanical advantage can be given to the brake pedal end of the system, and the foot pressure required to actuate the brakes can be reduced by making surface area of the master cylinder pistons smaller than that of any of the pistons in the wheel cylinders or calipers.

The master cylinder consists of a double reservoir and piston assembly as well as other springs, fittings etc. Double (dual) master cylinders are designed to separate two wheels from the others. Your car's braking system is separated diagonally. That is, the right front and left rear use one reservoir and the left front and right rear use the other.

Steel lines carry the brake fluid to a point on the car's frame near each wheel. A flexible hose usually carries the fluid to the disc caliper or wheel cylinder. The flexible line allows for suspension and steering movements.

The rear wheel cylinders contain two pistons each, one at either end, which push outward in opposite directions. The front disc brake calipers contain one piston each.

All pistons employ some type of seal, usually make of rubber, to minimize fluid leakage. A rubber dust boot seals the outer end of the cylinder against dust and dirt. The boot fits around the outer end of the piston on disc brake calipers, and around the brake actuating rod on wheel cylinders.

The hydraulic system operates as follows: When at rest, the entire system, from the piston(s) in the master cylinder to those in the wheel cylinders or calipers, is full of brake fluid. Upon application of the brake pedal, fluid trapped in front of the master cylinder piston(s) is forced through the lines to the wheel cylinders. Here, it forces the pistons outward, in the case of drum brakes, and inward toward the disc, in the case of disc brakes. The motion of the pistons is opposed by return springs mounted outside the cylinders in drum brakes, and by internal springs or spring seal, in disc brakes.

Upon release of the brake pedal, a spring located inside the master cylinder immediately return the master cylinder pistons to the normal position. The pistons contain check valves and the master cylinder has compensating ports drilled in it. These are uncovered as the pistons reach their normal position. The piston check valves allow fluid to flow toward the wheel cylinders or calipers as the pistons withdraw. Then, as the return springs force the brake pads or shoes into the released position, the excess fluid goes into the reservoir through the compensating ports. It is during the time the pedal is in the released position that any fluid that has leaked out of the system will be replaced from the reservoirs through the compensating ports.

The dual master cylinder has two pistons, located one behind the other. The primary piston is actuated directly by mechanical linkage from the brake pedal. The secondary piston is actuated by fluid trapped between the two pistons. If a leak develops in front of the secondary piston, it moves forward until it bottoms against the front of the master cylinder. The fluid trapped between the piston will operate one side of the diagonal system. If the other side of the system develops a leak, the primary piston will move forward until direct contact with the secondary piston takes place, and it will force the secondary piston to actuate the other side of the diagonal system. In either case the brake pedal drops closer to the floor board and less braking power is available.

The brake system uses a switch to warn the driver when only half of the brake system is operational. This switch is located in a valve body which is mounted on the firewall or the frame below the master cylinder. A hydraulic piston receives pressure from both circuits, each circuit's pressure being applied to one end of the piston. When the pressures are in balance, the piston remains stationary. When one circuit has a leak, however, the greater pressure in the circuit during application of the brakes will push the piston to one side, closing the switch and activating the brake warning light.

In disc brake system, this valve body contains a metering valve and, in some cases, a proportioning valve or valves. The metering valve keeps pressure from traveling to the disc brakes on the front wheels until the brake shoes on the rear wheels have contacted the drums, ensuring that the front brakes will never be used alone. The proportioning valve controls the pressure to the rear brakes to avoid rear wheel lock-up during very hard braking.

Warning lights may be tested by depressing the brake pedal and holding it while opening one of the wheel cylinder bleeder screws. If this does not cause the light to go on, substitute a new lamp, make continuity checks, and finally, replace the switch as necessary.

The hydraulic system may be checked for leaks by applying pressure to the pedal gradually and steadily. If the pedal sinks very slowly to the floor, the system has a leak. This is not to be confused with a springy or spongy feel due to the compression of air within the lines. If the system leaks, there will be a gradual change in the position of the pedal with a constant pressure.

Check for leaks along all lines and at wheel cylinders or calipers. If no external leaks are apparent, the problem is inside the master cylinder.

Disc Brakes

BASIC OPERATING PRINCIPLES

Instead of the traditional expanding brakes that press outward against a circular drum, disc brake systems utilize a disc (rotor) with brake pads positioned on either side of it. Braking ef- fect is achieved in a manner similar to the way you would squeeze a spinning phonograph record between your fingers. The disc (rotor) is a casting with cooling fins between the two braking surfaces. This enables air to circulate between the braking surfaces making them less sensitive to heat buildup and more resistant to fade. Dirt and water do not affect braking action since contaminants are thrown off by the centrifugal action of the rotor or scraped off by the pads. Also, the equal clamping action of the two brake pads tends to ensure uniform, straight line stops. Disc brakes are inherently self-adjusting.

Your car uses a pin slider front wheel caliper. The brake pad on the inside of the brake rotor is moved in contact with the rotor by hydraulic pressure. The caliper, which is not held in a fixed position, moves slightly, bringing the outside brake pad into contact with the disc rotor.

Drum Brakes (Rear)

BASIC OPERATING PRINCIPLES

Drum brakes employ two brake shoes mounted on a stationary backing plate. These shoes are positioned inside a circular drum which rotates with the wheel assembly. The shoes are held in place by springs. This allows them to slide toward the drums (when they are applied) while keeping the linings and drums in alignment. The shoes are actuated by a wheel cylinder which is mounted at the top of the backing plate. When the brakes are applied, hydraulic pressure forces the wheel cylinder's actuating links outward. Since these links bear directly against the top of the brake shoes, the tops of the shoes are then forced against the inner side of the drum. This action forces the bottoms of the two shoes to contact the brake drum by rotating the entire assembly slightly (know as servo action). When pressure within the wheel cylinder is relaxed, return springs pull the shoes back away from the drum.

The rear drum brakes on your car are designed to self-adjust themselves during application. Motion causes both shoes to rotate very slightly with the drum, rocking an adjusting lever, thereby causing rotation of the adjusting screw or lever.

Power Brake Boosters

BASIC OPERATING PRINCIPLES

Power brakes operate just as standard brake systems except in the actuation of the master cylinder pistons. A vacuum diaphragm is located on the front of the master cylinder and assists the driver in applying the brakes, reducing both the effort and travel he must put into moving the brake pedal.

The vacuum diaphragm housing is connected to the intake manifold by a vacuum hose. A check valve is placed at the point where the hose enters the diaphragm housing, so that during periods of low manifold vacuum brake assist vacuum will not be lost.

Depressing the brake pedal closes off the vacuum sources and allows atmospheric pressure to enter on one side of the diaphragm. This causes the master cylinder pistons to move and apply the brakes. When the brake pedal is released, vacuum is applied to both sides of the diaphragm, and return springs return the diaphragm and master cylinder pistons to the released position. If the vacuum fails, the brake pedal rod will butt against the end of the master cylinder actuating rod, and direct mechanical application will occur as the pedal is depressed.

The hydraulic and mechanical problems that apply to conventional brake systems also apply to power brakes, and should be checked for if the tests below do not reveal the problem.

Test for a system vacuum leak as described below:

1. Operate the engine at idle without touching the brake pedal for at least one minute.

2. Turn off the engine, and wait one minute.

3. Test for the presence of assist vacuum by depressing the brake pedal and releasing it several times. Light application will produce less and less pedal travel, if vacuum was present. If there is no vacuum, air is leaking into the system somewhere.

Test for system operation as follows:

1. Pump the brake pedal (with engine off) until the supply vacuum is entirely gone.

2. Put a light, steady pressure on the pedal.

3. Start the engine, and operate it at idle. If the system is operating, the brake pedal should fall toward the floor if constant pressure is maintained on the pedal.

Power brake systems may be tested for hydraulic leaks just as ordinary systems are tested.

Anti-Lock Brake System (ABS)
Continental only
BASIC OPERATING PRINCIPLES

The Continental is equipped with a four wheel Anti-lock Brake System (ABS). The system prevents wheel lockup by automatically modulating the brake pressure during an emergency stop. The driver has much more control over the vehicle when the wheel are moving during an emergency stop. ABS enables the driver to steer and stop the vehicle in the shortest amount of distance under most conditions.

The ABS controls each front brake separately, and the rear brakes as a pair whenever the wheel lockup begins. The force needed to engage the anti-lock function may vary with the road surface conditions. Dry surfaces require a higher force and slippery surfaces require less force to stop the wheels.

During the ABS operation, a pulsation can be felt in the brake pedal. This feeling while be accompanied by a rise in the pedal height and a clicking sound. The pedal will feel the same as a conventional brake system during normal braking.

The ABS system consists of the following major components: electronic controller, electric pump assembly, brake fluid reservoir and level indicator assembly, solenoid valve block assembly, hydraulic actuation unit, brake control valve and pressure switch, and proportioning valve.

The hydraulic pump maintains a pressure between 2000-2600 psi (14,000-18,000 kPa) in the accumulator. The electronic controller monitors the electromechanical components of the system. Malfunctions in the ABS system will cause the preliminary self check on the ABS electrical system. The self check indicator is a three to four second illumination of a amber CHECK ANTI-LOCK BRAKES lamp in the instrument cluster. During normal operation the electronic controller monitors all anti-lock functions and many hydraulic performance characteristics.

Brake Adjustment
FRONT DISC BRAKES

Front disc brakes require no adjustment. Hydraulic pressure maintains the proper pad-to-disc contact at all times.

REAR DRUM BRAKES

The rear drum brakes, on your car, are self-adjusting. The only adjustment necessary should be an initial one after new brake shoes have been installed or some type of service work has been done on the rear brake system.

REAR DISC BRAKES

The Continental and 3.0L SHO Taurus are equipped with rear disc brakes. The main difference is that the rear caliper houses the emergency brake actuator. The rear disc brakes are self-adjusting. Hydraulic pressure maintains the proper pad-to-disc at all times.

NOTE: *After any brake service, obtain a firm brake pedal before moving the car. Adjusted brakes must not drag. The wheel must turn freely. Be sure the parking brake cables are not too tightly adjusted.*

A special brake shoe gauge is necessary for making an accurate adjustment after installing new brake shoes. The special gauge measures both the drum diameter and the brake shoe setting.

Since no adjustment is necessary except when service work is done on the rear brakes, we will assume that the car is jacked up and safely supported by jackstands, and that the rear drums have been removed. (If not, refer to the appropriate sections of this Chapter for the procedures necessary).

Adjustment

Measure and set the special brake gauge to the inside diameter of the brake drum. Lift the adjuster lever from the starwheel teeth. Turn the starwheel until the brake shoes are adjusted out to the shoe setting fingers of the brake gauge. Install the hub and drum.

NOTE: *Complete the adjustment by applying the brakes several times. After the brakes have been properly adjusted, check their operation by making several stops from varying forward speeds.*

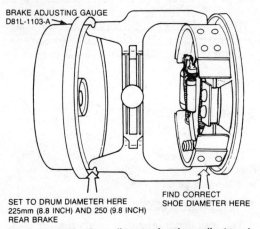

BRAKE ADJUSTING GAUGE
D81L-1103-A

SET TO DRUM DIAMETER HERE
225mm (8.8 INCH) AND 250 (9.8 INCH)
REAR BRAKE

FIND CORRECT
SHOE DIAMETER HERE

Measuring brake drum diameter for shoe adjustment

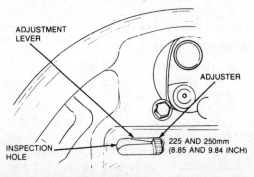

ADJUSTMENT
LEVER

ADJUSTER

INSPECTION
HOLE

225 AND 250mm
(8.85 AND 9.84 INCH)

Star wheel adjuster location

Adjustment for Brake Drum Removal

If the brake drum will not come off for brake servicing, pry the rubber plug from the backing plate inspection hole and use the following procedure:

Remove the brake line to axle retention bracket. This will allow sufficient room for the use of a thin screwdriver and brake adjusting tool. Push the adjuster lever away from the adjuster wheel with the screwdriver and release adjustment with the brake tool.

Master Cylinder

The fluid reservoir of the master cylinder has a large and small compartment. The larger serves the right front and left rear brakes, while the smaller serves the left front and right rear brakes.

Always be sure that the fluid level of the reservoirs is within 6mm of the top. Use only DOT 3 approved brake fluid.

REMOVAL AND INSTALLATION

Taurus/Sable

1. Disconnect and plug the brake lines from the master cylinder.
2. Disconnect the electrical connector (brake warning lamp) from the master cylinder.
3. Remove the master cylinder-to-power booster nuts and the master cylinder from the vehicle.

To Install:

4. Position the master cylinder over the booster pushrod and onto the two studs on the booster assembly.
5. Install the brake lines to the master cylinder and the pressure control valve outlet ports.
6. Install the nuts and tighten to 13-25 ft. lbs.
7. Fill the master cylinder with DOT 3 brake fluid to the MAX line on the side of the reservoir. Bleed the brake system as follows.

It is necessary to bleed the brake system of air whenever a hydraulic component, of the system, has been rebuilt or replaced, or if the brakes feel spongy during application.

Your car has a diagonally split brake system. Each side of this system must be bled as an individual system. **Bleed the right rear brake, left front brake, left rear brake and right front brake. Always start with the longest line from the master cylinder first.**

CAUTION: *When bleeding the system(s) never allow the master cylinder to run completely out of brake fluid. Always use DOT 3 heavy duty brake fluid or the equivalent. Never reuse brake fluid that has been drained from the system or that has been allowed to stand*

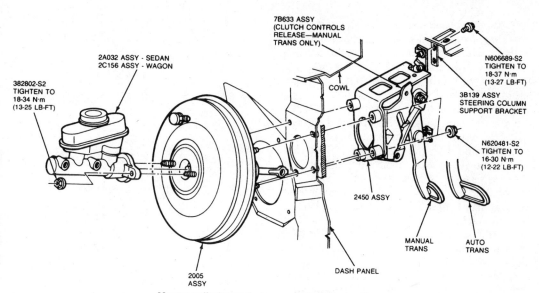

382802-S2
TIGHTEN TO
18-34 N·m
(13-25 LB-FT)

2A032 ASSY - SEDAN
2C156 ASSY - WAGON

7B633 ASSY
(CLUTCH CONTROLS
RELEASE—MANUAL
TRANS ONLY)

COWL

N606689-S2
TIGHTEN TO
18-37 N·m
(13-27 LB-FT)

3B139 ASSY
STEERING COLUMN
SUPPORT BRACKET

N620481-S2
TIGHTEN TO
16-30 N·m
(12-22 LB-FT)

2450 ASSY

MANUAL
TRANS

AUTO
TRANS

DASH PANEL

2005
ASSY

Master cylinder and vacuum booster mounting

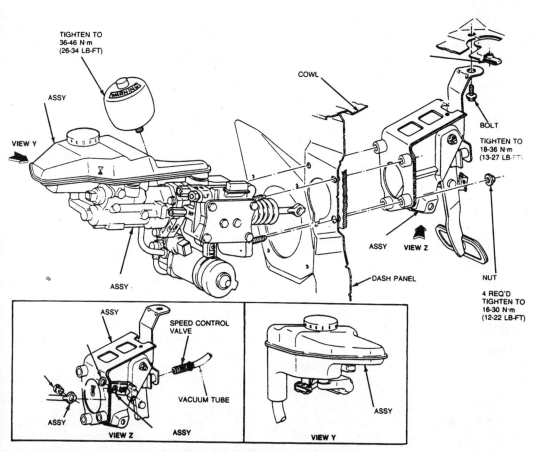

TIGHTEN TO
36-46 N·m
(26-34 LB-FT)

ASSY

COWL

BOLT

TIGHTEN TO
18-36 N·m
(13-27 LB-FT)

VIEW Y

ASSY

ASSY

VIEW Z

DASH PANEL

NUT

4 REQ'D
TIGHTEN TO
16-30 N·m
(12-22 LB-FT)

ASSY

SPEED CONTROL
VALVE

VACUUM TUBE

ASSY

VIEW Z

ASSY

ASSY

VIEW Y

Anti-lock brake system—Continental

in an opened container for an extended period of time. Remove the reserve vacuum stored in the booster by pumping the brake pedal several times before bleeding the brakes.

1. Clean all of the dirt away from the master cylinder filler cap.

2. Raise and support the car on jackstands. Make sure your car is safely supported and it is raised evenly front and back.

3. Starting with the right rear wheel cylinder. Remove the dust cover from the bleeder screw. Place the proper size box wrench over the bleeder fitting and attach a piece of rubber tubing (about three feet long and snug fitting) over the end of the fitting.

4. Submerge the free end of the rubber tube into a container half filled with clean brake fluid.

5. Have a friend pump up the brake pedal and then push down to apply the brakes while you loosen the bleeder screw. When the pedal reaches the bottom of its travel close the bleeder fitting before your friend release the brake pedal.

6. Repeat Step 5 until air bubbles cease to appear in the container in which the tubing is submerged. Tighten the fitting, remove the rubber tubing and replace the dust cover.

7. Repeat Steps 3 through 6 to the left front wheel, then to the left rear and right front.

NOTE: *Refill the master cylinder after each wheel cylinder or caliper is bled. Be sure the master cylinder top gasket is mounted correctly and the brake fluid level is within 6mm of the top.*

8. After bleeding the brakes, pump the brake pedal several times, this ensures proper seating of the rear linings and the front caliper pistons.

MASTER CYLINDER OVERHAUL

WARNING: *Because of the safety hazards involved in rebuilding brake master cylinders, it is advised not to rebuild this component. A new replacement master cylinder or a rebuilt master cylinder from a reputable rebuilder is recommended.*

ABS Unit Actuation Assembly
REMOVAL AND INSTALLATION
Continental (only)

CAUTION: *Before the actuation assembly is removed, it is mandatory that the hydraulic pressure is discharged from the system. To discharge the system, turn the ignition OFF and pump the brake pedal a minimum of 20 times until and increase in brake pedal force is clearly felt.*

1. Disconnect the negative (–) battery cable.

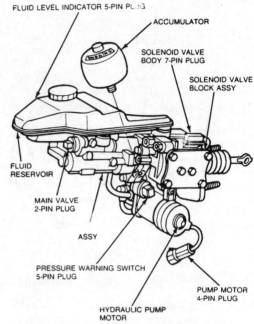

Electrical connector hock-up (ABS)—Continental

2. Remove the air cleaner housing and duct assembly.

3. Disconnect the electrical connectors from the fluid level indicator, main valve, solenoid valve block, pressure warning switch, hydraulic pump motor , and ground connector from the master cylinder portion of the actuation assembly.

4. Disconnect the three brake tube fittings. Immediately plug each threaded port to prevent fluid loss and contamination.

CAUTION: *Do not allow brake fluid to come in contact with any of the electrical connectors.*

5. Remove the trim panel from under the steering column and disconnect the actuation assembly pushrod from the brake pedal by removing the hair pin connector next to the stop lamp switch. Slide the switch, pushrod, and plastic bushings off the pedal pin.

6. Remove the four actuator assembly-to-brake pedal support bracket retaining nuts.

7. Remove the assembly from the vehicle.

To install:

1. Install the actuation assembly with the rubber boot and foam gasket to the engine side of the dash panel.

2. Loosely start the four retaining lock nuts attaching the actuation assembly to the pedal support.

3. Connect the pushrod to the brake pedal pin by sliding the flanged plastic bushing, pushrod, and washer onto the brake pedal pin. Install the stop lamp switch to the slot on the bracket and install the hairpin retainer.

4. Torque the four actuator assembly-to-brake pedal support bracket retaining nuts to 13-25 ft. lbs.

5. Connect the solenoid valve block brake tubes one at a time. Torque the brake tube lock nuts to 13-25 ft. lbs.

6. Connect the electrical connectors to the fluid level indicator, main valve, solenoid valve block, pressure switch, electric pump, and ground connector. Make sure the connectors are clean and all seals are in place.

7. Install the air cleaner and duct assembly. Connect the negative () battery cable. Bleed the system as outlined in the "Bleeding the ABS (Anti-lock Brake System" in this chapter.

Power Brake Booster

REMOVAL AND INSTALLATION

Taurus/Sable

1. Refer to the "Master Cylinder Removal And Installation" procedures in this section and remove the master cylinder from the power brake booster; it is not necessary to remove the brake tubes from the master cylinder.

2. Remove the vacuum hose from the power brake booster.

3. From under the instrument panel, remove the pushrod retainer and outer nylon washer from the brake pin.

4. Remove the power brake booster-to-pedal support nuts. Slide the booster pushrod and pushrod bushing off of the brake pedal pin.

5. Move the booster forward until the studs clear the dash panel and remove the it from the vehicle.

6. **To install:** reverse the removal procedures. Torque the power brake booster-to-brake assembly bracket nuts to 12-22 ft. lbs. and the master cylinder-to-power brake booster nuts to 13-25 ft. lbs. If the brake lines were disconnected, bleed the brake system as outlined in the "Bleeding the Brake System" section for Taurus/Sable.

ADJUSTMENT

1. Without disconnecting the brake lines, disconnect the master cylinder and set it away from the booster power unit.

NOTE: *The master cylinder must be supported to prevent damaging the brake lines.*

2. With the engine running, check and adjust the pushrod length as shown in the illustration. A force of approximately 5 lbs. applied to the pushrod with the gauge will confirm that the pushrod is seated within the power booster. If adjustment is necessary, grip the rod only by the knurled area.

3. Install the master cylinder on the power

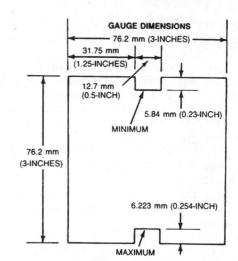

Power booster adjustment gauge

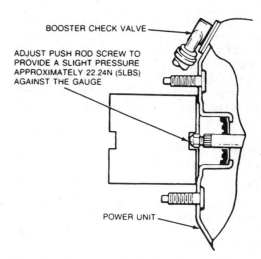

Power booster push rod adjustment

booster. Gradually and alternately tighten the retaining nuts to 13-25 ft. lbs.

TESTING THE POWER BRAKE BOOSTER

The power brake booster depends on vacuum produced by the engine for proper operation.

If you suspect problems in the power brake system, check the following:

1. Inspect all hoses and hose connections. All unused vacuum connectors should be sealed. Hoses and connections should be tightly secured and in good condition. The hoses should be pliable with no holes or cracks and no collapsed areas.

2. Inspect the check valve which is located in line between the intake manifold and booster. Disconnect the hose on the intake manifold side of the valve. Attempt to blow through the valve. If air passes through the valve, it is defective and must be replaced.

3. Check the level of brake fluid in the master cylinder. If the level is low, check the system for fluid leaks.

4. Idle the engine briefly and then shut it off. Pump the brake pedal several times to exhaust all of the vacuum stored in the booster. Keep the brake pedal depressed and start the engine. The brake pedal should drop slightly, if vacuum is present after the engine is started, less pressure should be necessary on the brake pedal. If no drop or action is felt, the power brake booster should be suspect.

5. With the parking brake applied and the wheels blocked, start the engine and allow to idle in Neutral (Park if automatic). Disconnect the vacuum line to the check valve on the intake manifold side. If vacuum is felt, connect the hose and repeat Step 4. Once again, if no action is felt on the brake pedal, suspect the booster.

6. Operate the engine at a fast idle for about ten seconds, shut off the engine. Allow the car to sit for about ten minutes. Depress the brake pedal with moderate force (about 20 pounds). The pedal should feel about the same as when the engine was running. If the brake pedal feels hard (no power assist) suspect the power booster.

Control Valve

REMOVAL AND INSTALLATION

Sedan

The control valve is mounted to the floorpan near the left-rear wheel. It utilizes a mechanical linkage to the lower suspension arm to vary the valve performance based on the rear weight of the vehicle.

1. Raise and support the rear of the vehicle on jackstands.

NOTE: *DO NOT raise or support the vehicle using the tension struts.*

2. Label and disconnect the brake tubes from the control valve assembly.

3. Remove the valve bracket-to-underbody screws and the control valve assembly from the vehicle.

NOTE: *The service replacement control valve will have a red plastic gauge clip on it, which MUST NOT BE removed until installation.*

4. **To install:** make sure that the rear suspension is in the Full rebound position and the control valve operating screw is loose, then reverse the removal procedures. Torque the control valve-to-underbody screws to 8-10 ft. lbs. Perform the control valve assembly adjustment procedures. Bleed the rear brake system.

Station Wagon

The control valves are screwed into the bottom of the master cylinder. They control the braking pressure to the rear wheels to minimize rear wheel skidding during hard braking.

1. Disconnect and plug the primary and/or secondary brake tube from the master cylinder.

2. Remove the pressure control valve(s) from the master cylinder.

3. **To install:** reverse the removal procedures. Torque the control valve-to-master cylinder to 10-18 ft. lbs. Bleed the brake system.

ADJUSTMENT

Sedan

1. Place the vehicle on a hoist or an alignment machine, so that the vehicle is at the curb load level and the wheels are on a flat surface.

2. At the control valve, loosen the adjuster screw.

3. Using a piece of rubber or plastic tubing 16.0-16.5mm long × 9.5mm OD × 6mm ID, slice it lengthwise (on one edge), then install it on the operating rod.

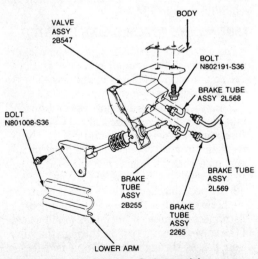

Control valve replacement—Sedan models

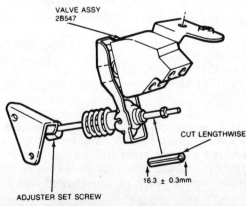

Control valve adjustment—Sedan models

4. Make sure that the adjuster is resting on the lower mounting bracket; tighten the set screw.

NOTE: *DO NOT change the position of the upper nut on the valve operating rod; the dimension will position the valve for normal operation.*

5. To decrease the rear brake pressure, perform the following procedures:

a. Make sure that the vehicle is at curb height.

b. Loosen the control valve set screw.

c. Move the piston Down the operating rod 1mm for each 60 psi pressure decrease.

d. Tighten the set screw in the desired position.

6. To increase the rear brake pressure, perform the following procedures:

a. Make sure that the vehicle is at curb height.

b. Loosen the control valve set screw.

c. Move the piston Up the operating rod 1mm for each 60 psi pressure increase.

d. Tighten the set screw in the desired position.

Bleeding the Brake System

Taurus/Sable

It is necessary to bleed the brake system of air whenever a hydraulic component, of the system, has been rebuilt or replaced, or if the brakes feel spongy during application.

Your car has a diagonally split brake system. Each side of this system must be bled as an individual system. **Bleed the right rear brake, left front brake, left rear brake and right front brake. Always start with the longest line from the master cylinder first.**

CAUTION: *When bleeding the system(s) never allow the master cylinder to run completely out of brake fluid. Always use DOT 3 heavy duty brake fluid or the equivalent. Never re-use brake fluid that has been drained from the system or that has been allowed to stand in an opened container for an extended period of time. If your car is equipped with power brakes, remove the reserve vacuum stored in the booster by pumping the brake pedal several times before bleeding the brakes.*

1. Clean all of the dirt away from the master cylinder filler cap.

2. Raise and support the car on jackstands. Make sure your car is safely supported and it is raised evenly front and back.

3. Starting with the right rear wheel cylinder. Remove the dust cover from the bleeder screw. Place the proper size box wrench over the bleeder fitting and attach a piece of rubber

tubing (about three feet long and snug fitting) over the end of the fitting.

4. Submerge the free end of the rubber tube into a container half filled with clean brake fluid.

5. Have a friend pump up the brake pedal and then push down to apply the brakes while you loosen the bleeder screw. When the pedal reaches the bottom of its travel close the bleeder fitting before your friend release the brake pedal.

6. Repeat Step 5 until air bubbles cease to appear in the container in which the tubing is submerged. Tighten the fitting, remove the rubber tubing and replace the dust cover.

7. Repeat Steps 3 through 6 to the left front wheel, then to the left rear and right front.

NOTE: *Refill the master cylinder after each wheel cylinder or caliper is bled. Be sure the master cylinder top gasket is mounted correctly and the brake fluid level is within 6mm of the top.*

8. After bleeding the brakes, pump the brake pedal several times, this ensures proper seating of the rear linings and the front caliper pistons.

Bleeding the ABS (Anti-lock Brake System) Continental

CAUTION: *When bleeding the system(s) never allow the fluid reservoir to run completely out of brake fluid. Always use DOT 3 heavy duty brake fluid or the equivalent. Never re-use brake fluid that has been drained from the system or that has been allowed to stand in an opened container for an extended period of time.*

Front Brakes (conventional method)

The front brakes can be bleed in the conventional way or by using a Rotunda Brake Bleeder part No. 104-00064 or equivalent with or without the accumulator being charged.

1. Remove the dust cap from the RH front caliper bleeder fitting. Attach a piece of rubber hose to the bleeder fitting and drain into a drain pan.

2. Loosen the bleeder fitting ¾ of a turn. Have an assistant push the brake pedal down slowly through the full travel and hold at that position.

3. In the down position, close the bleeder fitting, then return the pedal to the released position.

4. Wait five seconds then repeat operation 3 until all of the bubbles cease to appear in the drain pan.

5. Repeat the following operations at the LH caliper.

6. Procede to the rear brake bleeding procedures as outlined below.

Rear Brakes (conventional method)

The front brakes can be bleed in the conventional method or by using a Rotunda Brake Bleeder part No. 104-00064 or equivalent with or without the accumulator being charged.

1. Remove the dust cap from the RH rear caliper bleeder fitting. Attach a piece of rubber hose to the bleeder fitting and drain into a drain pan.

2. Loosen the bleeder fitting ¾ of a turn. Have an assistant push the brake pedal down slowly through the full travel and hold at that position.

3. In the down position, close the bleeder fitting, then return the pedal to the released position.

4. Wait five seconds then repeat operation 3 until all of the bubbles cease to appear in the drain pan.

5. Repeat the following operations at the LH caliper.

Front Brakes (Pressure Bleeder method)

1. Clean all dirt from the reservoir filler cap area and attach the Rotunda Pressure Bleeder part No. 104-00064 or equivalent.

2. Maintain 35 psi (240 kPa) pressure on the system.

3. Remove the dust cap from the RH caliper bleeder fitting and attach a piece of rubber hose to the fitting. Make sure the hose is snug around the bleeder fitting.

4. With the ignition switch in the OFF position and the brake pedal in the fully released position, open the bleeder fitting for ten seconds at a time until an air-free stream of fluid flows from the bleeder.

5. Repeat the above procedures on the LH bleeder fitting.

6. Turn the ignition switch to the RUN position and pump the brake pedal several times to complete the bleeding procedure and to fully charge the accumulator.

7. Siphon off the excess fluid in the reservoir to adjust the level to the MAX mark with a fully charged accumulator.

8. Proceed to the rear brake bleeding procedures

Rear Brakes (Pressure Bleeder method)

1. Clean all dirt from the reservoir filler cap area and attach the Rotunda Pressure Bleeder part No. 104-00064 or equivalent.

2. Maintain 35 psi (240 kPa) pressure on the system.

3. Remove the dust cap from the RH caliper bleeder fitting and attach a piece of rubber hose to the fitting. Make sure the hose is snug around the bleeder fitting.

4. With the ignition switch in the OFF position and the brake pedal in the fully released position, open the bleeder fitting for ten seconds at a time until an air-free stream of fluid flows from the bleeder.

5. Repeat the above procedures on the LH bleeder fitting.

6. Turn the ignition switch to the RUN position and pump the brake pedal several times to complete the bleeding procedure and to fully charge the accumulator.

7. Siphon off the excess fluid in the reservoir to adjust the level to the MAX mark with a fully charged accumulator.

FRONT DISC BRAKES

CAUTION: *Some brake pads contain asbestos, which has been determined to be a cancer causing agent. Never clean the brake surfaces with compressed air! Avoid inhaling any dust from any brake surface! When cleaning brake surfaces, use a commercially available brake cleaning fluid.*

Disc Brake Pads

INSPECTION

1. Loosen the front wheel lugs slightly, then raise the front of the car and safely support it on jackstands.

2. Remove the front wheel and tire assemblies.

3. The cut out in the top of the front brake caliper allows visual inspection of the disc brake pad. If the lining is worn to within 3mm of the metal disc shoe (check local inspection requirements) replace all four pads (both sides).

4. While you are inspecting the brake pads, visually inspect the caliper for hydraulic fluid leaks. If a leak is visible the caliper will have to be rebuilt or replaced.

DISC PAD REMOVAL

CAUTION: *Brake shoes contain asbestos, which has been determined to be a cancer causing agent. Never clean the brake surfaces with compressed air! Avoid inhaling any dust from any brake surface! When cleaning brake surfaces, use a commercially available brake cleaning fluid.*

1. Remove the master cylinder cap and check the fluid level in reservoir. Remove the brake fluid until the reservoir is half full. Discard the old fluid removed.

2. Raise the vehicle and support with jackstands. Remove the wheel and tire assem-

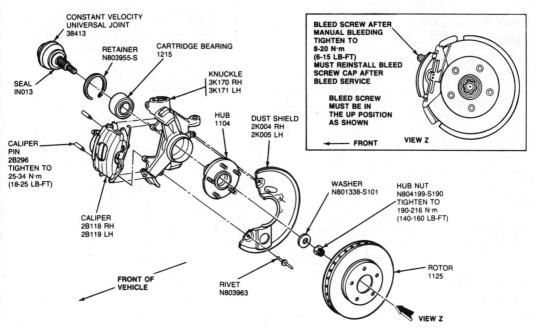

Front disk brake components

bly. Use care to avoid damage or interference with the caliper splash shield or the bleeder screw fitting.

3. Remove the caliper locating pins using Torx® Drive Bit D79P-2100-T40 or equivalent.

NOTE: *It is not necessary to disconnect the hydraulic connections.*

4. Lift the caliper assembly from the knuckle and the anchor plate and the rotor using a rotating motion. Do not pry directly against the plastic piston or damage will occur.

5. Remove the outer shoe and lining assembly from caliper assembly.

6. Remove the inner shoe and lining assembly.

7. Inspect both rotor brake surfaces. Minor scoring or buildup of lining material does not require machining or replacement of the rotor. Hand-sand glaze from both rotor braking surfaces using garnet paper 100A (medium-grit) or aluminum oxide 150-J (medium).

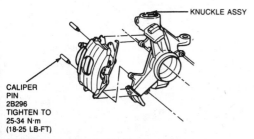

KNUCKLE ASSY

CALIPER PIN 2B296 TIGHTEN TO 25-34 N·m (18-25 LB-FT)

Caliper mounting pin locations

8. Suspend the caliper inside fender housing with wire.

WARNING: *Use care not to damage caliper or stretch brake hose.*

To install:

1. Use a 100mm C-clamp and wood block 70mm x 25mm and approximately 19mm thick to seat the caliper piston in its bore. This must be done to provide clearance for the caliper assembly to fit over the rotor during installation.

NOTE: *Extra care must be taken during this procedure to prevent damage to the plastic piston. Metal or sharp objects cannot come into direct contact with the piston surface or damage will result.*

2. Remove all rust buildup from inside of the caliper legs (outer shoe contact area).

3. Install the inner shoe and lining assembly in the caliper piston(s).

NOTE: *Do not bend the shoe clips during installation in the piston or distortion and rattles can occur.*

4. Install the correct outer shoe and lining assembly. Be certain the clips are properly seated.

5. Install the caliper over the rotor. Start the caliper locating pins. Using a Torx® drive bit D79P-2100-T40 or equivalent, torque the locating pins to 18-25 ft. lbs.

6. Install the wheel and tire assembly. Tighten the wheel lug nuts to 80-105 ft. lbs.

7. Pump brake pedal prior to moving vehicle to position brake linings.

8. Road test the vehicle.

Front Brake Caliper

REMOVAL

CAUTION: *Brake shoes contain asbestos, which has been determined to be a cancer causing agent. Never clean the brake surfaces with compressed air! Avoid inhaling any dust from any brake surface! When cleaning brake surfaces, use a commercially available brake cleaning fluid.*

1. Raise and support the vehicle with jackstands. Remove the wheel and tire assembly. Use care to avoid damage or interference with bleeder screw fitting during removal.

2. Mark the caliper assembly to ensure it is installed on correct knuckle during installation.

3. Disconnect the flexible brake hose from caliper. Remove the hollow retaining bolt that connects hose fitting to caliper. Remove the hose assembly from caliper and plug hose.

4. Remove the caliper locating pin using Torx® Drive Bit D79P-2100-T40 or equivalent.

5. Lift the caliper off rotor and the knuckle and the anchor plate using a rotating motion.
WARNING: *Do not pry directly against plastic piston, or damage to piston will occur.*

INSTALLATION

1. Retract the piston fully in the piston bore. Position the caliper assembly above rotor with the anti-rattle spring under upper arm of knuckle. Install the caliper over rotor with rotating motion. Be sure the inner shoe is properly positioned.
NOTE: *Be sure the correct caliper assembly, as marked during removal, is installed on the correct knuckle. The caliper bleed screw should be positioned on top of caliper when assembled on vehicle.*

2. Lubricate the locating pins and inside of the insulators with Silicone Grease D7AZ-19A331-A or equivalent. Install the locating pins through the caliper insulators and into the knuckle attaching holes.

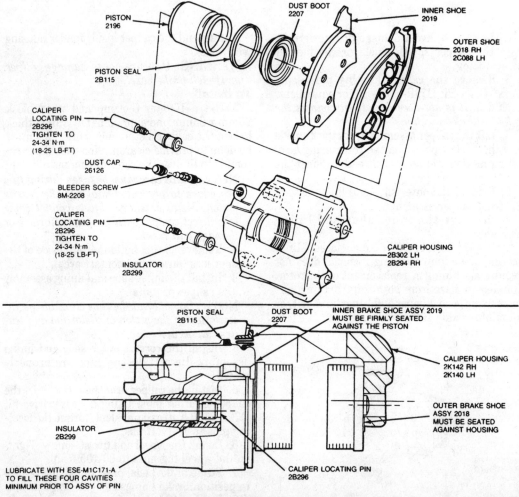

Disk brake shoe and caliper components

NOTE: *The caliper locating pins must be inserted and threads started by hand.*

3. Using a Torx® Drive Bit D79P-2100-T40 or equivalent, tighten the caliper locating pin to 18-25 ft. lbs.

4. Remove plug and install the brake hose on the caliper with a new copper washer on each side of fitting outlet. Insert the attaching bolt through washers and fittings. Tighten the bolts to 30-45 ft. lbs.

5. Bleed the brake system. Always replace rubber bleed screw cap after bleeding.

6. Fill the master cylinder as required.

7. Install the wheel and tire assembly. Tighten the wheel nuts to 80-105 ft. lbs.

8. Pump the brake pedal prior to moving the vehicle to position the brake linings.

9. Road test the vehicle.

OVERHAUL

After overhaul, pump the brake pedal and have a firm pedal before moving the vehicle. "Riding the brake pedal" must be avoided when driving the vehicle.

Disassembly

1. Remove the caliper assembly from knuckle and rotor as detailed above. Do not use screwdriver or similar tool to pry piston back into cylinder bore. Use a C-clamp. Remove the outer shoe by pushing shoe to move the "buttons" from the caliper housing and slipping down caliper leg until clip is disengaged. Remove inner shoe by pulling it straight out of piston.

NOTE: *Inner shoe removal force may be as high as 10-20 lbs.*

2. If further disassembly is required to service the piston, disconnect the caliper from the hydraulic system, and blow the piston out using air pressure.

WARNING: *DO NOT use a screwdriver or any similar tool to pry the piston out of the bore. It will result in damage to the piston. Cushion the piston's impact against the caliper when blowing it out of the bore by placing rags between the piston and the caliper bridge.*

Assembly

1. When assembling the caliper, examine the piston for surface irregularities or small chips and cracks. Replace the piston if damaged. Be sure to clean the foreign material from the piston surfaces and lubricate with brake fluid before inserting it into the caliper. Always install a new seal and dust boot.

2. When installing the piston back into bore, use a wood block or another flat stock, like an old shoe lining assembly, between C-clamp and piston. Do not apply C-clamp directly to the pis-

ton surface. This can result in damage to the piston. Be sure the piston is not cocked.

3. Be certain the dust boot is tight in boot groove on the piston and in the caliper.

4. To install the inner shoe with three-finger clip attached to the shoe into piston, grab each end of shoe, making it square with piston. Push firmly until the shoe clip snaps into the piston. Do not allow the shoe or the clip tangs to cock during installation.

Front Brake Disc (rotor)
REMOVAL

CAUTION: *Brake shoes contain asbestos, which has been determined to be a cancer causing agent. Never clean the brake surfaces with compressed air! Avoid inhaling any dust from any brake surface! When cleaning brake surfaces, use a commercially available brake cleaning fluid.*

1. Raise the front of the vehicle and support with jackstands. Remove the wheel and tire assembly. Be careful to avoid damage or interference with the caliper bleeder screw fitting and the rotor splash shield.

2. Remove the caliper assembly from rotor as described earlier.

NOTE: *If the caliper does not require servicing, it is not necessary to disconnect brake hose or remove caliper from the vehicle.*

3. Position the caliper out of the way and support it with a length of wire to avoid damaging the caliper and hose.

WARNING: *Handle the rotor and the caliper assembly in such a way as to prevent deformation of the rotor, and nicking, scratching or contamination of the brake linings/rotor surfaces.*

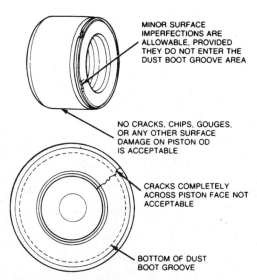

MINOR SURFACE IMPERFECTIONS ARE ALLOWABLE, PROVIDED THEY DO NOT ENTER THE DUST BOOT GROOVE AREA

NO CRACKS, CHIPS, GOUGES, OR ANY OTHER SURFACE DAMAGE ON PISTON OD IS ACCEPTABLE

CRACKS COMPLETELY ACROSS PISTON FACE NOT ACCEPTABLE

BOTTOM OF DUST BOOT GROOVE

Caliper piston inspection

4. Remove the rotor from hub assembly by pulling it off the hub studs.

NOTE: *If additional force is required to remove the rotor, apply Rust Penetrator D7AZ-19A501-A or equivalent on the front and rear rotor/hub mating surfaces. First, strike rotor between studs with a plastic hammer. If this does not work then attach a 3-Jawed Puller D80L-1013-A or equivalent and remove the rotor. If excessive force must be used during rotor removal, the rotor should be checked for lateral runout prior to installation.*

INSTALLATION

1. If the rotor is being replaced, remove the protective coating from the new rotor with carburetor degreaser. If the original rotor is being installed, make sure the rotor braking and mounting surfaces are clean. Apply a small amount of Silicone Grease D7AZ-19A331-A to the pilot diameter of the rotor.

2. Install the rotor on the hub assembly.

3. Install the caliper assembly on the rotor.

4. Install the wheel and tire assembly. Tighten the wheel nuts to 80-105 ft. lbs.

5. Pump the brake pedal prior to moving the vehicle to position brake linings.

6. Road test the vehicle.

REAR DRUM BRAKES

Taurus/Sable (except 3.0L SHO)

CAUTION: *Some brake shoes contain asbestos, which has been determined to be a cancer causing agent. Never clean the brake surfaces with compressed air! Avoid inhaling any dust from any brake surface! When cleaning brake surfaces, use a commercially available brake cleaning fluid.*

The rear brakes used on your car are of the non-servo leading/trailing shoe design. This means that the leading shoe does the majority of the braking when the car is going forward and the trailing shoe does the majority of the braking when the car is backing up.

The brakes are self-adjusting. The only time any adjustment should be necessary is during servicing of brake shoe replacement.

BRAKE SHOE INSPECTION

Two access holes, covered by a rubber plug, are provided in the brake backing plate. By removing the plugs the brake lining thickness and condition can be inspected.

Rear Brake Drum

REMOVAL

1. Remove the wheel cover, loosen the lugs, jack up the rear end of your car and safely support it on jackstands.

2. Remove the wheel ornament (wheelcover) and nut covers as required.

3. Remove the wheel lugs and the tire and wheel assembly.

4. Remove the grease cap from the hub. Remove the cotter pin, nut lock, adjusting nut and keyed flat washer from the spindle. Remove the outer bearing. Discard the cotter pin.

5. Remove the hub and drum assembly as a unit. Be careful not to damage the grease seal and the inner bearing during removal. Care must be taken not to drag the seal across the spindle threads during assembly and disassembly.

INSTALLATION

1. Inspect and lubricate the bearings as necessary. Replace the grease seal if any damage is visible.

2. Clean the spindle stem and apply a thin coat of wheel bearing grease.

3. Install the hub and drum assembly on the spindle.

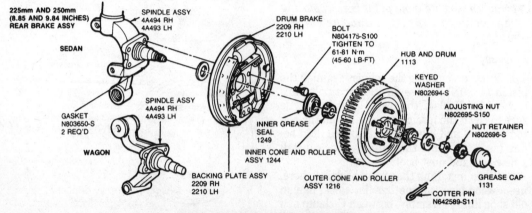

Rear brake drum and lining assembly

4. Install the outer bearings. Install the hub on the spindle.

5. Install the keyed flat washer and the adjusting nut. Tighten the nut finger-tight.

6. Adjust the wheel bearing as described below. Install the nut retainer and a new cotter pin.

NOTE: *The rear wheel uses a tapered roller bearing which may feel loose when properly adjusted; this feel should be considered normal.*

a. Back off the hub nut one full turn.

b. While rotating the hub/drum assembly, torque the adjusting nut to 17-25 ft. lbs. Back off the adjusting nut ½ turn, then retighten it to 10-15 in. lbs.

c. Position the nut retainer over the adjusting nut so that the slots are in line with cotter pin hole (without rotating the adjusting nut).

d. Install the cotter pin and bend the ends around the retainer flange.

e. Check the hub rotation. If the hub rotates freely, install the grease cap. If not, check the bearings for damage and replace as necessary.

7. Install the tire and wheel assembly.

8. Install the wheelcover and nut covers as required.

9. Lower the vehicle.

Rear Brake Shoes

REMOVAL

CAUTION: *Brake shoes contain asbestos, which has been determined to be a cancer causing agent. Never clean the brake surfaces with compressed air! Avoid inhaling any dust from any brake surface! When cleaning brake surfaces, use a commercially available brake cleaning fluid.*

1. Remove the wheel cover, loosen the lugs, jack up the rear end of your car and safely support it on jackstands.

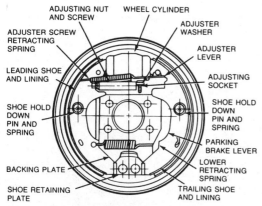

Rear brake lining components

2. Raise the vehicle and support with jackstands. Remove the wheel lugs and the tire and wheel assembly.

3. Remove the brake drum assembly as outlined in the "Rear Brake Drum" removal and installation procedures in this section.

4. Remove the two shoe hold-down springs and pins.

5. Lift the brake shoes, springs, and adjuster assembly off the backing plate and wheel cylinder assembly. Be careful not to bend the adjusting lever during assembly removal.

4. Remove the parking brake cable from the parking brake lever.

5. Remove the retracting springs from the lower brake shoe attachments and the upper shoe-to-adjusting lever attachment points. This will separate the brake shoes and disengage the adjuster mechanism.

6. Remove the horseshoe retaining clip and spring washer and slide lever off the parking brake lever pin on the trailing shoe.

To install:

1. Apply a light coating of Disc Brake Caliper Slide Grease D7AZ-19590-A or equivalent at the points where the brake shoes contact the backing plate.

2. Apply a thin uniform coat of multi-purpose lubricant to the adjuster screw threads and the socket end of the adjusting screw. Install the stainless steel washer over the socket end of the adjusting screw and install the socket. Turn the adjusting screw into the adjusting pivot nut to the limit of threads and then back off one-half turn.

3. Assemble the parking brake lever to trailing shoe and lining assembly by installing the spring washer and a new horseshoe retaining clip. Crimp the clip until it retains the lever to the shoe securely.

4. Attach the parking brake cable to the parking brake lever.

5. Attach a lower shoe retracting spring to the leading and trailing shoe assemblies and install to the backing plate. It will be necessary to stretch the retracting spring as the shoes are installed downward over the anchor plate to the inside of the shoe retaining plate.

6. Install the adjuster screw assembly between the leading shoe slot and the slot in the trailing shoe and parking brake lever. The adjuster socket end slot must fit into the trailing shoe and the parking brake lever.

NOTE: *The adjuster socket blade is marked R or L for RH or LH brake assemblies. The R or L adjuster blade must be installed with the letter R or L in the upright position (facing the wheel cylinder) on the correct side to ensure that the deeper of two slots in the adjuster sockets fits into the parking brake lever.*

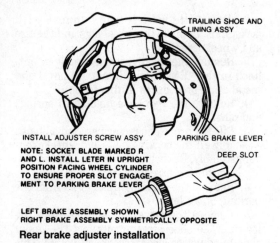

Rear brake adjuster installation

7. Assemble the adjuster lever in the groove located in the parking brake lever pin and into the slot of the adjuster socket that fits into the trailing shoe web.

8. Attach the upper retracting spring to leading shoe slot. Using an appropriate spring tool, stretch the other end of the spring into the notch on the adjuster lever. If the adjuster lever does not contact the star wheel after installing the spring, it is possible that the adjuster socket is installed incorrectly.

9. Install the brake hub and drum assembly and wheels as outlined.

10. Install the hub/drum and wheels.

11. Adjust the wheel bearing as described below. Install the nut retainer and a new cotter pin.

NOTE: *The rear wheel uses a tapered roller bearing which may feel loose when properly adjusted; this feel should be considered normal.*

a. Back off the hub nut one full turn.

b. While rotating the hub/drum assembly, torque the adjusting nut to 17-25 ft. lbs. Back off the adjusting nut ½ turn, then retighten it to 10-15 in. lbs.

c. Position the nut retainer over the adjusting nut so that the slots are in line with cotter pin hole (without rotating the adjusting nut).

d. Install the cotter pin and bend the ends around the retainer flange.

e. Check the hub rotation. If the hub rotates freely, install the grease cap. If not, check the bearings for damage and replace as necessary.

12. Install the tire and wheel assembly and torque the lugs to 80-105 ft. lbs.

13. Lower the vehicle. Pump the brakes several times before the vehicle is moved.

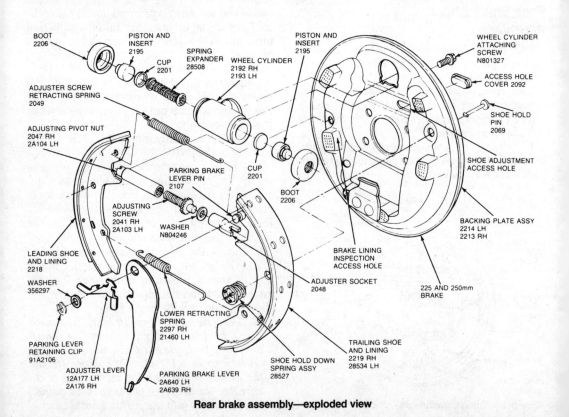

Rear brake assembly—exploded view

Rear Wheel Cylinder (Drum Brakes)

REMOVAL

CAUTION: *Brake shoes contain asbestos, which has been determined to be a cancer causing agent. Never clean the brake surfaces with compressed air! Avoid inhaling any dust from any brake surface! When cleaning brake surfaces, use a commercially available brake cleaning fluid.*

1. Remove the wheel cover, loosen the lugs, jack up the rear end of your car and safely support it on jackstands. Remove the wheel lugs and the tire and wheel assembly.

2. Remove brake shoe assembly.

3. Disconnect the brake line from the wheel cylinder using a flare nut wrench.

CAUTION: *If a flare nut wrench is not used, the flare nut at the end of the steel brake line may be damaged.*

4. Remove the wheel cylinder attaching bolts and remove the wheel cylinder.

WARNING: *Use caution to prevent brake fluid from contacting brake linings or they must be replaced.*

INSTALLATION

NOTE: *Wipe the end(s) of the hydraulic line to remove any foreign matter before making connections.*

1. Position the wheel cylinder on the backing plate and finger-tighten the brake line to cylinder.

2. Secure the cylinder to the backing plate by installing the attaching bolts. Tighten the bolt to 7.5-10 ft. lbs.

3. Tighten the tube nut fitting (using a flare nut wrench).

4. Install and adjust brakes.

5. Install hub/drum and wheel assembly.

6. Bleed the brake system.

OVERHAULING THE WHEEL CYLINDER

Wheel cylinders need not be rebuilt unless they are leaking or seized. To check the wheel cylinder for leakage, carefully pull the lower edge of the rubber end boot away from the cylinder. Excessive brake fluid in the boot or running out of the boot, when the edges are pulled away from the cylinder, denotes leakage. A certain (slight) amount of fluid in the boot is normal.

1. It is not necessary to remove the cylinder from the brake backing (mounting) plate to rebuild the cylinder, however removal makes the job easier.

2. Disengage and remove the rubber boots from both ends of the wheel cylinder. The piston should come out with the boot. If not, remove the piston by applying finger pressure inward on one piston, the piston on the opposite end should come out. Take care not to splash brake fluid all over yourself when the piston pops from the cylinder.

3. Remove the rubber cups, center expander and spring from the wheel cylinder. Remove the bleeder screw from the back of the cylinder.

4. Discard all rubber boots and cups. Wash the pistons and cylinder in denatured alcohol or clean brake fluid.

5. Inspect the pistons for scratches, scoring or other visible damage. Inspect the cylinder bore for score marks or rust. The cylinder may be honed (with a brake cylinder hone) if necessary. Do not hone more than 0.076mm beyond original diameter. If the scoring or pitting is deeper, replace the cylinder.

6. After honing the cylinder, wash again with alcohol or clean brake fluid. Check the bleeder screw hole to make sure it is opened. Wipe the cylinder bore with a clean cloth. Install the bleeder screw.

7. Never reuse the old rubber parts. Always use all of the parts supplied in the rebuilding kit.

8. Apply a light coat of brake fluid, or the special lubricant if supplied with the rebuilding kit, on the pistons, rubber cups and cylinder bore.

9. Insert the spring and expander assembly into the cylinder bore. Put the cups, facing in, and the pistons into the cylinder. Install the

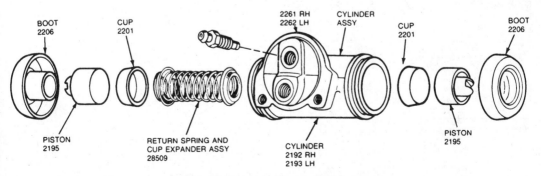

Wheel cylinder assembly—exploded view

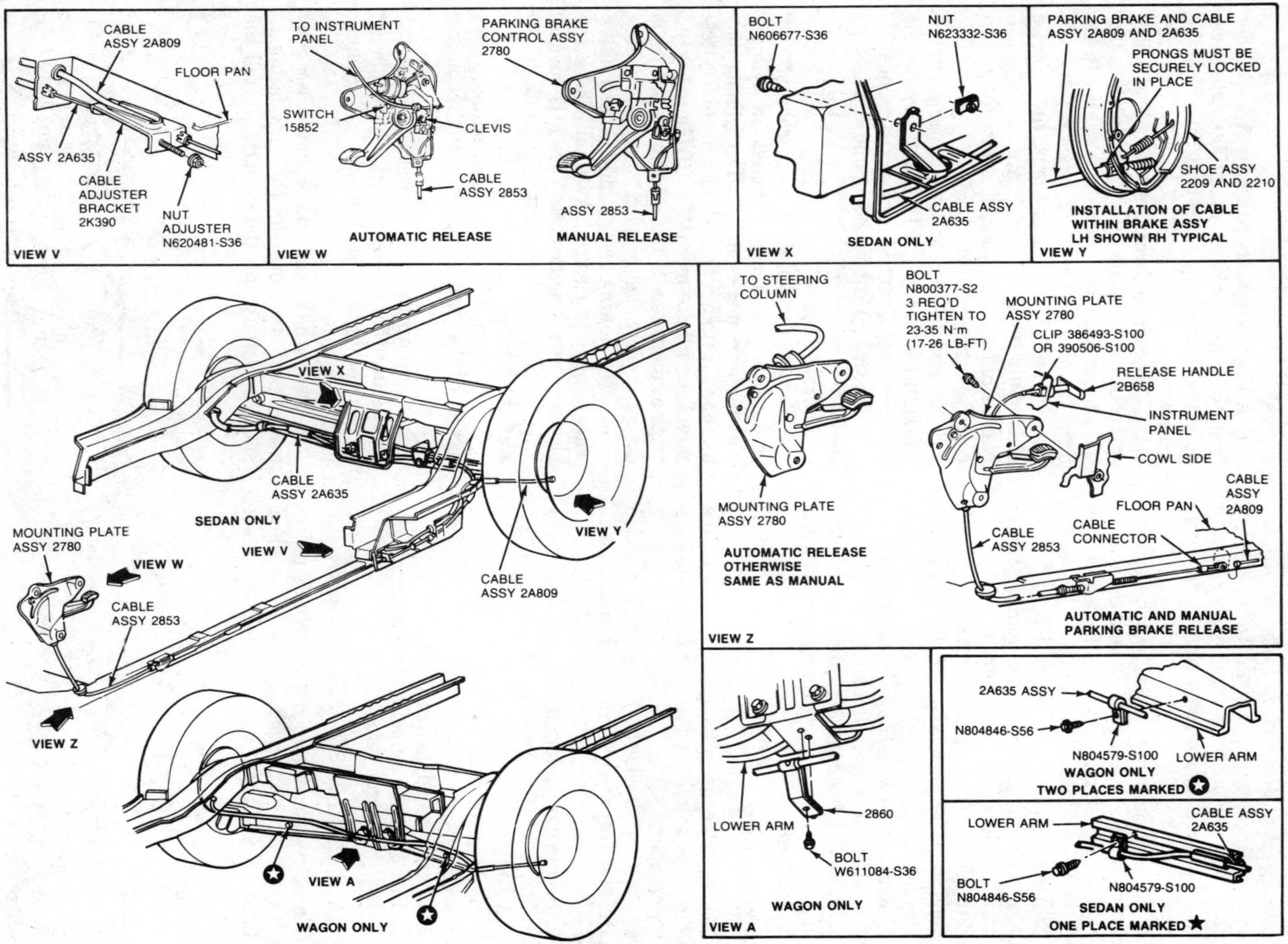

Parking brake cables and components

VIEW Y

PARKING BRAKE AND CABLE ASSY 2A809 AND 2A635

PRONGS MUST BE SECURELY LOCKED IN PLACE

SHOE ASSY 2209 AND 2210

INSTALLATION OF CABLE WITHIN BRAKE ASSY LH SHOWN RH TYPICAL

VIEW X

NUT N623332-S36

CABLE ASSY 2A635

BOLT N606677-S36

SEDAN ONLY

RELEASE HANDLE 2B658

INSTRUMENT PANEL

COWL SIDE

CABLE ASSY 2A809

FLOOR PAN

CABLE CONNECTOR

MOUNTING PLATE ASSY 2780

CLIP 386493-S100 OR 390506-S100

CABLE ASSY 2853

BOLT N800377-S2 3 REQ'D TIGHTEN TO 23-35 N·m (17-26 LB-FT)

AUTOMATIC AND MANUAL PARKING BRAKE RELEASE

TO STEERING COLUMN

MOUNTING PLATE ASSY 2780

AUTOMATIC RELEASE OTHERWISE SAME AS MANUAL

2A635 ASSY

N804579-S100

N804846-S56

LOWER ARM

WAGON ONLY

TWO PLACES MARKED ✪

LOWER ARM

CABLE ASSY 2A635

N804579-S100

BOLT N804846-S56

SEDAN ONLY

ONE PLACE MARKED ★

VIEW Z

LOWER ARM

2860

BOLT W611084-S36

WAGON ONLY

VIEW A

VIEW W

PARKING BRAKE CONTROL ASSY 2780

ASSY 2853

MANUAL RELEASE

TO INSTRUMENT PANEL

CLEVIS

CABLE ASSY 2853

SWITCH 15852

AUTOMATIC RELEASE

VIEW V

FLOOR PAN

CABLE ASSY 2A809

CABLE ADJUSTER BRACKET 2K390

NUT ADJUSTER N620481-S36

ASSY 2A635

VIEW Y

CABLE ASSY 2A809

VIEW X

CABLE ASSY 2A635

VIEW V

SEDAN ONLY

VIEW W

CABLE ASSY 2853

MOUNTING PLATE ASSY 2780

VIEW Z

VIEW A

WAGON ONLY

boots and fit the outer lips into the retaining grooves on the outer edges of the wheel cylinder.

10. Install the wheel cylinder onto the backing plate. Be sure that the inlet port (where the brake hose connects) is toward the rear of the car. Install the brake shoes, drum and wheel assembly. Adjust and bleed the brake system. Road test the car.

REAR DISC BRAKES

Continental and 3.0L SHO Taurus

CAUTION: *Brake shoes contain asbestos, which has been determined to be a cancer causing agent. Never clean the brake surfaces with compressed air! Avoid inhaling any dust from any brake surface! When cleaning brake surfaces, use a commercially available brake cleaning fluid.*

The Continental and 3.0L SHO Taurus are equipped with rear disc brakes. Except for the parking brake mechanism, the rear caliper assembly is similar to the pin slider front brake

caliper. The added parking brake lever on the back of the caliper is cable operated by the parking brake pedal located below the instrument panel. The parking brake cable is self-adjusting.

REAR DISC BRAKE INSPECTION

The rear disc brakes can be inspected through an oval hole in the back of the brake caliper. Raise the rear of the vehicle and remove the wheel and tire assembly to inspect the brake pads. If the brake lining thickness is less than 3mm the brake pads will have to be replaced.

Rear Brake Rotor

REMOVAL AND INSTALLATION

1. Raise the rear of the vehicle and support with jackstands.
2. Remove the wheel and tire assembly.

NOTE: *During service, handle the caliper assembly and rotor in such a way as to avoid nicking, scratching, or contamination of the brake linings and deformation of the rotor.*

3. Remove the retaining clip from the parking brake at the caliper. Disengage the parking brake cable end from the lever arm.

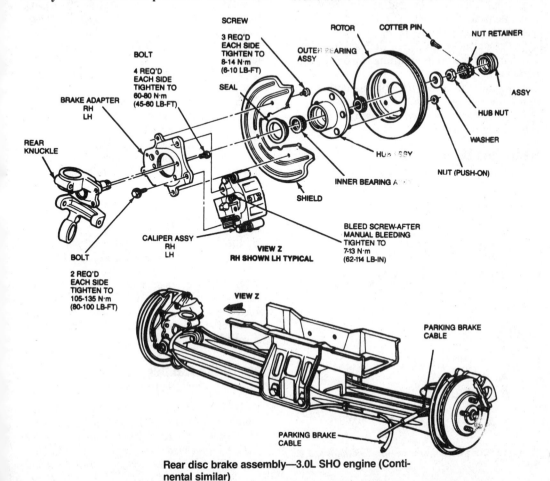

Rear disc brake assembly—3.0L SHO engine (Continental similar)

4. Hold the slider pin hex-heads with an open-end wrench and remove the pinch bolts.

5. Lift the caliper away from the anchor plate and remove the slider pins and boots from the anchor plate.

6. Support the caliper with a wire hooked to the body so that the flexible hose is not damaged.

7. Remove the anchor plate upper and lower attaching bolts.

8. Mark the flat sections of the rotors to distinguish the RH from the LH side rotors. Remove the rotor from the hub by pulling it off the hub. If the rotor is stuck, tap the center hub with a plastic hammer a few times and pull the rotor away from the hub.

To install:

1. Apply Silicone Dielectric Compound part No. D7AZ-19A331-A or equivalent to the inside of the slider pin boots and to the slider pin.

2. Install the anchor plate and torque the attaching bolts to 80-100 ft. lbs.

3. Position the slider pins and boots onto the anchor plate. Position the caliper onto the anchor plate. Make sure the anti-rattle springs are installed correctly.

4. Apply a drop of Threadlock and Sealer or equivalent to the pinch bolt threads. Torque the pinch bolts to 30-35 ft. lbs.

5. Attach the cable end of the parking brake lever. Install the cable retaining clip on the caliper assembly.

6. Install the wheel and tire assembly and lower the vehicle.

7. Pump the brake pedal a few times before the vehicle is moved.

Rear Disc Brake Pads

REMOVAL AND INSTALLATION

CAUTION: *Brake shoes contain asbestos, which has been determined to be a cancer*

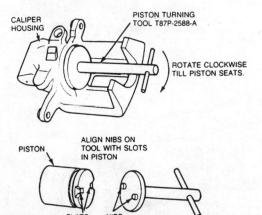

Turning caliper piston into bore—Continental and 3.0L SHO

causing agent. Never clean the brake surfaces with compressed air! Avoid inhaling any dust from any brake surface! When cleaning brake surfaces, use a commercially available brake cleaning fluid.

Continental and 3.0L SHO Taurus

1. Raise the rear of the vehicle and support with jackstands.

2. Remove the wheel and tire assembly.

3. Remove the screw retaining the brake hose bracket-to-shock absorber bracket.

4. Remove the retaining clip from the parking brake cable at the caliper and remove the cable end from the parking brake lever.

5. Hold the slider pin hex-heads with an open-end wrench. Remove the upper pinch bolt and loosen but do not remove the lower pinch bolt.

6. Rotate the caliper out of the way with a piece of wire and attach it to the body so that the flexible hose does not get damaged.

7. Remove the inner and outer brake pads and the anti-rattle clips from the anchor plate.

To install:

1. Using a Piston Turning Tool part No. T87P-2588-A or equivalent, rotate the caliper piston clockwise until the piston is fully seated. Make sure that one of the two slots in the piston face is positioned it will engage the nib on the brake pad.

2. Install the inner and outer brake pads on the anchor plate.

3. Rotate the caliper over the rotor into position on the anchor plate and make sure that the anti-rattle clips are installed correctly.

4. Apply Threadlock and Sealer or equivalent to the upper pinch bolt threads. Install the bolts and tighten the pinch bolts while holding the slider pins with an open-end wrench.

5. Attach the cable end of the parking brake lever and install the retaining clip on the caliper assembly.

6. Install the brake flex hose onto the shock absorber and torque the retaining screw to 8-11 ft. lbs.

7. Install the wheel and tire assembly and torque the lugs to 80-104 ft. lbs. Lower the vehicle.

8. Pump the brake pedal a few times before the vehicle is moved.

Rear Brake Caliper

REMOVAL AND INSTALLATION

CAUTION: *Brake shoes contain asbestos, which has been determined to be a cancer causing agent. Never clean the brake surfaces with compressed air! Avoid inhaling any dust from any brake surface! When cleaning brake surfaces, use a commercially available brake cleaning fluid.*

1. Raise the vehicle and support with jackstands. Remove the rear wheel and tire assemblies.

2. Remove the brake flex hose from the caliper assembly. Do not loose the hose sealing rings.

3. Remove the retaining clip from the parking brake at the caliper and disengage the parking cable end from the lever arm.

4. Hold the slider pin hex-head with an open-end wrench and remove the pinch bolts.

5. Lift the caliper assembly away from the anchor plate and remove the slider pins and boots from the anchor plate.

6. **To install:** apply Silicone Dielectric Compound D7AZ-19A331-A or equivalent to the inside of the slider pin boots and to the slider pins.

7. Position the slider pins and boots in the anchor plate. Position the caliper assembly on the anchor plate. Make sure that the brake pads are installed correctly.

8. Apply one drop of Threadlock and Sealer to the pinch bolt threads and torque the pinch bolts to 23-26 ft. lbs.

9. Attach the parking cable end to the brake lever and install the retaining clip on the caliper.

10. Using new flex hose washers, connect the brake flex hose to the caliper and torque the retaining bolt to 8-11 ft. lbs.

11. Bleed the brake system as outlined in the "Bleeding the Brake System" in this chapter.

12. Install the wheel and tire assembly and torque the lug nuts to 85-104 ft. lbs. Lower the vehicle and pump the brakes a few times before the vehicle is moved.

CALIPER OVERHAUL

1. Remove the caliper assembly from the vehicle as outlined in the previous section.

2. Mount the caliper in a vise. Using a Brake Piston Turning Tool T75P-2588-B or equivalent and turn the piston counterclockwise to remove the piston from the bore.

3. Using a snapring pliers, remove the

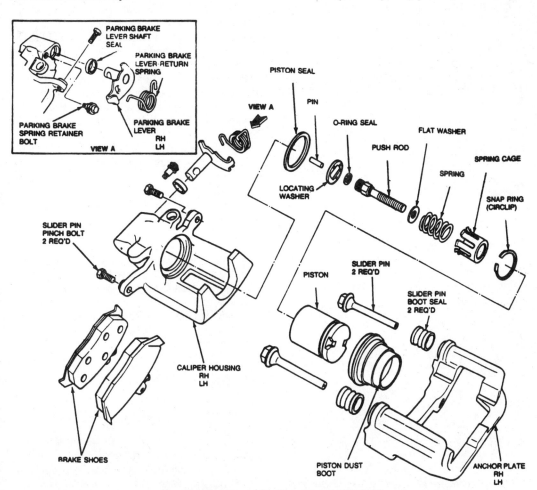

Rear brake caliper—Continental and 3.0L SHO

snapring retaining the pushrod from the caliper.

CAUTION: *The snapring and spring cover are under spring load. Be careful when removing the snapring.*

4. Remove the spring cover, spring, washer, key plate, and pull out the pushrod strut pin from the piston bore.

5. Remove the parking brake lever return spring, unscrew the parking brake lever stop bolt and pull the parking brake lever out of the caliper housing.

6. Clean all medal parts with isopropyl alcohol. Use clean dry compressed air to clean the grooves and passages. Inspect the caliper bores for damage or excessive wear. If the piston is pitted, scratched, or scored replace the piston.

ASSEMBLY

1. Lightly grease the parking brake lever bore and the lever shaft seal with Silicone Dielectric Compound or equivalent. Press the parking brake lever shaft seal into the caliper bore.

2. Grease the parking brake shaft recess and

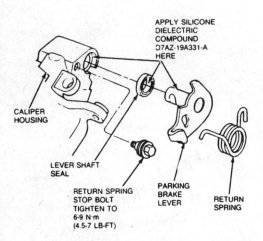

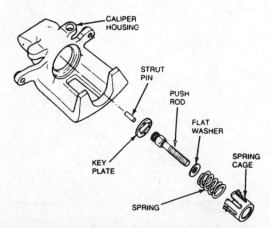

Parking brake assembly for rear brake caliper

slightly grease the parking brake lever shaft. Install the shaft into the caliper housing.

3. Install the lever stop bolt into the caliper housing and torque the bolt to 60-84 in. lbs.

4. Attach the parking brake lever return spring to the stop bolt and install the free end into the parking brake lever slot.

5. Install a new O-ring seal in the groove of the pushrod. Grease the pushrod end with Silicone Dielectric Compound or equivalent.

6. Position the strut pin into the caliper housing and in the recess of the parking brake lever shaft. Install the pushrod into the bore. Make sure the pin is positioned correctly between the shaft recess. Install the flat washer, pushrod, spring and spring cover in order.

PARKING BRAKE

Brake Cable

ADJUSTMENT

Taurus/Sable

1. Make sure the parking brake is fully released.

2. Place the transmission in NEUTRAL. Raise the vehicle and support the rear axle with jackstands.

3. Tighten the adjusting nut against the cable equalizer, causing a rear wheel brake drag. Then, loosen the adjusting nut until the rear brakes are fully released. There should be no brake drag. If the brake cables are replaced in a system having a foot-operated control assembly, stroke the parking brake control with approximately 100 lbs. pedal effort, then release the control and repeat this step.

4. Lower the vehicle and check operation of parking brake.

Continental

The Continental is equipped with an automatic (vacuum) release parking brake control that is standard. The vacuum unit is mounted on the control mounting bracket. Engine manifold vacuum activates the diaphram to release the parking brake whenever the engine is running and the transaxle is in the forward gear.

ADJUSTMENT

1. Make sure the parking brake is fully released.

2. Raise the vehicle and support with jackstands.

3. Tighten the adjusting nut against the cable adjuster bracket until there is a slight movement of the rear brake lever at the caliper.

4. Spin the rear wheels to ensure that the emergency brake is not binding.

5. Lower the vehicle and check for proper operation.

Parking Brake Manual Release Handle and Cable Assembly

REMOVAL AND INSTALLATION

Taurus/Sable

1. Disconnect the release cable from the parking brake control release arm and remove the release cable grommet from parking brake control.

2. From under the instrument panel using a screwdriver, pry off and remove the retainer clip securing the cable and handle to the instrument panel. Pull the handle and cable assembly out of instrument panel.

To install:

1. Start the cable and handle assembly through the locating hole in the instrument panel and install the retainer clip that secures the handle to the instrument panel.

2. Connect the release cable to the parking brake control release arm and install the release cable grommet to the parking brake control.

Continental

1. Disconnect the release cable from the parking brake control release arm and remove the release cable grommet from the parking brake control.

2. Remove the two screws attaching the release handle to the instrument panel and remove the handle assembly.

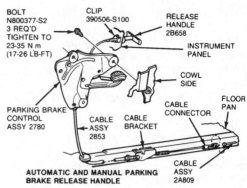

Parking brake cable release mechanism

To install:

3. Start the cable and handle through the slotted hole in the instrument panel and install the two retaining screws.

4. Connect the release cable to the parking brake control release arm and install the cable grommet.

Front Brake Cable

REMOVAL AND INSTALLATION

1. Raise the vehicle and support safely on jackstands.

2. Loosen the adjuster nut at the adjuster bracket.

3. Lower the vehicle.

4. Disconnect the cable from the control assembly at the clevis.

5. Raise the vehicle and support safely on jackstands.

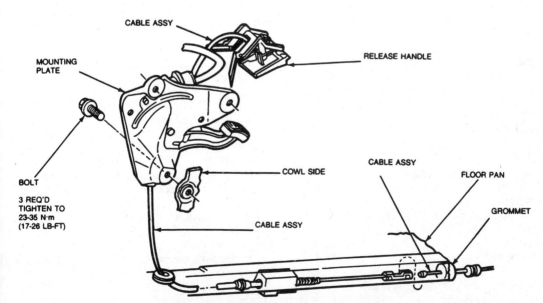

Parking brake control assembly—Continental

6. Disconnect the front cable from the rear cable at the cable connector.

7. Remove the cable and the push-in prong retainer from the cable bracket, using a 13mm box end wrench to depress retaining prongs. Allow the cable to hang.

8. Push the grommet up through floorpan.

9. Lower the vehicle.

10. Remove the LH cowl side panel.

11. Pull the carpet away from the cowl panel.

12. From inside the vehicle remove the cable end from the clevis and remove the conduit retainer from the control assembly.

13. Pull the cable assembly through floorpan hole.

To install:

1. Start the cable through the hole in floorpan and secure the grommet in place.

2. Push the prong retainer into the parking brake housing until the prongs are secure and connect the cable to the control clevis.

3. Install the carpeting and body side pad.

4. Raise the vehicle and position the cable through the front cable bracket at the frame side rail and push the prong into bracket.

NOTE: *The prongs must be securely locked in place.*

5. Connect the rear cable to the front cable connector.

6. Adjust the parking brake and lower vehicle.

7. Check the parking brake operation.

Left Side Rear Brake Cable

REMOVAL AND INSTALLATION

1. Raise the vehicle and support safely on jackstands.

2. Remove the parking brake cable adjusting nut.

3. Remove the rear cable end fitting from the front cable connector.

4. Remove the wheel and drum assembly. Refer to the "Rear Brake Drum" removal and installation procedures in this chapter.

5. Disconnect the brake cable end from the parking brake actuating lever. Using a 13mm box end wrench to depress the conduit retaining prongs, remove the cable end pronged fitting from backing plate.

6. Push the plastic snap-in grommet rearward to disconnect it from the side rail bracket.

7. Remove the pronged connector from the parking brake adjuster bracket. Remove the cable assembly.

To install:

1. Insert the cable through the side rail bracket and the adjuster bracket. Be sure the pronged connector is securely attached to the brake adjuster bracket.

2. Seat the plastic snap-in grommet inside the rail bracket.

3. Insert the cable end into the brake assembly backing plate and push the pronged cable end into the brake backing plate hole. Be sure the prongs are locked in place.

NOTE: *The cable must be located over the right cable.*

4. Attach the cable end to the parking brake actuating lever.

5. Attach the cable to the front cable connector.

6. Install the drum and wheel assembly.

7. Install the brake cable adjusting nut.

8. Adjust the parking brake and lower the vehicle. Refer to the "Parking Brake Adjustment" procedures in this chapter.

9. Check for proper operation.

Right Side Rear Brake Cable

REMOVAL AND INSTALLATION

1. Raise the vehicle and support safely on jackstands.

2. Remove the parking brake cable adjusting nut.

3. Using a 13mm box end wrench to remove the conduit retainer prongs and remove the cable from the frame side rail bracket.

4. Remove the wheel and drum assembly. Refer to the "Rear Brake Drum" removal and installation procedures in this chapter.

5. Disconnect the brake cable from the parking brake actuating lever. Using a 13mm box end wrench to depress the conduit retaining prongs, remove the cable end pronged fitting from the brake backing plate.

6. On sedan vehicles, remove the brake pressure control valve bracket at control arm.

7. **Sedan:** Remove the cable retaining screw and clip from the lower suspension arm and one screw from the cable bracket at the crossmember, and remove the entire right cable assembly.

Wagon: Remove the cable retaining clip and screw from each lower suspension arm, and one screw from the cable retaining clip on the lower suspension arm inner mounting bracket.

To install:

1. Insert the cable into the opening in the frame side rail bracket and the threaded end of cable in the adjuster, and start the adjuster nut on the threads. Be sure the pronged fitting is pressed into the frame side rail bracket and securely locked in place.

2. Route the cable under LH brake cable and lower suspension arms.

3. Secure the cable end into the parking brake actuating lever.

4. Insert the cable end pronged fitting into

the brake backing plate and securely lock in place.

5. Attach the bracket-to-crossmember bracket and install the nut.

6. Install the brake cable retaining clips (wagon) or the screw and clip (sedan). Tighten the retaining screws.

7. Install the brake pressure control valve assembly bracket to the control arm.

8. Install the drum and wheel assembly.

9. Adjust the parking brake.

10. Lower the vehicle.

11. Check for proper operation.

Brake Specifications

All measurements in inches unless noted

Year	Model	Lug Nut Torque (ft. lbs.)	Master Cylinder Bore	Brake Disc		Standard Brake Drum Diameter	Minimum Lining Thickness	
				Minimum Thickness	Maximum Runout		Front	Rear
1986	Sedan	80–105	0.828	0.896	0.005	8.85	0.125	1.49
	Wagon	80–105	0.828	0.896	0.005	9.84	0.125	1.49
1987	Sedan	80–105	0.875	0.896	0.005	8.85	0.125	1.49
	Wagon	80–105	0.875	0.896	0.005	9.84	0.125	1.49

Year	Model	Lug Nut Torque (ft. lbs.)	Master Cylinder Bore	Front Brake Disc		Rear Brake Disc		Standard Brake Drum Diameter	Minimum Lining Thickness	
				Minimum Thickness	Maximum Runout	Minimum Thickness	Maximum Runout		Front	Rear
1988	Sedan	80–105	0.875	0.974	0.003	—	—	8.85	0.125	0.149
	Wagon	80–105	0.875	0.974	0.003	—	—	9.84	0.125	0.149
	Continental	80–105	①	0.970	0.002	0.974	0.002	—	0.125	0.123
1989	Sedan	80–105	0.875	0.974	0.003	—	—	8.85	0.125	0.149
	Wagon	80–105	0.875	0.974	0.003	—	—	9.84	0.125	0.149
	Continental	80–105	①	0.970	0.002	0.974	0.002	—	0.125	0.123
	3.0L SHO Taurus	80–105	1.000	0.974	0.003	0.974	0.002	—	0.125	0.123

① The Continental is equipped with ABS (anti-lock Brake System) and does not have a master cylinder bore.

Troubleshooting the Brake System

Problem	Cause	Solution
Low brake pedal (excessive pedal travel required for braking action.)	• Excessive clearance between rear linings and drums caused by in-operative automatic adjusters	• Make 10 to 15 alternate forward and reverse brake stops to adjust brakes. If brake pedal does not come up, repair or replace adjuster parts as necessary.
	• Worn rear brakelining	• Inspect and replace lining if worn beyond minimum thickness specification
	• Bent, distorted brakeshoes, front or rear	• Replace brakeshoes in axle sets
	• Air in hydraulic system	• Remove air from system. Refer to Brake Bleeding.
Low brake pedal (pedal may go to floor with steady pressure applied.)	• Fluid leak in hydraulic system	• Fill master cylinder to fill line; have helper apply brakes and check calipers, wheel cylinders, differ-

Troubleshooting the Brake System (cont.)

Problem	Cause	Solution
Low brake pedal (pedal may go to floor with steady pressure applied.) (cont.)		ential valve tubes, hoses and fittings for leaks. Repair or replace as necessary.
	• Air in hydraulic system	• Remove air from system. Refer to Brake Bleeding.
	• Incorrect or non-recommended brake fluid (fluid evaporates at below normal temp).	• Flush hydraulic system with clean brake fluid. Refill with correct-type fluid.
	• Master cylinder piston seals worn, or master cylinder bore is scored, worn or corroded	• Repair or replace master cylinder
Low brake pedal (pedal goes to floor on first application—o.k. on subsequent applications.)	• Disc brake pads sticking on abutment surfaces of anchor plate. Caused by a build-up of dirt, rust, or corrosion on abutment surfaces	• Clean abutment surfaces
Fading brake pedal (pedal height decreases with steady pressure applied.)	• Fluid leak in hydraulic system	• Fill master cylinder reservoirs to fill mark, have helper apply brakes, check calipers, wheel cylinders, differential valve, tubes, hoses, and fittings for fluid leaks. Repair or replace parts as necessary.
	• Master cylinder piston seals worn, or master cylinder bore is scored, worn or corroded	• Repair or replace master cylinder
Decreasing brake pedal travel (pedal travel required for braking action decreases and may be accompanied by a hard pedal.)	• Caliper or wheel cylinder pistons sticking or seized	• Repair or replace the calipers, or wheel cylinders
	• Master cylinder compensator ports blocked (preventing fluid return to reservoirs) or pistons sticking or seized in master cylinder bore	• Repair or replace the master cylinder
	• Power brake unit binding internally	• Test unit according to the following procedure: (a) Shift transmission into neutral and start engine (b) Increase engine speed to 1500 rpm, close throttle and fully depress brake pedal (c) Slow release brake pedal and stop engine (d) Have helper remove vacuum check valve and hose from power unit. Observe for backward movement of brake pedal. (e) If the pedal moves backward, the power unit has an internal bind—replace power unit
Spongy brake pedal (pedal has abnormally soft, springy, spongy feel when depressed.)	• Air in hydraulic system	• Remove air from system. Refer to Brake Bleeding.
	• Brakeshoes bent or distorted	• Replace brakeshoes
	• Brakelining not yet seated with drums and rotors	• Burnish brakes
	• Rear drum brakes not properly adjusted	• Adjust brakes
Hard brake pedal (excessive pedal pressure required to stop vehicle. May be accompanied by brake fade.)	• Loose or leaking power brake unit vacuum hose	• Tighten connections or replace leaking hose
	• Incorrect or poor quality brakelining	• Replace with lining in axle sets
	• Bent, broken, distorted brakeshoes	• Replace brakeshoes
	• Calipers binding or dragging on mounting pins. Rear brakeshoes dragging on support plate.	• Replace mounting pins and bushings. Clean rust or burrs from rear brake support plate ledges

Troubleshooting the Brake System (cont.)

Problem	Cause	Solution
Hard brake pedal (excessive pedal pressure required to stop vehicle. May be accompanied by brake fade.) (cont.)		and lubricate ledges with molydi-sulfide grease. **NOTE:** If ledges are deeply grooved or scored, do not attempt to sand or grind them smooth—replace support plate.
	• Caliper, wheel cylinder, or master cylinder pistons sticking or seized	• Repair or replace parts as necessary
	• Power brake unit vacuum check valve malfunction	• Test valve according to the following procedure: (a) Start engine, increase engine speed to 1500 rpm, close throttle and immediately stop engine (b) Wait at least 90 seconds then depress brake pedal (c) If brakes are not vacuum assisted for 2 or more applications, check valve is faulty
	• Power brake unit has internal bind	• Test unit according to the following procedure: (a) With engine stopped, apply brakes several times to exhaust all vacuum in system (b) Shift transmission into neutral, depress brake pedal and start engine (c) If pedal height decreases with foot pressure and less pressure is required to hold pedal in applied position, power unit vacuum system is operating normally. Test power unit. If power unit exhibits a bind condition, replace the power unit.
	• Master cylinder compensator ports (at bottom of reservoirs) blocked by dirt, scale, rust, or have small burrs (blocked ports prevent fluid return to reservoirs).	• Repair or replace master cylinder **CAUTION:** Do not attempt to clean blocked ports with wire, pencils, or similar implements. Use compressed air only.
	• Brake hoses, tubes, fittings clogged or restricted	• Use compressed air to check or unclog parts. Replace any damaged parts.
	• Brake fluid contaminated with improper fluids (motor oil, transmission fluid, causing rubber components to swell and stick in bores	• Replace all rubber components, combination valve and hoses. Flush entire brake system with DOT 3 brake fluid or equivalent.
	• Low engine vacuum	• Adjust or repair engine
Grabbing brakes (severe reaction to brake pedal pressure.)	• Brakelining(s) contaminated by grease or brake fluid	• Determine and correct cause of contamination and replace brakeshoes in axle sets
	• Parking brake cables incorrectly adjusted or seized	• Adjust cables. Replace seized cables.
	• Incorrect brakelining or lining loose on brakeshoes	• Replace brakeshoes in axle sets
	• Caliper anchor plate bolts loose	• Tighten bolts
	• Rear brakeshoes binding on support plate ledges	• Clean and lubricate ledges. Replace support plate(s) if ledges are deeply grooved. Do not attempt to smooth ledges by grinding.
	• Incorrect or missing power brake reaction disc	• Install correct disc
	• Rear brake support plates loose	• Tighten mounting bolts

Troubleshooting the Brake System (cont.)

Problem	Cause	Solution
Dragging brakes (slow or incomplete release of brakes)	• Brake pedal binding at pivot • Power brake unit has internal bind	• Loosen and lubricate • Inspect for internal bind. Replace unit if internal bind exists.
	• Parking brake cables incorrrectly adjusted or seized	• Adjust cables. Replace seized cables.
	• Rear brakeshoe return springs weak or broken	• Replace return springs. Replace brakeshoe if necessary in axle sets.
	• Automatic adjusters malfunctioning	• Repair or replace adjuster parts as required
	• Caliper, wheel cylinder or master cylinder pistons sticking or seized	• Repair or replace parts as necessary
	• Master cylinder compensating ports blocked (fluid does not return to reservoirs).	• Use compressed air to clear ports. Do not use wire, pencils, or similar objects to open blocked ports.
Vehicle moves to one side when brakes are applied	• Incorrect front tire pressure	• Inflate to recommended cold (reduced load) inflation pressure
	• Worn or damaged wheel bearings	• Replace worn or damaged bearings
	• Brakelining on one side contaminated	• Determine and correct cause of contamination and replace brakelining in axle sets
	• Brakeshoes on one side bent, distorted, or lining loose on shoe	• Replace brakeshoes in axle sets
	• Support plate bent or loose on one side	• Tighten or replace support plate
	• Brakelining not yet seated with drums or rotors	• Burnish brakelining
	• Caliper anchor plate loose on one side	• Tighten anchor plate bolts
	• Caliper piston sticking or seized • Brakelinings water soaked	• Repair or replace caliper • Drive vehicle with brakes lightly applied to dry linings
	• Loose suspension component attaching or mounting bolts • Brake combination valve failure	• Tighten suspension bolts. Replace worn suspension components. • Replace combination valve
Chatter or shudder when brakes are applied (pedal pulsation and roughness may also occur.)	• Brakeshoes distorted, bent, contaminated, or worn • Caliper anchor plate or support plate loose • Excessive thickness variation of rotor(s)	• Replace brakeshoes in axle sets • Tighten mounting bolts • Refinish or replace rotors in axle sets
Noisy brakes (squealing, clicking, scraping sound when brakes are applied.)	• Bent, broken, distorted brakeshoes • Excessive rust on outer edge of rotor braking surface	• Replace brakeshoes in axle sets • Remove rust
Noisy brakes (squealing, clicking, scraping sound when brakes are applied.) (cont.)	• Brakelining worn out—shoes contacting drum of rotor	• Replace brakeshoes and lining in axle sets. Refinish or replace drums or rotors.
	• Broken or loose holdown or return springs	• Replace parts as necessary
	• Rough or dry drum brake support plate ledges	• Lubricate support plate ledges
	• Cracked, grooved, or scored rotor(s) or drum(s)	• Replace rotor(s) or drum(s). Replace brakeshoes and lining in axle sets if necessary.
	• Incorrect brakelining and/or shoes (front or rear).	• Install specified shoe and lining assemblies
Pulsating brake pedal	• Out of round drums or excessive lateral runout in disc brake rotor(s)	• Refinish or replace drums, re-index rotors or replace

EXTERIOR

Doors

REMOVAL

Front Doors

1. Support the door using padded jack or other suitable tool.

2. Remove the hinge attaching bolts and nuts from the door and remove the door.

3. Disconnect the wiring harness connectors, if so equipped.

4. If the door is to be replaced, transfer the following components to the new door if they are in usable condition: trim panel, watershield, outside moldings, clips, window regulators and the door latch components.

To install:

5. Position the door hinges and partially tighten the bolts.

6. Align the door and tighten the bolts securely to 13-21 ft. lbs.

Rear Doors

1. Remove the scuff plate.
2. Remove the center pillar trim panel.
3. Remove the seat belt assembly.

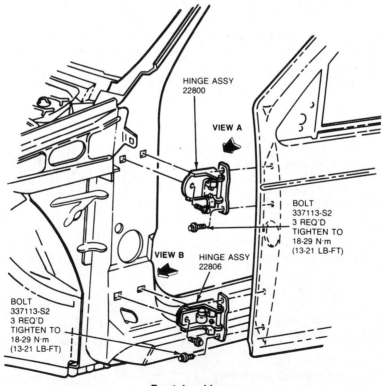

HINGE ASSY 22800

VIEW A

BOLT 337113-S2 3 REQ'D TIGHTEN TO 18-29 N·m (13-21 LB-FT)

VIEW B HINGE ASSY 22806

BOLT 337113-S2 3 REQ'D TIGHTEN TO 18-29 N·m (13-21 LB-FT)

Front door hinges

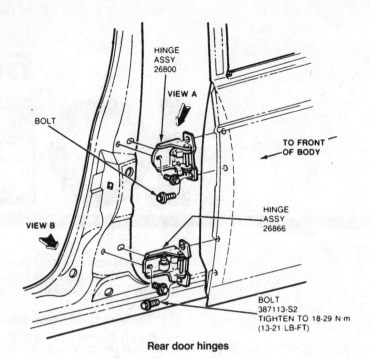

HINGE
ASSY
26800

VIEW A

BOLT

TO FRONT
OF BODY

HINGE
ASSY
26866

VIEW B

BOLT
387113-S2
TIGHTEN TO 18-29 N·m
(13-21 LB-FT)

Rear door hinges

4. Open the door and support it with a padded jack or other suitable tool.

5. Scribe the hinge location to the door for a reference point when reinstalling.

6. Remove the upper and lower hinge-to-door hinge attaching washer head bolts.

7. Remove the upper and lower hinge-to-body attaching bolts.

8. Remove the upper and lower hinge-to-body nut and washer assemblies. Remove the hinges.

To install:

9. Install the upper and lower hinge-to-body attaching bolts. Tighten to 13-21 ft. lbs.

10. Install the upper and lower hinge-to-body nuts and washers. Tighten to 13-21 ft. lbs.

11. Position the door to the hinges and install the upper and lower attaching washer head bolts. Tighten to 13-21 ft. lbs.

12. Install the seat belt assembly.

13. Install the center pillar trim panel.

14. Install the scruff plate.

ADJUSTMENT

Door Alignment

1. Determine which hinge bolts and nuts must be loosened to move the door in the desired direction.

2. Loosen the hinge bolts and nuts just enough to permit movement of the door with a padded pry bar.

3. Move the door the distance estimated to be necessary. Tighten the hinge bolts and nuts to 13-21 ft. lbs., and check the door fit to ensure

there is no bind or interference with the adjacent panel.

4. Repeat the operation until the desired fit is obtained, and check the striker plate alignment for proper door closing.

Door Latch Striker Adjustment

The striker pin can be adjusted laterally and vertically as well as fore-and-aft. The latch striker should not be adjusted to correct door sag.

The latch striker should be shimmed to get the clearance shown between the striker and the latch. To check this clearance, clean latch

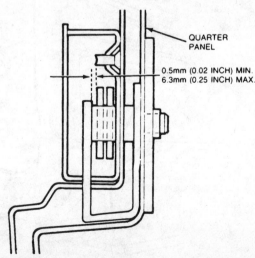

QUARTER
PANEL

0.5mm (0.02 INCH) MIN.
6.3mm (0.25 INCH) MAX.

Front and rear door latches

jaws and striker area. Apply a thin layer of dark grease to striker. As door is closed and opened, a measurable pattern will result on the latch striker. Use a maximum of two shims under the striker.

Move the striker assembly in or out to provide a flush fit at the door and pillar or quarter panel. Use the correct Torx® bit to loosen and tighten the latch striker. Tighten the striker to 24-33 ft. lbs.

Hood Latch Control Cable

REMOVAL AND INSTALLATION

1. From inside the vehicle, release the hood.
2. Remove the two bolts retaining the latch to the upper radiator support.
3. Remove the screw retaining the cable end retainer to the latch assembly.
4. Disengage the cable by rotating it out of the latch return spring.
5. To facilitate installing the cable, fasten a length of fishing line about 8 ft. long to latch the end of the cable.
6. From the inside vehicle, unseat the sealing grommet from the cowl side, remove the cable mounting bracket attaching screws and carefully pull the cable assembly out. Do not pull the "fish line" out.

To install:

9. Using the previously installed fish line, pull the new cable assembly through the retaining wall, seat the grommet securely, and install the cable mounting bracket attaching screws.
10. Thread the terminal end of cable into the hood latch return spring.
11. Route the cable through the V-slot on the latch and install the cable end retaining screw.
12. Check the hood latch cable release operation before the closing hood. Adjust if necessary.

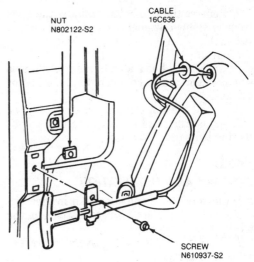

Hood latch control cable routing—interior

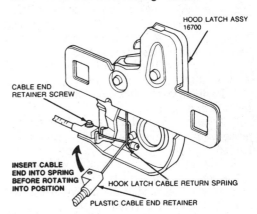

Hood latch assembly

Hood latch

REMOVAL AND INSTALLATION

1. From inside the vehicle release the hood.
2. Remove the two bolts retaining the latch to the upper radiator support.

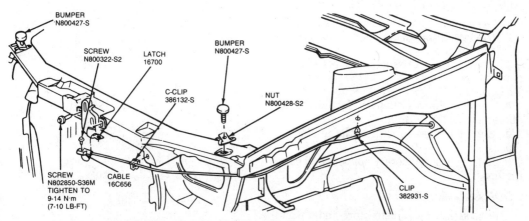

Hood latch control cable routing—engine compartment

3. Remove the two bolts retaining the hood latch assembly-to-radiator support and remove the latch.

To install:

1. Engage the hood latch to the control cable and position the hood latch to the radiator support.

2. Install the two attaching bolts.

3. Adjust the hood latch and torque the attaching bolts to 7-10 ft. lbs.

Hood

REMOVAL AND INSTALLATION

1. Open the hood and support it in the open position. Mark the hood hinge locations on the hood.

2. Protect the body with covers to prevent damage to the paint.

3. Disconnect the gas cylinders from hood.

4. Place thick rags under the corners of the hood. Remove the two bolts attaching each hinge to the hood, taking care not to let the hood slip when bolts are removed.

5. Remove the hood from the vehicle.

To install:

6. Position the hood-to-hood hinges. Install the attaching bolts.

7. Adjust the hood for even fit between the fenders and for a flush fit with the front of the fenders.

8. Adjust the hood for a flush fit with the top of the cowl and the fenders.

9. Adjust the hood latch, if necessary. Remove the protective fender covers.

10. Attach the gas cylinder to the hood.

Hood Gas Support

CAUTION: *Do not heat or try to disassemble the hood gas supports. The supports are gas charged and will explode if heated or disassembled.*

REMOVAL AND INSTALLATION

1. Open the hood and temporarily support it.

2. Disengage the gas support from the retainer at the top.

3. Remove the retaining pin at bottom. Remove the gas support.

To install:

4. Position the gas support. Install the retaining pin at the bottom.

5. Engage the gas support to the retainer at top.

6. Remove the temporary support and close the hood.

HOOD ALIGNMENT

The hood can be adjusted fore-and-aft and side-to-side by loosening two hood-to-hinge at-

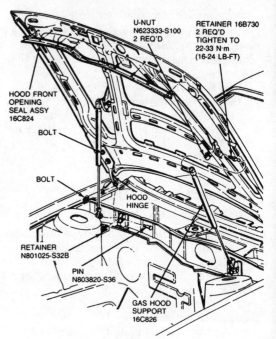

Hood gas support locations

taching bolts at each hinge. Then, reposition hood as required and tighten the hood-to-hinge attaching bolts. Always use protective fender covers.

To raise or lower the rear of the hood, loosen the hood hinge pivot nut. The pivot can now move up or down. Raise or lower hood as necessary to obtain a flush condition at the rear of the hood with the fenders. Then, tighten the hood hinge pivot nut to 16-25 ft. lbs.

HOOD LATCH ADJUSTMENT

Before adjusting hood latch mechanism, make certain that the hood is properly aligned.

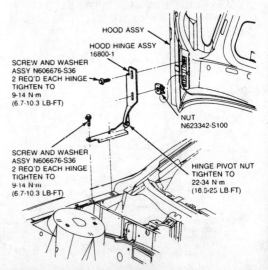

Hood hinge adjustment locations

The hood latch can be moved from side-to-side to align with the opening in the hood inner panel.

Adjust latch up and down to obtain a flush fit with front fenders.

1. Loosen the hood latch attaching bolts in the radiator support until they are just loose enough to move the latch from side-to-side.

2. Move the latch from side-to-side to align it with the opening in the hood.

3. Loosen the locknuts on the two hood bumpers. Lower the bumpers.

4. Move the hood latch up and down as required to obtain a flush fit between the top of hood and the fenders when upward pressure is applied to the front of the hood. Then, tighten the hood latch attaching screw to 7-10 ft. lbs.

5. Raise the two hood bumpers to eliminate any looseness at the front of hood when closed. Then, tighten the hood bumper locknuts.

6. Open and close the hood several times to check its operation.

Liftgate (Station Wagon)
REMOVAL AND INSTALLATION

WARNING: *The liftgate removal and install is a two person operation and should not be attempted alone.*

1. Before removing the hinge-to-roof frame attachments at both hinges, scribe the location of each hinge on roof frame and bolt locations.

2. Remove the hinge-to-roof frame screw and washer assembly at each hinge.

3. Remove the liftgate from the vehicle.

To install:

4. Position the hinges to the scribe marks on the roof frame and reverse the removal procedures. Torque the hinge-to-roof screw and washer assemblies to 16-25 ft. lbs.

ADJUSTMENT

The wagon liftgate latch has double-bolt construction, designed to be equivalent in function and load capacity to side door latches. The latch is non-adjustable. All movement for adjustment is accomplished in the striker which has a 5.5mm radial range. This latch system has a two-position latching system. The closing latch cycle consists of a secondary position which latches the liftgate but does not seal the door to the liftgate weatherstrip. The primary position holds the liftgate door firmly into the weatherstrip. Water leaks and rattles may occur because the liftgate appears closed. However, it may only be closed to the secondary (first) position. Be sure that positive primary engagement of the liftgate latch is achieved upon closing. To check it, use the following procedure:

Latch Function Test

1. Close the liftgate to an assumed primary condition.

2. Insert the key into the key cylinder. Place your left hand on the liftgate glass above and left of the key cylinder. Press firmly on the glass with your left hand and slowly turn the key until the latch is released. Return the key and release your left hand pressure. The liftgate should be in the secondary position.

3. If while performing the above test shows that the liftgate will not close to primary the position, adjust the striker rearward (to rear of vehicle) so that a positive primary engagement is obtained upon closing the liftgate.

Liftgate Support Cylinder
REMOVAL AND INSTALLATION

1. Open the liftgate and temporarily support it.

2. The lift cylinder end fitting is a spring-clip

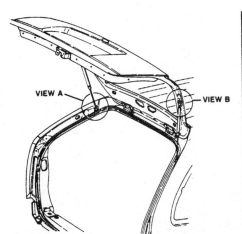
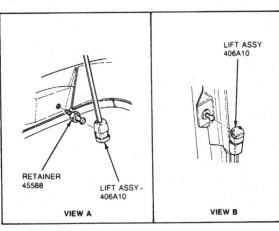

Liftgate support cylinder attachments

design and removal is accomplished by sliding a small screwdriver under it and prying up to remove it from the ball stud.

3. Remove the support cylinder.

To install:

4. Install each cylinder to the C-pillar and the liftgate bracket ball socket by pushing the cylinder's locking wedge onto the socket.

5. Close the liftgate. Check the support cylinder operation.

Trunk Lid (Sedan)

REMOVAL AND INSTALLATION

WARNING: *The trunk lid removal and install is a two person operation and should not be attempted alone.*

1. Remove the four hinge-to-trunk lid screws and remove the trunk lid.

2. **To install:** position the trunk lid to the hinges and install the four hinge-to-trunk lid retaining bolts.

3. Adjust for fit as outlined below.

4. Torque the retaining bolts to 16-25 ft. lbs.

ADJUSTMENT

The trunk lid door can be shifted fore and aft and from side to side on all models.

The trunk lid door should be adjusted for an even and parallel fit with the door opening. The door should also be adjusted up and down for a flush fit with the surrounding panels. Care should be taken not to damage the trunk lid door or surrounding body panel.

Fore-and-aft and up-and-down adjustment of the trunk lid is achieved by loosening the hinge-to-trunk lid attaching screw, shifting the trunk lid to the proper fit and tightening the attaching screw to 7-10 ft. lbs.

TRUNK LID TORSION BAR LOADING

1. Locally obtain the following materials.

a. A round flexible cable, 6mm in diameter by 1220mm long.

b. One ¼" cable clamp.

c. A water pipe, ½" diameter by 2" long.

d. A piece of heater hose, ⅝" diameter and 6" long.

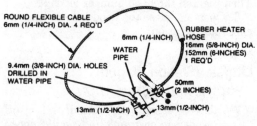

Trunk lid torsion bar adjusting tool

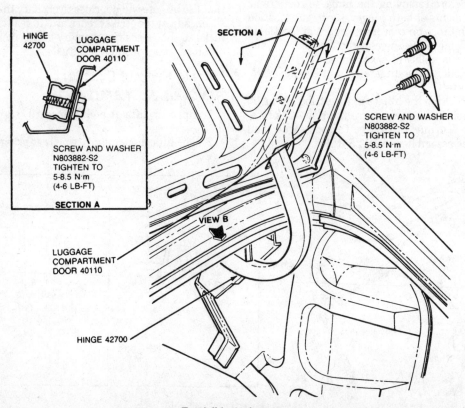

Trunk lid attachments

2. Assembly the materials as shown in the following illustration.

CAUTION: *Safety glasses* **MUST** be worn when performing this operation!

3. Install the torsion bar by inserting one end into the hole provided in the luggage compartment door hinge and resting the other end in the upper groove of the opposite hinge support.

4. Install the home made tool on the end of the torsion bar to be loaded.

5. With an assistant, place a long flat pry bar over the top of the torsion bar to be loaded. Pull on the torsion bar with the assistant holding the pry bar, guide the torsion bar down along the rear edge of the support into the lower groove of the hinge support and lock it in the lowest adjustment notch.

6. Using the home made tool, install the tool into the end of the torsion bar and unlock the bar by pulling toward you with the tool. Work the torsion bar into the second notch and release. If further adjustment is needed proceed to step 7.

7. Using a ⅜″ drive, ½″ deep well socket and a 6″ extension. Position the socket over the end of the torsion bar and unlock the bar. Reposition the torsion bar up the hinge support to the top notch and release.

Trunk Lid Latch and Lock

REMOVAL AND INSTALLATION

1. Open the luggage compartment door.
2. Remove the lever assembly and clip. If the

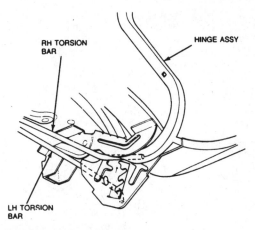

Trunk lid torsion bar positioning

clip breaks, replace with a new lever and clip assembly.

3. Remove the three latch attaching screws and disconnect the electric latch wire, if so equipped.

4. Remove the luggage compartment latch and rod from the vehicle with the retainer and seal.

5. Remove the screw and washer retaining the trunk lid lock cylinder plate-to-support and remove the plate and support.

6. Remove the lock cylinder and rod.

To install:

1. Position the lock cylinder and seal into the hole in the trunk lid. Push the lock cylinder retainer into position until it is locked.

2. Connect the electric latch wire, if so

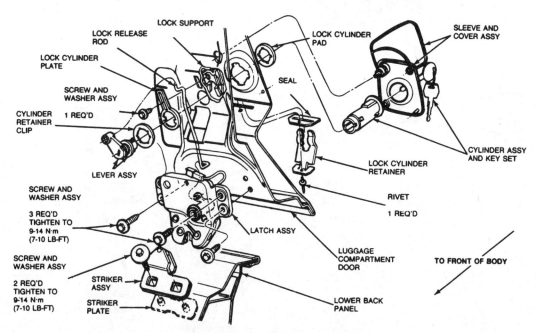

Trunk lid latch and lock assembly

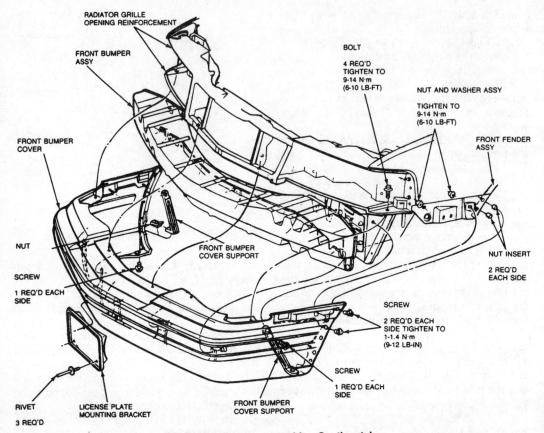

RADIATOR GRILLE
OPENING REINFORCEMENT

FRONT BUMPER
ASSY

BOLT
4 REQ'D
TIGHTEN TO
9-14 N·m
(6-10 LB-FT)

NUT AND WASHER ASSY

TIGHTEN TO
9-14 N·m
(6-10 LB-FT)

FRONT FENDER
ASSY

FRONT BUMPER
COVER

FRONT BUMPER
COVER SUPPORT

NUT INSERT

2 REQ'D
EACH SIDE

NUT

SCREW

1 REQ'D EACH
SIDE

SCREW

2 REQ'D EACH
SIDE TIGHTEN TO
1-1.4 N·m
(9-12 LB-IN)

SCREW

1 REQ'D EACH
SIDE

RIVET

3 REQ'D

LICENSE PLATE
MOUNTING BRACKET

FRONT BUMPER
COVER SUPPORT

Front bumper cover assembly—Continental

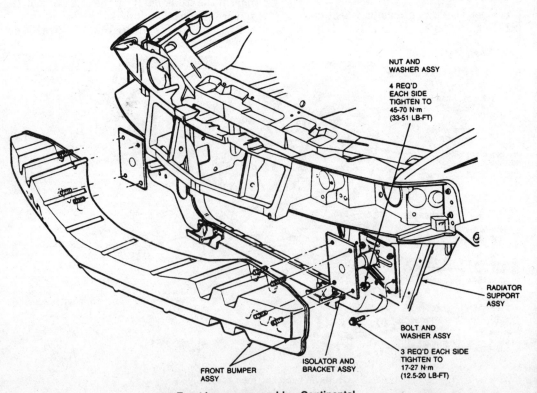

NUT AND
WASHER ASSY

4 REQ'D
EACH SIDE
TIGHTEN TO
45-70 N·m
(33-51 LB-FT)

RADIATOR
SUPPORT
ASSY

BOLT AND
WASHER ASSY

3 REQ'D EACH SIDE
TIGHTEN TO
17-27 N·m
(12.5-20 LB-FT)

FRONT BUMPER
ASSY

ISOLATOR AND
BRACKET ASSY

Front bumper assembly—Continental

equipped. Install the trunk lid latch and rod assembly. Install the three attaching screws and washers and torque to 7-10 ft. lbs.

3. Install the lever and clip assembly. Close the trunk lid and check for proper alignment and adjust if necessary.

Front Bumper

REMOVAL AND INSTALLATION

1. Remove the four screws attaching the front bumper to the fenders. There are two on each side.

2. Remove the four bolts attaching the front bumper cover-to-radiator grille reinforcement assembly and remove the front bumper cover.

CAUTION: *Never apply heat to the bumper*

energy absorbers! The heat may cause the material inside to expand and flow out of the absorbers or crack the metal!

3. Remove the four nut and washer assemblies attaching the isolator to the bumper. With an assistant remove the bumper assembly from the vehicle.

To install:

1. Install the front bumper onto the isolator and torque the six attaching bolt and washer assemblies to 12.5-20 ft. lbs.

2. Install the front bumper cover over the bumper assembly and attach the side bumper cover supports.

3. Install the four front bumper-to-radiator support bolts and torque to 6-10 ft. lbs.

4. Install the four front bumper cover-to-

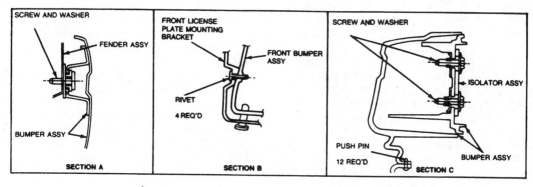

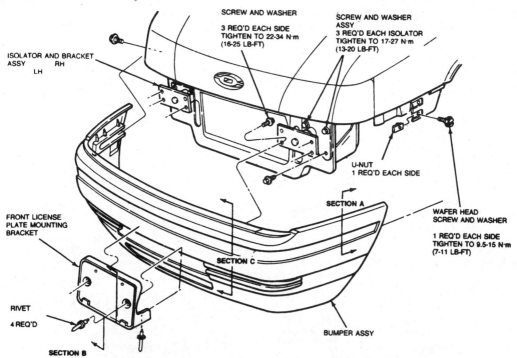

Front bumper cover assembly—Taurus (Sable similar)

fender attaching bolts and torque to 9-12 in. lbs.

Rear Bumper

REMOVAL AND INSTALLATION

1. Remove the four screws attaching the rear bumper cover-to-quarter panels.
2. Remove the luggage compartment side cover assemblies and the lower back trim panel.
3. Remove the nuts attaching the rear bumper cover-to-quarter panels and the lower back panel.
4. Remove the bumper cover. Remove the four nut and washer assemblies attaching each isolator to the rear bumper. With an assistant remove the rear bumper.

To install:

CAUTION: *Never apply heat to the bumper energy absorbers! The heat may cause the material inside to expand and flow out of the absorbers or crack the metal!*

1. With an assistant, install the rear bumper on the vehicle at the isolator and bracket.
2. Install the six bumper-to-isolator nuts and washer assemblies and torque to 33-51 ft. lbs.
3. Install the rear bumper cover over the bumper and install the bumper cover-to-quarter panels and the lower back panel.
4. Install the push pins attaching the rear bumper cover to the rear bumper.
5. Install the luggage compartment side cover and lower trim panels.
6. Install the four screws attaching the rear bumper cover-to-quarter panels and torque the screws to 6-10 ft. lbs.

Grille

REMOVAL AND INSTALLATION

Continental

1. Remove the two Phillips head screws and the three self-tapping bolts attaching the upper radiator sight shield.
2. Remove the Phillips head screws that fasten the grille to the grille opening reinforcement.
3. From behind the grille opening, release the two snap-in tabs located at the bottom of the grille.
4. While standing in front of the grille, pull the bottom of the grille toward you, disengaging the two upper snap-in tabs.

To install:

1. Position the two upper snap-in tabs in the slots shown in the grille opening reinforcement.
2. Once the upper tabs are positioned, snap in the bottom tabs. Apply enough pressure to ensure all the tabs are in securely.
3. Install the grille opening-to-grille Phillips head screws and torque the screws to 12-22 in. lbs.
4. Install the upper radiator sight shield with the two Phillips head screws and torque to 12-22 in. lbs.

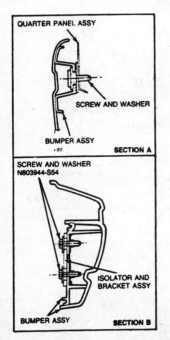

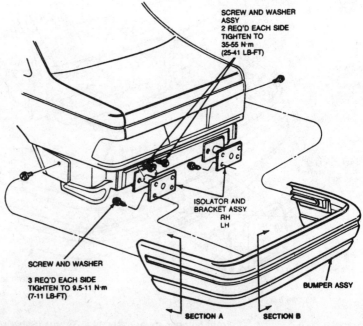

Rear bumper assembly—Taurus (Sable similar)

Taurus/Sable

1. Raise and support the hood.
2. Remove the two plastic retainers at the top corners with a cross-recessed pry bar.

3. Depress the tabs on the spring clips attached to the grille at both lower corners and pull the grille assembly from the vehicle.
To install:

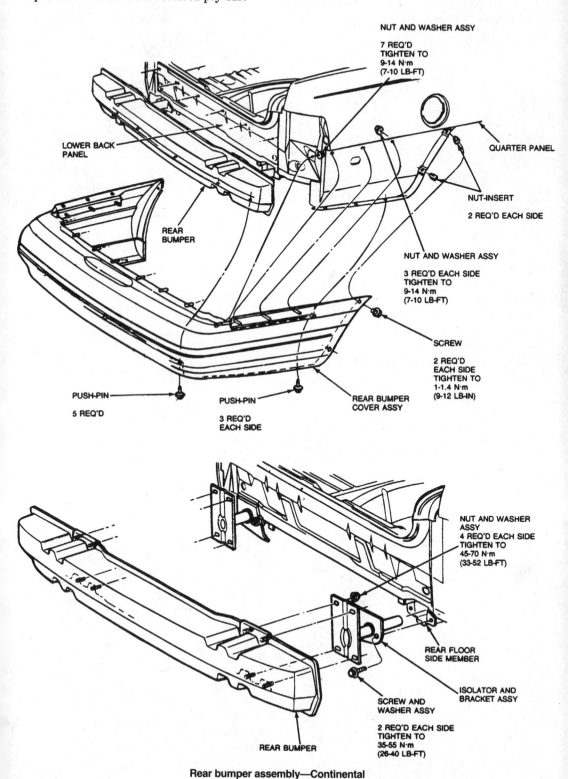

NUT AND WASHER ASSY

7 REQ'D
TIGHTEN TO
9-14 N·m
(7-10 LB-FT)

QUARTER PANEL

LOWER BACK
PANEL

NUT-INSERT

2 REQ'D EACH SIDE

REAR
BUMPER

NUT AND WASHER ASSY

3 REQ'D EACH SIDE
TIGHTEN TO
9-14 N·m
(7-10 LB-FT)

SCREW

2 REQ'D
EACH SIDE
TIGHTEN TO
1-1.4 N·m
(9-12 LB-IN)

PUSH-PIN

5 REQ'D

PUSH-PIN

3 REQ'D
EACH SIDE

REAR BUMPER
COVER ASSY

NUT AND WASHER
ASSY
4 REQ'D EACH SIDE
TIGHTEN TO
45-70 N·m
(33-52 LB-FT)

REAR FLOOR
SIDE MEMBER

ISOLATOR AND
BRACKET ASSY

SCREW AND
WASHER ASSY

2 REQ'D EACH SIDE
TIGHTEN TO
35-55 N·m
(26-40 LB-FT)

REAR BUMPER

Rear bumper assembly—Continental

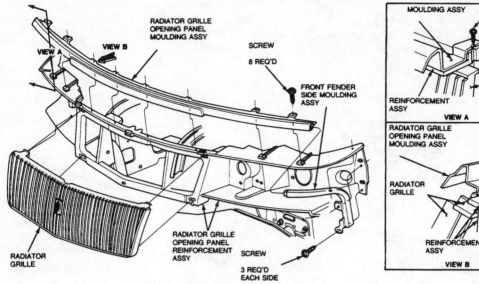

Grille assembly—Continental

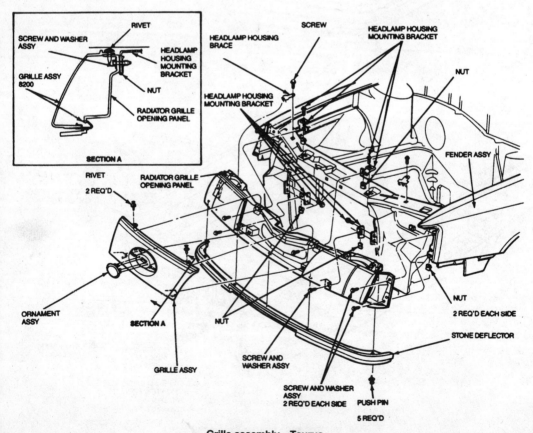

Grille assembly—Taurus

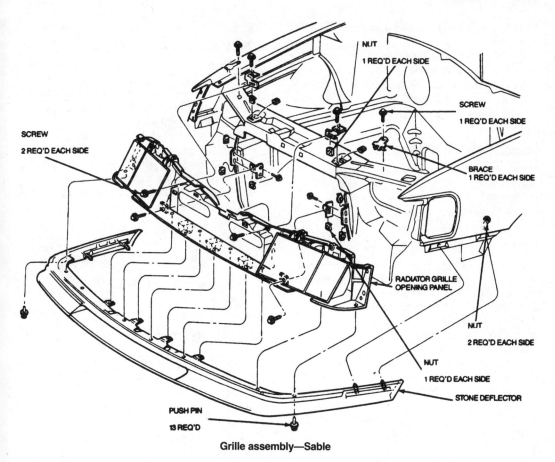

Grille assembly—Sable

1. Position the bottom of the spring tabs in the slots in the grille opening reinforcement.

2. Rotate the top of the grille toward the rear of the vehicle until the upper tab slots line up with the holes in the grille opening.

3. Install the two plastic retainers through the holes in the grille and grille opening. Retainers can be tapped in.

Manual Outside Mirrors

REMOVAL AND INSTALLATION

Standard Manual Type
Right Hand Only

1. Remove the inside sail cover.

2. Remove the nut and washer assemblies and lift the mirror off the door.

To install:

3. Install the mirror on door.

4. Install and tighten the nut and washer assemblies.

5. Install the inside sail cover.

Left Hand Remote Control

1. Pull the nob assembly to remove it from the control shaft.

2. Remove the interior sail cover retainer screw and remove the cover.

3. Loosen the setscrew retaining control assembly to the sail cover.

4. Remove the mirror attaching nuts, washers and grommet. Remove the mirror and the control assembly.

To install:

5. Seat the grommet in the outer door panel and position the mirror to the door. Install the attaching nuts and washer and tighten to 25-39 in. lbs.

6. Route the control mechanism through the

Manual remote control mirror assembly

door and position to the sail trim panel. Tighten the setscrew to 2-6 in. lbs.

7. Position the sail cover to the door and install the retaining screw.

8. Position the rubber knob onto the control shaft and push to install.

Power Outside Mirrors

CAUTION: *Outside mirrors that are frozen must be thawed prior to adjustment. Do not attempt to free-up the mirror by pressing the glass assembly.*

REMOVAL AND INSTALLATION

1. Disconnect the negative (−) battery cable.

2. Remove the one screw retaining the mirror mounting hole cover and remove the cover.

3. Remove the door trim panel. Refer to the "Door Trim Panel" removal and installation procedures in this chapter.

4. Disconnect the mirror assembly wiring connector. Remove the necessary wiring guides.

5. Remove the three mirror retaining nuts on the sail mirrors, two on door mirrors. Remove the mirror while guiding the wiring and connector through hole in the door.

To install:

6. Install the mirror assembly by routing the connector and wiring through the hole in the door. Attach with the three retaining nuts on the sail mirrors, two on the door mirrors. Tighten the retaining nuts.

7. Connect the mirror wiring connector and install the wiring guides.

8. Replace the mirror mounting hole cover and install one screw.

9. Replace the door trim panel. Refer to the "Door Trim Panel" removal and installation procedures in this chapter.

10. Connect the negative (−) battery cable.

Fog Lamp

REMOVAL AND INSTALLATION

1. Disconnect the negative (−) battery cable.

2. From inside the front bumper fascia, remove the two nuts retaining the springs and lamp mounting bracket-to-fascia bracket studs.

CAUTION: *Make sure that the spring compression is relieved before removing the nut from the stud.*

3. Disconnect the electrical connector from the back of the lamp assembly.

4. Slide the fog lamp and mounting bracket away from the studs.

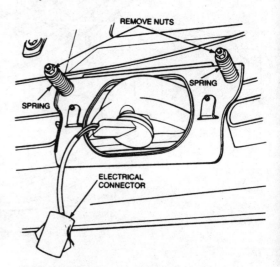

Fog lamp assembly—3.0L SHO Taurus

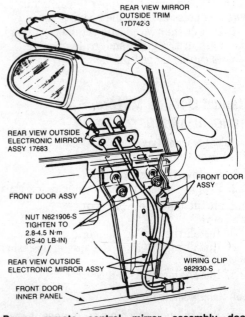

Power remote control mirror assembly—door mounted

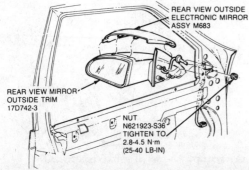

Power remote control mirror assembly—sail mounted

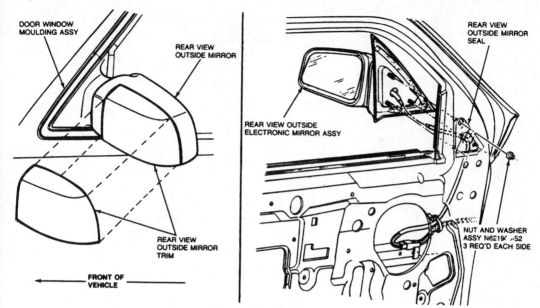

DOOR WINDOW
MOULDING ASSY

REAR VIEW
OUTSIDE MIRROR

REAR VIEW OUTSIDE
ELECTRONIC MIRROR ASSY

REAR VIEW
OUTSIDE MIRROR
TRIM

FRONT OF
VEHICLE

REAR VIEW
OUTSIDE MIRROR
SEAL

NUT AND WASHER
ASSY N62190 ~S2
3 REQ'D EACH SIDE

Power remote control mirror—Continental

5. Remove the two screws retaining the fog lamp-to-mounting bracket.

6. Remove the screws retaining the trim ring-to-fog lamp. Push the two trim ring retaining tabs outward to disconnect the trim ring from the lamp.

To install:

1. Install the trim ring-to-lamp assembly, engaging tabs.

2. Install the trim ring retaining screw.

3. Install the fog lamp assembly to the mounting bracket. Tighten the two retaining screws.

4. Position the fog lamp assembly over the studs on the rear of bumper fascia, and connect the wire connector.

5. Install the springs and retaining nuts to the mounting studs.

BULB REPLACEMENT

NOTE: When performing a bulb replacement only, it is not necessary to remove the mounting bracket or trim ring from the lamp assembly.

1. Peel back the rubber boot from the bulb housing.

2. Disconnect the bulb lead wire from the under rubber boot.

3. Push the bulb retaining wire in and to the side to release the bulb.

CAUTION: *When replacing the bulb, DO NOT handle the glass part of the bulb. The dirt on your hands may cause the bulb to burst when turned on.*

To install:

4. Install the bulb and socket assembly. Push the bulb retaining wire in and seat it in the slot.

5. Connect the bulb lead wire and reposition the rubber boot over the bulb housing.

6. Turn the fog lamps ON and check for proper operation.

Antenna

REMOVAL AND INSTALLATION

1. Push in on the sides of glove compartment door and place the door in the hinged downward position.

2. Disconnect the antenna lead from the RH rear of the radio and remove the cable from the heater or the A/C cable retaining clips.

3. Remove the RH front fender liner. Unplug the coaxial cable from the power antenna assembly or the manual antenna base assembly. Unplug the power lead from the power antenna.

NOTE: *The manual antenna mast is detachable from the base and cable assembly.*

4. Under the RH front fender, pull the antenna cable through the hole in the door hinge pillar and remove the antenna cable assembly from the wheel well area.

5. To remove the manual or power antenna base, remove the antenna nut and stanchion on the RH front fender.

6. Remove the lower antenna base screw and remove either the manual antenna base or the power antenna.

To install:

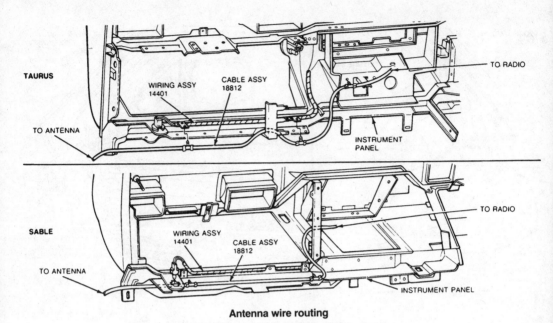

Antenna wire routing

1. Install the antenna assembly and base screw.

2. Install the antenna nut and stanchion on the RH front fender. Torque the antenna nut to 4 in. lbs.

3. Pull the antenna cable through the hole in the door hinge pillar. Attach the antenna cable lead to the RH rear of the radio.

4. Attach the cable to the heater and A/C housing. Install the front fender liner.

5. Install the glove compartment door and reposition the glove compartment.

INTERIOR

Door Trim Panels

REMOVAL AND INSTALLATION

Taurus/Sable

1. Remove the window regulator handle by unsnapping the handle cover from the base and expose the attaching screw. Remove the screw, handle and the wearplate.

2. Remove the door pull handle retaining screws and cover. Remove the handle.

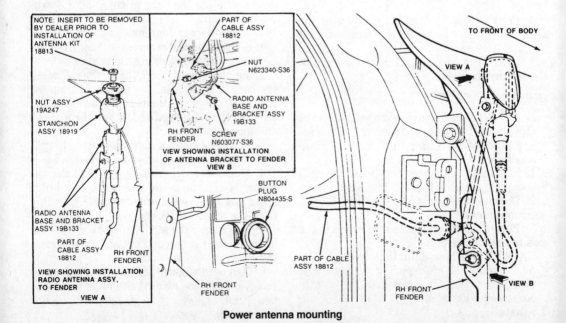

Power antenna mounting

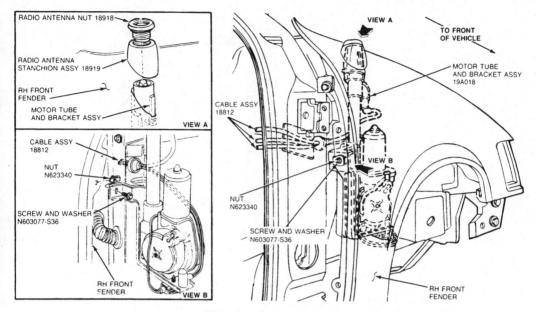

Manual antenna mounting

3. Remove the upper trim panel retaining screws and remove the panel.

4. On Taurus vehicles, remove the trim panel opening panel.

5. Remove the exterior rearview mirror mounting hole cover retaining screw and the cover.

6. Remove all the screws retaining door trim panel to the door, using a door panel removing tool, pry the trim panel retaining push pins from door inner panel.

7. If the trim panel is to be replaced, transfer all the push pins to the new panel. Replace any bend, broken or missing push pins.

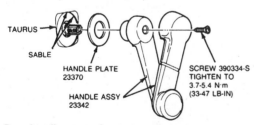

Door handle removal

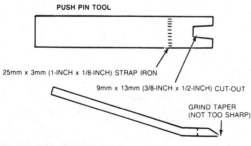

Door panel removing tool

To install:

1. Connect all door wiring and install the trim panel into position ensuring the upper ridge is seated properly in the door channel.

2. Snap the push pins in using your hand. Start at the top and move down the sides and make sure that the push pins align with the holes in the door before applying pressure.

3. Install all the screws retaining the trim panel-to-door.

4. Snap in the door handle retainer cover and install the retaining screws.

5. Snap in the front door lock control knob plate.

6. Install the outside rearview mirror mounting hole cover and retaining screws.

7. Install the window regulator handle (manual only) and snap in the handle cover.

Front Door Latch

REMOVAL AND INSTALLATION

1. Remove the door trim panel and the watershield.

2. Check all the connections of the remote control link and the rod and service if necessary.

3. Remove the remote control assembly and the link clip.

4. Remove the clip attaching the lock cylinder rod to the lock cylinder.

5. Remove the clip from the actuator motor, if so equipped.

6. Remove the clip attaching the push-button rod to the latch.

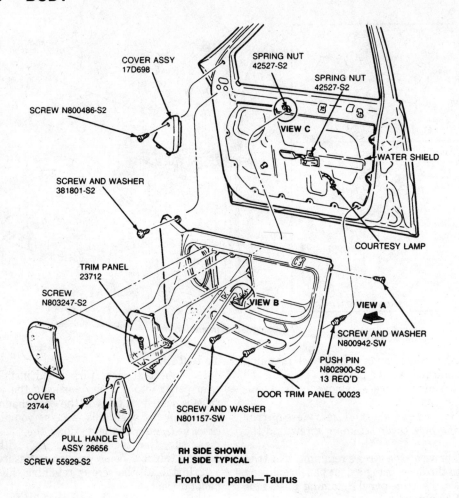

COVER ASSY
17D698

SCREW N800486-S2

SPRING NUT
42527-S2

SPRING NUT
42527-S2

VIEW C

WATER SHIELD

SCREW AND WASHER
381801-S2

COURTESY LAMP

TRIM PANEL
23712

SCREW
N803247-S2

VIEW B

VIEW A

SCREW AND WASHER
N800942-SW

PUSH PIN
N802900-S2
13 REQ'D

DOOR TRIM PANEL 00023

COVER
23744

SCREW AND WASHER
N801157-SW

PULL HANDLE
ASSY 26656

SCREW 55929-S2

RH SIDE SHOWN
LH SIDE TYPICAL

Front door panel—Taurus

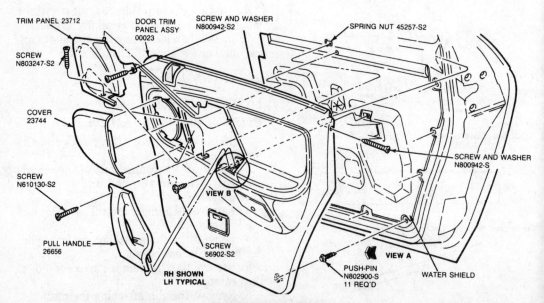

TRIM PANEL 23712

DOOR TRIM
PANEL ASSY
00023

SCREW AND WASHER
N800942-S2

SPRING NUT 45257-S2

SCREW
N803247-S2

COVER
23744

SCREW AND WASHER
N800942-S

SCREW
N610130-S2

VIEW B

PULL HANDLE
26656

SCREW
56902-S2

VIEW A

PUSH-PIN
N802900-S
11 REQ'D

WATER SHIELD

RH SHOWN
LH TYPICAL

Rear door panel—Taurus

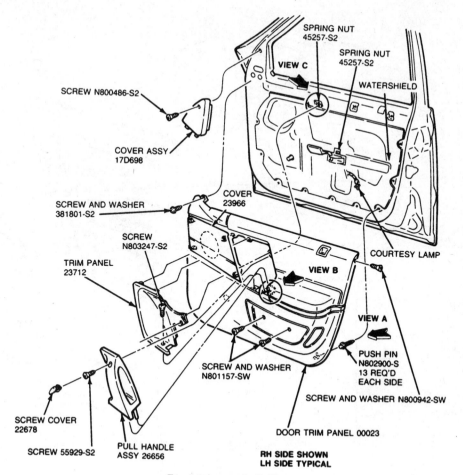

SPRING NUT
45257-S2

VIEW C

SPRING NUT
45257-S2

WATERSHIELD

SCREW N800486-S2

COVER ASSY
17D698

COVER
23966

SCREW AND WASHER
381801-S2

SCREW
N803247-S2

TRIM PANEL
23712

VIEW B

COURTESY LAMP

VIEW A

PUSH PIN
N802900-S
13 REQ'D
EACH SIDE

SCREW AND WASHER
N801157-SW

SCREW COVER
22678

SCREW 55929-S2

PULL HANDLE
ASSY 26656

SCREW AND WASHER N800942-SW

DOOR TRIM PANEL 00023

**RH SIDE SHOWN
LH SIDE TYPICAL**

Front door panel—Sable

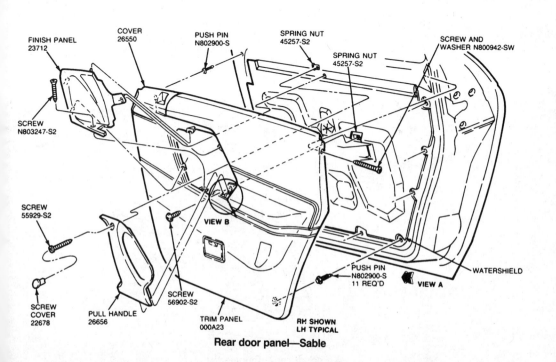

FINISH PANEL
23712

COVER
26550

PUSH PIN
N802900-S

SPRING NUT
45257-S2

SPRING NUT
45257-S2

SCREW AND
WASHER N800942-SW

SCREW
N803247-S2

SCREW
55929-S2

VIEW B

SCREW
COVER
22678

PULL HANDLE
26656

SCREW
56902-S2

TRIM PANEL
000A23

PUSH PIN
N802900-S
11 REQ'D

VIEW A

WATERSHIELD

**RH SHOWN
LH TYPICAL**

Rear door panel—Sable

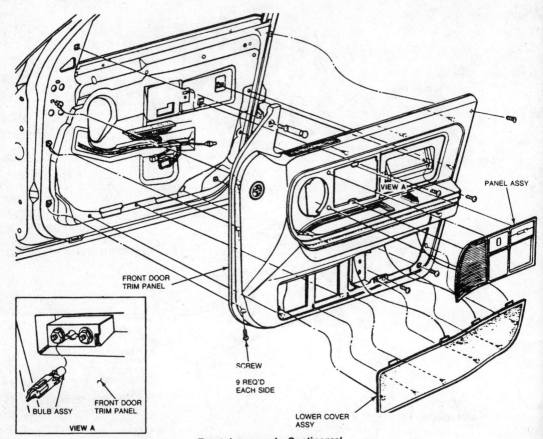

PANEL ASSY

VIEW A

FRONT DOOR
TRIM PANEL

BULB ASSY

FRONT DOOR
TRIM PANEL

VIEW A

SCREW

9 REQ'D
EACH SIDE

LOWER COVER
ASSY

Front door panel—Continental

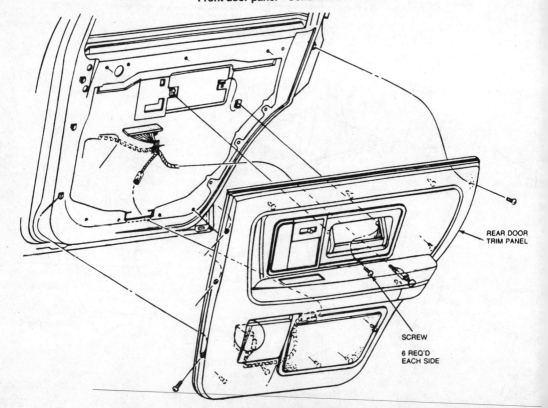

REAR DOOR
TRIM PANEL

SCREW

6 REQ'D
EACH SIDE

Rear door panel—Continental

CHILTON'S
AUTO BODY REPAIR TIPS

Tools and Materials • Step-by-Step Illustrated Procedures
How To Repair Dents, Scratches and Rust Holes
Spray Painting and Refinishing Tips

With a little practice, basic body repair procedures can be mastered by any do-it-yourself mechanic. The step-by-step repairs shown here can be applied to almost any type of auto body repair.

TOOLS & MATERIALS

You may already have basic tools, such as hammers and electric drills. Other tools unique to body repair — body hammers, grinding attachments, sanding blocks, dent puller, half-round plastic file and plastic spreaders — are relatively inexpensive and can be obtained wherever auto parts or auto body repair parts are sold. Portable air compressors and paint spray guns can be purchased or rented.

Auto Body Repair Kits

The best and most often used products are available to the do-it-yourselfer in kit form, from major manufacturers of auto body repair products. The same manufacturers also merchandise the individual products for use by pros.

Kits are available to make a wide variety of repairs, including holes, dents and scratches and fiberglass, and offer the advantage of buying the materials you'll need for the job. There is little waste or chance of materials going bad from not being used. Many kits may also contain basic body-working tools such as body files, sanding blocks and spreaders. Check the contents of the kit before buying your tools.

BODY REPAIR TIPS

Safety

Many of the products associated with auto body repair and refinishing contain toxic chemicals. Read all labels before opening containers and store them in a safe place and manner.

• Wear eye protection (safety goggles) when using power tools or when performing any operation that involves the removal of any type of material.

• Wear lung protection (disposable mask or respirator) when grinding, sanding or painting.

Sanding

1 Sand off paint before using a dent puller. When using a non-adhesive sanding disc, cover the back of the disc with an overlapping layer or two of masking tape and trim the edges. The disc will last considerably longer.

2 Use the circular motion of the sanding disc to grind *into* the edge of the repair. Grinding or sanding away from the jagged edge will only tear the sandpaper.

3 Use the palm of your hand flat on the panel to detect high and low spots. Do not use your fingertips. Slide your hand slowly back and forth.

WORKING WITH BODY FILLER

Mixing The Filler

Cleanliness and proper mixing and application are extremely important. Use a clean piece of plastic or glass or a disposable artist's palette to mix body filler.

1 Allow plenty of time and follow directions. No useful purpose will be served by adding more hardener to make it cure (set-up) faster. Less hardener means more curing time, but the mixture dries harder; more hardener means less curing time but a softer mixture.

2 Both the hardener and the filler should be thoroughly kneaded or stirred before mixing. Hardener should be a solid paste and dispense like thin toothpaste. Body filler should be smooth, and free of lumps or thick spots.

Getting the proper amount of hardener in the filler is the trickiest part of preparing the filler. Use the same amount of hardener in cold or warm weather. For contour filler (thick coats), a bead of hardener twice the diameter of the filler is about right. There's about a 15% margin on either side, but, if in doubt use less hardener.

3 Mix the body filler and hardener by wiping across the mixing surface, picking the mixture up and wiping it again. Colder weather requires longer mixing times. Do not mix in a circular motion; this will trap air bubbles which will become holes in the cured filler.

Applying The Filler

1 For best results, filler should not be applied over ¼" thick.

Apply the filler in several coats. Build it up to above the level of the repair surface so that it can be sanded or grated down.

The first coat of filler must be pressed on with a firm wiping motion.

Apply the filler in one direction only. Working the filler back and forth will either pull it off the metal or trap air bubbles.

REPAIRING DENTS

Before you start, take a few minutes to study the damaged area. Try to visualize the shape of the panel before it was damaged. If the damage is on the left fender, look at the right fender and use it as a guide. If there is access to the panel from behind, you can reshape it with a body hammer. If not, you'll have to use a dent puller. Go slowly and work the metal a little at a time. Get the panel as straight as possible before applying filler.

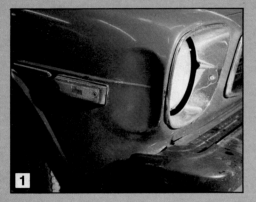

1 This dent is typical of one that can be pulled out or hammered out from behind. Remove the headlight cover, headlight assembly and turn signal housing.

2 Drill a series of holes ½ the size of the end of the dent puller along the stress line. Make some trial pulls and assess the results. If necessary, drill more holes and try again. Do not hurry.

3 If possible, use a body hammer and block to shape the metal back to its original contours. Get the metal back as close to its original shape as possible. Don't depend on body filler to fill dents.

4 Using an 80-grit grinding disc on an electric drill, grind the paint from the surrounding area down to bare metal. Use a new grinding pad to prevent heat buildup that will warp metal.

5 The area should look like this when you're finished grinding. Knock the drill holes in and tape over small openings to keep plastic filler out.

6 Mix the body filler (see Body Repair Tips). Spread the body filler evenly over the entire area (see Body Repair Tips). Be sure to cover the area completely.

7 Let the body filler dry until the surface can just be scratched with your fingernail. Knock the high spots from the body filler with a body file ("Cheese-grater"). Check frequently with the palm of your hand for high and low spots.

8 Check to be sure that trim pieces that will be installed later will fit exactly. Sand the area with 40-grit paper.

9 If you wind up with low spots, you may have to apply another layer of filler.

10 Knock the high spots off with 40-grit paper. When you are satisfied with the contours of the repair, apply a thin coat of filler to cover pin holes and scratches.

11 Block sand the area with 40-grit paper to a smooth finish. Pay particular attention to body lines and ridges that must be well-defined.

12 Sand the area with 400 paper and then finish with a scuff pad. The finished repair is ready for priming and painting (see Painting Tips).

Materials and photos courtesy of Ritt Jones Auto Body, Prospect Park, PA.

REPAIRING RUST HOLES

There are many ways to repair rust holes. The fiberglass cloth kit shown here is one of the most cost efficient for the owner because it provides a strong repair that resists cracking and moisture and is relatively easy to use. It can be used on large and small holes (with or without backing) and can be applied over contoured areas. Remember, however, that short of replacing an entire panel, no repair is a guarantee that the rust will not return.

1 Remove any trim that will be in the way. Clean away all loose debris. Cut away all the rusted metal. But be sure to leave enough metal to retain the contour or body shape.

2 Grind away all traces of rust with a 24-grit grinding disc. Be sure to grind back 3-4 inches from the edge of the hole down to bare metal and be sure all traces of paint, primer and rust are removed.

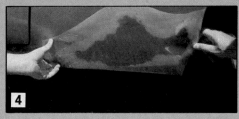

3 Block sand the area with 80 or 100 grit sandpaper to get a clear, shiny surface and feathered paint edge. Tap the edges of the hole inward with a ball peen hammer.

4 If you are going to use release film, cut a piece about 2-3" larger than the area you have sanded. Place the film over the repair and mark the sanded area on the film. Avoid any unnecessary wrinkling of the film.

5 Cut 2 pieces of fiberglass matte to match the shape of the repair. One piece should be about 1" smaller than the sanded area and the second piece should be 1" smaller than the first. Mix enough filler and hardener to saturate the fiberglass material (see Body Repair Tips).

6 Lay the release sheet on a flat surface and spread an even layer of filler, large enough to cover the repair. Lay the smaller piece of fiberglass cloth in the center of the sheet and spread another layer of filler over the fiberglass cloth. Repeat the operation for the larger piece of cloth.

7 Place the repair material over the repair area, with the release film facing outward. Use a spreader and work from the center outward to smooth the material, following the body contours. Be sure to remove all air bubbles.

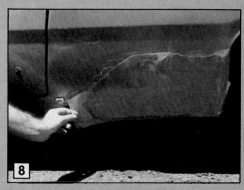

8 Wait until the repair has dried tack-free and peel off the release sheet. The ideal working temperature is 60°-90° F. Cooler or warmer temperatures or high humidity may require additional curing time. Wait longer, if in doubt.

9 Sand and feather-edge the entire area. The initial sanding can be done with a sanding disc on an electric drill if care is used. Finish the sanding with a block sander. Low spots can be filled with body filler; this may require several applications.

10 When the filler can just be scratched with a fingernail, knock the high spots down with a body file and smooth the entire area with 80-grit. Feather the filled areas into the surrounding areas.

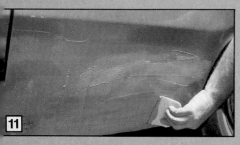

11 When the area is sanded smooth, mix some topcoat and hardener and apply it directly with a spreader. This will give a smooth finish and prevent the glass matte from showing through the paint.

12 Block sand the topcoat smooth with finishing sandpaper (200 grit), and 400 grit. The repair is ready for masking, priming and painting (see Painting Tips).

Materials and photos courtesy Marson Corporation, Chelsea, Massachusetts

PAINTING TIPS

Preparation

1 SANDING — Use a 400 or 600 grit wet or dry sandpaper. Wet-sand the area with a 1/4 sheet of sandpaper soaked in clean water. Keep the paper wet while sanding. Sand the area until the repaired area tapers into the original finish.

2 CLEANING — Wash the area to be painted thoroughly with water and a clean rag. Rinse it thoroughly and wipe the surface dry until you're sure it's completely free of dirt, dust, fingerprints, wax, detergent or other foreign matter.

3 MASKING — Protect any areas you don't want to overspray by covering them with masking tape and newspaper. Be careful not get fingerprints on the area to be painted.

4 PRIMING — All exposed metal should be primed before painting. Primer protects the metal and provides an excellent surface for paint adhesion. When the primer is dry, wet-sand the area again with 600 grit wet-sandpaper. Clean the area again after sanding.

Painting Techniques

P aint applied from either a spray gun or a spray can (for small areas) will provide good results. Experiment on an old piece of metal to get the right combination before you begin painting.

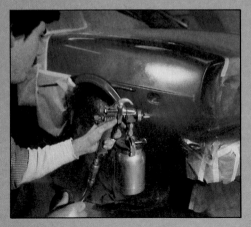

SPRAYING VISCOSITY (SPRAY GUN ONLY) — Paint should be thinned to spraying viscosity according to the directions on the can. Use only the recommended thinner or reducer and the same amount of reduction regardless of temperature.

AIR PRESSURE (SPRAY GUN ONLY) — This is extremely important. Be sure you are using the proper recommended pressure.

TEMPERATURE — The surface to be painted should be approximately the same temperature as the surrounding air. Applying warm paint to a cold surface, or vice versa, will completely upset the paint characteristics.

THICKNESS — Spray with smooth strokes. In general, the thicker the coat of paint, the longer the drying time. Apply several thin coats about 30 seconds apart. The paint should remain wet long enough to flow out and no longer; heavier coats will only produce sags or wrinkles. Spray a light (fog) coat, followed by heavier color coats.

DISTANCE — The ideal spraying distance is 8″-12″ from the gun or can to the surface. Shorter distances will produce ripples, while greater distances will result in orange peel, dry film and poor color match and loss of material due to overspray.

OVERLAPPING — The gun or can should be kept at right angles to the surface at all times. Work to a wet edge at an even speed, using a 50% overlap and direct the center of the spray at the lower or nearest edge of the previous stroke.

RUBBING OUT (BLENDING) FRESH PAINT — Let the paint dry thoroughly. Runs or imperfections can be sanded out, primed and repainted.

Don't be in too big a hurry to remove the masking. This only produces paint ridges. When the finish has dried for at least a week, apply a small amount of fine grade rubbing compound with a clean, wet cloth. Use lots of water and blend the new paint with the surrounding area.

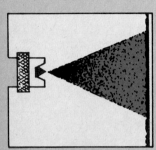

WRONG

Thin coat. Stroke too fast, not enough overlap, gun too far away.

CORRECT

Medium coat. Proper distance, good stroke, proper overlap.

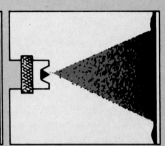

WRONG

Heavy coat. Stroke too slow, too much overlap, gun too close.

7. Remove the clip attaching the outside door handle rod to the latch assembly.

8. Remove the three screws attaching the latch assembly to the door.

9. Remove the latch assembly (with the remote control link lock cylinder rod) and anti-theft shield from the door cavity.

To install:

10. Install the new bushings and clips onto the new latch assembly. Install the anti-theft shield, remote control link and the lock cylinder rod onto the latch assembly levers.

11. Position the latch (with the link and rod) onto the door cavity, aligning the screw holes in the latch and door. Install the three screws and tighten to 36-72 in. lbs.

12. Attach the outside door handle rod to the latch with a clip.

13. Attach the push-button rod to the latch assembly with clip.

14. Remove the clip from the actuator motor (if so equipped).

15. Attach the lock cylinder rod to the lock cylinder with clip.

16. Install the remote control assembly (and the link clip).

17. Open and close the door to check the latch assembly operation.

18. Install the watershield and the door trim panel. Refer to the "Door Trim Panel" removal and installation procedures in this section.

Rear Door Latch
REMOVAL AND INSTALLATION

1. Remove the door trim panel and the watershield. Refer to the "Door Trim Panel" removal and installation procedures in this section.

2. Remove the door latch shield from the latch and check all the connections of the remote control links and rods. Service them as necessary.

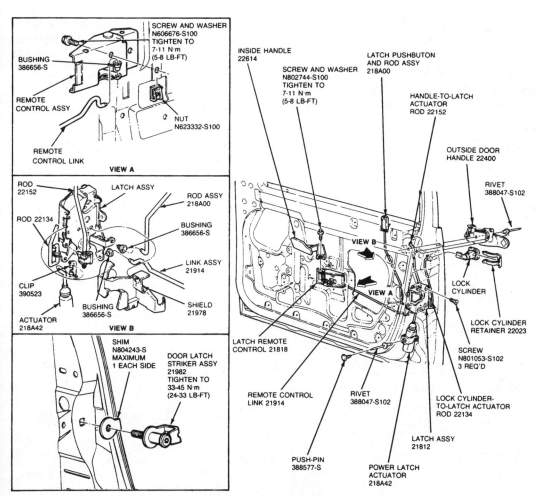

Front door latch assembly

3. Remove the remote control assembly (with the link retaining clip).

4. Remove the clip attaching the rod from the door latch bracket assembly from the latch assembly.

5. Remove the clip from the actuator motor (if so equipped).

To install:

6. Install new bushings and clip onto the latch assembly.

7. Install the clip on the actuator motor (if so equipped).

8. Install the remote control slide links onto the latch assembly. Install the latch with the links into the door cavity.

9. Position the latch assembly to the door, aligning the screw holes in the latch and door. Install the three screws and torque to 36-72 in. lbs.

10. Install the door latch shield.

11. Install the bellcrank to the inner door panel. Install the bellcrank attaching rivet.

12. Open and close the door to check the latch component operation.

13. Install the watershield and door trim panel.

Door Lock Assembly

REMOVAL AND INSTALLATION

NOTE: *When a lock cylinder must be replaced, replace both sides in a set to avoid carrying an extra set of keys.*

1. Remove the door trim panel and watershield as outlined in the "Door Trim Pan-el" removal and installation procedures in this chapter.

2. Remove the clip attaching the lock cylinder rod-to-lock cylinder.

3. Pry the lock cylinder out of the slot in the door.

To install:

1. Work the lock cylinder assembly into the outer door panel.

2. Install the cylinder retainer into the slot and push the retainer onto the lock cylinder.

3. Connect the lock cylinder rod to the lock cylinder and install the clip. Lock and unlock the door to check for proper operation.

4. Install the watershield and door trim panel as outlined in the "Door Trim Panel" removal and installation procedures in this chapter.

Lock Actuator (power)

REMOVAL AND INSTALLATION

1. Remove the door trim panel and watershield as outlined in the "Door Trim Panel" removal and installation procedures in this chapter.

2. Using a letter **X** and ¼" diameter drill bit, drill out the pop-rivet attaching the actuator motor to the door. Disconnect the wiring at the connector and the actuator rod at the latch assembly. Refer to the Door Latch Assembly illustrations in the previous section.

3. **To install:** attach the actuator motor rod to the door latch and connect the wire to the actuator connector.

4. Install the door actuator motor to the door with a pop-rivet or equivalent.

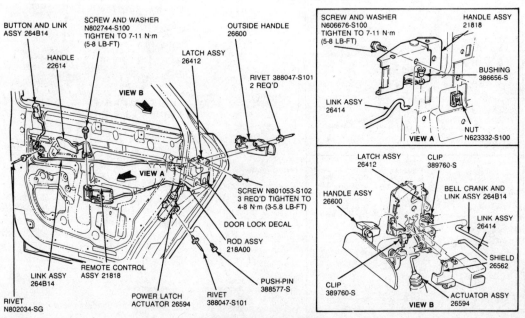

Rear door latch assembly

Front Door Glass
REMOVAL AND INSTALLATION

1. Remove the door trim panel and the watershield. Refer to the "Door Trim Panel" removal and installation procedures in this chapter.

2. Remove the inside door belt weatherstrip assembly.

3. Lower the glass to access the holes in the door inner panel. Remove the two rivets retaining the glass to glass bracket.

WARNING: *Prior to removing the center pins from the rivets, it is recommended that a suitable block support be inserted between the door outer panel and glass bracket to stabilizer glass during rivet removal. Remove the center pin from each rivet using a drift punch. Using a ¼" diameter drill, drill out the remaining rivets. Use care when drilling out the rivets to prevent enlarging the bracket and spacer holes and damaging the retainer.*

4. Loosen the nut and washer retaining the door glass stabilizer.

5. Remove the glass by tipping it forward then removing it from between the door belt opening to the outboard side of door.

6. Remove the drilling and pins the from bottom of door.

To install:

1. Snap the plastic retainer and spacer into the two glass retainer holes. Ensure that the metal washer within the retainer assembly is on the outboard side of glass.

2. Install the glass into the door at belt. Ensure that the glass is set within the front and rear glass run retainers.

3. Position the glass to the glass bracket. Install the two rivets to secure the glass to glass bracket.

NOTE: *Two ¼-20 x 1" bolts and two ¼-20 nuts and washer assemblies may be used as alternates for glass retention. However, torque must not exceed 36-61 in. lbs. Equivalent metric retainers may be used.*

10. Install the inside door belt weatherstrip assembly.

11. Raise the glass to within 75mm of the full-up position and adjust glass as outlined below.

12. Install the door trim panel and watershield.

FRONT GLASS ADJUSTMENT

1. Remove the door trim panel and the watershield. Refer to the "Door Trim Panel" removal and installation procedures in this chapter.

2. Lower the door glass approximately 75mm from the full-up position.

3. Loosen the nut and washer assemblies **A** and **B** retaining the equalizer bracket to the door inner panel. Refer to the following door glass adjustment illustration.

4. Loosen the nut and washer assembly **C** retaining the door glass stabilizer.

5. With the door open, place your hands on each side of the glass and pull the glass fully into the door glass run assembly at the B-pillar.

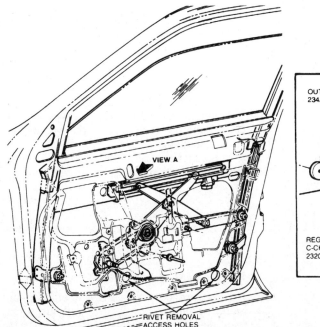

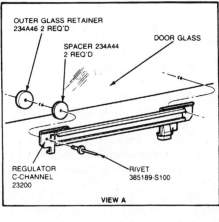

VIEW A

OUTER GLASS RETAINER
234A46 2 REQ'D

SPACER 234A44
2 REQ'D

DOOR GLASS

REGULATOR
C-CHANNEL
23200

RIVET
385189-S100

VIEW A

RIVET REMOVAL
ACCESS HOLES

Front door glass replacement

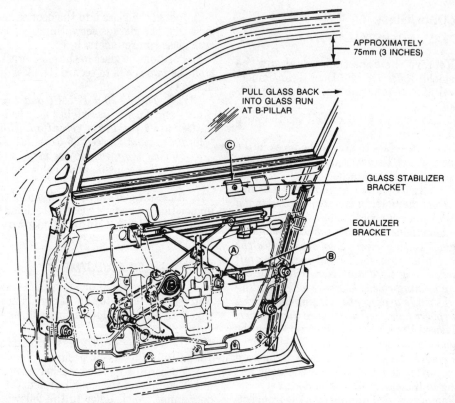

APPROXIMATELY
75mm (3 INCHES)

PULL GLASS BACK
INTO GLASS RUN
AT B-PILLAR

GLASS STABILIZER
BRACKET

EQUALIZER
BRACKET

Front door glass adjustment

6. Tighten the nut and washer **A**, then apply a downward pressure on the equalizer bracket and tighten the nut and washer **B** to 5-8 ft. lbs.

7. Set the door glass stabilizer so that it is slightly touching the glass and tighten the nut and washer assembly to 5-8 ft. lbs.

8. Cycle the door glass to ensure proper function and door fit.

Rear Door Glass

REMOVAL AND INSTALLATION

1. Remove the door trim panel and the watershield. Refer to the "Door Trim Panel" removal and installation in this chapter.

2. Remove the inner door belt weatherstrip by gently pulling the weatherstrip from the door flange.

3. Remove the glass-to-glass bracket attaching rivets.

WARNING: *Prior to removing rivet center pins, a suitable block support should be inserted between the door outer panel and glass to stabilizer the glass during rivet pin removal. Use a ¼" diameter drill to drill out remainder of rivet, using care not to enlarge sheet metal holes and damage the plastic retainer and spacer.*

4. Remove the glass stabilizer bracket retaining screw and the washer and bracket.

5. Lift the glass up between the door belt molding opening and remove it from the door.

To install:

6. Install the plastic spacer and retainers into the main glass. Install the main glass into the door.

7. Secure the glass-to-glass bracket using Heavy Duty Riveter D80L-23200-A or equivalent to install two rivets.

NOTE: *Two ¼-20 x 1" bolts and two ¼-20 nut and washer assemblies may be used as alternates for glass retention. However, the torque must not exceed 36-61 in. lbs.*

8. Install the inner door belt weatherstrip, using hand pressure to push the weatherstrip onto door flange.

9. Install the glass stabilizer bracket and the retaining screw and washer. Tighten to 36-61 in. lbs.

10. Cycle the glass to insure smooth operation.

11. Install the watershield and the door trim panel.

REAR GLASS ADJUSTMENT

The rear door glass has in-and-out and fore-and-aft adjustments. The in-and-out adjustment may be accomplished by loosening the two screws in the lower glass bracket assembly and

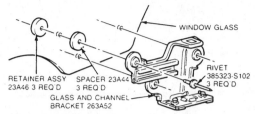

Rear door glass attachments

moving the glass in or out as required. The fore-and-aft adjustment is accomplished by loosening the tube run upper screw and washer assembly, and the lower nut and washer assembly attaching the rear door run and bracket assembly to the inner door panel, and adjusting the glass fore or aft as required.

When setting the glass to the window opening, lower the glass approximately 50mm from the full-up position with the four retention points loosely installed. Set the glass forward into the B-pillar and tighten lower run nut and washer number one, then numbers two, three and four.

Front Window Regulator
REMOVAL AND INSTALLATION

1. Remove the door trim panel and the watershield. Refer to the "Door Trim Panel"

removal and installation procedures in this chapter.

2. Remove the inside door belt weatherstrip and the glass stabilizer.

3. Remove the door glass as outlined above.

4. Remove the two nut and washer assemblies attaching the equalizer bracket.

5. Remove the three rivets (manual) or the four rivets (power) attaching the regulator base plate to the door inner panel.

6. Remove the regulator and the glass bracket assembly from the vehicle.

7. Working on a bench, carefully bend the tab flat to remove the arm slides from the glass bracket C-channel.

8. Install the new regulator arm plastic guides into the glass bracket C-channel and bend the tab back to 90° (use care not to break the tab, if the tab is cracked or broken, replace

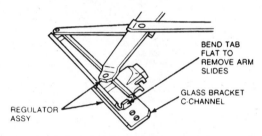

Removing the regulator from the C-channel

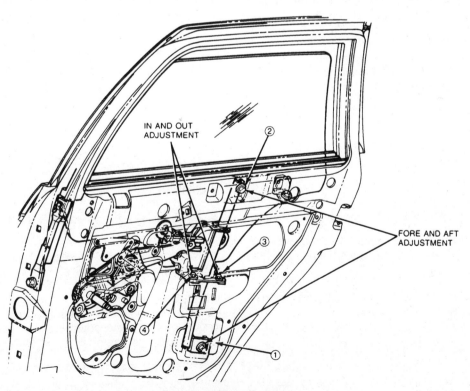

Rear door glass adjustment

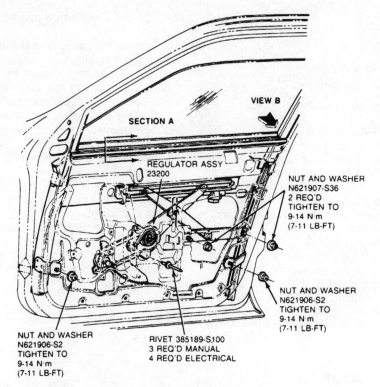

SECTION A

VIEW B

REGULATOR ASSY
23200

NUT AND WASHER
N621907-S36
2 REQ'D
TIGHTEN TO
9-14 N·m
(7-11 LB-FT)

NUT AND WASHER
N621906-S2
TIGHTEN TO
9-14 N·m
(7-11 LB-FT)

NUT AND WASHER
N621906-S2
TIGHTEN TO
9-14 N·m
(7-11 LB-FT)

RIVET 385189-S,100
3 REQ'D MANUAL
4 REQ'D ELECTRICAL

Front window regulator mechanism

the glass bracket assembly. Ensure the rubber bumper is installed properly on the new glass bracket, if a replacement is made.

WARNING: *If the regulator counterbalance spring must be removed or replaced for any reason, ensure that the regulator arms are in a fixed position prior to removal to prevent possible injury during C-spring unwind.*

The glass bracket assembly and regulator assembly are installed into the vehicle as one assembly. The glass bracket assembly may be disassembled from the regulator.

To install:

9. Install the regulator with the preassembled glass bracket into the vehicle. Set the regulator base plate to the door inner panel using the base plate locator tab as a guide.

10. Install the three (manual) or four (power) rivets (385189-S100) to attach the regulator to door inner panel.

11. Install the equalizer bracket.

12. Install the inside door belt weatherstrip and the glass stabilizer.

13. Lower the regulator arms to access holes in the door inner panel. Install the door glass.

14. Adjust the glass to ensure proper alignment with the glass run. Cycle the glass for smooth operation. Refer to the "Rear Glass Adjustment" procedures in this section.

15. Install the door trim panel and the watershield.

Rear Window Regulator

REMOVAL AND INSTALLATION

1. Remove the door trim panel and the watershield. Refer to the "Door Trim Panel" removal and installation procedures in this chapter.

2. Prop the glass in the full-up position.

3. Remove the three rivets (manual applications) or four rivets (power windows) attaching the regulator mounting plate assembly to the door inner panel.

4. Slide the regulator arm plastic guides out of the C-channel and disconnect the power wiring connector lift.

5. Remove the window regulator from door.

NOTE: *Use the access hole in the door inner panel for removal and installation.*

To install:

6. Install the window regulator through the access hole in the rear door and slide the regulator arm plastic guides into the glass bracket C-channel.

7. Install the rivets part No. 385189-S100 using Heavy Duty Riveter D80L-23200-A or equivalent, or ¼-20 x ½" screw and washer as-

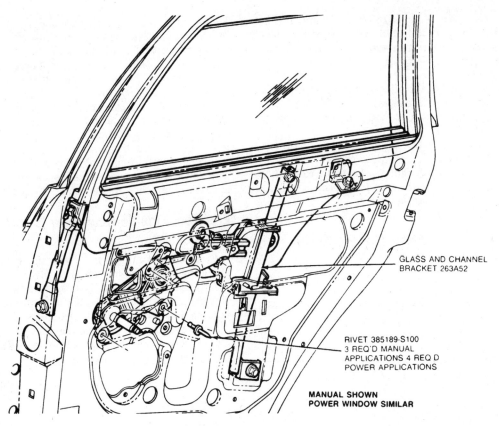

GLASS AND CHANNEL
BRACKET 263A52

RIVET 385189-S100
3 REQ'D MANUAL
APPLICATIONS 4 REQ D
POWER APPLICATIONS

**MANUAL SHOWN
POWER WINDOW SIMILAR**

Rear window regulator

semblies to secure regulator mounting plate to door inner panel.

8. Cycle the glass to check for smooth operation.

9. Install the watershield and the door trim panel.

Electric Window Motor

REMOVAL AND INSTALLATION

1. Raise the window to the full up position, if possible. If glass cannot be raised and is in a partially down or in the full down position, it must be supported so that it will not fall into door well during the motor removal.

2. Disconnect the negative (−) battery cable.

3. Remove the door trim panel and watershield. Refer to the "Door Trim Panel" removal and installation procedures in this chapter. Disconnect the window motor wiring leads.

4. Remove the two forward regulator mounting plate attaching rivets. Use a ¼″ drill bit and drill out the attaching rivets.

CAUTION: *Prior to motor drive assembly removal, ensure that the regulator arm is in a fixed position to prevent dangerous counterbalance spring unwind!*

5. Remove the three window motor mounting screws.

6. Push the regulator mounting plate outboard sufficiently to remove the power window motor.

To install:

7. Install the new motor and drive assembly. Tighten the three motor mounting screws to 50-85 in. lbs.

8. Install the two regulator mounting plate

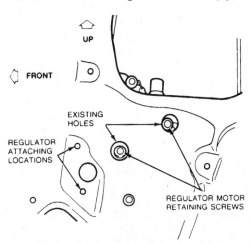

UP

FRONT

EXISTING
HOLES

REGULATOR
ATTACHING
LOCATIONS

REGULATOR MOTOR
RETAINING SCREWS

Electric window motor

rivets part No. 385189-S100 using a Heavy Duty Riveter No. D80L-23200-A or equivalent. A ¼-20 × ½″ screw and washer assembly may be used to secure the motor to the drive assembly.

9. Connect the window motor wiring leads.

10. Connect the negative (−) battery cable.

11. Check the power window for proper operation.

12. Install the door trim panel and the watershield.

NOTE: *Verify that all the drain holes at bottom of doors are open to prevent water accumulation over the motor.*

Manual Inside Rear View Mirror

REPLACEMENT

1. Loosen the mirror assembly-to-mounting bracket setscrew.

2. Remove the mirror assembly by sliding it upward and away from the mounting bracket.

3. If the bracket vinyl pad remains on windshield, apply low heat from an electric heat gun until the vinyl softens. Peel the vinyl off the windshield and discard.

To install:

4. Make the sure glass, bracket, and adhesive kit, (Rearview Mirror Repair Kit D9AZ-19554-B or equivalent) are at least at room temperature of 65-75°F (18-24°C).

5. Locate and mark the mirror mounting bracket location on the outside surface of the windshield with a wax pencil.

6. Thoroughly clean the bonding surfaces of the glass and the bracket to remove the old adhesive. Use a mild abrasive cleaner on the glass and fine sandpaper on the bracket to lightly roughen the surface. Wipe it clean with the alcohol-moistened cloth.

7. Crush the accelerator vial (part of Rearview Mirror Repair Kit D9AZ-19554-B or equivalent), and apply the accelerator to the bonding surface of the bracket and windshield. Let it dry for three minutes.

8. Apply two drops of adhesive (Rearview Mirror Repair Kit D9AZ-19554-B or equivalent) to the mounting surface of the bracket.

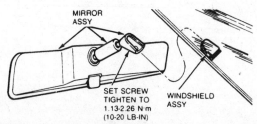

MIRROR ASSY

SET SCREW TIGHTEN TO 1.13-2.26 N·m (10-20 LB-IN)

WINDSHIELD ASSY

Interior rear view mirror mounting

Using a clean toothpick or wooden match, quickly spread the adhesive evenly over the mounting surface of the bracket.

9. Quickly position the mounting bracket on the windshield. The ⅜″ circular depression in the bracket must be toward the inside of the passenger compartment. Press the bracket firmly against the windshield for one minute.

10. Allow the bond to set for five minutes. Remove any excess bonding material from the windshield with an alcohol dampened cloth.

11. Attach the mirror to the mounting bracket and tighten the setscrew to 10-20 in. lbs.

Electronic Inside Rear View Mirror

REPLACEMENT

1. Remove the grommet from the garnish moulding above the mirror assembly.

2. Pull the wire assembly away from the garnish moulding opening until the connector is exposed and disconnect the wire.

3. Loosen the mirror assembly-to-mounting bracket setscrew and remove the mirror by sliding upward away from the bracket.

To install:

1. If the mounting bracket on the windshield has to be serviced, refer to the following procedures.

2. If the bracket vinyl pad remains on windshield, apply low heat from an electric heat gun until the vinyl softens. Peel the vinyl off the windshield and discard.

3. Make the sure glass, bracket, and adhesive kit, (Rearview Mirror Repair Kit D9AZ-19554-B or equivalent) are at least at room temperature of 65-75°F (18-24°C).

4. Locate and mark the mirror mounting bracket location on the outside surface of the windshield with a wax pencil.

5. Thoroughly clean the bonding surfaces of the glass and the bracket to remove the old adhesive. Use a mild abrasive cleaner on the glass and fine sandpaper on the bracket to lightly roughen the surface. Wipe it clean with the alcohol-moistened cloth.

6. Crush the accelerator vial (part of Rearview Mirror Repair Kit D9AZ-19554-B or equivalent), and apply the accelerator to the bonding surface of the bracket and windshield. Let it dry for three minutes.

7. Apply two drops of adhesive (Rearview Mirror Repair Kit D9AZ-19554-B or equivalent) to the mounting surface of the bracket. Using a clean toothpick or wooden match, quickly spread the adhesive evenly over the mounting surface of the bracket.

8. Quickly position the mounting bracket on the windshield. The ⅜″ circular depression in the bracket must be toward the inside of the

passenger compartment. Press the bracket firmly against the windshield for one minute.

9. Allow the bond to set for five minutes. Remove any excess bonding material from the windshield with an alcohol dampened cloth.

10. Position the mirror assembly over the mounting bracket after it has dried.

11. Tighten the mounting bracket setscrew to 10-20 in. lbs.

12. Connect the wire connector and push the wire back into the garnish moulding. Install the grommet to the garnish moulding.

Manual Front Seats

REMOVAL AND INSTALLATION

1. Remove the plastic shield retaining screws and remove the shield.

2. Remove the bolts and nut and washer assemblies retaining the seat tracks to the floor.

3. Remove the seat and track assembly from the vehicle and place on a clean working area.

WARNING: *Use care when handling seat and track assembly. Dropping the assembly or sitting on the seat not secured in the vehicle may result in damaged components.*

4. Remove the seat track-to-seat cushion attaching screws. Remove the seat cushion and assist spring from the tracks.

5. If the seat tracks are being replaced, transfer the assist springs and spacers, if so equipped, to the new track assembly.

To install:

1. Mount the seat tracks to the seat cushion.

2. Install the seat track-to-seat cushion retaining screws.

3. Place the seat assembly into vehicle and ensure proper alignment.

4. Install the screws, studs, plastic shields, and nut and washer assemblies.

Power Front Seats

REMOVAL AND INSTALLATION

1. Remove the heat shield covers to expose the nuts and washers and/or bolts.

2. Remove the nuts and washers, and bolts retaining the seat and track assembly to the floorpan.

3. Lift the seat and track assembly high enough to disconnect the wire harness. Remove the seat and track assembly from the vehicle.

4. Place the seat upside down on a clean bench. Remove the center occupant seat belt, if so equipped.

5. Disconnect the power seat switch-to-motor wire harness, if so equipped.

6. Remove the cushion side from the seat track assembly.

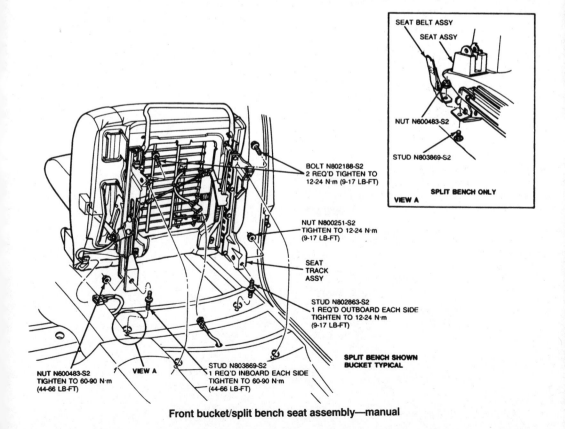

Front bucket/split bench seat assembly—manual

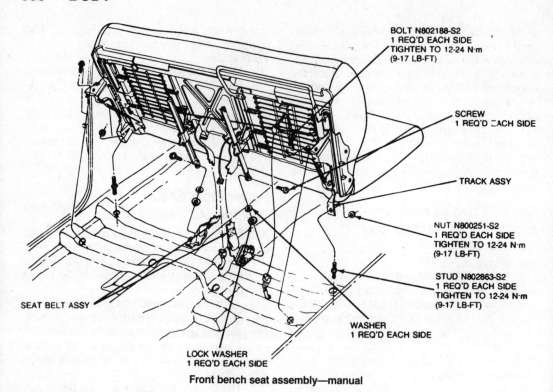

BOLT N802188-S2
1 REQ'D EACH SIDE
TIGHTEN TO 12-24 N·m
(9-17 LB-FT)

SCREW
1 REQ'D EACH SIDE

TRACK ASSY

NUT N800251-S2
1 REQ'D EACH SIDE
TIGHTEN TO 12-24 N·m
(9-17 LB-FT)

STUD N802863-S2
1 REQ'D EACH SIDE
TIGHTEN TO 12-24 N·m
(9-17 LB-FT)

WASHER
1 REQ'D EACH SIDE

LOCK WASHER
1 REQ'D EACH SIDE

SEAT BELT ASSY

Front bench seat assembly—manual

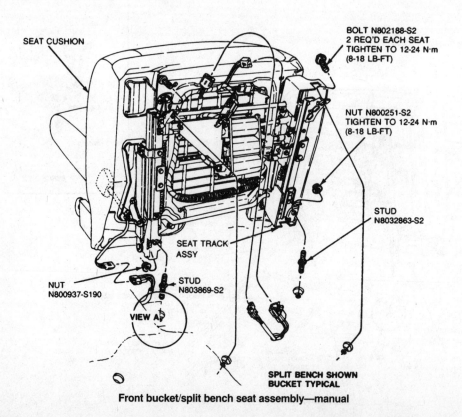

SEAT CUSHION

BOLT N802188-S2
2 REQ'D EACH SEAT
TIGHTEN TO 12-24 N·m
(8-18 LB-FT)

NUT N800251-S2
TIGHTEN TO 12-24 N·m
(8-18 LB-FT)

STUD
N8032863-S2

SEAT TRACK
ASSY

NUT
N800937-S190

STUD
N803869-S2

VIEW A

SPLIT BENCH SHOWN
BUCKET TYPICAL

Front bucket/split bench seat assembly—manual

7. Remove the two bolts retaining the clip mechanism to the the seat track.

8. Remove the seat back from the seat track.

9. Remove the outboard occupant seat belt.

10. Remove the four bolts retaining seat track to the seat cushion. Remove the track assembly.

WARNING: *Use care when handling seat and track assembly. Dropping the assembly or sitting on the seat not secured in vehicle may result in damaged components.*

To install:

1. Position the track assembly to the seat cushion.

2. Install the seat recliner-to-seat track retaining bolts.

3. Secure the outboard occupant seat belt to the seat track.

4. Secure the seat track assembly to the seat cushion using the four previously removed attaching bolts. Tighten the bolts.

5. Install the cushion side cover to the seat track assembly.

6. Connect the power seat switch to motor wire harness, if so equipped.

7. Install the center occupant seat belt to seat track.

8. Position the seat and track assembly in vehicle.

9. Lift the seat and track assembly high enough to permit the connection of the wire harness, then, connect wires.

10. Install the seat track-to-floorpan attaching nuts and washer and/or bolts. Tighten the bolts.

11. Install the heat shield covers.

12. Install the seat belt-to-floorpan attaching bolts.

13. Check the seat tracks for proper operation.

Power Seat Motor
REMOVAL AND INSTALLATION

1. Remove the seat and track assembly from the vehicle. Refer to the above "Front Seat" removal and installation procedures.

2. Remove the seat recliner mechanism and seat back from seat track.

3. Remove the seat belt.

4. Remove the seat track from the seat cushion.

5. Identify the cables and their respective locations.

6. Remove the motor bracket screw.

7. Lift the motor and deflect three left cables toward the left track assembly. Then, remove the three left hand cable assemblies from the motor.

8. Remove the two locknuts retaining the motor to the mounting brackets.

To install:

1. Secure the motor to the mounting bracket using the two previously removed locknuts. Tighten nuts to 8-10 in. lbs.

2. Lower the motor in place.

3. Position the three left hand drive cables to the motor, being sure to fully engage the square ends of cables into the motor armature.

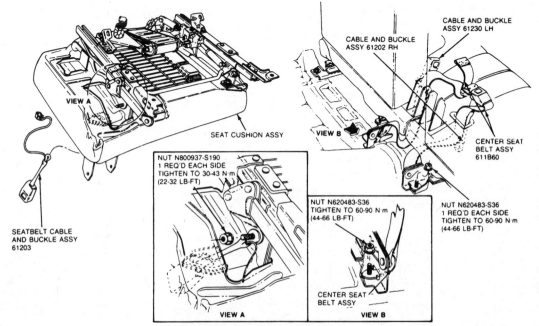

Front bench seat assembly—manual

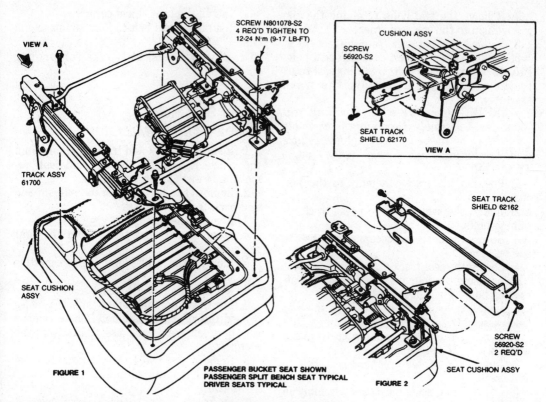

Power seat motor assembly

4. Align the right hand drive cable ends with the motor armatures.

5. With the three left hand cables engaged in the motor, lift the motor. Insert the right hand cable into the motor being sure to fully engage the square end of cable into the motor armature. Lower the motor into place.

6. Install the screw used to retain the motor bracket to the seat track. Tighten the screw to 54-70 in. lbs.

7. Install the seat track assembly to the seat cushion.

8. Install the seat recliner and the seat back to the seat track.

9. Install the seat belts.

10. Install the seat and track assembly in the vehicle.

Rear Seats

REMOVAL AND INSTALLATION

Seat Cushion

1. Apply knee pressure to the lower portion of the rear seat cushion. Push rearward to disengage the seat cushion from the retainer brackets.

NOTE: *The armrest is an integral part of the*

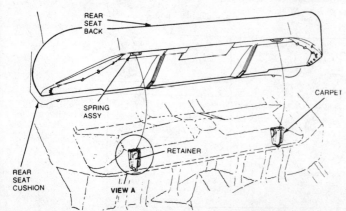

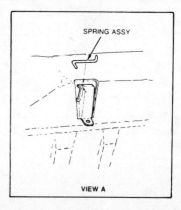

Seat cushion components

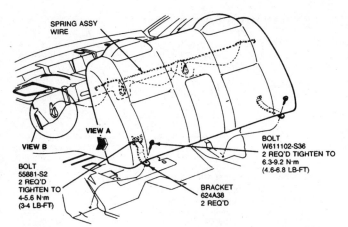

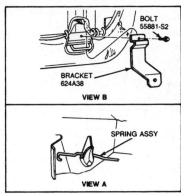

Rear seat back components

quarter trim panel. Its removal is not re-quired to remove rear seat cushion or back.

To install:

2. Position the seat cushion assembly into the vehicle.

3. Place the seat belts on top of the cushion.

4. Apply knee pressure to the lower portion of the seat cushion assembly. Push rearward

and down to lock the seat cushion into position.

5. Pull the rear seat cushion forward to be certain it is secured into its floor retainer.

Seat Back Rest

1. Remove the rear seat cushion.

2. Remove the seat back bracket attaching bolts.

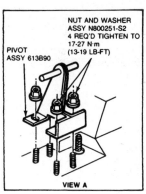

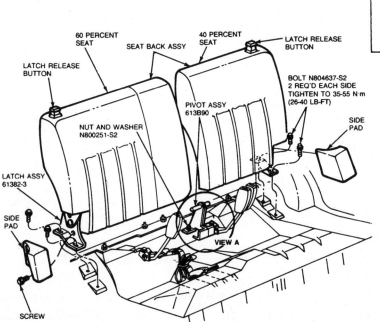

Rear split seat back components

How to Remove Stains from Fabric Interior

For rest results, spots and stains should be removed as soon as possible. Never use gasoline, lacquer thinner, acetone, nail polish remover or bleach. Use a 3' x 3" piece of cheesecloth. Squeeze most of the liquid from the fabric and wipe the stained fabric from the outside of the stain toward the center with a lifting motion. Turn the cheesecloth as soon as one side becomes soiled. When using water to remove a stain, be sure to wash the entire section after the spot has been removed to avoid water stains. Encrusted spots can be broken up with a dull knife and vacuumed before removing the stain.

Type of Stain	How to Remove It
Surface spots	Brush the spots out with a small hand brush or use a commercial preparation such as K2R to lift the stain.
Mildew	Clean around the mildew with warm suds. Rinse in cold water and soak the mildew area in a solution of 1 part table salt and 2 parts water. Wash with upholstery cleaner.
Water stains	Water stains in fabric materials can be removed with a solution made from 1 cup of table salt dissolved in 1 quart of water. Vigorously scrub the solution into the stain and rinse with clear water. Water stains in nylon or other synthetic fabrics should be removed with a commercial type spot remover.
Chewing gum, tar, crayons, shoe polish (greasy stains)	Do not use a cleaner that will soften gum or tar. Harden the deposit with an ice cube and scrape away as much as possible with a dull knife. Moisten the remainder with cleaning fluid and scrub clean.
Ice cream, candy	Most candy has a sugar base and can be removed with a cloth wrung out in warm water. Oily candy, after cleaning with warm water, should be cleaned with upholstery cleaner. Rinse with warm water and clean the remainder with cleaning fluid.
Wine, alcohol, egg, milk, soft drink (non-greasy stains)	Do not use soap. Scrub the stain with a cloth wrung out in warm water. Remove the remainder with cleaning fluid.
Grease, oil, lipstick, butter and related stains	Use a spot remover to avoid leaving a ring. Work from the outisde of the stain to the center and dry with a clean cloth when the spot is gone.
Headliners (cloth)	Mix a solution of warm water and foam upholstery cleaner to give thick suds. Use only foam—liquid may streak or spot. Clean the entire headliner in one operation using a circular motion with a natural sponge.
Headliner (vinyl)	Use a vinyl cleaner with a sponge and wipe clean with a dry cloth.
Seats and door panels	Mix 1 pint upholstery cleaner in 1 gallon of water. Do not soak the fabric around the buttons.
Leather or vinyl fabric	Use a multi-purpose cleaner full strength and a stiff brush. Let stand 2 minutes and scrub thoroughly. Wipe with a clean, soft rag.
Nylon or synthetic fabrics	For normal stains, use the same procedures you would for washing cloth upholstery. If the fabric is extremely dirty, use a multi-purpose cleaner full strength with a stiff scrub brush. Scrub thoroughly in all directions and wipe with a cotton towel or soft rag.

NOTE: *The seat belt bolts do not secure seat back to the vehicle.*

3. Grasp the seat back assembly at the bottom and lift it up to disengage the hanger wire from the retainer brackets.

To install:

4. Position the seat back in the vehicle so that the hanger wires are engaged with the retaining brackets.

5. Install the seat back bolts and tighten to 5-7 ft. lbs.

6. Install the rear seat cushion.

Split Folding Rear Seat Back

1. Remove the rear seat cushion.

2. Remove the seat back side pads by removing the attaching screws (one each) and sliding the pad upward.

3. Remove the four bolts (two each seat back) retaining the seat back assembly to the floorpan.

4. Remove the seat back from the inboard pivot pin by sliding the seat back toward the outboard side of the vehicle.

To install:

5. Position the seat back onto the inboard pivot pin in the full-up position.

6. Install the seat back-to-floorpan retaining bolts (two each side).

7. Check the seat back latch for proper operation.

NOTE: *A nut and bolt have been provided on the left hand (40 percent) seat back latch only, to align the right hand seat back to the fixed position (± 2° adjustment). To align the right hand seat back, loosen the nut and bolt and reposition the bolt in its slot. Tighten the bolt and nut to 30-40 ft. lbs. Check the seat backs for proper operation after alignment.*

8. Install the seat back side pads and the attaching screws.

Mechanic's Data

General Conversion Table

Multiply By	To Convert	To	
LENGTH			
2.54	Inches	Centimeters	.3937
25.4	Inches	Millimeters	.03937
30.48	Feet	Centimeters	.0328
.304	Feet	Meters	3.28
.914	Yards	Meters	1.094
1.609	Miles	Kilometers	.621
VOLUME			
.473	Pints	Liters	2.11
.946	Quarts	Liters	1.06
3.785	Gallons	Liters	.264
.016	Cubic inches	Liters	61.02
16.39	Cubic inches	Cubic cms.	.061
28.3	Cubic feet	Liters	.0353
MASS (Weight)			
28.35	Ounces	Grams	.035
.4536	Pounds	Kilograms	2.20
—	To obtain	From	Multiply by

Multiply By	To Convert	To	
AREA			
.645	Square inches	Square cms.	.155
.836	Square yds.	Square meters	1.196
FORCE			
4.448	Pounds	Newtons	.225
.138	Ft./lbs.	Kilogram/meters	7.23
1.36	Ft./lbs.	Newton-meters	.737
.112	In./lbs.	Newton-meters	8.844
PRESSURE			
.068	Psi	Atmospheres	14.7
6.89	Psi	Kilopascals	.145
OTHER			
1.104	Horsepower (DIN)	Horsepower (SAE)	.9861
.746	Horsepower (SAE)	Kilowatts (KW)	1.34
1.60	Mph	Km/h	.625
.425	Mpg	Km/1	2.35
—	To obtain	From	Multiply by

Tap Drill Sizes

National Coarse or U.S.S.

Screw & Tap Size	Threads Per Inch	Use Drill Number
No. 5	40	39
No. 6	32	36
No. 8	32	29
No. 10	24	25
No. 12	24	17
1/4	20	8
5/16	18	F
3/8	16	5/16
7/16	14	U
1/2	13	27/64
9/16	12	31/64
5/8	11	17/32
3/4	10	21/32
7/8	9	49/64

National Coarse or U.S.S.

Screw & Tap Size	Threads Per Inch	Use Drill Number
1	8	7/8
1 1/8	7	63/64
1 1/4	7	1 7/64
1 1/2	6	1 11/32

National Fine or S.A.E.

Screw & Tap Size	Threads Per Inch	Use Drill Number
No. 5	44	37
No. 6	40	33
No. 8	36	29
No. 10	32	21

National Fine or S.A.E.

Screw & Tap Size	Threads Per Inch	Use Drill Number
No. 12	28	15
1/4	28	3
6/16	24	1
3/8	24	Q
7/16	20	W
1/2	20	29/64
9/16	18	33/64
5/8	18	37/64
3/4	16	11/16
7/8	14	13/16
1 1/8	12	1 3/64
1 1/4	12	1 11/64
1 1/2	12	1 27/64

Drill Sizes In Decimal Equivalents

Inch	Decimal	Wire	mm	Inch	Decimal	Wire	mm	Inch	Decimal	Wire & Letter	mm	Inch	Decimal	Letter	mm	Inch	Decimal	mm
1/64	.0156		.39		.0730	49			.1614		4.1		.2717		6.9		.4331	11.0
	.0157		.4		.0748		1.9		.1654		4.2		.2720	I		7/16	.4375	11.11
	.0160	78			.0760	48			.1660	19			.2756		7.0		.4528	11.5
	.0165		.42		.0768		1.95		.1673		4.25		.2770	J		29/64	.4531	11.51
	.0173		.44	5/64	.0781		1.98		.1693		4.3		.2795		7.1	15/32	.4688	11.90
	.0177		.45		.0785	47			.1695	18			.2810	K			.4724	12.0
	.0180	77			.0787		2.0	11/64	.1719		4.36	9/32	.2812		7.14	31/64	.4844	12.30
	.0181		.46		.0807		2.05		.1730	17			.2835		7.2		.4921	12.5
	.0189		.48		.0810	46			.1732		4.4		.2854		7.25	1/2	.5000	12.70
	.0197		.5		.0820	45			.1770	16			.2874		7.3		.5118	13.0
	.0200	76			.0827		2.1		.1772		4.5		.2900	L		33/64	.5156	13.09
	.0210	75			.0846		2.15		.1800	15			.2913		7.4	17/32	.5312	13.49
	.0217		.55		.0860	44			.1811		4.6		.2950	M			.5315	13.5
	.0225	74			.0866		2.2		.1820	14			.2953		7.5	35/64	.5469	13.89
	.0236		.6		.0886		2.25		.1850	13		19/64	.2969		7.54		.5512	14.0
	.0240	73			.0890	43			.1850		4.7		.2992		7.6	9/16	.5625	14.28
	.0250	72			.0906		2.3		.1870		4.75		.3020	N			.5709	14.5
	.0256		.65		.0925		2.35	3/16	.1875		4.76		.3031		7.7	37/64	.5781	14.68
	.0260	71			.0935	42			.1890		4.8		.3051		7.75		.5906	15.0
	.0276		.7	3/32	.0938		2.38		.1890	12			.3071		7.8	19/32	.5938	15.08
	.0280	70			.0945		2.4		.1910	11			.3110		7.9	39/64	.6094	15.47
	.0292	69			.0960	41			.1929		4.9	5/16	.3125		7.93		.6102	15.5
	.0295		.75		.0965		2.45		.1935	10			.3150		8.0	5/8	.6250	15.87
	.0310	68			.0980	40			.1960	9			.3160	O			.6299	16.0
1/32	.0312		.79		.0981		2.5		.1969		5.0		.3189		8.1	41/64	.6406	16.27
	.0315		.8		.0995	39			.1990	8			.3228		8.2		.6496	16.5
	.0320	67			.1015	38			.2008		5.1		.3230	P		21/32	.6562	16.66
	.0330	66			.1024		2.6		.2010	7			.3248		8.25		.6693	17.0
	.0335		.85		.1040	37		13/64	.2031		5.16		.3268		8.3	43/64	.6719	17.06
	.0350	65			.1063		2.7		.2040	6		21/64	.3281		8.33	11/16	.6875	17.46
	.0354		.9		.1065	36			.2047		5.2		.3307		8.4		.6890	17.5
	.0360	64			.1083		2.75		.2055	5			.3320	Q		45/64	.7031	17.85
	.0370	63		7/64	.1094		2.77		.2067		5.25		.3346		8.5		.7087	18.0
	.0374		.95		.1100	35			.2087		5.3		.3386		8.6	23/32	.7188	18.25
	.0380	62			.1102		2.8		.2090	4			.3390	R			.7283	18.5
	.0390	61			.1110	34			.2126		5.4	11/32	.3425		8.7	47/64	.7344	18.65
	.0394		1.0		.1130	33			.2130	3			.3438		8.73		.7480	19.0
	.0400	60			.1142		2.9		.2165		5.5		.3445		8.75	3/4	.7500	19.05
	.0410	59			.1160	32		7/32	2188		5.55		.3465		8.8	49/64	.7656	19.44
	.0413		1.05		.1181		3.0		.2205		5.6		.3480	S			.7677	19.5
	.0420	58			.1200	31			.2210	2			.3504		8.9	25/32	.7812	19.84
	.0430	57			.1220		3.1		.2244		5.7		.3543		9.0		.7874	20.0
	.0433		1.1	1/8	.1250		3.17		.2264		5.75		.3580	T		51/64	.7969	20.24
	.0453		1.15		.1260		3.2		.2280	1			.3583		9.1		.8071	20.5
	.0465	56			.1280		3.25		.2283		5.8	23/64	.3594		9.12	13/16	.8125	20.63
3/64	.0469		1.19		.1285	30			.2323		5.9		.3622		9.2		.8268	21.0
	.0472		1.2		.1299		3.3		.2340	A			.3642		9.25	53/64	.8281	21.03
	.0492		1.25		.1339		3.4	15/64	.2344		5.95		.3661		9.3	27/32	.8438	21.43
	.0512		1.3		.1360	29			.2362		6.0		.3680	U			.8465	21.5
	.0520	55			.1378		3.5		.2380	B			.3701		9.4	55/64	.8594	21.82
	.0531		1.35		.1405	28			.2402		6.1		.3740		9.5		.8661	22.0
	.0550	54		9/64	.1406		3.57		.2420	C		3/8	.3750		9.52	7/8	.8750	22.22
	.0551		1.4		.1417		3.6		.2441		6.2		.3770	V			.8858	22.5
	.0571		1.45		.1440	27			.2460	D			.3780		9.6	57/64	.8906	22.62
	.0591		1.5		.1457		3.7		.2461		6.25		.3819		9.7		.9055	23.0
	.0595	53			.1470	26			.2480		6.3		.3839		9.75	29/32	.9062	23.01
	.0610		1.55		.1476		3.75	1/4	.2500	E	6.35		.3858		9.8	59/64	.9219	23.41
1/16	.0625		1.59		.1495	25			.2520		6.		.3860	W			.9252	23.5
	.0630		1.6		.1496		3.8		.2559		6.5		.3898		9.9	15/16	.9375	23.81
	.0635	52			.1520	24			.2570	F		25/64	.3906		9.92		.9449	24.0
	.0650		1.65		.1535		3.9		.2598		6.6		.3937		10.0	61/64	.9531	24.2
	.0669		1.7		.1540	23			.2610	G			.3970	X			.9646	24.5
	.0670	51		5/32	.1562		3.96		.2638		6.7		.4040	Y		31/32	.9688	24.6
	.0689		1.75		.1570	22		17/64	.2656		6.74	13/32	.4062		10.31		.9843	25.0
	.0700	50			.1575		4.0		.2657		6.75		.4130	Z		63/64	.9844	25.0
	.0709		1.8		.1590	21			.2660	H			.4134		10.5	1	1.0000	25.4
	.0728		1.85		.1610	20			.2677		6.8	27/64	.4219		10.71			

GLOSSARY OF TERMS

AIR/FUEL RATIO: The ratio of air to gasoline by weight in the fuel mixture drawn into the engine.

AIR INJECTION: One method of reducing harmful exhaust emissions by injecting air into each of the exhaust ports of an engine. The fresh air entering the hot exhaust manifold causes any remaining fuel to be burned before it can exit the tailpipe.

ALTERNATOR: A device used for converting mechanical energy into electrical energy.

AMMETER: An instrument, calibrated in amperes, used to measure the flow of an electrical current in a circuit. Ammeters are always connected in series with the circuit being tested.

AMPERE: The rate of flow of electrical current present when one volt of electrical pressure is applied against one ohm of electrical resistance.

ANALOG COMPUTER: Any microprocessor that uses similar (analogous) electrical signals to make its calculations.

ARMATURE: A laminated, soft iron core wrapped by a wire that converts electrical energy to mechanical energy as in a motor or relay. When rotated in a magnetic field, it changes mechanical energy into electrical energy as in a generator.

ATMOSPHERIC PRESSURE: The pressure on the Earth's surface caused by the weight of the air in the atmosphere. At sea level, this pressure is 14.7 psi at 32°F (101 kPa at 0°C).

ATOMIZATION: The breaking down of a liquid into a fine mist that can be suspended in air.

AXIAL PLAY: Movement parallel to a shaft or bearing bore.

BACKFIRE: The sudden combustion of gases in the intake or exhaust system that results in a loud explosion.

BACKLASH: The clearance or play between two parts, such as meshed gears.

BACKPRESSURE: Restrictions in the exhaust system that slow the exit of exhaust gases from the combustion chamber.

BAKELITE: A heat resistant, plastic insulator material commonly used in printed circuit boards and transistorized components.

BALL BEARING: A bearing made up of hardened inner and outer races between which hardened steel ball roll.

BALLAST RESISTOR: A resistor in the primary ignition circuit that lowers voltage after the engine is started to reduce wear on ignition components.

BEARING: A friction reducing, supportive device usually located between a stationary part and a moving part.

BIMETAL TEMPERATURE SENSOR: Any sensor or switch made of two dissimilar types of metal that bend when heated or cooled due to the different expansion rates of the alloys. These types of sensors usually function as an on/off switch.

BLOWBY: Combustion gases, composed of water vapor and unburned fuel, that leak past the piston rings into the crankcase during normal engine operation. These gases are removed by the PCV system to prevent the build-up of harmful acids in the crankcase.

BRAKE PAD: A brake shoe and lining assembly used with disc brakes.

BRAKE SHOE: The backing for the brake lining. The term is, however, usually applied to the assembly of the brake backing and lining.

BUSHING: A liner, usually removable, for a bearing; an anti-friction liner used in place of a bearing.

BYPASS: System used to bypass ballast resistor during engine cranking to increase voltage supplied to the coil.

CALIPER: A hydraulically activated device in a disc brake system, which is mounted straddling the brake rotor (disc). The caliper contains at least one piston and two brake pads. Hydraulic pressure on the piston(s) forces the pads against the rotor.

CAMSHAFT: A shaft in the engine on which are the lobes (cams) which operate the valves. The camshaft is driven by the crankshaft, via a belt, chain or gears, at one half the crankshaft speed.

CAPACITOR: A device which stores an electrical charge.

CARBON MONOXIDE (CO): a colorless, odorless gas given off as a normal byproduct of combustion. It is poisonous and extremely dangerous in confined areas, building up slowly to toxic levels without warning if adequate ventilation is not available.

CARBURETOR: A device, usually mounted on the intake manifold of an engine, which mixes the air and fuel in the proper proportion to allow even combustion.

CATALYTIC CONVERTER: A device installed in the exhaust system, like a muffler, that converts harmful byproducts of combustion into carbon dioxide and water vapor by means of a heat-producing chemical reaction.

CENTRIFUGAL ADVANCE: A mechanical method of advancing the spark timing by using flyweights in the distributor that react to centrifugal force generated by the distributor shaft rotation.

CHECK VALVE: Any one-way valve installed to permit the flow of air, fuel or vacuum in one direction only.

CHOKE: A device, usually a moveable valve, placed in the intake path of a carburetor to restrict the flow of air.

CIRCUIT: Any unbroken path through which an electrical current can flow. Also used to describe fuel flow in some instances.

CIRCUIT BREAKER: A switch which protects an electrical circuit from overload by opening the circuit when the current flow exceeds a predetermined level. Some circuit breakers must be reset manually, while other reset automatically

COIL (IGNITION): A transformer in the ignition circuit which steps of the voltage provided to the spark plugs.

COMBINATION MANIFOLD: An assembly which includes both the intake and exhaust manifolds in one casting.

COMBINATION VALVE: A device used in some fuel systems that routes fuel vapors to a charcoal storage canister instead of venting them into the atmosphere. The valve relieves fuel tank pressure and allows fresh air into the tank as fuel level drops to prevent a vapor lock situation.

COMPRESSION RATIO: The comparison of the total volume of the cylinder and combustion chamber with the piston at BDC and the piston at TDC.

CONDENSER: 1. An electrical device which acts to store an electrical charge, preventing voltage surges.
   2. A radiator-like device in the air conditioning system in which refrigerant gas condenses into a liquid, giving off heat.

CONDUCTOR: Any material through which an electrical current can be transmitted easily.

CONTINUITY: Continuous or complete circuit. Can be checked with an ohmmeter.

COUNTERSHAFT: An intermediate shaft which is rotated by a mainshaft and transmits, in turn, that rotation to a working part.

CRANKCASE: The lower part of an engine in which the crankshaft and related parts operate.

CRANKSHAFT: The main driving shaft of an engine which receives reciprocating motion from the pistons and converts it to rotary motion.

CYLINDER: In an engine, the round hole in the engine block in which the piston(s) ride.

CYLINDER BLOCK: The main structural member of an engine in which is found the cylinders, crankshaft and other principal parts.

CYLINDER HEAD: The detachable portion of the engine, fastened, usually, to the top of the cylinder block, containing all or most of the combustion chambers. On overhead valve engines, it contains the valves and their operating parts. On overhead cam engines, it contains the camshaft as well.

DEAD CENTER: The extreme top or bottom of the piston stroke.

DETONATION: An unwanted explosion of the air fuel mixture in the combustion chamber caused by excess heat and compression, advanced timing, or an overly lean mixture. Also referred to as "ping".

DIAPHRAGM: A thin, flexible wall separating two cavities, such as in a vacuum advance unit.

DIESELING: A condition in which hot spots in the combustion chamber cause the engine to run on after the key is turned off.

DIFFERENTIAL: A geared assembly which allows the transmission of motion between drive axles, giving one axle the ability to turn faster than the other.

DIODE: An electrical device that will allow current to flow in one direction only.

DISC BRAKE: A hydraulic braking assembly consisting of a brake disc, or rotor, mounted on an axle, and a caliper assembly containing, usually two brake pads which are activated by hydraulic pressure. The pads are forced against the sides of the disc, creating friction which slows the vehicle.

DISTRIBUTOR: A mechanically driven device on an engine which is responsible for electrically firing the spark plug at a predetermined point of the piston stroke.

DOWEL PIN: A pin, inserted in mating holes in two different parts allowing those parts to maintain a fixed relationship.

DRUM BRAKE: A braking system which consists of two brake shoes and one or two wheel cylinders, mounted on a fixed backing plate, and a brake drum, mounted on an axle, which revolves around the assembly. Hydraulic action applied to the wheel cylinders forces the shoes outward against the drum, creating friction and slowing the vehicle.

DWELL: The rate, measured in degrees of shaft rotation, at which an electrical circuit cycles on and off.

ELECTRONIC CONTROL UNIT (ECU): Ignition module, module, amplifier or igniter. See Module for definition.

ELECTRONIC IGNITION: A system in which the timing and firing of the spark plugs is controlled by an electronic control unit, usually called a module. These systems have not points or condenser.

ENDPLAY: The measured amount of axial movement in a shaft.

ENGINE: A device that converts heat into mechanical energy.

EXHAUST MANIFOLD: A set of cast passages or pipes which conduct exhaust gases from the engine.

FEELER GAUGE: A blade, usually metal, of precisely predetermined thickness, used to measure the clearance between two parts. These blades usually are available in sets of assorted thicknesses.

F-Head: An engine configuration in which the intake valves are in the cylinder head, while the camshaft and exhaust valves are located in the cylinder block. The camshaft operates the intake valves via lifters and pushrods, while it operates the exhaust valves directly.

FIRING ORDER: The order in which combustion occurs in the cylinders of an engine. Also the order in which spark is distributed to the plugs by the distributor.

FLATHEAD: An engine configuration in which the camshaft and all the valves are located in the cylinder block.

FLOODING: The presence of too much fuel in the intake manifold and combustion chamber which prevents the air/fuel mixture from firing, thereby causing a no-start situation.

FLYWHEEL: A disc shaped part bolted to the rear end of the crankshaft. Around the outer perimeter is affixed the ring gear. The starter drive engages the ring gear, turning the flywheel, which rotates the crankshaft, imparting the initial starting motion to the engine.

FOOT POUND (ft.lb. or sometimes, ft. lbs.): The amount of energy or work needed to raise an item weighing one pound, a distance of one foot.

FUSE: A protective device in a circuit which prevents circuit overload by breaking the circuit when a specific amperage is present. The device is constructed around a strip or wire of a lower amperage rating than the circuit it is designed to protect. When an amperage higher than that stamped on the fuse is present in the circuit, the strip or wire melts, opening the circuit.

GEAR RATIO: The ratio between the number of teeth on meshing gears.

GENERATOR: A device which converts mechanical energy into electrical energy.

HEAT RANGE: The measure of a spark plug's ability to dissipate heat from its firing end. The higher the heat range, the hotter the plug fires.

HUB: The center part of a wheel or gear.

HYDROCARBON (HC): Any chemical compound made up of hydrogen and carbon. A major pollutant formed by the engine as a byproduct of combustion.

HYDROMETER: An instrument used to measure the specific gravity of a solution.

INCH POUND (in.lb. or sometimes, in. lbs.): One twelfth of a foot pound.

INDUCTION: A means of transferring electrical energy in the form of a magnetic field. Principle used in the ignition coil to increase voltage.

INJECTION PUMP: A device, usually mechanically operated, which meters and delivers fuel under pressure to the fuel injector.

INJECTOR: A device which receives metered fuel under relatively low pressure and is activated to inject the fuel into the engine under relatively high pressure at a predetermined time.

INPUT SHAFT: The shaft to which torque is applied, usually carrying the driving gear or gears.

INTAKE MANIFOLD: A casting of passages or pipes used to conduct air or a fuel/air mixture to the cylinders.

JOURNAL: The bearing surface within which a shaft operates.

KEY: A small block usually fitted in a notch between a shaft and a hub to prevent slippage of the two parts.

MANIFOLD: A casting of passages or set of pipes which connect the cylinders to an inlet or outlet source.

MANIFOLD VACUUM: Low pressure in an engine intake manifold formed just below the throttle plates. Manifold vacuum is highest at idle and drops under acceleration.

MASTER CYLINDER: The primary fluid pressurizing device in a hydraulic system. In automotive use, it is found in brake and hydraulic clutch systems and is pedal activated, either directly or, in a power brake system, through the power booster.

MODULE: Electronic control unit, amplifier or igniter of solid state or integrated design which controls the current flow in the ignition primary circuit based on input from the pickup coil. When the module opens the primary circuit, the high secondary voltage is induced in the coil.

NEEDLE BEARING: A bearing which consists of a number (usually a large number) of long, thin rollers.

OHM: (Ω) The unit used to measure the resistance of conductor to electrical flow. One ohm is the amount of resistance that limits current flow to one ampere in a circuit with one volt of pressure.

OHMMETER: An instrument used for measuring the resistance, in ohms, in an electrical circuit.

OUTPUT SHAFT: The shaft which transmits torque from a device, such as a transmission.

OVERDRIVE: A gear assembly which produces more shaft revolutions than that transmitted to it.

OVERHEAD CAMSHAFT (OHC): An engine configuration in which the camshaft is mounted on top of the cylinder head and operates the valve either directly or by means of rocker arms.

OVERHEAD VALVE (OHV): An engine configuration in which all of the valves are located in the cylinder head and the camshaft is located in the cylinder block. The camshaft operates the valves via lifters and pushrods.

OXIDES OF NITROGEN (NOx): Chemical compounds of nitrogen produced as a byproduct of combustion. They combine with hydrocarbons to produce smog.

OXYGEN SENSOR: Used with the feedback system to sense the presence of oxygen in the exhaust gas and signal the computer which can reference the voltage signal to an air/fuel ratio.

PINION: The smaller of two meshing gears.

PISTON RING: An open ended ring which fits into a groove on the outer diameter of the piston. Its chief function is to form a seal between the piston and cylinder wall. Most automotive pistons have three rings: two for compression sealing; one for oil sealing.

PRELOAD: A predetermined load placed on a bearing during assembly or by adjustment.

PRIMARY CIRCUIT: Is the low voltage side of the ignition system which consists of the ignition switch, ballast resistor or resistance wire, bypass, coil, electronic control unit and pick-up coil as well as the connecting wires and harnesses.

PRESS FIT: The mating of two parts under pressure, due to the inner diameter of one being smaller than the outer diameter of the other, or vice versa; an interference fit.

RACE: The surface on the inner or outer ring of a bearing on which the balls, needles or rollers move.

REGULATOR: A device which maintains the amperage and/or voltage levels of a circuit at predetermined values.

RELAY: A switch which automatically opens and/or closes a circuit.

RESISTANCE: The opposition to the flow of current through a circuit or electrical device, and is measured in ohms. Resistance is equal to the voltage divided by the amperage.

RESISTOR: A device, usually made of wire, which offers a preset amount of resistance in an electrical circuit.

RING GEAR: The name given to a ring-shaped gear attached to a differential case, or affixed to a flywheel or as part a planetary gear set.

ROLLER BEARING: A bearing made up of hardened inner and outer races between which hardened steel rollers move.

ROTOR: 1. The disc-shaped part of a disc brake assembly, upon which the brake pads bear; also called, brake disc.
2. The device mounted atop the distributor shaft, which passes current to the distributor cap tower contacts.

SECONDARY CIRCUIT: The high voltage side of the ignition system, usually above 20,000 volts. The secondary includes the ignition coil, coil wire, distributor cap and rotor, spark plug wires and spark plugs.

SENDING UNIT: A mechanical, electrical, hydraulic or electromagnetic device which transmits information to a gauge.

SENSOR: Any device designed to measure engine operating conditions or ambient pressures and temperatures. Usually electronic in nature and designed to send a voltage signal to an on-board computer, some sensors may operate as a simple on/off switch or they may provide a variable voltage signal (like a potentiometer) as conditions or measured parameters change.

SHIM: Spacers of precise, predetermined thickness used between parts to establish a proper working relationship.

SLAVE CYLINDER: In automotive use, a device in the hydraulic clutch system which is activated by hydraulic force, disengaging the clutch.

SOLENOID: A coil used to produce a magnetic field, the effect of which is produce work.

SPARK PLUG: A device screwed into the combustion chamber of a spark ignition engine. The basic construction is a conductive core inside of a ceramic insulator, mounted in an outer conductive base. An electrical charge from the spark plug wire travels along the conductive core and jumps a preset air gap to a grounding point or points at the end of the conductive base. The resultant spark ignites the fuel/air mixture in the combustion chamber.

SPLINES: Ridges machined or cast onto the outer diameter of a shaft or inner diameter of a bore to enable parts to mate without rotation.

TACHOMETER: A device used to measure the rotary speed of an engine, shaft, gear, etc., usually in rotations per minute.

THERMOSTAT: A valve, located in the cooling system of an engine, which is closed when cold and opens gradually in response to engine heating, controlling the temperature of the coolant and rate of coolant flow.

TOP DEAD CENTER (TDC): The point at which the piston reaches the top of its travel on the compression stroke.

TORQUE: The twisting force applied to an object.

TORQUE CONVERTER: A turbine used to transmit power from a driving member to a driven member via hydraulic action, providing changes in drive ratio and torque. In automotive use, it links the driveplate at the rear of the engine to the automatic transmission.

TRANSDUCER: A device used to change a force into an electrical signal.

TRANSISTOR: A semi-conductor component which can be actuated by a small voltage to perform an electrical switching function.

TUNE-UP: A regular maintenance function, usually associated with the replacement and adjustment of parts and components in the electrical and fuel systems of a vehicle for the purpose of attaining optimum performance.

TURBOCHARGER: An exhaust driven pump which compresses intake air and forces it into the combustion chambers at higher than atmospheric pressures. The increased air pressure allows more fuel to be burned and results in increased horsepower being produced.

VACUUM ADVANCE: A device which advances the ignition timing in response to increased engine vacuum.

VACUUM GAUGE: An instrument used to measure the presence of vacuum in a chamber.

VALVE: A device which control the pressure, direction of flow or rate of flow of a liquid or gas.

VALVE CLEARANCE: The measured gap between the end of the valve stem and the rocker arm, cam lobe or follower that activates the valve.

VISCOSITY: The rating of a liquid's internal resistance to flow.

VOLTMETER: An instrument used for measuring electrical force in units called volts. Voltmeters are always connected parallel with the circuit being tested.

WHEEL CYLINDER: Found in the automotive drum brake assembly, it is a device, actuated by hydraulic pressure, which, through internal pistons, pushes the brake shoes outward against the drums.

ABBREVIATIONS AND SYMBOLS

A: Ampere

AC: Alternating current

A/C: Air conditioning

A-h: Ampere hour

AT: Automatic transmission

ATDC: After top dead center

μA: Microampere

bbl: Barrel

BDC: Bottom dead center

bhp: Brake horsepower

BTDC: Before top dead center

BTU: British thermal unit

C: Celsius (Centigrade)

CCA: Cold cranking amps

cd: Candela

cm^2: Square centimeter

cm^3, cc: Cubic centimeter

CO: Carbon monoxide

CO_2: Carbon dioxide

cu.in., in^3: Cubic inch

CV: Constant velocity

Cyl.: Cylinder

DC: Direct current

ECM: Electronic control module

EFE: Early fuel evaporation

EFI: Electronic fuel injection

EGR: Exhaust gas recirculation

Exh.: Exhaust

F: Fahrenheit

F: Farad

pF: Picofarad

μF: Microfarad

FI: Fuel injection

ft.lb., ft. lb., ft. lbs.: foot pound(s)

gal: Gallon

g: Gram

HC: Hydrocarbon

HEI: High energy ignition

HO: High output

hp: Horsepower

Hyd.: Hydraulic

Hz: Hertz

ID: Inside diameter

in.lb.; in. lb.; in. lbs: inch pound(s)

Int.: Intake

K: Kelvin

kg: Kilogram

kHz: Kilohertz

km: Kilometer

km/h: Kilometers per hour

kΩ: Kilohm

kPa: Kilopascal

kV: Kilovolt

kW: Kilowatt

l: Liter

l/s: Liters per second

m: Meter

mA: Milliampere

mg: Milligram

mHz: Megahertz

mm: Millimeter

mm^2: Square millimeter

m^3: Cubic meter

MΩ: Megohm

m/s: Meters per second

MT: Manual transmission

mV: Millivolt

μm: Micrometer

N: Newton

N-m: Newton meter

NOx: Nitrous oxide

OD: Outside diameter

OHC: Over head camshaft

OHV: Over head valve

Ω: Ohm

PCV: Positive crankcase ventilation

psi: Pounds per square inch

pts: Pints

qts: Quarts

rpm: Rotations per minute

rps: Rotations per second

R-12: A refrigerant gas (Freon)

SAE: Society of Automotive Engineers

SO$_2$: Sulfur dioxide

T: Ton

t: Megagram

TBI: Throttle Body Injection

TPS: Throttle Position Sensor

V: 1. Volt; 2. Venturi

μV: Microvolt

W: Watt

∞: Infinity

$<$: Less than

$>$: Greater than

Index

A

Air bypass solenoid, 163
Air cleaner, 6, 14, 160
Air conditioning, 22, 204
  Blower, 216, 220
  Charging, 25
  Compressor, 102
  Condenser, 23, 104
  Control panel, 204, 212
  Discharging, 23
  Evacuating, 25
  Evaporator, 23, 217
  Gauge sets, 24
  General service, 22
  Inspection, 204
  Leak testing, 24
  Operation, 22
  Preventive maintenance, 23
  Safety precautions, 23
  System tests, 24
  Troubleshooting, 26
Air pump, 156, 293
  air suspension, 291, 310
Alternator
  Alternator precautions, 63
  Operation, 59, 63
  Removal and installation, 64
  Specifications, 66
Alignment, wheel
  Camber, 302, 315
  Caster, 302, 315
  Toe, 302, 315, 318
Antenna, 383
Antifreeze, 23, 34
Anti lock brakes, 37, 343
Automatic transmission, 280
  Adjustments, 281
  Application chart, 247
  Back-up light switch, 260
  Filter change, 33, 280
  Fluid change, 33, 280
  Linkage adjustments, 280
  Neutral safety switch, 260
  Pan removal, 280
  Removal and installation, 282
  Troubleshooting, 288

B

Back-up light switch
  Automatic transmission, 260
  Manual transmission, 260
Ball joints
  Inspection, 295
  Removal and installation, 295
Battery, 16, 58
  Fluid level and maintenance, 17
  Jump starting, 41
  Removal and installation, 66
Bearings

Axle, 297
  Differential, 267
  Engine, 136, 141, 146
  Wheel, 37, 297, 316
Bellcrank, 389
Belts, 18, 112, 126
Boot (CV Joint), 254-260
  Replacement, 254
Brakes, 341
  Anti lock, 343, 349
  Bleeding, 349
  Brake light switch
  Disc brakes, 342, 359
    Caliper, 352, 360
    Description, 342
    Operating principals, 342
    Pads, 350, 360
    Rotor (Disc), 353, 354
  Drum brakes, 342, 354
    Adjustment, 344
    Drum, 354
    Operating principals, 342, 354
    Shoes, 355
    Wheel cylinder, 357
  Fluid level, 36
  Master cylinder, 36, 344
  Operation, 341
  Parking brake, 362
    Adjustment, 362
    Removal and installation, 363
  Power booster, 342
    Operating principals, 342
    Removal and installation, 347
  Proportioning valve, 348
  Specifications, 365
  Troubleshooting, 365
Bulbs, 234, 383
Bumpers, 376-378

C

Calipers
  Overhaul, 353, 361
  Removal and installation, 352, 360
Camber, 302, 315
Camshaft and bearings, 135
  Service, 131, 134
  Specifications, 74
Capacities Chart, 42
Caster, 302, 315
Catalytic converter, 155, 159
Charging system, 59, 65
Chassis electrical system, 194
  Circuit protection, 238, 240
  Heater and air conditioning, 204, 212-219
  Instrument panel, 207, 212
  Lighting, 230, 234
  Troubleshooting, 194
  Windshield wipers, 223
  Wiring diagrams, 212, 220, 222
Circuit breakers, 239

Clock, 230
Clutch, 275
    Adjustment, 275
    Cable, 276
    Operation, 275
    Pedal, 278
    Removal and installation, 277
    Troubleshooting, 286
Coil (ignition), 50, 61
Combination switch, 233, 319
Compact disc player, 221
Compression testing, 71
Compressor
    Removal and installation, 102
Condenser, 104
    Air conditioning, 23
Connecting rods and bearings
    Service, 136
    Specifications, 74
Console, 282
Constant velocity (CV) joints, 247, 254-60, 284
Control arm
    Lower, 296, 313
Cooling system, 23, 34, 102
Crankcase ventilation valve, 6, 15
    Service, 139
    Specifications, 74
Crankshaft damper, 124
Cylinder head, 107, 114
Cylinders
    Inspection, 137
    Reboring, 137

D

Damaged threads, 70
Disc brakes, 342
Distributor, 48, 50
    Removal and installation, 50, 60
Door glass, 391
Door locks, 385, 390
Doors, 369
Door trim panel, 384
Drive axle (front), 247, 284
    Application chart, 247
    Axle shaft, bearing and seal, 284
    Fluid recommendations, 33, 247, 280
    Front hub and wheel bearings, 297
    Lubricant level, 33
    Removal and installation, 250
Driveshaft
    Front, 247
Drive Train, 247
Drum brakes, 354
Dwell angle, 199

E

EGR valve, 161
Electrical, 58
    Chassis, 194
        Battery, 16, 41, 58, 66
        Bulbs, 234

        Circuit breakers, 238, 240
        Fuses, 238
        Heater and air conditioning, 212
        Jump starting, 41
        Spark plug wires, 46
    Engine, 82
        Alternator, 59, 63
        Coil, 50, 61
        Distributor, 48, 60
        Electronic engine controls, 47, 161, 164
        Ignition module, 62
        Starter, 58, 67
Electronic Ignition, 47, 164
Emission controls, 156
    Air pump, 156
    Applications chart, 162
    Catalytic Converter, 155, 159
    Exhaust Gas Recirculation (EGR) system, 161
    Fuel Return system, 173
    Fuel Tank Vapor Control system, 16, 160
    Oxygen (O_2) sensor, 164
    PCV valve, 15, 158
    Thermostatically controlled air cleaner, 159
    Troubleshooting, 166
Engine
    Application chart, 6, 73
    Camshaft, 31
    Compression testing, 71
    Connecting rods and bearings, 136
    Crankshaft, 139
    Crankshaft damper, 124
    Cylinder had, 107
    Cylinders, 137
    Design, 69
    Electronic controls, 47, 161, 164
    Exhaust manifold, 98
    Fluids and lubricants, 31
    Flywheel, 149
    Front (timing) cover, 122
    Front seal, 124
    Identification, 6, 73
    Intake manifold, 94, 180
    Main bearings, 146
    Mount, 78, 81, 86
    Oil pan, 117
    Oil pump, 121
    Overhaul, 58, 69, 149
    Piston pin, 136
    Pistons, 136
    Rear main seal, 146
    Removal and installation, 72
    Rings, 138
    Rocker cover, 89
    Rocker shafts and studs, 91
    Spark plug wires, 46
    Specifications, 73
    Thermostat, 93
    Timing belt, 112, 126
    Timing chain and gears, 127, 130
    Tools, 69, 150
    Troubleshooting, 54
    Valve guides, 117
    Valves, 115

Valve seats, 117
Valve springs, 115
Valve timing, 112, 126, 129
Water pump, 104
Evaporative canister, 16, 160
Evaporator, 23, 217
Exhaust Manifold, 98
Exhaust pipe, 155
Exhaust system, 150

F

Filters
    Air, 6, 14, 160
    Crankcase, 6
    Fuel, 7
    Oil, 32
Firing orders, 46
Flashers, 233, 238
Fluids and lubricants, 31
    Automatic transmission, 33
    Battery, 17
    Coolant, 34
    Drive axle, 247
    Engine oil, 31
    Fuel, 31
    Manual transmission, 33
    Master cylinder
        Brake, 36
    Power steering pomp, 36, 33
    Steering gear, 36
    Steering knuckle, 297
    Windshield washer, 37
Flywheel and ring gear, 149
Front bumper, 377
Front cover, 122
Front drive axle, 247
    Application chart, 247
    Axle shaft, bearing and seal, 284
    Fluid recommendations, 33
    Front hub and wheel bearings, 297
    Lubricant level, 33
    Removal and installation, 250
Front brakes, 342
Front hubs, 297
Front suspension, 289
    Ball joints, 295
    Description, 289
    Knuckles, 297
    Lower control arm, 296
    Shock absorbers, 308
    Springs, 294
    Stabilizer bar, 295
    Struts, 290, 300
    Wheel alignment, 302
Front wheel bearings, 297
Fog lights, 382
Fuel injection, 171, 176, 181, 185
    Fittings, 171, 189
    Fuel body, 175, 179, 183, 188
    Fuel pressure regulator, 173, 176, 181, 185
    Fuel pump, 169
    Injectors, 173, 177, 180, 182, 184, 186, 189

Throttle body, 53, 173, 183, 187
    Throttle position sensor, 175, 181
Fuel filter, 7
Fuel pump, 169
Fuel system, 169
    Fuel injection, 52, 172, 176
    Troubleshooting, 193
Fuel tank, 190
Fuses and circuit breakers, 238, 241
Fusible links, 239, 241

G

Gearshift linkage adjustment
    Automatic, 281
    Manual, 277
Generator
    Operation, 59
    Removal and installation, 64
Glossary, 406-411
Grille, 378

H

Halfshaft, 247, 254-260, 284
Hazard flasher, 233, 238
Headlights, 230, 234
Heater
    Blower, 216, 220
    Control panel, 204, 212
    Core, 204, 214
Hinges, 369, 371
Hoisting, 38
Hood, 371
    Coolant, 21
    Fuel, 171, 189
How to Use This Book, 1
Hubs, 297

I

Identification, 5
    Axle, 6, 247
    Engine, 6
    Model, 6
    Serial number, 5
    Transmission, 6, 247
        Automatic, 247
        Manual, 247
    Vehicle, 5
Idle speed and mixture adjustment, 52
Ignition
    Electronic, 47, 163
    Lock cylinder, 319
    Module, 62
    Switch, 232, 319
    Timing, 48, 112, 126, 129
Inertia switch, 72
Injectors, fuel, 173, 177, 180, 182, 189
Instrument cluster, 227
Instrument panel, 207, 210
    Cluster, 227
    Console, 282
    Panel removal, 207

Radio, 206, 209, 220
Speedometer cable, 232
Intake manifold, 51, 94, 180

J

Jacking points, 38
Jump starting, 41

K

Knuckles, 297
Knuckle oil seal, 297

L

Lighting, 382
    Headlights, 234
    Signal and marker lights, 234, 236
Liftgate, 373
Liftgate glass, 228
Liftgate lock, 373
Linkshaft, 252
Lubrication, 9, 39
    Automatic transmission, 33, 247
    Body, 38
    Differential, 33
    Engine, 31
    Manual transmission, 33, 247

M

MacPherson struts, 289, 294, 300, 309
Main bearings, 139, 147
Maintenance intervals, 8, 42
Manifolds
    Intake, 51, 94, 180
    Exhaust, 98
Manual transmission
    Application chart, 247
    Linkage adjustment, 277
    Operation
    Overhaul, 263-275
    Removal and installation, 261
    Troubleshooting, 248
Marker lights, 234
Master cylinder
    Brake, 36, 344
Mechanic's data, 404
Mirrors, 381
Model identification, 5
Module (ignition), 62
Muffler, 155
Multi-function switch, 233, 319, 323

N

Neutral safety switch, 260

O

Oil and fuel recommendations, 31, 39
Oil and filter change (engine), 32
Oil level check, 32

Differential, 33
Engine, 32
Transmission
    Automatic, 33
    Manual, 33
Oil pan, 117
Oil pump, 121
Outside vehicle maintenance, 38
    Lock cylinders, 38
    Door hinges, 38, 369
    Tailgate, 38
    Body drain holes, 38

P

Parking brake, 362
Piston pin, 136
Pistons, 136, 138
PCV valve, 15, 158
Power brake booster, 347
Power seat motor, 399
    Adjustments, 36, 329
    Removal and installation, 327
    Troubleshooting, 337
Power steering pump, 329
    Removal and installation, 329, 331
    Troubleshooting, 332
Power seats, 397
Power windows, 395
Preventive Maintenance Charts, 8, 42
Pushing, 42

Q

Quick Reference Specifications, 404

R

Radiator, 35, 102
Radiator cap, 23, 35
Radio, 206, 209, 220, 383
Rear axle
    Axle shaft bearing, 37, 38, 316
Rear brakes, 354, 359
Rear bumper, 378
Rear main oil seal, 146
Rear suspension, 304
    Control arms, 313-315
    Shock absorbers, 308
    Springs, 306
    Sway bar, 315
    Tension strut, 315
Rear wheel bearings, 37, 316
Regulator
    Removal and installation, 66
Ride height, 302
Rings, 138
Rocker arms or shaft, 89, 91
Rotor (Brake disc), 353, 359
Routine maintenance, 6, 42.

S

Safety notice, iv, 1, 4, 150, 194
Seats, 397

Serial number location, 5
Serpentine belt, 19
Shock absorbers, 308
Smog systems, 156
Spare tire carrier, 30
Spark plugs, 43
Spark plug wires, 46
Special tools, iv, 5, 150, 195, 203
Specifications Charts
    Alternator and regulator, 66
    Brakes, 365
    Camshaft, 74
    Capacities, 42
    Carburetor
    Crankshaft and connecting rod, 74
    Fastener markings and torque standards, 404
    Fuses and Circuit Breakers, 240
    General engine, 73
    Generator and regulator, 66
    Piston and ring, 75
    Preventive Maintenance, 8, 42
    Starter, 68
    Torque, 76
    Tune-up, 43
    Valves, 73
    Wheel alignment, 304, 315
Speedometer cable, 232, 262
Springs, 294, 306
Spout connector, 49
Stabilizer bar, 295, 315
Stain removal, 403
Starter, 58
    Drive replacement, 68
    Overhaul, 67
    Removal and installation, 67
    Specifications, 68
    Troubleshooting, 67
Steering column, 321
Steering gear
    Power, 327
Steering knuckles, 297
Steering knuckle oil seal, 284
Steering linkage, 327
    Tie rod ends, 326
Steering lock, 319
Steering wheel, 318
Striker plate, 370
Stripped threads, 70
Suspension, 289, 304
Switches
    Back-up light, 260
    Headlight, 230
    Ignition switch, 232
    Multi-function switch, 233
    Rear window wiper, 223
    Windshield wiper, 223

T

Tailgate, 228, 373
Tailgate lock, 373
Tailpipe, 150
Tension struts, 296, 315

Thermostat, 93
Throttle body, 53, 175, 178, 183
Tie rod ends, 326
Timing (ignition)
    Electronic systems, 48, 112, 126, 129
Timing belt, 112, 126
Timing chain and gears, 127, 130
Timing gear cover, 122
Tires, 29
    Rotation, 30
    Troubleshooting, 29, 31
    Wear problems, 29
Toe-in, 302, 315, 318
Tools, 2, 69, 150, 195, 203
Torque specifications, 76
Towing, 39, 40
Trailer towing, 39, 237
Transmission
    Automatic, 280
    Manual, 261
    Routine maintenance, 33, 280
Troubleshooting Charts
    Air conditioning, 26
    Automatic transmission, 288
    Brakes, 365
    Clutch, 286
    Engine mechanical, 54
    Engine performance, 54
    Fuel system, 193
    Gauges, 245
    Heater, 246
    Ignition switch, 336
    Lights, 243
    Lockup torque converter, 287
    Manual transmission, 248
    Power steering gear, 337
    Power steering pump, 339
    Starting system, 67
    Steering and suspension, 332
    Steering column, 333
    Tires, 29, 31
    Transmission fluid indications, 286
    Turn signals and flashers, 244
    Turn signal switch, 244, 335
    Windshield wipers, 246
Trunk lid, 374
Tune-up
    Distributor, 48, 50
    Idle speed, 52
    Ignition timing, 48
    Procedures, 43, 46
    Spark plugs and wires, 43
    Specifications, 43
    Troubleshooting, 54
Turn signal flasher, 238
Turn signal switch, 233, 319, 323

V

Vacuum diagram, 165, 204
Valve cover, 89
Valve guides, 117
Valve lash adjustment, 51

Valve seats, 117
Valve service, 115
Valve specifications, 73
Valve springs, 115
Valve timing, 112
Vehicle identification, 5
Voltage regulator, 66

W

Water pump, 104
Wheel alignment
  Adjustment, 302, 318
  Specifications, 304, 315
Wheel bearings, 37
  Front drive axle, 297

Rear wheel, 37, 38, 316
Wheel cylinders, 357
Window glass, 391
Window regulator, 393
Windshield wipers, 27, 223
  Arm, 223
  Blade, 27, 223
  Inspection, 27
  Motor, 223
  Rear window wiper, 226
  Rear window wiper switch, 223
  Windshield wiper switch, 223
Wire sets
Wiring, 200, 212, 220, 237
  Spark plug, 46
  Trailer, 39, 237